"*Plain Speaking* is the real thing; there has never been a book like it and never will be again. Not that future journalists won't be capable of matching Miller's efforts, but there will not ever again be a subject like Harry Truman, at least not in the White House."

Robert Alan Aurthur, *Esquire*

✿   ✿   ✿

". . . in a time of national psychic dislocation and trauma, PLAIN SPEAKING provides an instant and badly needed rehabilitation from the spreading sickness of cynicism; it restores us to our senses, to what we know, if for the moment only in our bones, to be true and right."

Eliot Fremont-Smith,
New York Magazine

✿   ✿   ✿

"How do you describe a book whose every page jumps at you with deliciously simple language about world-shaking events that happened several decades ago but which still affect all of us?

To borrow two favorite expressions of Harry Truman's: This book is a 'crackerjack,' and 'no two ways about it.' "

Fort Wayne News-Sentinel

"This is the Truman idiom, vigorous, without cant or inhibition and valid for no one could possibly make it up. It's a rich taste of a better past."

John Kenneth Galbraith

❁　❁　❁

"Congress may have to pass a law making it mandatory that before anyone can run for any office above Dog Catcher, he or she must read PLAIN SPEAKING and prove an understanding of it by passing an oral examination monitored by Diogenes."

Variety

❁　❁　❁

"I know of no other work in which an ex-President speaks so bluntly of his experiences from childhood to retirement, so candidly of his contemporaries and successors . . . the work is engagingly human."

Los Angeles Times

❁　❁　❁

"PLAIN SPEAKING is an 'oral biography' so alive it will seem warm to the touch. Both a human document and political history, there has never been another book quite like it. Its shrewdness would please Plutarch; its wit would delight Mark Twain."

Harriet Van Horne,
Book-of-the-Month Club News

"At a time when the White House seems to be dominated by the ethics of the advertising industry, it is a joy to go back to Truman and his simple creed. Miller has provided a superb portrait of a feisty President. He has brought an American original to life."

John P. Roche, *Saturday Review/World*

✿ ✿ ✿

"This is the most refreshing book that has ever been written about an American president."

Christian Science Monitor

✿ ✿ ✿

"Harry Truman talked into Merle Miller's tape recorder, and the result is almost as fascinating as the White House transcripts."

The *New York Times Book Review*

DEDICATION

❊　　❊　　❊

A NOTE ON THE LANGUAGE

The diligent reader will notice that sometimes Mr. Truman is quoted as saying "fella" and sometimes "fellow," that sometimes he confuses "like" and "as" and sometimes does not, and that while he usually has "dinner" at twelve noon, he occasionally has "lunch" at that hour. There are other inconsistencies. Mr. Truman talked that way, inconsistently, like the rest of us.

He was a self-educated man, and he mispronounced a reasonable number of words, which in the beginning puzzled me. Then I realized that while he had often read them, he had seldom, if ever, spoken them aloud, not even in many cases heard them spoken aloud. It's like that if you're one of the few readers in town.

❊　　❊　　❊

For, the noblest deeds do not always shew men's virtues and vices, but oftentimes a light occasion, a word, or some sport makes men's natural dispositions and manners appear more plain, than the famous battles won, wherein are slain ten thousand men, or the great armies, or cities won by siege or assault.

　　　　　　　　　—Plutarch, *Alexander the Great, i*

Plain Speaking
an oral biography of
Harry S. Truman
by
Merle Miller

A BERKLEY MEDALLION BOOK
published by
BERKLEY PUBLISHING CORPORATION

Parts of this book have appeared in ESQUIRE,
HOLIDAY, SHOW, *and* VISTA.

Grateful acknowledgment is made to the following sources for
permission to reprint:

Bernard Geis Associates: *Mr. Citizen* by Harry S. Truman ©
1960 by Harry S. Truman.
Harcourt Brace Jovanovich, Inc.: *The American Presidency*
by Clinton Rossiter © 1956, 1960 by Clinton Rossiter.
Harper & Row: *Sketches from Life, Of Men I Have Known*
by Dean Acheson © 1961 by Dean Acheson.
Dell Publishing Company, Inc.: *America Comes of Middle
Age* by Murray Kempton © 1967 by Murray Kempton.
Macmillan Publishing Co., Inc.: *Truman Presidency* by Cabell
Phillips, © 1966 by Cabell Phillips.
W. W. Norton and Company, Inc.: *Present at the Creation:
My Years in the State Department* by Dean Acheson © 1969
by Dean Acheson.
G. P. Putnam's Sons: *The Man from Missouri* by Alfred Stein-
berg © 1962 by Alfred Steinberg.
The Viking Press, Inc.: *The Patriot Chiefs: Chronicle of
American Indian Leadership* by Alvin M. Josephy, Jr. © 1961
by Alvin M. Josephy, Jr.

CONTENTS

Preface

It has been good to think about Harry Truman this spring and summer, the twentieth summer since he left the White House, the summer after his death, the summer of Watergate. The memory of him has never been sharper, never brighter than it is now, a time when menacing, shadowy men are everywhere among us.

There was never anything shadowy about old Harry, never anything menacing. He was never less than four-dimensional; he was always a person, a human being.

I once wrote that Harry Truman might be the last human being to occupy the White House, and considering, as he would say, "the four fellas that succeeded me," I see no reason to change my mind.

As you will see in reading this book, Harry's words were never fancy, but they were never obscure either. You never had to try to figure out what Harry was up to; he told you what he was up to. And, as they said of him back in Independence, he was a man of his word. There was not a duplicitous bone in his body. He was without guile, and when it was all over, when he and Bess came back home, after eighteen years in Washington, more than seven of them in an unbugged,* unshuttered White House, neither of them thought of bringing any of the trappings of the Presidency with them. In fact, that last day in Washington, in January, 1953, Harry had thought that since the relations between himself and the incoming

---

* The week it was revealed that Nixon's White House was extensively bugged Major General Harry Vaughan, Truman's military aide, remembered that during Truman's first week in office he took some FBI phone taps (an extensive practice during the Roosevelt years) to the new President and asked if he was interested. Harry took a look at two pages of transcript of the doings of the wife of one member of the White House staff and then told Vaughan, "I haven't time for any such foolishness as that. Tell them I don't authorize any such thing."

President were, to state it gently, strained, he and Bess might have to walk from the White House to the railroad station. Or perhaps take a taxi.

"But that wouldn't have bothered me," he told me years later. "I was there more or less by accident you might say, and I just never got to thinking that I was anything *special*. It's very easy to do that in Washington, and I've seen it happen to a lot of fellas. But I did my best not to let it happen to me. I tried never to forget who I was and where I'd come from and where I was going back to. And if you can do that, things usually work out all right in the end."

As nearly as he could remember, Harry's last act in the White House was returning a pencil or maybe it was a pen to the desk of the man he had borrowed it from.

"Everything," he said, "all of it belongs to the people. I was just privileged to *use* it for a while. That's all. And since it was only *lent* to me, and by that I'm includin' the power of the Presidency, such as it is, I had to try to use whatever it was with great care so that I could pass it on to the next fella in the best condition possible. And for the most part I think you can say I succeeded."

Mr. President, it's been said that the Presidency is the most powerful office in the world. Do you think that's true?

"Oh, no. Oh, my, no. About the biggest power the President has, and I've said this before, is the power to persuade people to do what they ought to do without having to be persuaded. There are a lot of other powers written in the Constitution and given to the President, but it's that power to persuade people to do what they ought to do anyway that's the biggest. And if the man who is President doesn't understand that, if he thinks he's too big to do the necessary persuading, then he's in for big trouble, and so is the country."

So Harry and Bess took the train back to Independence, and people in Independence found them unchanged; it was as if they had never been away, and as a neighbor says in this book, maybe Harry never really left Independence; maybe he just sort of commuted to Washington.

Anyway, people back home found that they were as

Bernard Berenson, yes, Bernard Berenson, said, "Both as natural, as unspoiled by high office as if he had risen no further than alderman of Independence, Missouri."

And you remember the day after Mr. Truman got back home, he took his usual morning walk, and Ray Scherer, the television reporter, asked him what was the first thing he did when he walked in the house at 219 North Delaware the night before, pausing for some monumental statement suitable for engraving on the side of Mount Rushmore.

"I carried the grips up to the attic," said Harry.

That house on North Delaware Street had served as the summer White House various times during the more than seven years that Harry Truman was President, but somehow it never occurred to him to have it all fancied up at the expense of the taxpayers. In fact, he didn't even own the place. He and Bess had put up with mother-in-law Wallace from the time of their marriage in 1919 until her death in 1952. They had fed her and clothed her and housed her, including in her last years a room of her very own in the White House. But Madge Gates Wallace never stopped ruminating, aloud and whenever possible in the presence of her son-in-law, about all the people who would have made better Presidents than Harry. And why did he have to fire that nice General MacArthur? The general was a man she could have felt socially at ease with; for one thing, he was a gentleman to the manor born. He was a five-star general, not like some dirt farmers who shall be nameless. And don't track up the kitchen with your muddy feet, Harry.

When she died, that impossible old woman, she didn't even leave the house to Harry. She left it to Bess and the Wallace boys, and Harry had to buy out their share.

But, as it says in these pages, in all those years, Harry never once complained. He never once answered back. Mrs. W. L. C. Palmer, who taught him Latin and mathematics, says, "You must remember Harry is a reticent man."

Ethel Noland, Harry Truman's first cousin, put it another way. She said that both of them grew up at a time when if people asked how you were, you said, "I'm fine. And you?" You wouldn't have *dreamed* of discussing with anybody, except possibly the family doctor, how you really were. One accepted one's fate, never bemoaned it. For one thing, you didn't have time.

Whatever happened to old-fashioned reticence, do you suppose? Is there any way of getting it back? I've looked everywhere, asked everybody; nobody seems to know; nobody seems to care even, and when you ask, it's difficult to keep the asked from telling you why he doesn't care and how he feels. None of them feels good, not ever.

All right then. This is a book about Harry Truman, and most of it is in his own words and the words of people who knew him before he went to Washington and after and while he was there. It should be said instantly that the words were not spoken with a book in mind. They were spoken in the hope that out of them would come ideas for God-alone-knew how many television programs that would explain to the eager millions what it had been like to be President and what as President Mr. Truman had done.

As Mr. Truman used to say, "I'm mostly interested in the children. The old folks, mostly they're too set in their ways and too stubborn to learn anything new, but I want the children to know what we've got here in this country and how we got it, and then if they want to go ahead and change it, why, that's up to them. But I want them to understand what it's all about first. I want to make a historical record that has never been made before in the history of this country, and if it turns out all right, I'll be very happy indeed."

The way it turns out comes later.

But it began in the summer of 1961, continued that fall and winter into the cold, very cold, never colder, months of 1962.

I first went to Independence as the writer and, as

my friend Robert Alan Aurthur* describes it, "the general
organizer" of the series. As I say, the programs were to
deal largely with Mr. Truman's years in the White House.
We're inclined, I am anyway, to think of those years as
being simpler times, but maybe we were only young.
Maybe it was that things seemed soluble then, and who
among us didn't think he would become what he dreamed
of becoming?

But looking back on them, the years don't seem simple
at all. Think of it—the dropping of the Bomb, the forma-
tion of the UN, the Korean decision, the Hiss case, the
firing of MacArthur, the birth of Israel, NATO, the Marshall Plan, McCarthyism, Point Four, and so on and endlessly on. And through it all, for almost eight years, Harry
Truman was *there,* not in the eye of the storm, he *was* the
eye of the storm. He did it, all of it. He asked his associates
to tell him how long he had to decide whatever was to be
decided, and when the deadline came, the decision had
been made. And no regrets, no looking back, no wondering
if-I-had-to-do-it-all-over-again, would I have? Dean Ache-

* Aurthur's beady-eyed account of some parts of our involvement with Mr. Truman appeared in two issues of *Esquire*
in 1971. He wrote, "You wonder how I ever got to hang
around Mr. Truman . . . ? Simply put, I was supervising a
series of films for television independently produced and fi-
nanced by David Susskind and his company, Talent Associates.
At the birth of the project, then uninvolved except as a friend,
I had suggested to David that the man to bring the perfect
creative spark as writer and general organizer was another
close friend, Merle Miller. To supplement Merle's obvious literary qualifications I felt he and Mr. Truman had much in
common: both were from the Midwest; both had strong
mothers, weak eyes, and early dreams of glory—which only
Mr. Truman had realized."

As Huck Finn says of Mark Twain and *The Adventures of
Tom Sawyer* at the beginning of his own adventures, ". . . he
told the truth, mainly. There was things which he stretched,
but mainly he told the truth."

The things which Bob stretched largely had to do with me.

son wrote that Harry Truman was totally without what he called "that most enfeebling of emotions, regret."

Regret was self-indulgent, as bad as, maybe worse than, telling people how you *felt*. No time for it. "If you can't stand the heat, stay out of the kitchen." Like that sign on Harry's desk when he was in the White House. "The buck stops here," it said, and that's where it stopped. The mistakes were Harry's, and he never blamed anyone else for them.

The triumphs were Harry's, too, but he was a modest man. There was nothing of Uriah Heep about him; he was just genuinely modest. Speaking of what Winston Churchill has called "the most unsordid act in history," the Marshall Plan, Mr. Truman once told me, "I said to General Marshall, I said, 'General, I want the plan to go down in history with your name on it. And don't give me any argument. I've made up my mind, and, remember, I'm your Commander in Chief."

And that other sign on his desk, that quotation from Mark Twain that his sister had at the little house out at Grandview the last time I saw her: "Always do right. This will gratify some people & astonish the rest."

Harry Truman always did what he thought was right. Can you imagine a member of his Cabinet seriously telling a committee of the U.S. Senate that he had *shielded* Harry from the truth?

One's blood congeals at the thought of how far we have gone since those days, and it's been downhill all the way.

Once Harry found out that a couple of his appointees had been "influence peddling"—how archaic those guys on the take for 5 percent seem these days—and, without hesitation, he threw them downstairs, right out in front of God, the electorate, and everybody.

When the fella that succeeded him, *whatever* his name was, Harry never could remember that bird's name, but when he had to get rid of *five* of his appointees for more or less the same thing, he *accepted their resignations* with letters so flattering that the resigners no doubt had them framed in gold and hung on their living-room walls. For one the President-General even had the troops pass in review.

When Harry was asked what he thought of such goings-on, he said, "I see why he had to fire them, but I don't see why he had to kiss them on both cheeks."

You can see what I mean by four-dimensional and why the memory of him is so luminous. Take the business of what you are willing to do to win an election.

In October, 1948, less than a month before the election almost nobody but Harry thought he could win, plans were made to send his old friend Fred Vinson, then Chief Justice of the United States Supreme Court, on a dramatic special mission to Moscow "to find some common ground with the Russians."

The journey just before the election would demonstrate to the electorate that Harry was a President who could be counted on to do anything to keep the peace. For a generation? Hell, maybe forever.

The President was to announce the Vinson trip on a national radio hookup. In fact, the speech had already been written, and the Chief Justice was packing his bags. Harry's exuberant adviser—not very much exuberance up to then—told him that this was what they'd been hoping for all through the campaign. This would do it. There were millions, maybe tens of millions of votes in it.

Harry listened, and then he went off to the communications room of the White House to discuss the mission with General George C. Marshall, who was then his Secretary of State and was attending a meeting of the Foreign Ministers in Paris. The general said that he, of course, was a subordinate of the President and that he didn't *know* that such a trip as Vinson's might make his work more difficult, but it might. He left the decision up to the President.

Harry came back to the meeting of his associates and said no. There would be no Vinson mission to Moscow, politically appealing as the idea might be.

His advisers said he was crazy. They asked what was

more important, *maybe* making old Marshall's work more difficult or winning the election. Jonathan Daniels, who was there, has written: "They talked to him as President and more sharply as candidate, too.

"He listened. His magnified eyes seemed almost slate gray. Then he said very quietly, 'I have heard enough. We won't do it.'

"He got up and went out of the glass-paneled door to the terrace by the rose garden and walked alone—very much alone that day—back toward the White House. . . ."

When in 1961 I mentioned that lonely night to Mr. Truman, he said, "Why, of course, I didn't know for sure whether it would help win the election or not, but after talking to General Marshall, I decided it wouldn't be the right thing to do, and so I didn't do it."

I waited for more, but there wasn't any more, and there really didn't need to be.

Harry Truman, a buck-stopper, a doer-of-right, alone, but his own man, never anybody else's. They said he was Tom Pendergast's man, but that wasn't true either. You'll see. Harry Truman never belonged to anybody. He once said, "Old Tom Jefferson wrote that, 'Whenever you do a thing, though it can never be known but to yourself, ask yourself how you would act were all the world watching you, and act accordingly.' "

Old Harry was far too modest a man to make any comparison between himself and old Tom.

I first went to Independence in the summer of 1961, and I must confess that up to then Harry hadn't been any-where near the top of my list of favorite ex-Presidents. True, I'd voted for him in 1948, but reluctantly, most reluctantly. I had never quite forgiven him for not being Franklin Roosevelt, for being plain instead of patrician. Besides, Bob Aurthur is perfectly right. There were a lot of things about Harry Truman that reminded me of things about me that I wanted to forget. My childhood, just to start out.

But then how many chances had I had to be the Boswell

of an ex-President? Besides which, Bob Aurthur had promised me that the project would make me very, very rich and my name a household word, two things I had had on my personal agenda for all of my life.

So I went to Independence, along with two associates; the associates kept changing, but they all had two things in common, incompetence and stupidity. We had been told before leaving New York that the President would not be able to see us until the next morning, but we went out to the Truman Library anyway, and while we were still looking at the huge Thomas Hart Benton mural just inside the public entrance to the library, a member of the staff came up and said that the President had heard we were there and wanted to see us.

We were taken into Mr. Truman's private office, and when he came in, he was wearing the familiar double-breasted suit with the usual neatly folded handkerchief in the breast pocket, a white shirt that could have come from J. C. Penney, and a Sulka—or was it Countess Mara? —tie. His skin was pink and healthy-looking, and his blue eyes were amused and active, enhanced rather than diminished by the thin-rimmed glasses. He looked just as feisty and mischievous and forthright as I'd expected. He looked like a man who enjoyed himself hugely and who, if he did not, kept that knowledge to himself. I'm fine. And you?

Since I hadn't expected to see Mr. Truman, I was wearing an unpressed pair of slacks and a sports shirt, and I apologized.

"Oh, that's all right," he said, a sentence he was to repeat many times in many different contexts.

"Besides," he added, "I'm just an old Missouri farmer, and you're just an Iowa farmer. So don't worry about a thing like that."

The President had taken the trouble to find out a good deal about all three of us. I doubt, though, that he had used whatever influence he had with the Kennedy administration to get any secret FBI reports on us or had detectives hired to bug our phones or our bedrooms. You will see later how he felt about such things. He was a very private man who respected the privacy of others, all others.

In my case he had taken the trouble to read two of my novels, and I'm sure they weren't his kind of books. So it was a measure of his forbearance that he was willing to let me handle the series. He was a very forbearing man. "You'll never find me in any way criticizin' or jumpin' on the people who are trying to help me. If a fella can't be patient and considerate of the people who are actually doin' the work for him, then he's not any good, and I don't like him."

David Susskind said that Mr. Truman was corny, and it's true. He often was, and sometimes I deplored it. But looking back now on those weeks we spent together, reading over and listening to his words, to the words of his friends, it all comes out beautifully refreshing. We need more of it.

David also said that Mr. Truman was an elemental man, the most elemental he, David, had ever met, and that's true, too. Mr. Truman was the most elemental man I've ever met, except maybe for my grandfather, and I think we could use more of that as well. My grandfather never voted for a Democrat his whole life through, and I don't know that he'd have voted for Harry Truman, but he'd have liked him. They were both elemental, and they were both men of whom it could be said that they never met a stranger.

That first afternoon with Mr. Truman we talked for a few minutes about plans for the television series, and then I said, "Mr. President, could I ask you a question that you might consider impertinent?"

"Go right ahead," he said. "If I want to stop you, I'll stop you."

"Well, sir, I've been wearing glasses since I was three years old, and I know you had to wear glasses when you were a boy. I wonder, sir, did they ever call you *four-eyes?*"

The President smiled. It was a good smile, warm and

welcoming, holding nothing back. I was never sure whether the even teeth were false.

"I've worn glasses since I was six years old," he said, "and of course, they called me *four-eyes* and a lot of other things, too. That's hard on a boy. It makes him lonely, and it gives him an inferiority complex, and he has a hard time overcoming it."

He paused a moment, still smiling, then said, "Of course, we didn't know what an inferiority complex was in those days. But you can overcome it. You've got to fight for everything you do. You've got to be above those calling you names, and you've got to do more work than they do, but it usually comes out all right in the end."

That last sentence was another the President was to repeat many times.

"I always had my nose stuck in a book," he said, "a history book mostly. Of course, the main reason you read a book is to get a better insight into the people you're talking to. There were about three thousand books in the library downtown, and I guess I read them all, including the encyclopedias. I'm embarrassed to say that I remembered what I read, too."

That was how our relationship, I like to think our friendship, began. It continued, as I say, until the winter months of 1962, when it ended, not because there was ever any trouble between the President and me but because the three television networks to which we all owe so much were having no part of a series on Mr. Truman's Presidency.

In the months after our meeting, however, Mr. Truman and I had days, sometimes weeks, of conversations, interviews if you insist, many of them on tape, many not. The more formal of them were in Mr. Truman's office, often with the inhibiting presence, inhibiting I felt to Mr. Truman and certainly inhibiting to me, of two associates. One was David Noyes, a wealthy former vice-president of Lord & Thomas who had been a speechwriter during the 1948 campaign. Except for Mr. Truman, he had been the only man who that year thought he could win the election. He clearly loved Mr. Truman and was very protective of him. I felt he was too protective.

The other was William Hillman, a former foreign correspondent of the Hearst newspapers. He was a large, shambling man, a cigarette forever dangling from his full lips, his ample stomach forever covered with ashes. A somewhat more benign version of Sidney Greenstreet with a suitably gravelly voice.

Bob Aurthur reports that he and Hillman once had lunch at the airport restaurant in Kansas City, all by itself a hazardous undertaking, and while Hillman described the way he had got an exclusive interview with Adolf Hitler, he ate *two* orders of pig's knuckles and sauerkraut.

Noyes and Hillman, Hillman in particular, had worked with Mr. Truman in writing the *Memoirs* and on his other writing chores. I felt that they had dejuiced and dehumanized him in everything that was written. They had laundered his prose, flattened his personality, and made him pontifical, which was the last thing I found him to be. Their mere presence in a room made him self-conscious, caused him to clean up his language and soften his opinions. With them around Mr. Truman came out bland, another thing he just wasn't.

But, happily, they were away a good deal of the time, and the best of the conversations in this book were when Mr. Truman and I were alone or were waiting for somebody to change the film in a camera or do something or other to one of the tape machines. A lot more time was spent doing things like that than was spent actually filming or recording. Mr. Truman never understood why, and neither did I. The crews all came from New York, union rules, and they were all bumbling incompetents. All.

Mr. Truman was invariably patient with them, though, and with me. The only time he ever got angry with me was once in New York when we were filming an episode of the series having to do with Korea. I had suggested that since even then Korea was very vague in the minds of those in the television audience who were under thirty, we should

perhaps try to *dramatize* what. . . . *Dramatize*. That did
it. Mr. Truman's eyes grew cold, and he drew his mouth
into a tight, unpleasant line and said—for a second I felt
some sympathy for the late Douglas MacArthur—"Now
you look here, young man, you asked me to tell you the
facts, and I'll do it, but I'm not going to be any playactor.
Now what's your next question?"

Anyway, I suppose the ineptitude of the technical crews
had its value; it gave me a lot more time to talk with Mr.
Truman and with the two dejuicers out of the room.

Most of the time I would suggest the day before what
we would discuss the following day, hoping that that night
he would bone up on whatever the subject was. For all I
know he did, and we returned to some subjects again and
again, amplifying, adding color and detail.

While I was working on this book, a reviewer in the
Village Voice dismissed a book about Mr. Truman as
well as Mr. Truman himself, "the one after FDR and before General Eisenhower." One of Mr. Truman's observations particularly infuriated him. He treated it as if it had
been the raving of an idiot child. The sentence was: "There
is nothing new in the world except the history you do not
know."

And all by itself it doesn't make much sense. But as
Mr. Truman explained it to me, the whole thing goes like
this:

"There's nothing new in human nature. The only thing
that changes are the names we give things. If you want
to understand the twentieth century, read the lives of the
Roman emperors, all the way from Claudius to Con-
stantine. . . . And go back to old Hammurabi, the Baby-
lonian emperor. Why, he had laws that covered everything,
adultery and murder and divorce, everything.

"Those people had the same troubles as we have now.
Men don't change. The only thing new in the world is the
history you don't know."

Not the most profound idea in the world, perhaps, but
it's true.

To Harry Truman history was the men who made it, and he spoke of Marcus Aurelius or Henry of Navarre or old Tom Jefferson or old Andy Jackson as if they were friends and neighbors with whom he had only recently discussed the affairs of the day, their day:

". . . his real name was Marcus Aleius Aurelius Antoninus, and he was one of the great ones. He was a great field general, and he was a great emperor, one of the six great emperors of Rome.

"Some people think they're old-fashioned, but I don't. What he wrote in his *Meditations,* he said that the four greatest virtues are moderation, wisdom, justice, and fortitude, and if a man is able to cultivate those, that's all he needs to live a happy and successful life. That's the way I look at it anyway." *

* Mr. Truman's copy of *Meditations,* which he lent to me to take back to the hotel one night, was by the look of it one of the most read books in his library. He was a great underliner, a great writer of marginal comments, usually about things with which he disagreed, *"Bunk!" "He doesn't know what he's talking about!"* "That's not True!!" "Where did he ever get a damn fool notion like that?" And so on.

I was interested to see that these passages in *Meditations* were underlined:

"If it is not right, do not do it; if it is not true, do not say it."

"First, do nothing thoughtlessly or without a purpose. Secondly, see that your acts are directed to a social end."

"Today I have got out of all trouble, or rather I have cast out all trouble, for it was not outside, but within, in my opinions."

"It is not fitting that I should give myself pain, for I have never intentionally given pain even to another."

"Always be sure whose approbation it is you wish to secure, and what ruling principles they have. Then you will neither blame those who offend involuntarily, nor will you want their approbation, if you look to the sources of their opinions and appetites."

"When another blames or hates you, or when men say injurious things about you, approach their poor souls, penetrate within, and see what kind of men they are. You will discover that there is no reason to take trouble that these men have a good opinion of you. However, you must be well disposed to-

About Mr. Truman's memory. In Cabell Phillips' book *The Truman Presidency*, he says that in 1951, when Hillman was interviewing the President for the book *Mr. President*, Mr. Truman was talking about Alexander the Great, who had, he said, made the mistake of overextending himself.

Phillips writes:

"And then the people around him," he told Hillman, "made him think he was immortal, and he found that thirty-three quarts of wine was too much for any man, and it killed him at Babylon."

Working over the proofs of his book later, Hillman paused to puzzle over the President's mention of the thirty-three quarts of wine. Obviously, he thought, it was some sort of allegory; he, himself, had never heard of it, nor was he sure what it meant. He called the Library of Congress and asked their scholarly assistance in running the item down. A few days later they called back to say, sorry, they could find no link, real or poetic, between Alexander and thirty-three quarts of wine. Hillman was convinced that the President had mixed either his metaphors or his kings and was about to challenge him on it when, a few days later, he received another call from the researcher at the Library. In the manner of librarians everywhere, this one had not given up the search after the first admission of failure. He had pursued his quarry behind the locked doors of the Rare Books Section, and into an obscure and long-out-of-print volume of the history of the ancient Greeks, and, by golly, the President was right after all!

"And you know what?" the researcher added. "That book has been checked out of the shelves only twice in the last twenty years, and the last time was for Senator Harry Truman in 1939."

---

wards them, for by nature they are friends. And the gods, too, aid them in all ways, by dreams, by signs, toward the attainment of their aims."

In the margin of this particular paragraph Harry Truman had written, *"True! True! True!"*

When I was talking with him, Mr. Truman's memory was best during the first two or three hours in the morning—we usually got started around eight—but frequently after lunch it was no good at all. That was partly due, I imagine, to the fact that an old man's mind tires easily. I'm sure another reason, though, was the fact that before going home for "dinner," always a few minutes before noon, he had I would have what he always called a "slight libation," scotch or bourbon. "The Boss doesn't think I ought to," he would say, winking. The Boss was Mrs. Truman. When we had lunch at the Howard Johnson's near the library, we would always have two or three before setting out, and they were never slight, although they were libational.

In any case, in the mornings we talked about history, that made by Mr. Truman and by other men, and in the afternoons we talked, if we talked at all, about more personal matters. Mr. Truman's views of people, large and small, that he'd been associated with. Adlai Stevenson, with whom he had long since become disenchanted. Stevenson was a man who could never make up his mind whether he had to go to the bathroom or not. And Henry Wallace was a fellow "who wanted to be a great man but didn't know how to go about it." And there were two men he hated, "held a grudge against." One of them was Richard Nixon. I don't think he hated "the fella that succeeded me in the White House." He thought he was a lousy President and a moral coward for, among other things, taking out praise for General Marshall that had been written into a speech Eisenhower was going to deliver in Wisconsin during the 1952 campaign. As you'll see, Harry Truman couldn't understand the kind of man who would do such a thing.

Or we'd talk about things like the day Eddie Jacobson, the man who'd been Mr. Truman's partner in the famous failed haberdashery, came to the Oval Room to persuade Mr. Truman to see Chaim Weizmann, who was to become the first President of Israel.

Or Mr. Truman's boyhood. His memory of that never

dimmed, and about his remarkable mother and, he insisted, his equally remarkable father. Or his sister, Mary Jane. Mr. Truman was very sentimental about the women in his life. Mary Jane, Bess, and Margaret. One day I asked him if he would read on camera one of the letters he had written during his first days in the White House to Mamma and Mary Jane.

The President didn't get angry, but I could see that I had made a suggestion almost as bad as asking him to *act*.

"I can't do a thing like that," he said. "You know I can't do a thing like that, and you shouldn't ask me."

He added that the letters belonged to Mary Jane, and he said that when he was President, "and we had three-cent stamps when I was in the White House," he had never franked the letters.

I asked him why, and he said, "Because they were personal. There was nothing official about them."

All clear?

Mr. Truman's memories were always cheerful, always. He had, God knows, had his share and more of frustration, of failure, of disappointment, of poverty, of mortgage foreclosures, of heartbreak. My God, at forty he hadn't succeeded at anything, and he had a wife and a baby and an insupportable mother-in-law to support. And he went ahead and did it. No job was too menial, if it was necessary.

Did he weep? Did he curse the fates? Did he shake his fist at the thunder? If ever he did, he did it in private. Lincoln was an outwardly melancholy man; Harry Truman was not. His melancholy, if any, was all buttoned up inside him. He never, to use a phrase several of his contemporaries used in describing him, wore his heart on his sleeve. How are you? I'm fine. And you?

Mr. Truman was cheerful, because who wants to have a grouch hanging around? He felt that he had lived a remarkable life, which he had, and he liked to talk about it, and I liked to listen. He was a remarkable man, and the fact that he had been President wasn't the only reason,

not even the most important reason. William Howard
Taft wasn't up to much when it came to making memorable observations, but he once said that in every American
town with a population of more than 5,000 there is at
least one man qualified to serve on the Supreme Court of
the United States. I think that's true, and in Independence,
Missouri, there was a man qualified to be President, and
he got to be it, and he turned out to be one of the great
ones. Remarkable.

In *The American Presidency* the historian Clinton Rossiter wrote:

> . . . I am ready to hazard an opinion, to which I
> came, I confess manfully, with dragging feet, that Harry
> S. Truman will eventually win a place as President
> alongside Jefferson and Theodore Roosevelt. There will
> be at least a half-dozen Presidents strung out below him
> who were more able and large-minded, but he had the
> good fortune to preside in stirring times and will reap
> large credit for having survived them. . . . Harry S.
> Truman is a man whom history will delight to remem-
> ber. Those very lapses from dignity that made him an
> object of scorn to millions of Republicans—the angry
> letters, testy press conferences, whistle stops, impossible
> sports shirts, and early-morning seminars on the streets
> of dozens of American cities—open his door to immor-
> tality. It is a rare American, even a rare Republican,
> who can be scornful about a man one hundred years
> dead, and our descendants will be chuckling over his
> Missouri wit and wisdom long after "the five-per-cen-
> ters" have been buried and forgotten. They will read
> with admiration of the upset he brought off in 1948,
> with awe of the firing of General MacArthur, and with a
> sense of kinship of the way he remained more genuinely
> "home folks" than any other President. . . . He was
> fascinating to watch, even when the sight hurt, and he
> will be fascinating to read about. The historians can be
> expected to do their share to fix him securely in history,
> for he provides a classic study of one of their favorite
> themes: the President who grows in office.

As I've said, I had hoped that the conversations in these pages would provide me with the material for a series of hour-long television programs with Mr. Truman and others talking about his years before, during, and after the White House and talking about this country and its past. But for reasons I'll explain in a minute, that was not to be.

I still had the tapes, though; I still had the mountains of notes I made at the earliest possible moment after each conversation, and I still had all those marvelously warm memories. I had planned in a vague sort of way to use them as the basis for a full-scale biography of Harry Truman, but at the time of his death last winter I decided I would never have the patience or make the time to do that. I am in my fifties, that dangerous decade (see the obituary pages of this morning's *Times*), and so, urged on by my friend Judy Freed, and with the assistance every step of the way of a brilliant young writer and friend, David W. Elliott,* I have organized them into this book.

It is a book about the thirty-second President of the United States in his own words and in the words of his friends; there is not an enemy anywhere in these pages. I have added a few observations here and there, and I asked all the questions, not that that was much of an accomplishment.

The justification for this volume, if such is needed, comes from Mr. Truman himself. He was talking about libraries, and he said, "The worst thing in the world is when records are destroyed. The destruction of the Alexandrian Library and also the destruction of the great libraries in Rome. Those were terrible things, and one was done by the Moslems and the other by the Christians, but there's no difference between them when they're working for propaganda purposes.

"Now as for the Presidency, every piece of paper a President signs, every piece of paper he touches even has

---

* Elliott is the author of the critically acclaimed *Listen to the Silence* and *Pieces of Night* and the forthcoming *A Flaw in My Character*.

to be saved. You take Lincoln and Fillmore. Millard Fillmore's son burned all his father's papers because he was
ashamed of his father, who had come from the very bottom line right to the top. And Robert Todd Lincoln
burned about half to two-thirds of his father's papers for
the same reason, because he was ashamed of him. A
thing like that ought to be against the law."

If every piece of paper the President signs or touches
is important, surely these wide-ranging conversations with
Harry Truman are essential to our history. I also happen
to think, perhaps immodestly, that the voice of Harry Truman that emerges from these pages is louder and clearer
than it has ever been.

And as I say, during the summer of Watergate, there is
a special kind of purity in what he has to say. Mary Mc-
Grory wrote some years back: "Since Harry Truman left
town almost nobody has spoken his mind. Mr. Truman
took the tradition of plain speaking back to Missouri with
him."

Now the purists may wonder how accurate Mr. Truman's memory was when we talked, and didn't he touch
things up a bit at times to give himself a more heroic
stance? The answer to both questions is yes, possibly. Mr.
Truman told it the way he remembered it, no doubt giving
himself the benefit of as much doubt as with his basic
honesty he could. I figured ten years ago and do now that
at seventy-seven a man who'd been through what Mr.
Truman had been through was entitled.

So, as I think Mr. Truman would have said, the hell
with the purists. There are already hundreds of books and
there will be hundreds more to clear up those small details
that Mr. Truman and his friends may have misremem-
bered.

I should perhaps warn the unsuspecting that a possibly
disproportionate part of this book deals with the memories
of people who knew Harry Truman when he was growing
up, knew him as a farmer, when he was a captain in Bat-

tery D, as an unsuccessful haberdasher, and as a man who needed a job and although he had no special aptitude or taste for it went into politics.

I do not apologize for that disproportion, if such it is. By listening to the voices of those people who knew Mr. Truman before 1935, when at the age of fifty he went off to Washington for the first time, the reader may gain some insight into why, being the kind of man he was, he was able to do what he did between that January and the January in 1953 when he and Bess came back to Independence.

In the Preface to the first volume of *Abraham Lincoln, The Prairie Years,* Carl Sandburg wrote, "Perhaps poetry, art, human behavior in this country, which has a need to build on its own tradition, would be served by a life of Lincoln stressing the fifty-two years previous to his Presidency. Such a book would imply that if he was what he was during those first fifty-two years of his life it was nearly inevitable that he would be what he proved to be in the last four."

To understand Harry Truman you must understand something about Independence, in particular the Independence in which he grew up. Mr. Truman was fond of saying that to him Independence was what Hannibal, Missouri, was to Mark Twain. He liked to quote what Twain said late in his life in a speech in India, "All the *me* in me is in a little Missouri village halfway around the world."

And Mr. Truman would add, "I wouldn't think much of a man that tried to deny the people and the town where he grew up. I've told you. You must always keep in mind who you are and where you come from. A man who can't do that at all times is in trouble where I'm concerned. I wouldn't have anything to do with him."

When Harry Truman was growing up, Independence was still pretty much of a frontier town. There were men who proudly said that they had helped Quantrill when he made his murdering raid on Lawrence, Kansas. There were others who remembered Jesse James, or said they did. And people spoke fondly of Frank James, who for a time was a prisoner in the town jail.

That jail changed hands five times in the bitter border war between Kansas and Missouri that started long before the rest of the Civil War. There were also people still alive who had been in what Harry later in these pages calls "concentration camps" in Kansas City, interned there by the Federal troops. Harry's mother was among those internees, and she, not surprisingly, thought it was a good thing when Lincoln was shot, and when at ninety-two she broke her hip and shoulder after tripping in her kitchen, Harry, who was then President, flew out to see her. She looked up at him from her bed of pain and said, "I don't want any smart cracks out of you. I saw your picture in the paper last week putting a wreath at the Lincoln Memorial."

Mary Jane Truman told me that when their mother said things like that, she was joking. It doesn't really matter one way or the other. She was a woman of great spirit. She taught her son to do what was right, and he never forgot it.

But in his boyhood Independence was not an easy place for a little boy who wore glasses, who always had his nose stuck in a book, whose contemporaries can scarcely ever remember seeing him without a music roll under his arm (". . . of course, they called me *four-eyes* and a lot of other things, too. That's hard on a boy"). The thing about Harry Truman is that he never forgot what it was like being a kid who was lonely, who was teased, who because he might break his glasses never played any games with his brother, Vivian, and the boys of the neighborhood.

And because he remembered, he was marvelous with children. When I was in Independence, his favorite hours were those spent in the auditorium of the library when it was filled with children. He would, for instance, tell them what it had been like during the summer of 1787 when those fellas, the Founding Fathers, met to write the Constitution. The fellas really came alive when Harry de-

scribed them. Washington and Alexander Hamilton and
Madison and old John Adams. It was never like that in
school.

One day he read them the opening paragraphs of one
of his favorite books, Catherine Drinker Bowen's *John
Adams and the American Revolution:*

"On the Fourth of July, 1826, America celebrated its
Jubilee—the Fiftieth Anniversary of Independence.
John Adams, second President of the United States, died
that day, aged ninety, while from Maine to Georgia,
bells rang and cannon boomed. And on that same day,
Thomas Jefferson died before sunset in Virginia.

"In their dying, in that swift, so aptly celebrated
double departure, is something which shakes an American to the heart. It was not their great fame, their long
lives or even the record of their work that made these
two seem indestructible. It was their faith, their bound-
less, unquenchable hope in the future, their sure, immortal belief that mankind, if it so desired, could be
free."

As he read that day, there was a grandeur in Mr. Truman's voice that I had never heard before and, for that
matter, never heard again. And while he was far too modest a man to say it, even to think it, there was at least one
person in the auditorium that day who thought that Harry
Truman shared with those two monolithic figures of our
past a feeling of indestructibility. I know that he shared
their hope in the future as well as their sure, immortal
belief that mankind, if it so desired, could be free.

At the end of Mr. Truman's speeches there was always
a question period, and on one day I like to remember the
last question came from an anxious small boy with red
hair whose ears had grown up, but not his face.

"Mr. President," he said, and his future and the world's
depended on the reply, "was you popular when you was
a boy?"

The President looked at the boy over the glasses that
always made him look like an irritated owl. "Why, no,"

he said, "I was never popular. The popular boys were the ones who were good at games and had big, tight fists. I was never like that. Without my glasses I was blind as a bat, and to tell the truth, I was kind of a sissy. If there was any danger of getting into a fight, I always ran. I guess that's why I'm here today."

The little boy started to applaud, and then everybody else did, too. It was an eminently satisfactory answer for all of us who ever ran from a fight, which is all of us.

Later the dejuicers asked me to—their wishes were often commands—see to it that that question and the answer be removed from the tape "before any public use is made of the tape." "Especially the sissy part," said one of them.

I refused. As I say, I'm fond of that moment. We need more Presidents who have run from fights and admit it. We must run from more fights. That's our only hope.

Yes, when Harry was growing up, Independence was a rough town, but having said that, I must add something else. It was also a town in which people read books and listened to music, and at "supper"—that was and is at five, five thirty at the latest—they discussed ideas. As Ethel Noland put it, "There was conversation. I mean by that talk about what was going on in the world, talk about ideas."

America was not then and is not now, as a high school classmate of mine once put it, "a great big, oblong statistical blur, which is what most people in New York seem to think."

True. Thought and literacy are not confined to a narrow strip of land on the Eastern seaboard. Read in these pages the weekly activities, since her retirement, of Miss Noland. And consider Mr. Truman's friends the three Chiles sisters, anxiously wondering why it is that nobody reads Dickens and Thackeray anymore.

In school Harry and Charlie Ross, who when Harry was President was to become his press secretary, were both fond of Latin, and during the whole of one April they spent every spare moment, along with Elmer Twyman, who came from a family of doctors, building a bridge that was said to be an exact replica of one of the bridges that Caesar built across the Rhine. They had found a description of the bridge in Caesar's *Commentaries*.

Harry and Charlie Ross and Elmer Twyman knew a lot about Caesar, and, of course, Harry went on to be President, and he was able to make some use of that knowledge:

"His [Caesar's] big trouble was that he didn't know when to stop. As I've told you, Alexander suffered from the same thing, and you'll find men like that all through history, most recently, of course, Hitler, and if we'd let him get away with it, Stalin had the same thing in mind."

I don't know about Elmer Twyman, who became a doctor, but Harry and Charlie Ross were also fond of the works of Cicero, and for a time they worked on their own translation of some of his works. "The good of the people is the chief law. . . . The harvest of old age is the recollection and abundance of blessings previously secured."

Harry and Charlie never finished the translation. Charlie went off to the University of Missouri, and Harry, whose father, John, had fallen on bad times—he was a man who failed at things—had to take a job in what was called "the zoo" of a bank in Kansas City, salary $35 a month.

"Old Cicero," as Harry called him, "his full name was Marcus Tullius Cicero, you know," wrote: "If you aspire to the highest place it is no disgrace to stop at the second, or even the third."

Harry never aspired to high place, but he got it, and he described it the way he described everything else in terms that were, I suppose, corny, but elemental as well, simple, pure: "That job I had in the White House, it wasn't so very different from other jobs, and I didn't let it worry me. Worrying never does you any good. So I've never worried about things much. The only thing that I ever do worry about is to be sure that where I'm responsible that the job is properly done. I've always tried my best and to some extent have succeeded in doing the job as well as it's been done before me.

"When I was in school, I used to always sit around for a week or two . . . I skipped a grade or two while I was going through school . . . before I found out what it was all about, and then I'd go on from there."

When you got that job as you call it in the White House, you didn't really have any time to sit around and find out what it was all about.

"No, no. Like I told you, I was sworn in one night, and the next morning I had to get right on to the job at hand. I was plenty scared, but, of course, I didn't let anybody see it, and I knew that I wouldn't be called on to do anything that I wasn't capable of doing. That's another thing you learn from reading your history. People in the past have had much bigger burdens than you've ever been asked to assume, and somehow, the best of them just went ahead and did what they were called upon to do. And they usually made out all right."

Yes, *remarkable.*

Early in 1962 it became painfully apparent that the networks were not interested in what we then called *The Truman Series.* A cardinal reason for the lack of interest on the part of the networks was that Harry Truman was then still "a controversial figure." The fearsome years of the blacklist were not yet quite over. And Mr. Truman somehow intuitively sensed that long before the rest of us were ready to admit it.

While I was still seeing him with some regularity in Independence, he made a trip to Los Angeles, where he spoke at one of the universities, and I had been briefed by Noyes on an incident that happened off campus. I said, *Mr. President, I understand that you had a little exchange with General Sarnoff* [then chairman of the board and president of the Radio Corporation of America, which, of course, includes the National Broadcasting Company] *out in Los Angeles.*

The President was delighted that I'd heard. He said,

"Yes. We both got on the same elevator at the Beverly Hilton Hotel out there, and I looked down, and he'd broken his leg. Or his toe. I forget which. But it was in a big cast and was all bandaged up.

"I just looked at him kind of sideways, and I said, 'Well, General, I guess now for a while you'll have to kick people in the ass with the other leg, won't you?' He was so nervous that he got off at the next stop, although I don't think that's what he had in mind doing."

That particular session ended with what I guess you'd call the sound of general merriment. The President laughed the most of all; he almost always did.

No, Harry Truman was not impressed with wealth and power. One day I said, *Mr. President, I understand you had a little exchange with Henry Luce at the time he published your* Memoirs *in* Life *magazine.*

"That's true. I did. His magazines never did tell the truth about me. And in 1948 during the campaign they took all those pictures at places I spoke trying to prove there weren't any crowds turning out for my speeches, which was a damn lie, of course. They say pictures don't lie, but they do. Pictures can lie just as much as words if that's what the big editors and publishers set out to do.

"And those Luce magazines are just too damn big anyway. They've got too much power over people and what they think, and I've always been against that. And the big publishers have always been against me. It started out with the Kansas City *Star.* It was always against me, and I guess it still is, although they had to admit when I was presiding judge that I'd done some good things for the county. But as I say, big publishers, I've always been against them, although maybe I shouldn't say that because my son-in-law, who is just the nicest boy he can be, is associated with a big paper himself, the New York *Times.*

"But what you asked me about. Old Luce and I met at the time *Life* magazine had agreed to buy the *Memoirs,* and there was a party given to celebrate.

"Luce and I were introduced, and he said he was very glad to meet me. I said, 'Mr. Luce, a man like you must have trouble sleeping at night. Because your job is to inform people, but what you do is misinform them.'

"Well, old Luce got red in the face, and Sam Rosenman came up to me—he was Roosevelt's friend and mine and he was one of the lawyers in charge of drawing up the papers—and he came up to me and said, 'Harry, be careful. We haven't signed all the papers yet. If you make him mad, maybe he won't sign up.' I said that wasn't true, that Luce needed us a hell of a lot more than we needed him, and in the end it turned out that was true.

"I talked to Luce once more that same night. A little later, maybe when I was leaving. I don't remember. He came over, and he said that he thought if he and I just had the time to talk things over, we'd find we agreed on most things.

"I told him I doubted that very much, and I did, and I I still do."

The last time I talked with Mr. Truman was in a projection room in New York. I was leaving the following day for Spain, and some friends were giving me a farewell party that night. Without telling me, they had sent a note to the Carlyle asking the President to attend.

They thought it would be great fun if he walked in unannounced. "After two drinks," they said that night, "everybody would have thought he was that actor in *Call Me Madam*. They'd have started slapping him on the back, and. . . ."

When I found out about the invitation, I was embarrassed, but I needn't have been.

"I'd very much like to come," said the President. "But the Boss and I are leaving for Independence this evening. Please apologize to your friends for me.

"We don't get out very much when we're in New York," he said.

I almost had the feeling that maybe he would have liked to come.

Was I going to Spain to write a book?

Well, I said, not exactly, though out of my experience

might, I hoped, come several books. Actually, though, I was just going to look and loaf.

For how long?

"Three months," I said, "maybe a little more, maybe a little less."

The President made no comment, but by then I knew enough about him to realize that he was shocked at the idea of a man in his forties taking three months off to "look around and loaf."

I thanked him for his patience and said that I hoped all the time we spent together wouldn't turn out to have been wasted.

"It couldn't possibly be," said the President. "I think you learned a little something, and I enjoyed teaching it to you. I've told you, if I hadn't got into this other business, I might have turned out to be a teacher, and if I do say so, I don't think I'd have been so bad at it."

That was the last time I spoke to the President. The last time I saw him was in September, 1969. I was in Independence to write a profile of the town for *Holiday,* and at the library I was told that he saw almost nobody anymore and except when the weather was good no longer went on his morning walks. Miss Sue Gentry, the gentle woman who until her recent retirement had been writing about the Trumans for the Independence *Examiner* since 1929, always with affection, had seen him a few mornings before, and the sight had saddened her. "He used to be such a joyful man. No matter where he was or what he had to do, even in the White House, he was never too busy to make a joke. But now—" She hesitated a moment to choose the exact words. "There is no smile in him anymore."

I saw the President the last day I was there.

It was a little after 8 A.M., and the September air was immaculate. About half a block from the Truman house I saw the President coming toward me. He had shrunk in size, as old men do (I was told he weighted fifty pounds less than when he was in the White House, less certainly

than when I had talked with him), and his clothes hung
loosely on the frail body. He was walking very slowly, no
longer the one hundred and twenty-two steps a minute
he'd learned in the Army and followed so many years
thereafter. He was leaning on the once-jaunty cane as if
without its support he would fall. His head was bowed, his
shoulders slumped; clearly, there was no smile in him
anymore.

I was across the street, and the President passed me,
and though shrunken, he still seemed to me to be very
large against the sky.

I did not call out to him. He would not have wanted
that. On the morning of his eightieth birthday he told
reporters, "Remember me as I was, not as I am."

Myself, I would remember a bitter cold morning in
November, 1961. It was below zero, and there was a hint
of snow in the air. The President had just returned from
visiting his old friend Sam Rayburn, who was Speaker of
the House longer than any man in American history. Mr.
Sam was dying of cancer at his home in Bonham, Texas.
The news had been an awful blow to the President. He had
said sometime before with, I felt, a mingling of rue and
regret, "It sometimes seems to me that all I do anymore
is go to funerals."

In any case, when he returned from Texas, he looked
very much older and sadder.

On this particular inhospitable morning the inept film
crew, every member of it, gathered outside the house at
219 North Delaware at 4:30 A.M.

Miss Gertrude Stein may have been perfectly right
when she said that a dawn can be very beautiful depending
on which end of the day you see it from. But surely she
was speaking of Parisian dawns, summer Parisian dawns.
A November dawn in Independence was not beautiful,
never ever.

But we were through some miracle ready when, as
planned, the light went on in the President's bedroom. A
few minutes later he was to appear at the front door, come

down the steps, pick up the morning newspaper, and go back inside the house.

When the door opened, however, Mrs. Truman came out on the porch. She said that the President was not feeling well, and she was afraid he wouldn't be on hand for the walk we had been planning to film later that morning. Moreover, she was certain that he would not be able to come to the library for the filmed interview we had set up for that afternoon.

The director thanked her and quietly dismissed the crew.

After I'd had breakfast, I went out to the library to do some research. I was sitting in a room next to the President's office when, at a few minutes after eight, he walked in.

The pink complexion was white, and his eyes were tired and faded. He came up to me and said, "I'm very sorry I wasn't out there this morning."

There were sudden tears in my eyes, but I managed to say, "That's all right, Mr. President. You were ill."

"I know," he said, "but I like to live up to my obligations."

1

The Happiest Childhood

One week in Independence I didn't talk to anyone who was less than seventy-five years old, and it was one of the pleasantest weeks of my life. People live a long time in and around Independence, and they have long memories. What's more they seem to have, all of them I talked to anyway, something in common with Mr. Truman. They have character.

I guess my favorite among them was Miss Ethel Noland, who was then seventy-nine years old, two years older than the President. She had lived her entire life in a house across the street from 219 North Delaware. Miss Noland, the Truman family historian, was a retired teacher, and if her sentences seem to have a certain sweep and grandeur to them that is perhaps because she not only read Gibbon's *Decline and Fall of the Roman Empire* with frequency, but also read, for pleasure, mind you, *The Iliad* and *The Odyssey* in the original Greek.

The only uneasy time I had with Miss Noland was when I had to tell her that it would be necessary for me to reach inside her bodice to hook up a throat microphone that she was to wear during one filming session.

I mentioned the matter to her with suitable diffidence, and after a moment she smiled and said, "Oh, that's quite all right. I do have a male doctor, after all, and this is almost the same thing, isn't it?"

I asked Miss Noland how she managed to keep busy since her retirement. That was not really a problem, she said. There was, first of all, her diary. She had been keeping it daily for more than sixty years. I said that that would surely be a valuable historical document, but Miss Noland said, "Oh, no, I have no intention of allowing it to be published, even should someone wish to do so. I kept it for my own satisfaction only, and that is the way it will remain. We are all very private people around here."

In addition to keeping the diary, Miss Noland went on, there were the meetings of the Historical Society, the Browning Society, the Tennyson Club, the group that discusses current events, and the Mary Paxon Study Class. That's for ladies who find themselves going stale."

In addition, she was taking a course in modern drama taught by a young professor from the University of Kansas City. She mentioned having read the plays of Beckett, Arthur Miller, John Osborne, and Ionesco. She liked both Miller and Beckett. Of Osborne she said only, "Are things really that bad in England?" Of Ionesco, "I'm very much afraid that he escaped me completely."

I asked if her class had yet read any of Tennessee Williams.

"No," said Miss Noland, with a saintly smile, "that we still have to look forward to."

One day I asked Miss Noland, *Do you think Harry Truman had a happy childhood?*

"Well, of course, happiness, that is not easy to say about anyone really, is it? It is so close to being an indefinable word, and one is never quite sure—is one?—whether one is really quite happy. But Mr. Truman and I are first cousins, and I have known him, have observed him all his life, and I should say that, yes, I believe he had a happy childhood and one that was secure. Secure in the love of those, his family first, of course, but all of those who knew him. His family were all of them loving people.

"It should, I believe, be pointed out that his early environment was not nearly as poverty-stricken as many of the biographers have for some reason felt it necessary to portray. I think he has suffered a little bit from the image that has been put before the public. The fact that he did not come from a very rich family has, I think, been exaggerated.

"What has not been pointed out is that they were always very comfortable, very free of financial anxiety.

"And, of course, the picture of Mr. Truman's mother that people have been given is simply not true at all. She has been portrayed as, I believe you could say, a country bumpkin, and that is simply not the case.

"Mr. Truman's mother studied art and music at the Baptist Female College down in Lexington, Missouri. She played the piano, and she had a most remarkable idea of the proper values in life. One of them was music. Another was books. If she thought that money should be spent for a piano or for music lessons, she spent it that way.

"She never deviated from her idea of what was right, and she didn't let her children do that either. She had just about the finest set of values I have ever known. She was the type of mother that you would think would furnish a President for the United States. Her principles were so sound. Her discipline was so fine that greatness seemed to grow out of it.

"These days more and more people are beginning to act like Jimmy Hoffa, and it sometimes seems to me that a great many people are beginning to look like him, too.

"There are many things about this modern time that are desirable and good and amazing. But there are things that are fine and substantial and eternal about the nineteenth century that we will do well to hold on to. And Harry Truman is very much a man of the nineteenth century. His mother I think represented the best of those values.

"She was a most unusual woman."

Mary Jane Truman: "I suppose all of us think that we have . . . a most unusual mother, but I think it truly can be said that our mother was a very fine woman. I don't believe that she had an enemy in the world, and even after my brother Harry got to be President, she couldn't resist inviting everybody in. If anybody came to our door, why, they were always welcome. Mamma would go to the door, and regardless of who they might be, she would ask them in. And sometimes we had a little difficulty because people who came were sometimes not what they should have been mentally. So we decided it was time to put up a fence and have the gate locked.

"Sometimes it wasn't really very convenient. But it was

really the best thing that could have been done under the circumstances because my mother was in her nineties, and we just had to protect her from everybody seeing her, although she didn't like it at all. She just wanted to be friendly with everybody in the entire world.

"When my mother and I went to Washington not long after Harry got to be President, my brother went to the plane to take her out, and when she saw all those people, she said, 'My goodness, Harry, if I'd known this was going to happen, I wouldn't have come.' Of course, everybody quoted that, and we all laughed at her, and everybody thought she was serious. But I saw that she had a twinkle in her eye, and she had a fine sense of humor just generally, and a lot of the time when people took her seriously, she was making a joke. I don't know why people couldn't see that."

Harry Truman: "When my mother and sister came to Washington at the time I was . . . in the White House, my brother had told my mother that the one bed that was not occupied was the one in the Lincoln Room, and she said, 'You tell Harry if he tries to put me in Lincoln's bed, I'll sleep on the floor,' and she would have. But I had reserved the Rose Room, which is where the queens and princesses and everybody stay, and I took her back there when she arrived, and my sister was with her. And I said, 'Mommy, here's your room.' And there was a great four-poster bed that takes a stepladder to get into—it's that high above the floor—and she looked at me and said, 'Harry, do you expect me to sleep in that thing? Is that the only bed you've got in this big house?' I said, 'No, there's several more.'

"She went around and looked in the adjoining room where the maid to the queens and princesses and that sort of thing stayed, and there was a nice little single bed in there. She said, 'That's where I'll stay,' and she did.

"She was always a woman who did the right thing, and she taught us, my brother and sister and I, that, too. We were taught that punishment always followed transgression, and where she was concerned, it always did. I was punished, and it hurt, and I tried never to do whatever it was again. They say that isn't the way to do it now, and they may be right. I don't know. All I know is that's the way I was brought up."

Judge Albert A. Ridge of the U.S. District Court in Kansas City and a veteran of Battery D: "Harry Truman grew up in a society in which a man's word was his bond. If a man's word could be trusted there was no place he couldn't go. Nobody around here ever doubted Harry Truman's word.

"When Harry was a boy, it seems to me there was more a sense of moral values than there is now, more a sense of community life. Harry Truman was brought up in that kind of life—as almost all of us were, even though we lived here in Kansas City instead of in Independence. What I'm getting at, when someone on the block got sick, my mother would go and take care of them. And if she would get sick, the neighbors would come and take care of her.

"And we weren't too proud to go next door and borrow a cup of sugar. And if we had anything that the people next door needed, why, they were welcome to it. That was the sort of era I'm talking about. Mr. Truman grew up to be a man who's devoid, I think—as men generally were in those days—of an ability to hide their faults and pretensions under that cloak of public attitude that so many public men take refuge in. Harry Truman never learned to put on a public face, and he never had a public manner. He just never learned how to be anybody except himself."

Mr. President, Judge Ridge says that in this part of the country a man's word was very important when you were a boy. A man had to stand by his word, and that's the way you were brought up.

"That's true. Unless you were a man who stood by what he said, you were not well thought of around here and you never got very far, never got anywhere at all in this part of the country.

"And you never had to sign a piece of paper when you made a bargain. If you made a trade with a man, if you said you'd take so much for so many head of cattle, why, that was what you agreed on, and if the fella you'd made the bargain with came along later, it never did matter how much time had passed or if the price might have changed in the meantime, you just lived up to what you had agreed on at that earlier time. That's what your word meant.

"In those days, in the time I was growing up and when I was a young man, people thought more of an honest man than any one thing, and if a man wasn't honest, he wouldn't stay long in the neighborhood. They would run him out.

"And I have never changed my mind since. You have to stick by your word. Trust is . . . why, it has always seemed to me that unless you can trust a man and he can trust you, why, everything breaks down."

You seem to be saying that trust is like a cement that holds everything together, holds society together.

"That's a very good way to put it, yes, trust is absolutely fundamental in every possible kind of relationship, and in government. . . . If the people can't trust their government, the people in their government, the whole works will fall apart."

Edgar Hinde, the former postmaster of Independence and a veteran of Battery D: "Around here if a man gives his word, we expect him to keep it, and Harry Truman always kept his word. I never heard of him breaking his word to anybody. When he told you something, you could go home and sleep on it. That was it."

Harry Truman: "I had just the happiest childhood that could ever be imagined. My brother, Vivian, and I and two or three of the neighborhood boys used to have a great time playing in the pasture south of the house out at Grandview. There was forty acres in bluegrass, and it had a little draw that ran through it, and there was a spring right in the middle. And we used to catch tadpoles and have a big time over that.

"It was a wonderful place for small boys to enjoy themselves. There wasn't any place they could go that they'd get lost, although once in a while one of them would wander over in the cornfield and get lost. I did myself. I had a dog, a little black and tan dog named Tandy, and I also had a big Maltese cat named Bob. The reason he was called Bob is that he was sleeping in front of the fireplace in the old house one time, and a coal popped out and burned off his tail.

"Bob and Tandy always followed me everywhere I went, so when I got lost over in the cornfield, my folks could watch this dog and cat working in and out among the cornstalks, catching field mice. I must have been three and a half or four years old, and I suppose I got a good spanking for running away. I don't remember the spanking, but I do remember the trip through the cornfield.

"Those were most pleasant periods of time. We had a great big swing out in the backyard in one of the big old elm trees that was there. It's gone now. And we had a hammock made out of barrel staves that hung on the north porch. And even after we moved to Independence and began to go to school, in the summertime we would go out to Grandview and spend some happy times during the vacation, my brother and I together and sometimes each one of us by himself.

"Then the rest of the kinfolk, cousins who were about our size, usually would come out there, and we would have a real time when that happened, celebrating the Fourth of July or Christmas or whatever it happened to be.

"I once read some place that a happy childhood is a very, very rare thing, and I'm sure that that is true, but I can honestly say I had one. . . . Of course, we didn't have all the places to go and things to do that kids do now, and a lot of them don't see how they can get along if they don't have them. But I guess if you don't know what you're missing, you don't miss it, and so, of course, when I was a boy, we didn't have cars and movies and television and radio, none of that. We played. My mother played, and my sister and I played the piano, and we always had a houseful of books, and we read.

"And of course, we all had our chores to do, and we went to bed early and got up early and were always busy."

Were you ever bored?

"Oh, my, no. We didn't know the meaning of the word, and I'll tell you another thing. I can't remember being bored, not once in my whole life. How in the world can you be bored if you have things to think about, which I must say I always have?"

Mr. President, do you think those were better times, when you were a boy?

"Oh, I don't know about that. Comparisons like that. They're so easy to make, but I'm not sure they're ever right."

He thought for a moment, and then he said, "The only thing I'm sure of: People weren't so *nervous* then. All these things people have now that are supposed to entertain them and all. They just seem to end up by making everybody *nervous*."

Mary Jane Truman: "I don't think I could have had two nicer brothers than my brother Vivian and my brother Harry. And I suspect that maybe I took advantage of it just a little. I think they used to think I was kind of hard to live with once in a while. But my brother Harry always saw to it that I could go where I wanted to go. If there wasn't anyone else to take me, he would take me. I sometimes think that's why I never did get married. I just never met anybody who was as nice to me as Harry.

"When I was a baby, Harry used to sit on a rocking chair and sing me to sleep, and he braided my hair, and when I was outdoors, he wouldn't let me out of his sight. He was so afraid I'd hurt myself.

"He just couldn't have been nicer—and Vivian, too, of course.

"We played almost all of the games that children played in those days, and we all three had a horse to ride and did quite a bit of horseback riding. I remember one horse in particular—we called him Old Bill—and he wouldn't let the boys catch him. But I could go out and catch him in the pasture or anywhere else because I usually carried a biscuit or a piece of cake or something for him. He'd eat anything.

"He was the old buggy horse, and we drove him for years. We still had him when my brother Harry went to the First World War, and I drove him all during that time and then bought a car in the spring of 1919, shortly after my brother came home. But Old Bill was still there. We kept him as long as he lived."

One sunny summer afternoon Miss Mary Jane and I were standing on the tiny plot of land that was all that was left of the Truman home place at Grandview.

Most of the land had been turned into a neon-lighted shopping center that, naturally, is called Truman Corners. It was dominated by a large electric cat over a drugstore. The cat had malevolent brown eyes that lighted up at night, and it revolved endlessly behind the old barn in which Mary Jane, Vivian, and Harry used to play.

As Miss Truman and I stood in the field near the barn, the cat eyed us menacingly. An old C-47 groaned overhead, and there were the sounds and smells of trucks on their way to the grime and smog of downtown Kansas City. A voice on a loudspeaker shouted out a then-popular rock-and-roll song, and there was the competing noise of a disc jockey from the radio in a TV appliance store.

Miss Mary Jane listened for a moment.

"It used to be so quiet," she said, "and you could plow the north eighty without taking the plow out of the ground. It's all changed so much."

She looked around again.

"Well," she said. "That's progress. At least they say it is."

Ethel Noland: "Of course, really to understand Mr. Truman's boyhood, you must be aware that he was always reading. Just everything. He had a real feeling for history, that it wasn't something in a book, that it was part of life —a section of life of a former time, that it was of interest because it had to do with people.

"And I think that Harry had a sense of history during his entire career, that what he was living through was making history, not in a spectacular way. It was just a section of life. I think he understood a great deal about what it meant to be President that a person would not understand who had not had his background and his sort of boyhood and young manhood—serious but not dull. Thoughtful is the word that I would use. Harry was always thoughtful."

Henry Chiles, a childhood neighbor of Harry Truman: "Kids are always having an argument, and any kind of knowledge—well, Harry generally had it, and we didn't. We'd save up questions for him when he wasn't there. We'd play Dalton and the James gang, and Harry would set us straight on how many bank robbers there was and how many Daltons got killed. He'd tell us that. We didn't know. We didn't care. We was just shooting each other.

"And Harry always got good grades. Now don't ask me about mine because I just got by. That's probably the reason Harry got to be President and I'm just an old dirt farmer."

Morton Chiles: "I'm ashamed to admit it now, but we used to call Harry a sissy. He wore glasses and didn't play our games. He carried books, and we'd carry a baseball bat. So we called him a sissy."

One afternoon when I was discussing the decision to intervene in Korea with *General Omar Bradley* he said:
"President Truman was always reading things. I've been at his office when he was President at practically all hours, from six in the morning to as late as eleven o'clock at night, Saturdays, Sundays, weekdays, and I almost always found him at a desk with a bunch of papers in front of him, studying those papers.

"Now I know some people think that's going into too much detail. But from my own experience I found that even though I might be commanding a large unit, I had to know enough of the details to get a true picture of the big picture—the big problem. And I think that that was one of the attributes of President Truman. He always knew enough of the details to know what the big problem was.

"I did find him one time not behind a desk. This was about eleven o'clock at night when I took a message over to get clearance on it. I found him in his dressing room, reading a book. Before I left, I commented that I was glad to find him not working but reading a book. And he held up the book for me to see. The subject of it was the economics of government. So I still didn't catch him dead-beating it. He was thinking about his job."

Dean Acheson, Mr. Truman's Secretary of State, said, "Mr. Truman read, I sometimes think, more than any of the rest of us. It was never necessary to *digest* anything for him, to simplify, to make it understandable to the . . . shall I say *meanest* intellect. Mr. Truman read the documents themselves, and he understood and acted on them. It was, I believe, the habit of reading and, moreover and possibly more important, of *understanding* that followed all through his life, from his boyhood on."

I mentioned to Mr. Acheson that I had read that General Eisenhower wasn't much of a reader except for the Western novels of Zane Grey, and he said, yes, he had heard that, too, and added, "I doubt very much if a man whose main literary interests are in the works of Mr. Grey, admirable as they be, is particularly well equipped to be chief executive of this country—particularly where *Indian* affairs are concerned.

"Of course literacy is not an absolute essential for the Presidency. So far as I know it is not anywhere written into the Constitution as a requirement, but somehow, I do feel more *relaxed* with a *literate* man in the White House."

Mr. President, can you remember a time when you haven't read?

"No, I can't, not unless I was sick, and even then if I could manage it, I'd prop up a book and read on the sickbed. I read the Bible clear through twice before I went to school. My mother taught me to read, and my father, too, of course. I guess I read the Bible because the type was large, but then it developed about the time I was six years old, it was then that we first noticed it, that I had flat eyeballs. So my mother took me to a doctor, and he tested my eyes and gave me a pair of glasses, and I've worn them ever since.

"But glasses or not, I never stopped reading. I've never regretted it either, and I suppose considering the fact that I became President of the United States, it wasn't time wasted.

"And as I think I told you yesterday, when I was about ten, my mother gave me a little blackboard on the back of which was a column of about four or five paragraphs on every President up to that time, which included Grover Cleveland. And that's how I started getting interested in the Presidency and in the history of this country."

I mentioned that someplace not too long before, President Kennedy had made a speech in which he listed a whole series of books he had read recently. I said that to my knowledge Mr. Truman had never done that.

"Well, no. I never thought reading was something you went around bragging about. It was just something you did. And when I was a boy you kept as quiet about it as you possibly could. Reading wasn't any too . . . wasn't the most popular thing to do around these parts."

Mr. President, tell me about your first job.

"Well, when I was ten, maybe eleven years old, I got a job at Jim Clinton's drugstore on the northeast corner of the square in Independence. I had to get there at six thirty in the morning and set up the place so that when Mr. Clinton came down, he would find everything in order. I'd mop the floor and dust off the bottles and wipe off the counters, and then I'd wake Jim Clinton at seven."

Did you ever have any early-morning customers?

"Oh, yes, a great many. The people who were church members, the high hats in town, the ones who were afraid to go into a saloon and buy a drink, they'd come in, and I'd have to set out a bottle of whiskey, and they'd pay a dime for a drink before most people were up and around to see them. They'd put their dimes on the counter, and I'd leave all those dimes there until Mr. Clinton came in, and he'd put them in the cash register.

"All those fancy high hats, they'd say, 'Harry, give me a drink,' and I'd do it. And that's where I got my idea of what prohibitionists and high hats are. That's the reason some of them didn't like me. Because they knew I knew their background and their history.

"There were saloons all around the square, and the tough old birds who didn't give a damn about what people think, they'd go into the saloons and buy a drink when they wanted it. But as I say, the so-called *good* people, the fancy ones, they'd come in and buy a drink behind the prescription counter from a boy who didn't have any right to sell it to them.

"But that's the way I got to . . . well, feel a lack of respect for the counterfeits, and I don't care where they are. In Washington or wherever. There's a story they tell about this high hat that got to be Postmaster General of the United States. I think Mark Twain told it on him.

"He got to be Postmaster General, and he came back to his hometown to visit, and there wasn't anybody at the station to meet him but the village idiot. And the high hat wanted to know what people in the town had said when they found out he was Postmaster General.

"And the village idiot said, 'They didn't say anything. They just laughed.'

"That's what happens if you're a high hat and start taking yourself too seriously."

Do you think you ever did that, Mr. President?

"I tried not to. I did my level best not to, and if I had, the Boss and Margaret wouldn't ever have let me get away with it."

Mr. President, I understand that when you were still a boy, you got a job working as timekeeper for the Santa Fe Railroad.

"I worked for an old fellow named Smith, L. J. Smith his name was, and he was head of the construction company that was building the double track for the Santa Fe Railroad down here from Eaton Falls to where the Missouri Pacific comes into the Santa Fe down at Sheffield.

"I was eighteen years old, and I'd just finished high school and knew I wasn't going to get to go to West Point. So I took this job as a timekeeper. I took it to help out at home, to keep my brother, Vivian, and my sister, Mary, in school. My father was having a hard time with finances just then.

"Old man Smith had three camps, and there were about a hundred hoboes in each camp, and I got very well acquainted with them. My job was to keep tabs on them, to keep track of how much time they put in, and then I'd write out their paychecks for them. I'd usually write those checks in a saloon on the north side of the square in Independence here, a saloon called Pogunpo's or in old man Schmidt's saloon in Sheffield. I used to sit there and pay off those hoboes. And they weren't bad fellows. They'd work for two weeks. They'd get discounted if they drew their checks before that time. So they'd work two weeks, and then they'd spend all their money for whiskey in the saloon and come back to work the next Monday morning. I'd pay them off on Saturday night.

"But they weren't bad fellows. Not in any way. Most of them had backgrounds that caused them to be hoboes. Either they'd had family troubles or they'd been in jail for some damn fool thing that wasn't a penitentiary offense. But they weren't bad citizens at all. I remember one time I told the old man that ran the saloon, he was an old Dutchman and wore whiskers, I told him, I said, 'This old bastard is the blacksmith out there on the railroad, and we need him. So try to cut out on his whiskey.'

"Well, damn old Schmidt went out and told this blacksmith what I'd said, and I never got a better cussing in my life than I did for interfering with the freedom of an American citizen. And he was right. And that taught me something.

"But after that I guess the blacksmith was grateful for it because he took a file, a regular ordinary file about that long and made a butcher knife out of it and tempered it so that the edge would never come off. He made two of them for me, and I think one of them is still around the house somewhere. . . . So he didn't hold it against me that I was trying to keep him from getting drunk."

When you said camps, what were they, houses or tents?

"Tents mostly. There were tents, and I had a tricycle car on the railroad that I went up and down on. I had to make a list of the men that were working every morning at seven thirty, and then I had to go back at one thirty in the afternoon to be sure that they were still there. So when the time came for their being paid, I had the records. No one ever doubted the records I kept."

How much did those men make?

"They made eleven dollars for two weeks' work, and as I say, they'd get paid on Saturday, and by Monday morning most of them had drunk it all up. But it was one of the best experiences that I ever had because that was when I began to understand who the underdog was and what he thought about the people who were the high hats. They felt just like I did about them. They didn't have any time for them. And neither did I. I always liked the underdogs better than the high hats. I still do."

Weren't you ever uneasy? I mean, you were a reader of books and wore glasses and, as you say, you'd been called a sissy.

"No. No. I never had any trouble with those birds. They were just as nice as they could be, and when I left, the foreman down there in Sheffield said, 'Harry's all right from the navel out in every direction.' Which when you come to think of it is just about the highest compliment I ever have been paid.

"Some of those hoboes had better educations than the president of Ha-vud University, and they weren't stuck up about it either. The average of them was just as smart as the smartest people in the country, and they'd had experiences, and a lot of them told me about their experiences. I hope I profited from it, and I think I did. I had to quit at the end of the summer, but my goodness, that was a great experience for me."

I understand you learned a few cuss words that summer.

"I did. The words some of those men knew I'd never heard before, but later when I was in the Army, there was an occasion or two when those words came in handy, and I used them.

"That experience also taught me that the lower classes so called are better than the high hats and the counterfeits, and they can be trusted more, too.

"About this counterfeit business. My Grandfather Young felt the same way. We had a church in the front yard where the cemetery is now. And the Baptists and the Methodists and all of them used it. And Grandfather Young when I was six years old, he died when I was eight, he told me that whenever the customers in any of those denominations prayed too loud in the Amen corner, you'd better go home and lock your smokehouse.

"And I found that to be true. I've never cared much for the loud pray-ers or for people who do that much going on about religion."

Mrs. W. L. C. Palmer, retired teacher: "In 1898 Harry Truman came into my classes, taking Latin and mathematics, and also Bess Wallace was in the same class, and so was Charlie Ross, who was later Harry's press secretary.

"I had thought I was going to be a Greek teacher, but when it came time for me to go away to school myself, my father asked me where I wanted to go, and I said I wanted to go to Missouri University. 'Well,' he said, 'they dance and play cards down there, and you can't go.' So he sent me to a little Methodist school where I took four years of Greek and four of Latin and four years of mathematics, which were required before you could graduate.

"I came as a teacher of Latin and mathematics, and I remember in my first classes I had Nellie and Ethel Noland, cousins of Harry Truman, and they were both excellent pupils and both took Latin. When I finished college, I had thought I was going to be a Greek teacher, as I said, but I found there was no Greek in the local high school. But Nellie and Ethel were very much interested in Greek, so they organized a little private class, so I did have Greek for one year.

"I had Harry in my classes for the years 1898 and 1899 and 1900. And then I married the principal of the high school, Professor W. L. C. Palmer. And there was a rule against married teachers in the schools. So I'm sorry to say I wasn't a teacher the year he graduated. That was in 1901.

"The night they were graduated from high school—Harry, Bess, and Charlie Ross—Harry didn't get the highest grades, and he didn't win the English prize. Charlie Ross did, and at the end of the program, Miss Matilda Brown, the teacher of English, went up on the stage and kissed Charlie Ross. Harry Truman was standing nearby, and he said to Miss Brown, 'Don't I get one, too?' And Miss Brown said, 'Not until you've done something to deserve it.'

"Well, after Harry Truman became President of the United States, Charlie, who had been a correspondent for the St. Louis *Post-Dispatch,* became his press secretary. He wouldn't receive as high a salary, but nevertheless it was such an honor that he couldn't turn it down. And the first night they were together, Charlie said to Harry, 'Wouldn't Miss Tillie be glad to know we're together again?' And Harry picked up the phone and put in a call for Independence and Miss Matilda Brown, and he said,

'Miss Brown, this is the President of the United States. Do I get that kiss now?'

"And she said, 'Yes, come and get it.' But I understand that he never did go and get it, so Miss Brown told me. I think she was very much disappointed.

"The first high school paper was put out in 1901, and Harry had a good deal to do with seeing that it got out. When I think of the motto of that high school paper, *The Gleam*, from the poem *Merlin and the Gleam*, which had been published not too long before, in 18 and 89 I believe you will discover, when I think of that motto, I feel that Harry Truman all through the years of his life has followed that gleam, and I'd like to quote it for you:

> Not of the sunlight,
> Not of the moonlight,
> Not of the starlight!
> O young Mariner,
> Down to the haven,
> Call your companions,
> Launch your vessel
> And crowd your canvas,
> And, ere it vanishes
> Over the margin,
> After it, follow it,
> Follow the Gleam.*

"I believe that that is what Harry Truman has done his whole life through."

* Alfred, Lord Tennyson.

2

Some Ancestors

Mr. President, did your grandparents have slaves?

"Oh, yes. They all had slaves. They brought them out here with them from Kentucky. Most of the slaves were wedding presents."

Was that a custom at the time, to give slaves as wedding presents?

"Yes, it was quite common. When a young couple got married, they got a few slaves to start out housekeeping with."

How many would an average family have, would you say?

"Five or six. They'd have a cook and a nurse for the children and a maid-of-all-work. Then maybe they'd have a couple of field hands to go along with them."

Why do you think your grandparents came here?

"I don't know why except that they thought it was a good place to start a new life. As it turned out to be. . . . In those days, I'm speaking of the 1840's now, Independence was where people who were going West made their equipment secure and got ready to start. The trails all began here, the Santa Fe Trail and the Oregon and the Mormon trails. They all started here in Independence."

Why here?

"It was convenient. The Missouri River makes a big bend up here, about ten miles from here, and there was a landing place a little east of what is now Courtney. Then it was called Blue Hills.

"Then they had a landing place west of Courtney called Wayne City Landing, and Independence built a railroad from Wayne City Landing to the city up here. That was the first railroad west of the Mississippi River. We used to play out there when I was a youngster. They only tore up the last part of that old railroad in the 1890's."

Mr. President, what kind of people came up and down the river in steamboats? Or were there steamboats?

"All the best sort of people came here by steamboat. All my ancestors came out here that way. The steamboats plied regularly between Wayne City Landing and St. Louis, and my grandparents got on the Ohio River at Louisville, and the steamboats ran from Louisville to St. Louis. Then they changed boats, and the Missouri River boats ran from St. Louis to Wayne City Landing and eventually to Westport Landing at the foot of Grandview Avenue in Kansas City.

"Solomon Young and grandmother, Harriet Louisa Young, came here in 1841, and my other grandfather, Anderson Shippe Truman, came a few years later."

I read in Jonathan Daniels' book, The Man of Independence, *that it was in 1846.*

"That book is filled with a lot of bunk; I don't know what got into Daniels. He used to work for me when I was President, and he worked for Roosevelt, and I liked him. But when he wrote that book, he just seemed to go haywire in places.

"But if he said it was 1846, it probably was. He got most things like that right. . . . Now they say my grandmother, my maternal grandmother, Mary Jane Holmes, got here first and went all the way back to Shelbyville to find my grandfather and marry him. . . . Anyway, they got married back there, although they say my great-grandfather, William Truman, was against it. I don't know the truth of it.

"But all four of my grandparents did originally come here from Kentucky. They may have known each other back there. I'm not sure. They came from Shelbyville in Shelby County. But whether they knew each other or not, they became very well acquainted when they got here. They eventually settled as neighbors no more than three or four miles apart. And a distance like that made them close neighbors in those days.

"In those days you could enter land, buy it for a dollar twenty-five an acre, and most of those old pioneers entered a hundred and sixty acres, but both my grandfathers entered more than that.

"Grandfather Young kept buying land wherever he could get his hands on it, and at one time he owned five thousand acres out in the southwest corner of Jackson County. He also owned almost the whole of what later became Sacramento, California. He owned about forty thousand acres of land, although it was in Spanish leagues, I don't know how many leagues it was. But forty thousand acres, and if you go back far enough you'll find his name on the title of nearly every lot in Sacramento. It was just a bit ranch at the time he owned it, and he had to sell it because one of the partners of his wagon train went broke, and my Grandfather Young had to pay off his debts."

Mr. President, if he hadn't sold that land, I guess you would have been born rich.

"I guess that's true, but people who spend too much time thinking about things like that are likely to wind up feeling sorry for themselves. So I haven't given it much thought. . . . Anyway, if I'd been rich, I wouldn't have wound up President."

And given a choice. . . .

"I didn't have a choice. What's your next question?"

Yes, sir. How did your Grandfather Solomon Young get out all the way to Sacramento, California?

"Well, he was quite a man, a great big man with a beard, and he could do pretty much anything he set his mind to, and mostly he did. He ran a wagon train from here, from Independence and Westport to San Francisco and Salt Lake City and places like that. He'd have a wagon pulled by a dozen oxen or maybe that many mules, a huge wagon that could haul tons of freight, and there would be as many as twenty-four or thirty of them in a train. And the train would take all that goods to the West."

I believe Chief Justice Warren referred to that in his speech dedicating the library.

"He did. He spoke of my Grandfather Young, and he said that on trips like that, and I can quote him, on trips

like that 'the timid never started and the weak died along
the way.' And I don't see how it can be denied. Those trips
took a year at a time. They'd start one spring and they
wouldn't get back until the next. But Solomon Young did
it time and again."

Did he ever have any trouble with the Indians?

"I never heard him say that they bothered him. There
were two or three trainmasters that the Indians didn't disturb, and he was one of them. They were afraid of him.
That's why. They knew he had the ammunition and the
guns and he would shoot them if they commenced to
bother him."

Did he ever take your Grandmother Young with him?

"No, she never did go. She stayed here and raised a
family. They had nine children, seven of whom lived to be
grown. My Grandfather Young was out West in 1861
when she had to cook all those biscuits for Jim Lane's
Red Legs.*

"She was a strong woman, had the prettiest red hair I
ever saw on anybody, and there wasn't a thing in the
world that ever scared her. She lived until I was more than
twenty-one years old. She was ninety-one, and she was one
of the most charming ladies I have ever encountered."

*The other day Miss Ethel Noland said that your Grand-
mother Young was just as stern a taskmaster as your
mother. Taskmaster is Miss Noland's word.*

"As she always is, Miss Noland was perfectly right.
My Grandmother Young laid down the law, and nobody
ever questioned it. There was no need to. In those days
what was right was right, and what was wrong was wrong,
and you didn't have to *talk* about it. You accepted it."

*You never argued with either your mother or your
grandmother when they told you to do something?*

"Never. Not once. Oh, maybe when I was very young,
but I always got spanked for it."

Your mother spanked you?

"Of course she did. When I misbehaved, she switched

* See Chapter 4, *Independence and the War Between the
States.*

me, and I never thought anything of it. She didn't do it unless I deserved it."

Did your father ever spank you?

"No, never, but he got mad at you over something or other, he could give you a scolding that would burn the hide off of you. I'd rather have taken the licking."

How about your Grandmother and Grandfather Truman?

"Well, of course, my Grandmother Truman had been dead a long time. She died in 1879, and so none of us ever knew her. My Grandfather Truman was a farmer. He had two hundred acres of land out at Hickman's Mills. He was a very quiet man, and the two of us were very fond of each other. I was very fortunate when it came to my family. We were all very close.

"My Grandfather Anderson Shippe Truman had three girls and two boys, and when they were all married off, he sold his farm and went to live with my mother and father until he died. He died when they were running Solomon Young's old farm. And then we moved to Independence.

"We moved to Independence in 1890, and we came here so that Mary and Vivian and I would have the benefit of graded schools. They just had an old one-room schoolhouse out at Grandview, and my mother wanted us to go to graded schools, which, of course, we did. When we moved, I was six years old; my brother, Vivian, was three, and Mary Jane was one year old.

"We lived in a house on Crysler Street, and we always had a lot of livestock, cows and chickens and pigeons and everything of that kind, and the boys in the neighborhood always liked to congregate in our yard, front and back. My mother was always kind to them. She was always on the side of the boys if any of them got in trouble."

Did you ever get in trouble when you were a boy?

"Very, very seldom. I was too busy. I told you I'd read all three thousand books in the library by the time I was fourteen years old. And I went through the grade schools of Independence and the high schools, and I must have learned something that prepared me for what happened later."

Did you have any juvenile delinquency when you were growing up in Independence?

"We never heard of it. We didn't know anything about it because there was no advertising medium to tell us about something like that.

"We had bad boys but no bad girls. The girls were all above reproach and decent, but we had boys who were terrible. They usually came through all right, though, and some of them graduated at the head of their classes.

". . . But I was too busy reading books to be bad. Now the only reason you read books is so you'll get a better insight into people. The thing I found out from reading was that there is damn little information in most schoolbooks that was worth a damn. If you wanted to find out why France was against England during the Revolution and the why and wherefore of Jefferson's being able to buy Louisiana, you had to go and look it up for yourself. It didn't matter how good your teachers were. They never taught you things like that.

"And you had to find out for yourself that no two smart men ever agree on anything. Never. No two historians ever agree on what happened, and the damn thing is they both think they're telling the truth.

"But you had to find that out for yourself and that somebody with authority has to make them understand that their viewpoint and the other viewpoint can be brought together and an agreement can be reached.

"It takes a politician to do that, not a historian."

How would you define a politician?

"Why, a politician is a man who understands free government. That's all the definition there is. When he understands free government, he's a politician. If he doesn't understand it, he's a Mugwump or something, somebody who likes to cause trouble."

It seems odd, feeling as you do, that you didn't want to get into politics.

"Well, I never did. I got into politics by accident. In

1922 I had gone broke trying to run a haberdashery store, and I had to have a job. And I had a lot of good friends in Jackson County and was kin to everybody else, and so I ran for eastern judge, one of five, and I licked all the rest of them because I knew more people in the county than they did. That's all. . . . It's getting lunchtime, and the Boss is expecting me. I have time for one question more."

Mr. President, getting back to your Grandfather Solomon Young for a moment, I understand that in 1948, when you were speaking in towns of the West, you often mentioned that he had stopped his wagon train in that town. Somebody, some newspaperman, said that if Solomon Young had made that many stops, it's a wonder he ever got to Sacramento at all.

The President laughed. "Well, he never kept a record of where he stopped that I know of, and so I may have let my imagination go a little wild there every once in a while."

After all, he made several trips.

"Yes, he did, and on one of them he made a deal to sell some goods to Brigham Young, the founder of the Mormons. That was in Utah, and you can bet I made some use of that incident when I was campaigning in that state."

Do you think your grandfather would have minded?

"Of course not. He was a horse trader, you remember, and so was my father."

I understand that in 1940, when you were running for reelection to the Senate, one of your opponents said that Solomon Young was a Jew.

"Yes, they did. It wouldn't have mattered a speck if he had been, but he wasn't. They said he was a Jew, and they foreclosed the mortgage on my mother's farm. Why, there wasn't anything they didn't do to try to defeat me that year. And that's why when 1948 came along, nothing surprised me. I'd already won in 1940 against the worst campaign I can ever rightly remember. . . . But I can't get into any of that now because the Boss will skin me alive if I'm any later."

3

John Anderson Truman

Harry Truman's father was born in Jackson County in 1851 and died there in 1914 at the age of sixty-three. He was at one time or another a mule trader, a farmer, a night watchman, a grain speculator, and a road supervisor. He was a small, feisty man, fastidious in dress and manner. Everybody called him Peanuts, and while, like his son, no one ever questioned his word, he was never a financial success. He dreamed always of the lucky break, of sudden wealth, but it didn't happen.

I asked Ethel Noland if she had ever heard him lament his fate. She said, "The Trumans have never been a lamenting people."

One day I said, *Mr. President, it's quite obvious that your mother was a great woman.*

"And don't overlook my father. He was just as great as she was and had every bit as much influence on me, although my mother was naturally the one that took care of the children in the home and saw to it that they grew up in the right way.

"But my father was a fighter, and if he didn't like what you did, he'd fight you. He was an Andrew Jackson descendant, you understand, and those people are all fighters. He was five foot six and weighed a hundred and forty pounds, and he'd whip anybody up to two hundred if they got in his way.

"I've told you about counterfeits. Well, there was an old fellow who was one of the greatest orators in this part of the country. We called him Colonel Crisp. His name was Crisp, and he was a colonel by agreement. He was a real counterfeit, though, and people never did trust him.

"I was with my father when he drove out to old Crisp's place, and I held the lines, and my father said, 'Colonel, I've come to collect for that nine cords of wood. Twenty-seven dollars. Three dollars a cord.' And old Crisp says, 'You oughter have better sense than to sell me anything like that, John. You know I never pay my bills.'

"The old man hopped out of the wagon and said, 'All right. I'll take it out of your hide then.'

"Crisp says, 'Wait a minute, John. I'll pay you,' and he did. . . . He made one of his great speeches down at Lone Jack where we went to picnic the other Sunday. He was telling all about how the Battle of Lone Jack took place, and there happened to be an old man there, Abe Koger was his name. He was a friend of my father's, and he said, 'Colonel, that didn't happen that way. I was there, and I know what took place. You've misrepresented the facts.'

"Old Crisp says, 'Goddamn an eyewitness anyway. He always spoils a good story.' And then he went right on with his speech. It didn't bother him a bit. He ran for Congress time after time, but he never made it. People knew he was a counterfeit, and they wouldn't vote for him."

Did your father ever take you to hear any political speeches when you were a boy?

"Oh, yes. He never liked to miss a political meeting, and he often took me along with him. There used to be some big political meetings in this county. Before they got these things (the microphone) and the radio and the television. I remember the first good political story I ever heard. My father took me, and it was a speech by a Congressman named William S. Cowherd, who was from Kansas City. The meeting was in the southern part of the county, and there must have been—oh, I guess there were two thousand people there, and that was a good many for that time.

"I remember Cowherd talked about how the Republicans had ruined this country with their tariff acts and one thing and another. Then he proceeded to tell a story. He said an old fellow from out in these parts went to New York for some purpose, and they took him to one of those fancy restaurants, and then they brought him a bowl of consommé, and he looked at it and then drank it. And they brought him a couple stalks of celery, and he ate that, and then they brought him a lobster, and he called the waiter over and said, 'Look here, young feller, I drank your dishwater, and I ate your bouquet, but I'll be damned if I'll eat that bug.'

"And Cowherd said, 'That's what the Republicans have had to eat all this time.' [Laughter.]"

There weren't many Republicans in these parts when you were a boy.

"Not very many, and the ones there were had the good sense, most of them, to keep their mouths shut about it."

Were you always interested in politics?

"I was always interested. I didn't become old enough to vote until about 1908 or '09, but I was always a clerk of the election at the Grandview precinct in every election, and the Republican judges always depended on what I had to say about the situation because they knew I knew all the people and what they were fitted for and things of that kind. We had one old man in the neighborhood who was a Socialist, and it was necessary to count those votes the same as the others.

"But at one time there were two, and one of the judges said to me, 'Harry, do you reckon that old man voted twice?' And I said, 'No, his son's at home.'"

I understand that you feel you learned a good deal about politics from Plutarch's Lives *and that your father read it aloud to you when you were a boy.*

"He did. We saved our dimes, threw them into the tray of an old trunk, and they accumulated faster than you'd think even in those days, and then my father sent away, or maybe it was my mother, but one of them sent away, and we got the nicest set of Shakespeare you ever did see and a book of Plutarch's *Lives*. It had a bright-red cover, and you're right. My father used to read me out loud from that. And I've read Plutarch through many times since. I never have figured out how he knew so much. I tell you. They just don't come any better than old Plutarch. He knew more about politics than all the other writers I've read put together.

"When I was in politics, there would be times when I tried to figure somebody out, and I could always turn to Plutarch, and nine times out of ten I'd be able to find a parallel in there. In 1940, when I was running for re-election to the Senate, there was this big apple grower named Stark trying to beat me. I'd started him out in politics, but in 1940 he was out to lick me, and I couldn't figure it out.

"But the more I thought about him, the more he reminded me of what Plutarch said about Nero. I'd done a lot of thinking about Nero. What I was interested in was how having started as well as he did, he ended up in ruin. And Plutarch said the start of his troubles was when he began to take his friends for granted and started to buy his enemies.

"And I noticed some of those same traits in old Stark. That's how I decided I could lick him, and I did, of course. Nobody thought I could, but I did. I'll tell you about that campaign at another time. . . .

"But about Plutarch. It was the same with those old birds in Greece and Rome as it is now. I told you. The only thing new in the world is the history you don't know."

"I'll always be grateful to my father for introducing me to Plutarch. The things you happen on at an early age like that stay with you for the rest of your life."

Wasn't your father at one time an overseer of roads in Grandview?

"He was, and he was a good one. At the time every man in Missouri had to give two days' work or six dollars a year to keep up the roads. Now most of the overseers took the money, put it in their pockets, and let the roads go to hell.

"That sort of thing happens all through politics, the fellow who holds out his hand for a little money, a little bribe. And it always takes two, the briber and the bribee, and I don't know who is worse.

"It was the same when I got to be the chief presiding officer of the county. I came out of county government after ten years' service a damn sight worse off financially than when I got in, and it was the same in the Senate. There were bribes all over the place, and when I got into that committee work that I'll tell you about, during the war. Why, at one time or another I could have picked up a dozen fortunes. A lot of money was lying around loose in those days, billions of dollars, and the main people who weren't getting any of it were the kids who were off doing the fighting. They weren't getting rich; they were getting killed.

"I sent a few people to the penitentiary because of that, including two brigadier generals. I think the two of them are still over there at Leavenworth.

"But as I say it's the same in every branch of government. There are those who hold out their hand, and there are those who don't. My father never took a dishonest dollar in his life.

"And he was a determined cuss. One day, when he was road supervisor, there was a big boulder across the road, and he lifted it off all by himself. He wouldn't let his crew help him. That's the kind of man he was.

"Well, it hurt him, and when we finally got him to go to the doctor . . . the hospital, it was too late. I was with him when he died. I dozed off, and when I woke up, he was gone.

"I'll never forget him, though. He was quite a man."

Mr. President, I read some place that you had started to buy some Black Angus cattle for the farm at Grandview when your father died, but that you had to sell them to pay off the doctor's bills. Is that true?

"Yes, that's true. I had some Black Angus cattle, and I had to sell them, and I never owned any again. I've had a few setbacks in my life, but I never gave up. I went right ahead and did what was required of me. After my father died, somebody had to run the farm, and so I did it."

Were there other things you'd rather have done?

"Oh, there may have been, but I didn't give it any thought, because what would have been the use of it?"

Didn't you succeed your father as overseer of the roads?

"I did, and I didn't get any richer either. We just had good roads. In those days Grandview had the best roads in the county."

Would you say your father was a success?

"He was the father of a President of the United States, and I should think that that is success enough for any man."

Independence and the War
Between the States

As I've said, to understand Harry Truman it is necessary to understand Independence. One morning early on during our conversations I said that when I first came to Independence I'd expected that it would be rather like my hometown, Marshalltown, Iowa.

"Oh, no," said Mr. Truman. "Marshalltown is the Middle West, and Independence isn't like that at all. I've been in Marshalltown, though, several times. It's a fine town, and you've got that fine cemetery.

"I think it's hard for people in the Middle West to understand what the Civil War was really like in a place like Independence and how it divided people and left scars you might say both . . . it scarred up both the land and the people, too.* It left scars, and some of them it

---

* Historian Albert Castel has said of that war in American Heritage, "We like to think of the Civil War as the last romantic war—as a sort of gallant duel between gentlemen. There was a certain aura of 'swords and roses" in the East, but west of the Mississippi, that neglected area of Civil War history, quite a different atmosphere prevailed. Here the fighting was grim, relentless, and utterly savage—a 'battle to the knife, and the knife to the hilt.'

"Nowhere was this more true than in the bloody war-within-a-war that raged along the Kansas-Missouri border. There the people did not even wait for the bombardment of Fort Sumter. As early as 1855, armies of proslavery 'border ruffians' from Missouri and Anti-slavery Kansas 'jayhawkers' clashed in the fierce struggle which determined that Kansas would enter the Union as a free rather than as a slave state.

"This prelude to the Civil War engendered a mutual hatred and bitterness which, in 1861, flared into vicious reprisals and counterreprisals. As one Kansan later remarked, 'The Devil came to the border, liked it, and decided to stay awhile.' Led by Jim Lane, Charles Jennison, and Don Anthony, Kansas raiders swirled through western Missouri, looting, burning, and killing. Missouri 'bushwhackers' in turn made quick, devastating

took seventy-five years and longer to fade away, and in some cases I'm not at all sure they have to this day.

"Of course the people around Independence were very much involved on the Southern side of the thing, the Confederate side. The war here was a border war, what you might call a two-state war between Missouri and Kansas. The Federal troops, troops from Iowa and from Kansas, came in and wantonly destroyed houses, burned every house that they could get to and took everything out of it, furniture, fixtures, everything. My grandmother used to say, 'They stole everything loose that they could carry.' "

Mary Jane Truman: "When the Federal troops came to my Grandmother Young's house, they demanded food, and so my grandmother made biscuits. And I've heard her say that she made biscuits until her wrists were blistered from working with the dough and rolling the dough out. And then they killed hogs and just took the hams and the better part of it and left the rest.

"And I have a quilt. It was the first one that my grandmother pieced after she was married, around 1839 I think it was, and it's a beautiful old quilt, but the Federal troops took that out into the barn lot, and it was kind of wet, muddy weather, and they played cards on that quilt.

"It had to be washed so hard that it ruined the colors in the quilt, but the quilting. . . . You can still see . . . it's a star . . . what they called a star quilt, and it's a beautiful old thing. It's a keepsake but, of course, not what it would have been had it not been abused like that.

"I think I have heard my grandmother say that the place was raided at least two times during the war. And my Uncle Harrison, who was a boy of about thirteen at the time, was hanged because they thought he was telling a story about where his father was. His father was freight-

guerrilla forays into Kansas. Soon a border strip forty miles wide was a no man's land of desolate farmhouses, brush-grown fields, and prowling gangs of marauders."

ing across the plains and had started, I think, before the war was declared.

"So he was on his way out West, but they tried to make my uncle say that he was with the Southern Army. He told them the truth, but they wouldn't believe him. So they hanged him about three times, and he said the third time he thought he was a goner. But they finally let him down, and he lived to tell the story.

"The Federal troops tried the same thing with my Grandmother Young, tried to get her to say that my grandfather was in the Army. But she told them the same thing that my Uncle Harrison did. So they finally went away, but it was a very difficult time for all the members of our family who were alive at that time."

Harry Truman: "They tried to make my Uncle Harrison into an informer, but he wouldn't do it. He was only a boy, but he wouldn't turn informer. They tried to hang him, time and again they tried it, 'stretching his neck,' they called it, but he didn't say anything. I think he'd have died before he'd of said anything. He's the one I'm named after, and I'm happy to say that there were people . . . people around at the time who said I took after him."

Mrs. W. L. C. Palmer: "Everybody around here was very much involved in the War Between the States. My father was a native of Virginia. His name was Hopkins Hardin, and when the war came on, he joined up immediately with the Army of Northern Virginia, which was the army of Robert E. Lee, and my father was assigned to Pickett's Division [General George Edward Pickett]. My father went through many battles, all the famous battles before Gettysburg, and then at Gettysburg he was in Pickett's Charge.*

* Pickett's Charge is one of the bloodiest and most famous battles in American military history. Pickett's division was held in reserve at Gettysburg until July 3, 1863, when it led the attack on Cemetery Ridge. Three-quarters of Pickett's men were left dead or wounded in the field after the charge.

"I've heard him describe that charge so many times . . . until I can just see it. How they laid down in a wheatfield most of the morning until the order came to charge, and they did. They got up and charged. They had to go over a picket fence that they didn't know was there. I guess it was concealed by the wheat. And they were making for what was called Cemetery Ridge when my father was wounded. He'd been wounded twice, but the third time he fell on the battlefield, and he knew that General Lee's forces were defeated by the way the movement of the troops was going.

"He was on the battlefield for three days before he was found by the Sisters of Charity from Baltimore, who came out looking over the field. They took him to a hospital in Baltimore, where he recovered from a very severe wound in the hip.

"Federal officials, . . . officers from Washington, came out and asked him to take an oath of allegiance to the United States, but he refused to do it. Consequently he was kept in prison during the rest of the war, a dreadful prison down at Fort Pulaski in Georgia where there were six hundred men.

"He said he would have died if it hadn't been for my Aunt Lizzie McCurty, who had come out here to Independence in 1848. While he was in prison, Aunt Lizzie had sent him boxes of food. And when the war was over, in 1865, Aunt Lizzie wrote for him to come out here and not go back to his home in Virginia where everything was destroyed.

"So he came out here, and he met my mother, Susan Westmoreland, whose family had come from North Carolina. And they bought a farm south of town, the Pritchard Farm, and the old house is still standing there. I saw it a few days ago, and I was born on that farm, about five miles south of Independence in the year of 18 and 76.

"And of course, when I was a girl, everyone talked about the war and about the battle . . . the battles of Independence. Independence was captured three different times by the Federal troops and was recaptured each time.

The fighting . . . it was mostly guerrilla warfare, but in one battle . . . the Federal troops were very firmly entrenched in what is now the Christian Sawyer Bank downtown, and the Confederate troops were trying to take it. There were many shots fired on both sides. You can still see bullet holes in the bank where those troops fought, and then Quantrill, William Quantrill, came up, and he saw what was transpiring. And he said to whoever was in charge of the Confederate troops, he said, 'If you'll give me three hundred men, I'll get the Federal troops out of that building,' and he did. He got the three hundred men, and he drove out the Federal troops. Quite a number were taken prisoner, but the rest retreated to Kansas City. . . . But that is one of the reasons William Quantrill is a hero to many people in this part of the country."

William Clarke Quantrill was a dark, romantic-looking young man with hooded blue eyes who as a boy in Ohio was said to have enjoyed nailing snakes to trees and torturing dogs and cats; after he grew up, he emigrated to Kansas and then for unsavory reasons of his own crossed the border into Mr. Truman's Jackson County.

Among the many bloody exploits for which he was responsible was a raid on Lawrence, Kansas, during which almost the entire town was destroyed, including 150 men, most of them unarmed civilians.

As his men set fire to the town, Quantrill is alleged to have shouted, "Kill! Kill! Lawrence must be thoroughly cleansed, and the only way to cleanse it is to Kill, Kill."

That sounds like quite a mouthful to have been shouted from horseback at the beginning of a raid, but the evidence of Quantrill's bloodthirstiness is considerable. Historian Albert Castel has called him, "the bloodiest man in American history . . . in the company of Simon Girty and John Wilkes Booth as one of the great national villains."

On the other hand, the night before the Civil War conversation with Mr. Truman I was up until two drinking beer and sipping bourbon with an eighty-year-old admirer of both the President and Quantrill. The old man had a number of pictures of the President, one of them autographed, but an entire corner of his living room was devoted to a shrine to Quantrill. Among other items was a life-size photograph of him lighted the way some people light a statue of the Virgin Mary.

"If we'd had a few more like Quantrill, we'd of won the War Between the States," the old man said. "The history books are all written by Yankees. Why, Quantrill is one of the most misunderstood men in the War Between the States. I've known men who served with him, and they've said he wouldn't of hurt a fly if it wasn't that he was absolutely forced into it by the Yankees."

I asked Mr. Truman his opinion of Quantrill and his men, and he said, "I've told you that history is always written by the winners, and that's what happened in this case. In this whole border dispute the historians got only one side of it. As soon as the war was over, they had to justify what was done. Read up on the War of the Roses. It was the very same thing. It took hundreds of years before the real truth came out.

"There's a lot been written about what a terrible thing it was when Lawrence, Kansas, was destroyed, and it was a terrible thing. It never should have been allowed, but you hear very little about the towns that were destroyed here on the Missouri side, Osceola and Harrisonville and Independence. It's only now that the true facts are coming out, almost a hundred years, and it's a pity it took so long.

"But Quantrill and his men were no more bandits than the men on the other side. I've been to reunions of Quantrill's men two or three times. All they were trying to do was protect the property on the Missouri side of the line, and it was the same for the Red Legs. They were the Federal troops and were called Red Legs because they wore red leggings.

"And I've been to one or two of their reunions over in Kansas. I didn't let them know who I was, of course, but they were just the same as Quantrill's men. They set around telling lies to each other. Just like the reunions of the soldiers in the First World War and, I suppose, of every war there ever has been. The stories these fellas tell, they get taller and taller with every passing year, and after a time you can't believe a word any of them says.

"I remember one time when I came home from one of those reunions in Kansas, and my mother said, she was joking when she said, 'If you'd kept your eyes open, you'd probably have seen your grandmother's silver and you could have brought it home with you.'

". . . You can see that the War Between the States or the Civil War, whatever you want to call it, has had quite an impact on the people in these parts, and as I say, some of them aren't over it yet.

"And you have to keep in mind another thing. The Federal troops, after what happened over in Lawrence, a . . . General Ewing issued something called Order Number 11,* the order by which everybody in these parts was moved into what they called posts.

"There was one in Kansas City where all my family had to go.

"Everybody, almost the entire population of Jackson County and Vernon and Cass and Bates counties, all of them were depopulated, and the people had to stay in posts.

"They called them posts, but what they were, they were concentration camps. And most of the people had . . . were moved in such a hurry that they had to leave all their goods and their chattels in their houses. Then the Federal soldiers came in and took everything that was left and set fire to the houses.

"That didn't go down very well with the people in these parts; putting people in concentration camps in particu-

---

* General Thomas Ewing issued Order Number 11 in August, 1863, and Mr. Truman's grandmother, Harriet Louisa Gregg Young, loaded as many belongings as she could into an oxcart and with six of her children, among them Harry Truman's mother, made the long journey to a "post" in Kansas City. It was a journey that Martha Ellen Truman remembered all her ninety-four years.

lar didn't. And the general who issued Order Number 11 never did live it down. He was from Ohio, and he went back there after the war. And he tried to run for governor and for the Senate, but he never did make it.

"The Red Legs made people . . . tried to make people sign loyalty oaths, too, and that was just a bunch of damn nonsense as it always has been and always will be. You can't *force* people to be loyal by making them sign a piece of paper, and it was the experience of my people . . . my family that made me be against loyalty oaths. And I have always been, was when I was President and before and am now.

". . . But the bad feeling that these things cause dies a very slow death. I had to overcome some of that hatred when I was president of the National Old Trails Association,* which has branches from Baltimore to Los Angeles, and I had to go over Kansas on many occasions and got to know the people over there. And I found out that they didn't have horns and tails. They were the same kind of people as we have over here. . . . I've always felt that people were pretty much the same everywhere, but isn't it a pity that we have to be *taught* that?"

Mr. President, in view of the extreme Southern sympathies of most of the members of your family and most people you grew up with in Independence, in retrospect your civil rights program of 1948 now seems even more remarkable than it did at the time.†

---

* In 1925, after Mr. Truman's defeat in his second race for county judge, he needed a job; he was forty-one years old and, as he has said, "completely broke and without much prospect of being any other way." He first got a job selling memberships in the Kansas City Automobile Club and later became president of the National Old Trails Association, which involved traveling all over the country to promote the idea of building highways over the famous trails that had been so important in the various historical moves West.

† In 1945 Truman, against the advice and protests of almost every admiral and general, as well as most of his civilian advisers on military affairs, ordered the integration of the armed

"As you know, in 1948 some of the Southern states walked out of the Democratic Party, but I won the election without the Solid South and without New York. Nobody'd ever done it before, and it hasn't happened since.

"There was one old woman in 1948, one of the Democratic committee ladies from one of the Southern states; I forget which one,* and she said she was just sure I hadn't meant what I said in my message to Congress, and she wanted to go back down wherever it was and tell them I hadn't meant a word I said.

"Well, the first thing I did, I read her the Bill of Rights; I doubt that she'd ever read it, probably hadn't even heard of it.

"Anyway, I read it to her, and I says to her, 'I said what I said because I meant it, and I have no intention in any way whatsoever in taking back one word, and you can go back down there and tell them what I said. Those . . . the Bill of Rights applies to everybody in this country, and don't you ever forget it.'

"I guess I lost her support for sure, but I could . . .

---

forces. In December, 1946, Truman named a Committee on Civil Rights. The report of that committee was called "To Secure These Rights," and most members of his Cabinet advised him to forget all about it, at least until after the 1948 elections.

But on February 2, 1948, Truman sent a ten-point civil rights message to Congress, asking, among other things, for a federal law against lynching, a strengthening of existing civil rights laws, a Federal Fair Employment Practices Committee, an end to Jim Crow in interstate transportation, and the protection of the right to vote.

While these demands seem mild in 1973, in 1948 they created an uproar in the South that was unprecedented in American history.

* Mrs. Leonard Thomas, a Democratic national committeewoman from Alabama. In reporting a slightly different version of the incident in *The Man from Missouri, Life and Times of Harry S. Truman*, Alfred Steinberg adds, "A Negro White House waiter got so excited listening to the argument that he accidentally knocked a cup of coffee out of Truman's hands."

you can always get along without the support of people like that."

Mr. President, I've often wondered whether your experience in seeing the bitterness between Kansas and Missouri after the Civil War, the things we've just been talking about, had anything to do with your sponsoring the Marshall Plan after the Second World War.

"Oh, yes. Very much so. I think I told you the other day. You can't be vindictive after a war.

"After the Second World War, Europe had suffered in the same way we had suffered after the War Between the States, and that made me think that Europe had to be rehabilitated by the people who had destroyed it. And that's what happened.

"But we'll get into that tomorrow. I've got a date with the Boss in ten minutes, and she'll never let me hear the last of it if I'm late."

The President paused at the door, and he started laughing. He said, "I was just thinking of that old woman's face when I started reading her the Bill of Rights. It was quite a sight. . . . But you know something? It's not a bad idea to read those ten amendments every once in a while. Not enough people do, and that's one of the reasons we're in the trouble we're in."

Banking Days and Farming

Mr. President, in 1904 you went to work for the National Bank of Commerce in Kansas City, and in 1905 and 1906 you worked for the Union National Bank in Kansas City. Did you ever think of becoming a banker?

"No, I never did. I never liked it enough for that. I was good enough at it, I guess. I started out making thirty-five dollars a month and when I quit to go back to the farm, I was making fifty-five dollars a month, which was good money in those days. I still didn't like it much, though, and somehow it gave me a prejudice. Later I could never get myself to like very much people who make their living dealing with money. I don't like to say that, but I'm afraid it's true. We had this one old fellow, a vice-president I think he was, and he never did to my knowledge give anybody a raise. He kept a little book. I think it was a little book. Maybe it was all in his mind. But whatever it was, when anybody went to him for a raise, he could always remember something you'd done that he didn't like, and you never did get one. . . . Another thing I didn't like: I didn't have any responsibility. I just added up figures all day, and it didn't seem to me there was much of a future in it. . . .

"But that whole experience did cause me to realize that a lot of people in this world spend their time doing work they don't care much for, and that's a real pity."

I understand that you at one time lived in the same boardinghouse as General Eisenhower's brother Arthur.

"Yes, yes. We lived at a place called Mrs. Trow's boardinghouse, I believe it was called, and Arthur Eisenhower and I got along very well indeed. I'm sorry to report I can't say as much for his brother, the one you mention that went into the Army. It's too bad, too, what happened to him, because he had opportunities that no man I know had. But you take a man that has been educated in the professional military, especially if he comes from a section of the country where all the folks are plain folks the way that fellow did, it seems to go to his head some way or other. I don't know what causes it, but it's too bad. It oughtn't to happen.

"And then, when somebody like that gets into politics, it's even worse. They never make a go of it. You'll find that General Grant was in the same class exactly. Old Zack Taylor was, too, and so was Benjamin Harrison. As I say, I don't know how it happens, but when they get into politics, those fellows, all hell breaks loose; it kicks hell out of the country for a while, and it takes time to get over it."

Mr. President, several of your biographers have suggested that you have great admiration for military men and for the military. And one man whose name I won't mention suggests that the fact that you wanted to go to West Point proves it.

"Well, that's a damn fool thing to say, and whoever said it is a damn fool and I don't care how many degrees he has or even if he's a professor at Ha-vud (an epithet) College or some place like that. The only reason I wanted to go to West Point was because I wanted a free education; my father'd lost his money, and that was the only kind of education I could get. But because of my eyes, I didn't get to go, of course. So there's no point in getting into it. And even if I had gone, I'd have busted out in my third year probably when they started getting into the foreign languages. . . . The military man I liked best you might say was General George Marshall, and he'd have been a great man no matter what he was. It just wouldn't have mattered at all what he was; he'd have been the best there was at it."

Dean Acheson wrote: "The moment General Marshall entered a room, everyone in it felt his presence."

"Yes, that's true. He was one of the most remarkable men who ever lived, and one of these days I'm going to tell you about him. I never knew anyone like him and never will again."

Mr. President, didn't Theodore Roosevelt come to town while you were working at the bank in Kansas City?

"He did. It was in 1904 when he was President, and I went to hear him. I was working at the old National Bank of Commerce where the Commerce Trust Company is now, at Tenth and Walnut. Teddy made a trip to Kansas City and was scheduled to make a speech from the back end of a car at Tenth and Main, just a block down the street. When it came time for him to speak, half a dozen of us little clerks in 'the zoo' they called it, the cage where we worked, half a dozen of us left our desks and ran down the street to hear Teddy speak.

"He had a very high tenor voice, and it carried very well. He made a good speech, too, but nobody really wanted to hear him speak. They wanted to see him grin and show his teeth, which he did. He was a short man, only about five foot six. The Roosevelts were none of them very big people, and they all seemed to have a lot of teeth to show."

Did you like living in Kansas City?

"I liked some things about it. I went to every vaudeville show there was, and I saw some of the great ones, Weber and Fields and Eva Tanguay and Lillian Russell and 'The Four Cohans,' one of whom turned out to be the famous George M. Cohan himself. . . . I didn't have any too much spending money in those days. Arthur Eisenhower has been quoted as saying that after we'd paid all our expenses, we had a dollar left over. I don't remember how much, but I got a Saturday afternoon job either at the old Orpheum or the Grand as an usher, and I got to see the shows for free. I may have made a little bit extra, too. I don't remember. . . . I used to go to a lot of concerts in those days, too. People seemed to have more time to listen to music in those days."

Mr. President, speaking of music, I've read that when you were a boy taking piano lessons you got up at five every morning to practice. Is that true?

"Yes. When I was about seven or eight years old, we had a piano in the house, which wasn't usual at that time,

although my mother played. We had a piano, and I
wanted to learn how to play it. So I took a great many
lessons on it and finally wound up with one of the great
instructors in Kansas City. Her name was Mrs. E. C.
White, and I took two lessons a week and got up every
morning and practiced for two hours. . . . Mrs. White
had studied with a man, one of the great teachers of the
world, a man named Leschetizky, who was in Vienna and
who was the teacher of Josef Lhévinne and Paderewski.

"Paderewski was in Kansas City when I was about
twelve or thirteen and Mrs. White was giving me lessons
on various things, and I was studying the Chopin waltzes.
Chopin's A-Flat Opus 42 Waltz is one of the great pieces
of music for the piano, maybe the greatest, and I played
that, although never as well as I wished. . . . And I was
studying the Minuet by Paderewski. And when he got
through with his concert—which was a wonder—he
played that Chopin A-Flat Waltz, Opus 42, which has always been a favorite of mine. And he played the waltz
rendition of the 'Blue Danube,' and so on.

"When we went back behind the scenes, Mrs. White
took me with her, and it almost scared me to death. She
told him I didn't know how to make 'the turn' in his
minuet, and he said, 'Sit down,' and he showed me how
to do it. I played it at Potsdam for old Stalin. I think he
was quite impressed."

What about Churchill?

"I don't think he was listening. Churchill was a man
who didn't listen very often."

A few days later I said, *Sir, the other day, when you
were talking about Churchill, you said he didn't listen
very much. Could you tell me what you meant.*

"Well, he was more of a talker than a listener. He liked
to talk, and he was one of the best. But he didn't care
much for that kind of music.

"I was the only head of a state there at Potsdam. The
others were Prime Ministers, and so I always sat next to
the host. And the night Stalin was host I had some very
nice conversations with him. I liked him. I didn't like what

he did, of course, but I liked him. We talked about music. He was just like me about Chopin. He liked Chopin. Churchill didn't. He didn't care for that kind of music at all, and he told me that he wished I'd get up and go home because he couldn't do it until I did. But I stuck around there for a while because I was enjoying it, about an hour I guess. Stalin had some women from the Ukraine who sang and played the violin. It was quite a lengthy program."

Mr. President, did you ever think of being a concert pianist?

"Oh, I may have thought of it at one time or another, but that's as far as it ever went."

When did you give up the piano, studying the piano?

"About the time I was working at the bank I gave it up."

Why, Mr. President?

"Because I decided that playing the piano wasn't the thing for a man to do. It was a sissy thing to do. So I just stopped. And it was probably all for the best. I wouldn't ever have been really first-rate. A good music-hall piano player is about the best I'd have ever been. So I went into politics and became President of the United States.

"I guess it's too late to take it up now, playing the piano, although maybe I could become sort of the Grandma Moses of ex-Presidents."

Do you still listen to music?

"Oh, yes. I've got quite a collection of records. When I shipped them out of the White House, it took up most of the space in one whole truck. I guess what I've got most of is records by the great piano players of the world. Rubenstein, of course, and Horowitz. . . . And symphonies. Beethoven's First. I've got the Toscanini recording of that. And the Beethoven Concerto in D Major, the Francescatti recording with the Philadelphia orchestra."

Mr. President, do you ever regret giving up the piano?

"Young man, I've told you. I don't regret things like that. It's a waste of time."

When I'd recovered from that one, I said, *Mr. President, do you think Paul Hume knew much about music?*

"Not a damn thing. Not a goddamn thing. When he wrote what he wrote about Margaret in the Washington *Post*, he showed he didn't know a thing about music. He was just a smart aleck and a showoff. When she put on her singing program in Washington, it was a wonderful program. She was scared, of course, but she put on just the best program ever. And she had a nice young man for an accompanist who was a crackerjack. He played two or three pieces during the intermission.

"And then the next morning this Hume that you mentioned wrote the dirtiest, meanest critique you ever saw. And I wrote him a letter. I wrote him a letter saying that if I could get my hands on him I'd bust him in the jaw and kick his nuts out (chuckle). General Marshall thought that Margaret was his daughter; he was just crazy about Margaret. And when I told him what I'd done, he said, 'Well, I'm just as sorry as I can be that you couldn't get to him because that's what he deserved. He criticized everything but the varnish on the piano, and that's all that needed criticizing.' "

Mr. President, could you tell me a little about how you got the letter off? *

---

* It is generally forgotten that on the day of Margaret's concert, Charlie Ross, Mr. Truman's high school friend and his press secretary, died at his desk of a heart attack. Mr. Truman did not tell Margaret until after the concert.

Hume wrote, "She is flat a good deal of the time. . . . She cannot sing with anything approaching professional finish. . . . She communicates almost nothing of the music she presents."

As Bob Aurthur has written, "Now! You are Harry Truman, and you have a couple of problems: you'd surely like to destroy Douglas MacArthur, because on the front page of your newspaper the General, in the midst of a headlong retreat, is demanding the war be expanded into China; next, you want to lash out at a man you never heard of who, in the entertainment section of the same newspaper, is attacking your daugh-

"Why, I sent it by messenger, I guess, but I wrote it in long hand, and when he got to the *Post,* Hume—he didn't know much about *anything*—Hume couldn't believe it was from me, and he called in the music critic for the Washington *Star,* and they met in a coffee shop someplace, and Hume showed the letter to the man from the *Star.* He recognized my handwriting, but he told Hume he was sure I couldn't have written it, that it was written by somebody playing a joke.

"And then he went back to his office and wrote the whole story and scooped Hume [chuckle]. . . . I understand Hume's sold it. They tell me he's got several thousand dollars for it. . . . There was only one copy. I can't remember all that was in it, but it was pretty hot. When Margaret and Bess found out, they both wept and said that I'd ruined Margaret and I don't know what all. I said, 'Now you wait and see. Every man in this United

---

ter. Given the fact that you can do only one thing at a time, which item do you deal with first? Remember, it's before breakfast, and your best friend has just died.

"What Harry Truman did was snatch up a pen and pad of White House notepaper and address the following to Mr. Hume:

" 'I have just read your lousy review buried in the back pages. You sound like a frustrated old man who never made a success, an eight-ulcer man on a four-ulcer job and all four ulcers working.

" 'I never met you, but if I do you'll need a new nose and a supporter below. Westbrook Pegler, a guttersnipe, is a gentleman compared to you. You can take that as more of an insult than a reflection on your ancestry.'

"Refusing the advantage of his franking privilege—the note after all, was personal—Mr. Truman affixed his own stamp ("We still had 3 cent stamps in my administration"), went on his morning walk, and dropped the envelope in the nearest mailbox. Mr. Truman's vengeful words have been quoted in full here as they appear in the books, but Merle Miller has an audio tape where the former President says what he really told Mr. Hume was he'd 'kick his balls in.' After the incident Margaret said she was positive her father wouldn't use language like that. Surely not."

States that's got a daughter will be on my side,' and it turned out they were."

Mr. President, tell me how you felt when you went back to Grandview in 1906. I won't ask you if you regretted going back to the farm.

"I'm glad you're cleared up about that. There's nothing much to tell. In the year 1906 they needed me back on the farm, and I went. There was some talk that I wouldn't stay, but I did. I don't give up on what I start. I'm a stubborn cuss. They all found that out when I was President. I was stubborn. . . . I stayed on the farm until the war came, and I had to go. I could have got an exemption, of course, being a farmer, but I never even thought of it."

The farm must have been lonely compared with Kansas City.

"No, it wasn't. You say you grew up on a farm. You ought to know better than that. A farmer's life is not a lonely life at all. You have the best time in the world on a farm like ours. You've always got the stock to take care of, and you've got people coming in to talk to you about whether you can help them out in harvesting the wheat or planting the corn or whatever else is necessary in the neighborhood. I was very active in the Farm Bureau out there and later in the 4-H and other organizations of that kind.

"We had six hundred acres at the time, finest land you'd ever find anywhere. We raised everything—corn, wheat, oats, clover—and we rotated them. I was very much interested in the creation of things that come out of the ground.

"I helped my brother and my father to sow oats, plow corn, and sow clover. And in the long run we improved the production of the farm nearly fifty percent. . . . I had a gangplow made by the Henderson Manufacturing Company, and I used that with four horses or two horses and two mules, whatever we had available. That was the way we plowed.

"Then the land had to be harrowed, and I enjoyed that. It gave me plenty of time to think. Farmers really all have time to think, and some of them do it, and those are the ones who have made it possible for us to have free government. That's what Jefferson was writing about. Farmers have more time to think than city people do."

Mary Jane Truman: "Harry was always very particular about how he laid off the corn rows. He laid it so that you could plow it every way, crossways and straight, every way. And it was the same with the wheat. When he sowed the wheat in the fall, you almost never saw a skipped place where he had missed sowing the wheat.

"He was really very particular. He kept books on everything that he did, and he raised fine hogs and some very good cattle. He was just a good all-around farmer and proud of it. I think perhaps he might have enjoyed other things more. I wouldn't say for sure, but while he was on the farm, he gave it everything that he had, just as he did in everything that he went into."

Mr. President, suppose in those years you were on the farm, from 1906 to 1917, somebody had told you that someday you would be President of the United States. What would you have done?

The President laughed, not unkindly; he was never unkind. He laughed because he was amused. He said, "That's a damn fool question if ever I heard one. Who in the world would have done such a thing? It just never would have occurred to anybody.

"Nobody ever thought I was going to amount to much,* and that's why when people are always asking about the records of when I was a boy and so on, the answer is no-

---

* Miss Zuba Chiles, a retired schoolteacher, put it this way: "When Harry was in school, well, we all liked Harry, and he always got his lessons but never much beyond that, and we never thought—people deny it now; they say they knew it all along, his becoming President—but nobody did. Nobody thought that he'd go far at all.

"Not that we didn't like him. Harry was always just as nice as he could be, but that's another thing."

body kept any records because nobody thought it was
necessary.

"They say my grandfather, Anderson Shippe Truman,
said I was going to be President someday, but since he
died when I was only three years old, that doesn't seem
to me very likely. You know how people sometimes are
inclined to remember things after the fact."

*And you yourself were never tortured by ambition to
be head of the whole shebang?*

"No, no, no. Those are the fellas that cause all the
trouble. I wanted to make a living for my family and to
do my job the best I could do it, and that's about the size
of it."

6

On Battery D

One morning the President said that after lunch he was going to Kansas City.

"I've got to go in and see my haircutter at two thirty or something like that. My wife said it would be much better if I'd go to New York and get it done. She doesn't like my haircutter, but he's one of my boys. He's one of the Battery D boys, and so is my dentist and my tailor. You cain't quit them. You just cain't quit them.

"They're just like your family, your sisters and your cousins and your aunts. I had a hundred and eighty-eight men and a hundred and sixty-seven horses in Battery D, and my haircutter was one of my men, and I've stayed with him ever since. He's retired now, but he comes down a couple of days a week and takes care of the old-time customers, which I guess you might say I'm one of.

"Why, he cut my hair under a tree in the St.-Mihiel drive and the Meuse-Argonne drive, and he cut it under fire sometimes, and what are you going to do? You have to stick with them. What else is there to do?"

I guess what you do depends on the kind of man you are, Mr. President. Would you tell us a little about Battery D?

"Well, when I was still in Kansas City, I joined the old Battery B in Kansas City; it was a field artillery outfit, and we drilled once a week in the armory there."

I understand you had to pay twenty-five cents a week to drill there.

"We did. I believe that was for the upkeep, to keep it clean and so on, but I'm not sure why. I really don't remember.

"But I was a private in Battery B and finally became a sergeant and a corporal in that battery. And when the B Battery went to the border in Texas in 1916, chasing old Pancho Villa, well, I couldn't go because I was harvesting wheat and had a hundred and sixty acres that had to be cut, so they didn't require me to go to the border.

"But when the battery in Kansas City and Battery C here in Independence were expanded into a regiment, I helped to organize it. And it became the Hundred and Twenty-ninth Field Artillery, part of the Thirty-fifth Infantry Division, and I got a lot of those boys to join by promising them that if they'd join the artillery, they'd ride. But they never rode a mile. They walked every inch of the time.

"I'd expected to be a sergeant in F Battery when it was organized, but instead, they elected me to be a first lieutenant. In those days the enlisted men elected their officers.

"And after I got to be a first lieutenant, why, they sent me down to Camp Doniphan in Oklahoma. Near Fort Sill, the place where they kept that old Indian chief, Geronimo, in prison.

"They sent me to the school of fire down there, and they tried to give me . . . well, a college education in three months, and my head has never recovered from it since."

Mary Jane Truman: "When my brother Harry went off to enter the service during the First World War, he said I'd have to look after Mamma and the farm, and so I did. My brother Vivian was on another farm east of here.

"I ran the farm, but I did have one good man. He had a house down on the other part of the farm where he and his family lived. Our trouble was getting good help to help him. But we got through, and we raised wheat and oats and corn and came out very well with it."

Wasn't that pretty hard work for you?

"Well, not too hard. I didn't do any work in the field, of course, but I did help, and we cooked for the threshers and the hands that shocked the wheat and all that. Of course we didn't have the conveniences that you have today, you know, even in 1918, but it worked out just fine, and I got along."

Mr. President, didn't you meet Eddie Jacobson down at Camp Doniphan?

"Oh, no. I'd known Eddie long before that; I'd known him ever since I worked in the bank in Kansas City, and he was working in a clothing store, I believe, over at Eighth and Walnut streets. But we became very close friends when we opened the canteen down at Doniphan.

"Eddie was not in my battery. He was in Battery F. He was a sergeant in Battery F. And then the colonel gave me the job of canteen officer in addition to the other things I had to do, and I was dead sure he did it because he wanted to get rid of me. Because none of those canteens made money, and a lot of officers got in trouble with handling the money.

"But Eddie and I had the most successful canteen in the Thirty-fifth Division. We—Eddie and I went to Oklahoma City and got the merchandise we needed for the canteen, and every man in the regiment—there were eleven hundred men in the regiment—put in two dollars apiece, making a total of twenty-two hundred dollars. And within six months we returned their original investment and paid out fifteen thousand dollars in dividends.

"Then I had to go overseas, and Eddie ran the canteen from then on."

Eddie Jacobson's widow, Bluma Jacobson: "Before Harry went overseas . . . Well, Harry, had been a farm boy, but I believe he always wanted to go into business, and before he went overseas, he said to my husband, Eddie, 'If we come back alive and in good shape, let's go into business together.' And they shook hands on it.

"There was never anything signed. In all their relationship there was never anything signed. They just felt that close to one another that they could trust each other, which they did all through their lives.

"Once in the canteen they had some sweaters that they

wanted to get rid of, and the two of them let it out that they'd be doing the men in the battery a favor by letting those sweaters go at six dollars apiece.

"I've been told that those men were like a bunch of women at a bargain basement sale. They just mobbed the canteen and bought up every sweater there was. And later one of the officers was going over the books, and it turned out Harry and Eddie had only paid three dollars apiece for those sweaters, and so the profit was exactly one hundred percent."

Harry Truman: "I got kidded a lot about those sweaters, but I always said, 'Well, that's the reason we made a profit, and we were there for that purpose.'

"Besides, those boys couldn't have bought those sweaters anyplace else for less than fifteen dollars. So I was doing them a favor."

When you went overseas, you went to France.

"We went to France. We landed at Brest, France, on April 13, 1918, and just twenty-seven years later on that same day you may remember I spent my first full day in the White House.

"I told you. I went to a French artillery school, and then I went to Camp Coëtquidan for some more instruction in French artillery, and then in July—the rest of the Hundred and Twenty-ninth had come over by that time—in July the colonel called me in and told me I was going to be the new captain in charge of Battery D, which was known as Dizzy D, and it had, to say the least, a very bad reputation indeed. They'd had four commanding officers before that, and none of them could control those Irish boys. They were most of them Irish boys from Kansas City, many of them college boys from Rockhurst College, which is a Jesuit school in Kansas City. They were very well educated, many of them, but they were wild.

"I told the colonel; I said he might just as well send me home right then and there. I was never so scared in my life, not even later when we were under fire, but I—well, it was one of the things I had to do, and I did it."

Judge Albert A. Ridge of the federal district court in Kansas City, a veteran of Battery D: "The first recollection I have of Harry Truman actually taking over the battery was the day he succeeded Captain Thatcher.

"Thatcher had been well loved by all the men in the battery, and there was a general feeling of unrest, of anger when he was relieved of duty. The men in the regiment . . . in the battery just didn't want to lose Captain Thatcher, and when it was learned that Captain Truman had been assigned to Battery D, there was a good deal of talk about mutiny, about causing trouble.

"I remember it was at retreat when he came before the battery, and I can visualize even now the emotion of that time. There was a stirring among the fellows in rank. Although they were standing at attention, you could feel the Irish blood boiling—as much as to say, why, if this guy thinks he's going to take us over, he's mistaken.

"I think perhaps Captain Truman could feel it, too.

"He looked the battery over, up and down the entire line, about three times, and the men were all waiting for the castigation that they really knew they were entitled to receive from a new commander. Because of their previous conduct.

"But Harry Truman . . . he just . . . continued to look at them, and then . . . his only command to the battery was—*Dismissed.*

"Well, of course, the dismissed battery went toward their barracks. But I think that that command to that Irish group was a sort of benediction. He had not castigated them. He had dismissed them as much as to say—like the Good Lord said to Mary Magdalene, 'Go and sin no more.'

"From that time on I knew that Harry Truman had captured the hearts of those Irishmen in Battery D, and he never lost it. He has never lost it to this day."

Eugene Donnelly, a veteran of Battery D and a Kansas City lawyer: "We were a pretty rough bunch of boys; anyway, we thought we were. We'd already got rid of four commanding officers when Harry came along. He looked like a sitting duck to us. He was sort of small and with four eyes.

"And then he called all the noncoms together, and he said, 'Now, look, I didn't come here to get along with you guys. You're going to have to get along with me, and if any of you thinks he can't, why, speak right up, and I'll give you a punch in the nose.'

"He was tough, but he was fair; he was a good officer.

"I remember once a bunch of us were going to Paris on a furlough, and we didn't have any money. Harry found out about it, and he lent us the money we needed. We'd have done anything for him then, and nobody that I know has changed his mind."

Mike Flynn, a Kansas City livestock dealer: "I first got acquainted with Harry Truman in 1917. I was transferred from Battery D to Battery E, but I saw a lot of him during the war. He was very much respected.

"He used to get a lot of letters from the old Irish mothers of the boys in the outfit, and most battery commanders, company commanders, wouldn't pay any attention, but not Harry. I don't think he ever went to bed at night before he answered every one of those letters.

"I used to come in, maybe late, maybe toward nearly dawn even, and I'd see him in his tent writing letters, answering the letters he'd got that day.

"And he never changed. Even after he got to be President.

"In 1948, in December, 1948, we had a bad accident. My only son . . . he had just been married two years, and we were driving down here when a . . . when an oil truck skidded in front of us, and my son . . . he was very badly hurt, and he lasted . . . lasted only five days.

"And during the time that we were praying for his

funeral [clears throat] I received a telegram of condolence from Harry Truman. I don't know how he was notified. I don't think he ever was. I think he saw it in the paper.

"He told me later that he kept in close touch with things [clears throat] while my son lived, and I thought it was very kind of him to remember us at that time, when he was President of the United States and had just won the election. And he must have . . . I always felt that he must have had many other things on his mind as well.

"I would say. If you were to ask me, I would say Harry Truman was the kindest and most thoughtful man I have ever known. Bar none."

Eddie Meisburger, a veteran of Battery D and a retired Kansas City newpaperman: "The men trusted him to get them through the war and to get them back home. And he went out of his way to help them.

"That was illustrated I think by something that happened when we were on the march in the Vosges Mountains on our way into the St.-Mihiel sector.

"The men would be walking all day and leading their horses, and the infantry would ride by in trucks and yell at us to join the infantry and ride.

"Anyway, they were riding, and we were walking. And we were pretty well fagged out. And the colonel of the regiment came by, and by the way, he had a fine mount. He came down the road one afternoon and started sounding off about how we were just straggling along and were a sight to behold and so on, and he wanted to know whose outfit it was.

"Captain Truman was walking at the time because he had put his own horse into the harness to help pull the guns. That's how bad things were. They had to have that horsepower. So he was walking with us, and when the colonel came up, Captain Truman said that this was his outfit, Battery D.

"And the colonel said it was a hell of a looking outfit and that he wanted the men to be called to attention and fall in and double-time up a hill about half a mile or half a kilometer, it being France, away.

"Captain Truman realized that the men were out on their feet, and instead of giving the men a double-time order, he took us off the road, gave us a right turn, and took us into a forest with instructions to put the horses on the picket line and to bed the men down.

"And he said that he would go down and see the colonel, which he did. And he risked a court-martial by his action. But he told the colonel that his men weren't going to go any farther. They were going to rest that night. And he said if the colonel wanted his job, why, to court-martial him.

"The result was, he came back with the orders that we'd stay right there that night, and the whole outfit bedded down.

"The next day word spread around that he'd gone to bat for us, and things of that nature happened all the time.

"And it has been the same way in civilian life. Men have gone to him; they still do. Men from Battery D. Only the other day a certain man from the outfit needed some help, and I went to Mr. Truman and told him, and he said that he always had a lot of people from his old outfit who came crying on his shoulder when they needed help, and he said that he had that shoulder ready to help them. And that in this case he would do what he could. And he did. He always does what he can."

Mr. Meisburger, I understand there's a bottle of 3-Star Hennessy somewhere. Could you tell me about that?

"It's customary in all outfits to . . . most of them have a 'last man's club,' and these clubs have something put away, generally a bottle of some refreshment for the last man to drink.

"In this case there's a bottle of 3-Star Hennessy which was purchased in France in 1919, when we held our first reunion after the Armistice. I don't know whether it was a contribution from the outfit or who purchased it. But we know that it is still in existence, and Harry Truman has vouchsafed us that it is in good hands. Locked up in a box in a vault. And we know that if it comes to a show-down, that bottle is there.

"We're sure that it is because Harry Truman told us that it is."

Edgar Hinde, a veteran of Battery D and the former postmaster of Independence: "He was a wonderful officer. I don't . . . I would never have described him as tough, but he was thoughtful. He always saw to it that his men were well taken care of. Where he was concerned, his men came before everything, and in the Army I've always felt that that's about ninety-five percent of what makes a good officer."

Mr. President, can you tell me about the Battle of Who Run?

"What they called . . . what the men called the Battle of Who Run. We were in the Vosges Mountains in posi-tion on a place called Mount Herrenberg, and the Ger-man artillery began to fire on us; it had been a very quiet sector up to then, but the Germans started firing, and one of the sergeants got panicked, you might say, and he started yelling about how the Germans had a bracket on us, and he said that everybody ought to run, and some did, including the sergeant.

"I stood right there, and I called them every name I could think of, which was plenty, and they came sneaking back and got the horses and the battery in a position of safety.

"Later they wanted me to court-martial the sergeant, but I wouldn't do it. I busted him to private, and later I got him transferred to another battery, where I under-stand he did very well for all the rest of the war.

"I tried never to get anybody court-martialed. When we had troubles, we handled them ourselves, and that's the way to do it. Why put a man through the disgrace of a court-martial, something that will follow him all the rest of his life, unless you absolutely have to? And ninety-nine times out of a hundred you don't.

"You have to have faith in a man—that if he makes a mistake, and if you treat him like a man, you'll find that he won't repeat that mistake. That's been my experience in any case, and it was the same in the Army and in politics."

You mean you have a basic trust in people.

"You have to. If you don't, what's the use of living? My goodness, if you don't have trust in your fellowman, how can you expect him to have trust in you?

Those are very old-fashioned sentiments, Mr. President. A lot of people don't feel that way anymore.

"I know they don't, and it's a pity. That's the reason we're in the shape we're in."

Tell me about Father Tiernan [L. Curtis Tiernan].

"I used to walk at the head of my battery and lead my horses, and Father Tiernan, the Catholic chaplain, would walk with me. There were only five or six Protestants in my battery, and I was one of them. All the rest were Catholics.

"The father and I would walk along and discuss the history of the world and I don't know what all. And I'd corner him on the things that were done by the Jesuits in the Spanish Inquisition, and he always had an answer for me. Of course it was never the right answer as far as I was concerned [much laughter]."

I believe you saw him again at Potsdam.

"I did. He was chief of the Army chaplains in Europe during the Second World War.

"Well, when we landed in Antwerp on our way to Potsdam, General Jesus Christ Himself Lee was there to meet us. Do you remember him?"

I said, "Vividly."

Lieutenant General J. C. H. "Jesus Christ Himself" Lee was commanding general of the Communications Zone of the Supreme Headquarters of the American Expeditionary Forces during the Second World War. We were, you might say, both stationed in Paris at the same time.

I was editor of the Army weekly *Yank* in Paris, and the general threatened me with court-martial at least three times, largely because of material that appeared in the magazine, although we once had something of a disagreement over housing for the *Yank* staff. The general won the latter argument. As I say, he was a lieutenant general, and I was a master sergeant.

The general was a demanding martinet, and among other things that later got him into trouble—he retired in disgrace—was the fact that during the war and after he frequently sent an empty bomber from Paris to North Africa to bring back oranges for his breakfast mess.

I mentioned this to the President, who said, "Oh, yes. He was a regular son of a bitch and no two ways about it.

"But when I got to Antwerp on the way to Potsdam, he was appointed as my aide, and I said to him, 'There are two people I want to see.' I wanted to see a major general who'd been a private in my battery and finally retired a major general.

"I wanted to see him, and I said, 'And I want to see that damned priest that's the chief of chaplains down in Paris.'

"Old Lee said, 'Who?'

"And I said, 'Tiernan. That damn chief of chaplains that used to be in my battery.'

"He said, 'You mean *Monsignor* Tiernan?' I said, 'Yes. Go and get him.' And he did.

"And Tiernan came to Potsdam, and he brought along all his fancy vestments and one thing and another, and he and I had the best time you ever saw in your life. He sat up half the night with Charlie Ross [the President's press secretary], and the two of them drank a quart of cognac or whatever a bottle of cognac is in France.

"And the next morning he came to see me, and he said, 'Mr. President, I want to put on a high mass for you.'

"I said, 'All right. You can do it. But there's one thing you've got to do. You've got to get every Protestant in this outfit to be sure and be there at that mass because if they're not, they're going to be in trouble with me.'

"Well, they were all there, and it was just a wonderful service.

"That priest was a grand fella. Never was anybody like him. When I used to walk along with him in the First War, he'd talk about the religious history of the world and how the differences between the religions had caused all the trouble. He knew most of the answers, and I said, 'Padre, you know what? If all the damn priests were like you, there wouldn't be any Protestants.'

"And he said, 'I know that. And I ain't' [laughter].

"Oh, you know. Petty larceny things like religious differences and political differences never made any difference with me. And with people I like I don't care what they believe if they honestly believe it. It's up to them. . . . But I wish you could have known that priest. He was in a class by himself."

Judge Ridge: "Father Tiernan gave the best summing up of Harry Truman I have ever encountered. He said, 'Harry Truman had integrity and much more than normal intelligence, and there is no limit in a free society to what men with those attributes can attain.'

"Whenever the boys in Battery D would see Captain Truman, they would salute him, and that salute meant that they were saying to him—I'm with you. And he would salute back—I know you are. I'm with you also."

Harry Truman: "We finally worked up the battery to be one of the best batteries in the regiment. And we could always hit the target when the time came.

"I had quite a great time with those youngsters. We were in a great many engagements, fired eleven thousand rounds of seventy-five ammunition, came back here, and marched in a parade downtown, and even now there are about sixty or seventy of those men who are still alive and living in Kansas City, and we're still friends, and I'm just as proud of that as I am of having been President.

"It's quite a satisfaction to a fellow who's commanded men during a tour of duty on the front where there was a lot of shooting. It's not often that the men feel kindly toward the fellow who commanded them. Because he had to make them do things they didn't like.

"I've always felt that the best definition of a leader, and it doesn't matter where it is, in the military or in the White House. It doesn't matter. The best definition of a leader is a man who can make the people who served with or under him do what they don't want to do and like it."

That certainly can be said of you and the men of Battery D.

"Yes, I think it can be, and, hell, you know. They say I was ambitious, but I was never ambitious. If the only thing I'd ever done in my life was be the best damn battery commander I could be, I'd have settled for that.

"And now let's go to lunch. I told you we were going to the cheap place. Bess told me I ought to take you to lunch in New York, but I said to her, 'Why do that? I can do it a lot cheaper here.'"

As we went into the Howard Johnson's for lunch, several children standing outside recognized Mr. Truman and asked for his autograph, which he gave them.

As we walked away he said, "These kids and their autographs are just like a bunch of pups. One of them does it on a fire hydrant, and then they've all got to do it."

Harry Truman, Madge Gates Wallace, and the Haberdashery

On June 28, 1919, shortly after Harry Truman returned from France, he married Elizabeth Virginia Wallace.

I never asked Mr. Truman about his personal life; I felt that it would have been presumptuous to do so, and now, more than ten years later, I still think so.

I met Mrs. Truman several times, always briefly. She was a courteous woman with an enormous sense of personal dignity. A few days after Mr. Truman had told me that he liked to live up to his obligations Mrs. Truman agreed, I am sure with great reluctance, that for four hours the film crew—it seems to me its members numbered in the hundreds—could come inside the house at 219 North Delaware Street.

The house was built in 1867 by Bess Truman's grandfather, General Porterfield Gates, who made a fortune milling Queen of the Pantry flour, which in my youth was still popular throughout the Middle West.

The Gates family may not have been the richest family in Independence, but they were by far the fanciest, and Madge Gates Wallace, Bess' mother, certainly fancied herself as the grandest lady in town. David W. Wallace, Bess' father, was not, in the language of Independence, nearly as "well fixed" as the Gateses. He was a handsome man with long sideburns, a mustache that drooped over his wide mouth, and a charming manner that everybody in Independence remembered with affection.

But he was never quite able to make a living for his four children and his imperial wife, and again in the language of Independence, he "took to drink." And in 1908 he seated himself in a bathtub and shot himself in the head with a pistol.

After his death, Madge Gates Wallace, perhaps understandably, became not less imperious; she became more so. She was called "the queenliest woman Independence ever produced." I always felt that when Harry Truman talked, as he often did, never with affection, about "the high hats and the counterfeits" of Independence, he had the Gateses and the Wallaces in mind.

He had known Bess since they met at Sunday school in the First Presbyterian Church in 1890, but they were not married until twenty-nine years later. That may not have been the longest courtship in history, but it is certainly in the running.

Janey Chiles, a retired Independence schoolteacher: "I thought that they never would get married. I think Bess wanted to, although I'm not sure, but Mrs. Wallace. . . . Nobody was ever good enough for her, or so it seemed. She was a very, very difficult person, and there wasn't anybody in town she didn't look down on. And Harry Truman was not at that time I believe a very promising prospect."

Harry Truman was thirty-five years old; his only experience up to that time had been as a bank clerk, a farmer, and a soldier, and now he was proposing to go into the haberdashery business with, of all things, a Jew named Eddie Jacobson.

Bluma Jacobson: "Eddie and I were never at the Truman house. We went maybe two or three times on picnics and on the Fourth of July, but the Trumans never had us at their home. The Wallaces were aristocracy in these parts, and under the circumstances the Trumans couldn't afford to have Jews at their house."

Susan Chiles, another retired schoolteacher: "The Gateses, the whole Gates family, were all topnotchers here. If there was anybody in town that was high society, it was the Gates family."

Henry Chiles, a retired farmer: "I knew Bess long before I knew Harry. Bess lived over on Delaware Street, and it's just a block and a half away.

"Bess' brother Frank was just a little younger than I, but we played together. And her other brother George. It was altogether, the Wallaces were, one girl and three boys, and she straightened those boys out. Physically she could do whatever she wanted to do. She was just as good a ballplayer as they were, and they knew it.

"The Wallaces lived next door to the Paxtons, and the Paxtons were all boys and outweighed the Wallace boys just a little bit. But when the Wallaces were losing, Bess would come over, and she'd decide the battle right then and there. She was quite a tomboy, but she turned out to be a real Southern lady.

"Harry didn't play any of the rough games the way Bess did. He was wearing glasses, and he was afraid of breaking them. Vivian never paid much attention to the books. He was more like me in that."

Mary Jane Truman: I had taken over the farm when Harry went into the Army, and I had a hundred acres in wheat and sixty in oats, and the day of the wedding, I'll never forget, my mother and I cooked dinner for twelve threshers, and then we had to clean up and hurry to the wedding.

"It *couldn't* have come at a worse time. I remember the night before I went with Harry to pick some daisies in a field where they grew wild. I didn't have anything to do with decorating the church, but I certainly will never forget where the daisies on the altar came from."

After their marriage and brief honeymoon in Chicago and Detroit, Harry and Bess moved into the house on North Delaware Street with Mrs. Wallace, and the three of them lived together until her death in December, 1952. She was ninety years old, and in the thirty-two years between the marriage and Mrs. Wallace's death they lived not only in Independence but in Washington, D. C. At the time Harry Truman became President, she was sharing a bedroom with Margaret in the apartment on Connecticut Avenue, after which came Blair House and the White House.

But in all that time, I was told, she never quite reconciled herself to the marriage. In Mrs. Wallace's mind Bess had clearly married beneath herself. The Trumans were dirt farmers, and Mrs. Wallace said so, frequently in the presence of her son-in-law.

Henry Chiles: "I don't think Harry ever really *liked* Independence. Well, he liked it all right, I guess, but Grandview was always more like home to him, and Independence has always been more what you might call a *Wallace* town, and Mrs. Wallace never let him forget that for a minute."

Susan Chiles: "I probably shouldn't say this, but there just didn't seem to be any way in the world to get along with Mrs. Wallace. Bess put up with her, though, stuck with her through thick and thin, although I understand that even in the White House there was just not any way of satisfying her.

"But Harry was always as nice as he could be to her. It was just a most remarkable thing, and I think people around here respect him as much for that as anything else."

No matter what his job was, Harry Truman always took home a briefcase full of work, but the house on North Delaware never seemed to be quiet. Floors were forever being waxed, curtains hung, ceilings painted, and walls papered, particularly it seemed in exactly the places where Harry Truman was trying to concentrate. There were also Madge Gates Wallace's guests, frequently her sons and their wives, who also never seemed completely content with Bess' husband.

As I've said, even while she was living at the White House, Mrs. Wallace seldom failed to make it clear that Harry Truman was not what she had in mind as a son-in-law. Or as a President. As late as 1948 she was often heard to remark that she could not for the life of her understand why Harry was running against that nice man, Thomas E. Dewey.

"And in all those years," said Mrs. W. L. C. Palmer, "Harry Truman never once answered back. Never once. You must remember Harry is a reticent man."

Mrs. Truman said that while she would allow the film crew in the house, she would not take part in the filming and would not be interviewed.

The house was immaculate. There are fourteen large rooms with old-fashioned high ceilings, many with damask wallpaper. There are seven bedrooms, three fireplaces with marble mantels, and a dining room large enough to seat thirty. I was pleased to see on one end table, a book, undoubtedly Mrs. Truman's, called *The Corpse in the Snow*. Otherwise, only history and biography, hundreds of volumes of both.

We filmed the President reading the morning paper in his study, then rising, going through one of the large living rooms and into the hall, where he picked up his hat, opened the front door, and went outside.

It might seem that this simple episode would take only a few minutes to film, but it took the entire four hours, and if there had been more time, it would have taken more time.

At one point during the interminable waits between takes a member of the crew whose job I never figured out turned to Mrs. Truman and said, "I wonder if you'd mind running out to the kitchen and getting me a glass of water?"

Mrs. Truman, a woman of whom I believe it could be said, does not run, went to the kitchen and got him a glass of water.

I gave her a chance to recover, then asked her whether she ever went to the door with the President when he started on his morning walks. She said that sometimes she did and sometimes she didn't. I asked whether she would agree to accompany the President to the door and allow us to film her doing that.

She hesitated a moment and looked with dismay at the chaos around her, at the heavy cameras and the coiled wires and the unshaven men and short-haired women. She sighed, and then she said that she would. She said it without joy.

I should have stopped then, but I didn't. I said, "And I wonder if you'd mind saying whatever you might normally say to the President and let us record that." And I added, "We really ought to record it for posterity's sake."

Mrs. Truman gave me a look that Madge Gates Wallace might have envied, and she said, "I have no desire to have my voice recorded for posterity."

Later that morning during another long delay and after, I suspect, a few more "small libations," Mr. Truman turned on the hi-fi and played excerpts of several pianists, including, as I recall, Glenn Gould and, I think, Rubenstein playing Beethoven's *Appassionata*.

"I can play that," said the President, and he went to the piano that he had bought for Margaret one Christmas when she was a girl, sat down, and played a few halting bars.

"Now, Harry," said Mrs. Truman, who was standing near the piano, "we all know it's not the same."

She said it with kindness, though, and she smiled.

8

The Haberdashery

Not long before Harry Truman's marriage he met Eddie Jacobson on the streets of Kansas City—"How the hell are you, you baldheaded old son of a bitch?"—and they decided that since they had both come back from the war physically intact and since neither was overburdened with attractive job offers, they would indeed go into business together, the haberdashery business.

Mr. Truman told me, "We'd done so well in the canteen, we didn't see why we couldn't do just as well in civilian life, and it looked like we were a pretty good combination. I'd do the selling and keep the books, and we had a clerk part of the time, and Eddie would do the buying. Of course the way things turned out we both did everything, a little of everything. We were open six days a week at first, twelve hours or more a day, and the first year we kept busy until late in the evening, and sometimes I'd take the books home and Mrs. Truman would help me with them."

Bluma Jacobson: "There were slack days as well as good days, and if Harry wasn't around, you could always look up in the balcony, and, Harry would be up there with a book, reading or studying. He studied law a good deal in those days. Just picking it up, not going to law school at that time. He later went to night school in Kansas City and studied law, but at that time you would always find him reading a book.

"The first year was a good year in the store. I believe they sold as much as eighty thousand dollars' worth of merchandise, because everybody coming back from the war, all the men, needed new clothes, and they had very good merchandise. Expensive shirts that were very good . . . everything. Eddie had very good taste in men's furnishings.

111

"Perhaps . . . it may be that they were overstocked; they had over thirty-five thousand dollars' worth of stock, or forty thousand dollars, and in the second year the price of the stock went down until it was worth only ten thousand dollars or less.

"When you speak of the depression these days, everybody thinks of the depression of the 1930's, but the depression in 1922 was just as bad, although it didn't last as long.

"The depression came, and there wasn't enough fuel. There was a coal shortage, and the store had to close at two or three in the afternoon. They couldn't stay open as they had the first year. I don't think Eddie ever worked as hard as he did that first year, or Harry either I guess."

Mary Jane Truman: "Harry and . . . and Mrs. Truman, they used to come out to the farm here at Grandview on a Sunday when Harry was in business. That was his only day off, and they'd drive out here to see Mother and me, and sometimes we, . . . Harry and I, would play duets on the piano, which my mother always very much enjoyed. She knew a great deal about music, and she liked to hear it.

"When Harry was in the haberdashery business, she very much wanted, we all did, for him to succeed, but when it did not work out that way, we knew it wasn't Harry's fault.

"Later, when Harry got into politics, the newspapers liked to make out that he had been a poor businessman, but that was not the case at all."

Judge Albert A. Ridge: "I believe I was working in a neighborhood grocery store at the time, and I didn't have much of a career in mind.

"But in the evenings I'd go over to the haberdashery, and there were always a lot of men from the battery hanging around, doing nothing much, but Harry was always busy. He was always being asked for advice of one kind or another. He was only thirty-five years old, but he was an old man to us kids who were in our early twenties at the time.

"And then I got a job in the courthouse in Kansas City, as a clerk in one of the courts. And I got to thinking about going to law school at night, and I talked to Harry Truman about that.

"He encouraged me to go to night school and study law, but he said that just knowing the law wasn't enough. He said that was the trouble with far too many lawyers, that they knew the law but did not know much of anything else. He said . . . he encouraged me to also study about the nature of man and about the culture and heritage of Western civilization in general.

"I was just a young . . . a not very serious young man, and I'd never studied any of those things; I'd never even thought of most of them, and they sounded a little profound to me, a little difficult.

"But Harry Truman always said that I . . . that a man could do anything he set his mind to, and that encouraged me. I once asked him. . . . No, I believe he volunteered once to give me a list of about ten or so books that I ought to read. I don't know what happened to that list, although I treasured it greatly. But I can remember that it included Plutarch's *Lives*. And Caesar's *Commentaries*. And Benjamin Franklin's *Autobiography*. He used to say, 'Al, you'll find a good deal in there about how to make use of every minute of your day and a lot of horse sense about people.' And he was always talking about the Roman lawgivers. He knew all about them. And he had read all of Gibbon's *Decline and Fall of the Roman Empire* several times. He was . . . himself he was always reading two or three books at a time and always making notes in the margins, especially in history books. Frequently . . . very often he knew much more than the writer, the historian, and he would . . . his favorite word was 'bunk,' and I guess it still is.

"He told me to read a book called *Bunker Bean* and one called *Missouri's Struggle for Statehood*. The Bible. I remember he said even back then that the King James

Version was the best and that he doubted it could be improved on. I believe he still thinks that. . . . Plato's *Republic*. Shakespeare. He said I'd have to read all of Shakespeare, but he recommended *Hamlet* and *Lear* and *Othello* in particular, and the sonnets. He insisted on the sonnets.

"He recommended to me the complete works of Robert Burns, which he was always reading himself. And Byron. All of Byron, too, I believe, although his favorite was *Childe Harold,* which is a poem most people who do not, did not, know Harry Truman would not have expected him to choose. It's a very . . . you might say it is not an easy poem.

"There was a book called *Fifteen Decisive Battles of the World.* Harry Truman felt that you had to understand war to understand mankind. Because man was always getting into wars, and if you didn't understand how wars happened, you couldn't be expected to understand how to prevent them.

"And I remember Charles Beard had just come out with a book on the history of the Constitutional Convention: *An Economic Interpretation of the Constitution.* I believe that book was a best seller at the time, and Harry and I each got a copy."

Bluma Jacobson: "Harry always kept in mind the other person's point of view. I remember not long after Harry got to be President, he came back here to Kansas City, and he and Eddie and some of the others were playing poker. Eddie lost. I don't know how much, but he lost, and the next morning Harry came into the store and bought eighteen or twenty pairs of socks. I don't think he actually needed that many pairs, size eleven, I think. It was just something he wanted to do for Eddie. Harry Truman has always been very, very aware of how other people feel about things."

Tom Murphy, a veteran of Battery D and a Kansas City salesman: "Our hang-around was the old haberdashery store. It's possible we scared out some customers by just hanging around like that.

"Harry was counselor for all the boys. In the war he was Captain Harry, not Captain Truman. And even after the war, if anybody was going to get married or go into business, they talked to old Captain Harry to ask his advice.

"Of course, now you know Battery D is the largest in the country. Since Harry became Senator and then Vice President and President, we got many more people in the battery. . . . Everybody claims they were in Harry Truman's battery.

"We were a rough outfit; we'd drink and get into fights, but we weren't mean. There wasn't much swearing, and we weren't brutal.

"Later we had occasion to see Harry at our reunions. The first reunion cost him some money. It was during Prohibition, and everybody came to the reunion with a jug of liquor. Not a bottle. A jug. And they got going and started throwing plates and saucers and things, and when it was all over, Harry paid for it. He just grinned and paid the bills. He never did drink.

"Like I said, we may have scared some customers away from the haberdashery, but Harry would never say a word, let a word be said against anybody who was in his outfit."

The store closed in 1922, and although Harry was advised to go into bankruptcy, he refused. It took him fifteen years to pay off his debts, but in 1937 he finally did it.

I once asked Mr. Truman what he felt he had learned from his experience in the haberdashery, and he said, "Well, I learned, although I'd never had much doubt about it, never to elect a Republican as President. [Warren G. Harding had been elected President in 1920.] Because he'll look out for the rich and squeeze out the farmer and the small businessman. And when you get a man like old Mellon as Secretary of the Treasury—Andrew Mellon was Secretary of the Treasury in the cabinets of Harding,

Calvin Coolidge, and Herbert Hoover from 1921 to 1931
—you've got somebody who'll do everything in his power
to make the rich richer and the poor poorer, and that's
exactly what happened. There just wasn't anybody in a
position of power in Washington at that time who gave a
good goddamn what happened to people. Except for the
very rich."

Mr. President, did you like being in the retail business?

"To tell the truth, I never had a chance to spend any
too much time thinking about things like that. What I did
was what I had to do or thought I had to do . . . to
make a living most of the time. I had a wife and later a
daughter to support, and I had to make a living for them.
And I always went ahead and did it as best I could without taking time out to worry about how it would have
been if it had worked out another way. Or to complain
about what happened.

"You'll notice if you read your history, that the work of
the world gets done by people who aren't bellyachers."

I had other questions, but somehow that didn't seem
the time to ask them.

Early Politics

Mr. President, what's the first Presidential election you can remember?

"In 1892. [He was eight years old.] Grover Cleveland was running for his second term." Cleveland, who had been President from 1885 to 1889 ran for a second term in 1892 and was elected.

"Cleveland was running for President, and Adlai Stevenson, not the one we've been talking about, his grandfather. He was running for Vice President on the Democratic ticket, and I had a white cap that said on it 'Cleveland' and 'Stevenson,' 'Grover Cleveland' and 'Adlai Stevenson' on the visor."

I gather you liked the first Adlai Stevenson better than you liked his grandson.

"Yes, I did. Old Adlai wasn't any reluctant debutante. They didn't have to beg him to make up his mind whether he wanted to run for office. You know if a man doesn't enjoy running for office and doesn't think he can do something good for people by doing it, I don't know what the hell he's in politics for in the first place.

"Anyway, Grover Cleveland ran against Benjamin Harrison in 1892, and when he was elected, my father climbed up on the roof of the old house out in Grandview. It had a tower on the corner with a rooster as a weather vane, and my father climbed up, after the election returns came in, and decorated it with red, white, and blue bunting. Then he rode a gray horse and carried a torch in a torchlight parade, and so did everybody else in town if he could get a gray horse. Everybody was very pleased that Cleveland had won the election.

"But in his second term Cleveland was a great disappointment. Between his first term and his second he'd worked for one of the big life insurance companies, as a lawyer. I believe it was the Prudential Life Insurance

Company that he worked for, and in his second term he was more interested in the big-money people than he was in the common people, and he accomplished very, very little. It's a shame when that happens to a man, but it sometimes does."

Why do you think some men are more—I guess suscep-tible to that kind of thing than others are?

"Some men are greedier than others, and they get to thinking they *are* the power rather than the instrument of power."

You were quite an admirer of William Jennings Bryan, I believe. Bryan was the Democratic Presidential nominee in 1896, 1900, and 1908; he was best known for being a proponent of the free coinage of silver, which he felt would help farmers and small businessmen.

"Old Bill Bryan was a great one, one of the greatest."

A good many people don't think as much of Bryan as they used to, largely, I believe, because of his opposition to the teaching of evolution in Tennessee. In 1925, wasn't it?

"Yes, yes. I think it was, around that period anyway, and he was an old man then. What he said then shouldn't be held against him because of . . . because of the things he said and stood for when he was at the height of his powers.

"My goodness, the things he stood for—he was one of the first to come out for the popular election of Senators, you know; Senators used to be elected by state legis-latures, and you know how state legislatures are always, almost always controlled by the money people. And old Bill Bryan was one of the first supporters of an income tax, and he was for woman suffrage and I don't know what all.

"And in 1912 when the Democratic Party was split every which way—why, he held it together behind Wood-row Wilson. If it hadn't have been for Bill Bryan, there wouldn't be any liberal outfit in the country at all now. At least that's what I think. Old Bryan kept liberalism alive, kept it going.

"I don't know whether you ever heard him speak or not, but I used to drive a hundred miles to hear that old man speak; I didn't care what the subject was.

"I was at lunch with him one time in Kansas City, and he had a bowl of radishes and a plate of butter in front of him, and he'd butter the radishes and eat them. And that was his whole lunch.

"Nobody had a voice like old Bill. They didn't have any . . . things like this . . . like this microphone in those days. You didn't need them.

"And he made a statement here I'll never forget. You know what he said?

"It was just an ordinary luncheon. He just happened to be in town, and they invited him, and he came. And he said, 'I've been in this political game since 1896 when I got myself nominated for President, and I got licked, as I did twice after that.'

"But he said, 'You know, I've often thought of my first visit to a Democratic convention, which was in 1876' [Bryan was sixteen] and he said, 'They had to bring me up a side stair outside the building, and then they had to poke me in at a window, and you know, they've been trying to put me out over the transom ever since.' And then he went on and made a beautiful speech.

"And another time I heard him. In 1900 the Democratic convention was here in Kansas City, and I was a page. The hall there could hold . . . oh, thousands of people, maybe seventeen thousand people, and I was up in the roof garden. From where I was watching he didn't look more than a foot high, and as I told you he didn't have a microphone, but I could hear every word he said. I never will forget it."

Why do you think he never got elected?

"I don't know. I don't know. I've given it a great deal of thought, but I've never figured it out. I think . . . the best I've come up with is that he was just too far ahead of his time, and the people in the East, the big-money people, were against him and did everything they could to defeat him. Three different times they did it.

"And the first time, in 1896, we got McKinley. He got the Republican nomination, and he ran what they called a front-porch campaign. He didn't go anywhere. He just sat on his front porch in Canton, Ohio, and they brought people to meet him.

"He didn't *say* a damn thing, of course, which in a way reminds me of the fellow who ran against me in 1948. He talked a lot, but he didn't ever *say* anything.

"People said that old McKinley had his ears so close to the ground he got grasshoppers in them.

"The whole campaign was run by a man named Mark Hanna, who was a rich old man whose only interest was in getting richer, and that is what happened when McKinley got elected. He was another one of those who was good for the rich and bad for the poor.

"They say he was a nice man, and I'm sorry he got shot. But he was still a damn poor President.

"And then we had—for almost two terms we had Teddy Roosevelt, and he was just one of our best Presidents."

How did a man like Teddy Roosevelt get to be President, elected President on a Republican ticket?

"Well, in 1898 he got back from Cuba, and he and his Rough Riders, his soldiers, had just won some great victories in the Spanish-American War, and he was a great hero. About the most popular hero since Andy Jackson won the Battle of New Orleans against the British in the War of 1812.

"He got back, and the old Republicans, the Republican bosses, couldn't stop him; he practically got unanimously elected governor of New York in 1899. And he made just a wonderful record in favor of the common people, the same kind of record that Franklin Roosevelt made later. And the bosses were scared of him. They didn't want him to be reelected, which is what he had in mind. And that old boss in New York, whatever his name was, was scared of what Teddy might do in a second term."

Actually, there were two political bosses in New York who were opposed to Roosevelt's renomination and re-election as governor of New York. They were Richard Croker of Tammany Hall and Tom Platt, a reactionary Republican leader. Roosevelt's ideas and programs terrified both of them. Platt wrote of him that he had "various altruistic ideas and was . . . a little loose on the relations of capital and labor, on trusts and combinations and the right of a man to run his own business in his own way." Another boss, one "Tim" Campbell, appealed to Roosevelt not to "let the Constitution stand between friends." He couldn't understand why Roosevelt first was angry and then laughed.

In any case, as Mr. Truman said, the bosses of New York were willing to go to any lengths to prevent Teddy Roosevelt from being governor for a second term.

Mr. Truman continued: "And so they arranged for him to get the Vice Presidential nomination. They figured he couldn't do any harm there.

"Then, of course, we know what happened. McKinley and Roosevelt were elected in November and inaugurated in March, and in the fall, September 4, McKinley was up in Buffalo at the Pan American Exposition, and he got shot, and Roosevelt wound up being President.

"I'll bet those old birds were plenty scared when that happened, and they should have been. . . . That's one of the things you have to keep in mind in picking a Vice Presidential candidate . . . It's a place . . . well, as you know I've had some experience in that line."

Whoever it is may end up being President.

"That's right, and some have made good, and some haven't. Someday I'll tell you which is which. But Teddy . . . he was just a crackerjack. He didn't do all he had in mind doing, of course. You never can do that, but there've just been very few Presidents who've done as much for the country as he did. . . . The biggest mistake he made was picking William Howard Taft to succeed him. He picked Taft, and Taft beat Bill Bryan in 1908.

"Taft was the father of the man [Robert A. Taft, Republican Senator from Ohio] I had so much trouble with when I was in the Senate and in the White House. And as Vice President, too. There wasn't anybody who was more against what I stood for as Taft was.

"And his father, the fat old man who was President. Roosevelt handpicked him to be his successor in the White House, and he was no damn good at all. He didn't have the slightest idea of what being President meant. At least that's my opinion.

"And the minute Teddy Roosevelt got out of the White House, the moneybags took over again, as they always do if you don't keep your eyes and ears open. Taft wasn't even *in* Washington most of the time, and he didn't have any understanding at all of the office."

I understand he wanted to be a judge.

"Maybe so, and he might have been a good one, but I'm talking about the Presidency of the United States. And the fact that during the four years Taft was in the White House the country started going to hell."

I gather you think the system can take a bad President now and again and still survive.

"Oh, yes. That's the . . . beauty of what those men who wrote the Constitution did. You can have a bad President. Why, I'll tell you— There was a time when we had five bad Presidents in a row, and it . . . we might not have had a Civil War if it hadn't been for those five fellas, but the government survived. It's just a miracle is all, what this government is."

Getting back to William Jennings Bryan, Mr. President. Do you think he understood the system?

"I haven't the slightest doubt of it, and he understood the people, too, and in my opinion he knew what the people wanted, needed.

"And I told you. He was a real honest-to-goodness orator. I've got a book on him here with all his principal speeches, and it was a wonder what he knew, the things he knew. He was a Congressman, but he didn't like Congress because he felt . . . he thought he didn't have any power in Congress and couldn't get his ideas across.

"He ran for the Senate and was beat. Maybe if he'd been elected to the Senate, he'd have become President the way I did. He'd have been a good one.

"Of course most of the things that he was for were what eventually happened anyway, even though he was never elected.

"My father was a violent Bryan man, but my old Uncle Harrison Young, he thought that the country would be ruined if we had free and unlimited coinage of silver.

"But you know what happened. In the Wilson administration they set up the Federal Reserve Board, the Federal Reserve System, which obtained the authority, and they still have it of issuing money against the commodities. And that's exactly what Bryan had been fighting for in 1896 and all along. That's the whole background of the Federal Reserve Bank.

"So you see even though he was never elected President, he still did the country a lot of good, and that's what you have to remember about him. That thing about his being against the teaching of evolution, that was when he was an old man. And I don't think . . . what an old man said should be held against him as long as his record was good when he had the power."

Mr. President, I understand you were very interested in the Presidential election of 1912 when Woodrow Wilson was elected for the first time.

"I was, and so was my father, and we were both also interested in the Democratic convention that year.

"My father was for old Champ Clark, who was the Speaker of the House and was quite a man. . . . The blood in the family was running quite a little thinner when his son, . . . the one that nominated me for Vice Pres-

ident, came along. Besides, he was drunk half the time and
more. . . . Still, after he got defeated for reelection to
the Senate and I got to be President . . . well, he had a
law firm in Washington that wasn't doing at all well; I
could have told him why it wasn't, but I didn't. I appointed him to be an associate justice of the circuit court
of appeals. He was no damn good, though."

*Mr. President, why—I hope you won't think me im-
pertinent, but under the circumstances and considering
the way you felt about him—why did you do that?*

"I . . . felt I owed him a favor; that's why, and I
thought as a judge he couldn't do too much harm, and he
didn't. That . . . he wasn't the worst court appointment
I ever made. By no means the worst. But we'll talk about
that at another time. I'm none too proud of it. I'll tell you
that."

*We were talking about 1912. I gather Bennett Clark's
father, Champ Clark, was a better man.*

"Much better. My father was for him, as I say, for the
Democratic nomination in 1912. And during the convention, which was in Baltimore, Maryland, I believe, I was
binding wheat, driving a binder. Binding a hundred and
sixty acres of wheat where that business proposition, . . .
where what they call Truman Corners, is now.

"The little railroad station was just about a quarter mile
from the corner where I had to turn the team to go back
to the other end of the half-mile field, and in the afternoon
I tied up the horses, and I ran over to the station to find
out what had happened at the station."

How did they know?

"There wasn't any radio in those days, of course, and
those old birds, those old stationmasters had teletype machines in every station, and when the machines weren't
being used to send over railroad information, they'd send
news over them.

"Out at Grandview we didn't get the Kansas City
papers until the next morning, and so if you wanted to
find out what was going on, that was the only way you
could do it."

How did your father feel about the fact that Wilson won the nomination?

"Well, of course, when Wilson got the nomination, my father was all for him. He was always for the Democratic candidate, didn't matter who it was, and so was my mother, and I've been pretty much a Democrat, you might say, for most of my life [much laughter]."

Mr. President, it seems almost incredible that with your having such a deep interest in politics, you never really . . . well, yearned to run for office yourself.

"Well, I never did. Oh, I might have thought about it, wondered how it would be to run for office, but that's about all.

"But then as I have said I went broke trying to run a haberdashery, and I had to have a job, and when it was suggested that I might . . . run for county judge [an administrative job in Missouri, similar to a county commissioner in most other states] of the eastern district of Jackson County, I decided to do it. I had a lot of good friends in that part of the county and was kin to most of the rest. So I ran. There were five; I was one of five candidates. I licked all the rest of them because I knew more people in the county than they did. That's all.

"And after that, why things just happened. That's about the size of it. Things just happened, and I wound up being President of the United States, which was the last thing in the world I had in mind."

Did you know Tom Pendergast when you first ran for office, Mr. President?

"No. I'd known his nephew Jim, of course; he was a lieutenant in the war with me in the 129th, but I did not know Tom at that time. It was Jim, and it was Tom's brother Mike who agreed that I might be a good candidate.

"And I had an old Dodge roadster, and I drove all over the county and went to each of the seven townships in the district and met people, and I spoke wherever I could find anybody to listen to me, you might say."

Could you tell me about your first speech?

"My first speech was out at the town of Lee's Summit, as I recall, and I was so scared I couldn't say a word. So I just got off the platform. It was good for me because I began to learn how to make an appearance before a crowd. It took time, but I learned.

"And in 1948, in the campaign of 1948 I made quite a few speeches, you may recall, and when I . . . well, just talked to people without anything being written down, just stood there and talked, people seemed to understand what I was getting at, and the result was the same as it was here in Jackson County in 1922."

Edgar Hinde: "Harry learned how to make a speech, but it was slow going, and in that first campaign, the first time I heard him speak, it was . . . I think it was the most painful thirty minutes of my life. I just couldn't wait for him to finish."

Mr. Hinde, I understand you tried to persuade Mr. Truman not to run in that first campaign.

"I did. He came to see me; I believe he came to see most of his old buddies of Battery D, of which I was one. And he told me he was planning to run for county judge. I said to him, 'What do you want to do a thing like that for, Harry?' And he said, 'I've got to eat, don't I?'

"I still tried to discourage him, though; to me . . . he just wasn't the politician type. The kind who would slap somebody on the back; he was just not that sort of man, and it seemed to me he should . . . stay out of politics.

"He paid no attention to me, of course, and I suppose you might say he didn't do too bad a job of it."

Tom Evans, an old friend of Mr. Truman's, owner of a chain of drugstores and radio and television stations: "The first time I met Harry . . . I was a soda jerk, not a soda squirt, a soda jerk at the drug store at Twenty-Sixth and Prospect streets in Kansas City. And that was where the headquarters of the Tenth Ward Democratic Club was. It was headed by Mike Pendergast, brother of Tom

Pendergast, and it was a good thing to belong to that club if you were in the neighborhood, and everybody did belong.

"Harry came, this was at a time when he was in the haberdashery business, he came to the club, and he was different from most of the others. They were most of them out for a good time. But Harry wasn't that type at all.

"I remember that at first I thought he was a school-teacher. He struck me as a schoolteacher type, and then when the rest would go out on the town for drinks and things like that, Harry never joined in. He always went home. He was a very sturdy type of young man.

"So when I heard that he was running for office, I wasn't too surprised, and I wasn't surprised when he got elected. There was something about him that you . . . that you wanted to trust and knew you could."

Did you ever think he would wind up being President?

"A thing like that never occurred to me, but Harry . . . Harry Truman was always the type of man you felt could do whatever he set out to do, and one other thing about him: He never got discouraged. He never showed it anyway if he did. He kept his feelings to himself, and he was always very, very cheerful when you met him, and he was always interested in you and in your . . . welfare."

Tom Murphy, a veteran of Battery D and a Kansas City salesman: "I used to box in France, and I lost one big match there with a guy who was fifteen or twenty pounds heavier than I was. Harry bet money on me, and he lost it all.

"After the armistice he had a furlough to go to Paris, and he did, and while he was gone, some of the men found some bottles of green cognac, and we all got very drunk and disorderly.

"When Harry first came back, he didn't say a word, and I had . . . well, I had started oversleeping and missing reveille, and he called me in. I was a sergeant, and he called me in and said, 'Sergeant, that business with the cognac was pretty disgusting, and I understand you've been missing reveille. I'm going to bust you.'

"I said, 'Well, sir. I certainly do deserve it.' He looked at me in the eye and paused for a minute, and then he said, 'Okay. You go back and behave yourself now.'

"I'm sure if I'd pleaded to keep my rank, he'd have busted me. But he appreciated the fact that I didn't do it, and after that . . . I'd, . . . like most of the rest of Battery D, would do whatever we possibly could for Harry Truman.

"I fought in Boston in 1920 and won the national AAU boxing championship. And in 1922, when Harry first ran for office, I was still boxing, and I helped him open his campaign out at Lee's Summit. I went out there with a boxing partner and gave an exhibition to help draw a crowd.

"A lot of men in the outfit helped him in the campaign. They'd go out in cars and tack up campaign posters for him, and we'd go to the rallies and cheer and applaud.

"We'd do whatever was necessary to help Harry. We were that loyal to him."

Harry Truman: "If you're going to be in politics, you have to learn to explain to people what you stand for, and learning to stand up in front of a crowd and talk was just something I had to do; so I went ahead and did it.

"You might say I never got in a class with old Bill Bryan, but . . . well, by the last meeting of that campaign in 1922 there was a meeting up in front of the courthouse here on the square in Independence. I guess there must have been five thousand people there, and they had to listen to all five candidates, all of them supposedly more qualified than I was, but I maneuvered it . . . I was friendly with the chairman and the secretary of the county committee, and I maneuvered the thing so that I was the last one on the program, and I got the ovation and won the election. I won by about five hundred votes over all the other four, and from then on I had no difficulty in getting along before an audience."

Mr. President, in the theater the star always maneuvers to have the last act in the show. Did you know that when you arranged to be last?

"Of course not. How would I know a thing like that? I was just using common sense, which if you've got it helps in getting what you want."

What if you haven't got it?

"If you haven't got it, the best thing to do is not get out of bed in the morning."

The Only Defeat—and
Then Victory

Mr. President, in 1924 when you ran for reelection as county judge, you were defeated. Why was that?

"The two factions of the Democratic Party in this county [the Rabbits under a boss named Joe Shannon and the Goats under Pendergast] were more interested in fighting each other than they were in winning the election. That was the biggest reason. I was defeated by an old Republican, an old harnessmaker named Henry Rummel. That was a great time for Republicans. Calvin Coolidge was in the White House, and a lot of people thought the prosperity was going to last forever. I knew better than that, but it didn't do any good . . . not that year."

Wasn't another reason for your defeat the fact that the Ku Klux Klan was against you?

"The Klan was against me. That's true."

I've read that the members of the Klan in Jackson County weren't only one hundred percent Americans. They thought of themselves as two hundred percent Americans, and they didn't just hate Catholics, Jews, and Negroes. They hated everybody.

Mr. Truman laughed. "That's what they were all right. They claimed . . . later it was claimed that I was a member, but I never was. I've told you; most of the boys in Battery D were Catholics, so how could I be a member of something like the Klan? I told them to go to hell. They were a bunch of damn cowards hiding behind bedsheets.

"Here in Jackson County the Klan was a Republican adjunct, just like it was after the Civil War. And it was used politically to cause a great many good people in Missouri, Democrats, to be defeated. And they had several meetings in Jackson County when I was running for county judge and also when I was running for presiding judge and the Senate.

"And in 1924 I went to one of their meetings; it was in

the daytime down in the eastern part of the county. I guess there must have been a thousand people there, and I knew every durned one of them."

They weren't wearing their sheets?

"Oh, no. This was in the daytime. And I got up and told them exactly what I thought of them. Got down off the platform, walked right down through the center of them, and started home.

"And I got about halfway home, and I met two carloads of my Democratic boys coming out from Independence with shotguns and baseball bats, and I made them turn around and go back. I said, 'You don't need to use guns. Those guys are scared when they don't have their sheets on.' And that's all there was to it."

Did you have any thoughts before you went that you were risking a thousand votes?

"No, no. I went down there to tell them what I thought of them, and I did, and half of them voted for me."

How do you explain that?

"Because they knew what they were doing wasn't right. I told them that anybody that had to work behind a sheet was off the beam and that my partner in the haberdashery business, Eddie Jacobson, had told me that the fellow that was organizing the Ku Klux had to be a Jew because nobody but a Jew could sell a dollar ninety-five-cent nightgown for sixteen dollars. That's what it cost them to get in."

Mr. President, under the circumstances mightn't it have been wiser not to go out and tell off those Klanners?

"It might have been, yes, but once a man starts thinking that way, about what it's wise to say and what isn't, why, he might just as well cash in his chips and curl up his toes and die.

"I tried never to act that way, and for the most part I think you can say I succeeded. Sometimes I was advised to hold my fire on this and that because they said telling the truth would *offend* people. But whenever I took such advice I never thought much of myself.

"If you keep your mouth shut about things you think

are important, hell, I don't see how you can expect the democratic system to work at all.

"I wouldn't want you to say this . . . not as long as the boy [John F. Kennedy] is in the White House, but in 1952 I was out campaigning for the fellow we've talked about [Adlai Stevenson] and I made some speeches up in Massachusetts. The Kennedy people got the word to me that they'd very much appreciate it if I'd hold my fire on Joe McCarthy. I believe . . . I was told that they were afraid I might say something against old Joe that would cost the ticket some votes up there, but I didn't pay any attention to that. I went right ahead and said what I had on my mind, and I believe you'll find that in the long run it did more good than it did harm.*

* "The shadow of Joe McCarthy hangs like a great pall over the Democrats of Massachusetts. At Joe's lightest breath they button their coats to the chin and shiver. John Kennedy, the Massachusetts' Democrats' great hope for the Senate, never mentions Joe's name.

"It is Kennedy's view that the Irish core of his party likes Joe McCarthy and will grievously punish any man who traduces him.

"The Democrats of Massachusetts sent that message to Harry Truman just before he went into New England week before last. Take it a little easy with McCarthy, they said; talk about Hoover. The people up here don't have to be told why they hate Hoover.

"A few weeks ago the Republican National Committee gave Eisenhower the lay-off McCarthy warning for Wisconsin. Eisenhower took their orders like a soldier.

"But Harry Truman marched into Boston's Symphony Hall last Friday with his lips tight and his eyes hot. Just before he got there, Jack Kennedy had completed a nice, alliterative, in-offensive assault on the 'Capeharts and the Cains, the Brickers, and the Butlers.' . . .

"Mr. Truman looked Boston in the face and read it a lecture about McCarthy. He could speak without shame, he said, of his administration's record against Communism.

"He told them what McCarthy had done in pillorying the innocent. He spoke of 'those moral pygmies, Senators Jenner and McCarthy,' and he fairly spat their names. He reminded

"I cussed out old McCarthy every chance I got. He was nothing but a damn coward, and he was afraid of me. The only thing he ever did that I approved of was when he knocked down Drew Pearson.

"And when Eisenhower let McCarthy get away with calling General Marshall a traitor. Why that was one of the most shocking things in the history of this country.

---

them that in a choice between McCarthy's favor and his debt to General Marshall, Eisenhower had gone with McCarthy.

" 'I stand by my friends,' said the President, and suddenly Boston's cheers came pounding back at him. He spat out McCarthy's name again, and they were booing it. Mr. Truman had taken his chances on Boston, and Boston had come through.

"For Harry Truman, wherever he goes, is campaigning unafraid against the McCarthys and the Jenners. He is telling his party to meet them beard to beard. He singed the Connecticut Republicans for coddling them. In New Jersey, last Tuesday, he singled out that ancient fraud, Senator Smith, for 'his sad lack of backbone' in caving in before McCarthy.

"Not even for campaign purposes would Harry Truman blanch or quail. Yesterday in Cumberland, Maryland, where McCarthy is generally credited with deciding the 1950 Senate election, the President called Joe 'a political gangster,' a denizen of the 'political underworld,' a dealer in 'the big lie.' His audience listened open-mouthed and then applauded.

"The President of the United States, a man nobody writes off as a political scientist, is gambling that McCarthy is an overrated punk. And, even if he isn't, Mr. Truman will not bow before him, and none of the faint-hearted can tell him to.

"You cannot write about this little man with thick glasses in the language of politics. The words are the sparse words of a military citation—the citation, for example, of a soldier named Charles Kelly, who stood off a German battalion in Italy. The sergeant who wrote it remembered leaving Corporal Kelly with his machinegun burned out and rifle useless.

" 'When last seen,' the sergeant said, 'Corporal Kelly was observed loading and firing a rocket launcher at the advancing enemy.' A soldier like Harry Truman fights the enemy on the ground of the enemy's choosing. He'll run on your own terms —any track, anywhere, any time and distance and who in the hell are you?"

—Murray Kempton, Washington, D.C.,
October 15, 1952

The trouble with Eisenhower . . . he's just a coward. He hasn't got any backbone at all, and he ought to be ashamed for what he did, but I don't think there's any shame in him."

Mr. President, I believe that in 1926 when you ran for presiding judge of the county, you were elected.

"Yes. In 1926 they got together, the two factions of the Democratic Party got together, and I ran for presiding judge, which is the chief executive officer of the county, and I held that position for eight years.

"The county was in debt when I got in because the previous occupants of the job were the kind who were always standing with their hands out when contracts were let for buildings or roads or anything at all.

"I put a stop to it, and I came out of the county courts after ten years of service a damn sight worse off than when I went into it. No man can get rich in politics unless he's a crook."

Edgar Hinde: "I have had the President tell me many, many times that Tom Pendergast never asked him to do anything that wasn't absolutely all right. And I think he gave the President a free hand while he was in county politics, and he ran his job as he saw fit. There was never any hint of graft or skulduggery all the time he was in office in Jackson County. . . .

"In 1931 I believe it was they voted a bond issue. They voted seven million dollars to build a road system in Jackson County, and every one of those contracts, with I believe the exception of one, was let to out-of-state contractors. There was only one contractor in the state of Missouri that got a job here. That was because Harry never let politics enter into a thing of that kind. He gave the bid to the lowest bidder, didn't matter who he was as long as he could do the job.

"And when they finished they had about twenty-five miles more of road than they had contracted for and about two hundred and thirty thousand dollars left in money. So I don't think you could say there was any graft in that deal.

"In fact, when Harry started that bond issue, he appointed a bipartisan board of supervisors to oversee things under his supervision, and there was not a bit of graft in this expenditure of ten million dollars."

Mrs. W. L. C. Palmer: "My husband, who was principal of the high school, was one of the few people who thought Harry was going to be President someday. I have to admit I didn't. I was just too young and flighty at that time, so that I didn't think anybody was going to be President would be going to school with me.

"But my husband did. That was when Harry was presiding judge of the county, and he built—oh, I think ten million dollars' worth of roads. Up to that time the roads in Jackson County were in dreadful condition. You couldn't get anywhere except through mud.

"But Harry got a bond issue approved, and he built those roads. I've heard it said those were the finest roads of any county in the country except Westchester County in New York.

"I remember Harry came to see us one afternoon, and he got out a book showing different parts of the county and what he had done. He gave my husband one of the books and wrote in it, 'To my good friend and preceptor, Professor W. L. C. Palmer, whose ideals were impressed upon me at the right time. Harry S. Truman.'

"I wanted a book, too, of course, and Harry had another one, and he wrote in it, 'To Mrs. W. L. C. Palmer, who tried to teach me to do what I ought. Harry S. Truman.'

"After Harry had gone, Mr. Palmer said to me, 'That boy is going to be President of the United States someday.' So I'm very proud to tell you that while I didn't predict Harry would be President, my husband did."

Harry Truman: "Mrs. Palmer, Miss Hardin her maiden name was, Ardelia Hardin, used to quote that proverb from the Bible, 'Seest thou a man diligent in his business? He shall stand before kings.' I was always diligent enough, I guess. Maybe that's why I've stood before a few kings. I've even sat down with one or two.

"About this getting rich in politics. Like I said, you just can't do it unless you're a crook. After being in politics in the county here, I went to the Senate and stayed there for ten years, and the same thing was true. There were fellas that had their hands out for crooked money. So you could do the same thing in the Senate. You could do the same thing as President of the United States. But I didn't believe in it."

Mr. President, have we ever had a President who was financially dishonest?

"No, no. We've had Presidents who've had crooked men around them. Grant and Harding and perhaps some others who don't come to mind at the moment. But so far as I know, we have never had one who was himself dishonest. And we have never had one who tried to be a man on horseback. We've been very lucky in that regard, and I just hope our luck holds out."

Mr. Truman continued: "When I took office I found the county with two million three hundred thousand dollars in protested warrants, which would bring six percent. And so I went to Chicago. I went to the Harris Trust Company and the First National Bank of Chicago and got them to refinance those warrants on a three percent basis, and that was accomplished. Then I succeeded in getting the court to agree with me to raise the tax enough to meet the county income, and on that basis eventually the county was no longer in debt.

"And when I quit the county, we had a road system that was one of the best in the United States at that time. . . . The protested warrants had all been paid; the county was out of debt, and I was, . . . a fella doesn't like to say this about himself, but I was pleased with what I had done.

"Then I got fooled into running for the United States Senate, and you know what happened after that."

I understand Tom Pendergast once asked you to come into Kansas City to meet some contractors who were unhappy that they weren't getting awarded contracts while you were in office.

"He did, and I went, and here were all these birds in his office, local contractors, and they said they *deserved* to get the bids for building the roads because they were local people and local taxpayers and that sort of thing.

"And I said I didn't give a damn who they were or where they were from. I said I was going to give the bids to the lowest bidders who could do the job, and I didn't care if they were from California or China or where.

"And old Tom Pendergast told them, he said he'd warned them that I was the contrariest goddamn mule in the world. And they left. They were sore as hell and were mumbling and carrying on, but they left, and afterwards Tom Pendergast said to me that I was to go ahead and carry out my commitments as best I saw fit, and that is what I did."

And you never had any more trouble with Mr. Pendergast on that score?

"No, nor on any other. I've said many times that he never asked me to do a dishonest deed, and that's the God's truth. I did my job in the way I thought it ought to be done. And he never interfered, not even when he was in deep trouble himself."

Mr. President, I understand you built a courthouse while you were presiding judge.

"I did. I built a courthouse in Kansas City, and I remodeled the courthouse here in Independence. It was in 1931, and I was in my second term, and it was in the depth of the Depression. Nobody thought I could do it, but I wanted . . . I proposed a bond issue of close on to eight million dollars to build more roads and a new courthouse and make other improvements in the county. And to provide jobs, of course; a lot of people were out of work.

"As I say, nobody thought the voters would approve, but I simply told them what I had in mind, and I told them that not a penny would be wasted, and they understood, and the bond issue was approved."

I understand you've always been interested in architecture.

"Yes, I always have been. I might even have studied architecture if I'd gone off to college, which, as you know, didn't happen. But I've always felt that architecture was most important. You can tell a lot about a country by the kind of building it has.

"And so when we were about to build the courthouse in Kansas City I wanted the best-looking one you could get for the money, built by the best architect. So I got in a car, and I traveled a good distance before I ended up in Shreveport, Louisiana, in Caddo Parish down there, and that was the courthouse I liked. It had been designed by a man named Edward F. Neild, and I hired him to come to Kansas City and build the courthouse there, and it's twenty-two stories high, and it's a beauty.

"And after I became President and we had to rehabilitate the White House because it was falling apart, Neild was in charge of that, too. And he did a crackerjack job."

Who paid for that trip to Shreveport?

"I did. There wasn't anything in the budget to take care of a thing like that, but I felt it was necessary, and so I went ahead and did it. I must have traveled—oh, twenty-five thousand to thirty thousand miles. I went down to Texas and up to New York and out to Denver and Wisconsin. Wherever I heard there was a good courthouse, I went to look at it."

I hear there wasn't a stone that went into the courthouse in Kansas City that you didn't watch being put into place.

"There were some. I had a few other things to do, but there were very few working days when I wasn't there.

That courthouse was costing the people of Jackson County a lot of money, and I didn't want anybody, the workers or the contractors or anybody, to lay down on the job. When you're spending the taxpayers' money, you've got to have a sense of responsibility."

That was pretty much the same thing that motivated you when you started the Truman Committee in the Senate, wouldn't you say?

"It was. And I've said this so often people get sick of hearing it, but the only way free government works is if the men in charge of it have got the welfare of the people in mind at all times. If a man loses sight of that even for a minute, you don't have free government anymore.

"That's why I was never any too happy about the fellow that succeeded me in the White House. He didn't give a damn about the welfare of the people."

How about the Vice President?

"Now let's not get into that. I've told you, all the time I've been in politics there's only two people I hate, and he's one. He not only doesn't give a damn about the people; he doesn't know how to tell the truth. I don't think the son of a bitch knows the difference between telling the truth and lying."

Mr. President, I understand you also took considerable pains to find a sculptor to design the statue of Andrew Jackson in front of the Kansas City courthouse.

"I did. We had a little . . . some money left over from building the courthouse, and I wanted it to go into a statue of old Andy. And I wanted it to be a statue of a real man on a real horse. The one of Andrew Jackson on the horse in Lafayette Square is a ridiculous man on an impossible horse. Every time I looked out of the window in the White House and saw it over there it made me angry. I don't know what got into them, allowing a statue like that across the street from the White House.

"And . . . so to get the right statue, when I was on my trip about the courthouse, I went to see a man named Charles Keck. He'd done a statue of Stonewall Jackson that's down in Charlottesville, Virginia, which is one of the best equestrian statues in this country and maybe the world.

"I went to see him, and I got him to do the Andrew Jackson statue that's in Kansas City. I also went to Andy Jackson's old place, the Hermitage down near Nashville. They've got some of old Andy's uniforms there, and I measured them and gave the measurements to Keck so they'd be just right. And I got the War Department to send him the information on what a general like old Andy would be wearing. They did, and Keck made use of that information."

Mr. President, did you have to do any of those things?

"Of course I didn't, but I wanted to. I wanted that courthouse and that statue to be the best they could be. . . . When I was a boy, that was the way everybody went about things. Or so it seems to me. Nowadays in politics and just about everywhere else all anybody seems to be interested in is . . . not how much he can do but how much he can get away with. And I don't like to see it. I don't know what's going to become of us if everybody starts thinking and acting that way."

Since we were talking about architecture, I asked about the balcony.

In January, 1948, President Truman announced that he was going to build a balcony off his second-floor study in the White House. Those were days when nothing he did went without criticism, and in this instance the outcry was immediate. The New York *Herald Tribune* angrily said that Mr. Truman was only a part-time President of the White House and that he had "a lamentable penchant for meddling with an historic structure which the nation prefers as it is."

I said, *Mr. President, how did you feel when there was so much criticism of your putting that balcony on the White House?*

"It didn't surprise me a bit. That was an election year if you recall. And anyway people get in an uproar whenever any change is suggested in the White House. My goodness, when Mrs. Fillmore wanted to put in bathtubs, the way people screamed and carried on you'd have thought it was the end of the world, but, of course, eventually everybody calmed down."

And the Fillmores were a lot cleaner.

"That's right. They were, and I knew the furor over the balcony would calm down, too. If you read Jefferson's idea of the White House, that balcony ought to have been there in the first place. And that's where I got the idea, from old Tom Jefferson."

I pointed out that now the balcony seemed to be widely admired.

"Well, of course, and that's the way it ought to be. And I never spent any time on that balcony. They claimed I built it so I could sit on it, but I never did. I never had time. I put it there because I thought that it belonged there."

Mr. President, I've read that Chester Arthur sold a lot of White House furniture when he was President.

"He had an auction sale right in the front yard of the White House, and I believe he sold twenty-four or more wagonloads of furniture. He sold a pair of Lincoln's pants and some of Jackson's furniture, and I don't know what all he sold. The whole thing only brought in about four or five thousand dollars, and there were some things that were just invaluable.

"I don't know why he did it. But then he was a President I couldn't ever figure out. They say he kept a whore in the White House, but I don't suppose I ought to say that. He's got some relatives still living out in San Francisco, and they wouldn't like it a bit."

Mr. President, could you tell me about the cheese some of Andrew Jackson's admirers sent him from New York? While he was in the White House, wasn't it?

"It was some people up in Herkimer County, New York, which used to be, maybe still is, cheese country. And some people there wanted to show old Andy how much they liked him, and so they decided to send him the biggest cheese in the world. It weighed about two thousand pounds and was round and as big as a silo, and they brought it down to Washington in a wagon, and naturally, it got a little riper every day.

"And then on the day of old Andy's last reception in the White House. He didn't invite people. He just opened up the doors and let people pour in, and they did, and they started cutting into that cheese, and when they were finished, there was hardly any left over for old Andy. Just about enough to go with a piece of pie, I believe.

"And then what happened? People trampled that cheese all over the White House, into the drapes and the rugs and everything, and when old Van Buren moved into the White House, he wasn't a man of the people like Jackson, and they had to spend I don't know several thousand dollars cleaning up the mess left by that cheese."

I said, still thinking of architecture, that I had recently built a house near Brewster, New York, that was half glass and half brick.

"Like one of those damn things Lloyd Wright used to put up?" asked the President, his lips drawn in a thin line.

Mr. Truman said, "I don't understand fellows like Lloyd Wright. I don't understand what gets into people like that. He started this whole business of chicken-coop and hen-house architecture, and I don't know why in the world he did it.

"I think what the building people do shows what they are thinking for that period, and that's why I hope that one of these days we'll get back to some real architecture."

So much for modern architecture.

On the way back to Kansas City that afternoon my associates were making fun of Mr. Truman's architectural taste, and I went along with the crowd. But that night I walked over to the courthouse and stood there for quite a long while, looking at it and at the statue of Andrew Jackson. And I thought of a man pushing fifty with no money except a salary of $6,000 a year getting into his car and at his own expense driving 25,000 to 30,000 miles so that he could build a courthouse and have a statue that were the best that in his mind they possibly could be. And paying not a cent more than they were worth because he had some old-fashioned idea about his *duty* as a public servant. Duty. Obligations. And what was it Dean Acheson had said of him, that he was a man of rectitude?

And I thought, those things are more important than his opinions of Frank Lloyd Wright. I haven't changed my mind either.

The First Race for the Senate

Mr. President, in 1934 you went from being presiding judge of Jackson County to being a candidate and a successful candidate for the U.S. Senate. How did that happen?

"In 19 and 34 I was finished with the county; I'd done my job, and there wasn't any more reason for my staying on around here than there was for me to stay in the White House in 1952 after I'd finished what I set out to accomplish. Besides which, I felt somebody else deserved a chance. . . . But as you know, I was very much disappointed in the Democratic campaign and in the way the candidate ran it. And I was also very disappointed in the way the election turned out that year.

"But in 1934 there was a new Congressional district . . . a couple of years before the state legislature had redistricted the state, and one of the districts included my old stamping ground, the eastern part of Jackson County. I had intended to run for that seat, but that just didn't happen. And so I went down and filed for the Senate, running against two fine Congressmen who later became friends of mine, Tuck [Jacob L. Milligan] and Jack [John J. Cochran].

"And, oh, the newspapers made quite a bit of fun of me, especially the St. Louis *Post-Dispatch* and the Kansas City *Star* and the St. Joseph *News-Press* and the Springfield *Leader-Press*—they made quite a big to-do about a little country judge who wasn't even a lawyer running for the U.S. Senate. Especially the Kansas City *Star*, which never has liked me and doesn't to this day. The *Star* has always supported the big-business interests of this community . . . , this area and no doubt will continue to do so.

"But when the time came for the campaign to start, I went into sixty counties, and I talked in all kinds of places

. . . any place there was any kind of audience at all, in the little towns and in the country stores, and I shook people's hands, and sometimes, why, sometimes there weren't more than two or three people, but I'd go in, and I'd shake hands, and I'd tell people that I was a farmer and a failed businessman and that I understood the problems that the common people were facing because I was one myself, and they could see that despite what the newspapers were saying, I didn't have horns and a tail. And Roosevelt . . . the Roosevelt New Deal was just getting under way at that time, and I told the people that I was a supporter of Roosevelt and his policies, and I told them why.

"I told them that . . . I said that it was the first time since Woodrow Wilson had been in the White House . . . the first time in more than ten years that there was a President who had the people's welfare at heart. I must have made . . . oh . . . sometimes as many as fifteen or twenty speeches a day. And it was the same kind of deal as I had in 1940 when I ran for reelection to the Senate and there wasn't a person who thought I had a chance to get back to Washington in any way whatever. And in 1948, when as you may recall I ran for reelection as President, and my prospects were not considered any too . . . very likely.

"I just stood there, and I didn't have to make any fancy speeches or put on any powder or paint. I just told people the facts, and the people believed me and didn't pay any attention to what some of the newspapers said about me. They could see for themselves that I was telling the truth as I saw it.

"And I spent time seeing the county courts like the one here in Jackson County, and I saw the clerks who make the appointments for the judges, and there wasn't a precinct in the whole of Missouri where I didn't have a friend, where there wasn't somebody to see to it that I got the votes that had been voted for me. They didn't have to cheat; that wasn't necessary. The votes were there. All they had to do was see to it that they got added up properly. And I came out ahead. I had a plurality of forty thousand votes in the primary, and after that I went ahead and won the election.

"We didn't have a lot of money to spend. But I never stopped talking to people and explaining the issues. I even had a car accident and sprained some ribs. I didn't stop campaigning, though, and, as I say, I got myself elected to the U.S. Senate.

"And so . . . eventually we moved to Washington. Margaret wasn't any too happy about it, and neither, I believe, was Mrs. Truman, but that was how it had to be."

Tom Evans: "I don't think Harry was looking forward to going to Washington that first time . . . or moving to Washington, but in 1940 he certainly wanted to go back, to be reelected, and nobody except maybe Harry himself thought he had a chance to do it."

Mrs. W. L. C. Palmer: "I believe he was somewhat nervous about going to Washington the first time. I remember he talked about the Senate and what an important body of lawmakers it was, and he talked about the Roman Senate and some of the Roman Senators and how grateful he was that I had taught him Latin and something of Roman history.

"He was not the quickest to learn; I believe Charlie Ross was quicker than he, and I believe you could say Bess was, too. But what Harry did learn it seemed he never did forget.

"Even after he became President, he was having a discussion with Chief Justice Vinson about some bill that was being debated in Congress, and Chief Justice Vinson quoted Marcus Porcius Cato about that Carthage must be destroyed. Except he said it in Latin. I forget how he said it, but I remember Harry said, 'That's the idea, but you didn't say it right. You should have said, 'Ceterum censeo Carthaginem esse delendum.' And Harry was right, of course.

"The newspapermen who wrote the story up wondered how Harry Truman knew anything about Latin. So they went to the encyclopedia and took it out and found that it was exactly as Harry Truman had said it was. So when I read that, I wrote to him, and I said, 'I want to congratulate you on your Latin. I don't suppose I taught it to you. You probably got it out of the *Encyclopaedia Britannica.*'

"He answered my letter and set me a photograph, and on it was inscribed 'To Mrs. W. L. C. Palmer, from her old Latin publicity man.'"

The last time I saw Mrs. Palmer the autographed photograph was hanging on the wall of the living room, slightly to the right of the horsehair sofa.

When I mentioned what Mrs. Palmer had said about Cato and the quotation from Cato, Mr. Truman said, "Mrs. Palmer—she was Miss Ardelia Hardin when I was in school—was a crackerjack of a teacher. She was so interested in what she was teaching that you just couldn't think of letting her down.

"I don't remember what Fred Vinson and I were talking about, what bill, but it was probably something to do with that damn Eightieth Congress. The majority of those fellows were just as bad as Cato was. He was against just about every progressive idea that came up in his whole lifetime, and they called him 'The Censor' because he was opposed to new ideas and tried to suppress them. And he was jealous of Carthage because it was more prosperous than Rome. That's why for years he ended every speech by saying, *'Ceterum censeo Carthaginem esse delendum.'*

"But I'll tell you one good thing about him, Cato. He wrote one of the best books about farming in Rome and farming anywhere else that I've ever come across. *De Agricultura* it's called. I read it in Latin before the war, when I was on the farm out at Grandview. I think I've got a copy in the library here someplace.

"I've told you. The only thing new in the world is the history you don't know. And that's true because human nature doesn't change. I sometimes wish it did, but I'm afraid it just isn't possible. At least that's what I've learned from studying history.

"And it's the same with farming. It hasn't changed from Roman times until now. We've got a few more machines now, but that's about the only difference."

Returning to the time Harry Truman went to Washington as a freshman Senator from Missouri, Mrs. Palmer said, "Mr. Palmer said to him, 'Harry, of course, this is just the first step for you. You have just started on your way, and I remember Harry said, 'Oh, no,' he said. 'The Senate is going further than I have any right to expect.'

"Harry Truman was a very modest boy and a modest man, and I believe that that is why he has been so successful in whatever he has done. People always felt they could count on him, and he has never disappointed them. At least if he has, I have never heard of it, and neither has anyone else in Independence.

"I don't believe that it is true, about a prophet being without honor in his own land. I think Harry Truman has always been very much honored by the people of Independence. There is not a man of his time who in this town has been so much revered."

Harry Truman: "Before we moved to Washington and after we got there, I studied up on the lives of each Senator, and by the time the session started I knew pretty much the history of every man. So I felt sure that when I got there, got to Washington, I'd understand all those men and why they acted the way they did."

Is that what happened?

"Oh, no. Oh, my, no. I guess you might say that is . . . was really the first time I realized that there is often a considerable difference between what people write about themselves and what is written about them . . . even when the writer has set out to tell the truth . . . and the way things really are.

"There were some very good men in the Senate; most of them were, but there were some who were not so good, who were lazy, who never did any work but who got the headlines every time they made a speech, and some of them got sent back to the Senate time after time."

In other words, you can fool some of the people some of the time.

"Yes. Old Abe was right about that. As he was about most other things. But most of the Senators were very good men and worked very hard at their jobs."

Were you happy in the Senate?

"At first I wasn't. At first I was not very comfortable at all. And one day old Ham Lewis [J. Hamilton Lewis of Illinois, then the Democratic whip of the Senate] came over to me, and he said, 'Harry, the first six months you're here you'll wonder why . . . you'll wonder how the hell you got here, and after that you'll wonder how the hell the rest of us got here.' And that's pretty much the way it turned out. Old Ham pretty much hit the nail on the head."

Mr. President, is it true that when you were in the Senate your mother used to write you letters telling you how she felt you ought to vote on certain legislation?

"She very often did that. She read the *Congressional Record* every day, and she understood what was going on a lot better than some Senators I could mention. And she was one of my constituents, in addition to being my mother, and she had every right to write to me."

Did you always agree with her and follow her suggestions?

"Most of the time, yes; she was very strong for Roosevelt, and so was I, and so we agreed most of the time, but when she thought I'd voted wrong, you can bet I heard from her in no uncertain terms. She was a woman who knew her own mind."

Did you ever have the feeling that some people in Washington are convinced that people in the western part of the country can't read at all? And don't think?

"I did. Oh, my, yes. That's why when there was some talk that Washington might be bombed, while I was President, I wanted to move the capital out to Colorado so the people in the Senate, in the government, many of whom had never been west of the Appalachians would have to come across the country—they'd have to drive; I wouldn't let them fly—would come across and see the country and get to meet people who aren't suffering from what I call Potomac Fever."

What's Potomac Fever?

"It was Woodrow Wilson who coined the phrase. He said that some people came to Washington and grew with their jobs, but he said a lot of other people came, and all they did was swell up. Those that swell up are the ones that have Potomac Fever. They're the people who forget who they are and who sent them there."

Does that happen very often?

"I'm afraid so. Washington is a very easy city for you to forget where you came from and why you got there in the first place."

Did you ever feel you were in any danger of doing that?

"No, no. I always came back to Independence every chance I got because the people in Independence, the people in Missouri had been responsible for sending me to Washington. And that's why when I ended up at the White House, after I had finished the job, I came back here. This is where I belong."

Mr. President, I understand that during your first term in the Senate, you met Justice Brandeis.

Justice Louis D. Brandeis was appointed to the Supreme Court by Woodrow Wilson and was the first Jew to serve. He was a man of awesome intellect, a graduate of the Harvard Law School, and along with Justice Oliver Wendell Holmes one of the great and most consistent liberal dissenters on the Court until the New Deal came along. Until his retirement in 1939 he was an almost equally consistent supporter of New Deal legislation.

"I did know Justice Brandeis, and he was a great old man. I went to his place very often, and we seemed to have no trouble in hitting it off. We had many a long talk. I had read many of his decisions and his books, two of them. I believe there were two. One was called *Other People's*

Money, and I've forgot, don't remember, the name of the other. But he was very pleased that I had read his books."

I said, "Writers often are," and the President laughed.

Did you in general agree with Justice Brandeis' philosophy?

"Oh, yes. Very largely yes. He was one of the great Justices. He and Oliver Wendell Holmes were my favorites. And Justice Brandeis and I were certainly in agreement on the dangers of bigness, and my goodness . . . I cannot . . . I have often wondered what Justice Brandeis would think of these great combines of business now. He wouldn't have liked it. Of that I am sure, and neither do I."

I'm not sure the word "conglomerate" was in general circulation in 1961; it certainly was not in Harry Truman's vocabulary, and he would have despised it, both the word and the idea. We will come to what Mr. Truman thought about the Pentagon.

Mr. President, I've been told that you made a largely forgotten speech on the floor of the Senate during your first term in which you blasted big business.

"There were . . . I've got them. There were two speeches, and they are in one of the books here."

The speeches were in a collection of Mr. Truman's speeches. One was delivered in June, 1937, and it said in part:

"Some of the country's greatest railroads have been deliberately looted by their financial agents. . . . Speaking of Rock Island reminds me that the first railroad robbery was committed on the Rock Island in 1873 just east of Council Bluffs, Iowa. The man who committed that robbery used a gun and a horse, and he got up early in the morning. He and his gang took a chance of being killed, and eventually most of them were killed. The loot was $3,000. That railroad robber's name was Jesse James. The same Jesse James held up the Missouri Pacific in 1876 and took the paltry sum of $17,000 from the express car.

"About thirty years after the Council Bluffs holdup, the Rock Island went through a looting by some gentlemen

known as the 'Tin Plate Millionaires.' They used no guns,
but they ruined the railroad and got away with seventy
million dollars or more. They did it by means of holding
companies. Senators can see what 'pikers' Mr. James and
his men were alongside of some real artists."

In the speech Senator Truman delivered on the floor of
the Senate in December, 1937, he said in part:

"One of the difficulties as I see it is that we worship
money instead of honor. A billionaire in our estimation is
much greater in the eyes of the people than the public
servant who works for the public interest.

". . . It makes no difference if the billionaire rode to
wealth on the sweat of little children and the blood of
underpaid labor. . . . No one ever considers the Carnegie
libraries steeped in the blood of the Homestead steel workers, but they are. We do not remember that the Rocke-
feller Foundation is founded on the dead miners of the
Colorado Fuel Company and a dozen other performances.
We worship Mammon. Until we get back to the . . .
fundamentals and return to the Giver of the Tables of the
Law and His teachings, these conditions are going to remain with us.

"It is a pity that Wall Street with its ability to control
all the wealth of the nation and to hire the best brains of
the country has not produced some statesmen, some men
who could see the dangers of bigness and of the concentration of the control of wealth. Instead of working to meet
the situation, they are still employing the best law brains
to serve greed and selfish interest.

"People can only stand so much, and one of these days
there will be a settlement. We shall have one receivership
too many, one unnecessary depression out of which we will
not come with the power still in the same old hands.

"I believe this country would be better off if we did not
have sixty per cent of the assets of all insurance companies
concentrated in four companies. I believe that a thousand
insurance companies with $4,000,000 each in assets would
be just a thousand times better for the country than the

Metropolitan Life with $4,000,000,000 in assets. The average brain is not built to deal with such astronomical figures.

". . . a thousand county seats of 7,000 each are a thousand times more important to this Republic than one city of 7,000,000. Our unemployment and our unrest are the result of the concentration of wealth, the concentration of population in industrial centers, mass production, and a lot of other so-called modern improvements.

"We are building a tower of Babel."

After reading the two speeches, I said, *Mr. President, you said some pretty strong things in those speeches. You sound like a Populist.*

The President had been rereading the speeches with, I felt, considerable pleasure. He said, "Maybe I do. I don't like giving names to things if I can help it, but that's the way I felt at the time and still do.

"That's one of the things I try to tell these youngsters when I talk to them. That people have to keep their eyes and ears open at all times or they'll be robbed blind by the Mugwumps in politics and by the big-business interests.

"Every generation seems to have to learn that all over again, and it's a shame. I've wondered and I've wondered and I've wondered why. It's a human trait, I guess. Every youngster as he grows up knows he was a darned sight smarter than his daddy was, and he has to get to be about forty before he finds out the old man was smart enough to raise him.

"But as I say, I don't know why it is. Why the next generation can't learn from the one before until they get knocked in the head by experience.

"I'll tell you one thing for sure. The only things worth learning are the things you learn after you know it all."

During your first term in the Senate you served on a committee under Senator Wheeler [Burton K. Wheeler of Montana] to investigate the railroads.

"Senator Wheeler set up a subcommittee to look into railroad finances. They were in bad shape and going bankrupt because the more money that was poured into them, mostly by the government, the more 'the tin-plate millionaires' that I mentioned in that speech, the more they and the rest of the big-money boys and their lawyers stole.

"Wheeler wanted me to look into that. At first I wasn't a member of the committee, but I was allowed to sit in on the hearings, which I did every day."

I understand that you did a lot of reading, too, and at one time you took fifty books on railroads and railroad history out of the Congressional Library so that you could bone up on the subject.

"I don't remember that I did, but I wouldn't doubt it a bit. As I've told you, I like to be thorough, to have a thorough knowledge of whatever I'm involved in."

You spent a lot of time in the Congressional Library?

"I used it a great deal, and the people there were just as nice, as helpful, as they possibly could be. My goodness the trouble they'd go to if you asked them a question, to look something up.

"What surprised, what disappointed me about the Congressional Library was how few members of Congress ever seemed to use it; I used to go in there, and there sometimes wouldn't be anybody else there except a few young people and the librarians. Seldom any . . . very seldom any members of Congress.

"I couldn't understand it then, and I still can't."

Eventually you were appointed to the Wheeler committee, weren't you?

"Yes, eventually when there was a vacancy on the committee, Wheeler appointed me, and . . . I believe a year or so later, when he was out of Washington a good deal of the time, making speeches against what was called the Roosevelt court-packing plan, I became vice-chairman of the committee."

You liked Senator Wheeler, didn't you?

"I did. Later, of course; we always disagreed on many things, and we were in almost total disagreement on the

Second World War. He was an isolationist, and as you know, I was not.

"But on other issues he was just as valuable as he could be, and he was honest as the day is long. When I first came to Washington, he was one of the first Senators to be . . . who took the trouble to be kind to me, and I never forgot a thing like that."

You presided over a good many meetings of that committee.

"I did, and it was very good training for what came later when I presided over what people called for whatever reason the Truman Committee.

"I presided, and one of the first investigations I conducted was into the affairs of the Missouri-Pacific Railroad, and my goodness, the telegrams I got, and the phone calls and letters. And visitors, quite a number of visiting firemen who asked me to call off my dogs. I was threatened with political ruination of every kind you can imagine if I didn't call off the investigation, but, of course, I didn't do it."

Max Lowenthal, who was counsel to the committee, has said that there were very few if any other Senators out of all the ninety-six who could or would have withstood the pressure you withstood.

"That may be, but it didn't make any difference. I had undertaken to do a job, and I was not about to give up without finishing it no matter what was said. So we went ahead with the hearings, and my, the lies I listened to from all those lawyers with their Ha-vud accents. It just seemed they didn't make any bones about telling lies, and a lot of people believed them. You dress a man up in a fancy suit and give him a fancy accent, and a lot of people seem to think he has to be telling the truth, but I never did.

"I went right ahead and found out the truth, and the result was that I was able to present to the Senate a new law regulating railroad finances, and oh, my, the shouting and screaming that went on from the big corporations and the holding companies.

"I was called every name in the book that they could

think of, including that I was a Socialist and a Communist and an anarchist and I don't know what all. And every Senator and every Congressman got a number of telephone calls and telegrams.

"But we went right ahead, and after some time . . . it took some time to do it, but after a while we got the law passed. It was called the Transportation Act of 1940, and at that time it represented a very good piece of legislation that had the interests of the people at heart, and I was happy to have had some part in getting it . . . enacting it into law."

Mr. President, I'm an occasional victim of the New York Central Railroad. Do you feel that railroad management perhaps needs looking into again perhaps?

"Yes, yes, of course. Those lawyers with their Ha-vud accents are always thinking up new ways to take advantage of people, and you need a new investigation every five, every ten years or so."

And now it's been more than twenty years since there was one.

"It has, and it's a great pity."

As of this writing it has been more than thirty years since such an investigation was held, and the corrupt New York Central has become the even more corrupt and bankrupt Penn Central, but there is no Harry Truman to conduct an investigation. To care even.

It *is* a great pity.

Another major achievement of Harry Truman's first term in the Senate was his fight for the Wheeler-Rayburn bill in 1935; that bill, also known as the Public Utility Holding Company Act, had at its heart what was called the Death Sentence clause, which proposed dissolving all public utility holding companies on the grounds that they drained off the profits from the utility companies themselves, thus causing consumers to be charged higher rates.

In opposing the bill as a whole and that clause in particular the utility companies put on what was said to be the most extensive and expensive lobbying campaign in history up to then.

I said, *Mr. President, I understand that you got as many as thirty thousand letters from people in Missouri asking that you vote against the Public Utility Holding Company Act.*

"I did. Twenty-five to thirty thousand, something like that, and I had them burned."

You had them burned?

"I most certainly did. Those letters and telegrams . . . were caused by the lobbyists who'd been sent out to Missouri to tell people lies. You have to watch out for the people's interest in that kind of thing, and the people's interest, for the vast majority of the poor and middle-class people, it was in their interest to get that bill passed into law. So I didn't pay any attention to all those letters.

"And they sent a . . . the utility people sent a lot of high-powered people down to Washington to stir up things. One of them was a fella by the name of John Foster Dulles who later wound up in the Cabinet of the fella that succeeded me. And Mr. Wendell Willkie was another. So when in a year or so in 1940, when he ran for President against Roosevelt and told the people how he was out to protect their interests, I wasn't much impressed."

I believe Harold Ickes [Roosevelt's Secretary of the Interior] called Willkie "the barefoot boy from Wall Street," because he'd, . . . Willkie, had made so much of being from Indiana, although he'd lived in New York for twenty years or so and he was head of a big utility company [Commonwealth and Southern].

"Did he? I'd forgot that. . . . Sometimes Harold Ickes got off a good one. Not too often, though. He was mad too much of the time."

The controversial Death Sentence section of the utility bill was passed by the Senate 45–44, and the complete bill was passed by a vote of 56–32. Truman was paired in favor of the bill.

Mr. President, in 1940 did you want to return to the Senate?

"No question about it at all. For one thing there were too many people around who didn't want me to run.

"I knew it was going to be a hell of a fight, but I've never backed away from a fight. Roosevelt got word to me that I could be on the Interstate Commerce Commission if I'd get out of the race and support Lloyd Stark." Stark was then the Democratic governor of Missouri.*

"Well, I wouldn't. I wouldn't at all, and I got word back to Roosevelt that if the only vote I got was my own, I'd still run. Roosevelt was a fine man and a great President, but he sometimes made mistakes, just like the rest of us."

Mr. President, would you describe yourself as a stubborn man?

The President smiled, and he said, "What I am . . . I don't know if I'm stubborn or not, although I've been called that from time to time, but when I make up my mind to do something, I believe you'll find I usually carry through on it.

"Lloyd Stark is a no good son of a bitch, and I don't care what anybody says. He's the president of Stark Orchards, which is the biggest in the country. He and his cousins and his brother run it, and they're all fine people. But Lloyd's a nut. He couldn't make up his mind what he wanted to be, and then he tried to run for everything at the

* During his first term in the Senate Mr. Truman was often referred to as "The Senator from Pendergast." It was thought that he had been elected by a corrupt machine and must, therefore, be corrupt himself. Thus, many Senators ignored him, and so for a very long time did the White House. Lloyd C. Stark, the nurseryman who was to be Truman's opponent in his 1940 race for the Senate, was often a guest on the Roosevelt yacht on the Potomac; Truman never was. Stark, of course, was a graduate of Annapolis and a man of polish and sophistication. Harry Truman was not, and Roosevelt, despite his political programs for the common man, was a considerable snob socially.

Truman liked to remember being closer to Roosevelt than he ever was.

same time.* He's sort of like that fellow we were talking about downstairs [Adlai Stevenson]. Couldn't make up his mind what he wanted to do.

"I had more to do with making him governor than anybody else in the state, and then he turned around and ran against me for the Senate.†

"He'd come to my office in Washington. He was always dropping in to ask some favor or other. I don't think he ever once visited me without wanting a handout of some kind, and in those days if I could give it to him, I did.

"One day long before the primary [the Democratic primary to choose a nominee for the Senate which in Missouri at that time was tantamount to election] he came into my office. I forget what he wanted on that occasion, but he said some people in Missouri wanted him to run against me for the Senate.

"But he said [imitating Stark's voice], 'I'm not a gonna do it, Harry.' He says, 'You know I'm a friend of yours, Harry, and I wouldn't do anything in the world to hurt your feelings.'

"When he left my office I said to my secretary [Victor

---

* In 1940, at the same time that Stark was threatening to run for the Senate, he showed up at the Democratic convention in Chicago with a number of Stark Delicious apples to hand out to the delegates and an announcement that he was *available* for the Vice Presidential nomination on the ticket with Roosevelt. He withdrew before the balloting for that office began, but a good many potential supporters from Missouri felt that he had made a fool of himself and of them by running for two offices at the same time.

† In the summer of 1935 Harry Truman and Senator Bennett Clark, the senior Senator from Missouri, at his request took Stark to New York to introduce him to Tom Pendergast, who was about to sail for Europe. Stark begged for Pendergast's support in his race for governor. Truman has reported that Pendergast said of Stark, "He won't do, Harry. I don't like the so-and-so. He's a no-good."

Nevertheless, with the urging of Truman and Clark, Pendergast did support Stark, and he was elected.

Messall], I said, 'That son of a bitch is gonna run against me,' and sure enough I was right. That's exactly what happened.

"I believe I mentioned that Lloyd Stark is one of the two people I have ever held a grudge against."

12

The 1940 Campaign

The historic triumph was in 1948, of course, the year
Mr. Truman astounded everybody, friends and enemies
alike, and he did it with the whole world looking on and
a good part of it delighted with the miracle he had somehow managed.

But in 1940 when he ran for reelection to the Senate,
with nobody much watching and everybody who mattered
against him, he was even more of an underdog, and he
won that time, too.

That looked like a bad year for a man turned fifty-six
years old who, if he didn't get reelected, would be out of
a job, permanently it looked like. His old friend Tom Pendergast was in jail, convicted of income-tax evasion. He
had failed to report almost half a million dollars, a bribe
given him by various insurance companies.

They had tried to dig up dirt on Harry, but there just
wasn't any. Still, he suffered from old Tom's downfall.
Birds of a feather, the newspapers said. And, anyway, if
Harry wasn't involved, why didn't he denounce Pendergast? That would clear the air.

"No," said Harry. "I wouldn't kick a friend who was
in trouble no matter what it might do to win me votes."

And Harry was broke, as usual. His mother was eighty-
eight years old, and they were threatening to foreclose the
mortgage on her farm, which later, as you'll see, did happen. But Harry couldn't give her any financial help. Hell,
at the beginning of the campaign he couldn't even afford
stamps to write to people, old friends, asking for money.
Later, he did manage to borrow $1,000 from a St. Louis
contractor, which was repaid after the Democratic primary.

Harry had two opponents in the primary, Maurice Milligan, the prosecutor who had earned a name for himself
by sending Pendergast to jail, and Lloyd Stark.

Both Milligan and Stark vigorously campaigned against Tom Pendergast, and they indicated that Harry Truman was no more than his crooked errand boy. If the truth be known, they said Harry ought to be in jail himself, and when the whole truth came out, he no doubt would be.

All the important papers of the state were against him. The St. Louis *Post-Dispatch* just never let up on the man, and one cartoon showed two heavy trucks, one named Milligan, the other named Stark, with Harry in a toy car between them. The caption was: "No Place for a Kiddy-car."

After he got to be President, the cartoonist sent Mr. Truman the original of that cartoon, and it is in the library at Independence now.

The campaign began at Sedalia, Missouri, a town of 20,000 people in the center of the state, and Mr. Truman and his supporters had trouble getting enough money to pay for the posters advertising the meeting. Quite a few people turned out, though, and that proud Rebel Martha Ellen Truman sat in the front row. And it was there, on the courthouse steps in Sedalia, of all places and all times, that Harry Truman made a speech on civil rights. By 1973 standards it may not seem like much, but by 1940 standards it was quite something.

I wondered why, why then, why there. Of course the record of his administration on civil rights was clear enough. Clinton Rossiter has written that of two major accomplishments of Mr. Truman as President: "One was domestic in character: the first real beginnings of a many-sided program toward eliminating discrimination and second-class citizenship in American life." True. And we remember that at the 1953 inaugural blacks were invited to all the social events for the first time in American history. But that was public, that was *politics;* people were watching, and the black vote was getting to be important.

But in 1940 in Sedalia, Missouri, before an audience mostly of farmers, many of them ex-Ku Kluxers, and not a black face anywhere, Harry Truman spoke out on civil rights. While the words were not eloquent, the man's words were never eloquent, they were unequivocal, and they had a simple beauty of their own:

"I believe in the brotherhood of man, not merely the brotherhood of white men but the brotherhood of all men before law.

"I believe in the Constitution and the Declaration of Independence. In giving Negroes the rights which are theirs we are only acting in accord with our own ideals of a true democracy.

"If any class or race can be permanently set apart from, or pushed down below the rest in political and civil rights, so may any other class or race when it shall incur the displeasure of its more powerful associates, and we may say farewell to the principles on which we count our safety.

"In the years past, lynching and mob violence, lack of schools, and countless other unfair conditions hastened the progress of the Negro from the country to the city. In these centers the Negroes never had much chance in regard to work or anything else. By and large they went to work mainly as unskilled laborers and domestic servants.

"They have been forced to live in segregated slums, neglected by the authorities. Negroes have been preyed upon by all types of exploiters from the installment salesmen of clothing, pianos, and furniture to the vendors of vice.

"The majority of our Negro people find cold comfort in shanties and tenements. Surely, as freemen, they are entitled to something better than this. . . . It is our duty to see that Negroes in our locality have increased opportunity to exercise their privilege as freemen . . ."

Mr. President, when I came across that speech in Jonathan Daniels' book last night, I found it surprising. It seems to me to have been very courageous.

"I don't know why. That sort of thing, whether what I was saying was courageous or not, never did occur to me. And you have to understand what I said out there at Sedalia wasn't anything *new* for me to say. All those Southern fellas were very much surprised by my program for civil rights in 1948. What they didn't understand was that I'd been for things like that all the time I was in politics. I believe in the Constitution, and if you do that, then everybody's got to have their rights, and that means *everybody*, doesn't matter a damn who they are or what color they are.

"The minute you start making exceptions, you might as well not have a Constitution. So that's the reason I felt the way I did, and if a lot of folks were surprised to find out where I stood on the colored question, well, that's because they didn't know me."

On the same page in the Daniels book that quotes your speech there's something Lincoln said about the Know-Nothings that I guess you'd agree with.

"If Lincoln said it, the chances are ninety-nine out of a hundred that I'd agree with it. What's that? Read it to me."

Well, he said, "As a nation we began by declaring that 'all men are created equal.' We now practically read it 'all men are created equal except negroes.' When the Know-nothings get control, it will read 'all men are created equal except negroes and foreigners and Catholics.' When it comes to this, I shall prefer emigrating to some country where they make no pretense of loving liberty,—to Russia, for instance, where despotism can be taken pure, and without the base alloy of hypocrisy."

"Well, that's just as true these days as it was in Lincoln's time, both about this country and Russia, too. I've always known it and always said it. That's what they never seemed to get right when they were writing me up in the newspapers. I always meant what I said, especially about the Constitution. You'll never find me playing fast and loose with that. Never."

Getting back to the 1940 campaign, tell me about that.

"Well, what we've been talking about. The first meeting was at . . . in the town of Sedalia, and Lew Schwellenbach [U.S. Senator from Washington] made a pitch for me, and there was quite a good crowd, friendly, but that was just the first step. I realized that if I was going to win, I had to go out and beat the bushes, which I did. Missouri's got a hundred and fourteen counties, and I got into seventy-five of them and finally won by a very close shave when you take into consideration that nearly four hundred thousand votes were cast in the primary and I won by about eight thousand. Altogether it was one of the toughest, maybe *the* toughest campaign I ever went through."

I understand your mother was at the meeting at Sedalia.

"She was. I couldn't have kept her away if I'd tried."

I've read that when people were taken up to meet her, she could always tell who was your friend and who wasn't.

"She was a very good judge of people, and although she was eighty-eight years old, her eyes were just as sharp as ever they had been, and she never had any trouble sizing up who was going the right way and who was going the wrong way as far as I was concerned. And she did not like Lloyd Stark. She said she'd just like to get her hands on Lloyd, and there were times when I wouldn't have minded if she could have.

"I've been called a lot of things in my life, but some of the things Lloyd said about me—(imitating Stark) 'I'm your friend, Harry, and I wouldn't do anything to hurt you'—some of those things I never will forget. Never in a hundred years."

Mr. President, is it true that at the same time that Stark was attacking you for accepting Pendergast support you had a letter signed by him, thanking you for introducing him to Tom Pendergast so that he could get such support?

"Oh, yes, I did."

But you didn't use that letter in the campaign—despite Stark's vicious attacks on you. Why?

"I didn't think it would be right to do a thing like that."

Rufus Burrus, Mr. Truman's Independence lawyer and longtime friend: "I campaigned for him when he was running for reelection to the Senate in 1940. Things were very, very difficult; it was like 1948, when he was running for reelection to the Presidency. Nobody around here, including me, thought he had a chance.

"The two candidates running against him were talking about their virtues and waving their names in front of the people. And all Harry talked about was Roosevelt and the New Deal and how it ought to be supported. And I said, 'Mr. Truman, don't you think it's about time you said something for Harry Truman? Or if you don't, let me say something for you.'

"'No,' he says. 'I'm talking about the Democratic achievements in Congress and the Democratic program, and people will catch on and know I've had some part of it. Those other fellows are doing enough blowing their own horns.'"

Mr. Burrus, I understand there wasn't much money to toss around in that campaign.

"No, no, there wasn't. Mr. Truman . . . part of the time I believe he didn't have enough money for a hotel room, and I believe he slept in the car. A United States Senator . . . sleeping in his car. And they were . . . his opponents were accusing him of being dishonest and of having a slush fund and I don't know what all.

"But the people he met . . . they could see just by looking at him that what was said about him was a bunch of lies. There wasn't anybody who saw him or listened to him talk who ever thought there was a dishonest bone in Harry Truman's body. He was . . . was just about the worst speaker ever, but people never doubted he was telling them the truth.

"But that campaign in 1940 was very, very difficult. He never complained, though. He went right ahead and did it, and of course he won."

Mr. Burrus, how has your relationship been with Mr. Truman as his attorney all these years?

"Mr. Truman is just the best kind of client there is or ever could be. He never tells you what to do or how to do it the way so many people do. He just says, 'Would you please see about getting this taken care of?' And of course I do, and that's how our relationship works.

"Mr. Truman and I never talk about money. I'm always glad to do Mr. Truman's legal chores and errands for him without discussing money. He's endeavored to make me take some money at times, but I don't see fit to do that.

"That would be like taking money from my own family members that I do things for. And I've always considered my relationship with Mr. Truman as being a family relationship rather than as attorney and client. And here in Missouri we don't charge our kinfolks with fees like we would do if they were strangers."

Mr. President, I understand they foreclosed the mortgage on your mother's farm during that campaign.

"Yes, they did. They did foreclose it. Had an old squint-eyed guy that was head of the county government, and he thought that would be a good way to help in my defeat, but nearly everybody in Missouri had a mortgage, so it didn't do me a bit of harm.

"But it was a sad thing to see. We had to move my mother and the furniture and everything else off the old farm, and not long after she moved, she fell and broke her leg, which I don't think would have happened in the old place.

"It wasn't a pretty thing to see . . . to have to move an old lady of eighty-eight out of her home place, but they went ahead and did it. Some people will do anything to win an election, and it's a sorry thing to see. If you have to do something . . . pull a thing like that, I've never seen the use of winning."

You don't think the end justifies the means then?

"No and never have. Never."

How much money do you think you spent in that campaign, Mr. President?

"I didn't have any of what you'd call real money, didn't have any at all. I finally raised about eight or nine thousand dollars. We sent out some letters saying that if people wanted to see me go back to the Senate, they ought to send one dollar each, and we got a good deal in small contributions like that.

"But that's about all. I think we had one fifteen-minute radio broadcast in St. Louis a few days before the election, but the St. Louis organization paid for that.

"The whole thing made me convinced that it isn't money that wins elections, although in some instances I know it has."

Like in the last Presidential campaign, for instance. (I meant the 1960 campaign when John F. Kennedy was said to have spent a fortune in the primary campaigns in particular.)

"You said that; I didn't. But it's a very bad thing spending hundreds of thousands of dollars . . . trying to buy the votes of the people.

"I was always very particular about where my money came from. Very few people are going to give you large sums of money if they don't expect to get something from it, and you've got to keep that in mind.

"At least that's the way I've always felt."

Did you make your last campaign appearance in Independence that year?

"Oh, yes, same as usual. It didn't matter what I was running for; I always ended up the campaign back here in Independence, and we had a rally out at the football field of the high school, and there were some stands selling hot dogs and the like and quite a good crowd of people. And I ended up the program by telling the people what I stood for, and that was that.

"I came back home, and I started getting calls. Everybody thought for sure I was beat, and I wasn't too sure myself how it would turn out that time. And when I went to bed, Stark was eleven thousand votes ahead, so I thought for sure I was a goner."

But you went to bed anyway, and I suppose went to sleep.

"Yes, I did. Of course I did. But along about three o'clock in the morning an old man called me from St. Louis. And he had a Dutch accent I think it was, and he said [imitating the accent], 'I want to congratulate you.' And I said, 'Quit kidding. What are you congratulating me about?'

" 'Well,' he said. 'You're five thousand votes ahead, and the St. Louis *Post-Dispatch* says you're elected.' And that's what happened."

Truman carried St. Louis by 8,411 votes, which put him ahead of Stark by about 8,000 votes in the state and won him the primary. The Truman victory in St. Louis was made possible by a young Irishman named Bob Hannegan, who four years later as chairman of the Democratic national committee played an important part in getting the Vice Presidential nomination for Harry Truman.

Mr. President, I understand that being a Mason helped you win the election over your Republican opponent that November.

"I was . . . I had just been made Grand Master for the whole state of Missouri, and the Republican candidate for the Senate [Manvelle Davis] was cussing me out every time he opened his mouth. He said I was guilty of every crime in the book, and then one day at a meeting down at Wellsville a friend of mine was down there, and so was the fella running for governor on that ticket. His name was Forrest Donnell, and he was a Mason, as I was.

"So my friend said to Donnell that if I was as bad as Davis was saying, how was it possible that I could be Grand Master of the Masons? And Donnell said, 'He couldn't be.'

"Well, that word got around the state, and it did me no harm at all at the polls."

Mr. President, I understand that when you got back to the Senate the next year, following that election, you got a standing ovation from the Senators of both parties.

Mr. Truman was a sentimental man; his eyes misted over, and it was a moment before he could speak. Then he said, "It was one of the . . . it impressed me very much indeed, and that's one of the reasons when they mentioned that other job to me [the Vice Presidency], I didn't want to take it. Because the Senate of the United States is one of the greatest, maybe *the* greatest legislative body in the history of the world.

"It takes a long time for a person to reach a position of influence in the Senate. Eight or ten Senators really run the whole thing. And you have to have their confidence to get anything done, and I think it can be said that eventually I did have. Just to . . . as an example, the Senate was considering the approval of one of those admirals, Admiral Land [Emory S.] as chairman of the Maritime Commission I think it was.

"And when I came into the Senate, I'd been over to the House, and I came in the door and stopped by Vandenberg's desk [Arthur H. Vandenberg, Republican of Michigan], and he turned to me and said, 'Harry, what do you think of Admiral Land?'

"I said, 'Senator, I think he's all right. I think he'll do a good job.' And I went around to my seat, and Vandenberg got up and said, 'When the junior Senator from Missouri makes a statement like that, it's worth agreeing to.' And they did. The Senate approved of Land for the job.

"But that's what I mean. That shows you that if you have a fundamentally honest background with the Senators, you can get things accomplished. The whole thing, our whole government works on trust. If you can't trust a fellow Senator or anybody else in our government, the whole thing breaks down.

"And of course there are always those on the other side of the fence, the ones whose word you know isn't worth a good goddamn. Like Huey Long [Senator from Louisiana] who was later assassinated. He was a liar, and he was nothing but a damn demagogue.

"It didn't surprise me when they shot him. These demagogues, the ones that live by demagoguery. They all end up the same way.

"One day I was sitting in the chair. I was the only one there because the minute he started talking the other Senators started leaving. But I had to stay in the chair. And he was carrying on. And he had a big stack of books, you know. He always read the newspapers and books and everything else he could lay his hands on when he was carrying on a filibuster.

"I adjourned the Senate when he closed his book, and we walked across the street from the Senate, and he said, 'What did you think of my speech, Harry?'

"I said, 'Hell, Huey, I had to sit there and listen to it.' And he never spoke to me after that. Not that I was missing much."

As I said the other day, the extraordinary thing to me is the amount of homework you did while you were in the Senate.

"Well, as I told you, I did that just like I did everything else. Whenever I had to have information on a subject that was to come up before any of the four or five committees that I belonged to, I made it a point to find out exactly what I needed to know to vote the right way. The way that would benefit the most people."

The Truman Committee

Mr. President, tell me about the Truman Committee.

"That wasn't the name of it. It was called the Committee to Investigate the National Defense Program. Of course later they gave it that shorter name, and I didn't like it at all, but I couldn't put a stop to it.

". . . the way the committee started . . . I've said before. My Jackson County experience gave me an idea of how contractors and people who are dealing with government funds, whether they are local, state, or national, have very little respect for them. I had made some investigations of county government and state government before I went to the Senate. And so when the first draft act was passed and all the construction of those camps got under way, I felt that we would be in serious trouble if the matter wasn't investigated. At that time nobody seemed to care much, so I decided I'd have to do it.

"It's an amazing thing. Every ten cents that was spent for those work relief projects, the WPA and the PWA and those, every dime was looked into, and somebody was always against spending a nickel that would help poor people and give jobs . . . to the men that didn't have any.

"But the minute we started spending all that defense money, the sky was the limit and no questions asked. The 'economy boys' never opened their mouths about that, and I don't understand it. I don't now, and I didn't then.

"I do know from my experience that all . . . that no military man knows anything at all about money. All they know how to do is to spend it, and they don't give a damn whether they're getting their money's worth or not. There are some of them . . . I've known a good many who feel that the more money they spend, the more important they are.

"That's because of the education they get. I told you.

It's like putting blinders on a man. He can't see on either side of him, and he can't see ahead of him beyond the end of his nose.

"So somebody has to keep tabs on the military and all the time, too. That's the reason our government is set up the way it is."

Mr. President, there are those who think, and I must say I'm one of them, that since there's much more profit in spending money for arms and Army installations and bombs than there is in feeding the hungry or giving jobs to the unemployed, that's why the military usually has first priority on spending.

Harry Truman didn't speak for quite a time. I'm not sure why. It was certainly not that such a simple idea had never occurred to him before. After all, he understood the system very well. See the speeches he made on the Senate floor about 'the tin-plate millionaires' and the railroads. Maybe it was just that nobody had ever said it in quite that way to him.

In any case after a moment he said, "Of course that's true, and we shouldn't ever forget it. All through history it's the nations that have given the most to the generals and the least to the people that have been the first to fall."

Getting back to the committee, Mr. Truman said: ". . . Around that time Gene Cox [Congressman Eugene Cox, a Georgia Democrat who was a rabid Roosevelt hater] wanted to set up an investigating committee in the House, but that never happened. And anyway all he wanted to do was embarrass Roosevelt.

"Like the Committee on the Conduct of the War. That was the committee that was set up during the Civil War, and it wasn't so much interested in finding out what was going wrong as they . . . its members wanted to cause trouble for Lincoln, which they succeeded in doing. Lee [General Robert E. Lee, commander of the Confederate Army] later said that committee was worth at least two divisions to the Confederate cause, and I think he was right. Except I wouldn't doubt the committee did more harm than that.

"I'd read the hearings those birds had, every damn one of them. They only had one copy in the Library of Congress, and I guess it must have been . . . all those books must have been about so long (indicating a five-foot shelf), but I read them all to learn what *not* to do.

"And I am happy to say that so far as I know our committee did not make any of those mistakes. We were never an embarrassment to Roosevelt, not at any time.

"The chairman of that Civil War committee [Benjamin Franklin Wade, U.S. Senator from Ohio] was a mean old man, a real son of a bitch, one of those radical Republicans that was more interested in his own career than he was in anything else. And he interfered with Lincoln and his conduct of the war in every way you can possibly imagine.

"Once he told Lincoln he had to get rid of General McClellan, and Lincoln asked him who he'd get in McClellan's place. Wade says, 'Anybody.'

"And Lincoln says to him, 'Well, Senator, anybody may be all right with you, but I've got to have somebody.'

"Later Wade was one of those who was in the lead to convict Andrew Johnson of impeachment, and the reason he was so hot for it was that he was President pro tem of the Senate, and if Johnson had been convicted, Wade would have been President of the United States. . . . I don't like to think what would have happened to the country. Because Wade was a man . . . he was just a no-good son of a bitch."

So you weren't going to set up a committee like that.

"No, no, I wasn't. And I knew that after the First World War there'd been a hundred and sixteen investigating committees *after* the fact, and I felt that one committee *before* the fact would prevent a lot of waste and maybe even save some lives, and that's the way it worked out."

I understand that prior to setting up the committee, you got some letters from people in Missouri saying that there was a lot of waste at Fort Leonard Wood.

"I did, and so I decided . . . just the way I'd done in

Jackson County, I decided to take a look for myself, and I got in an old broken-down Dodge and drove down there and saw for myself. There were buildings—this was all cost plus, you understand—being built, barracks, mess halls, all kinds of building, and they were costing three to four times what they should have. I've told you before. Contractors and people who deal with government funds have very little respect for them.

"And at Fort Leonard Wood in Pulaski County there were . . . was material of all kind that was out in the snow and the rain, getting ruined, things that could never be used, would never be used. Some of them had been bought because somebody knew somebody who. . . . Well, you know what I mean.

"And there were men, hundreds of men, just standing around and collecting their pay, doing nothing. And I made notes on everything that I saw . . . and what people said, and after that I drove twenty-five thousand to thirty thousand miles or so, all over the country, looking at what money was being spent for, and it was the same everywhere. Millions of dollars were being wasted.

"And then I went back to the Senate, and I saw to it that the committee you were speaking of was set up, and you know what happened after that. It got me into all kinds of trouble."

I speak here in ignorance, Mr. President, but how do you go about setting up a Senatorial committee? How do you get approval?

"In the first place I made a speech [on February 10, 1941] telling the Senate what I had seen, and then I introduced a resolution calling for a committee to be set up. And after that was passed, it is customary for the author of the resolution to be made chairman of the committee, and that was done.

". . . Eventually the committee was authorized to spend fifteen thousand dollars and we took it from there.

"As soon as I was made chairman, I called up Jackson, who was Attorney General [Robert H. Jackson, later chief counsel of the War Crimes Trials at Nuremberg], and I said to him, 'I want the best investigator that you have on your payroll, and I'd like to interview him if you'll send him to see me down here at the Senate Office Building.

"So Jackson picked out the fella who had sent a couple of federal judges to jail for misuse of their positions. His name was Hugh Fulton. He was a great big, fat, nice-looking fella. Wore a derby hat. And he had kind of a high-pitched voice, and at first I didn't know what to think, but I looked him over, and finally I decided to take Jackson's recommendation. So I said to Fulton, 'I want you to make an investigation for me on the expenditures in the national defense program. What salary are you getting?'

"He said, 'I'm getting eight thousand dollars a year.'

"I said, 'All right. I'll give you eighty-five hundred.'

"And he said, 'Are you . . . is your committee just interested in getting headlines or is this going to be a real investigation?'

"I said, 'It's going to be real, and all you have to do is get the facts and nothing else. Don't worry about another thing. We haven't got any sacred cows around here. If you do your job, I'll do mine. You've got my word on that.'

"So he said, 'Okay. I'll take the job,' and we shook hands on it, and he did a very good job all the time he worked for me. But later . . . later he got too big for his breeches, which as I've told you happens time and again around Washington.

"Eventually we had about a dozen or so investigators, and the committee went from five members to nine, and we went ahead and did our job.

"After we ran out of money they gave us another sixty thousand dollars, and the next appropriation that was made was for three hundred thousand dollars. Those were the only appropriations that were ever made, and I guess you could say it was money well spent because it was said . . . I believe it was established that we saved the tax-payers about fifteen billion dollars. And the lives of some

kids. I don't know how many. It was said . . . some reporters estimated we may have saved the lives of a few
thousand kids.

"I can tell you the story of the airport between Fort
Worth and Dallas. Myself and a couple of Senators went
down there because the payrolls were outrageous.

"But they heard we were coming, and so they straightened things out, and everything looked perfectly fine. But
under a great big hangar was a kind of basement which
was above ground.

"And I said, 'What's under there?' And they said, 'Oh,
that's just a basement for storage.'

"So I said, 'Fine. Raise up the trapdoor and let's see.'
And I counted over six hundred men come out of there.
They were hiding. They were on the payroll, but they
weren't doing a day's work.

"And that's what you run into. Of course that contractor had to restore the overpayments which he had
received, and he didn't get any more contracts.

"But dozens, hundreds of things like that and worse
happened. They . . . Glenn Martin was making B-26
bombers, and they were crashing and killing kids right
and left. So I said to Martin, 'What's wrong with these
planes?'

"He said, 'The wingspread isn't wide enough.'

"So I said, 'Then why aren't you making it wider?'

"And he said, 'I don't have to. The plans are too far
along, and besides, I've got a contract.'

"So I said, 'All right. If that's the way you feel, I'll see
to it that your contract is canceled and you won't get another.'

" 'Oh,' he says, 'if that's the way it's going to be, we'll
fix it,' and he did.

"I just don't understand people like that. He was killing
kids, murdering kids, and he didn't give a damn. I never
will understand people who can do a thing like that."

Well, greed is one of the seven deadly sins.

"And I guess maybe it's the worst. Down at Curtiss-
Wright at the airplane plant in Ohio, they were putting de-

fective motors in planes, and the generals couldn't seem to find anything wrong. So we went down, myself and a couple other Senators, and we condemned more than four or five hundred of those engines. And I sent a couple of generals who'd been approving, who'd okayed those engines to Leavenworth, and I believe they are still there. I certainly hope so."

Did you put many people in jail?

"We only had to jail about three or four people. The whole time only about three or four people went to jail.

"Just the fact that there was such a committee, that there was an investigation going on caused a lot of people to be more honest than they'd had in mind being. I wish it didn't have to be that way, but I'm afraid that's the way it is."

How did the President, did Roosevelt, feel about the committee?

"At first Roosevelt hadn't been any too fond of the idea, but as things went along, he saw that we were out to help him and not hinder the war effort, and he'd call me in from time to time, and he'd tell me there was something I ought to look into.

"He'd say, 'I can't do a thing with the sonsabitches. See what you can do.' And I would, and I . . . we were very often quite effective in clearing up whatever it was. And the Secretary of War and General Marshall would call me in. That's the first time I got to know General Marshall really well, and I got to know that you could depend on every word that he said, that he just never would lie to you, and that he always knew what he was talking about.

"Eventually, as I've told you, we saved the taxpayers fifteen billion dollars. And what frightens me . . . what I often think about: What if somebody hadn't been there looking after the interest of the taxpayers who were putting up all the money?

"And another thing I'm proud of. We didn't give a hoot in hell about publicity. My goodness, if I'd got into that committee to make headlines, I could have made enough to cover the whole of this room, but I didn't do it. We didn't give anything to the reporters unless the case was closed down tight. Nobody got his case before the public until we had the goods on him, and that's what I'm proudest of.

"And also the fact that we never issued a report that wasn't unanimously approved by every single member of the committee, and we had five members at one time and then seven and then nine."

Mr. Truman was succeeded as chairman of the committee by Senator James Mead, a New York Democrat. But nothing much happened, ever again.

Mr. President, why do you suppose it is that after you left the committee, it was more or less allowed to die?

"I'm afraid that's true. As soon as a war's over, nobody gives a good goddamn anymore. Of course the war went on for a time after I got that job I didn't want, but the fellow that took my place as chairman, well, he was as nice a fella as he possibly could be, but he just didn't have much get-up-and-go.

"And when the war ended . . . as I say, nobody gave a damn anymore. And all the Mommies wanted to get their little boys home. During a war they're men, but the minute it's over they're all of a sudden babies, and their Mommies want to get them home. I suppose it's . . . I suppose it's understandable, but it's a shame.

"Once there's an armistice, *everybody* gets selfish all of a sudden."

William James said that there ought to be a way to find the moral equivalent of war in peacetime.

"There ought to be, but I'd be greatly surprised to see it come about."

You don't think man is perfectible then?

"No, no. He can be improved on, but that's about it."

Mr. President, how do you feel about all the money that's being spent now by the military, without a Truman Committee to keep an eye on what's being done with it?

"It's a crime and disgrace. I'll bet you . . . I'll bet billions of dollars are being wasted over there at the Pentagon. Billions of dollars lining somebody's pocket.

"The thing I've always felt about the Pentagon is that while it was probably necessary . . . it's not right to have all those people in one building without a single watchdog. There ought to be somebody looking into every penny that's spent, but there isn't. And we're all in trouble when that goes on, when the generals get that much power."

Mr. President, you'll pardon my mentioning it, but earlier this year the fellow that succeeded you in the White House warned people against what I believe he called the military-industrial complex and its growing power in peacetime, what we've just been talking about. I believe he said that if we weren't careful that complex would engulf democracy and the people as well. Something like that.

Mr. Truman paused for a long time, very long. Finally, and with difficulty (it was not easy for him to say anything good about Dwight D. Eisenhower), he said, "Yes, I believe he did say something like that. I think somebody must have written it for him, and I'm not sure he understood what he was saying, but it's true. And I don't know why people aren't more concerned. Why the Congress isn't, but they aren't . . . don't seem to be anyway."

Mr. President, you once said you might run for reelection to the Senate when you were ninety. If you did and if you were reelected, as I'm sure you would be. . . .

The President laughed. He said, "That's one of the first damn things I'd look into. They'd probably try to stop me, but at ninety I'm still going to be a contrary goddamn cuss."

Unhappily, Mr. Truman died before he was able to run for reelection to the Senate. And the military-industrial complex continues to grow unchecked.

The Convention and the Campaign
of 1944

In the summer of 1944 I was a sergeant in the Army and was in the United States between an assignment in the Pacific and another in Europe. I wrote in my journal of the Democratic convention that year—I seem to have expressed myself more dramatically in those days—"President Roosevelt has betrayed all of us who are fighting for freedom by endorsing a little machine politician, his name is Harry Truman, for the Vice-Presidential nomination.

"Naturally, with Roosevelt's backing Truman was forced down the throats of the delegates . . . and he got the nomination. Under the circumstances I thought Vice President Wallace took it very gallantly. But if anything should happen to President Roosevelt during his fourth term, I fear the direst consequences. We shall have as our leader a political hack when we could have had a great man."

Well.

Years later Henry A. Wallace had a farm not too far from the place I'd moved to in Brewster, New York, and we had several conversations. I decided, I think rightly, that he would have been a disaster as President of the United States. More on that later.

Franklin Roosevelt was not at his best in the summer of 1944. For one thing he was tired; he had, after all, been President since 1933, most of three four-year terms, and the strain was beginning to show. I had dinner at the White House that summer, a guest of Eleanor Roosevelt, and I was dismayed at the President's appearance. I hadn't seen him for two years, but it seemed to me that he looked twenty years older. His eyes were sunken and tired; he seemed to have shrunk in size, and his hands trembled as he ate.

The dinner was not a joyous one, although I was *on* a satisfactory amount of the time. Mr. Roosevelt wanted to know about the morale of the troops in the Pacific, and I told him. It was not an optimistic report, but he listened. A few weeks later, when I said some of the same things before a group of officers at the Special Services School in Lexington, Virginia, I almost got court-martialed.

Although it was generally agreed that Roosevelt knew all along that he was going to run for a fourth term, that indeed since there was a war going on he *had* to run for a fourth term, he did not announce his candidacy until a few days before the Democratic convention in Chicago, which began on July 19.

As for his running mate he not only allowed total confusion to reign; he seemed to insist on it. Henry Wallace, his former Secretary of Agriculture and by his own choice Vice President since 1940, went to Chicago convinced that it was to be the same ticket again. And somehow James F. Byrnes, the small, feisty South Carolinian, a former Senator who was then head of the Office of War Mobilization, got the idea that he was Roosevelt's first choice, and so did Harold Ickes, who was Secretary of the Interior, and Alben Barkley, who was then majority leader of the Senate.

After Roosevelt's death Harry Hopkins told Robert E. Sherwood, "I'm pretty sure that Jimmy Byrnes and Henry Wallace and Harold Ickes are saying right now that they'd be President if it weren't for me. But this time I didn't have anything to do with it. I'm certain that the President had made up his mind on Truman long before I got back to the White House last year. I think he would have preferred Bill Douglas, because he knew him better, and he always liked Bill's toughness. But nobody really influential was pushing for Douglas. I think he'd gone off fishing out in Oregon or someplace. And Bob Hannegan [then chairman of the Democratic National Committee] was certainly pushing for Harry Truman, and the President believed he could put him over at the Convention. So the President told him to go ahead and even put it in writing when Bob asked him to. People seemed to think that Truman was just suddenly pulled out of a hat—but that wasn't true. The President had had his eye on him for a long time. The Truman Committee record was good—he'd got himself known and liked around the country—and above all he was very popular in the Senate. The President wanted somebody that would help him when he went up there and asked them to ratify the peace." *

Recently some historians have said that Harry Truman really lusted after that Vice Presidential nomination. If that is so, he certainly kept it a secret from everyone, and he said the opposite to everyone, including his mother, and Harry Truman was not a man who lied to his mother.†

Sue Gentry, the reporter for the Independence *Examiner* who covered the Trumans for so many years, told me the last time I was in Independence, "Mr. Truman was never ambitious for power. He never went after it in that sense, but when he got it, he certainly knew how to use it."

Mrs. Ralph Truman, the wife of Harry Truman's first cousin Brigadier General Ralph Truman, remembered that July this way:

"We had been getting reports from all over the country that Harry Truman was going to be the choice for Vice President. And the day he was leaving for the 1944 convention, a niece of the general was visiting us here in Kansas City, and I took the niece, and we went out to

* See Robert E. Sherwood's *Roosevelt and Hopkins.*

† At lunch one day at the Carlyle, I forget in what context, too many slight libations, Mr. Truman said, I remember the tone being one of complete incredulity, "What kind of a man would lie to his mother?"

Later at that same lunch he returned to the subject of Adlai Stevenson; Stevenson had said what Mr. Truman considered some damn fool thing at the United Nations the day before.

"The real trouble with Stevenson is that he's no better than a regular sissy," said Mr. Truman.

Grandview to have lunch with Harry and Mary Jane and Aunt Mat [Harry Truman's mother].

"And during the course of our conversation at lunch, I said to Harry, 'Well, when you come back, the next time we see you, you'll be the nominee for Vice President.'

"And he said, 'God forbid.' He said, 'I don't want the job.' And he says, 'In fact I have a speech right here in my pocket. I'm going to nominate Jim Byrnes for Vice President.'

"And I said, 'Well, nevertheless, when you come back you'll be Vice President—the nominee for Vice President. And Aunt Mat said that she knew Harry didn't want that. But she says, 'Harry, if they nominate you, I know you'll do a good job because you've always been a good boy.' And that was the way she always talked. . . . She always talked about Harry that way, that he'd always been a good boy.

"Of course as I found, after I was in the Truman family for a number of years, they were a very close-knit family. And they all looked to Aunt Mat for advice and counsel because she kept a firm hand on the family, always."

It's one thing to be firm and another to be just. Generally, would you say she was pretty just?

"She was very just. She was one of the most broad-minded women I ever knew. And even up to the date of her death, when she was ninety-four years old, she had a very clear mind and she was very much interested in everything—in world affairs and everything. And even though she'd got where she couldn't see to read herself, she insisted that newspapers and the *Congressional Record* and things of that kind be read to her every day so she could keep up with what was going on because she didn't want to be left out."

General Ralph Truman: "Harry said he didn't want the nomination, and I have known Harry since 1891 when he was seven years old, and I knew one thing. I knew that Harry had never told me a lie, and I have never told him one."

Do you remember, sir, anything about the first time you met Mr. Truman?

General Truman: "No, I can't say I formed much of an impression of him at that age. As I say, he was only seven years old, but I do remember one thing about that day. Aunt Mat served biscuits. That was very unusual. In those days, in my family at any rate, the only time we had biscuits was when the preacher came, about once a month. The rest of the time we were accustomed to eating corn bread. And we liked it. I still do. . . . But I remember Aunt Mat made biscuits that day."

Sir, do you remember anything about the summer of 1944, before Harry Truman got the Vice Presidential nomination?

General Truman: "I remember Harry said he was happy right where he was in the Senate, and he said he was doing his best for the country right there, and he didn't want to change. And I said to him, I remember I said to him, I says, 'Harry, whoever gets that Vice Presidential nomination is going to be President because there is no man alive who can be in that job for sixteen years.' And Harry said, says, 'I know. I know, and that is why I do not want the nomination.' He says, 'The responsibility is just too great.'

"And so the night when President Roosevelt passed on, I had great emotion. I thought, 'The responsibility. The awful responsibility,' and I am afraid that I shed tears."

Mary Jane Truman: "Harry said, he said, 'I'll bet you can't name the names of half a dozen Vice Presidents,' and I had to admit that I couldn't, and he said, 'No,' he said. 'The Vice Presidency is simply not a place I wish to be.' And Harry was always very serious about things like that. I remember once he said, I'm not sure when it was, he said, 'Being President is not a job a man should go after. There is too much involved for one man to do.'

"And I believe he still felt that way after he became President, but then it was too late, of course, and he had to do what he could. Whatever he did, he always did well, and he was conscientious and worked hard, and I believe that can be said of what he did as President."

Mr. President, in 1860, before the Republican convention in Chicago, Lincoln said that he did not want the nomination, but when he was pressed, he said, "The taste is in my mouth a little." Was the taste for the Vice Presidency ever in your mouth a little in 1944?

"No, no, not a bit, not at all.

"I was home here in Independence getting ready to go to Chicago, and the phone rang, and it was Jimmy Byrnes, and he said, 'Harry, the old man is backing me; I'm going to be the Vice Presidential nominee. Will you make the nominating speech?' I said that I'd be happy to.

"And a little later Alben Barkley called and wanted me to nominate him. I said, 'I'd be glad to, Alben, but I've already promised Jimmy Byrnes.' "

Had Roosevelt really backed Byrnes?

"No, he hadn't, and I never did know how Jimmy got that idea, but he did. Maybe Roosevelt just had never said he *wouldn't* back him. Jimmy was a man who sometimes heard things that hadn't been said at all. I found that out later when he was my Secretary of State. He sometimes claimed I said things I hadn't said, and I don't think he was lying, didn't know he was lying anyway."

What would you say he was doing?

"He was fooling himself."

How is that different from lying?

The President smiled. "I'll tell you. Some men when they *taste* wanting to be President, they can fool themselves without much trouble. There's something about the Presidency that causes that to happen to some men.

"After I got to be President, I knew every time Jimmy and I talked that he thought it ought to be the other way around. He ought to be sitting where I was sitting. That happens, and in a way you can understand it."

Would Byrnes have made a good President?

"He was a good Senator. I didn't agree with him on a lot of things, but he was a damn good Senator.

"But you never can tell what being President will do to a man. It's made some, and it's broken some. There's no way to tell unless you know a lot more about a man than the people ever have a chance to know."

We just have to leave it to chance—and maybe pray a little?

"That's about right. Of course you have to find out as much as you can about a man, and we have been very lucky in this country up to now. We have had some damn poor Presidents, I've told you about them, but we have never had a man who was totally dishonest in the White House."

What about Henry Wallace? Would he have made a good President?

"I don't know about being President, but he was a damn poor Vice President. Why, hell, he'd been there presiding over the Senate for almost four years, and I'll bet there weren't half a dozen Senators who'd call him by his first name. He didn't have any friends in the Senate, and that's the way things get done in the Senate . . . in politics. You may not like it, but that's the way it is.

"If you don't like people, you hadn't ought to be in politics at all, and Henry talked a lot about the common people, but I don't think he liked them, couldn't get along with them anyway.

"The fellow we were talking about from Illinois [Adlai Stevenson] could never understand that either, how you have to get along with people and be equal with them. That fellow was too busy making up his mind whether he had to go to the bathroom or not [much laughter]."

I was never much impressed by Wallace's speeches. Most of the time I couldn't decide what he was getting at.

"I'm not sure he could either, and long-winded. . . . Those long-winded birds. They're all the same. The less they have to say, the longer it takes them to say it."

I understand that you had a little experience in that line in 1940 with the man who was running for the Democratic nomination for governor.

"That's true. In 1940 when I was running for reelection, going around the state and meeting people, shaking their hands, I never talked more than twenty minutes, twenty-five.

"A fellow named Larry McDaniel was running for governor, to get the governor nomination as you say, and he couldn't stop talking. I guess his speeches must have got up to two hours long and more, and people were walking out on him in droves, but you couldn't stop him. I told him he was losing votes, but he just couldn't stop.

"And that November, although he got the nomination, he lost the election. I knew he would. . . . It's the same way out there in California now. With Pat Brown."

Edmund "Pat" Brown, then governor of California, was running for reelection; his opponent was Richard Nixon.

"I talked to Pat on the phone the other day, and I told him every time he makes a speech he loses ten thousand votes.

"If you're running against Nixon you don't have to say *anything*. You don't even have to get out of bed in the morning to beat him. My goodness, if I'd ever had a chance to run against *him,* it would have been the easiest campaign I ever had." *

Bob Aurthur once described the President as chuckling dryly, and I guess that is as good a description as any of what Mr. Truman did then. He chuckled dryly.

"I could have stayed right in Washington and licked him," he said, still chuckling.

How do you explain that, Mr. President?

"Because Nixon is a shifty-eyed, goddamn liar, and people know it. I can't figure out how he came so close to getting elected President in 1960. They say young Kennedy deserves a lot of credit for licking him, but I just can't see it. I can't see how the son of a bitch even carried one state."

Mr. President, would it be fair to say that you dislike Richard Nixon?

* Pat Brown must have stopped talking because he won the election; after his defeat his opponent told the press that it wouldn't have Dick Nixon to kick around anymore.

More dry chuckling. "Yes, I guess you could say that.
. . . Now I never carried personal grudges. Only two,
only two. There are only two men in the whole history
of the country that I can't stand. And . . . I've told you
. . . one of them was the former governor of Missouri,
Lloyd C. Stark, who followed me around like a poodle
dog to get the support of the organization of which I was
a member so that he could be governor of the state.

"Then he forgot where he got that support, and he did
everything he possibly could to beat me for the Senate
the second time I ran.

"And Nixon is in that same class exactly. He went down
to Texarkana, Arkansas, and he called General Marshall
and me traitors. And I knew it, and the big fat Leonard
Hall, when he was chairman of the Republican National
Committee, he said he'd give a thousand dollars to any
charity I wanted if I could prove it, prove Nixon said
that.

"Well, I sent down there and got the reports verbatim
from the Texarkana paper and sent them to Hall, and I
said, 'Now you can send that one thousand dollars to the
Korean Red Cross.' But I never heard from him."

Do you know whether he ever sent it?

"He didn't, of course. He didn't think I could find it.

"But those are the only two, Nixon and Stark. I've often
said around the country that if General Marshall and the
former President of the United States are traitors, then
the country's in one hell of a fix.

"You can't very well forget things of that kind, and
that's why I don't trust Nixon and never will." *

* According to an Associated Press dispatch from Texarkana on October 2, 1952, Nixon said that Truman, Acheson,
and Stevenson were all three "traitors of the high principles
in which many of the nation's Democrats believe." These "real
Democrats," he was quoted as saying, were "outraged by the
Truman-Acheson-Stevenson's gang's toleration of and defense
of Communism in high places."

But what he really said may remain as forever disputed as
what his friend Senator Joseph R. McCarthy really said that

I gather you don't think he's much of a campaigner either.

"He's one of the few in the history of this country to run for high office talking out of both sides of his mouth at the same time and lying out of both sides."

Do you think he talks too long?

"Any talk at all from him is too damn long."

Some people think Senator Humphrey talks too much sometimes.

"Hubert has that same difficulty, but I wouldn't want to

---

dark afternoon in February, 1950, when he made a Lincoln Day address before the Republican women of Wheeling, West Virginia.

The climax of the speech came when McCarthy waved a sheaf of papers in his hand and said, "I have here in my hand a list of. . . ."

After that, confusion. Either he said a list of 205 members of the Communist Party who were working for the State Department and whose names were known to the Secretary of State. Or else he said he had in his hand a list of 57 people who *probably* were or *appeared to be* card-carrying members of a party they *seemed* to be *loyal to*. Or else he said he had in his hand a list of 110 Communist sympathizers or anti-anti-Communists, which was pretty much the same thing.

In any case, the speech in Wheeling was delivered on February 9. On February 20 when it or something like it was placed in the *Congressional Record*, there was no list of any kind. The speech McCarthy read into the *Record* said, "The reason why we find ourselves in a position of impotency . . . is the traitorous actions of whose who have been treated so well by this nation. It is not the less fortunate or members of minority groups who have been selling this nation out but rather those who have had all the benefits the wealthiest nation on earth has had to offer—the finest homes, the finest college educations, the finest jobs of the government that we can give. This is glaringly true of the State Department. There the brightest young men who were born with silver spoon in their mouth [*sic*] are the ones who have been worse [*sic*]."

Quite a different speech, and so in Texarkana Nixon may have said Truman and Marshall or Truman and Acheson and Stevenson were *traitors* to their party or to their country. No matter, really. *Traitors* was the operative word.

say it in public. . . . You can't win many votes if people are either asleep or walking out on you."

How did you learn that? Did you know that in your first campaign?

"I had to learn it the hard way like everything else. I learned it in a lot of campaigns, and I learned it by keeping my eyes and ears open. That's the only way you learn anything. But some men just never do it. I can't figure out why."

Anyway, you don't think Henry Wallace would have made a good campaign in 1944?

"No, he would not have, and what campaigning he did do he was no good at.

"Roosevelt didn't want him to have the nomination, but he couldn't tell Wallace to his face. Roosevelt wasn't much good at telling things like that to people's faces. He told somebody, I forget who it was, 'I'm afraid Henry just hasn't got it,' and he was right, of course.

"As I say, Henry's speeches ran on and on; he didn't say anything, but you couldn't get him to stop talking."

Tell me about the 1944 Democratic convention.

"I went there to nominate Jimmy Byrnes, and as I told you, I had no thought at all of accepting the job and no idea it would be offered me. If it'd been an *offer*, I'd have turned it down."

Truman with Bess and Margaret drove to Chicago from Independence; they got there on Friday, July 14; the convention was to open the following Wednesday at noon.

The day the Trumans left Independence Roosevelt got on a special railroad car that would take him from Washington to San Diego. There he would board the U.S.S. *Baltimore* and go to Pearl Harbor for conferences with Admiral Chester Nimitz and General Douglas MacArthur to discuss the future strategy of the war in the Pacific.

The President agreed, apparently with reluctance, to stop off in Chicago and have a conference in the railroad yard there with Bob Hannegan and Ed Pauley, a California oilman and Democratic kingmaker. I have read at least a dozen different versions of what happened during that conference, but it is certain that Pauley and Hannegan emerged with a note from Roosevelt saying:

July 19 1944

DEAR BOB:

You have written me about Harry Truman and Bill Douglas. I should, of course, be very glad to run with either of them and believe that either of them would bring real strength to the ticket.

Always sincerely
FDR.

Since Douglas had no apparent support at the convention and since Wallace had been conveniently ignored by the President, with Byrnes never taken seriously by anyone much except himself, it was clear that the nominee would be Truman. It was, on the second ballot.

Mr. President, did you know that there was a lot of activity on your behalf going on behind the scenes?

". . . The only thing I knew: I had breakfast on Sunday with Sidney Hillman." Hillman had been co-chairman of the wartime Office of Production Management and was in Chicago as head of what was then the CIO's new Political Action Committee. "I had breakfast with Sidney Hillman, and I told him I was going to nominate Jimmy, and he said, 'Harry, that's a mistake. Labor will never support Byrnes. He's against labor. His whole record proves it.'

"And I said, 'Who the hell do you want then?'

"He said, 'We're supporting Wallace, but we have a second choice, and I'm looking right at him.'

"I had breakfast with Phil Murray [head of the CIO] the next morning, and he said pretty much the same thing. And I talked . . . I saw every political leader and every labor leader. I knew them all, and not a single one of them would be for Jimmy Byrnes. They said—there'd only be two people they'd be for: 'That's you and Henry Wallace.'

"And I said, 'You needn't be for me. I'm not going to be a candidate.'

"Well, on the afternoon of the day the President was nominated, would be renominated for the fourth term, they had a meeting up at the Blackstone Hotel. Suite 560 or 570 or wherever it was. If you're ever up there some time, I'll show you where it took place.

"And Bob Hannegan was there. He was an Irishman from St. Louis and a particular friend of mine. I made him Postmaster General before he died.

"The room was crowded. Every damn political boss in the country was there, any of them you would want to name, and half a dozen governors.

"And they all said, 'Harry, we want you to be Vice President.' I said, 'I'm not gonna do it.'

"Well, Bob Hannegan had put in a call to Roosevelt who was . . . down at San Diego. They finally got him on the phone. And with Roosevelt you didn't need a phone. All you had to do was raise the window and you could hear him.

"I was sitting on one twin bed, and Bob was on the other in this room, and Roosevelt said [Mr. Truman gave a near-perfect imitation of Roosevelt, Harvard accent and all], Roosevelt said, 'Bob, have you got that guy lined up yet on that Vice Presidency?'

"Bob said, 'No. He's the contrariest goddamn mule from Missouri I ever saw.'

" 'Well,' Roosevelt said, 'you tell him if he wants to break up the Democratic Party in the middle of the war and maybe lose that war that's up to him.' Bang."

Did Roosevelt know that you could hear him?

"No, no, he didn't. But hell, he'd been through Chicago a couple or so days before that, and I made my call on him, and he never said a word to me about the situation. And I said to Bob, 'Why in hell didn't he tell me that when he was here or before I left Washington? He knew I was coming here.'

"Bob said, 'I don't know, but there it is.'

"Well, I walked around there for about five minutes, and

you should have seen the faces of those birds. They were just worried to beat hell.

"Finally, I said, 'All right, Bob, if that's the way the old man feels, I'll do it, but who in hell's gonna nominate me now? I've told everybody here that I'm not a candidate, and every member of my committee and everybody else is committed to somebody else.'

" 'Well,' Bob says, 'maybe your colleague will do it.' *

"I said, 'All right, Bob, but where is he?'

"He said, 'Damned if I know. We'll have to find him.' So I spent the afternoon and half the night trying to find Bennett Clark. At about five o'clock in the morning I found him in the penthouse of the Sherman Hotel, which was Democratic headquarters, and he wasn't—well, he had a lot of whiskey in him. And I got a pot of coffee, and I put it on the table next to the empty whiskey bottle, and I said, 'Bennett, they want you to nominate me for Vice President. Will you do it?'

Mr. Truman then imitated a drunken Senator Clark. "He said, 'Yeah, Harry. I'll do it.' So I called Bob and said, 'I found your boy. He's cockeyed. I don't know whether you can get him ready or not, and I hope to Christ you can't.'

"Well, Bob did get him ready, and he was ten minutes late, but he nominated me, and then half a dozen fellas around over the country did it, too. And that was the worst time I ever spent in my life."

I read some place that after you were nominated the crowds started pressing in on you and trying to reach you, and you got in the street and there were more crowds, and Mrs. Truman turned to you and said, "Harry, are we going to have to go through this all the rest of our lives?"

"Yes, she did say that, something like that. It's an awful thing, crowds and the way they want to grab hold of you and all of that, and it's frightening. I did my best to keep the Boss and Margaret out of it as much as I could, but

---

* Bennett Clark, then senior Senator from Missouri.

that didn't always happen, and that's why we were glad to get back here to Independence."

Where people leave you alone?

"They don't leave us alone exactly. A fella like me who's been notorious and who's been what I've been and been *through* what I've been through, well, there are always curiosity seekers waiting out there, and you sometimes can't even go out to get the papers. You have to send the old nigger cook out to do it for you." *

What happened after the 1944 convention in Chicago?

"I went to see Roosevelt in August after . . . after he got back from Hawaii, and we had lunch in the backyard of the White House—there's a picture of that in that stack somewhere—and he said, 'I want you to do some campaigning. I don't feel like going everywhere.' I said, 'All right. I'll make some plane reservations to go around over the country anywhere you want me to go.' He says, 'Don't fly. Ride the trains. Can't both of us afford to take chances.' "

I understand you had trouble sometimes raising money for that train ride.

"Yes, yes, we did. We ran out of money a few times, but Tom Evans, who was chairman of the finance committee, he and Eddie Jacobson always managed."

Tom Evans: "Eddie was really a whiz at raising money. I don't know how he did it, but he'd pick up the phone and call somebody, and while we never got great amounts, we always got enough money to get the train moving again. That was the trouble. We'd be in some town, and we

* Privately Mr. Truman always said "nigger"; at least he always did when I talked to him. That's what people in Independence said when he was growing up. Of course, Independence was a Southern town, a border town, one of whose more prominent organizations has been the United Daughters of the Confederacy.

Considering his use of the word his civil rights program is even more remarkable.

wouldn't have enough money to pay to get the train to the next town. But with Eddie—we managed to have enough to make the full journey."

Mrs. Eddie Jacobson: "I don't think there was anything in the world that Eddie wouldn't have done for Harry, and raising money in that campaign—he was, I think he was only sorry he couldn't do *more.* . . . He and Harry never quarreled. Even when the haberdashery, even when business was bad, when it was going to go broke, they never quarreled. The newspapers always said that Harry had a very quick temper, but we never saw it around here."

Tom Evans: "Harry wouldn't take money from just anybody. He always told me, any contribution, to clear it with him. Harry was particular about where the money came from.

"One of the things we had to try to do, we had to get him to bed early at night because he had always been an early riser, and he had a lot of work to do, but one night in the hotel in Boston—we had a suite, a living room here, a bedroom over there, which was Senator Truman's room, and another bedroom off from that, which was Mrs. Evans and I.

"And we got him to bed, and we frankly thought he was sound asleep, and Matt Connelly, who'd worked with the Senator on the committee, and Ed McKim, one of his overseas buddies in Battery D, and Mrs. Evans and I were in the living room having a few drinks.

"And the door opened, and here was the Senator in his bathrobe, and he said, 'Can I please come in and have a little fun, too?' We said no. We said he had to go get some sleep, but he came in for a few minutes, and then he said that he'd go and let us have a good time. He said he had to wash his socks, and Mrs. Evans jumped up and said, 'You're a candidate for Vice President of the United States, and you won't wash your socks,' and she did it for him."

Mrs. Tom Evans: "He always said that that was one thing everybody had to do himself, wash his own socks and his own underwear, and I believe he always did. Even after he became President I believe he still did."

Tom Evans: "My biggest job in the campaign. We had a special car, the 'Henry Stanley,' it was a club car and a sleeping car, and it was attached to a regular train. And of course everybody knew when the train was coming through and that the candidate for Vice President would be on the train.

"We couldn't stop in the smaller towns, of course, and Senator Truman gave me the job of standing outside, on the back of the platform and waving at the people as we went through. Of course I'm much taller than President Truman, but I do have gray hair, and I wear glasses, and I can wave. And we went through so fast that people never knew the difference.

"But that was the big job I had in the campaign of 1944."

Harry Truman: "That day Roosevelt and I had lunch under old Jackson's magnolia tree, he looked very sick and tired. I knew he was a sick man. And what he said about both of us not being able to take chances, why, what more did you need?"

I understand that you and Ed McKim went to a movie at the White House that September. Tell me about that.

"It wasn't a movie. It was a reception for the actors that were in a movie about Woodrow Wilson, early in September this was, and Eddie and I went, and afterwards, when we went outside, Eddie said he'd been looking at the President, and he said something like I was going to be living in the White House before long. And I said, 'Eddie, I'm afraid I am, and it scares the hell out of me.'

"But after that lunch with Roosevelt, that's when the real train ride began, and we went just everywhere. New Orleans, Los Angeles, San Francisco, Seattle.

"And when we were in Uvalde, Texas, we saw old Jack Garner (Roosevelt's first Vice President), and he came down to see me, and we talked a little about this and that;

he'd been out in the cornfields that day I remember, and he said, 'Harry, do you think there's any chance you'd find the time to strike a blow for liberty? Somewhere in the world it must be twelve o'clock.'

"So I knew what he wanted. He wanted a slight libation, and I took him on the train, and we both had one. . . .

"But that campaign. That was the meanest campaign I ever can remember. I think it was even meaner than the campaign in 1948—the things they said about me. Most of the newspapers didn't hesitate to lie, and there was a whispering campaign—I've always thought it was organized—that Roosevelt—well, that his mind was gone and he was senile and I don't know what all.

"That about his mind was a damn lie. He wasn't well, but his mind—his mind was just as sharp as ever it had been, and that was the case whenever I saw him right up to the end.

"And Mrs. Luce—well, she said things about Mrs. Truman that I never will forgive her for, and that's another reason I never had the Luces to the White House. I don't care what they say about me, but when you get into saying things about Mrs. Truman and Margaret, you're bound to have some trouble on your hands.

"And before the campaign was over, the Hearst papers said I'd been a member of the Ku Klux Klan, which was a damn lie as I told you. But as I say, that was the worst campaign I ever can remember. They even claimed I was Jewish because I had a grandfather named Solomon."

What kind of audiences did you have?

"I had every kind of audience there was from those big auditoriums in places like Boston and Madison Square Garden to . . . one time in a little town in Idaho there were just three people showed up, three schoolteachers as I recall it."

Did you give them a speech anyway?

"Of course I did. It wasn't their fault that only three people were there, and they deserved the same consideration as the audience at Madison Square Garden, and I believe I can safely say that I gave it to them.

". . . As I say, we went just everywhere, Los Angeles and San Francisco and then up the coast, stopping at various places as we went along, and we stopped in Seattle and in St. Paul and Minneapolis and in Chicago, and we were in Boston.

"And when we were in Boston, Bob Hannegan was in a suite at the Ritz-Carlton Hotel, and who should be in his suite but old man Kennedy, the father of the boy that's in the White House now?

"Old man Kennedy started throwing rocks at Roosevelt, saying he'd caused the war and so on. And then he said, 'Harry, what the hell are you doing campaigning for that crippled son of a bitch that killed my son Joe?'

"I'd stood it just as long as I could, and I said, 'If you say another word about Roosevelt, I'm going to throw you out that window.'

"And Bob grabbed me by the arm and said, 'Come out here. I'm gonna get ten thousand dollars out of the old son of a bitch for the Democratic Party.' And he did.

"That is absolutely correct and the way it happened. I haven't seen him since. . . . When they asked me down in Richmond, I was down in Richmond, Virginia, delivering a lecture on the Constitution to the law school down there, and one of the smart-aleck kids got up—this was before the 1960 election—got up and said, 'What's going to happen when the Pope moves into the White House?' I says, 'It's not the Pope I'm afraid of, it's the Pop.' And that's still true. Old Joe Kennedy is as big a crook as we've got anywhere in this country, and I don't like it that he bought his son the nomination for the Presidency."

He really did buy it?

"Of course he did. He bought West Virginia. I don't know how much it cost him; he's a tightfisted old son of a bitch, so he didn't pay any more than he had to, but he bought West Virginia, and that's how his boy won the primary over Humphrey.

"And it wasn't only there. All over the country old man Kennedy spent what he had to to buy the nomination. . . . Of course, he didn't buy the Presidency itself. He didn't have to. I told you. When you're running against a man like Nixon. . . . Oh, my, I do regret I never had the chance to run against him." *

* Mr. Truman and I never got back to the subject of Joe Kennedy buying the Democratic nomination for his son in 1960, but Robert Alan Aurthur recalls a conversation among Truman and two advisers, David Noyes, and William Hillman. The conversation took place at about the same time as the above during a ride between Independence and Kansas City, as dreary a stretch of road as there is anywhere in the world:

". . . Mr. Truman reiterated his disappointment when Kennedy had taken the nomination from Lyndon Johnson in 1960. In response to my question as to what specifically had set him against Kennedy, Mr. Truman answered abruptly, 'I felt he was too immature.'

" 'The Boss doesn't like wealthy Northeast elitists,' Hillman told me, sotto voce, to which I commented that Franklin Roosevelt had been exactly that.

" 'But one of the greatest politicians that ever lived,' Mr. Truman said, putting the art of politics above anything else.' "

Noyes observed that at least Jack Kennedy was willing to listen, and he seemed to be maturing fast. Mr. Truman laughed.

" 'The Presidency will make a man out of any boy,' he said."

Hillman wondered if anyone could fault the Kennedys as practical politicians, citing their extraordinary gift for organization, and Mr. Truman mumbled something half under his breath to the effect that ". . . if you have enough money you can buy almost anything.

"With Mr. Truman no more than two feet from us, Hillman whispered loudly to me, 'He hates the idea that Joe Kennedy bought the nomination for his son Jack.'

". . . Mr. Truman stared straight ahead, thin lips pressed tightly together to indicate his residual disapproval of Joe Kennedy. It was quiet for a moment, and then the participant [Aurthur] asked hesitantly how one would go about buying the Presidency.

"Not the Presidency," Mr. Truman said. "The nomination. You can't buy the office itself . . . at least, not yet."

". . . One has to know where the local power is, Hillman said, then be prepared to use leverage as ruthlessly as necessary. Like in West Virginia, the muscle is in the counties, exercised by the individual sheriffs. With tight, tough organization,

More sustained laughter and dry chuckling here and something about "as easy as shooting fish in a barrel."

Did you think you and Roosevelt would win in 1944, Mr. President?

"Never doubted it for a moment. I knew he'd win because the country wouldn't want to change Presidents while there was a war on. Besides, there was something about that other fellow [Thomas E. Dewey, the Republican candidate for President, then governor of New York] that people just never did trust. He had a mustache, for one thing, and since in those days, during the war, people were aware of Hitler, that mustache didn't do him any good.

"I also made use of that mustache during the 1948 campaign. I never mentioned him by name, but I kept

---

and a maximum of a thousand dollars a sheriff in the key counties, a wealthy man could bag the primary for his son.

"Money, Mr. Truman mused; just knowing there's an unlimited money available is often enough to cause the opposition to cut and run.

"And a Midwestern politician, not a Kennedy man to begin with, and with the power to control his delegation, who was also running for governor of his state. One phone call, just one phone call from old Joe with the threat to throw a million and a half dollars into this man's opponent's campaign, was enough to swing his support into the camp of the future leader of the New Frontier.

"(". . . ask not what your country can do for you. . . .")

"Oh, said Noyes, Whatsisname—another local politico who held sway over his delegation—had sold out for a measly $14,-500, just enough to pay off his house mortgage. The marvelous acumen of old Joe, finding each man's price, never spending more than he had to.

"Wide-eyed and slack-jawed, your hang-about, a self-admitted cynic, had never conceived of such political opportunities in the Presidential arena, but Mr. Truman reacted with contempt for that local nabob's cheap price. The damn fool could have held out and got at least a hundred thousand, Mr. Truman said.

"Maybe more, Noyes said, and Mr. Truman nodded. Probably. The state was worth a hundred and fifty to the Kennedys."

mentioning that I had a feeling I was being followed, and I'd make a motion of stroking a mustache. People got the idea. And I said, 'There's one place he's not going to follow me, and that's into the White House.' That got a considerable round of applause."

In your 1944 speech at Madison Square Garden, I understand there was some feeling that, since it was New York, Wallace might get more applause than you did.

"There was some talk like that, yes, and it was finally decided . . . that Henry and I ought to walk in together so that nobody would know who was getting the most applause.

"Well, we waited, and we waited, and I think maybe Henry had found out what we planned because he didn't come and he didn't come until about five minutes before we were supposed to go in, but we waited him out, and the two of us went in together. There was plenty of applause to go around for everybody that night, but Henry was not any too friendly.

"I tell you. I always thought Henry was more interested in the pe—he kept talking about the pee-pul—the pee-pul this and the pee-pul that. I always thought he was more interested in the pee-pul's applause than he was in the people themselves.

"You take a fella that carries on too much about the pee-pul—it's like what I told you about folks that pray too loud. You better get home and lock the smokehouse, and that's the way I always felt about Henry Wallace. I didn't trust him."

You came back to Independence on election day.

"Oh, yes. No matter where I was I always came back to Independence on election day, and we had . . . we had some of the fellows from Battery D and some others up in the penthouse of the Muehlebach (a hotel in Kansas City), and we were waiting for the returns, and they were worried to beat hell.

"I understand Roosevelt was, too. Old man Leahy [Admiral William D. Leahy, Chief of Staff both to Roosevelt and Truman] told me. He was staying with Roosevelt up

at Hyde Park on the night of the election. And he told me
he came downstairs about four in the morning to raid the
icebox or something, and Roosevelt was still up, sitting
there in front of the radio, and Roosevelt says to Leahy,
'I've been waiting for two hours for the son of a bitch to
concede.'

"He didn't concede until three forty-five in the morning,
you know, and it was the same in 1948. I have never
understood why that fellow was such a slow conceder."

*I understand you played the piano while waiting for the
returns.*

"I did. I wasn't scared, but everybody else was, and so
I said, 'I guess what we need is a little piano music,' and I
played a little while we were waiting."

Do you remember what you played?

"No. I don't remember. A little Mozart, I guess, and
maybe some Chopin. I always played Chopin every chance
I got."

*Mr. President, when you knew the election was won,
did you think about the fact that now you were almost
surely going to be President?*

"Oh, yes. I was scared. Ever since that interview with
him in the garden, in the backyard of the White House
. . . I was worried about it all the time, and when it
finally happened, it was a terrible thing to have to take
over after a three-term President who had been so nearly
unanimously elected every time. It was something to worry
about, and I did worry about it.

"Maybe that was just as well. Maybe that made me
work harder."

The End and the Beginning

Harry Truman became Vice President of the United States on January 20, 1945, and he became President less than three months later, on April 12.

After the January inaugural Harry went back to the Capitol and called his mother in Grandview. Had she heard it on the radio, he asked, heard old Henry Wallace administering the oath of office to him and heard Chief Justice Harlan F. Stone swear in Franklin Roosevelt?

She said she had; she'd heard it all. "Now you behave yourself up there, Harry," she said. "You behave yourself."

"I will, Mamma," said the Vice President of the United States.

In his last years, as I've said, Harry liked to remember that he and Franklin Roosevelt were closer than they were; Roosevelt hadn't been close to any of his Vice Presidents. Truman liked to believe that Roosevelt had prepared him to take over, but that really hadn't happened. Not at all.

The truth is Roosevelt knew very little about Mr. Truman. Apparently he felt he didn't need to know much. Truman had done a good job as head of that investigating committee in the Senate; he was popular up there on the Hill, as poor Henry, "poor Henry just doesn't have it," had not been. When the time came to call on the Senate to ratify the kind of peace agreement that he in his wisdom had made or to get the Senators to agree to the setting up of the United Nations, Harry Truman could manage it for him.

It never seemed to occur to Franklin Roosevelt that he wouldn't be running things. Like most of the rest of us at the time, Franklin Roosevelt couldn't imagine anybody else as President. He began to think of himself as immortal.

The Trumans hadn't even been invited to the White House to break bread with the Roosevelts, not that that was any treat. The Roosevelts didn't set much of a table. Frances Perkins, who was Secretary of Labor, remembered that Mr. Roosevelt could and did carve seventeen to eighteen helpings from *one* side of a *small* turkey. See below what the Roosevelt boys have to say about meals at the White House in those days.

Well, as I say, we were lucky. Harry Truman was better prepared for the job than anybody, including, perhaps, Mr. Truman himself, would have guessed.

There are a few things that all of us of a certain age remember, and chief among them, I think, is where we were the night, the day Franklin Roosevelt died, what we did, what we said, what we thought. I was in Paris in the shabby office on the rue de Berri, where the European edition of *Yank* was, always haphazardly, put together. We were playing poker, with the radio turned low.

Suddenly the music—was it "Don't Sit Under the Apple Tree"?—was interrupted, and the sorrowing voice of a sergeant on the Armed Forces Network said, "President Franklin D. Roosevelt died this afternoon at. . . ."

As I wrote sometime back, "We put down the cards and, wrapped in our separate silences, went our separate ways. I walked up the Champs Elysées to the Arc de Triomphe. It was one of those bleak hours before dawn, and even the whores had retired for the night. I stood for a time in front of the light of the Unknown and, it seems, Eternal Soldier, and in the grim and ghostly dawn I prayed. I do not believe in God or gods, but I prayed to the promising sunrise.

"For nearly three years, first in the Pacific and then in Europe, I had seen killing and destruction, suffering and starvation that even in my darkest melancholy I could not imagine. I did not think that we had made the world safe for anything at all, none of us did, but we had bought ourselves a little peace, had we not, a time of quiet?

"In the twenty-five years since that April dawn a new war has broken out in the world every five months."

So much for what I thought that dawn or what in my better moments I like to think I thought. By noon chow that day I was feeling somewhat less melancholy and more realistic—but frightened. I remember saying, again like millions of others, "My God, now we're left with Harry Truman. Are we in trouble?"

That was one of the biggest things wrong with Harry Truman, that he wasn't Franklin Roosevelt. With Roosevelt you'd have known he was President even if you hadn't been told. You'd have known he was head of whatever he wanted to be head of. He looked imperial, and he acted that way, and he talked that way.

Harry Truman, for God's sake, looked and acted and talked like—well, like a failed haberdasher. He *certainly* wasn't any Roosevelt, and another trouble with him, for people like me anyway, was that he wasn't Henry Wallace.

And that first day, naturally, it was Friday the thirteenth, after Harry went up to the Capitol for lunch with some of his former colleagues ("cronies" was soon to become the word to describe any associate of Truman's), he said to the newspapermen, "Boys, if you ever pray, pray for me now. I don't know whether you fellows ever had a load of hay fall on you, but when they told me yesterday what had happened, I felt like the moon, the stars, and all the planets had fallen on me."

My God. Pure cornball. I had left Marshalltown, Iowa, at the earliest possible age to get away from people who talked like that, thought like that, and now we had one of them in the White House.

Where had all the poetry gone?

Mrs. Ralph Truman: "After the election, I decided that I would like to go to the inauguration. The general was busy and couldn't go. So I went to Washington to attend the inauguration ceremonies.

"It was during the war, and it was very short because of the war, and Mr. Roosevelt took the oath of office on the south porch of the White House. The weather was bad, and they didn't want to have too much display. And so on January 20 Mr. Roosevelt came out to take the oath of office. Everybody, myself included, was horribly shocked. You could tell he was a very sick man. I was close enough to him so that I could see how sick he was.

"And after the inauguration I came back to Kansas City, and I told the general, I said, 'President Roosevelt cannot possibly live more than three months because,' I said, 'he's terribly ill.' And I said, 'It's going to mean that Harry is going to be President,' and, of course, I missed it by eight days. He died on the twelfth of April, and if it had been the twentieth, it would have been three months.

"Of course it was a tragic thing for the world and the country, and it put a tremendous burden on Harry Truman to have to take over then.

"I couldn't help thinking what a responsibility it was—what an awful responsibility."

Mary Jane Truman: "After my brother Harry got nominated as Vice President, Mother and I talked about what would happen after he got elected. We never doubted that Mr. Roosevelt would be reelected, and we realized that he was not well, but I don't think we really thought about his passing away. And I know we didn't think it would come as soon as it did.

"When it did happen, when we realized that Harry had become President we felt—oh, sorry that Mr. Roosevelt was dead, but we also felt sorry for Harry.

". . . At the time Mr. Roosevelt died I had been at Joplin, Missouri, at an Eastern Star meeting, and I had to come home to get some things so that I could go back to Joplin that same evening.

"While I was getting ready to go, my mother was at my brother Vivian's, and my sister-in-law, Mrs. Vivian Truman, called me and asked me if I had the radio on, and I told her no. And she said, well, it had just come over that Mr. Roosevelt had passed away.

"And it was really, oh, it was really quite a shock. But then, just as quickly as I could, I went down to my brother's and brought my mother home. And shortly after that —why, of course the callers began to come.

"I shall never forget what my mother said later on. Someone asked her if she wasn't proud of the fact that her son had become President. I believe she stated she was not happy about it. 'Well,' she said, 'I can't say that I'm happy because I wouldn't want Mr. Roosevelt to die for him to be President, but if he is ever elected President, I'm going to get out and wave a flag.'

"She never did do that, of course, because by . . . in 1948 when Harry was elected President, she had passed away."

Mr. President, I have read that even though it was short, President Roosevelt had worked very hard over his fourth inaugural address. Do you remember anything about that day? And what Roosevelt said?

"Never will forget any part of it. I got sworn in by Henry Wallace, and then Roosevelt was sworn in by Chief Justice Stone, and he stood there on the south portico. He stood there. You remember later, when he made that speech before Congress on Yalta, he sat in the wheelchair the whole time, but at the inauguration he stood. He had on his braces, and you could see from his face that it was hard on him. He was in pain, I think, considerable pain, but he stood there, and he took the oath. He wasn't wearing an overcoat or a hat, nothing but a thin suit, and it was a cold day. It may even have snowed a little that day. I don't remember. But it was cold, and he said. . . . It's right here. Read it."

The President handed me a book with, as I recall, various inaugural addresses. Roosevelt's address was very short; it lasted only about five minutes and, among other things, said, "We have learned to be citizens of the world, members of the human community. We have learned the simple truth, as Emerson said, that 'the only way to have a friend is to be one.' "

Mr. Truman continued, "He stood there in the cold, very, and his hands shook, and his voice was not steady. I remember Frances Perkins [Secretary of Labor in Roosevelt's Cabinet] was crying, I think. But she was careful not to let Roosevelt see her.

"It was a very sad sight to see, especially if you remembered how he had sounded in former days."

He was about to go off to Yalta?

"He was. In a few days. And, of course, later I learned all about Yalta, and there's very little in our history that's been lied about as much. They said Roosevelt sold out the United States, which was a damn lie, of course; if the Russians'd lived up to their agreements that they made at Yalta, there wouldn't have been any trouble at all, but they didn't; they never lived up to an agreement they made ever, and that's what caused the trouble, and we all know what happened as a result."

I understand one of the things you did during the eighty-two days you were Vice President was to convince the Senate to agree to Wallace's confirmation as Secretary of Commerce.

"Yes, Roosevelt wanted to get rid of old—he called him Jesus H. Jones." [Jesse H. Jones was Secretary of Commerce and Federal Loan Administrator; he was a Texas financier and became a firm enemy of the New Deal.] "Jesus H. Jones, and he wanted to get Henry in both jobs, but I knew the Senate would never sit still for that, and . . . we had to concentrate on the Secretary of Commerce situation, and that was hard enough to do. I told you. Henry was not at all liked in the Senate. And I had to break two ties to get the son of a bitch confirmed. I didn't want to do it, but if that's what the old man wanted, I did it."

It was about that time that Tom Pendergast died, wasn't it?

"Tom Pendergast died on January 26, and everybody . . . everybody said I shouldn't go to the funeral. They said I should send a note or something, but I couldn't do that. Tom Pendergast was a good and loyal friend, and he never asked me to do a dishonest deed, and so I went to his funeral. I've said that time and again, and I say it now.

"I got into an Army plane, and I went to the Catholic church in Kansas City, and I attended his funeral.

"You should have heard the squawks. Headlines in the newspapers and editorials and I don't know what all. And they said some very mean things, but I didn't care. I couldn't have done anything else. What kind of man would it be . . . wouldn't go to his friend's funeral because he'd be criticized for it?"

After a while I said, *Mr. President, how many times did you see Mr. Roosevelt between the inauguration and his death? I've read that there's a record of only two such meetings: March 8 and March 19.*

"There were more meetings than that. Those were *scheduled* meetings, but there were other times . . . several other times when I wouldn't go in the front way at the White House, but I went. And there were Cabinet meetings. I attended the Cabinet meetings, not that Roosevelt ever did much at his Cabinet meetings. He did it, tried to do it all himself, which was one of his troubles.

"But when I saw Roosevelt, it was usually about something that was coming up in the Senate."

Mr. President, some historians feel that you might have been better prepared for the Presidency and some of the enormous problems that you inherited if Roosevelt had told you more about them, had been more frank.

Mr. Truman's mouth became a very thin line, and he said, "He did all he could. I've explained all about that, and I told you that's all there is to it, and it is."

I had learned by then that there were times when it was useless to pursue a subject. This was clearly one of them, and so I adjourned the session for the day and went back to Kansas City. Evenings are longer in Kansas

City than in any other city in the United States, with the possible exception of Los Angeles.

A few days later I said, *Mr. President, can you tell me about the day Franklin Roosevelt died?*

"It is a day . . . it's a time I can even now not think about without feeling very deep emotion.

"It was an ordinary day in the Senate, and I presided. I usually presided most of the time when I was Vice President. Senator Wiley [Alexander Wiley, a right-wing Republican from Wisconsin] was making a speech about something. I forget what it was about; it didn't make any difference with Wiley. He could go on forever about nothing. And so I wrote a letter to Mamma. . . .

Dear Mamma and Mary:

I am trying to write you a letter from the desk of the President of the Senate while a windy Senator is making a speech on a subject with which he is in no way familiar. . . .

. . . Turn on your radio tomorrow night at 9:30 your time, and you'll hear Harry make a Jefferson Day address to the nation. . . . It will be followed by the President, whom I'll introduce.

"Along about, oh I guess it was probably half past four or a quarter of five, Sam Rayburn called. He'd been in Texas, and he called and said there was a meeting of the Board of Education."

The Board of Education was the name of a group of legislators who dropped into Rayburn's private office from time to time after a legislative session to share stories and drink a little bourbon and tap water. Rayburn, a bachelor from Texas, was Speaker of the House.

". . . the Board of Education, and so I went over, and before I could sit down, Sam told me. Before I could even begin a conversation with the half a dozen fellows that were there, Sam told me that Steve Early (Roosevelt's press secretary) had called and wanted me to call right back. I did, and Early said to come right over to the White House and to come to the front entrance, and he said to come up to Mrs. Roosevelt's suite on the second floor. I didn't think much about it. I just supposed that the President had come back from Georgia [Roosevelt died at Warm Springs, Georgia] and was going to be at Bishop Atwood's funeral. [Julius W. Atwood, the former Episcopal Bishop of Arizona, was a friend of Roosevelt's.] Roosevelt was an honorary pallbearer, and I just supposed that was what had happened.

"And so I went over to the White House, and Mrs. Roosevelt . . . Mrs. Roosevelt . . . she told me that . . . the President . . . was dead."

For a moment Mr. Truman was unable to continue.

When he could, he said, "I was able . . . I told Steve Early to call the Cabinet, and they started phoning for the Chief Justice [Harlan F. Stone] and members of Congress.

"I went over to the office of the President in the West End of the White House and tried to call my wife and daughter. I had a hard time getting them, but I finally did, and they came, and the Chief Justice was there, and all the others, including the Cabinet, and everybody was crying.

"They had just an awful time finding a Bible. I'm sure there were plenty of them in the family living quarters of the White House, but down in the executive wing they had a terrible time finding one, and the Chief Justice was waiting to swear me in.

"Finally, they found one in the office I believe it was of Bill Hassett, who was Roosevelt's secretary.

"It had a red cover I remember. It looked sort of like a Gideon Bible, but I don't think it was. . . . Anyway, that's the one I was sworn in on, and there were half a dozen people that were sworn in on it. Dean Acheson and two or three other Cabinet members, and the flyleaf is covered with the signatures of Chief Justices, Chief Justice Stone, Chief Justice Vinson, and so on. . . .

"I gave it to Margaret, and she kept it for two or three

days, and then she insured it and sent it back and said, 'Put this in the safe in the library; I'm afraid to keep it.' And it's now . . . now on display in the library.

"I was sworn in—there was a clock on the mantel—and I was sworn in at 7:09. Exactly at 7:09 on April 12, 1945, and that's all the time it took for me to become President of the United States.

What happened next?

"Well, Margaret and Mrs. Truman went back to our apartment; they were both crying, and all the members of the Cabinet were there, I believe, except the Postmaster General, Frank Walker; I forget where he was. And we all sat down around the Cabinet table, and then Steve Early or Jonathan Daniels [another Presidential press secretary] came in and said the newspapermen were outside, and they all wanted to know if there was going to be the United Nations meeting in San Francisco in April as had been planned, and I said it most certainly was. I said it was what Roosevelt had wanted, and it had to take place if we were going to keep the peace. And that's the first decision I made as President of the United States.

"And we sat there for a little while. I told them . . . I told the Cabinet that I wanted them all to stay on as long as they could. Harry Hopkins later told me that was a mistake. He didn't call it a mistake. He didn't really advise me to do anything in particular, but he said that it would be difficult for some of the members of the Cabinet to understand a change in policy and administration, and I believe he did say that some of them might be comparing me to Roosevelt, but I said, well, I said, 'Harry, I am not gonna fire anybody. Those fellows have been working their heads off. There's a war going on, and I'm going to keep the same outfit. I'll keep the press secretaries and the other people on as long as they want to stay. Whenever they want to quit, why, they can,' and that's the way it worked."

Nobody talked about quitting that night?

"No, no, they were all so broken up and upset that they didn't . . . none of them did much talking. I did say, did emphasize that the decisions to be made . . . I was President, and they could . . . tell me if they thought I was wrong, but in the long run, I said . . . I told them I'd make the final decisions, and I'd expect them to support me. And that was about all that happened."

Didn't you have a conversation with Secretary Stimson?

Henry Stimson, then seventy-seven, had been Roosevelt's Secretary of War.

"Yes, Secretary Stimson stayed behind, and he said that the most destructive weapon in history was being built, and that is about all he said that night.

"I already knew something was going on. The committee . . . what they called the Truman Committee sometime before had learned that a good deal of money was being spent on what I thought then was two projects, one in the state of Washington and the other in Tennessee. I had sent some people out to look into the projects, to investigate what was going on. And Stimson came to see me. He said that one of the biggest, most significant projects in the history of the world was going on, and he asked me not to investigate. He said that the whole thing could be ruined if it was made public in any way.

"And I said, 'Mr. Secretary, if you tell me that, the dogs are called off.' And that is exactly what I said and what I did. And I was never sorry for it because Stimson was a man you could trust. One hundred percent.

"When I got to be Vice President, Jimmy Byrnes told me something was going on that was a tremendous explosive that would surely end the war, which is exactly what it did."

And that was the first you knew of the atom bomb.

"I didn't know, had no idea from what Byrnes said or Stimson told me that it was a bomb of any kind, and the night we're talking about I must confess I had some other matters on my mind as well."

Did you go back to your apartment after that?

"I went to the apartment at 4701 Connecticut Avenue, and Margaret and Bess were at the apartment of General Davis [General Jeff Davis, a retired brigadier general], and I had a sandwich with them there. And they were all very upset about Roosevelt's death.

"They were also concerned about what would happen in the apartment house while we were still there, living next door to a President.

"And I said, 'Well, it'll cause you plenty of trouble. Don't worry about that.' But I said, 'As soon as we can, we'll move out. So you won't be disturbed.'

"And I'd say within a week, maybe less than that, we moved to Blair House and stayed there three weeks until Mrs. Roosevelt had time to move her things out of the White House.

"After I finished the sandwich, I went back to our apartment and called Grandview. My mother, of course, knew what had happened. I told her, I said, 'Mamma, everything is all right,' and I told her not to worry. I said I was busy, and I said she probably wouldn't hear from me for a little while. And after I talked to her, I went to bed."

Did you sleep?

"Of course."

Right away?

"Of course. I knew I had a big day coming up. I had to sleep."

Mr. President, I've read—I find it almost impossible to believe—that General Marshall went right to sleep at the usual time the night before D Day.

"Knowing General Marshall, I wouldn't doubt it a bit. If you've done the best you can—if you have done what you have to do—there is no use worrying about it because nothing can change it, and to be in a position of leadership . . . you have to give thought to what's going to happen the next day and you have to be fresh for . . . what you have to do the next day. What you're going to do is more important than what you have done."

If you've done the best you can.

"That's right. That's the main thing. A man can't do anything more than that. You can't think about how it would be . . . if you had done another thing. You have to decide."

Mr. President, how do you think Hamlet would have been as President?

"He'd have made a damn . . . a poor President, and old Lear. That's a good play, great play, but old Lear couldn't even handle his daughters, let alone the country."

Mr. President, now that you've been out of the White House for a number of years, do you ever look back, have you ever looked back and wished you had done something different when you were President?

"No. Never. Not one time that I can recall. What would be the use of it?" *

. Mr. President, when you put it that way, there wouldn't have been any use of it at all. . . . Could you tell me what happened, if you'd be good enough, on the first full day when you were President, April 13, 1945?

"I got up a little later than usual, around six thirty, and I didn't take my morning walk. I had breakfast with . . . I'd just as soon not mention the gentleman's name.†

"The car was setting out there waiting for me, and as

---

* For an exception see Chapter 19, "My Biggest Mistake."

† That morning Mr. Truman had breakfast with Hugh Fulton, who had been chief investigator for the Truman Committee. Fulton went into private practice in Washington and had sent out announcements advertising that fact, which Mr. Truman felt was unethical.

Mr. Truman had strong feelings about using one's official position, past or present, for gain. He was extremely fond of General Omar Bradley, the fellow Missourian who at one time during Mr. Truman's administration was Chief of Staff. After Bradley returned, he took a job as chairman of the board of the Bulova Watch Company, and one day in discussing General Bradley, Mr. Truman said, "I hold it against him, taking that job. They weren't hiring him; what they thought they were doing was buying some influence in the Pentagon, and I don't care at all for that sort of thing, and I can't understand how General Bradley could bring himself to do it."

Being an admirer of General Bradley, I said, no doubt apologetically, "He probably felt he needed the money."

And Mr. Truman said, "Nobody ever needs money that bad."

we drove down Connecticut Avenue past Chesapeake Street, which is on the east side of 4701, there was Tony Vaccaro [an Associated Press reporter] leaning against a telephone pole, and he was the saddest-looking kid you ever saw. He'd been assigned to me by the Associated Press when I was Vice President.

"And I said, 'Stop the car. Come on. Get in, Tony. I'm on my way to the White House. What are you so sad about?'

"And he said, 'Mr. President, I've lost my job, and I'll probably get fired. There's nobody for me to cover anymore.'

"I said, 'I wouldn't worry.' I said I doubted very much if he would lose his job, and sure enough he got assigned to the White House, and the next week he got a thirty-five-dollar raise in salary.

"But that morning Tony and I rode to the White House, and he got out of the car, and I believe he wished me luck.

"I went in, and then the business began.

"I saw more people that day than anybody in the history of the Presidency up to then. The first person I saw was the Secretary of State [Edward R. Stettinius], and he told me and later gave me a memo saying that Churchill was very upset. The Russians weren't living up to their agreements. And they hadn't been since Yalta.

"He [Stettinius] said that before his death Roosevelt had been upset, too. Later a lot of people said that before Roosevelt died, everything was going along just fine with the Russians and that I was to blame for the whole thing that happened, but that is a damn lie. All they have to do is read their history to know that's a damn lie.

"They weren't living up to their promises, especially in Poland, as I've said."

At Yalta Roosevelt, Churchill, and Stalin had agreed to a compromise government in Poland that would include all the anti-Fascist parties in Poland, as well as Polish diplomatic leaders living abroad, to be followed by a free election based on a secret ballot and with universal suffrage. But the Russians were sabotaging that agreement in every way possible.

"That same morning I saw the Secretary of the Navy and Secretary Stimson, and old man Leahy, Admiral Leahy. He was Chief of Staff to the President, and I saw the other Chiefs of Staff."

They were . . . I know because I read about it at the hotel last night. They were Admiral Ernest J. King of the Navy, Lieutenant General Barney M. Giles of the Air Force, and General George C. Marshall of the Army. That wasn't the first time you ever saw General Marshall, was it?

"Oh, no. No. I believe I'd seen them all before in one way or another when I was working with the committee and when I was Vice President. But General Marshall, I've told you, I knew him in France in the First World War. I didn't know him well, of course, because he was a colonel, and I was only a captain.

"He was General Pershing's aide [General John J. Pershing, head of the American Expeditionary Force in France during the First World War]. But I met him. He made the inspections around the AEF, and he came to the school where I was going when I went over there to study French artillery."

Where was that?

"At Chatillon-sur-Seine and at Coëtquidan, which was Napoleon's artillery headquarters in his time. I went down there and worked as an instructor part of the time, and that's where I met General Marshall for the first time. And everybody knew that he was just about the best of the young officers in France at the time. And I believe that even then he was a man who knew exactly what he wanted to do at all times.

"And when he got to be Chief of Staff at the beginning of that other war I knew that things were in good hands. When Marshall said, 'This is it,' that was it. I had some dealing with him in the Senate when I was . . . head of that committee, and he'd listen to whatever it was I told him. He'd listen until you got through. And then I'd say, 'What about it?'

"He'd say, 'Go ahead. You're on the right track.' He never wasted words. Never argued with me at all. Although in the middle of the conversation if he thought of something that would add to the efficiency of the program, in it went.

"And later, as you know, I made him Secretary of State and Secretary of Defense. There never was a man like him."

Mr. President, I understand that when you were still in the Senate, you went to see General Marshall and told him that you wanted to be in the Army. Could you tell us about that?

"That's right. I did. I went to him, and I said, 'General, I'm a colonel in the field artillery, and I've kept it up, and I've trained a lot of these youngsters since the First World War, and I'd like to command a group, or a regiment, or whatever a colonel has in this war.'

"And he looked at me—he could look right through you if he wanted to, although he was the kindest man that ever was—he looked at me, and he said, 'Senator, how old are you?' I said, 'I'm fifty-six.' He says, 'You're too damn old.'

"I said, 'I'm four years younger than you are.' And he said, 'Yes, but I'm already in.'

"Well, I went back and started on this other thing [the Truman Committee] which was as helpful to him I guess maybe as if I'd been a colonel in the field artillery.

"And one day he came to see me after I got to be President, and some visiting fireman was in the Oval Room with me, and he sat outside for a while and talked to Matt Connelly [the President's appointments secretary], and Matt said, 'General, what about the fact that you wouldn't let the old man be a colonel of field artillery in this war? Don't you wish you'd a done it?'

"Marshall kinda grinned at him, and he says, 'All of us make mistakes, but I don't think that was one.'"

I said, *Getting back to that first morning you were President. Wasn't it Friday the thirteenth?*

"Yes, it was, Friday the thirteenth, 1945, and I keep going off . . . getting off the subject."

Mr. President, that's not possible. Whatever you say is very much on the subject.

"No, no, it's not, and when I do it, you've got to stop me. I said, was saying that I had a meeting with the Chiefs of Staff of each of the services, the four of them, and they said that the war . . . the war in Europe was going to last another six months and the war in Japan, they said would go on for another year and a half."

Germany surrendered unconditionally only twenty-five days later, Japan four months later. I said, *Were the Chiefs of Staff always so wrong?*

"You always have to remember when you're dealing with generals and admirals, most of them, they're wrong a good deal of the time. Even Washington knew that; he kept warning the people, and Jefferson, too, warning the people against letting the generals give you too much advice. I told you. They're most of them just like horses with blinders on. They can't see beyond the ends of their noses, most of them."

Would you say that General Marshall was an exception to the rule?

"General Marshall was wrong about when the war would end; at least if he didn't agree with the others, he didn't let on. Not the day we're talking about here, but General Marshall was an exception to every rule there ever was."

What were some of the other things that happened that day, the first full day you were President?

"Well, I went up to the Senate, and I had lunch there, and I asked them to support me. I wanted to make a speech to a joint session of Congress just as soon after the Roosevelt funeral as I possibly could. And I did, on the following Monday.

"I wanted Congress to . . . well, to see the new President and to hear him, and I wanted the people to hear him, too. I thought it was important. People were very, very confused, and some of them . . . well, they were frightened, and I wanted to tell them that the Roosevelt policies would go on.

"Later, that afternoon, of course, I saw Byrnes. He'd been to Yalta, and he'd made a good many notes, and I wanted him to tell me what he remembered and later to transcribe the notes he'd made, which he did. And I told him I was going to ask him to be Secretary of State. And at that time he seemed to be very pleased. Of course later he changed his mind, and as I say, I always felt sure that he thought he ought to be President and that he'd have done . . . possibly a better job of it, and maybe he would have. . . . If I'd have died while he was Secretary of State, of course he would have been President. When there is no Vice President, the Secretary of State is next in line for succession."

Did you think that first day would never end?

"Yes, yes, I did, but of course, even when it did, even when I went home, I had a lot of reading still to do.

"And there was all that fuss, of course, with the Secret Service, and before anybody could get into the apartment house, they had to present their identification, and we felt, Mrs. Truman and I felt that the sooner we could move, the less trouble our neighbors would be put to."

Mr. President, a great many people will find it difficult to believe that at a time like that with everything else you had on your mind after your first full day as President of the United States, you were thinking about the convenience of your neighbors.

"I don't know about that, but that is what happened. I told Mrs. Roosevelt that she should take all the time she needed to move out of the White House and that we would move into Blair House across the street, and that is what we did."

Did you work after you got back to 4701 Connecticut Avenue, to your apartment that night?

"Oh, yes. I had quite a good deal to do that same night. I always thought . . . all the time I was President I thought it would let up, but it never did. It never got any easier.

"On the fourteenth [Saturday, April 14, 1945, Mr. Truman's second full day as President] I got up a little earlier than usual, around five in the morning I think it was, and I worked on my speech that I was going to give to Congress, and later that morning we had to go up to Union Station to bring . . . to escort Roosevelt's body back to the White House, and I asked Byrnes and Wallace to go with me, which they did do."

Why was that?

"Because I knew, as I told you, that they both thought they ought to be sitting where I was. A lot of people in the country also thought so, and so I thought asking them was the proper thing to do, and I did it.

"We went up to Union Station to meet the body, and when we started back to the White House, the streets were just jammed. People on both sides of the streets when we brought the body back, people were crowded together, and people were crying. I saw one old nigger woman sitting down on the curb with her apron up to her eyes just crying her eyes out.

"It was a very sad occasion. I'll tell you that, and before . . . as soon as we got back to the White House, I had to slip away, and I went to my . . . to the President's office in the west wing of the White House.

"I knew Harry Hopkins [Roosevelt's top adviser during the whole of his White House career] had been out at the Mayo—no, it wasn't the Mayo Clinic. It was a hospital in Rochester, Minnesota, but it wasn't the Mayo Clinic. I don't remember which hospital it was.

"Anyway, I went to my office in the west wing of the White House, and I called him in. He looked just like a ghost, pale and thin. Like a ghost."

I believe you'd known Harry Hopkins before.

"Oh, yes. I first met him back in 1933, when I was presiding judge of the county and I was also head of the federal relief program for the state. I believe I got a dollar a year for that, but I don't believe I ever did collect it.

"Harry came out to Kansas City to see me, and we couldn't have got along better."

I've read that the two of you had a good deal in common, that you both came from families that weren't rich, that you were both Midwesterners, and that no matter what happened to you, how much power you got, you never forgot your origins.

"I don't . . . I wouldn't care to comment on myself, but I believe Harry Hopkins was from Grinnell, Iowa, and his father was . . . I believe was a harnessmaker.

"We agreed that when we first met . . . a lot of people were out of work, and our job . . . my job in Missouri was to see to it that they got work . . . and enough to eat. Some people said and the newspapers said that that relief money was wasted, but it wasn't. Some of the finest buildings in the state of Missouri were built with that money.

"The only people who objected were the damn rich, and I didn't pay any attention to them, and neither did Harry Hopkins.

"We stayed friends through the years. When I was operating the committee, he was one of the men in Washington that I knew I could go to, and he'd tell me the truth. He always told the truth. Never tried to fool you.

"After I was sworn in as Vice President, one of the first people that came to see me was Hopkins. He said, 'I'm going to tell you something. I've been around the old man for a long time, and I'll tell you exactly the approaches that he likes,' and he gave me a steer that was exceedingly useful in the dealings that I had with the White House.

"He was just as fine a man as I've ever met, and his word was perfectly good. Better than most bankers' bonds."

What did you talk about that first day, the day of Roosevelt's funeral?

"Well, I asked him to come in. I told you how bad he looked, and I apologized for calling him in, but I said I wanted as best he could tell me about our relations with Russia. He'd been to all those conferences with Roosevelt, to Yalta and the ones at Casablanca and Teheran and I believe Cairo, and he filled me in. He told me everything that he could, and it was very helpful indeed.

"He said he was going to resign; he didn't have a cent to his name. After all those years in the government, in the service for Roosevelt he never made any money, and he said he had to make some. I'm sorry to say that I don't think he ever did. I think he died before he ever had a chance, and it's a pity.

"But he really understood Stalin. He told me that first afternoon that Stalin . . . he said you could talk to him, and I knew *he* could, and so in May, when we were having trouble with Stalin, Molotov [Vyacheslav Molotov, Russian Foreign Minister] was threatening not to sign the United Nations Charter. I called Hopkins in again, and I said, 'Harry, are you physically able to go to Moscow? If you are, I want you to go over there and tell Stalin to make Molotov sign this Charter.'

"And he got in a plane and went. He had a three-hour conference with Stalin, and about an hour and a half after that Molotov signed the Charter."

Why do you think Hopkins was so successful in talking to the Russians?

"I don't know. I don't know, but he knew exactly how to do it. He talked tough to them all the time. I don't know how he did it, but he got it done. That was the main thing. He always did whatever he promised to do.

"And when he got back from Russia, he made a report to me, and he said, 'Old Stalin seemed to be very happy to see me, and he said to give his best regards to the President of the United States.'

" 'Well,' I said, 'I'm exceedingly obliged to you for what you did, and I want to thank you for it.'

"Harry Hopkins, as he went out, said to Steve Early or whoever was out there, he said, 'You know, I've had something happen to me that never happened before in my life.'

"Steve Early or whoever it was looked at him and said, 'What's that?'

" 'Why,' he said. 'The President just said, "Thank you" to me.' "

You mean in all those years he'd worked for Roosevelt he'd never been thanked for all he did?

"Now I told you what he said. And that's all I told you."

A few minutes later I said, *But on the afternoon of Roosevelt's funeral, Hopkins mostly filled you in on the . . . on what had happened at the various conferences and told you the kind of man Stalin was.*

"That's right. He answered all my questions just as fully and completely as he could, and I was very grateful to him for it. But I felt very, very sorry for him because he had worked a very long time and contributed to the victory as much as any man, and, well, he hadn't got much out of it."

Except historically, perhaps. I mean his place in history seems very firm.

"Yes, yes. I suppose, but you can't read what they say about you in the history books if you're not around to read it."

I believe you went on the funeral train to Hyde Park.

"Yes, yes, we went, on Saturday night, and every place we stopped there'd be a crowd just as if . . . well, you'd think the world had come to an end, and I thought so, too. So there you are.

"On the way back I heard old Harold Ickes [Secretary

of the Interior] carrying on about how the country would go to hell now that Roosevelt was gone. He said there wasn't any leadership anymore, something like that. He went on and on. He was a man who carried on a good deal."

Did he know that you could hear him?

"I think yes, I think that is what he had in mind, that I'd hear him."

You didn't fire him when you heard him talk like that?

"No, no. I didn't have to. I knew he'd talk himself out of a job sooner or later. I knew the kind of man he was. He was a resigner. He reminded me of old Salmon P. Chase, who was Secretary of the Treasury in Lincoln's Cabinet, and he thought he ought to be President, that he'd be a better President than Lincoln, and he was always resigning. He must have resigned a dozen times, and he caused Lincoln more trouble than all the generals put together, and that was not an easy thing to do.

"Lincoln said some place that old Chase wasn't happy unless he was unhappy, and that was just about the case with Ickes. I knew he'd turned in his resignation a few times while Roosevelt was President. So I knew I could wait.

"The trouble with Ickes was . . . well, he was no better than a common scold. I don't like saying that about a man, but it's true, and he wanted to be President the worst way. That's about the size of it. Lincoln said about Chase that he thought he was indispensable to the country, and he didn't understand why the country didn't realize it."

Did Ickes think he was indispensable?

"I don't think he ever doubted it for a minute.

"About a year after I became President I was going to appoint Ed Pauley [a California oilman and Democratic Party leader] Undersecretary of the Navy, which was exactly what Roosevelt had intended to do before he died.

"Well, old Ickes—'Honest Harold' they called him— he went up to the Senate, and he called Pauley every name he could think of, including some things that were not facts and he knew it.

"Pauley asked me to withdraw his nomination, and that is what happened. But I said at a press conference that I was still behind Pauley, and Ickes fired off a letter saying he was resigning. As I say, it wasn't the first time. Roosevelt had just never accepted those letters of resignation, but I did. I told him he could go right away. He wanted to stay on for another couple months I think it was, but I got word to him that he could leave the next day.

"The whole thing . . . . it was a great pity because he'd been a good man in his day."

What happened to him?

"He got to thinking he was more important than he was. I told you. I've seen that happen time and again in Washington.

"I think when old Honest Harold left, he thought the government couldn't run without him."

But you managed.

"Yes, we managed."

Mr. President, can you remember anything else about coming back on the train from Hyde Park, after Roosevelt was buried?

"Well, we came back on the special train, and Mrs. Roosevelt and two of the boys, Franklin, Jr., I think it was, and Elliott, they came in to see us, and they said to Mrs. Truman with their mother sitting right there, they said, 'The first thing we want you to do. We want you to fire the housekeeper at the White House. She's starved us to death. She wouldn't give us anything at all to eat.'

"And Mrs. Roosevelt said, 'Why, you boys had enough to eat, and you know you did.'

" 'Well,' the boys said to Mrs. Truman, 'she's no good as you'll find out.'

"Well, that woman. Her name I believe was . . . I can't for the life of me remember her name."

I believe it was Mrs. Nesbitt.

"Mrs. Nesbitt. I believe that she several times said to Mrs. Truman that Mrs. Roosevelt had done it, whatever it was, had done it in a different manner, and after a time

Mrs. Nesbitt left. I believe she decided, suddenly, to resign."

Did the food improve after she left?

"When Mrs. Truman took charge, the food was always good."

Mr. President, last night I was reading a book by Alonzo Fields, who for twenty-one years was a butler at the White House.

"He was. He was a fine old fellow. He had wanted to be a singer, but it hadn't worked out, and he worked at the White House, and he was just as nice, just as dependable as he could be. We were always good friends."

He says in his book, My Twenty-one Years in the White House, *that of all the Presidents he served under, from Herbert Hoover to your successor in the White House, you were the only one who took the trouble to understand him as a person.*

"I know he did. I know he did. He sent me a copy of the book; it's in there somewhere, and he was just as generous as he possibly could be.

"But I've never understood how to do anything else except try to understand the other fellow, and most of the time I've succeeded to some degree, I believe.

"But as Fields says, whenever I'm in Boston—he's retired and living in Boston now—whenever I'm there, he comes up to my hotel, and we have a long talk.

"You see the thing you have to remember. When you get to be President, there are all those things, the honors, the twenty-one-gun salutes, all those things, you have to remember it isn't for you. It's for the Presidency, and you've got to keep yourself separate from that in your mind.

"If you can't keep the two separate, yourself and the Presidency, you're in all kinds of trouble."

Jonathan Daniels says in one of his books that—I hope you'll forgive me—he was very upset when he was a boy, and he and a friend were passing the White House, and his friend reminded him that the President—I believe

*it was Coolidge at the time—the President had to go to
the bathroom just like everybody else.*

"That's right. We've had a few Presidents who've not
remembered a thing like that, and the minute it happens,
you can't possibly do the job.

"I've told you before. The fella that succeeded me, it
got so he didn't see anybody but millionaires and more.
He forgot all about the common people, and it had very
bad results for the country.

"But we go through those periods, and it always comes
out all right in the end."

16

Israel

Mr. Truman was speaking of April 20, 1945, the eighth day of his Presidency. He said, "I remember that day very well. I was still having trouble with the boys in the Secret Service; they wanted to drive me from Blair House to the White House in one of those damn limousines. Can you imagine being *driven* across the street?

"Of course I wouldn't allow it, and so that morning at a little after seven—I was *late*—I walked across the street, and I think I had three briefcases full of papers. Two or three. I forget which, but that wasn't anything new, of course. It seems to me all the time I was in Washington and a good part of the time when I was an old country judge back in Independence I always had papers to work on at night, always had a briefcase. Mrs. Truman once told me that a briefcase was as much a part of my outfit as my suit and hat.

"I had a long list of appointments that day, and one of them, you were asking earlier about Palestine, one of them was with Rabbi Wise [Dr. Stephen S. Wise, chairman of the American Zionist Emergency Council]. I saw him late that morning, and I was looking forward to it because I knew he wanted to talk about Palestine, and that is one part of the world that has always interested me, partly because of its Biblical background, of course.

"I told you. I've always done considerable reading of the Bible. I'd read it at least twice before I went to school. . . . I liked the stories in it. I never cared much for fairy stories or Mother Goose, not that I'm sure we had any Mother Goose at our house, but I just didn't care for that *kind* of thing.

"The stories in the Bible, though, were to me stories about real people, and I felt I knew some of them better than *actual* people I knew.

"I liked the New Testament stories best, especially the

Gospels. And when I was older, I was very much interested in the way those fellas saw the same things in a different manner. A very different manner, and they were all telling the truth. I think that's the first time I realized that no two people ever see the same thing in quite the same way, and when they tell it the way they saw it, they aren't necessarily lying if it's different.

"I think I told you, in school we usually had only one man's point of view of the history of something, and I'd go to the library and read three or four, sometimes as many as half a dozen, versions of the same thing, the same incident, and it was always the *differences* that interested me. And you had to keep in the mind that they were all telling what for them was the truth.

"And that is one of the reasons that when I got into a position of power I always tried to keep in mind that just because I saw something in a certain way didn't mean that others didn't see it in a different manner. That's why I always hesitated to call a man a liar unless I had the absolute goods on him."

There was a brief interruption while the President left the room; I later learned that sometimes when he left, he refreshed himself with a small "libation" or two, and I think that is what happened this morning because the President, when he returned, was more loquacious than he was in any other conversation.

Of course it may simply be that he was, as he says, vitally interested in the area and in the subject of Israel.

In any case he said, "We were talking about the Bible, and I always read the King James Version, not one of those damn new translations that they've got out lately.*

"I don't know why it is when you've got a good thing, you've got to monkey around changing it. The King James Version of the Bible is the best there is or ever has been

---

* The first edition of the New Testament of the New English Bible had just been published, and I believe Oxford University Press, the publishers, had sent him a copy asking for a quote.

or will be, and you get a bunch of college professors spending *years* working on it, and all they do is take the poetry out of it.

"The next thing they'll do, they'll probably appoint some committee of college professors to rewrite Shakespeare.

"But as I started to say . . . it wasn't just the Biblical part about Palestine that interested me. The whole history of that area of the world is just about the most complicated and most interesting of any area anywhere, and I have always made a very careful study of it. There has always been trouble there, always been wars from the time of Darius the Great and Rameses on, and the pity of it is that the whole area is just waiting to be developed. And the Arabs have just never seemed to take any interest in developing it. I have always thought that the Jews would, and of course, they have. But what has happened is only the beginning of what could happen, because potentially that is the richest area in the world.

"But getting back to what you were asking about, that morning I saw Rabbi Wise. It was late in the morning, and I remember he said, 'Mr. President, I'm not sure if you're aware of the reasons underlying the wish of the Jewish people for a homeland.'

"He was just as polite as he possibly could be, but I've told you in those days nobody seemed to think I was *aware* of anything. I said I knew all about the history of the Jews, and I told the rabbi I'd read all of Roosevelt's statements on Palestine, and I'd read the Balfour Declaration [Britain's statement in favor of a Jewish homeland, issued in 1917], and of course, I knew the Arab point of view.

"I also said that I knew the things that had happened to the Jews in Germany, not that I . . . at that time I didn't really know what had happened. At that time I couldn't even have *imagined* the kind of things they found out later.

"But I said as far as I was concerned, the United States would do all that it could to help the Jews set up a homeland. I *didn't* tell him that I'd already had a communica-

tion from some of the 'striped pants' boys warning me
. . . in effect telling me to watch my step, that I didn't
really understand what was going on over there and that
I ought to leave it to the *experts*.*

"The rabbi—he was just about the most courteous man
I've ever seen—said he believed me, but he said he was
sure a great many people, including some State Department
people, wouldn't go along with me. The *experts* on
the Middle East, he said.

"I told him I knew all about *experts*. I said that an
expert was a fella who was afraid to learn anything new
because then he wouldn't be an *expert* anymore.

"And I said that some of the *experts*, the career fellas
in the State Department, thought that they ought to make
policy but that as long as I was President, I'd see to it that
I made policy. Their job was to carry it out, and if there
were some who didn't like it, they could resign anytime
they felt like it.

"The rabbi thanked me very much for my time and my
assurances, but I knew that wasn't the . . . I knew it
would be a very, very long time before matters in that area
got themselves sorted out, and that proved to be the case."

* As reproduced in the *Memoirs*, the State Department
communication read: "It is very likely that efforts will be made
by some of the Zionist leaders to obtain from you at an early
date some commitments in favor of the Zionist program which
is pressing for unlimited Jewish immigration into Palestine and
the establishment there of a Jewish state. As you are aware,
the Government and people of the United States have every
sympathy for the persecuted Jews of Europe and are doing all
in their power to relieve their suffering. The question of Palestine is, however, a highly complex one and involves questions
which go far beyond the plight of the Jews in Europe.

". . . There is continual tenseness in the situation in the
Near East, largely as a result of the Palestine question, and as
we have interests in that area which are vital to the United
States, we feel that this whole subject is one that should be
handled with the greatest care and with a view to the long-
range interests of the country."

Mr. Truman is perfectly right; the tone is that of a wise and
wealthy uncle writing to a nephew who is none too bright.

Mr. Truman had masterfully understated the case. Almost three years later, in March, 1948, not only were matters in the Middle East not yet sorted out, but it looked very much as if open warfare between the Arabs and the Jews might break out at any minute, and Israel was not yet a state.

As Mr. Truman says in the *Memoirs*, ". . . the matter had been placed in the United Nations and, true to my conviction that the United Nations had to be made to work, I had confidence that a solution would be found there." But pressure on the White House from American Zionists was, as Mr. Truman told me, so great that: "Well, there'd never been anything like it before, and there wasn't after. Not even when I fired MacArthur, there wasn't. And I said, I issued orders that I wasn't going to see anyone who was an extremist for the Zionist cause, and I didn't care who it was. There were . . . I had to keep in mind that much as I favored a homeland for the Jews, there were simply other matters awaiting . . . that I had to worry about."

And then late on the morning of March 13 Mr. Truman got a telephone call from the Statler, where his old friend and business partner Eddie Jacobson was staying. Eddie wanted to come to the White House to see the President.

"I said to him, 'Eddie, I'm always glad to see old friends, but there's one thing you've got to promise me. I don't want you to say a *word* about what's going on over there in the Middle East. Do you promise?' And he did."

A little later Eddie was ushered into the Oval Room, and this is the way Harry Truman described what followed:

"Great tears were running down his cheeks, and I took one look at him, and I said, 'Eddie, you son of a bitch, you promised me you wouldn't say a word about what's going on over there.' And he said, 'Mr. President, I haven't said a word, but every time I think of the homeless Jews, homeless for thousands of years, and I think about Dr.

Weizmann [Chaim Weizmann, head of the World Zionists and the first President of Israel], I start crying. I can't help it. He's an old man, and he's spent his whole life working for a homeland for the Jews, and now he's sick, and he's in New York and wants to see you. And every time I think about it I can't help crying.'

"I said, 'Eddie, that's enough. That's the last word.'

"And so we talked about this and that, but every once in a while a big tear would roll down his cheek. At one point he said something about how I felt about old Andy Jackson, and he was crying again. He said he knew he wasn't supposed to, but that's how he felt about Weizmann.

"I said, 'Eddie, you son of a bitch, I ought to have you thrown right out of here for breaking your promise; you knew damn good and well I couldn't stand seeing you cry.'

"And he kind of smiled at me, still crying, though, and he said, 'Thank you, Mr. President,' and he left.

"After he was gone, I picked up the phone and called the State Department, and I told them I was going to see Weizmann. Well, you should have heard the carrying-on. The first thing they said—they said Israel wasn't even a country yet and didn't have a flag or anything. They said if Weizmann comes to the White House, what are we going to use for a flag?

"And I said, 'Look here; he's staying at the Waldorf-Astoria hotel in New York, and every time some foreign dignitary is staying there, they put something out. You find out what it is, and we'll use it. And I want you to call me right back.' "

On March 18 Chaim Weizmann came to the White House, but no flag was necessary. He came in through the east gate, and the fact of his visit was not known until later.

In any case, only eleven minutes after Israel became a state in May, its existence was officially recognized by the United States.

A year later the Chief Rabbi of Israel came to see the

President, and he told him, "God put you in your mother's womb so that you could be the instrument to bring about the rebirth of Israel after two thousand years."

At that, great tears started rolling down Harry Truman's cheeks.

On Herbert Hoover

One day I said, *Mr. President, I think one of the reasons that so many people have such a special feeling for you is that after you left the White House you didn't go to the Waldorf Towers [the home of former President Herbert Hoover]. And you didn't go to Gettysburg [the home of former President Eisenhower].*

"Leave the Waldorf Towers out of it; you're making a reflection there. You can use Gettysburg."

Tell me about your relations with Mr. Hoover.

"Well, not long after I got the job as President I read in the morning paper [May 28, 1945], that he was in Washington, and was staying at the Shoreham Hotel, and so I picked up the phone—I told you a lot of times I didn't bother to go through the switchboard—I picked up the phone and called the Shoreham and got through to him.

"And I said, 'Mr. President, this is Harry Truman.'

"Well, Hoover was just flabbergasted. He said, 'Mr. President, I don't know what to say.'

"And I said, 'Mr. President, I want to talk to you. If I may, I'll come right up there and see you.'

"He said, 'I couldn't let you do that, Mr. President. I'll come to see you.' *

* From Alfred Steinberg's *The Man from Missouri, The Life and Times of Harry S. Truman*: "On May 10, 1945, Truman felt lonely in his position and sought advice in an eight-page longhand letter to Eleanor Roosevelt. In her reply, Mrs. Roosevelt scolded him for wasting time writing longhand letters. Her advice was that he should quickly get on a personal footing with Churchill. 'If you talk to him about books and let him quote to you from his marvelous memory, everything on earth from Barbara Frietchie to the Nonsense Rhymes and Greek Tragedy, you will find him easier to deal with on political subjects. He is a gentleman to whom the personal element means a great deal.'

"The tone of her reply made it clear to Truman that he had to depend solely on himself for answers to the problems he

"So I said, 'That's what I figured you'd say, and I've got a limousine on the way to pick you up.'"

"A few minutes later they brought him into the Oval Room, and I said to him, 'Mr. President, there are a lot of hungry people in the world, and if there's anybody who knows about hungry people, it's you. Now there's plenty of food, but it's not in the right places. Now I want you to—' *

"Well, I looked at him. He was sitting there, just as close to me as you are, and I saw that great big tears were running down his cheeks. I knew what was the matter with him. It was the first time in thirteen years [since Hoover left the Presidency in 1933] that anybody had paid any attention to him.

"He said, 'Excuse me a minute, Mr. President,' and he went in the other room there for a few minutes, and when he came back, everything was all right, and we went on

------

faced. Indeed, his self-assurance grew with practice, though it took time. On May 28, for instance, when Herbert Hoover called on him to discuss the devastation and hunger in Europe, Truman kept addressing Hoover as 'Mr. President,' to the former President's embarrassment."

* Shortly after the outbreak of the First World War, with Belgium and northern France occupied by the Germans, almost 10,000,000 Belgians and Frenchmen faced starvation. Hoover arranged a Commission for Relief in Belgium and in four years of war got a billion dollars' worth of food to those people.

After the United States entered the war Hoover was appointed Food Administrator by Woodrow Wilson and, once again, got great quantities of much-needed food to the Allies. After the Armistice he continued to head both governmental and private organizations that fed and clothed millions of cold and hungry Europeans in twenty-three countries, including millions of children.

It was those widely publicized humane activities in Europe that caused Hoover to be so powerful a candidate in the 1928 Republican convention and strongly influenced his getting nominated and elected. When the Depression began while he was President, many people felt that Hoover was less understanding of the hungry in his own country.

from there. I wanted him to find out how our European relief program was going and how to get the food from the places where there was more than enough to the places where there wasn't any, and he agreed to do that.

"But don't you ever cast any aspersions on Mr. Hoover because he's done some very important things for this country and the world."

Early in 1946, when large parts of both Europe and Asia were threatened with a famine, Truman made Hoover honorary chairman of a Famine Emergency Committee, and in that capacity Hoover traveled 35,000 miles to twenty-two countries threatened with famine. As a result of his recommendations, the United States in five months shipped more than 6,000,000 tons of bread grains to the people of the hungry nations.

Hoover's friendship with Truman continued until the end of his life in 1964.

Did you and he ever talk politics?

"No, no, we never did. Because we never could have agreed, and besides, there were always plenty of other things to talk about."

Could you give me an example?

"Well, of course, we'd had one great experience in common. We'd both been President of the United States, and we talked a good deal about that experience. We talked about what it was like being President."

Mr. Truman stopped there, and I wanted to say, "What *was* it like, for God's sake?" Because how can any of us who has not been President possibly understand what it was like? Come even close to understanding?

But I didn't ask that question; I couldn't somehow; it didn't seem proper.

18

Los Niños Heroes

In March, 1947, at the invitation of President Miguel Alemán, President Harry S. Truman visited Mexico, and while in Washington there had been considerable concern about a possible "incident," there was none. To the contrary, everywhere Truman went, mingling with crowds of cheering people, he seemed to diminish whatever resentment of "gringos" there might have been.

And in the afternoon he made an entirely unexpected appearance at Chapultepec Castle, where a hundred years before General Winfield "Old Fuss 'n' Feathers" Scott's troops stormed the heights and captured the castle. The only survivors in the castle, which was the West Point of Mexico, were six cadets, and they committed suicide rather than surrender.

Truman went to the monument to "Los Niños Heroes," placed a wreath on it, and bowed his head in tribute. The cadets in the color guard burst into tears. Later it was said that in the history of the two countries, nothing has ever been done that was so helpful in cementing their relationship. Even now in Mexico City if you mention Harry Truman's name, taxi drivers of a certain age will weep.

I asked Mr. Truman about the incident at Chapultepec Castle, and he said, 'Well, when I first suggested it, everybody, *everybody* said I couldn't do it. They trotted out all the so-called protocol experts, and they all said no. Those birds, all they know how to say is, 'You can't do this, and you can't do that.' And if you ask them *why* you can't, all it ever adds up to is, 'It's never been done before.'

"And then they went on to say that if I did it, it would remind the Mexicans of the war with the United States, and they'd resent that. And some others said that if I paid tribute to those Mexicans' boys, it was going to alienate the Texans.

"I said, 'What the hell. Any Texan that's damn fool

enough to be put out when a President of the United States pays tribute to a bunch of brave kids, I don't need their support.'

"So I went out there, and I put a wreath on that monument, and it seemed to work out all right."

My Biggest Mistake

What do you consider the biggest mistake you made as President?

"Tom Clark was my biggest mistake. No question about it."

I'm sorry, sir. I'm not sure I understand.

"That damn fool from Texas that I first made Attorney General and then put on the Supreme Court [Thomas C. Clark, Attorney General, 1945–1949, Justice U.S. Supreme Court, 1949–1967]. I don't know what got into me. He was no damn good as Attorney General, and on the Supreme Court . . . it doesn't seem possible, but he's been even worse. He hasn't made one right decision that I can think of. And so when you ask me what was my biggest mistake, that's it. Putting Tom Clark on the Supreme Court of the United States.

"I thought maybe when he got on the Court he'd improve, but of course, that isn't what's happened. I told you when we were discussing that other fellow [Nixon]. After a certain age it's hopeless to think people are going to change much."

How do you explain the fact that he's been such a bad Justice?

"The main thing is . . . well, it isn't so much that he's a *bad* man. It's just that he's such a dumb son of a bitch. He's about the dumbest man I think I've ever run across. And lots of times that's the case. Being dumb's just about the worst thing there is when it comes to holding high office, and that's especially true when it's on the Supreme Court of the United States.

"As I say, I never will know what got into me when I made that appointment, and I'm as sorry as I can be for doing it."

I had hoped that when Mr. Truman began considering the biggest mistake he had made as President he might have something new to say about dropping the Bomb, perhaps some second thoughts on the Berlin Airlift, the Marshall Plan, the creation of NATO. But no, it was Tom Clark and the Supreme Court.

And to be sure, Clark's career on the Court was, to be charitable, lacking in distinction. It was characterized by its illiberality, by the Justice's apparent inability to figure out what was going on most of the time, and the fact that he wore outrageous bow ties under his judicial robes.

Tom Clark was at one time described as the oldest Eagle Scout in America, which is a pretty fair summation.

His son, Ramsey Clark, was Lyndon Johnson's Attorney General, a job which, despite perhaps some blemishes in the field of civil liberties, he held with honor.

20

The Bomb

There had to be a program on the Bomb, the Bombs really, the one that was dropped on Hiroshima on the morning of August 6, 1945, and the one that was dropped on Nagasaki on August 9. I had written a book about the latter, deploring it. I don't know whether Mr. Truman had read that book; I doubt it. To my almost certain knowledge nobody had after the proofreader had finished with it.

But if there was one subject on which Mr. Truman was not going to have any second thoughts, it was the Bomb. If he'd said it once, he'd said it a hundred times, almost always in the same words. The Bomb had ended the war. If we had had to invade Japan, half a million soldiers on both sides would have been killed and a million more "would have been maimed for life." It was as simple as that. That was all there was to it, and Mr. Truman had never lost any sleep over *that* decision.

Well, yes, and since Mr. Truman had made the decision to drop the Bomb all by himself, no one else was around when he made up his mind, it wouldn't be possible to bring other people into the program as we did with the Korean decision. Besides which, except for Brigadier General Leslie R. Groves, who had been head of the Manhattan Project that produced the Bomb,* most of the peo-

---

* I have elsewhere described my single encounter with General Groves, an experience I had, as you will see, no wish to repeat:

"In 1945, shortly after my Army discharge, I was for reasons I prefer to forget in the Grand Ballroom of the Waldorf-Astoria listening to a speech by Brig. Gen. Leslie R. Groves. . . . The general stood a little way from where the fillet of beef had been, and he said, the words loud and clear, that the United States didn't need to worry about the Russians ever

ple who had had anything to do with it were dead. Or they were in one way or another unacceptable to the President. J. Robert Oppenheimer, for instance, a man who had had as much as any other to do with making the Bomb, had, in Mr. Truman's mind, ". . . turned into a crybaby. I don't want anything to do with people like that."

No further questions.

The film on Mr. Truman as a man of Independence and/or independence was still being assembled in a cutting room on Broadway, a process that took months and, as I recall, the services of hundreds. David Susskind had, however, *described* the program to the officials of all the networks, and they had scarcely been able to stay awake. "Who cares? That old man?"

So for the second program we needed something dramatic, and what was more dramatic than the Bomb? We'd bomb the bastards awake.

All right, but we needed a format for the program, and that was what I was being paid for. Not only was I being paid, but I was already more or less responsible for the

———

making a bomb. 'Why,' he said, smiling, 'those people can't even make a jeep.'

"You should have heard the applause; thunderous is the only way to describe it; a great many people stood and cheered.

". . . I hesitate to think how many months of my life, maybe years, I've spent in the Grand Ballroom of the Waldorf, how many overdone fillets of beef I've eaten, how many Cherries Jubilee, how many idiot statements I've listened to, sometimes, too often, applauded.

"As I left the Waldorf that night a woman with blue hair and the face of a parakeet in distress looked at me with a snarl; she was wearing mink; they always wear mink; it's wrong about tennis shoes. You don't have to kill anything to make tennis shoes. The woman, her voice that of a finger on a blackboard, said, 'Now that we've got the Bomb let's hope we use it again and the sooner the better, and we could start out with some of the Commies right here at home.'"

spending of at least $100,000 of David's money, the money of his company, Talent Associates, anyway. I never knew which was which, a problem I'm sure David never had.

In any case, on September 27, 1961, I wrote a long and diplomatic memorandum to David, one that would, I was sure, end up in the hands of Mr. Truman; hence, the diplomacy:

"I have given deep and serious thought to the A-bomb program or programs, and it seems to me that there is only one way to deal with the subject tastefully and dramatically. As I said yesterday, Mr. Truman should himself go to Hiroshima, and he should speak in the museum there, preferably to a group of local schoolchildren. Essentially he would have to say only one thing, that the bomb must never be used again. There is no need for him to justify his decision to drop it. It was a simple, necessary military decision. Thus, to justify it or in any way to apologize for it would be repugnant.

"I think we might open the program by seeing the President enter Hiroshima, and as he does so, he might recall the events leading up to the decision to drop the bomb. We would see film of the explosion at Alamogordo, New Mexico, then film of the President at Potsdam, then of the notes that were sent to Japan asking them to surrender, then the unsatisfactory Japanese reply, then the city of Hiroshima itself, then the explosion, and the President's explanation of how and why he felt the decision was necessary. Then we go back to the President entering the city as it is today; then we talk with some Japanese people, a military man, perhaps, explaining that regrettable as the bombing was, the military of any other country would probably have decided the same thing, a Japanese intellectual saying that the Japanese now feel no bitterness toward the United States or toward the President, another intellectual who is still bitter over the A-bomb and still resents Mr. Truman because of his role in its use, a Japanese child talking about what the bomb means to him. And so on.

"Finally, the President arrives at the museum; we go through it with him, and he goes to the auditorium and speaks to the children gathered there.

"MERLE MILLER"

Of course, Mr. Truman never went to Hiroshima. I'm not sure whether he ever saw the diplomatic, duplicitous if you will, memorandum. If he did, he never mentioned it.

But when Bob Aurthur joined the project in November, taking David Susskind's place as producer, having Mr. Truman go to Hiroshima was one of the two suggestions he made for a program to follow the one that was on the cutting-room floor. The other was for a film on the Korean decision.

Bob writes of his first meeting with the President: "When I went into my outline of the Korean film, he stared at me, unblinking, his face, deeply lined, set in Rushmore-like granite, and all at once the participant realized whom he was conning, what this man was and what he had been, and the words sounded trivial, the idea infantile. But when I finished, Mr. Truman nodded sharply once, saying, 'All right, sounds pretty good,' and I knew Noyes and Hillman had already briefed him and gotten his approval.

" 'Just one thing,' Mr. Truman warned, 'don't try to make a playactor out of me.'

"Swearing this was the last intention possible, the participant needed only to flee, but Hillman held me back. 'Tell the President your idea for the atom-bomb film,' he said.

"Mr. Truman looked at me with quick suspicion; this was something he hadn't been told. No way out for me; I explained my desire to film the basic framework for the hour in Hiroshima.

"It was the only time I ever saw him blink. He was silent for a moment as Noyes studied the rug pattern and Hillman shuffled some papers, and then he said something surprising to me, if not to Noyes and Hillman.

" 'I'll go to Japan if that's what you want,' he said. 'But I won't kiss their ass.'

"Unhappily, we never got a chance to find out what he meant."

I expect what Mr. Truman meant was that while he was perfectly willing to explain why he had decided to drop the Bomb, he wasn't going to apologize for it, wasn't going to say that he had been wrong. And for all I know he wasn't wrong. Maybe it did save lives, ours and theirs.

My only insight into Mr. Truman's feeling about the Bomb and its dropping, and it isn't much, came one day in his private library at the Truman Memorial Library. In one corner was every book ever published on the Bomb, and at the end of one was Horatio's speech in the last scene of *Hamlet*. Mr. Truman had underlined these words:

. . . let me speak to the yet unknowing world
How these things came about: So shall you hear
Of carnal, bloody, and unnatural acts,
Of accidental judgements, casual slaughters,
Of deaths put on by cunning and forced cause,
And, in this upshot, purposes mistook
Fall'n on the inventors' heads. . . .
But let this same be presently perform'd,
Even while men's minds are wild; lest more mischance,
On plots and errors, happen.

Mr. Truman had underlined the last line twice. Which would indicate, I guess, that while he may not have lost any sleep over his decision, he had certainly given it a good deal of thought.

21

General Marshall and the Marshall Plan

. . . not the discovery of atomic energy but the solicitude of the world's most privileged people for its less privileged as vested in Truman's Point 4 and the Marshall Plan . . . this will be remembered as the signal achievement of our age.

—ARNOLD TOYNBEE

. . . it [the Marshall Plan] was the most unsordid act in history.

—WINSTON CHURCHILL

Mr. President, today if we may I'd like to talk again about General Marshall and your relationship with him and then get into the Marshall Plan itself. In his new book, Sketches from Life, *which I'm sure you've read Dean Acheson says that the general always insisted on complete frankness from his subordinates. He quotes him as saying, "I have no feelings except those I reserve for Mrs. Marshall."*

And Mr. Acheson says that's the way it always worked out with him. I wonder, sir, if that's the way it worked out with you, too, his Commander in Chief?

"It didn't matter what you were as far as General Marshall was concerned, didn't matter a damn. I've told you. I knew him long before I got that job in the White House, knew him in France when he was a young colonel . . . and kept track of him as best I could from then on, and he was always outstanding in every way.

"General Pershing wrote a book I read some time ago, and in it he said that General Marshall, Colonel Marshall then he was, did one of the most remarkable jobs on the entire western front when he was responsible for moving about a million men and God knows how many horses and mules and ammunition from the battlefield at St.-Mihiel to the Meuse-Argonne for the offensive there.

"And as you know I was around there at the time. The Germans were caught completely by surprise, and the man responsible for planning and executing that whole thing was Marshall. Pershing said it was one of the most remarkable things of the war.

"So Marshall always was the man everybody knew was going to have a wonderful future. No one who worked with him ever doubted it.

"So it wasn't any surprise at all when in 1939 Roosevelt made him Chief of Staff of the Army. He was only a brigadier general, wasn't even near the top of the list of brigadiers eligible for promotion, but Roosevelt reached right down there and brought him up, one of the smartest things Roosevelt ever did. Because General Marshall, more than any other man, was responsible for winning that war. At least that's my opinion.

"Of course he wanted a field command, and he'd have been wonderful at it, but Roosevelt convinced him his job was in Washington as Chief of Staff, and so that's what he did, and he did it without a single complaint.

"A lot of them had big parades after the war, a lot of the generals, but there was never a parade for General Marshall, and he deserved it more than all the rest put together.

"I gave him a decoration or two, but there wasn't a decoration anywhere that would have been big enough for General Marshall.

"But what you started to ask me, about him wanting to be told the truth. He was the kind of man who always insisted that he be told exactly what was on your mind, and he never failed to tell you exactly what was on his. Always, when I was a Senator and again when I was President. He was one of the men you could count on to be truthful in every way, and when you find somebody like that, you have to hang onto them. You have to hang onto them.

"When I first got that job in the White House, General Marshall was Chief of Staff of the Army, of course, and I saw him several times a week, which was always a pleasure because he never said much, but what he said was always exactly to the point. He never made any speeches at you. He told you what you wanted to know, and that was all he told you.

"And when you're in the kind of position I was in at the time, you appreciate that.

"And then he . . . he had no more than announced his retirement, and he and Mrs. Marshall had moved down to a new home in Virginia when I had to call on him to undertake another job."

In November, 1945, Major General Patrick J. Hurley, a reactionary, mean-spirited man from Oklahoma who was then ambassador to China, returned to the United States for conferences with various State Department officials and with President Truman. While he was in Washington, it became clear that relations between the Chinese Communists and the forces of Chiang Kai-shek were developing into a full-scale civil war. The alternatives open to the United States seemed to be either to pour further huge sums of money, weapons, and possibly soldiers into China to support Chiang or to try to convince Chiang and the Communists to work out some kind of compromise agreement. Mr. Truman favored the latter course and so instructed General Hurley, who said he agreed with him.

As Mr. Truman described it, "Old Hurley came to see me one morning [November 27, 1945], and he said he was sure everything would work out all right over there, and I said, 'Will you go back and finish the job?'

"He said that he would, and that was about eleven thirty or so in the morning, and then, I'd say it must have been somewhere between twelve thirty and one, why, Tony Vaccaro [Associated Press White House correspondent] called me up from the press club, and he said, 'Hurley's down here abusing you in every way he can think of.'

"I said, 'He just told me he was going back to China.'

"And Tony said, 'Well, he just told these people that he *won't* go back.'

" 'Well,' I said, 'all right. He won't.'

"And then I called up General Marshall, and I said, 'General, Hurley's conked out on me. And I want you to go to China. Will you go?'

"He said, 'Yes, Mr. President.' And bang went the phone. I thought he'd argue with me because I'd told him that since he'd retired, I wasn't going to bother him, that he was going to have a chance to rest.

"When he came in the next morning, I said, 'General, what did you cut me off so short for? I thought you'd argue with me.'

"'Well,' he said, 'Mrs. Marshall and I were just unpacking and getting things ready to live in that house down there, and I thought I'd break the news gently. But before I could get to Mrs. Marshall, the radio was on and blared out, "Marshall goes to China."'

"He said, 'I was in the grease sure enough then.'"

Marshall served in China until January, 1947; then he was called back to Washington and shortly thereafter became Secretary of State. He retired two years later, after a series of operations. He was then seventy, but in September, 1950, President Truman called on him once again.

As Mr. Truman remembered it, "I had the same kind of experience with him when I wanted to make him Secretary of Defense. He had to have a kidney stone taken out, and of course, after that he didn't come back.

"But I needed him. I was having a terrible time with this Secretary of Defense thing.* And I knew he was the only man in the country who could handle the job, getting everybody together, and I knew if I asked him, explained to him how necessary it was, he'd say yes because he was

---

* The Secretary of Defense had been Louis Johnson, a man of many limitations, who, before Truman sacked him, had publicly criticized the State Department's China policy and was said to have been giving material critical of Dean Acheson to at least two of Acheson's Senate enemies. With the war in Korea only recently under way Truman had to have a man of Marshall's stature to succeed Johnson.

a man who never turned down a job that needed to be done.

"So I called up Mrs. Marshall, and I said, 'Where's the general?'

"She says, 'He's fishing up in Michigan. I guess you want to get him in trouble.'

"I said, 'Yes, I do.'

" 'Well,' she said, 'go ahead. He'll go anyhow.'

"So I called him up, took me a long time to get him. He was about five or six miles from a telephone, maybe further. He finally returned the call, and I said, 'General, I want you to be Secretary of Defense. Will you do it?'

"He said, 'Yes, Mr. President.' And he did the same thing to me, banged down the receiver.

"When he came back, he said, 'I want to tell you why I had to hang up in such a hurry. I was . . . it was a general store, and all the cracker-barrel experts were sitting around there waiting to see what I was going to get from the President.' "

At the time of his appointment as Secretary of Defense Marshall was attacked by, among others, Senator Robert A. Taft of Ohio, who accused him of having "encouraged" the Chinese Reds. Senator William Jenner, an Indiana Republican, went considerably further. He said, "General Marshall is not only willing, he is eager to play the role of a front man, for traitors.

"The truth is this is no new role for him, for Gen. George C. Marshall is a living lie.

". . . [As a result], this government of ours has been turned into a military dictatorship, run by a Communist-appeasing, Communist-protecting betrayer of America, Secretary of State Dean Acheson. . . .

"Unless he, himself [General Marshall], were desperate, he could not possibly agree to continue as an errand boy, a front man, a stooge, or a co-conspirator for this administration's crazy assortment of collectivist cutthroat crackpots and Communist fellow-traveling appeasers. . . .

"It is tragic, Mr. President, that General Marshall is not enough of a patriot to tell the American people the truth of what has happened, and the terrifying story of what lies in store for us, instead of joining hands once more with this criminal crowd of traitors and Communist appeasers who, under the continuing influence and direction of Mr. Truman and Mr. Acheson, are still selling America down the river."

As Dean Acheson writes in that admirable book *Present at the Creation,* "Immediately, an honorable gentleman from Massachusetts, Senator Saltonstall, followed by Senator Lucas, rose to rebuke such words as being as contemptible as any ever uttered in that place of easy standards."

Mr. President, how do you explain a man like Jenner?

"There's no explaining him. Birds like that are just part of the dirt that comes up when we're in for a run of hysteria in this country.

"He's just one of the dirty sonsabitches that gets elected to the Senate and elsewhere when we're going through one of those periods.

"But I told you. I don't worry so much about them as I do about the ones that kiss their ass and let them get away with it. Eisenhower got his picture taken with him, sitting right next to him on the same platform. Kissing the ass of a man who said things like that about General Marshall when General Marshall had made Eisenhower, helped him at every point in his career.

"The whole thing was something I just never will forget. There are some things people do that you have to forgive them for, but there are some . . . a few that you just can't. I can't anyway."

Mr. President, do you feel that despite attacks like Jenner's, do you think history always catches up, that the true facts always eventually emerge? As in the case as we've discussed of Andrew Johnson and some others?

"No question about it. It always does, and in my opinion General Marshall will go down in history as one of the great men of his time. And of course, people like Jenner, they aren't even a footnote in history.

"And I am sure that General Marshall knew that. We never did discuss it, but he knew that. I'm sure it still hurt some, though. When they stand up and call you names, it always hurts some, and I don't care how old or how young you are, what age you are."

Mr. President, did you ever see General Marshall ruffled, lose his temper?

"No, no. He was a man you couldn't ruffle. And I never saw him lose his temper. When they were cussing him out in Congress, like Jenner, calling him every name in the book that they could think of, he never lost his temper, and he never answered back.* He wouldn't take the time. He performed . . . I'd say he performed more important jobs for this country than any other man I can think of, and I don't know where we'd be if we hadn't had him."

Mr. President, how do you explain the fact that you and General Marshall and Dean Acheson, who are so widely different in background, formed one of the most remarkable and to me awesome trios in all our history?

"I don't know about that. I don't know about that, and I don't like to talk about myself in terms like that, in that way. But I'll tell you this. Dean Acheson and General Marshall were men who went ahead and did what had to be done. And they both realized that if you are going to keep the government running, you have to make decisions, and you have to meet the deadlines, whatever they are.

* In *Sketches from Life* Dean Acheson has written: "General Marshall never answered his critics. It would have been wholly out of character for him to have done so. But more than this, he had a sort of sympathy with them. His decisions, he said more than once, were adopted and were largely successful. Why should he now try to prove that his critics' views would not have succeeded? If they wished to justify their views, it was their privilege. This tolerance of criticism, this willingness to let the record speak for itself with interpretation by him, is supremely typical of him."

"That's what some of these fellas that sit on the sidelines and criticize never do seem to realize, that you have got to do your best to keep things moving. And you hope you're moving in the right direction, moving forward. Because the minute things start slipping in the other direction, the country is in trouble. And so is the world."

And it would be true, I think, that you three men had something else in common. You were all unselfish.

"You said that. I didn't."

I'll tell you something else they had in common, the members of that remarkable trio. Dean Acheson expressed it more eloquently than either Mr. Truman or General Marshall could have managed, but I am certain they totally agreed with what he said in a speech to the Associated Harvard Clubs of Boston when he was Undersecretary of State in 1946:

"For a long time we have gone along with some well-tested principles of conduct: That it was better to tell the truth than falsehoods; that a half-truth was no truth at all; that duties were older than and as fundamental as rights; that, as Justice Holmes put it, the mode by which the inevitable came to pass was effort; that to perpetuate a harm was always wrong, no matter how many joined in it, but to perpetuate it on a weaker person was particularly detestable. . . . Our institutions are founded on the assumption that most people will follow these principles most of the time because they want to, and the institutions work pretty well when this assumption is true.

"It seems to me the path of hope is toward the concrete, the manageable. . . . But it is a long and tough job, and one for which we as a people are not particularly suited. We believe that any problem can be solved with a little ingenuity and without inconvenience to the folks at large. . . .

"And our name for problems is significant. We call them headaches. You take a powder and they are gone. These pains about which we have been talking are not like that. They are like the pain of earning a living. They will stay with us until death. We have got to understand that all our lives the danger, the uncertainty, the need for alertness, for effort, for discipline will be upon us.

"This is new to us. It will be hard for us. But we are in for it, and the only question is whether we shall know it soon enough."

That is what we have got to get back to or move forward to, those well-tested principles of conduct. As the dean says, it will be hard for us. No other way to get the institutions working again, though.

Mr. President, why was the Marshall Plan called the Marshall Plan?

"It was called that because I realized that it was going down in history as a very great, very important thing, and I wanted General Marshall to get credit for it, which he did. I said to him, 'General, I want the plan to go down in history with your name on it. And don't give me any argument. I've made up my mind, and, remember, I'm your Commander in Chief.' "

How would you describe the plan to those who don't know what it was?

"It was a plan after the Second World War to prevent the kind of thing we had happen in this part of the country after the War Between the States. I think I told you the other day you can't be vindictive after a war. You have to be generous. You have to help people get back on their feet.

"After the Second World War, Europe had suffered the same way we had, and that made me think that we had to help rehabilitate Europe. It had to be rehabilitated by the people who had helped destroy it.

"The reports from Europe that I got in the winter and spring of 19 and 47 . . . it's easy to forget, but I doubt if things in Europe had ever been worse, in the Middle Ages maybe but not in modern times. People were starving, and they were cold because there wasn't enough coal, and tuberculosis was breaking out. There had been food riots in France and Italy, everywhere. And as if that wasn't bad enough, that winter turned out to have been the coldest in history almost.

"And something had to be done. The British were broke; they were pulling out of Greece and Turkey, and they couldn't put up money to help the people on the Continent. The United States had to do it, had to do it all, and the people and the Congress had to be persuaded that it was necessary.

"I had a chance to make a speech in Mississippi—in the spring of 1947, May, I think it was, and I couldn't do it. So Dean Acheson made it for me, and that was one of the first places we started laying out what the facts were and what had to be done.

"We had several conferences on what he was going to say."

The President had promised to make a speech to a gathering of several thousand farmers and their families at the annual meeting of the Delta Council in Cleveland, Mississippi, on May 8. But for a number of reasons, partly political, partly personal, the continued illness of his ninety-four-year-old mother, who had broken a hip in February, he was unable to go.

Dean Acheson went in his stead.

Dean Acheson: "It was quite clear that in the President's mind the speech was to be a major statement on foreign policy, and we had several meetings on its contents.

"I was to say, as I did say, that Europe and Asia were totally exhausted after a terrible war and after two horrible winters. It was necessary for the United States to help them recover, and to do that, huge sums of money would have to be appropriated. And it must all be done soon.

"That was the way the President saw it, and that was the way it was. As Mr. Truman has very often said of very many things, that was all there was to it.

"I have never known a man who kept so clearly in mind what were first things. Mr. Truman was unable to make the simple complex in the way so many men in public life tend to do. For very understandable reasons, of course. If one makes something complex out of something simple, then one is able to delay making up one's mind. And that was something that never troubled Mr. Truman.

"The speech I was to make was only one of several dozen, no doubt several hundred matters with which the President was concerned at that time. In many ways it was surely one of his lesser concerns, and yet every time we went back to the speech he seemed to remember every word.

"Now having a precise memory may not be one of the major virtues, but it is, I submit, in every way preferable to having an imprecise memory.

"And Mr. Truman was never troubled by hindsight, feeling, as I do, that it is a waste of time. Hindsight only tells you what did happen. It never tells you what did not happen and what might have occurred if you had taken action you did not take."

Mr. Secretary, speaking of memory, in Joe Jones' book on the Marshall Plan, The Fifteen Weeks, *he writes about a time in 1949 when Mr. Truman's knowledge of the history of the Dardanelles and that whole area astonished both you and Mrs. Acheson, especially Mrs. Acheson. Could you tell me about that?*

"We had been in New York for the dedication of the United Nations Building, and on the train going back to Washington, Mr. Truman for reasons I don't remember began talking about Central Asia and the Middle East. We had just finished dinner, and I remember that as he talked, he drew outline maps with a spoon to demonstrate what he was saying.

"It was one of the most lucid presentations I have ever heard, beginning with the travels of Marco Polo up through the conquests of Genghis Khan, the rise and fall of the Ottoman Empire, and in modern times the increasing Russian ambitions in the area, including control of the Dardanelles.

"Of course I was quite familiar with the President's wealth of historical knowledge and his ability to apply it to the problem at hand, but Mrs. Acheson was very much impressed with his profound knowledge of what to most people is a puzzling and obscure part of the world.

"He told her that it wasn't surprising at all, that he had spent a good part of his life reading history and that for reasons he really could not explain Central Asia and the Middle East had always held a very special interest for him.

"But there were very few subjects on which Mr. Truman did not have a detailed and accurate knowledge and which he could not explain with complete lucidity."

There's another episode in Joe Jones' book about a meeting in August, 1946, a meeting with some people from the State Department and from the armed services, including you as Undersecretary of State and General Eisenhower, who was Chief of Staff of the Army. The Russians had recently made demands on the Turkish government which would, I gather, have meant the virtual abandonment of its independence.

I believe that at that meeting there was an exchange between the President and General Eisenhower.

"No, I wouldn't describe what happened as an exchange. The President conducted that meeting as he conducted all such meetings. He elicited the point of view of everyone present at the meeting, and then he said it would, of course, be necessary to take a firm stand against the Russian demands and that to make sure that everyone realized we were serious in our support of the Turks, we were sending a considerable naval force to rejoin the USS *Missouri,* which was already in Istanbul. That had been the recommendation, and he approved it and directed that it be carried out, fully realizing that such action could lead to armed conflict.

"General Eisenhower, who was seated next to me,

leaned over and in a stage whisper asked whether I thought the President realized the implications of what he had done.

"With as benign a smile as I could under the circumstances manage I suggested that the general ask the President that question, which he did do.

"The President reached in a drawer, took out a large and clearly much-studied map of the area, and proceeded for the next fifteen or twenty minutes once again to give a detailed account of the history of the area up to the present day. It was once again a masterful performance, and when it was over, Mr. Truman turned to the general and asked whether or not he was satisfied that the President understood the implications of what he was saying.

"I believe the general did have the grace to join in the laughter that followed, although I would not say that in general he was burdened with a sense of humor."

Mr. Secretary, I gather you don't have too high a regard for General Eisenhower.

Mr. Acheson smiled, no doubt as benignly as he could manage, and we went on to other matters, but in *Present at the Creation* he says that during the 1952 Presidential campaign:

General Eisenhower began discussing foreign policy in terms surprising for him. The great chain of events begun under his benefactor, General Marshall, he called a 'purgatory of improvisation.' In the same speech, relating what he termed some 'plain facts' about the period leading up to the attack on South Korea, the General grossly distorted my Press Club speech, and, when I publicly set the record straight, severed all relations with me. It appears to be true that one who unjustly injures another must in justification become his enemy. During the eight years of his Presidency I was never invited into the White House or to the State Department or consulted in any way. However, this involved no invidious discrimination, since my chief, President Truman, was treated the same way.

Mr. Secretary, what was the reaction to your speech in Mississippi?

"The reaction was quite favorable and widespread, particularly in the foreign press.

"What I was doing, of course, was really no more than preparing the way for what General Marshall was to say at Harvard the following month. The President always called my remarks at Cleveland 'the prologue to the Marshall Plan.' "

Mr. President, why was it that General Marshall announced the Marshall Plan at Harvard?

"General Marshall told me about a month before, maybe more, that he was going up there. They were going to give him an honorary degree, and he said to me, 'I've got to make this damn speech, and you know how I hate to make speeches. And I don't know what to talk about.'

"I said, 'I want you to spell out the details of this plan that's being worked out over in the State Department to save Europe from going under.' And I said, 'This plan is going down in history as the Marshall Plan, and that's the way I want it.'

"He blushed. He was just about the most modest man I ever did know, and he said, 'I can't allow a thing like that to happen, Mr. President.'

"And I says to him, 'You won't have anything to do with it, but that's what will happen, and that's what I want to happen.' And I was right. It did." *

* General Marshall made his speech on June 5, 1947, at the 296th Harvard commencement. In presenting him with an honorary degree President James B. Conant compared Marshall to that other general who was also a George, Washington, "An American to whom freedom owes an enduring debt of gratitude, a soldier and statesman whose ability and character brook only one comparison in the history of this nation."

In his short speech Marshall described the horrors of the winter in Europe that had just passed and, further, what would surely happen in the months ahead—the increasing shortages

Winston Churchill has called the Marshall Plan "the most unsordid act in history."

"Well, there wasn't anything selfish about it. We weren't trying to put anything over on people. We were in a

of food and fuel and money, the physical wreckage, the dislocated economies.

Then he said, "The truth of the matter is that Europe's requirements for the next three or four years of foreign food and other essential producers—principally from America—are so much greater than her present ability to pay that she must have substantial additional help or face economic, social, and political deterioration of a very grave character. The remedy lies in breaking the vicious circle and restoring the confidence of the European people in the economic future of their own countries and of Europe as a whole. The manufacturer and the farmer throughout wide areas must be able and willing to exchange their products for currencies the continuing value of which is not open to question. . . .

"It is logical that the United States should do whatever it is able to assist in the return of normal economic health in the world, without which there can be no political stability or secured peace. Our policy is directed not against any country or doctrine but against hunger, poverty, desperation, and chaos. Its purpose should be the revival of a working economy in the world so as to permit the emergence of political and social conditions in which free institutions can exist. Such assistance, I am convinced, must not be on a piece-meal basis as various crises develop. Any assistance that this government may render should provide a cure rather than a palliative. Any government that is willing to assist in the task of recovery will find full cooperation, I am sure, on the part of the United States government. Any government which maneuvers to block recovery of other countries cannot expect help from us. Furthermore, governments, political parties, or groups which seek to perpetuate human misery in order to profit therefrom politically will encounter the opposition of the United States. . . .

"An essential part of any successful action on the part of the United States is an understanding of the character of the problem and the remedies to be applied. Political passion and prejudice should have no part. With foresight, and a willingness on the part of our people to face up to the vast responsibility which history has clearly placed upon our country, the difficulties I have outlined can and will be overcome."

General Marshall did not mention the Soviet Union or

position to keep people from starving and help them preserve their freedom and build up their countries, and that's what we did."

Mr. President, the plan called for expenditures of sixteen billion dollars. Didn't that cause a lot of concern in Congress?

"Yes, it did, but it had to be done, and so I called in all the favors I was owed, and we got it through. I called in Sam Rayburn and when I told him what we had in mind, he just wouldn't believe it. His first reaction was just like everybody else's. He said we couldn't afford it. He said, 'Mr. President, it will bust this country.'

"And I said to him, 'Sam, if we don't do it, Europe will have the worst depression in its history, and I don't know how many hundreds of thousands of people will starve to death, and we don't want to have a thing like that on our consciences, not if it's something we can prevent, we don't.

"And I said, 'If we let Europe go down the drain, then we're going to have a bad depression in this country. And you and I have both lived through one depression, and we don't want to have to live through another one, do we, Sam?'

"He says, no, we didn't. And then he kind of swallowed hard, and he says, 'Harry, how much do you figure this thing is going to cost?'

"And I looked him right in the eye. I never told Sam anything less than the whole truth at all times. That's the kind of relationship we had. I looked him right in the

Communism in his speech; the only enemies he enumerated by name were the abovementioned "hunger, poverty, desperation, and chaos."

It could not have occurred to the general that some years later revisionist historians would see that speech as a bomb-rattling threat to the peace by a dedicated cold warrior. Nor did it occur to me when talking to Mr. Truman and Mr. Acheson about General Marshall and the Marshall Plan in 1961 and 1962.

eye, and I said, 'It's going to cost about fifteen, sixteen billion dollars, Sam.'

"Well, his face got as white as a sheet, but I said to him, 'Now, Sam, I figure I saved the people of the United States about fifteen, sixteen billion dollars with that committee of mine, and you know that better than anyone else.

" 'Now we're going to need that money, and we can save the world with it.'

"And he says to me, 'Harry, I'll do my damnedest. It won't be easy, but you can count on me to help all I can.' And he did, too, and so did a lot of others in both parties. There wasn't anything partisan about any part of this or anything else where foreign policy was concerned. Not when I was in the White House there wasn't.

"We always went ahead and did what had to be done, and the Marshall Plan saved Europe, and that's something I am glad I had some part in helping accomplish."

22

The 1948 Victory

Mr. President, you said the other day that you decided you were going to run for reelection the first day you were President, in April, 1945, but you didn't go into any detail about that. What were some of the reasons you decided so soon?

"I always knew that from April, 1945, until January, 1949, what I would really be doing was filling out the fourth term of Roosevelt, who was a great President, but I had some ideas of my own, and in order to carry them out I had to run for reelection and be reelected, and that is exactly what happened.

"Of course I didn't say I was going to run for quite some time. It didn't do any harm that I could see to keep people guessing for a while. I knew I'd be able to win, though. I knew that all along."

You knew?

"Of course I knew. I knew the Republicans would come up with somebody like Taft or Dewey, and I knew that the people of this country weren't ready to turn back the clock—not if they were told the truth, they weren't.

"The only thing we . . . I had to figure out was how to tell them the truth, in what way, and I decided that, the way I'd always campaigned before was by going around talking to people, shaking their hands when I could, and running for President was no different. The only difference was instead of driving to the various communities where people were, I went by train. But otherwise, it was exactly the same experience. I just got on a train and started across the country to tell people what was going on. I wanted to talk to them face to face. I knew that they knew that when you get on the television, you're wearing a lot of powder and paint that somebody else has put on your face, and you haven't even combed your own hair.

"But when you're standing right there in front of them

and talking to them and shaking their hands if it's possible, the people can tell whether you're telling them the facts or not.

"I spoke I believe altogether to between fifteen and twenty million people. I met them face to face, and I convinced them, and they voted for me."

Did you think it would be a three-way race, that Henry Wallace would run against you?

"Never had the slightest doubt of it. All through 1947 Henry went around the country making speeches saying that I was trying to get this country into war with Russia, which, of course, was the opposite of what I was doing. I was doing everything in the world to prevent a war, and I succeeded.

"But Henry said I was trying to start a war, and he also kept saying that he was still a loyal Democrat, and the more he said it, the more I was sure he was going to run against me on a third-party ticket."

Why?

"Because Henry was like Lloyd Stark, the fella that ran against me for the Senate. What he said he wasn't going to do was exactly what I knew he was going to do. I don't know, in Henry's case, if you'd say he was a liar as much as that he didn't know the difference between the truth and a lie.

"And anyway the way he . . . the way Henry talked to you, you had to listen very hard to understand what he was getting at, and half the time I was never sure if Henry knew. He was a very difficult man to follow what he meant." *

* As I said earlier, some years after the 1948 election I moved to Brewster, New York, not far from Mr. Wallace's large farm at South Salem. At one time I thought of writing something about him, maybe a biography, although I felt his campaign in 1948 had been a shambles and a shame.

In any case, I made several trips to South Salem and had several conversations with him. I have never been more disappointed in a public figure. He was a muddled, totally irrational man, almost incapable of uttering a coherent sentence. He was also the bitterest man I have ever encountered.

Mr. President, you have quite a reputation as a poker player. Would you say there's any resemblance in politics and poker in that in both you seem to have to size up your opponent pretty well if you want to win?

"I was never much of a poker player. Roosevelt was more of a poker player than I was. But they never wrote anything in the papers about it. But they were always writing about me playing poker.

"Newspapermen, and they're all a bunch of lazy cusses, once one of them writes something, the others rewrite it and rewrite it, and they keep right on doing it without ever stopping to find out if the first fellow was telling the truth or not.*

"But it is true that you have to size up the other fella, in politics, too. And I'd sized up Henry as a fella that would say one thing and do another. So it didn't surprise me a bit when he came out with a third party.

"And I knew another thing. He was like the other fella that ran against me that year. I knew the more he talked, the more votes he'd lose."

Do you mean he was dishonest?

"It wasn't so much that. It was that half the time and more he just didn't seem to make sense."

---

* Dr. Wallace Graham, the President's personal physician in the White House and until the time of his death, said, "When Mr. Truman was in the White House, we would play poker sometimes in the evening. I don't think he really enjoyed it much. He played more to find out about people. Often he'd play with someone he was considering for some office or other, some appointment. He'd ply him with champagne, and then General Vaughan [Colonel Harry Vaughan, a veteran of Battery D who followed Harry Truman right into the White House and was his most-criticized associate] would rib whoever it was, and the President would watch to see what the reaction would be. If the guy got flustered, if he couldn't take the ribbing or got too tight, Mr. Truman would feel, I believe, that he shouldn't be given whatever the appointment was.

"But I don't think he ever played much for his own enjoyment. He'd never give up, though. The way we'd play you couldn't lose more than eighty dollars or so, but Mr. Truman would stay in every hand, always."

*Were you surprised when the Dixiecrats walked out of
the convention and Strom Thurmond, who I believe then
was governor of South Carolina, became another third-
party candidate?*

"No. When 1948 was coming along, they said that if I
didn't let up with my asking for a Fair Employment Practice Commission and asking for a permanent commission
on civil rights and things of that kind, why, some of the
Southerners would walk out.

"I said if that happened, it would be a pity, but I had
no intention of running on a watered-down platform that
said one thing and meant another. And the platform I
did run on and was elected on went straight down the line
on civil rights.

"And that's the beautiful thing about it. Thirty-five votes
walked out of that convention and split up the Solid South,
and because of Wallace, Dewey was able to carry New
York State by sixty thousand votes.

"So I always take a great deal of pleasure in saying I
won without the Solid South and without New York,
which wasn't supposed to be able to be done. It was never
done before, and it hasn't been done since.

"People said I ought to pussyfoot around, that I
shouldn't say anything that would lose the Wallace vote
and nothing that would lose the Southern vote.

"But I didn't pay any attention to that. I said what I
thought had to be said. You can't divide the country up
into sections and have one rule for one section and one
rule for another, and you can't encourage people's prejudices. You have to appeal to people's best instincts, not
their worst ones. You may win an election or so by doing
the other, but it does a lot of harm to the country.

"Another thing about that election. I won it not because
of any special oratorical effects or because I had any help
from what you call 'the Madison Avenue fellas' but by a
statement of fact of what had happened in the past and
what would happen in the future if the fella that was running against me was elected.

"I made three hundred and fifty-two speeches that were

on the record and about the same number that were not. I traveled altogether thirty-one thousand seven hundred miles I believe, and it was the last campaign in which that kind of approach was made, and now, of course, everything is television, and the candidates travel from one place to another by jet airplane, and I don't like that.

"You get a real feeling of this country and the people in it when you're on a train, speaking from the back of a train, and the further you get away from that, the worse off you are, the worse off the country is. The easier it gets for the stuffed shirts and the counterfeits and the fellas from Madison Avenue to put it over on the people. Those people are more interested in selling the people something than they are in informing them about the issues."

You didn't have any Madison Avenue people on the campaign-train with you?

"No, no. We couldn't afford their services to speak of. In Detroit the day when I was going to make the Labor Day address from Cadillac Square they had quite a time raising the money for a radio broadcast, fifty thousand I think it was, and we were always running short of money throughout the campaign just paying to keep the train going from station to station.

"But we didn't have any advertising men along. I never felt the need for any."

Mr. President, speaking of money, in Jack Redding's book,* which I know you've read because some of your marginal comments were printed in the book, he says that Senator Howard McGrath said in 1948 that if you had just invited some potential contributors to take a cruise aboard the Presidential yacht, the Williamsburg, *the Democratic National Committee would have had no trouble at all raising a lot of money but that you wouldn't*

---

* Jack Redding was director of public relations for the Democratic National Committee in 1948; his book, published in 1958, was called *Inside the Democratic Party*. Howard McGrath was a Senator from Rhode Island, as well as chairman of the Democratic National Committee in 1948.

agree to that, to inviting them. Although, as you say, the party was nearly broke during the entire campaign.

"That's true. I wouldn't."

Why?

"Because it's the Presidential yacht. It belongs to the President."

That was another time when I waited for more, knowing there would be no more.

I gather you have no faith in advertising men in politics.

"None at all. I'm sure they're very good at what they're trained to do, but in politics what you're doing, and I've said this a few times before, what you're doing or ought to be doing is discussing ideas with people so they can decide which is better, yours or the other fellow's.

"And as I say, you don't have to have any oratory to put it over. You just have to set down the facts, which is what I always did.

"The thing I never could understand about the fella that ran on the Democratic ticket in 1952 [Stevenson], he always spent a lot more time worrying about *how* he was going to say something than he did on *what* he was going to say. I told him once, I said, 'Adlai, if you're telling people the truth, you don't have to worry about your prose. People will get the idea.'

"He never did learn that, though. He was a very smart fella, but there were some things he just never got through his head, and one of them was how to talk to people."

That's not uncommon in politics, would you say?

"No, and it's a pity. It seems to get more that way all the time. The more time goes on, it seems people running for public office just don't tell what they have on their minds. There was a lot of that in the last campaign [1960]. The candidates for President didn't talk any less, but they said a lot less."

Mr. President, early in 1948, long before the convention there was a lot of talk among some Democrats about

trying to nominate or draft the fellow who in 1952 suc-
ceeded you in the White House. Did that bother you?

"Not a bit. It didn't make any sense at all. They didn't
know what party he belonged to even or how he stood on
any issue at all."

There are those, myself among them, who would say
that after eight years in the White House you still didn't
know, the country didn't know, where he stood on almost
any issue at all.

The President laughed, and then he said, "All that
carrying-on before the convention in 1948, I knew nothing
much would come of it, and it didn't."

What did you think of the Democrats who did it, the
two Roosevelt boys, among others, James and Elliott, I
believe?

"Well, their father was a great politician, but none of
his sons seem to have inherited his abilities in that line.
They just never seem to have what it takes to get people
to vote for them. I told one of them, James I think it was,
and I was out in California making a speech. I told him
he was a goddam fool for trying to get rid of somebody
who was just carrying out his father's policies. Trying to
anyway.

"Of course, later, after the convention, he came around
and supported me, but I never did forget what went on
earlier.

"I never did anything about it, but the old man never
forgets."

Weren't you a little bitter?

"No, no. I didn't have time for that. Being bitter . . .
that's for people who aren't busy with other matters."

Mr. President, didn't you make what you called a "non-
political tour" across the country before the Democratic
national convention?

"I did. I had to dedicate some things. I think I dedicated
the Grand Coulee Dam two or three times. I forget which,
and it was, as you say, 'nonpolitical.' But on the way I
made a few stops and told the people what was going on

in Washington, and they showed up in large numbers and listened and seemed to appreciate what I had to say. About a million people were lined up on the streets of Los Angeles alone, but they never took any pictures of that. They took pictures to prove . . . at times when there weren't big crowds."

Could you tell me how the phrase "whistle-stop" originated?

"Robert Taft [Republican Senator from Ohio] started it, and he wished he hadn't. Somebody asked him what was happening on my tour, and he said that I was lambasting Congress at all kinds of 'whistle-stops across the country.'

"Of course some of the boys at the national committee picked that right up and got word out to towns all across the country about what Taft had said, and the mayors of those towns didn't like it a bit. It did us no harm at all at the polls in November, of course."

What he was saying was, "Well, where the President is going is just to all these tiny towns that are of no importance."

"That's right, and some of those towns had populations of a hundred thousand people and more, including Los Angeles, of course, and, after that, the whole campaign became what was called a whistle-stop campaign, and I saw to it in my speeches that people remembered what Taft had said about their towns."

Why is it do you suppose that Republicans so often make mistakes like that? Or seem to. Is it stupidity?

"No. Most of them are smart enough. It's just—this is only my opinion, of course—it's just that they don't seem to know or care anything about people. Not all of them but a lot of them don't.

"The fella they nominated to run against me was a good example of that. People could tell he wasn't open and above board, and the more he talked, the more he showed that he didn't have any program at all in mind if he got elected. Except to set things back a few dozen years or more. So he didn't get elected. It was as simple as that."

Mr. President, you said the other day you hadn't given much or any thought to what you were going to say at the convention, but it says in the Memoirs *that I believe you had made some informal notes.*

"Yes, I'd written down some notes when Margaret and the Boss and I were coming from Washington to Philadelphia, and they were in a big black notebook that I carried to the podium with me when I made my acceptance speech. There were two things I was sure of that I was going to say. I was going to tell them that Alben Barkley [Truman's Vice Presidential running mate] and I were going to win the election, and I'd made up my mind that after I lambasted into the do-nothing Eightieth Congress that I was going to call them back into a special session, which is what I did do.*

* "On the twenty-sixth of July, which out in Missouri we call 'Turnip Day,' I am going to call Congress back and ask them to pass laws to halt rising prices, to meet the housing crisis—which they are saying they are for in their platform.

"At the same time I shall ask them to act upon other vitally needed measures, such as aid to education, which they say they are for; a national health program; civil rights legislation, which they say they are for; an increase in the minimum wage, which I doubt very much they are for; extension of the Social Security coverage and increased benefits, which they say they are for; funds for projects needed in our program to provide public power and cheap electricity. By indirection, the Eightieth Congress has tried to sabotage the power policies the United States has pursued for fourteen years. The power lobby is as bad as the real-estate lobby, which is sitting on the housing bill.

"I shall ask for adequate and decent laws for displaced persons in place of this anti-Semitic, anti-Catholic law which the Eightieth Congress passed.

"Now, my friends, if there is any reality behind the Republican platform we ought to get some action from a short session of the Eightieth Congress. They can do this job in fifteen days, if they want to do it. They will still have time to go out and run for office.

"They are going to try to dodge their responsibility. They are going to drag all the red herrings they can across this campaign, but I am here to say that Senator Barkley and I are not going to let them get away with it."

"That really stirred things up. It was in the middle of my speech, and I said, 'The Republicans have agreed on a platform. Now I'm gonna call a special session of the Congress and give them a chance to put their platform into effect.

"And of course they didn't do a damn thing. If they had been smart and even passed one measure along the lines they'd promised in their platform, I'd have been up a creek, but I knew damn well they wouldn't do it, and of course, they didn't."

Mr. President, you said you were calling that special session for Turnip Day. What's Turnip Day?

"The twenty-sixth of July, wet or dry, always sow turnips. Along in September they'll be four, five, maybe six inches in diameter, and they're good to eat—raw. I don't like them cooked."

Turnip greens are pretty good.

"Well, yes, but the only way to get turnip greens is in the spring. You take out the turnips that you've kept in the cellar all winter and set them out in the garden, and then they come up. You grow them, and the greens that have come up when they're both, oh, about four or five inches long you mix them with dandelions and mustard, and they make the finest greens in the world. Spinach isn't in it.

"That's what the country people used to have in the spring. Turnip greens with dandelions and mustard and things of that kind.

"But you have to know which is which with plants like that. Plenty of those things are violent poison. You take poke berries, pokeroots. When they're so long, they're good to go into greens, but you wait a little longer, and you might as well order your coffin. Because you're done. They're as poisonous as cyanide."

How do you find out when to pick them?

"Your grandmother has to tell you."

Mr. President, during the campaign, how did you decide where to go, where to speak? For instance, you spoke at

*a plowing contest I think it was in Dexter, Iowa. I'm from
Iowa, and I don't even know where Dexter is. How did
you happen to decide to go there?*

"Well, there were ninety-six thousand farmers at Dexter, Iowa [I-uh-way], and somebody had to go there and
talk to 'em, and I went."

How do you know there were ninety-six thousand?

"There was a lot of disagreement in the papers and
the newsmagazines about how many people were there.
Nobody asked me, but I could have told 'em. Some said
fifty thousand, some said seventy-five thousand, and some
said ninety thousand.

"But there were ninety-six thousand people there. There
was ten acres, and the place was jammed full. Now figure
two to the square yard and you'll see how many there
were. Figure it out yourself."

*How do you think those farmers felt about what you
said?*

"I don't know, but they voted for me. I've told you
time and again. You've got to know how to talk to people.
That's the whole thing, and you've got to convince them
that you know what you're talking about. They don't go
for high hats, and they can spot a phony a mile off.

"I stopped one time in a place in either Montana or
Idaho. And I guess there must have been two or three
hundred people there, and I got off the train, and some
smart aleck on a horse rode up and said, 'Mr. President,
how old is this horse?' I said, 'Which end do you want me
to look at, his tail or his mouth?' I looked at his mouth,
and I said, 'He's so old.' The fella said, 'Jesus Christ, he
knows, doesn't he?'

"If you don't think I had that vote committed.

"Some of these smart alecks are always saying that to
tell how old a horse is you can look either at his tail or his
mouth, but that isn't true. You have to look at his teeth,
and this horse had teeth that long. I said, 'This old son of
a bitch must be fifteen or twenty years old, and he ought
to be taken out to pasture.' The fella turned and rode him
off."

I read someplace that when you were in Dexter, you talked at some length about the differences between mules and machines.

"I did. I don't remember what I said, but all those speeches were recorded. They're in a book in there. But what I probably said is that there's a hell of a lot of difference between riding behind a mule and riding behind a tractor.

"The most peaceful thing in the world is riding behind a mule, plowing a field. It's the calmest and most peaceful thing in the world, and while there's some danger that you may, like the fella said, get kicked in the head by a mule and end up believing everything you read in the papers, the chances are you'll do your best thinking that way. And that's why I've always thought and said that farmers are the smartest people in the world.

"My father used to trade mules, and he knew a lot about them. He didn't have to look at a mule's teeth to tell how old he was. All he had to do was look at him, and he was never wrong.

"A tractor will never be as . . . satisfactory as a mule. It makes a noise, for one thing, and noise interferes with a man's thoughts.

"But plowing a field with a mule is the most satisfying thing a man can do. And at the end of the day, looking over what you've done, you can feel a real sense of accomplishment, and that's a very rare thing."

Mr. President, I see by Jack Redding's book that not all your speeches in 1948 were for votes, that when you were in Dallas, you stopped at an orphanage and talked to the children there.

"Yes, I did. Yes, I did. I just told them to stop the cars, and I went inside and talked to those children."

Why?

"I thought that, well, being spoken to by the President of the United States was something they'd remember all their lives. It's a very lonely thing being a child. It was for me, and I had a family, including, as I think I told you, thirty-nine first cousins, and I was the only one they all spoke to.

"So I was very lucky when I was a child, and I had a happy childhood, but sometimes . . . well, I was lonesome, and I felt that it must be twice as bad for boys and girls who are orphans. So I went inside and talked to them.

"I was glad I did it, and I guess they were, too."

And when you were in Dallas, Texas, you had the first integrated rally in the history of the state.

"Oh, yes, and there was quite a to-do over that. They said I'd lose votes, and they said there'd be race riots, and I don't know what all they said.

"But that rally was just as peaceful as any of the others. If you just give people a chance to be decent, they will be. If the fella that succeeded me had just given people a little leadership, there wouldn't have been all that difficulty over desegregating the schools, but he didn't do it. He didn't use the powers of the office of the President to uphold a ruling of the Supreme Court of the United States, and I never did understand that.

"If he'd got out in front and told people that they had to uphold the law of the land, it's my opinion that they'd have done it. But he didn't; he shillyshallied around, and that's the reason we're in the fix we're in now."

Mr. President, didn't your train run out of money in Oklahoma someplace?

"In Oklahoma City. We ran out of money, and some of them got in a panic again and said we'd have to call off the campaign and go back to Washington, but we raised it. We never had much, but we raised enough to finish the trip. And then we got up enough money for a second trip."

It sounds as if it was always nip and tuck as far as money was concerned, though.

"It was, but that's the way it ought to be. I think I've told you. When people are anxious to give you a lot of money in a political campaign, you always have to ask yourself what the reason for it is. People just don't give money away for no reason."

What are some of the other highlights of that remarkable campaign that you remember?

"Well, in an auditorium in Seattle that holds seven thousand people, they had eight thousand or more crowded in, and some bird way up in the balcony shouted, 'Give 'em hell, Harry. We'll take 'em.' And that's where that whole thing started. After that a lot of people started shouting it."

Was that spontaneous?

"Oh, yes. None of those things was ever worked up. I didn't believe in that. The minute you start planning things, why, the next step is powder and paint, and they want you to become a playactor, and I believe I've told you a time or two how I feel about that."

Yes, sir, I remember. . . . Could we try a typical day on the campaign train? What would happen? What time would you get up in the morning?

"Five o'clock."

And would you take a walk?

"The first time where there was a stop I'd get off and take a walk. And of course, they had to hold the train as long as I wanted it held. I was President."

And after the walk? What happened next?

"We'd go on, and whenever the train got to a spot where there were enough people on the platform to be talked to, we'd stop, and I'd talk to them."

What did you consider enough people?

"Ten to a thousand."

Did you ever actually speak to an audience as small as ten people in 1948?

"Many a time, many a time. They'd come out to hear me, and I talked to them."

And did you lambaste the Republicans at every stop?

"Most of the time, but there were some exceptions, and they got me into trouble with some of the local politicians. When I was in Michigan, they wanted me to light into

Senator Vandenberg [Arthur Vandenberg, Republican Senator from Michigan]. But I wouldn't do it. He'd supported the Marshall Plan; if it hadn't been for him, it might never have been approved in the Senate, and I wasn't about to forget that and start attacking him, and I didn't. It made a lot of those birds in Michigan unhappy, but I wouldn't do it.

"And in California I wouldn't say anything against Governor Warren [Earl Warren, Republican candidate for Vice President] because he was a friend of mine.

"If you can't win an election without attacking people who've helped you and who're friends of yours, it's not worth winning. I think I've told you. You can't pay too high a price to win an election."

Didn't Mr. Dewey have a little trouble with the engineer of his train out in Illinois?

"He said something about how maybe he ought to have the engineer shot at sunrise because he backed up the train too far. We managed to get that news around the country, and it didn't help him much with the working people. The trouble was he'd forgot what it was like to have to work for a living, and it showed on him, which is why he lost the election." *

Someplace I read that Lester Biffle [Secretary of the Senate] went around during the campaign disguised as a chicken peddler and made a poll that was the only poll that showed you were going to win.

---

* In his illuminating book on 1948 *The Loneliest Campaign,* Irwin Ross writes of that incident, which took place in Beaucoup, Illinois, on October 12: "As Dewey began to speak from the rear platform, the train suddenly moved backward into the crowd. It stopped after a few feet and no one was hurt. Dewey momentarily lost his poise. 'That's the first lunatic I've had for an engineer,' he told the crowd. 'He probably ought to be shot at sunrise but I guess we can let him off because no one was hurt.' The flash of temper was forgivable under the circumstances, but it was to cost Dewey dearly. Before the campaign was over, the Democrats inflated the remark to the dimensions of a cause célèbre, charging that it proved that Dewey was unfeeling and hostile to the workingman."

"That's right. He went around in a spring wagon and dressed in overalls, and he got more information for me than anybody else in the business. He said, 'Now listen, Harry, you don't have to worry. The common people are for ya.' And they were."

What's a chicken peddler?

"Well, in every neighborhood in the country where they raise chickens there was always a fella who drove around either in a truck or an old spring wagon with a team of mules who bought the surplus chickens and eggs.

"That's what a chicken peddler is, and in the old days there were a tremendous number of them. There used to be an old man with whiskers who'd come out to our farm, and my mother would sell him eggs and butter, and with the money she got she'd buy all the coffee and sugar and everything else we needed.

"They called him Old Folks, and he was always honest with my mother. He'd give her a fair price for the chickens by weight and eggs by the dozen, and he was always welcome because people knew he was honest.

"But I don't think they have them anymore. I think they're gone. I think they're gone."

So Mr. Biffle's poll was the only one that had it right?

"The only one. The rest of them, what they were doing was polling each other, and I didn't let it worry me. What I did was keep on giving the facts to the people."

Weren't you worn out at the end of the campaign?

"I felt better at the end of the campaign than I had at the beginning, and I'll tell you why. I got the feeling . . . a real feeling of the kind of country we've got here and the kind of people, and it sort of you might say renewed my faith."

Especially since you won the election.

"No, no, no. Even if I'd lost the election, my feeling for the common people of this country wouldn't have changed. You know what Lincoln said. 'The Lord must have loved the common people he made so many of them.' Well, the feeling I got in that campaign was that most of the people in this country are not only, like I said, decent people, they want to do the right thing, and what you have to do is tell them straight out what the right thing is.

"And feeling . . . like that, I didn't get tired."

Mr. President, I guess everybody in the United States who was alive at the time remembers what he did on election day, November 2, 1948. For one thing, the radio networks had sent out word to expect Mr. Dewey's victory announcement around nine in the evening. So we all planned to listen to that and then go to bed and get a good night's sleep. Instead of which, we stayed up all night, and, as you may recall, Mr. Dewey didn't concede until almost noon the next day. I wonder, sir, could you tell me what you did that day?

"Nothing very special. I got up at the usual time and took my morning walk, and then later, of course, we voted, and I had a nice, long lunch at the country club. Mayor Sermon [Roger T. Sermon, mayor of Independence] gave a little party out there, and we all had a good time. Just a few old friends was all it was, but we had a good time."

Rufus Burrus, Harry Truman's personal attorney: "We had lunch . . . and Mr. Truman said, 'Now, fellows, don't worry. I'm going to get elected. You can depend on it. But you'd better go out in the precincts and do a little work, see that the vote gets out.

"None of us believed it, believed that he was going to win, but he did. He was as sincere in his belief that he was going to be reelected President as he was at any time when he was running for judge of the county or the Senate of the United States.

"And before that lunch was over, speaking only for myself, of course, he'd brought me around to thinking that way, too."

Tom Evans, an old friend of Harry Truman's: "He called me from the country club, and he said he was having dinner there but that he was going to escape out the back door and go down to Excelsior Springs [about thirty miles north of Independence]. Which is what he did."

Mr. Truman: "We drove down to Excelsior Springs, and I had a bath in the hot springs and a little something to eat and went to bed, about six o'clock in the evening I think it was."

And you went to sleep, of course.

"Oh, yes, and about midnight I tuned in the little radio there, and old H. V. Kaltenborn was carrying on about how while I was ahead, he didn't see how I could win."

Tom Evans: "I called him about midnight. He had just lost New York State to Dewey, and I knew he had to carry Ohio, Illinois, and California. And when I called him to tell him that he said, 'Tom, I'm going back to sleep. Now don't call me any more. I'm going to carry all three of those states.' Which he did." *

Mr. Truman: "The Secret Service, one of the Secret Service men woke me up the next morning around four thirty, and I was elected. So I got up and got dressed, and we drove over to the Muehlebach Hotel to celebrate."

---

* Truman carried Ohio by 7,107 votes, California by 17,-865, and Illinois by 33,612.

23

The Korean Decision

Dean Acheson was understandably proud of a hand-written note from Mr. Truman. It was, in Mr. Acheson's words, "written on scratch-pad, with *The White House* at the top of it . . . dated the 19th of July 1950, when the first phase of the Korean operation was over. . . . I think it throws some light on the type of man that I worked for and the kind of relationship we had:

"Memorandum to Dean Acheson. Regarding June 24 and June 25. Your initiative in immediately calling the Security Council of the United Nations on Saturday night and notifying me was the key to what developed afterward. Had you not acted promptly in that direction we would have had to go into Korea alone. The meeting, Sunday night, at the Blair House, was a result of your action Saturday night. The results thereafter attained show that you are a great Secretary of State, and a diplomat. Your handling of the situation, since, has been superb. I am sending you this for your records. Harry S. Truman."

Bob Aurthur and I tried to persuade Mr. Truman to read that note on camera, but he refused. It was the old business of trying to make a playactor out of him. "I'm not putting on a show. I'll tell you the facts *as they occurred*. I'm not gonna try to put on any show. If I have to put on a show . . . it'll be a failure."

The President asked Mr. Acheson to read the note, which he did. He added, "I should have preferred to have President Truman read this note rather than to have to read it myself. The problem, of course, is who is more embarrassed by it. Is it more embarrassing for me to read a note praising me, or is it more embarrassing for him to read a note that shows what a great man he is? He chose that I should be embarrassed—and I am happy to abide by his orders once again."

That note sums up how the United Nations and not just the United States got into the Korean War or "police action," they are hard to tell apart, about as well as is possible. Largely but not wholly because of Dean Acheson's quick thinking and action, we did not have to go it alone in Korea. That happened in Vietnam. We went it alone, and it was perhaps the costliest disaster in our history.

But in Korea, in Mr. Truman's words, "For the first time in history, an aggressor was opposed by an international police force, and it worked. It saved the free world."

I guess all but a handful of revisionist historians would agree that it worked, but as you will see in following the way it all began, it wasn't just what Mr. Acheson and the President did. A lot of it was pure luck. *If* Jacob Malik, the Soviet delegate, had come to the meeting of the United Nations Security Council and exercised his veto power. . . . And *if* Dean Acheson hadn't been at his farmhouse in Maryland that Saturday night. And *if* Harry Truman out in Independence hadn't said, "Dean, we've got to stop the sons of bitches no matter what. . . ."

But all that is hypothesis, idle speculation, and as I believe I've explained Harry Truman thought all such exercises were "a damn waste of time."

He was probably right, too. Besides, what did occur that June weekend and on the Monday and Tuesday that followed reads like an exercise in high adventure. A cliffhanger. An eerie whodunit involving the fate of the world. All you have to keep in mind is that it all really happened and no so long ago either.

What's more, the story has a happy ending, and that all by itself is rare enough these days to make it worth telling.

As Mr. Acheson told Bob Aurthur and me in the winter of 1962, "Fate never selected a more unlikely place to plant the seeds of great events than in Korea as it appeared in the late 1940's and the beginning of the 1950's."

Korea, which in English means "the land of the morning calm," has had a tempestuous history, and Harry Truman knew it as well as he knew the history of the Dardanelles. One afternoon at the Carlyle Hotel in New York Mr. Truman spent more than an hour tracing the history of that never-calm peninsula from about 57 B.C. when it was known as the kingdom of Silla until the present day. It was depressing but fascinating, and for our purposes I think we can safely begin with the end of the Second World War. Later that month, January, 1962, in Washington Dean Acheson said, "When the Japanese indicated that they were ready to surrender, the question arose as to whom they should surrender.

"On about the twelfth of August, 1945, the Pentagon sent over to us in the State Department—I was then an Assistant Secretary of State—a memorandum dealing with many affairs, but among them it said that the Japanese troops north of the thirty-eighth parallel in Korea should surrender to the Russians and those south should surrender to a representative of General MacArthur.

"This was exactly what it purported to be. It did not intend to be a boundary. It did not intend to be zones of occupation. It was merely that for convenience troops north of this dividing line should surrender to one commander, those south of it to another. And this was done.

"Immediately afterward we discovered in Korea, as we discovered in Germany, that when one dealt with the Russians any sort of dividing line meant much more than one had supposed it was going to mean. It meant that an Iron Curtain descended at that point and that everything north of the thirty-eighth parallel became completely Russian and everything south under Allied or American control."

And that is the way things nervously remained until the weekend we're coming to. True, in 1947 Mr. Truman ordered General Eisenhower, Admiral Leahy, Admiral Nimitz, and General Spaatz to study the military value of Korea, and their report, issued in September of that year, said, "The Joint Chiefs of Staff consider that, from the standpoint of military security, the United States has little strategic interest in maintaining the present troops and bases in Korea."

General MacArthur agreed. Moreover, he said that anyone who advocated a land war on the Asian continent had clearly gone bonkers.

For the way the general changed his mind, changed it several times and in several different ways, read on.

In January, 1950, Dean Acheson, then Secretary of State, made a speech at the National Press Club in which, as he put it almost exactly twelve years later, "I pointed out that we had established our own troops in what I called a defense perimeter and that this perimeter, beginning in Alaska, running along the Aleutian Islands, then touched Japan, where we had a garrison, went from there to the Ryukyu Islands, where we had both a military garrison and an Air Force base—from there to the Philippines. And I said that in this way we had established ourselves in the Western Pacific rather than in the Central and Eastern Pacific as we had before the war.

"I said, 'So far as the military security in the other areas of the Pacific is concerned, it must be clear that no person can guarantee those areas against military attack. . . . But should such an attack occur, the initial reliance must be on the people attacked to resist it and then upon the commitments of the entire civilized world under the Charter of the United Nations.'"

It all *seems* clear enough, and indeed it all was clear enough until the Presidential campaign of 1952, when the Republican right, the China Lobby idolators, and the superhawks who are always among us dug up that speech to *prove* that Mr. Acheson by its words had *invited* the North Koreans to invade South Korea.

At one point a bill was introduced in Congress to cut off his salary.

Mr. Acheson, like General Marshall, never answered his attackers. He maintained throughout his remarkable calm. I once asked him how he managed, and he said,

"I am something of a stoic both by nature and by in-
heritance. And I learned from the example of my father
that the manner in which one endures what must be en-
dured is more important than the thing that must be en-
dured. I am inclined to agree with Sir Francis Bacon that:
'The good things which belong to prosperity are to be
wished, but the good things that belong to adversity are
to be admired.' "

We come now to Saturday, June 25, 1950.
Dean Acheson: ". . . I had gone from the State Department around noontime, expecting to have a relaxed
and quiet weekend at my farm, in a quiet old Maryland
farm house about twenty miles north of the capital. The
house was built in the nineteenth century and is very simple, very small, very quiet, and very secluded.

"I was sitting there reading with my wife when about
ten o'clock I received a telephone call on what we called
the white telephone. I had in my office and also in my
house a white telephone which was connected directly with
the switchboard of the White House. If one lifted the receiver, one got the switchboard in the White House and
could be directly connected with the President or through
that switchboard with any other department or Cabinet
officer in Washington.

"The telephone rang, as I say, about ten o'clock, and I
answered it to find on the wire Assistant Secretary of State
Jack Hickerson, who had charge of international organization affairs, including the United Nations. He said he was
in the State Department with Assistant Secretary Dean
Rusk, who is now Secretary of State, and that they had
just received an alarming message from Ambassador [John
Joseph] Muccio in Seoul. This message was to the effect
that there was a serious attack along the whole northern
border of South Korea. They were not sure whether this
was a determined effort of the North Koreans to penetrate
South Korea or whether it was a larger than usual border
incident.

"But the military mission was alarmed. The Korean

forces were alarmed, and the ambassador was standing by to confer with the head of our military mission and let us know more details during the course of the night.

"I asked him what recommendations they had, and he said that it was their view that we should call for a meeting of the Security Council of the United Nations for the following afternoon, Sunday, and obtain a resolution requesting or ordering all parties to return within their borders, to cease any aggression, and calling upon all members of the UN to assist in this endeavor.

"I said that they were to get in touch with our representatives to the United Nations, have them available in New York the next day, and that in the meantime I would call the President, who was then at his home in Independence. And if the President approved this action, they would already have started on it. If he disapproved it, they could stop it at once. But I thought that time was so pressing that we should not even delay while I spoke to the President.

"I told them that I would call them back, but immediately to get in touch with people in the Pentagon to set up a working force which would be there all night . . . so that we could find out more about this situation and be prepared to take further action in the morning.

"I then called the President. I gave him this message and told him what I had done, saying that I had done it entirely subject to his approval and that I wished further orders or instructions from him. The President said he approved this action entirely and that I was to proceed with it with the utmost vigor."

Mr. Truman: "It was about ten thirty on Saturday night, and I was sitting in the living room reading. The phone rang, and it was Dean Acheson calling from his home in Maryland. He said, 'Mr. President, I have serious news. The North Koreans are attacking across the thirty-eighth parallel.'

"I wanted to get on the plane and fly to Washington right that night, but he said that I shouldn't, that a night flight wasn't necessary. He said that I should stand by for another call from him when he'd have more details. And I agreed.

"I also gave my approval to his suggestion to call an emergency session of the United Nations Security Council to consider a declaration that active aggression had been committed against the Republic of Korea.

"I went to bed, and that was one night I didn't get much sleep."

John Hickerson, Assistant Secretary of State for United Nations Affairs: "I knew that Ambassador Warren Austin, our permanent representative to the United Nations, was in Rutland, Vermont, for the weekend. So . . . after talking to Secretary Acheson, I called Ambassador Ernest Gross, who was our deputy representative to the United Nations. I called him at his house and was told that he was out to dinner somewhere on Long Island and they did not have the telephone number. I asked that he call me urgently at the State Department as soon as he came in. . . .

"At twelve o'clock, not having heard from Ambassador Gross, it seemed to me it would be a good idea to call the Secretary-General of the United Nations, Trygve Lie, and alert him. . . . I got him on the phone at five minutes past twelve. He had been listening to the midnight news, and there was something I had not heard about disturbances on the Korean border. He had some inkling of it but no idea of whether it was simply a minor clash or what. I told him that it was an all-out massive attack from the North Koreans against South Korea.

"I shall never forget his words. He listened. And then— Trygve Lie speaks perfect English but with a Norwegian accent—and he said, 'My God, Jack, that's war against the United Nations!'

"I regret to say that I couldn't think of anything more original to reply than, 'Trygve, you're telling me!'

"We ended the conversation. He said he would alert his boys—find out where every member of the Security Council was—and would wait further word from Ambassador Gross."

Ernest A. Gross, who was acting chief of the U.S. delegation to the United Nations: "Jack Hickerson called me at a friend's house where a dinner party was just breaking up. He told me that it seemed quite certain that the forces of North Korea had suddenly mounted an offense across the thirty-eighth parallel, and he instructed me to return immediately to my home on Long Island to wait further word.

"He also said that because of some slight difficulty in tracing me, he had called Trygve Lie and told him what had happened.

"He said that I would be expected to take it from there and would be in communication with Trygve Lie during the night.

"I went back to my home, and my teen-age daughter was having what was then called in the adolescent vocabulary a slumber party. A dozen or so of her teen-aged friends were sprawled all over the living room, and I had to stagger over the recumbent bodies to get to the telephone.

"And they clustered around the phone and began to get very excited. I imagine for them it was a memorable night, but they didn't get any more sleep than I did.

"I talked with Trygve Lie I think four times between midnight and five A.M. And in the meantime I telephoned virtually all the members, at least seven or eight of the members of the Security Council at their homes.

"I called them all in the middle of the night and got them out of bed, and I can say . . . that they were all profoundly shocked by what had happened. They felt that the United Nations had to do something about it, that this was an attack on the UN itself. There was no question about that.

"And they were ready to act even though many of them would not . . . there would not be time to get instructions from their governments.

"We did not know whether the Soviet Union would show up for the emergency meeting on Sunday. It may be recalled that the Soviet delegation had walked out of the Security Council in early January on the ground that the Council was illegally composed because the Chinese Communist regime did not occupy the seat of the Republic of China. The Soviet delegate had not attended any Security Council sessions between that time and the moments of our impending meeting on Sunday, June 25. It was obvious that if the Soviet delegate were to attend the meeting, any resolution would be vetoed, and the Security Council would be precluded from action, as had happened so many other times by the abuse of the Soviet veto.

"But we went ahead and did what we had to do, and I was instructed by Mr. Hickerson to notify the other members of the Security Council . . . to communicate a formal request to Secretary General Trygve Lie to convene a meeting on that day . . . an emergency meeting for two o'clock that Sunday afternoon."

Dean Acheson: "On Sunday morning I drove immediately to the State Department and found that my colleagues there had been working throughout the night with representatives in the Department of Defense. And they had brought together all the information available and necessary for decisions as to what should be done.

"In the first place, it was clear that this was not an isolated border incident. This was a general attack which extended all across the border and therefore was a matter of the utmost seriousness. And in the second place, it was established that it was an attack in very considerable force. The South Korean forces were falling back. They had not yet lost contact with one another. The retreat was orderly, but it was precipitant, and it seemed fairly clear that before long the capital of South Korea would be overrun. Therefore, we knew that we had a critical military situation to handle. We then had reports on enemy strength insofar as our intelligence was able to gather them. They indicated that these forces were well trained. Many of them had been within the Soviet Union for some time. They were well equipped, and this was a dangerous attack.

"We then had an up-to-date report on our own forces. The nearest available, of course, were in Japan. These, for the most part, were untried divisions. The veterans had all been mustered out. A few of the soldiers had had battle experience but not many. The Navy was in the Philippines at Cavite. There were Air Force planes available. So we knew that much. We knew what we had available.

"We knew that the United Nations was convening at two o'clock, and that was about all the information that we had. We then began to get to work on recommendations to the President, and I called him on the telephone in Independence."

Mr. Truman: "I'd been out to my brother Vivian's farm, and when I got back, a little while after I got back, the telephone rang, and Margaret went to answer it. She came back and said, 'Daddy, it's Dean Acheson, and he says it's important.'

"I went to the phone and said, 'What is it, Dean?' And he said, 'Mr. President, the news is bad. The attack is in force all along the parallel.' And I said, 'Dean, we've got to stop the sons of bitches no matter what.'

"He said he agreed with me, and he told me that an emergency meeting of the Security Council was all set for two o'clock that afternoon.

"I said fine, and I said I was returning to Washington immediately, and we were on our way back in less than an hour. In fact we left in such a hurry that two of my aides were left behind.

"The flight took about three hours, and on the way I thought over the fact that what the Communists, the North Koreans, were doing was nothing new at all. I've told you. The only thing new in the world is the history you don't know.

"And it was always the same, always had the same results. Hitler and Mussolini and the Japanese were doing exactly the same thing in the 1930's. And the League of

Nations had let them get away with it. Nobody had stood up to them. And that is what led to the Second World War. The strong got away with attacking the weak, and I wasn't going to let this attack on the Republic of Korea, which had been set up by the United Nations, go forward. Because if it wasn't stopped, it would lead to a third world war, and I wasn't going to let that happen. Not while I was President.

"That's what a lot of people never understood, including the general we had over there at the time. This was a police action, a limited war, whatever you want to call it to stop aggression and to prevent a big war. And that's all it ever was. I don't know why some people could never get that through their heads.

"When my plane, the *Independence,* landed in Washington, the Secretaries of State and Defense were there to meet me, and we rushed to the Blair House for the conference. We had a quick dinner. We were living at Blair House at the time, and this dinner was in the dining room in the Lee House, which joins the Blair House. After it was over and the dishes were cleared away, I asked Dean Acheson to give me the joint recommendations of the State and Defense departments." *

Dean Acheson: "This I did. The recommendations were three. They were, first of all, that Americans should be evacuated from the Seoul area. Those Americans consisted of most of the people attached to the political mission there, the military mission—that is, the wives and children, all the people who were not required to be there.

---

* According to Dean Acheson those present at the meeting, "Aside from the President and myself . . . were the Undersecretary of State James Webb, Assistant Secretary Dean Rusk . . . , Ambassador Philip Jessup, Assistant Secretary of State John Hickerson, Secretary of Defense Louis Johnson, Secretary of the Army Frank Pace, Secretary of the Air Force Thomas K. Finletter, Secretary of the Navy Matthews, General Vandenberg, Chief of Staff of the Air Force, General Collins, Chief of Staff of the Army, Admiral Sherman, Chief of Naval Operations, and General Bradley, who was Chairman of the Joint Chiefs of Staff."

"And in order to do this and to allow any other people who wished to leave to go, General MacArthur was asked to give air protection to the airport to prevent any North Korean troops or soldiers or air forces from interfering with it.

"The second recommendation was that General MacArthur should be instructed to air-drop supplies—food, ammunition, weapons, whatever he could to the Korean forces to strengthen them.

"The third recommendation was that the fleet should be ordered to move north from Cavite at once and to take up a position between Formosa and the mainland. And we added along with that the recommendation that the President should announce that we would not permit any attack, either upon Formosa or from Formosa upon the mainland. The idea being that we wanted strictly to limit the sphere of military operations and did not want to have several wars on our hands at the same time.

"The President, when I had finished making these recommendations, asked each person in the room to make his own statement of how the situation appeared to him and his own view as to these recommendations. Each person did so. They all agreed with the recommendations made and the President, therefore, who had been considering all of this while the discussion was going on, said that he would adopt the three recommendations which I made and the orders should be prepared immediately for his signature with the proviso that he would not that night make any statement as to what the fleet would do until the fleet was in a position to do it.

"This was rather typical of President Truman. It is extremely unwise to say what is going to happen when one is not in a precise position to do it. I realized at once that he was right and that our recommendation was wrong.

"The fleet did a remarkable job. It was a time of peace. Men were ashore in Cavite Harbor. They had no expectation of leaving on any kind of a mission at all. But steam was gotten up, or whatever is the equivalent of steam today in the Navy, and by the time the orders to sail came every man was aboard. Battle stations were maintained, and the fleet was moving northward. This was an extremely praiseworthy operation.

"That concluded our operations for Sunday night. The President told us to stand ready to meet again on Monday night, when the situation became clearer. I told all my people to go home and get some sleep, which they needed very badly, having missed one night entirely."

That afternoon, as the President was flying to Washington, the Security Council, as planned, held an emergency meeting. Calling the session to order, Trygve Lie said, "The present situation is a serious one and is a threat to international peace. . . . I consider it the clear duty of the Security Council to take the steps necessary to reestablish peace. . . ."

Mr. Gross then spoke, saying that the attack on South Korea was "of grave concern to the governments of all peace-loving and freedom-loving nations" and that it "openly defies the interest and authority of the United Nations." The hastily written resolution he introduced asked the Security Council to accuse North Korea of the "armed invasion" of South Korea, asked that it order an immediate cease-fire and withdraw all its troops south of the thirty-eighth parallel. Finally, it asked every member of the UN "to render every possible assistance to the United Nations in the execution of this resolution."

The resolution that was passed at the end of the afternoon, by a vote of 9 to 0, with Yugoslavia abstaining, was somewhat weaker. The words "armed invasion" were changed to "armed attack," and both North and South Korea were called on to order a cease-fire.

Jacob Malik had not been at the meeting, but how long could his absence be counted on? Already in Washington a much-stronger resolution was being drawn up, to be presented at another meeting of the Security Council, it was hoped, on Tuesday, June 27. Suppose Malik showed up for that and exercised the Soviet veto? The United States would then face two extraordinarily difficult decisions. It could take the matter to the General Assembly and ask that the veto be overridden, but that could only be done by a two-thirds majority, a most unlikely prospect at that moment, not to mention the considerable time such an action might take.

Or the United States could unilaterally enter the Korean conflict. But that might easily deal a death blow to the UN. Would Harry Truman risk that? * After all, minutes after he took the oath of office as President back in 1945 his first order of business was to announce that the United Nations Charter Conference would go forward in San Francisco just thirteen days later. And on Monday, June 26, the fifth anniversary of the signing of the Charter would be observed.

Was the possibility of unilateral action discussed by the men in Washington making those monumental decisions that weekend?

Dean Acheson: "I've been asked several times whether in these critical meetings we considered what would be done in the event that the United Nations refused to take any action. . . . I think in asking these questions, those who do so have not participated in decisions of this sort. This business of making decisions is a continuous process. One does not say, 'We will do this,' then someone else says, 'Suppose this doesn't work, what do you do?'

"This is not the way it is done if the action is as vague and general as proceeding through the United Nations as against proceeding unilaterally.

"For instance, it was perfectly clear that the United Nations would and must denounce an aggression. It could not do otherwise. The Charter prohibited an aggression, and this was clearly one. Moreover, there was a report from the United Nations Commission itself in Korea branding this as an aggression from the north.

* Mr. Acheson's answer to that question is coming up. I once asked Mr. Truman if the United States was prepared to go it alone, and his answer, as usual, was short and to the point. He said, "No question about it."

"Therefore, it was certain that the United Nations, in some form or other, would denounce this action, would state that opposing it was a good thing and that continuing it was bad. This we knew would occur.

"It was doubtful that it would go further, that it would call on its members to fight. However, it would have gone far enough so that those who wanted to fight would be fighting with its blessing and not against it.

"But one says, suppose Mr. Malik appeared and interposed a veto? He might have appeared. It was extremely unlikely. The very fact that it was unlikely underlined the importance of immediate action. One thing that one can be fairly sure about in the Soviet system is that they are not capable of making instantaneous decisions. There has to be even more palaver in the Soviet system than there does in the democratic system. They can make decisions over a long period of time, so that action appears to be peremptory—but it really isn't. . . . And here was something that they had undoubtedly inspired. And undoubtedly they had not expected us to take the action that we did.

". . . To have reversed their boycott of the UN would have taken a major decision of the Politburo. So the betting was all in favor of Malik's not returning, *if* we acted fast. If we didn't act fast, why, anything could have happened.

"Therefore, I think to all of us it would have been a waste of time to spend the precious minutes that we have saying what we'll do if Malik appears.

"The answer is, 'Let's wait and see. Chances are seventy-five out of a hundred that he won't. We haven't got time to fool with the twenty-five percent chance. Let's get forward with the job.'

"If he had appeared, we would immediately have adjusted ourselves to that and taken some other action, either through the General Assembly or unilaterally. I think Mr. Truman was quite right that the interest of the United States and its allies and of the free world was so great in defeating this aggression . . . that it had to be done. And if through some sort of legal mechanism one operation was blocked, then another operation would have to be found to do it.

"My own view was not to worry about things that were *not* likely to happen. And therefore, I was in favor of Admiral Farragut's advice, 'Full steam ahead and damn the torpedoes.' "

Do you wonder that I never felt more inarticulate than in the days I spent with Mr. Acheson?

To continue. Monday, June 26:

Dean Acheson: ". . . We prepared a new resolution to lay before the Security Council, feeling that the earlier one did not go far enough in branding the North Korean invasion as an aggression and declaring that it was a violation of the Charter and calling upon its members to stop it."

On Monday, June 26, the news from Korea was very bad indeed. The South Korean forces were in headlong retreat. North Korean tanks were near Seoul, and the government had retreated to Taegu, 150 miles to the south.

John Hickerson: "By Monday it was apparent that massive United States assistance would be necessary if Korea was to be saved. And on Monday night we had another meeting at Blair House, at about nine o'clock. Again the President heard reports from Secretary Acheson, from the diplomatic front, and from the military representatives on the military situation.

"It was at this meeting that a decision was reached for us to give all-out air and naval support, under the United Nations, to Korea. The necessary directions were given by the President.

"Again let me emphasize the fact that he went around the table and asked everybody present to state his views. There was unanimity of opinion, but the President took the action. He was the only one who could do it, and he unhesitatingly did it.

"I never shall forget at the end of the meeting Secretary

Acheson and I left together to go back to the State Department, and I had to check with the President and Secretary on one or two points of phraseology on the draft resolution which we had prepared to be introduced to the Security Council on Tuesday.

"We very quickly disposed of those minor things, and the President said to Secretary Acheson and me, with great earnestness, in effect, these words, 'I've been President a little over five years, and I've spent five years trying to avoid making a decision like the one I've had to make tonight. What I want you to know is that this is not a decision just for Korea. It's a decision for the United Nations itself.'

"I went back to the State Department and put the necessary steps in motion to get ready for the Security Council meeting the following afternoon."

Ernest A. Gross: "Prior to the session of June 27 when the American resolution was passed, it happened that a luncheon had been arranged by the Soviet delegation, arranged about a month before Korea, to say good-bye to Malik, who was going back to the Soviet Union, either permanently or for a rest cure. You never knew.

"This was to be a farewell luncheon at the Stockholm Restaurant in Syosset, Long Island. Trygve Lie had been invited, and a number of other delegates were there.

"I was seated between Trygve Lie and Jacob Malik, and, naturally, I tried to discuss with Malik what was happening, what was behind this whole business in Korea. He, of course, as was to be expected, was noncommittal. He said nothing.

"But Trygve Lie felt it expedient to urge Malik to drive back to Lake Success with us and take his seat in the Security Council. I think that Trygve felt this would be a great thing for the organization and might be a step toward a resumption of peace. I don't know what was in his mind, but it made me very unhappy, and I kept glaring at Trygve and urging him to stop inviting Malik back.

"Fortunately, of course, Malik didn't come back, and

Trygve Lie and I got into his car and drove back to Lake Success. I rather sternly reprimanded him, as an old friend, for what he had done. And I expressed my relief that he'd been such a poor advocate that he hadn't persuaded Malik to return. I said, 'Trygve, can you imagine what would have happened if he *had* accepted your invitation?' "

As a result, I told you luck was with us that week, at ten forty-five that night the Security Council passed a resolution recommending that "members of the United Nations furnish such assistance to the Republic of Korea as may be necessary to repel the armed attack and to restore international peace and security in the area."

For the first time in recorded history a world organization had voted to use armed force to stop armed force. Lucky or not, it was a considerable victory for Harry Truman.

Dean Acheson: "On Tuesday morning, before the Security Council meeting, the President called in the Congressional leaders and informed them of the decisions we had made the night before.

"We had supposed the resolution we had drawn up was to be laid before the Security Council in the morning. But the Indians had asked for a postponement until the afternoon.

"We were unaware of this when we were meeting with the Congressional leaders. But we had no doubt that in the absence of the Russian delegate, it would pass.

"Therefore, as the Congressional leaders were leaving, knowing that there would soon be in the press as many different views of what was said as there were Congressional leaders, it seemed to us desirable that an exact statement be made as to what the President had decided the previous night and what he had said to the Congressional leaders.

"Such a statement was made public. However, the United Nations had not passed the resolution, and the Russians had a good deal of fun with this, saying that we had decided to use military force before the United Nations had called on us to do it. This was a debating point to which they were entitled but no more than that because the previous resolution had done practically the same thing, and, as I say, there was no doubt that the stiffer resolution would also pass.

"Also on Tuesday we sent a note . . . to the Soviet government asking them to use their good offices with the North Korean government to bring this aggression to an end. It seemed to us that it might be possible that they would do it, but in any event they should be asked to do it. The Russians replied on Thursday. This reply said that the real aggressor was South Korea; therefore, there were no good offices for them to use, but we must use *our* good offices to prevent the South Koreans from continuing their aggression.

"Since the South Koreans had already lost their capital, this seemed to be slightly an ironic thing to do. We noted, however, that the Russian note was not vitriolic, and it seemed to us a good sign that they intended to disengage from this operation and at least not be caught publicly having anything to do with it.

"Meantime, the situation in Korea was deteriorating very rapidly. It was clear that the retreat had become a rout. The Korean Army was throwing away its weapons and was moving fast . . . as fast as it could go.

"On Wednesday Washington time General MacArthur flew over the battlefields, saw what was going on, talked to President Syngman Rhee, talked to the American military mission, and on the night of the twenty-ninth and thirtieth, between Thursday and Friday, General MacArthur put in what is known as a telecon. This is a form of communication which is highly secure and consists of two typewriters and two screens. In one place a message is typed out which appears immediately thousands of miles away in typewritten form on the screen before the audience receiving it. They consider this message; then they type out and send back the reply. This appears on your own screen and on the recipient's screen. So the whole conversation remains constantly before you and is not subject to any of the difficulties which come from oral talk and can so easily be misunderstood.

"General MacArthur got General Collins on the telecon and told him that it was a disaster in Korea, a complete rout. The Korean Army had ceased to exist. That if there was to be any resistance on the ground, it had to be by American troops. And he requested permission to bring over from Japan a regimental combat team as the initial point of a twelve-division buildup to try and hold the area around Pusan, until stronger measures could be taken to defend South Korea.

"General Collins suggested that this would be put up to the President when he was awakened a little bit later. But General MacArthur said there was not time to do that. And therefore, General Collins called General Bradley [Chairman of the Joint Chiefs of Staff] and the President at five o'clock in the morning to discover that Mr. Truman was already up, dressed, and at work. They put this to him, and the President gave his approval at once. Therefore, before the rest of us were awake, the regimental combat team was on its way to Korea.

"Friday morning . . . at the Friday morning Cabinet meeting the President reported to us what had occurred. He had thought what he did was the right thing to do. But he asked us if we had any comments to make about it. There was no doubt in any of our minds that this was the correct step.

"We all voiced our strong endorsement and approval of it, and I haven't the slightest doubt that every member of the Cabinet would have done that if he had been asked in advance. This is one of the situations in which the course of events really determines action. And having decided that we were going to meet this aggression, we could not flinch even though the course of the aggression turned out to be much more serious than it had first appeared to be.

"About this same time we were offered by Generalissimo Chiang Kai-shek thirty thousand Chinese troops for use in Korea. The President asked for a recommendation in regard to this from the Defense and State departments. And after conferring about it, we agreed that the offer should not be accepted. It seemed to us that these troops were not reliable, were not very good troops, were not well armed, and would perhaps cause more trouble than they would be helpful. They were not too sure of their loyalty, and we did not want to get into that difficulty."

Mr. President, Dean Acheson has said that there was some consideration of using Chiang Kai-shek's troops in Korea. How serious was that consideration, on your part, I mean?

"Not very damn serious. What would have been the use of it? They weren't any damn good, never had been. We sent them about three billion five hundred million dollars' worth of matériel, sent that to the so-called free Chinese, and then about five million of Chiang's men between Peking and Nanking surrendered to three hundred thousand Communists, and the Communists used that matériel to run Chiang and his men out of China. I told you. He never was any damn good.

"They wanted me to send in about five million Americans to rescue him, but I wouldn't do it. There wasn't *anything* that could be done to save him, and he was as corrupt as they come. I wasn't going to waste one single American life to save him, and I didn't care what they said. They hooted and hollered and carried on and said I was soft on Communism and I don't know what all. But I never gave in on that, and I never changed my mind about Chiang and his gang. Every damn one of them ought to be in jail, and I'd like to live to see the day they are." *

Dean Acheson: "Another reason for not using Chiang's troops. . . . If one had to use other than European and American troops, the troops required were Koreans. This was their country. They had been defending it. And it seemed to us that we could far better get the equivalent of

---

* For more of Mr. Truman's observations on Chiang and his Madame and others in their crew, see the next chapter.

thirty thousand troops from reorganizing the Korean Army
and using them.

"And finally, we did not wish to raise the political complications which would have been raised, if we had introduced the Nationalist–Red Chinese controversy into the
battle in Korea. We were going to ask many of our European allies to take part in this battle. Some recognized
Chiang Kai-shek; some recognized the Red Chinese. And
it would have been a divisive and not a unifying action, if
we took it.

"Therefore, we thought it wise to decline, and the President did decline."

*Sir, the other day you mentioned, when you were dis-
cussing the Tuesday meeting between Mr. Truman and the
Congressional leaders you mentioned that there was some
talk about asking for a Congressional resolution.*

"Toward the end of our meeting on Tuesday with the
Congressional leaders, Senator Alexander Smith of New
Jersey, who was a member of the Senate Committee on
Foreign Relations, asked the President whether or not he
thought it would be a good idea if the Congress would
pass a resolution approving what the President was doing
in Korea or what the United States was doing in Korea.
The President said he would take that under advisement.

"After the meeting broke up, he asked me to consider
it and meet with him later and discuss it. I gave it a good
deal of thought and then gave the President this advice,
which he followed. It seemed to me that this should not
be done. At the moment the troops of the United States
were engaged in a desperate struggle in and around Pusan.
Hundreds, thousands of them were being killed. The outcome of the battle was not at all clear. It seemed to me if,
at this time, action was pending before the Congress, by
which hearings might be held, and long inquiries were being entered into as to whether or not this was the right
thing to do, or whether the President had the authority to
do it, or whether he needed Congressional authority for
matters of that sort—we would be doing about the worst

thing we could possibly do for the support of our troops and for their morale.

"I felt that we were in this fight—and it was a desperate fight—and we had better concentrate all our energies in fighting it and not in trying to get people to formally approve what was going on.

"The President accepted this advice. This is what was done. In other words we did not follow up Senator Smith's suggestion. This may well, in the light of events, have been a wrong decision. I don't think so myself. But it can be argued that it was wrong. If the Congress had promptly and without debate passed a resolution endorsing vigorously what had happened, this, of course, would have been fine, and it would have nipped in the bud all the statements about the Korean War being Mr. Truman's war and so on.

"But that is hindsight, and I have said that I think hindsight is nonsense. It proves nothing."

Mr. Secretary, as you know, Mr. Truman has said that the Korean decision was his most important decision. Do you agree with that?

"Yes. In this I think he is wholly right. It was a critically important decision, and I think it was important for this reason. This was an occasion upon which a perfectly clear alternative was presented to the United States, an alternative between withdrawing, retreating in front of Russian pressure brought through a satellite, or standing up and fighting and taking the consequences, and Mr. Truman did not shrink from that decision. The United States, under his leadership, decided to fight and did fight. And I think that this has changed the whole history of events since then.

"I think that if we had continued to negotiate, discuss, to take measures which were not the ultimate measures of physical resistance, if we had gone before the United Nations, gotten resolutions condemning the North Koreans . . . if, after the event was over, we'd had all kinds of commissions appointed for the relief of Korea, this would have been a disaster. But when the Russians, to their great surprise, found that they had started something which the

United States met absolutely squarely and hit with the ut-most vigor, I think they stopped, looked, and listened. And the whole history of the world has since changed. . . . We have not had to fight a third world war, which, as Mr. Truman has often said, would destroy us all. What we did in Korea, fighting a limited war for limited objectives, was not an easy thing for many people to understand. Never-theless, it was what had to be done and what was done."

That is the way it began in Korea, or the way in 1961 and 1962 the men responsible for that beginning remem-bered it. Now, the revisionist historians are saying we should never have gone into Korea. Myself, I go along with Mr. Acheson. Hindsight is nonsensical, and as nearly as I can make out revisionist history is all hindsight.

Mr. Truman was fond of the work of Horace, that most civilized of Romans, who wrote "The man who is just and firm of purpose can be shaken from his stern resolve neither by the rage of the people who urge him to crime nor by the countenance of the threatening tyrant."

Both Mr. Truman and Mr. Acheson had to endure the rage of those who urged them to crime as well as the countenances of an extraordinary number of threatening tyrants, at home and abroad, and they were never shaken from their stern resolve.

24

Firing the General

What happened in 1948 was wonderful to behold, but in this summer of Watergate with its reports of secret bombings and the generals' falsified communiqués, something else old Harry did seems even more miraculous—when he gave the biggest general of all, Douglas MacArthur—his comeuppance.

Mr. President, I know why you fired General MacArthur, but if you don't mind, I'd like to hear it in your own words.

"I fired him because he wouldn't respect the authority of the President. That's the answer to that. I didn't fire him because he was a dumb son of a bitch, although he was, but that's not against the law for generals. If it was, half to three-quarters of them would be in jail. That's why when a good one comes along like General Marshall . . . why, you've got to hang onto them, and I did.

"But MacArthur . . . well, to understand what happened and what I think most people don't understand is that the so-called China Lobby was very strong in this country when I was in the White House. They had a great many Congressmen and Senators lined up to do pretty much what they were told, and they had billions of dollars to spend, and they spent it. They even had some newspapers lined up, some big ones at that.* I'm not saying that they bought anybody out, but there was a lot of money floating around, and a lot of people in Washington were following what I call the China Lobby Line.

"You used to hear a lot about the Communist Party

---

* Unfortunately, we never did get to the Congressmen, the Senators, and the newspapermen the China Lobby had lined up, but, as Harry would say, if you want to find out, all you have to do is read your history.

Line, but the China Lobby Line was a lot . . . had a lot more people going along, powerful people, too. And what they wanted, they wanted to put old Chiang back in power. And the first step in that direction was getting . . . was trying to get Chiang's army into the war in Korea, which I was not about to let happen in any way.

"It wasn't only that I didn't want . . . had no intention whatsoever of starting a third world war. I knew Chiang's forces wouldn't be any damn good.

"Whatever they did, they'd be more trouble than they were worth, and any money we spent to support them would end up . . . a good deal of it would end up in the pockets of Chiang and the Madame and the Soong and Kung families.

"They're all thieves, every damn one of them."

Mr. President, did you ever meet Chiang Kai-shek?

"No, I never met him. I met the Madame. She came to the United States for some more handouts when I was President [in 1948]. I wouldn't let her stay at the White House like Roosevelt did. I don't think she liked it very much, but I didn't care one way or the other about what she liked and what she didn't like."

I've read in Alonzo Fields' book [a White House butler; his book was called My Twenty-one Years in the White House] *that she brought her own silk sheets and they had to be changed from top to bottom as many as four or five times a day. They had to be changed even if she took a ten-minute nap. And he says she was very mean to the help in the White House. He says, "Any opinion of the Great Lady of China . . . depended on what status of life the observer might happen to belong to."*

"If Fields says it, it's true, because he doesn't lie. I didn't know that . . . what he says, but I knew that the Madame is a very difficult lady. She just didn't make much of an impression on me, but I never met him. He never was in this country, and I was never in China.

"But ole 'Vinegar Joe' Stilwell [General Joseph W. Stilwell, commander of U.S. troops in the China-Burma-India theater during the Second World War; he was recalled

in 1944 because of his inability to get along wtih Chiang],
he came to see me. He was stationed over there, and he
made that famous march down . . . along the Burma
Road. He came to see me, and he said, 'You know, Mr.
President, that Chiang Kai-shek is nothing but a damn
son of a bitch, and he's gonna lose that war just as sure
as you're sitting here. Because his head's made out of
iron, and you can't tell him a goddamn thing.'

"Chiang wouldn't do what ole Joe wanted him to, which
if he had, he'd of been out of trouble."

*In the Army they used to call him, the GI's who were
over in China called Chiang Chancre Jack. And in England during the war they had a radio program; I believe it
was a radio program with a character named Cash-my-
Check. A Chinese general.*

"That's exactly the way it was, and that kind of put
me off the whole works. I discovered after some time that
Chiang Kai-shek and the Madame and their families, the
Soong family and the Kungs, were all thieves, every last
one of them, the Madame and him included. And they
stole seven hundred and fifty million dollars out of the
thirty-five billion that we sent to Chiang. They stole it,
and it's invested in real estate down in São Paulo and
some right here in New York. [This conversation was
held at the Carlyle Hotel.] And that's the money that was
used and is still being used for the so-called China Lobby.
I don't like that. I don't like that at all. And I don't want
anything to do with people like that."

Because of the way Truman and for that matter all
his advisers, including the Joint Chiefs of Staff, felt about
Chiang and his army, only a little more than a month after
hostilities in Korea began, MacArthur was sent to Formosa to tell Chiang that the use of his troops "would be
inappropriate."

Only God, MacArthur, and Chiang know what happened at that meeting, but it is assumed that MacArthur
delivered the message. Nevertheless, no sooner had he left
the island than Chiang's spokesmen were on the radio
telling the world that he and MacArthur were in total

agreement. Formosa should not be neutralized, as Mr. Truman had insisted. Not only that. MacArthur felt that Chiang's troops should be "unleashed," but they shouldn't bother with Korea at all. They should immediately go to the mainland.

I said, *Mr. President, what did you think when that happened?*

"I didn't know what to think. One of them was lying, but since I wouldn't have trusted either of them as far as I could throw them, I decided to wait and see. Sometimes that's the best policy. I sent Averell Harriman to Tokyo to see MacArthur and get him cleared up on anything he maybe didn't understand."

You called on Mr. Harriman a good many times to undertake delicate missions.

"Yes, I did, because he was completely trustworthy. He'd do what you asked him to do, and you could depend on him to tell you the complete truth about what had happened. As you know I wanted him to be the Democratic nominee for President in 1956 and I still think he'd have done a hell of a lot better than the fella that got it.

"So I sent the right man to see MacArthur, but, Christ, you couldn't depend on a word MacArthur said, and when he got back, Harriman warned me about that."

After a series of conferences with MacArthur Harriman wrote a long memorandum to Truman saying that MacArthur had told him he had no doubts at all about the wisdom of the Korean decision. He quoted MacArthur as saying, ". . . It was an historic decision which would save the world from communist domination and would be so recorded in history."

Moreover, MacArthur said he had no intention of letting Chiang drag the United States into a war with the Chinese Communists. According to Harriman he said that ". . . he would, as soldier, obey any orders that he received from the President. . . .

"I pointed out to him the basic conflict of interest between the U.S. and the Generalissimo's position as to the future of Formosa. . . . Chiang had only the burning ambition to use Formosa as a stepping-stone for his re-entry to the mainland. MacArthur recognized that this ambition could not be fulfilled, and yet thought it might be a good idea to let him land and get rid of him that way."

So much for Douglas MacArthur's devotion to Chiang Kai-shek.

"I thought it was all worked out with him," said Mr. Truman, "but I should have known that he was a man you couldn't depend on. Roosevelt had all kinds of trouble with him in that other war. He was just a man who couldn't sleep easy at night without thinking up ways and means of getting himself and everybody else into trouble."

He certainly seemed to do just that. In late August the general sent a message to the annual encampment of that farsighted patriotic group the Veterans of Foreign Wars outlining his very own foreign policy for the entire Pacific. If his ideas were adhered to, said MacArthur, that small ocean would turn into "a peaceful lake." And just to begin, he proposed a United States defense line that would stretch from Vladivostok to Singapore, all of which would be protected by United States air, naval, and ground forces, presumably with himself in complete charge.

Then, once again swearing eternal fealty to Chiang, he said that Chiang should be encouraged, not discouraged. Anything less was "appeasement . . . a fallacious and threadbare argument."

Mr. Truman was reported at the time as being in "a cold fury."

More than ten years later I asked him, *Mr. President, how can you explain a man like that?*

Mr. Truman, who was then seventy-seven, said of Mac-Arthur, who in 1950 was seventy, "I've given it a lot of thought, and I have finally concluded . . . decided that there were times when he . . . well, I'm afraid when he wasn't right in his head.

"And there was never anybody around him to keep him in line. He didn't have anybody on his staff that wasn't an ass kisser. He just wouldn't let anybody near him who wouldn't kiss his ass. So . . . there were times when he was . . . I think out of his head and didn't know what he was doing, and I'm sorry as I can be about a thing like that.

"That's the day I should have fired him, though. And I'll tell you this. After that day, I knew it was only a matter of time before there'd be a showdown."

The next morning there was an emergency conference at the White House with the Secretaries of State and Defense and the Joint Chiefs of Staff.

"I told them I wanted to fire him, and I wanted to send over General Bradley to take his place. But they talked me out of it. They said it would cause too much of an uproar, and so I didn't do it, and I was wrong."

Mr. President, suppose you had done it that morning in August instead of the following April?

"I don't know. I do not know. We might have got out of Korea six months earlier and not been at one time on the brink of a third world war. But I don't know for sure.

"The only thing I learned out of the whole MacArthur deal is that when you feel there's something you have to do and you know in your gut you have to do it, the sooner you get it over with, the better off everybody is.

"But one thing I did do that morning. I got him [MacArthur] to withdraw that statement. I said to Lou Johnson [Louis Johnson, who was in his last days as Secretary of Defense], 'I want that damn thing withdrawn immediately, and you tell MacArthur that's a direct order from me and make sure he understands it.' "

MacArthur did "recall" the statement, but since it was already in print in newspapers all over the world, that didn't really matter much.

For a time the hostility between the President and the general quieted down. In mid-September MacArthur made a surprise landing on the west coast of Korea at Inchon. His troops made a victorious march toward the thirty-eighth parallel, and within two weeks almost 130,000 North Koreans were taken prisoners. MacArthur's generals were in complete control of the area below the thirty-eighth parallel.

Truman sent the general a telegram:

"Few operations in military history can match either the delaying action where you traded space for time in which to build up your forces, or the brilliant maneuver which has now resulted in the liberation of Seoul. . . . Well and nobly done."

Truman made it clear, at least thought he had made it clear that while ". . . we have to fight a while longer in order to convince the North Koreans that they are vanquished and that further aggression doesn't pay," MacArthur was to go north of the parallel only if he was sure there were no large-scale Red Chinese or Soviet forces there. He was not to cross the Soviet or Manchurian borders by land or by air and he was to rely solely on South Korean troops near those borders.

That was a very complex order, particularly for a general who no matter what the condition of his head at any given moment had never fought less than a total war for anything less than total victory. And almost immediately there were rumors, not yet accredited to MacArthur himself, that his effectiveness was being limited. True, it was supposed to be a limited war for a limited objective, but there is no evidence anywhere that the general ever understood that or that he even tried to understand it.

Up to that time President Truman and General MacArthur had never met.

"I decided it was about time that we do so. The damn fool hadn't been back in the United States for fourteen years or more, and the messages I'd sent him through other people he somehow or other never seemed to understand. And so I decided that he ought to come back to the United States. To Washington. I thought we'd meet in the White House.

"I talked to General Marshall about it. [General Marshall had just returned from his retirement to become Secretary of Defense.] But the general advised me against having him come to Washington. He said, 'That man has become a kind of living legend with certain groups and especially with certain members of Congress, and if you brought him back here, I think it might do more harm than good. He'd stir up the China Lobby and all those people, and I don't know what all might happen.'

"He was right, of course; I told you. He was always right, ninety-nine percent of the time anyway. So we decided . . . I decided to meet him at some halfway point, and that's why we chose Wake Island."

Actually, the President had to fly more than 4,700 miles from San Francisco, while the general flew only 1,900 miles from Tokyo.

Dr. Wallace Graham, Mr. Truman's personal physician when he was President and after his return to Independence until his death: "I was with the President when he was going to meet MacArthur on Wake Island. And MacArthur was always a showman type. He deliberately tried to hold up his landing so that we would go in and land ahead of them.

"Harry caught it right away, and he told MacArthur, 'You go ahead and land first. We've got plenty of gas. We'll wait for you.' And that's what happened. That's what we did."

Mr. Truman: "MacArthur was always playacting, and he wasn't any damn good at it. I knew what he was trying to pull with all that stuff about whose plane was going to land first, and I wasn't going to let him get away with it.

"So I let . . . I made it quite clear that he was to go in first, and he did."

I understand that when you did get on the ground, there was another delay.

"There was. After we landed, there was a welcoming party there on the ground, but I looked out the window, and MacArthur wasn't there.

"Even after we stopped the engines and they opened up the door of the plane, the bastard still didn't show up.

"So I just sat there. I just waited. I'd have waited until hell froze over if I'd of had to. I wasn't going to have one of my generals embarrass the President of the United States.

"Finally, the son of a bitch walked out of one of the buildings near the runway there. He was wearing those damn sunglasses of his and a shirt that was unbuttoned and a cap that had a lot of hardware. I never did understand . . . an old man like that and a five-star general to boot, why he went around dressed up like a nineteen-year-old second lieutenant.

"I'll tell you this. If he'd been a lieutenant in my outfit going around dressed like that, I'd have busted him so fast he wouldn't have known what happened to him.

"But I . . . I decided to overlook his getup, and we shook hands and arranged . . . we had a meeting. I got there on time, but he was forty-five minutes late, and this meeting—it was just between the two of us, you understand, and was the only one like that.

"When he walked in, I took one look at him, and I said, 'Now you look here. I've come halfway across the world to meet you, but don't worry about that. I just want you to know I don't give a good goddamn what you do or think about Harry Truman, but don't you ever again keep your Commander in Chief waiting. Is that clear?'

"His face got as red as a beet, but he said . . . he indicated that he understood what I was talking about, and we went on from there.

"I didn't bring up what he'd written to the Veterans of Foreign Wars; I didn't have to. He did it. He said he didn't know what had got into him, and that it had been a mistake, and nothing like that would ever happen again.

"I didn't mention 1948* either, but he did. He says, 'Mr. President, I was just taken in by the politicians, and I apologize for that, too. It won't happen again. I've learned my lesson.' "

He seems to have been very apologetic and contrite that morning.

"He was. He was. When you were alone with him, he was a very different kind of fella. Butter wouldn't melt in his mouth. But . . . I've known a few other fellas like that, and when they're out in public, it's an entirely different story. They're always playacting out in public.

"I asked MacArthur point blank if the Chinese would come in, and he said under no circumstances would they come in. He says, 'Mr. President, the war will be over by Thanksgiving and I'll have the American troops back in Tokyo by Christmas,' and he went on like that.

"We must've talked for an hour or so, just the two of us, and I believe I made it more than abundantly clear to him that I was his Commander in Chief and that he was to obey orders and keep . . . not issue any public state-

---

* That year nobody knew much about MacArthur's views on anything, but the Chicago *Tribune* and the Hearst press thought they knew enough to be sure he wasn't one of your left-wingers and to start trying to drum up support for him.

In mid-March MacArthur, with his usual flair for understatement, allowed as how, "In this hour of momentous importance . . . I can say, and with due humility, that I would be recreant to all concepts of good citizenship were I to shirk any public duty to which I might be called by the American people."

Since he was on active duty in Japan, he couldn't do any active campaigning. His name, nevertheless, was entered in the Wisconsin Republican primary. He had, after all, once gone to school in Wisconsin and was appointed to West Point by a Congressman from that state, although he hadn't been in Wisconsin or anyplace else in the United States for eleven years. Some people even said he was the state's favorite son.

On primary day, however, the general got only eight of the twenty-seven delegates, and that more or less finished off talk about the duty the general wouldn't be able to shirk.

ments of any kind that hadn't been approved by me personally.

"He was just like a little puppy at that meeting. I don't know which was worse, the way he acted in public or the way he kissed my ass at that meeting." *

Mr. President, at the second meeting with MacArthur, the one with General Bradley, Dean Rusk from the State Department, Philip Jessup, Ambassador Muccio, and all the others, I believe he said that no more than sixty thousand Chinese troops could be got across the Yalu River because the Chinese didn't have any air power to protect them. And he also said that he had had complete cooperation. The official statement of what he said reads, "No commander in the history of war has ever had more complete and adequate support from all agencies in Washington than I have."

"I believe he did say something like that, yes."

The complete account of that meeting came in very handy the next spring after you'd relieved MacArthur and he was denying that he'd said, among other things, that the Chinese wouldn't come into the war with any force. It was very fortunate that a Miss Vernice Anderson was next door to the Quonset hut taking notes, although nobody knew that she was taking notes. Officially, that is.†

* In Mr. Truman's *Memoirs* the last of three paragraphs describing that meeting states: "The general seemed genuinely pleased at this opportunity to talk with me, and I found him a most stimulating and interesting person. Our conversation was very friendly—I might say much more so than I had expected."

I wanted to ask Mr. Truman about that discrepancy and many others, but I never did. The reason I never did was that I wanted our conversations to continue.

† Those notes worked out very well for everybody—except, maybe, the general, who claimed in April that he didn't know any such transcript was made, although a staff member had signed a receipt for the transcript at MacArthur's Tokyo headquarters.

The notes did not, however, surface until the general was appearing before a Senate committee that in April was looking

"No, nobody knew that she was taking notes; as you say, nobody *officially* knew it," said the President, and he smiled, and I believe he winked. The President was not

---

into the reasons for MacArthur's recall. Then the top-secret classification on them was somehow lifted, and they turned up in a front-page story in the New York *Times,* written by Anthony Leviero. Leviero received a Pulitzer Prize for his daredevil enterprise in the matter.

After all, he had been at Wake Island himself, and he described the meeting as giving the appearance of one between that of an "insurance salesman who has at last signed up an important prospect . . . while the latter appeared to be dubious over the extent of the coverage." Mr. Truman was the salesman, the general the insured.

In the *Memoirs* Mr. Truman and his ghost, Bill Hillman, say of those notes: "It was not until much later that I learned that Miss Vernice Anderson, the secretary to Ambassador Jessup, was next door and, without instructions from anyone, took down stenographic notes. This fact further became known during the hearings following General MacArthur's recall, and there was a good deal of noise about it. I can say that neither I nor Mr. Jessup nor anyone else had given Miss Anderson instructions to take notes; as a matter of fact, she was not brought along to take notes but merely to have a secretary available for the drafting of the communiqué that would have to be issued at the end of the meeting."

An awful lot of protesting about accidental note taking in those few words, and I yearned to ask Mr. Truman whatever happened to Mrs. Anderson. I hope at the very least she got a raise.

But, for reasons already noted above, I kept my silence on the subject.

As Bob Aurthur has written of the matter, "While the participant nods vigorously at Mr. Truman's injured denial that he had anything to do with stashing the secretary, or even knew she was there, the observer reflects how critical world events are sometimes conducted in Graustarkian, wondrous, and—dare I say?—simple minded ways. And why does Mr. Truman smile a little when he thinks back on how those notes suddenly surfaced when needed most?"

Bob's remarks were written back in those innocent days when Watergate meant nothing more than the name of a swank apartment house in Washington, D.C.

much of a winker, and when he did, the wink was always so fleeting that you weren't sure you'd seen it.

"You run into good luck like that sometimes," he added.

Mr. President, I believe that at the very moment General MacArthur was telling . . . was saying that the Chinese wouldn't come into Korea in any force a hundred and twenty thousand members of the Chinese Communist Fourth Field Army had already crossed the Yalu, a lot of them with Russian artillery and tanks made in Russia.

"That's right, and of course, that was only the beginning."

Mr. President, do you think the general was lying when he made the assurances he made you, or was his intelligence just bad?

"You'd have to ask him that, but I think . . . my feeling is that he just never learned the difference between the truth and a lie. That was one of his troubles, and another was. . . .

"Well, there's a story. On his ninetieth birthday, I think it was, somebody asked Justice Holmes, Oliver Wendell Holmes, how he figured he'd done all he'd done, been a Supreme Court Justice and a soldier in the Civil War and all of that.

"The fella that asked him, a newspaper fella, says, 'What's the secret of your success, Justice Holmes?'

"And Old Holmes says, 'Young man, the secret of my success is that at a very early age I discovered that I'm not God.'

"I told you. MacArthur never did find that out. And that was his trouble. That was one of his troubles."

Mr. President, before we're through with this series, we're going to make you one of the great storytellers of our time.

"Now, no. Don't try that. Don't try anything like that on me. Don't try to make a playactor out of me because if you do, it'll fail. I'll tell you the facts, and I know what the facts are because I was there. But that's all I'll do."

Yes, sir.

Only a few days after President Truman's return to Washington from Wake Island and from MacArthur's assurances of everlasting loyalty, the general directly countermanded the President's orders to use only South Korean troops near the northern borders. He personally ordered American forces into the vanguard of the drive north to the Yalu.

And on November 6, the day before the 1950 Congressional elections, which followed one of the bitterest campaigns in recent history, MacArthur sent a message saying that hordes of Chinese troops and matériel were crossing the bridges of the Yalu from Manchuria. He asked for permission to bomb the bridges and with characteristic rhetoric added, "Every hour that this is postponed will be paid for dearly in American and other United Nations blood."

Mr. President, do you think it was a coincidence that that message arrived just the day before an important national election?

"I leave that to you, whether it was a coincidence or not?"

Assuming that it wasn't, that it was deliberately done to affect the outcome of the election, has any other general in American history ever interfered with an American election in that way?

"Not to my knowledge, never. And it was a shocking thing."

In remembering the incident, the President still seemed to be in a state of shock. It was as if he were still feeling some deep personal sorrow over MacArthur's perfidy. Of course, I can't be sure what he was thinking. What is clear is that his resolve to avoid a war with Red China never wavered, election or not. In his answer he authorized attacks on the bridges only on the Korean side as a defensive measure. MacArthur wanted permission to invade China. Said permission was refused. "You are authorized to go ahead with your planned bombing in Korea near the frontier including targets at Sinuiju and Korean end of Yalu bridges. . . . The above does not authorize the

bombing of any dams or power plants on the Yalu River.
. . . Because it is vital in the national interests of the
U.S. to localize the fighting in Korea it is important that
extreme care be taken to avoid violation of Manchurian
territory and air space."

The not-surprising result of that particular exchange
was that the Republicans won sweeping victories at the
polls the next day. Not only were the Democrats in general and Harry Truman in particular preventing a heroic
general from using his full forces to defeat the Communists abroad, but they were at the same time conniving
with and being supported by Communists at home. Joseph R. McCarthy, the United States Senator from Wisconsin, had said so. "The Democratic label is now the property of men and women who have . . . bent to the whispered pleas from the lips of traitors . . . men and women
who wear the political label stitched from the idiocy of a
Truman, rotted by the deceit of a Dean Acheson, corrupted
by the red slime of a White [Harry Dexter White, a Treasury Department official]."

Of course, the voters turned large numbers of the trea-
sonous bastards out. And in California they voted Richard M. Nixon in, electing him to the Senate and defeating
Helen Gahagan Douglas, the Democratic "pink lady."
Nixon claimed she was sympathetic to Communism, and
his campaign manager, Murray Chotiner, issued the famous "pink sheet," which alleged that Mrs. Douglas' vot-
ing record very closely paralleled that of "the notorious
Communist party-liner Congressman Vito Marcantonio
of New York." In that campaign Nixon gave his full support to MacArthur, called for "unleashing" Chiang Kai-
shek and his troops, and denounced Truman as being
soft on Communism, both the domestic and the international variety. He did not actually get around to calling
Mr. Truman a traitor until almost two years later.

In any case, if MacArthur's message was politically
motivated, it was successful. But then an odd thing happened, very odd. On the day after the election, Novem-

ber 8, he sent another message. He'd been wrong. Hordes
of Chinese troops and Russian matériel were *not* flowing
across the Yalu on the still-unbombed bridges. Thus, although the general did not say so, no unnecessary American and other United Nations blood had been needlessly
shed, not because of the bridges anyway.

But now the general said that "hostile planes are operating from bases west of the Yalu River against our forces
in North Korea." He wanted to engage in "hot pursuit"
of those planes and—yet again—to bomb bases in Manchuria.

President Truman, with the full approval of the Joint
Chiefs of Staff, yet again denied him such permission.

MacArthur did, however, continue his drive to reach
the Yalu, and by November 24 he announced that the final
offensive was under way. "If successful," he said, "this
should for all practical purposes end the war, restore
peace and unity to Korea . . . and enable the prompt
withdrawal of United Nations forces."

Not only that, the boys would be home by—well, not
Thanksgiving but surely by Christmas.

As we all know, the Chinese do not celebrate Christmas, and they are notoriously unsentimental about American religious holidays. On November 26 more than 200,-
000 of them poured across the Yalu, and the United
Nations troops, most of them American, retreated in total
confusion. Some observers said it was the worst military
defeat in American history.

MacArthur said that what had happened was the result
of Washington's, meaning Truman's, restrictions on him.
He called them "extraordinary inhibitions . . . without
precedent in American military history."

By January, 1951, not only had Pyongyang, the capital
of North Korea, been captured by the Chinese Communists, but so had Seoul, the capital of the Republic of
Korea in the south.

But then MacArthur, still smarting, still issuing complaints about his treatment in Washington, regrouped his

forces and started north again. By March they were once more back at the thirty-eighth parallel, and it was here that the final, bitter showdown between the general and the President began.

Truman and the Joint Chiefs wanted MacArthur to stop at the thirty-eighth parallel so that the President, with South Korea now cleared, could, it was hoped, begin to negotiate a cease-fire.

MacArthur was having none of that. He proposed not to stop the war, but to expand it; only in that way, he said publicly, would lasting peace be achieved. Otherwise, he would be fighting what he called "an accordion war," moving back and forth until first one side, then the other moved too far ahead of its supplies. As an alternative he proposed bombing China's industrial cities, blockading its coast, and, once again, using Chiang Kai-shek's army in Korea and to invade South China as well.

It was one of the most extraordinary long-distance confrontations between a civilian leader and a general in all history. Lincoln's troubles with the nine generals who preceded Grant seem pale by contrast.

Reminding the President of that moment, I said, *Mr. President, you have the reputation of being a somewhat impatient man, somewhat quick on the draw, but it seems to me, sir, under these circumstances, that you displayed Job-like patience. How did you manage to keep silent?*

"In the first place I knew what was at stake. I knew that if the slightest mistake was made, we would find ourselves in a third world war, and as I've told you time and again, I had no intention in any way of allowing that to happen. General Bradley said at the time that that would be the wrong war at the wrong place, at the wrong time, and with the wrong enemy, and he was absolutely right.

"If what MacArthur proposed had happened . . . had been allowed to take place, we would have wound up being at war not only with Red China, but with Russia, too, and . . . the consequences would have been . . .

it might have meant the destruction of a good part of the world."

Mr. President, considering what you said earlier about what you felt might be the condition of General Mac-Arthur's mind at times, weren't you afraid of what might happen while he was still in charge?

"Yes, I was. I was very much concerned."

But you restrained yourself.

"I had no alternative. I had to act . . . whatever I did had to be done with extreme caution because I felt the fate of a good part of the world was at stake."

Was that possibly your most difficult time as President?

Mr. Truman once again paused for a very long time, and then he said, "I believe it was."

On March 26 the Joint Chiefs of Staff informed Mac-Arthur that the State Department was "planning a Presidential announcement shortly that, with the clearing of the bulk of South Korea of aggressors, the United Nations is now preparing to discuss conditions of settlement in Korea."

MacArthur paid no attention at all to the advice from Washington. Instead, four days later he issued a statement of his own.* He said that he personally was ready to meet with the enemy [Red China] to discuss a settlement in Korea. Barring that, he threatened a general attack against China. And he suggested that if North Korea were to be surrendered, it be surrendered to him personally.

---

* "The enemy [Red China], therefore, must by now be painfully aware that a decision by the United Nations to depart from its tolerant effort to contain the war to the area of Korea, through an expansion of our military operations to its coastal areas and interior bases, would doom Red China to the risk of imminent military collapse. . . . Within the area of my authority as the military commander . . . I stand ready at any time to confer in the field with the commander in chief of the enemy forces to find any military means whereby realization of the political objectives of the United Nations in Korea might be accomplished without further bloodshed."

Even now, more than twenty years later, MacArthur's statement is almost unbelievable. One can't help wondering if Mr. Truman wasn't right. Perhaps MacArthur was mentally unhinged at times. Statements like that one certainly bear the marks of a man far gone in paranoia and megalomania.

The revisionist historians who see Harry Truman only as the most hawkish of cold warriors have generally ignored these particular exchanges between Mr. Truman and Douglas MacArthur, but it seems to me they demonstrate the very essence of the two men, a President who not only understood his position as Commander in Chief and who was determined to prevent a worldwide atomic conflict and did and an aging general who did in fact seem to confuse his identity with that of God, a wrathful, destructive God. Terrifying.

The other chilling thought that passes through my mind is what would have happened if Richard Nixon had been President at that time, a time when he was calling for full support of MacArthur, calling him "the greatest American patriot."

Sometimes I think we are luckier than we realize. But there. As Dean Acheson says in another part of this book, it's a waste of time to speculate on what might have happened if. . . .

Harry Truman waited two weeks.

I didn't ask how he managed, but I did ask why.

"I wanted, if possible, an even . . . better example of his insubordination, and I wanted it to be one that the . . . that everybody would recognize for exactly what it was, and I knew that, MacArthur being the kind of man he was, I wouldn't have long to wait, and I didn't. He wrote that letter to Joe Martin.* And you've read it. He

---

* Joseph W. Martin was the House minority leader, and on April 5 he read to the House a letter he had received from MacArthur. Martin, a reactionary Republican from Massa-

repeated that *he* wanted to use Chiang Kai-shek's troops and repeated that . . . all that stuff about there being 'no substitute for victory.' "

Whatever that means.

"Yes, yes. Whatever that meant."

And then what happened?

"We had a series . . . several meetings with what they called the war cabinet;* I never called it that, but that's what the papers called it. I called everybody together, and I said, 'I'm going to fire the son of a bitch *right now.*' And they all agreed. All except General Marshall. He said he was afraid . . . it might cause a lot of trouble with Congress as far as the defense budget was concerned. And

---

chusetts, had asked MacArthur how he felt about the Truman administration's refusal to use Chiang Kai-shek's army against the Chinese Reds.

Here, Martin told the House, was the general's reply; he had not asked that it be kept confidential:

"My views and recommendations with respect to the situation created by Red China's entry into the war against us in Korea have been submitted to Washington in most complete detail. Generally those views are well known and generally understood, as they follow the conventional pattern of meeting force with maximum counterforce as we have never failed to do in the past. Your [Martin's] view with respect to the utilization of the Chinese forces on Formosa is in conflict with neither logic nor this tradition.

"It seems strangely difficult for some to realize that here in Asia is where the Communist conspirators have elected to make their play for global conquest, and that here we fight Europe's wars with arms while the diplomats there still fight it with words; that if we lose this war to Communism in Asia the fall of Europe is inevitable; win it and Europe most probably would avoid war and yet preserve freedom.

"As you point out, we must win. There is no substitute for victory."

* It included, among others, Averell Harriman; Secretary of State Dean Acheson, General Marshall, Secretary of Defense; and General Omar Bradley, Chairman of the Joint Chiefs of Staff.

there were some other arguments, but not too many. The only question was how to do it with the least fuss."

There wasn't any way that wouldn't cause some fuss.

"With a man like that no way at all."

Mr. President, is it true that neither General Bradley nor General Marshall liked General MacArthur?

"Oh, no. No, not at all. I don't know anybody that liked him except maybe some of the people on his staff, and it was hard to tell with them because as I've told you each and every one of them was nothing but a damn ass kisser."

I reminded the President of something Heywood Broun once wrote about Herbert Hoover when Hoover was President. Broun wrote, "No one in the entire world really likes Herbert Hoover except Mark Sullivan [a conservative columnist of the time] and, possibly, Mrs. Hoover."

For the first and last time that day Mr. Truman laughed; then he said, "You be careful what you say about Mr. Hoover, because he's a friend of mine."

You said General Marshall had some doubts about discharging MacArthur.

"Yes, he did; he was concerned about the reaction of . . . certain Congressmen, and he wanted to think over what he felt the reaction of the troops would be. And so at the end of the meeting I asked him, I said, 'General, you go over there and you read all the correspondence that's passed between MacArthur and me for the last two years. Then be in my office at nine in the morning, and if you still feel I shouldn't fire him, I won't.' "

And you wouldn't have, if General Marshall had told you you shouldn't?

"I've told you. I knew the general very, very well; we'd been through a lot together, and I knew how his mind worked, and there wasn't a doubt in the world in my mind that when he saw what I'd put up with, that he'd agree with me.

"And the next morning at eight fifteen when I got to my office, he was out there waiting for me, which was very unusual. General Marshall was usually a punctual man, but he . . . I had never known him to be ahead of time. He worked on a very tight schedule.

"But that morning he looked up at me, and he says, 'I spent most of the night on that file, Mr. President, and you should have fired the son of a bitch two years ago.'

"And so we went right ahead, and we did it. There were . . . a good many details to be worked out. I asked General Bradley to be sure we had the full agreement of the Joint Chiefs of Staff, which he got; they were all unanimous in saying he should be fired. And we had to arrange to turn the command over to General Ridgway.

"And then of course, we wanted to be sure that MacArthur got the news through official channels. We didn't want it to get into the newspapers first. But then . . . well, it was on a Tuesday I remember, and I signed all the papers and went over to Blair House to have dinner. Some of the others stayed behind at the White House to decide on exactly how to get the word to Frank Pace [Frank Pace, Jr., Secretary of the Army, then in Korea]. Pace was going . . . was supposed to notify the general.

"While I was still at Blair House, Joe Short [then White House press secretary] came in to where the others were, and he said . . . he had heard that the Chicago *Tribune* had the whole story and was going to print it the next morning.

"So General Bradley came over to Blair House and told me what was up, and he says if MacArthur hears he's going to be fired before he officially is fired, before he's notified, he'd probably up and resign on me.

"And I told Bradley, I says, 'The son of a bitch isn't going to resign on me, *I want him fired.*'"

As I've said, at the time of these conversations, Mr. Truman was seventy-seven years old, and while he was not noticeably enfeebled by age, he always struck me as being fragile. Not at that moment, though. At that moment his blue eyes blazed with fury. Harry Truman was right back there in the White House. He was ten years younger; he was once again President and Commander in Chief, and he wanted the son of a bitch *fired,* goddamn it.

The President continued, his eyes still angry, "And I told Bradley I wanted an hour-by-hour report of what was going on, and so he went back to the Pentagon, and he sent the message to Pace. But he couldn't get to him so General Bradley called me, and he asked my permission to send the message that he was . . . discharged right to MacArthur and telling him to turn his command over to Ridgway. I told him to go right ahead, the faster the better, I said, and he did it.

"And that's all there was to it. I went to bed, and Joe Short called a press conference and read my statement,* and it was all over but the shouting."

As I recall, there was plenty of shouting.

"No more than I expected. I knew there'd be a big uproar, and I knew that MacArthur would take every advantage of it that he could, but I knew that . . . in the end people would see through him, and it would all die down."

Mr. President, I'm not going to ask you if you slept that night.

"I'm very glad you're not going to ask me because if you did, I'd have to tell you the truth, which is that I did. The thing you have to understand about me is if I've done

---

* "With deep regret, I have concluded that General of the Army Douglas MacArthur is unable to give his wholehearted support to the policies of the United States government and of the United Nations in matters pertaining to his official duties. In view of the specific responsibilities imposed upon me by the Constitution of the United States and the added responsibility which has been entrusted to me by the United Nations, I have decided that I must make a change of command in the Far East. I have, therefore, relieved General MacArthur of his commands and have designated Lieutenant General Matthew B. Ridgway as his successor."

the right thing and I *know* I've done the right thing, I don't worry over it. There's nothing to worry over."

And in this case you were sure you were right.

"Didn't have a minute's doubt about it, and I knew that's the way history would judge it, too, and I guess you can say looking back on it now, that it has."

25

God Bless America

From the minute the news of MacArthur's dismissal appeared in the morning newspapers on April 11, there was a "fuss" that was unprecedented in American history. Never before and, for that matter, never since have so many millions of people been so instantly and deeply angry. And the man they were angry at was Harry S. Truman, who had fired the great man.

To a lesser degree, of course, Dean Acheson was blamed, but most people had known all along that he was a Communist, him and his haughty manner, his suspicious mustache, his phony accent, and his elegant tweed suits. Scarcely a day went by when Senator McCarthy didn't ask for *his* resignation.

I said, "Mr. Secretary, I understand that in this period, during the uproar over MacArthur's dismissal, a group of citizens in Ponca City, Oklahoma, burned a dummy of you in effigy. Do you remember that?

"I'm afraid not. It really would be a very difficult thing to remember all of the times things like that happened in those . . . troubled years. I became quite used to being vilified. It has its stimulating aspects, and for all I know, it may even be good for the liver.

"I believe it was sometime during this period that I got in a taxi someplace in Washington, and the driver turned to me and said, 'Aren't you Dean Acheson?'

"I said to him, 'Yes, I am. Would you like me to get out?' "

I told Mr. Acheson that I was in Europe at the time, working on a magazine piece about American troops stationed there, and one day in Marburg, Germany, I attended a lecture being given by the education officer on the dangers of Communism.

At one point he asked, "Who is head of the Communist Party in the United States?"

Only one hand was raised, that of a dark-haired young private who, judging by his accent, was from one of the states in the Deep South. Yes, he said; he knew who was head of the Communist Party in the United States. "Dean Acheson."

The dean was very pleased with that.

By noon of April 11 the Republicans had made plans to invite the deposed warrior to speak to a joint session of Congress the minute he got back to the United States. Did the Democrats object? Don't be silly. Most of them at the time were afraid to say anything really *mean* about Joe McCarthy, and the Senator from Wisconsin was at least human. To object in any way to the glorification of MacArthur—well, one might as well get up and blaspheme God on the floor.

Joe Martin said that in their meetings the Republican leaders had discussed "impeachments," meaning not only Harry Truman but, presumably, Acheson as well. McCarthy was less cautious, but that day he concentrated his fire on Truman. He said, "The son of a bitch ought to be impeached." And he added that the decision must have come "after a night of bourbon and benedictine."

The Gallup Poll found that only 29 percent of the people were in favor of what Truman had done, and the telegrams and letters pouring into the White House, 78,000 of them, were 20 to 1 against the dismissal. Most newspapers condemned what had been done, often vituperatively. And Harry Truman was burned in effigy by the indignant citizens of scores of towns in every part of the country.

And then, on April 17, MacArthur's Constellation, the *Bataan,* landed in San Francisco. He was back in his own, his native land for the first time since 1937. He was wearing a trench coat and a frayed battle cap; it may or may not have been the same cap that Mr. Truman found so objectionable at Wake Island. A man I know who was on MacArthur's staff insists that the general had an enlisted man, I believe a corporal, who did nothing but *fray* battle caps that had come straight from the Post Exchange, fray them so that they would look as if the general had just stepped out of some firing line or other.

Douglas MacArthur, the deposed Commanding General of the U.S. Armed Forces, U.S. Commander in Chief, Far East Command, Supreme Commander for the Allied Powers in Japan, and Commander in Chief, United Nations Command, paused dramatically at the head of the landing ramp, allowing the spotlights to play over the uniform, the jet-black hair, and the oddly unwrinkled face.

The crowd roared its approval, and the next day when the general went to a reception in front of the San Francisco City Hall, he spoke for the first time. He said, "The only politics I have is contained in a single phrase known well to all of you—God Bless America."

A hundred thousand people went wild at the wisdom of that remark; it seemed the cheers and shouts would never stop. Strong men were not ashamed to be seen weeping; women were hysterical, and hundreds of people were seen to cross themselves.

And when the general got to Washington, it was the same. Cheering crowds lined every street. It was estimated that there were 300,000 people on Pennsylvania Avenue alone, and there were another quarter of a million at the Washington Monument. Not a dry eye anywhere.

The general later appeared before the Daughters of the American Revolution and spoke to the ladies for about three minutes. "I have long sought personally to pay you the tribute that is in my heart. . . . In this hour of crisis, all patriots look to you."

As he spoke, all the daughters took off their hats so that their view of the mighty warrior would not be impaired by millinery. And the next day, when the recording secretary-general read from her minutes that the general's remarks

were "probably" the most important event in the history
of Constitution Hall, the word "probably" was immediately struck out.

When the general, Mrs. MacArthur (Jeannie), and little Arthur MacArthur went to New York, it was said that
7,500,000 people were out to greet them. Almost 800
tons of confetti and ticker tape were showered on them.
The reception was bigger by far than that given to Charles
A. Lindbergh when he got back from flying to Paris in
1927; it was greater than that accorded Dwight D. Eisenhower when he returned from victory in Europe in 1945.

As Eric Goldman points out in *The Crucial Decade*,
MacArthur's welcome wasn't all cheers and tears. Writing
of MacArthur's appearance in New York, Goldman says,
"Amid all the uproar a quite different kind of feeling kept
expressing itself. As MacArthur's limousine went by, men
and women would cross themselves. The handkerchiefs
came out. And sometimes there were patches of quiet, a
strange, troubled, churning quiet."

The day after the conversation about the firing of Mac-
Arthur I said, *Mr. President, when you discharged General MacArthur, weren't you afraid that he might become
a martyr, that in fact you might be helping him become
President of the United States?*

"I didn't give a damn what became of him. He dis-
obeyed orders, and I was Commander in Chief, and either
I was or I wasn't. So I acted as Commander in Chief and
called him home.

"I knew that he was one of those generals that wanted
to be President, and there are a lot of them, more than
you'd think. Some of them . . . one of them in particular
that I can think of and I'm not naming any names. He
thought he *deserved* to be President."

*I believe the one you mean made it, didn't he? And re-
cently, too.*

"The one I'm thinking of was a . . . lived in the White
House for eight years, but I don't think he was ever *President*.

"But about this general situation. What you have to

understand is that the President of the United States has to act as Commander in Chief at *all* times. A civilian executive just has to run the armed forces. The men who wrote the Constitution understood that, and it's been the same all through history.

"The Romans had the same sort of arrangement with two consuls who were in charge of running the army in the field. It just has to be that way. Other ways have been tried, but they never have worked. Somebody has to be in charge who has been freely and legally chosen by the people . . . by a majority of the people.

"France tried . . . you remember . . . tried a different way with the Committee of Five Hundred in the French Revolution. They couldn't make up their minds what they wanted to do. And Napoleon finally got tired of fooling around with them and took over and became the head of the French state.

"But about MacArthur. I'll say this to you. What I did I didn't do to injure anybody or head off any political opposition or anything of that kind. If he had had any background in politics at all instead of being completely military, he could have made good use of the situation, but he didn't do it."

How do you mean, he could have made use of it?

"Why, when he landed in the United States, he should have come in and reported to his Commander in Chief. That was the first thing he should have done, and then if people around over the country wanted to listen to him make speeches, that would have been all right. But he didn't do it.

"He made a lot of speeches . . . including that speech to both Houses of Congress. At the time of that speech . . . well, the minute I found out he was going to make it, I wanted to get a copy of it.

"So we were having a Cabinet meeting, and I knew somebody had to get it for me. So I looked around, and there was Frank Pace, and I said to him, I said, 'Frank, you get a copy of that speech and bring it to me.'

"Well, I've told you how he was. He was all right when

there wasn't any trouble, but the minute there was . . .
he'd be hiding in a goddamn tent someplace. So he started
stuttering and stammering, and he says [imitating Pace],
'Please, Mr. President, it would be very embarrassing for
me to ask the general or one of his aides. . . . I'd really
rather not.'

"I said to him, I said, 'Frank, I don't give a good goddamn what you'd rather. I want you to get me that speech
and bring it to me. On the double,' I said.

"He went and got it, and I read it. It was nothing but a
bunch of damn bullshit."

In *The Truman Presidency* Cabell Phillips says of that
speech, "one of the most memorable orations ever heard
in the Capitol, before a joint meeting of the House and
Senate and radio-television audience of untold millions.
He [MacArthur] was a stirring, romantic figure out of the
pages of a Kipling or a Richard Harding Davis as he
mounted the rostrum in the House of Representatives and
with a benevolent smile waited for the two-minute ovation
to subside. He was handsome, proud, resonant of voice,
confident of manner, and yet humble in a magisterial sort
of way. . . .

" 'I address you with neither rancor nor bitterness in the
fading twilight of life, with but one purpose in mind. To
serve my country. . . . "Why," my soldiers asked of me,
"surrender military advantage to an enemy in the field?"
[Long pause] I could not answer.

" '. . . I am closing my fifty-two years of military service. When I joined the Army, even before the turn of the
century, it was the fulfillment of all my boyish hopes and
dreams. . . .' "

Hunter S. Thompson, the political reporter for *Rolling
Stone,* author of *Fear and Loathing in the Campaign Trail
'72,* says that when he first heard a recording of the speech,
not knowing the circumstances or whose voice he was listening to, he rolled on the floor; he thought it was one of
Lenny Bruce's put-ons.

But it wasn't like that on April 19, 1951. According to

Phillips, "Nearly every sentence he spoke was punctuated by applause.

"There were tears in his eyes when, at last, he uttered his peroration:

" 'Since I took the oath at West Point, the hopes and dreams [of youth] have all vanished. But I still remember the refrain of one of the most popular barracks ballads of that day, which proclaimed most proudly that old soldiers never die, they just fade away.

" 'And like the old soldier of the ballad, I now close my military career and just fade away, an old soldier who tried to do his duty as God gave him the light to see that duty.

" 'Good-bye.' "

I said to Dean Acheson, *Mr. Secretary, I understand that after General MacArthur's speech before Congress there was a full-dress Cabinet meeting and that until you livened it up, it had been a pretty gloomy meeting.*

"Everybody, except I must say the President, was greatly upset by the speech; it was thought to have been extremely effective. But I could not agree. I thought it was more than somewhat bathetic, and this was at a time when bathos was less common and less popular in American political oratory than it is today.

". . . The President asked each of us what we thought the effect of the speech would be, and I said that . . . it was difficult to gauge with any precision, but I said that the whole thing reminded me of a man who had an extraordinarily beautiful daughter, and her father did everything he could to protect her. He let her go out only rarely and then only with young men of whom he approved and whose backgrounds were impeccable.

"At last, when she was twenty, she came to her father and said that she had a terrible thing to confess. She said, 'I'm pregnant.'

"At that her father threw up his hands and shouted, 'Thank heaven it's over. I've been afraid of something like this all my life.' "

I said, *Mr. Secretary, do you remember the President's comment on that speech?*

"No, no. You would have to ask him about that, but as I recall, it was a short comment. He described the speech with two Anglo-Saxon words, I believe, but as I say you must ask him about that."

Mr. Truman told me, "I said it was nothing but a bunch of bullshit. . . . There was a lot of carrying-on about that speech, and some of those damn fool Congressmen were crying like a bunch of women, but it didn't worry me at all."

Mr. President, did you listen to the speech on the radio or watch it on television?

"I'd already read the damn thing. And there wasn't any law that I knew of that could make me listen to it, too. Let alone watch it on television.

"It certainly didn't worry me, and neither did the ticker-tape parades they gave for him. Because I knew that once all the hullabaloo died down, people would see what he was.

"And somehow, wherever he went he just didn't make an impression on people that would make him President or much of anything else. Down in Houston, Texas—there are more damn fools down there than just about anyplace I can think of—they tried to raise five thousand dollars to buy him a Cadillac car. I don't think it's paid for yet."

After his triumph before both houses of Congress and the ticker-tape smash in New York, MacArthur retreated to a $130-a-day suite at the Waldorf, where for a week he said nothing, although an aide, when asked about the general's availability for a Presidential draft, referred reporters to the Book of John, especially the part where Thomas expresses some doubts about the Resurrection.

Reporters, most of whom are not vigilant Bible readers, hurried to their Gideons and to the Book of John, but about the best anybody could come up with was the part where Thomas says, "Except I shall see in his hands the print of the nails, and put my finger into the print of the nails, and thrust my hand into his side, I will not believe."

When Jesus finally shows up, He says to Thomas, "Reach hither thy finger, and behold my hands; and reach hither thy hand, and thrust it into my side: and be not faithless, but believing.

"And Thomas answered and said unto him, 'My Lord and my God.'

"Jesus saith unto him, 'Thomas, because thou hast seen me, thou hast believed: blessed are they that have not seen, and yet have believed.' "

That seemed to pretty much wrap up how MacArthur felt about the 1952 Republican national convention.

A few days later MacArthur emerged from his cave at the Waldorf and took off on a "crusade" that took him first to Chicago and Milwaukee and then to Washington again, this time for an appearance before joint hearings of the Armed Services Committee of the House and the Senate Foreign Relations Committee into the reasons for his dismissal. Simple disobedience of his Commander in Chief was not enough.

The hearings ran from May 3 until June 25, and there were many witnesses besides MacArthur, although he was clearly the star performer. In a three-day period he spent twenty-one hours and ten minutes on the stand.

Any oratorical flourishes were considerably diluted, however, because the hearings, despite Republican protests, were closed, and only what was supposedly non-classified material was released each day. The total words spoken during the seven weeks were estimated at 7,000,-000, and, although newspapers devoted a good deal of space to them, they were almost universally unread.

MacArthur was not resurrected by the hearings. Indeed a nation of MacArthur idolators turned into a nation of doubting Thomases. As Harry Truman had predicted, people began to see MacArthur for what he was—vain, arrogant, jealous, petulant, more than a little foolish, and, above all, boring:

". . . the insidious forces working from within would lead directly to the path of Communist slavery. . . . We must not underestimate the peril. It must not be brushed off lightly. It must not be scoffed at, as our present leadership has been prone to do, by hurling childish epithets such as 'red herring,' 'character assassin,' 'scandal monger,' 'witch hunt,' 'political assassination,' and like terms designed to confuse or conceal. . . ."

Stuff like that was putting most people under sixty to sleep wherever MacArthur appeared. And people who a few weeks before had applauded when Harry Truman was being burned in effigy now began to see him as a plucky little man who had defended the Constitution, their Constitution, against an old warrior who once may have been powerful but was now only pompous.

When MacArthur first got back, Harry Truman had told newspapermen that it would take about six weeks for the "fuss" to die down, and that is exactly what happened.

In late May MacArthur returned to New York, and he, Mrs. MacArthur, and little Arthur MacArthur went to the Polo Grounds to see a Giant-Phillies game. A recording of a seventeen-gun salute was played; the general stood at attention in a box decorated with the Stars and Stripes and a five-star flag. Then he paid tribute to "the great American game of baseball that has done so much to build the American character."

At the end of the game, while the band played "Old Soldiers Never Die," the three MacArthurs and the rest of their party rose and started walking across the diamond to the center-field exit.

Just before they got there, a man who had to be from the Bronx shouted from the stands, "Hey, Mac, how's Harry Truman?"

The spectators burst into spontaneous laughter and applause, and that was it. That was the end. It was a beautiful moment, and after that except for a few little old ladies in tennis shoes and the Chicago *Tribune,* there was no more serious talk about Douglas MacArthur and the Presidency.

I reminded the President of that afternoon, and he laughed and said, "Well, of course. The American people always see through a counterfeit. It sometimes takes a little time, but eventually they can always spot one. And MacArthur. I'll tell you. If there ever was to be a Counterfeit Club, he would have been president of it. That is one position he wouldn't have had to run for; he would have been elected, unanimously."

Mr. President, what was your overall impression of the general, besides the fact that he was a counterfeit and that he thought he was God?

Mr. Truman didn't have to give any thought at all to that one. He said, "He struck me as a man there wasn't anything real about."

26

On Generals in General

Mr. President, I gather you're not the only one of our Chief Executives who's had difficulties with generals.

"Oh, no. By no means. James Madison had a terrible time with his generals. He just sort of stumbled into the War of 1812. It never would have happened if it hadn't been for a few hotheads like Henry Clay."

Clay was a Congressman from Kentucky, Speaker of the House, and one of the leading proponents of the war.

"Clay was an expansionist, wanted to extend the country west, and wanted to take over everything that wasn't tied down, and . . . he even wanted to annex Canada, and that is the reason . . . one of the reasons he was so much for getting into war with Britain. He thought we'd gain a lot of new territory.

"But most of the people along the east coast, and that was a good part of the country at that time, they weren't for that war at all. Silliest damn war we ever had, made no sense at all.

"And like I say, Madison didn't want it, but he was a very weak President. A very valuable man when he . . . when they wrote the Constitution, but as President, he just couldn't seem to make up his mind about anything.

"And when he blundered into the War of 1812, except for Andy Jackson he didn't have a general who was worth a good goddamn. They not only weren't any good, they wouldn't do what he told them. And that's the reason the British were able to take Washington and burn the White House. When Madison heard the British were coming, he ran around like a chicken with its head cut off. It wasn't that he was a *coward;* he just didn't know what to do.

"What has always made me feel sorry for Madison is that he became President at all. The work he did on the Constitution and in writing the Federalist Papers with

343

Alexander Hamilton, that was more than enough to justify any man's life.

"But in the War of 1812 . . . Jackson won the only great victory, in the Battle of New Orleans, and it was fought three weeks after the peace treaty, the Treaty of Ghent, but because of bad communications, Jackson didn't know the war was over.

"That victory restored some of Madison's popularity, but he was still hurting over all those generals he'd had trouble controlling. So when the time came, he was very glad to retire to Montpelier [the Madison estate in Virginia], and as I told you, he died broke. And his widow, Dolley, she had to sell Montpelier, and she had to move to . . . had to move in with relatives in Washington, and Daniel Webster had to send her food. And Madison's son was a drunkard, his stepson that was, and he sold his father's papers to buy himself a drink.

"It was an awful thing to see. I don't know *why* this country isn't more grateful to its leaders."

Who were some of the other Presidents who had trouble with generals?

"James K. Polk, for one. He had trouble with 'Ole Fuss 'n' Feathers' [General Winfield Scott] during the war with Mexico. Couldn't get him to move. He stayed down there in Puebla in Mexico from April until August, wouldn't move an inch. Just sat on his ass. Churchill told me he had the same kind of trouble with Montgomery [Bernard Law Montgomery, British field marshal] in France in that other war. Couldn't get him off his ass.

"Of course, Scott finally got moving, and he finally took Mexico City, but he could have done it in May or June at the latest instead of in September, which is when it happened.

"One of the troubles with Scott was that he had in mind being President, which a lot of generals do. MacArthur, of course, was one, and Eisenhower was another, and he's the one I never would have believed it of. He's sat as close to me as you're sitting right this minute and swore up and down that he would never run for any political office and given me the reasons why a military man shouldn't be in politics, and I believed him."

But you didn't believe Lloyd Stark when he told you he wouldn't run against you for the Senate.

"I knew Lloyd was a goddamn liar; I thought I could trust Eisenhower."

You were saying that General Scott wanted to be President.

"He did, and he tried again and again, and, finally, in 1852, the Whigs nominated him. But he made a damn fool of himself every time he opened his mouth. So he didn't get very far. He retired in 1861, so Lincoln didn't have to put up with him during the Civil War. Retiring when he did was one of the few good things Scott ever did. Lincoln had enough trouble with generals without having to contend with 'Ole Fuss 'n' Feathers.' "

Did President Polk have any trouble with Zachary Taylor in the Mexican War?

"Not too much. Taylor, 'Ole Rough 'n' Ready,' he won the Battle of Buena Vista, and he was a pretty good general. Claimed he had no political ambitions. Just like Ike. Claimed he didn't want to be President, and he may even have meant it at one time. They say when somebody started to toast him as the next President of the United States, he told whoever it was, 'Stop your damn nonsense and drink your drink.'

"But later he sort of, apparently, changed his mind. That's the way it almost always happens. There are very few men who when they start thinking about the Presidency don't start thinking how maybe they'd do better at it than the fellow who's then in office, and then they start telling themselves that they'd probably be able to do the job as well as anybody else who's had the job except maybe for . . . oh, Washington and Lincoln and Jefferson maybe.

"And then the first thing you know they are . . . wondering what they are going to say when they get the nomination.

"In Taylor's case . . . finally, in 1848, he was nominated by the Whigs. They didn't know a damn thing about him, didn't know what party he belonged to even or how he stood on any of the issues, but they went ahead and did it.

"They always reminded me a little of some of those smart-aleck Democrats in 1948 who wanted to nominate Eisenhower for President without knowing a thing about him. Didn't even know what party he belonged to.

"But the Whigs nominated Taylor, and of course, he got elected because he was a great military hero. But he was no damn good in office. He was too old, and he didn't know anything about it. He only lived about sixteen months after he got in office, but that was plenty long enough to tell that he was very much out of place in the White House.

"Somebody, I forget who, said war is too important to be left to the generals, and that's true. But politics . . . we ought to try to devise a way to keep them out of politics altogether."

Tell me about Lincoln and his generals.

"Lincoln had more trouble than any President with the general proposition. He had to fire McClellan twice, and then he had to fire all the rest of them or demote them in rank until he finally got Grant in charge, and the war came to a successful conclusion."

Why did he have to fire McClellan twice?

"McClellan was a very difficult man. He was young, about thirty-five, thirty-six, I believe, and after the First Battle of Bull Run, when the streets of Washington were filled with stragglers and deserters, and nobody seemed to know what to do, why, McClellan organized the Army of the Potomac, and he did a very good job of it. He was always very popular with the soldiers.

"But as I say, he was a young, very young man, and just like MacArthur after he organized the Army of the Potomac, McClellan got blown up by the papers out of all proportion, and he got to thinking that the whole fate

of the Union was on his shoulders. Lincoln liked him;
they'd known each other back in Illinois when McClellan
was head of one of the railroads there and Lincoln was
one of its lawyers. The Illinois Central, I believe.

"But when he got to Washington, McClellan had a hard
time getting it into his head that Lincoln was President.
He seemed to think that Lincoln was still . . . that he
was still Lincoln's boss somehow. He was very rude to
the President, used to come late to meetings, and once
when Lincoln went to visit him at *his* house, McClellan
came in, and he saw Lincoln, but he didn't say hello or
anything. He went straight upstairs and went to bed.

"But as you know, Lincoln was a very patient man,
and he overlooked these . . . this rudeness. When some
of Lincoln's Cabinet members objected to the way Mc-
Clellan was acting, Lincoln told them . . . he said,
'Never mind.' He says, 'If he brings us success, if he
brings success to the Union side, I will gladly hold Mc-
Clellan's horse for him.' But that didn't happen. McClellan
didn't *move*. Same trouble Polk had with 'Ole Fuss 'n'
Feathers' and Churchill had with Montgomery. McClellan
just sat on his ass.

"One day somebody in the War Department came and
told Lincoln that there didn't seem to have been any
firing in McClellan's sector since after sunset. And Lincoln says that that didn't surprise him a bit. He says what
he really wanted to know was had there been any firing
in that sector *before* sunset. He says it reminded him about
the fellow who went around saying that he had come
across a really unusual child that was black from the
hips down. And when somebody asked him what color the
child was from the hips up, the fellow said, 'Why, black,
of course.'

"And it wasn't only that Lincoln couldn't get McClellan
to *move*. The general was always issuing statements about
. . . concerning political matters, and they always indicated that whatever it was, McClellan could do it a lot
better than Lincoln was doing it.

"Of course that meant that McClellan was aiming to be

President, and they asked Lincoln if he was going to issue a reply to something or other McClellan had said.

"Lincoln said, 'No,' he wasn't. He said he wouldn't do that, but he said the whole thing reminded him of the fella whose horse started kicking around and got his foot stuck in the stirrup. The fella looked at the horse, and he said, 'Look here, if you want to get on, I'll get off.'

"Of course, in 1864 the Democrats nominated McClellan for President, and at the same time they adopted a platform saying that the war was a failure and that they were willing . . . would probably make a deal with the South.

"McClellan refused to support the platform, and then the Union victories at Mobile Bay and Atlanta lost him a lot of support. But Lincoln . . . Lincoln was a man who suffered greatly, and he was inclined, always, to look on the dark side of things. He was convinced that he would be . . . that he would lose the election in 1864, and he felt that that would mean the end of the Union.

"He drew up a statement that was signed by every member of his Cabinet saying that after losing the election, he would do everything he could between the election and the inauguration to save the Union. But he said after the inauguration, the successful candidate would have made promises to win the election that would mean the end of the Union.

"Of course that didn't happen. Lincoln was reelected, and afterward Lincoln told Seward [William Henry Seward, Lincoln's Secretary of State] that if McClellan had been elected, he'd have said to him, 'General, you are more popular with the American people than I am. Now let us both use our influence to try to save the country. I'll help you raise all the troops you need to end the war as quickly as possible.'

"Old Seward, who had never liked McClellan, said, 'And the general would have said, "Yes, yes," and kept on saying, "Yes, yes," and he would never done a damn thing at all.' Which is probably true. Because McClellan was a man who fought more with his mouth than he did with . . . than he used his troops to fight.

"Lincoln also had trouble with a fella named Pope [General John L. Pope]. He was another bombastic fellow who made all kinds of promises that he never did live up to, and he never had any intention of living up to them.

"When Lincoln put him in command of the Army of the Potomac, Pope said he wouldn't *rest* until the war was won. He said he would have his headquarters in his saddle. But after the Second Battle of Bull Run, which was one of the worst Union defeats of the war, there were hundreds, maybe thousands of wounded and dying men in the streets of Washington and on the floor of the Capitol and everywhere else where there was empty space.

"It was just an awful defeat, and Lincoln removed Pope from his command and sent him up in the northeast someplace to keep an eye on some tame Indians. And old Horace Greeley said in the New York *Tribune* . . . said that in the Second Battle of Bull Run, 'Pope evidently had his headquarters in his saddle, and he sat on his brains.' "

Mr. President, how do you explain the success of General Grant? Especially after all those other generals had been such terrible failures?

"Grant was a very . . . had a very simple idea of how you go about winning a war. He wasn't much . . . didn't know much about strategy. A lot of other generals on both sides, they had all studied the same books at West Point, and Grant . . . well, he wasn't much of a reader or scholar. There was one book by some Frenchman. I forget his name.* And the high-ranking officers on both sides of the fence were studying this book and using the same strategy, and it wasn't working.

---

* Baron Henri Jomini, actually Swiss, whose military writings attracted Napoleon, who gave him an important position in the French Army. The book which summarized all of Jomini's military theories was published in 1838 and was called *Précis de l'art de la guerre*.

And one day some young lieutenant asked Grant if he'd read that book, and Grant said, 'Hell, no.' Of course he hadn't. He said he didn't have to. He said what you have to do to fight a war, you have to find the enemy, and you have to hit him with everything you've got, and then you've got to keep right on going. And that's what he did. He never stopped to issue fancy statements about this and that. He just kept right on going."

Mr. President, last week when I was back in Brewster I was reading W. E. Woodward's biography of Ulysses S. Grant, and he says that when Grant went back into the service in 1861, he took over a very unruly regiment that I believe two previous officers had been unable to manage. This was in Galena, Illinois.

And when Grant arrived, wearing an old felt hat and a beat-up coat and his beard needing a trim, the men expected he'd give them a long lecture, eat their tails out, as they used to say when I was in the Army.

But Grant didn't. He just stood up in front of them, of the regiment, and all he said was, "Men, go to your quarters."

And that very much reminded me of what you said when under very similar circumstances you took over Battery D. All those men expected that you'd give them a very hard time, but all you said was, "Dismissed."

I hope you won't think my question is impertinent.

"I've told you before. If I think you're impertinent, I'll let you know."

I was just wondering if you'd read that about General Grant before in the First World War you said what you said to the troops in Battery D.

"Well, you might say that at that time I was familiar with the history of the Civil War or the War Between the States, whatever you want to call it, and so I *may* have happened on that incident. I've told you. One of the reasons for reading history is to learn from it and, if possible, make use of it."

That was the second and last time that I believe Mr. Truman winked.

I gather you feel some admiration for General Grant, as a general at least.

"Well, you have to remember that all my people were on the other side, were on Lee's side. But I have always felt that Grant was a very good general; they both were, and Lee was one of the kindest men who ever lived. After the war, he became president of Washington and Lee University down in Virginia. Only then it was just called Washington University, and they say he knew the name of every boy in that school.

"And he was a very gentle man, never got angry or, if he did, never did show it. When he was marching up the Shenandoah Valley on his way to Gettysburg, he kept waiting for Jeb Stuart to show up. Stuart was a fine cavalry officer but a very undependable sort of fellow. And he was another one of those who was always out to make as many headlines as he possibly could. Lee didn't know where he was when he was going to Gettysburg. Stuart finally did show up, on the first day of the battle, which meant that he hadn't done his job, finding out, as the cavalry was supposed to, how strong the enemy was. And I think that was a very big factor in losing that battle, if it was lost. More of a draw, I think.

"Anyway, when he did show up, Lee didn't say what he . . . . all that he must have had in his mind. He just said, 'I see you are here at last, General Stuart.'

"Lee was a tactician and a scholar, and he had studied every battle in history, I think, and he'd learned from what he'd studied. If he'd been on the other side in that war, he'd probably have more the reputation he deserves. I told you. History is always written by the winners. And if Lee had been on the other side, he'd probably have wound up being President of the United States."

How do you think he'd have been as President?

"We've done about enough guesswork for one time. Lee was a professional military man and a West Point graduate. I've told you how professional soldiers are in politics, no damn good at all."

Mr. President, the way you feel about West Point, or

seem to feel, you don't seem to think too much of it, and yet you wanted to go there yourself.

"Yes, but that was because I needed to, wanted to, get a free education. I didn't necessarily say it was a good one. I'll tell you. It seems to give a man a narrow view of things, and if you're going to be a soldier and nothing else, that may work out all right. But not for any other line of work and especially not politics. They never seem to teach them anything at all about understanding people up there." *

Getting back to General Grant, he certainly seemed to demonstrate at Appomattox that he was a very generous man, wouldn't you say?

"One of the most generous who ever was. Lee was all dressed up fit to kill that day, you know, wearing his best uniform and wearing a sword. Grant showed up in . . . I believe it was an enlisted man's uniform, and his boots hadn't been shined, and as you were saying about that incident up at Galena, Illinois, his beard probably needed a trim. I'm not even sure he had a sword. They say that during the Battle of the Wilderness he just stood there whittling away on a piece of wood with a jackknife.

* I'm aware that we have already discussed Mr. Truman's feelings about a West Point education, but his answer this time was somewhat different and seemed to me to be worth preserving.

And there is this, from *The Man from Missouri*, by Alfred Steinberg; speaking of Mr. Truman's first term in the Senate:

"Despite his lack of major influence, requests for aid poured into his office. When he could do something, his approach was to favor the underdog. 'One morning,' Messall [Victor Messall, the Senator's Secretary] said, 'I brought him fifty folders of applications for appointments to West Point from Missouri boys. The folders were thick and contained recommendations from judges, state legislators, mayors, et cetera. We went through each folder methodically, and finally we got down to a folder that contained no letters of recommendation—only a single-page application written in pencil on a sheet of cheap, rough paper. Truman read it and then he turned to me and ordered, 'Give him the appointment.' "

"One thing you have to understand about Grant. He was very familiar with defeat, with failing at things, and he knew about being poor. His father was a tanner, you know, and he grew up working as a plain dirt farmer. They never had much money, the Grants, and after he'd been to West Point, he said that what he'd learned there wasn't nearly as important as what he'd learned as a boy, which was that if you undertake a job, you have to finish it. And of course, knowing that is . . . was why he was so successful in the war.

"After he finished at West Point, he was in the Mexican War and made a very good record for himself, and then . . . he finally wound up stationed out in California; he had to send his wife and children back to Ohio, and he missed them. He and Mrs. Grant, they were . . . very fond of each other.

"While in California, he and the colonel in charge, a Colonel Buchanan, they didn't hit it off, and Grant was drinking. He was always a drinking man his whole life through.

"The colonel was going to bring him up on charges, but instead, Grant resigned. He came back East, and his father-in-law gave him some timberland down near St. Louis, which Grant cleared, about sixty acres, I believe, and he built his own log cabin. Called it Hard Scrabble, and of course, it has since become a national monument.

"He tried to farm the land, but the panic of 18 and 57 and 58 wiped him out, and after that he never made much of a go of anything he seemed to undertake. When the war came along, he was working for his brother in Galena, working in a leather store. He was thirty-nine, forty years old, and nobody thought he'd ever amount to a tinker's dam.* Except his wife, Julia. Julia Dent her

---

* In speaking of this part of Grant's career, which he did with great warmth and understanding, I always felt that Harry Truman felt a real sense of identity with him. After all, at forty, Harry Truman, having already gone broke in the haberdashery, had just suffered his first political defeat, and Margaret had just been born.

name had been. She never lost faith in him, and in the
war it turned out she was right.

"What I'm saying is that Grant was always a very humble, very understanding man, and down there at Appomattox he realized that he wasn't any different from those
Southern boys who'd been on the wrong side. And he felt
just the way Lincoln did, that the South should be treated
as a disobedient child and not a conquered nation. Some
of the Radical Republicans in Washington were talking
about hanging Lee or convicting him of treason, but
Grant said that nothing like that was going to be allowed
to happen. The kids . . . the boys in Lee's army were
hungry, and they had to be fed. That was the first thing.
And it was spring; it was April the ninth, and the . . .
those boys were going to need horses and mules to plant
their spring crops. They were not going to be put in
prison camps . . . the way some of the Radical Republicans were suggesting. They were going home. All
they had to do was sign paroles, and as long as they lived
up to them, they would be left strictly alone.

"That was all. It was a very good thing that he did.
As I said, Grant was a very generous, kind man, and if
he hadn't got into politics, he might not have gone down.
. . . His place in history would have been . . . more
secure. But when he got into the White House, he turned
out to be the weakest President we have ever had, and
his administration was the most corrupt in all our history
up to now. He wasn't crooked himself, but everybody
around him was.

"And the biggest trouble was that he just had no understanding at all of what to do. He didn't have the
slightest understanding of free government.

"I've told you what happens with these generals. They
think being President is some kind of reward for services
rendered in the war, and they think the White House is
like some Army post they can retire to and take life easy.

"Grant had the idea that Congress was supposed to
run things, and he thought being President was just sort
of . . . like that other fella we've discussed, some kind

of ceremonial job where all you had to do was entertain visiting royalty and pin medals on people and shake hands and getting your picture taken with a big grin on your face.

"I'm pretty sure he'd never read the Constitution; he wasn't much of a reading man, and he'd only voted once in his life and that was in 1856, when he voted for the Democrats. After he'd had a misunderstanding with Andrew Johnson,* the Radical Republicans took him over, claiming he was one of them, which he wasn't. He wasn't one of anything, of any party. He just didn't understand what was going on.

"And after he got elected in 1868, why the people around him were stealing the country blind. Old Gould and Fisk [Jay Gould and Jim Fisk, New York financiers and scoundrels] wined and dined him and tried to convince him to keep the government out of the gold market so they could clean up on it, and for a while they did.

---

* In 1867 during the height of Andrew Johnson's troubles with Congress he appointed Grant to succeed Edwin M. Stanton as Secretary of War. Stanton was an ally of the Radical Republicans in Congress, who favored the severest penalties for the Southern states; Johnson and Grant agreed with Lincoln's policy, which was, as Mr. Truman says, to treat the Southern states as disobedient children. "Let 'em up easy," Lincoln once said.

At the time of Grant's appointment Congress, then in recess, had already passed the Tenure of Office Act, which asserted that no member of the President's Cabinet could be discharged without the Senate's approval, a clearly unconstitutional measure.

When Congress re-convened at the end of 1867 one of its first acts was to refuse to consent to Stanton's dismissal. Grant immediately resigned. He had no real understanding of the issues involved. He just thought that Congress was boss, no matter what, and that confusion was unfortunate then and even more so when he himself became President.

In any case, Johnson, a man of monumental rages at times, felt that he had been betrayed. It was his understanding that Grant would stay on until the Tenure of Office Act had been tested in the courts. Grant then felt that *his* honor had been impugned, and the two men became lifelong enemies.

And there was the Credit Mobilier scandal in which speculators made tens of millions of dollars by bilking the Union Pacific Railroad, which had been subsidized by the federal government. And it resulted in a great scandal that involved several members of Congress who had accepted gifts of stock as a bribe to keep their mouths shut.

"As I say, Grant wasn't involved in any of those things personally, but he has gone down in history as head of the crookedest government we have ever had.

"But he was reelected, mostly because the Democratic candidate was Horace Greeley, the fellow I've told you was editor of the New York *Tribune*. Greeley was also nominated by the Liberal Republican Party, but somehow he just didn't come across in the campaign. He just couldn't seem to project himself to the electorate the way he should have. For some reason I never have been able to figure out he came across as kind of a nut. People didn't care much for Grant as President, but they reelected him rather than take a chance on Greeley. His defeat and the death of his wife just before the election drove him crazy, and he died in less than a month. A very interesting man, though; he's worth reading about, because for one thing as you will see a lot of his ideas were way ahead of their time.

"But Grant got reelected, and his second term was even worse than his first. A lot more fraud and corruption were uncovered, and there was the panic of 18 and 73, and through it all Grant just sat there, not knowing what to do. It was just an awful period of American history. Grant's indecisiveness and his letting the Radical Republicans run things led to difficulties between the North and South that haven't been settled to this day."

After Grant got out of office, didn't he go on a round-the-world cruise?

"Yes, after he got out of office, he went over to see his daughter who'd been married in the White House to an Englishman, and they made quite a bit over him in England, which he liked, and so he just kept on going, and everywhere he went he was greeted by the kings and queens and prime ministers and what have you, and there were parades for him, and they gave him a lot of decorations.

"When he got back to the United States, he'd been gone two years or so, and he landed at San Francisco and was greeted with considerable enthusiasm. And then he tried to go back to Galena, Illinois, for a while, but somehow things didn't work out there. Nothing seemed to go right for him there."

Unlike your returning to Independence after being President. I mean, things seem to have worked out very well indeed.

"If you want to make that comparison, I suppose you could make it, yes."

And eventually didn't Grant wind up in New York?

"He went to New York, and he didn't have much money left, but then he went flat broke with a Wall Street firm named Grant and Ward. He was the only President who tried to promote the Presidency in business, and I don't like that fact in his history. That is exactly what he was doing, though.

"But Ward, Ferdinand Ward his name was, took him for every penny he had. And he'd borrowed money from old man Vanderbilt [William Henry Vanderbilt, son of Cornelius Vanderbilt], and since he couldn't pay it back, Vanderbilt took what little real estate he owned and everything else poor old Grant had, including even his ceremonial swords. I believe they ended up down at the National Museum.

"But that's an awful thing, to see a former President humiliated like that. It shouldn't happen. You might say Grant brought it on himself by acting like a damn fool, but it still isn't right. It shouldn't be allowed to happen to an ex-President.

"When Grant realized that Ward had taken advantage of him, he said, 'I have always trusted men long after other people gave up on them, but I never will trust another human being as long as I live.' "

And did he?

"Oh, I don't know. I suppose so. He was a trusting fella, and you either are or you aren't, and there's not much you can do about it.

"He seems to have trusted old Mark Twain. He was desperately in need of money, and that's when he got tied up with Twain and wrote his memoirs. In two volumes. I think Mark Twain helped him write them. Some of it. I don't know how much, but some of it sounds a lot funnier than Grant ever was, and a lot of what is said doesn't compare at all with what really happened. Those books are very interesting reading, but they are very inaccurate." *

Do you think that's carelessness or deliberate?

"Oh, I think he told Mark the things, just like I'm talking to you, the things that he remembered the way he remembered them. And of course, no man's memory is absolutely perfect.

"I think the principal thing he was trying to do was to make a good front before the country because he was, even in that day, considered the worst President that ever was in the White House. Although he came very near to being nominated and elected a third time. Did you know that?"

No, I didn't. Tell me about it.

"It was in 1880, and the Republican convention was in Chicago, and there was . . . there were several different splits in the party. The first person nominated was John

---

* I couldn't find any evidence that Twain actually helped Grant write the two volumes of his *Personal Memoirs;* indeed, the last pages, in Grant's own weakening hand, were written only forty-eight hours before he died.

There are places, though, where Grant does come through wittier than anyone ever suspected he could be. And Twain certainly had a hand in editing the manuscript.

In any case the memoirs are very good books, not much read any more, which is a pity. Harry Truman felt that Grant was, despite his failure as President, a complex and interesting man, and judging by the memoirs, he was right.

Sherman, who was a Senator from Ohio and a brother of the old general who took Atlanta. Sherman didn't have the chance of a snowball in hell, but he was nominated by James A. Garfield, who had just been elected to the Senate from Ohio, and he gave what turned out to be the best speech of the convention. He was quite a great orator, Garfield was. On the day Lincoln was shot he was in New York, and the crowds were running wild, and they asked him to speak, someplace down in Wall Street, I believe. Asked him to speak to quiet people down, and he did. He said that . . . told people that sad as Lincoln's death was, he said something like the Republic would survive. It's in one of the books in the library here. You could look it up.*

"The second person named was James G. Blaine, who was from Maine and had been Speaker of the House for several terms. And then he was elected to the Senate, and he almost got the nomination for the Presidency in 1876, but he was . . . he had been accused of making a personal profit out of the sale of some railroad stocks and bonds and using his position in Congress to swing it."

Railroad corruption keeps turning up, it appears, all through American history. Why is that, do you suppose? Is it because . . . well, there used to be a man named Willie Sutton who robbed banks, and they asked him why he did it, and he said, "Because that's where the money is."

"That's part of it. That's part of it. The railroads have always been subsidized by the government, and they have always made enormous profits, and as we were talking

* Lincoln's assassination inspired one of Garfield's most memorable speeches. He stood on the steps of the Sub-Treasury building in New York and to the uneasy crowd below said, "Clouds and darkness are around Him; His pavilion is dark waters and thick clouds; justice and judgment are the habitations of His throne; mercy and truth shall go before His face! Fellow citizens, God reigns and the Government at Washington still lives!"

. . . saying the other day, very little looking into it is ever done. It's not like Wall Street and the Securities and Exchange Commission. The railroads just keep on being looted, and the greedy do it and get away with it."

Maybe the railroads should be socialized.

"That may be."

I waited for more, but there was no more. I guess that Harry Truman at that stage of his life wasn't going to let himself be accused of being a Socialist, not again.

I didn't press the issue, and we continued.

What kind of man was Blaine?

"Well, I've never thought he was much of any kind of man. He was in the Senate in 1880, and he was known as 'The Plumed Knight' because of his very fancy way of talking. He was one of those men . . . who just seem to spend their whole lives doing nothing but running for President, and it's been . . . I've always felt that the ones who want it too much and let it show too much, they never do make it for some reason or other.

"That was what happened in 1948, among other things. The fella that was running against me wanted to be President so much his tongue was hanging out, and it showed.

"The trouble with people like that, and there have been a lot of them in our history, if they ever . . . if by some chance they ever do get *elected,* they don't know what the hell to do. A lot of them haven't thought beyond just getting elected. Grant was a good example of that type, and there've been others more recently. They get elected, and they don't have a program.

"Once you get in the White House those—what-do-you-call-them—those Madison Avenue fellas can't bail you out, not all the time they can't.

"Anyway, in 1884 Blaine finally did get the Republican nomination, and he might have made it, too; he was running against Grover Cleveland, and everybody thought he'd be elected until a few nights before . . . maybe the night before the election some minister* in New York City introduced him as the candidate who was against 'Rum, Romanism, and Rebellion' and, of course, Cleveland's people made good use of that, and Blaine never did repudiate it for some damn reason, and he was licked.

"He lost New York State, and that was the end, except he did serve in the Cabinet of Benjamin Harrison and didn't do too bad a job of it, especially in Latin American affairs.

"He was a lightweight, though; at least that's my opinion."

But getting back to the Republican convention of 1880, he did not get the nomination that year.

"No, he did not. You've got to stop me from getting off the beam here; I get carried away some times."

Keep going right ahead and doing it. I've learned more American history during the time we've been talking than all the time I was in school, including college. More world history, too. And I must say it's a lot more interesting.

"Well, I'm glad you feel that way. I told you. If I hadn't got mixed up in politics, I might have been a history teacher. . . .

"But at that 1880 convention of the Republicans it finally got down to a race between Blaine and Grant. The big city bosses, Conkling of New York† and the bosses from Pennsylvania and Illinois, I forget their names, they wanted Grant again because they were pretty sure they could reelect him, and they knew that once he got in again, they could control him. Just as they always had.

---

* On October 29, 1884, the Reverend Samuel Dickinson Burchard in a speech introducing Blaine referred to the Democrats as the party of "Rum, Romanism, and Rebellion." The following Sunday Catholics in every church in New York City and a great many other places heard about that speech. Very few of them voted for Blaine.

† Roscoe G. Conkling, a U.S. Senator from New York who controlled all the federal patronage of the state when Grant was President. He placed the general's name in nomination at the convention.

They were called the Stalwarts, and the other side, the folks that were supporting Blaine, were called the Half-Breeds.

"The convention was completely deadlocked. They had thirty-five ballots, I believe, and finally Hayes [President Rutherford B. Hayes] got in touch with the fella that was running the convention and suggested to him that Garfield had made the best speech of the convention and why didn't they nominate him. And so on the thirty-sixth ballot they did.

"Garfield made the first of the front-porch campaigns; people came down to that little town in Ohio, whatever it's called [Mentor] to see him, and he got elected but by a very small margin, about ten thousand votes, I believe.

"And then, of course, after he was inaugurated in March, he only served until July, when he was shot in the back in the Baltimore and Ohio station in Washington. By a disappointed office seeker.

"And he was succeeded by Chester Arthur, the guy with the side whiskers and striped pants."

The one that was supposed to have kept a whore in the White House.

"That's what they tell on him, yes. . . . But getting back to where we started out, you can see how near Grant came to being nominated for a third term and, as I say, automatically practically reelected.

"But of course that didn't happen, and that's . . . after that he and Twain got together on his memoirs, and while they were working on them, Grant got cancer of the jaw, and he died a very painful death. But he was a stubborn cuss; he was in great, great pain, but he wouldn't . . . you might say he wouldn't *allow* himself to die until he'd finished. It's just like he was in the war and everything else he undertook. He wouldn't give up. He said once someplace in the war that he'd fight it out if it took all summer on the same front line, and that's the way it was with the memoirs.

"Of course, the funny thing about it. Grant. He was

living on borrowed time, you might say, for the last twenty years of his life, because if he'd . . . Lincoln asked him to go to the Ford Theater with him the night he was assassinated, but Grant and Mrs. Grant didn't go. They went up to visit their children someplace in New Jersey.

"If they had gone, though, Grant would have been shot because he was on the list of John Wilkes Booth."

I believe those memoirs turned out to be very successful, didn't they?

"Yes, they did. They made a lot of money for Twain, though he managed to lose it later, but they made a lot for Mrs. Grant, which always pleased me very, very much. Because otherwise, she'd have been under very hard circumstances. As she had been a good part of her life."

Mr. President, what really astounds me—if Grant had been nominated again in 1880, you say he'd have been reelected. Even though everybody knew that he'd been a very bad President.

"That's right."

How could such a thing happen? How could they even consider nominating him when he'd had such a poor record?

"How could they nominate Eisenhower for a third term and elect him? And that's what would have happened if the Republicans hadn't cut their own throats with that amendment [the twenty-second] they passed to stop another Roosevelt and limit the President to two terms. The damn thing wasn't ratified until 1951, and only nine years later, when 1960 came along, if it hadn't been for that damn amendment, they could have had Eisenhower in the White House for another four years. So instead they had to make *do* with somebody like Nixon.

"I would like to have been a mouse in the corner at some of the carrying-on I'll bet they did in private. I would just like to have been there and heard it."

Mr. Truman thought over that delicious possibility for a moment, and then he started laughing. He laughed for quite a long time. Or else he was chuckling dryly.

One thing I am sure of. He was enjoying himself hugely.

A little later I said, *Do you think Eisenhower could have defeated Jack Kennedy? We may have discussed this before; at the moment I can't remember.*

"Yes, I do. If Nixon came as close as he did to doing it, Eisenhower could have done it in a walk."

Mr. President, you said earlier this morning that you thought General Grant had never read the Constitution. Do you think Mr. Nixon has?

"I don't know. I don't know. But I'll tell you this. If he has, he doesn't understand it."

27

A Few Further Observations
on "Ike"

Mr. President, yesterday you said that if it hadn't been for the Twenty-second Amendment, Eisenhower would have been nominated in 1960 and reelected for a third term. Do you think the Republic could have survived another four years of him?

"Oh, yes. We survived those five poor Presidents that I'm going to tell you about, even though if they'd been stronger, we might not have had a Civil War. But what you have to understand is that the system we have under the Constitution that was set up by those fellows in Philadelphia has survived worse things than Eisenhower. Not much worse but some worse."

Getting back to Grant for a moment, do you think there are other parallels between Grant and Eisenhower, beyond the fact that they were both professional Army men and poor Presidents?

"For one thing, Grant was a hell of a lot better soldier than Eisenhower. What they never seem to say about Eisenhower is that he was . . . very weak as a field commander. When they had to fire that general* at Kasserine Pass, after the Kasserine Pass, Ike was in charge, but Marshall had to do the firing. Ike didn't have the guts to do it.

"Bradley was a great field soldier, but Ike wasn't. That job he had over there in London and in Paris [Supreme Allied Commander in Europe] what he was, what he did,

---

* After the fiasco at Kasserine Pass Major General Lloyd R. Fredendall was relieved of duty as commander of the II Corps. He was returned to the United States, actually fired. The official reason was that he would be of more value as a trainer of troops. I was unable to track down exactly who did the firing, although, again officially, it was Eisenhower. In any case he was replaced by General George C. Patton. Omar Bradley became Patton's deputy.

he presided at meetings mostly, and he approved strategy that had been drawn up by other people, but he never did *originate* anything. General Marshall was just the kindest man that ever was or ever will be, but he told me that Eisenhower had to be led every step of the way.

"But he, apparently, did well enough at that presiding job. They seemed to like him, but that's one of his troubles. He wanted, as President he wanted everybody to like him, and you can't have that.

"A President who's any damn good at all makes enemies, makes a lot of enemies. I even made a few myself when I was in the White House. And I wouldn't be without them. I wouldn't be without them."

Mr. President, as you know, there has been considerable debate about what was said between you and General Eisenhower at his headquarters in Frankfurt in 1945, at the time of Potsdam, about your volunteering to support him for President in 1948 if he wanted it.

"There's no reason for any debate about it. I saw him there in Frankfurt, and I told him how grateful the American people were for the job he'd done, and we talked about the fact that a lot of wartime heroes get into politics and get elected. And he said that under no circumstances was he going to get into politics at any time. And that's all there was to it. He said I said it, but I didn't.

"I've told you time and again how I feel . . . how I've always felt about professional military men in politics. It wouldn't have made any sense for me to promise a thing like that, would it? It would be against my whole philosophy, wouldn't it?"

Yes, sir. Totally against it.

"And it was the same thing in 1948; he said I offered him the Presidency, which I didn't. In the first place, it wasn't mine to offer. What happened, before he retired as Chief of Staff to go up there to Columbia we had a talk, and *again* he assured me he had no intention whatsoever of going into politics. I told him I thought that was the right decision, and it was. If he'd just stuck to it.

"There's a letter in my file in here which was written

by Eisenhower to the old man who runs the paper in Manchester, New Hampshire,* that is the best analysis I know of on why a military man can't possibly make a good President. I never pulled it on him, but it's the best possible analysis of why a military man can't be an executive in a republic. It's a crackerjack. It's just exactly what the facts are.

"But I wouldn't have *ever* supported Eisenhower under any circumstances for President even if I didn't . . . hadn't known about his personal life."

I'm sorry, sir. What do you mean about his personal life?

"Why, right after the war was over, he wrote a letter to General Marshall saying that he wanted to be relieved of duty, saying that he wanted to come back to the United States and divorce Mrs. Eisenhower so that he could marry this Englishwoman."

It took me a moment to recover from that one, and then I said, *Do you mean Kay Summersby, who I believe was his jeep driver?* †

* Leonard Finder, then publisher of the Manchester *Union Leader,* placed Ike's name in the Republican primary, but Eisenhower wrote him: "I could not accept nomination even under the remote circumstances that it would be tendered me. . . . The necessary and wise subordination of the military to civil power will be best sustained when life-long professional soldiers abstain from seeking high political office."

† Miss Summersby, a member of the British Women's Auxiliary Corps, which later became the Women's Army Corps, began her association with General Eisenhower as his jeep driver. In *Crusade in Europe,* his single mention of her comes when he discusses putting together his personal staff in Algiers in December, 1942. He states, "Kay Summersby was corresponding secretary and doubled as a driver."

But he does go on to pay tribute to women in wartime: "Until my experience in London I had been opposed to the use of women in uniform. But in Great Britain I had seen them perform so magnificently in various positions, including service in active anti-aircraft batteries, that I had been converted. . . . From the day they first reached us their reputation as an efficient, effective corps continued to grow. Toward

"I think that was her name, yes. But I don't care what her name was. It was a very, very shocking thing to have done, for a man who was a general in the Army of the United States.

"Well, Marshall wrote him back a letter the like of which I never did see. He said that if he . . . if Eisenhower even came close to doing such a thing, he'd not only bust him out of the Army, he'd see to it that never for the rest of his life would he be able to draw a peace-

---

the end of the war the most stubborn die-hards had become convinced—and demanded them in increasing numbers. At first the women were kept carefully back at GHQ and secure bases, but as their record for helpfulness grew, so did the scope of their duties in positions progressively nearer the front."

In any case, Miss Summersby stayed with the general until November, 1945, and in 1948 her book was published— *Eisenhower Was My Boss*. On the jacket it says, "Hers is a portrait of General Eisenhower as few could see him, continuously, at moments of tension, making great decisions, during long hours of routine work, and while he relaxed at bridge or horseback riding.

"As the General's chauffeur, she was the guide who introduced him to wartime London and conducted him safely through pea-soup fogs. With him in Africa, Italy, France, and Germany, she first piloted his car to important conferences and on arduous inspection tours over roads scarred by battle and crowded with the matériel of war. Later, at headquarters, she was his receptionist, personal secretary, and aide."

Miss Summersby describes the end of their long relationship rather cryptically: ". . . on the last day of October, he gave me the nicest present of the war . . . or the peace: an empty seat on his plane, headed for Washington on official business.

"I took out my first papers toward becoming an American citizen.

"Arriving back in Germany after the short trip, I found the General packing. He was taking over from General Marshall [as Chief of Staff], who had postponed his retirement in order to carry out a Presidential assignment in China.

" 'I'm going to Washington tomorrow,' General Ike said as I entered the office. 'But I'll be back.'

"He didn't come back."

ful breath. He said it wouldn't matter if he was in the Army or wasn't. Or even what country he was in.

"Marshall said that if he ever again even mentioned a thing like that, he'd see to it that the rest of his life was a living hell. General Marshall didn't very often lose his temper, but when he did, it was a corker."

Mr. Truman was silent for a moment, and then he said, "I don't like Eisenhower; you know that. I never have, but one of the last things I did as President, I got those letters from his file in the Pentagon, and I destroyed them."

That was the first mention and the last of Miss Summersby and the exchange of letters between Generals Marshall and Eisenhower.

A little later I said, *Mr. President, the other day when we were making our first tour of the library, you showed me the copy of* Crusade in Europe *that General Eisenhower inscribed to you. I'm sure you've read it, but I was wondering, of the things you know about, how accurate is it?*

No answer. That was the only time in all our conversations that Mr. Truman didn't respond at all to a question. So I waited a moment, then said, *Have you read General Bradley's book* A Soldier's Story?

"Yes, I have, and that is a very good book. Bradley was perhaps our greatest field general in the Second World War, and in his book, he has . . . so far as I can make out, he hasn't told a single lie. Of course he's a Missourian, so maybe I'm prejudiced."

Mr. President, were you surprised when Eisenhower finally did become a Presidential candidate in 1952?

"No, no. I could see it coming a long way back. I told you. Once the bug bites a man, there are very few, generals or not, who can resist. And I never thought Eisenhower was one of those who could. He had . . . a very high opinion of himself. Somewhere along the line he seemed to forget all about the fact that he was just a poor boy from Kansas."

After he got the nomination, did you think he'd be elected?

"When I saw the way the fellow that was running against him acted, I did. That fellow didn't know the first thing about campaigning, and he didn't learn anything either. He got worse in 1956."

Still you helped . . . Eisenhower's opponent out in 1952.

"Yes, I did. After Eisenhower got his picture taken with that fella from Indiana—what's his name?—the one that called General Marshall a traitor?"

Senator William Jenner.

"He got his picture taken with him, and then when he was in Milwaukee, he took out what . . . he was going to pay a tribute to General Marshall, but he took it out rather than stand up to McCarthy. It was one of the most shameful things I can ever remember. Why, General Marshall was responsible for his whole career. When Roosevelt jumped him from lieutenant colonel to general, it was on Marshall's recommendation. Three different times Marshall got him pushed upstairs, and in return . . . Eisenhower sold him out. It was just a shameful thing." *

---

* On October 3, 1952, Eisenhower made a speech in Milwaukee, Wisconsin, the home state of Senator Joseph R. McCarthy, then at the height of his influence and popularity.

Eisenhower spoke of freedom; he was all for it. He said, "To defend freedom . . . is—first of all—to *respect* freedom. This respect demands, in turn, respect for the integrity of fellow citizens who enjoy their right to disagree. The right to question a man's judgment carries with it no automatic right to question his honor."

Then, according to Emmet John Hughes, who wrote the speech, the general was to have said, "Let me be quite specific. I know that charges of disloyalty have, in the past, been leveled against General George C. Marshall. I have been privileged for thirty-five years to know General Marshall personally. I know him, as a man and a soldier, to be dedicated with singular selflessness and the profoundest patriotism to the service of America. And this episode is a sobering lesson in the way freedom must *not* defend itself."

Did you ever discuss it with General Marshall?

"Oh, no. Oh, my, no. You didn't discuss things like that with General Marshall. He would have been very much embarrassed if you'd even try."

I understand there were a few controversies between you and General Eisenhower about the inauguration in 1953.

"Yes, there were. . . . Eisenhower's got a reputation —and I don't see how it happened—of being an easygoing fella, but he isn't. He is one of the most . . . difficult people I have ever encountered in my life. I'm told that when he was in the White House, he treated the staff worse than a bunch of enlisted men.

"But on this inaugural business. He wanted . . . he was going to treat the President the way MacArthur did at Wake Island, and I was still President until he was sworn in, and I wasn't going to stand for it.

"He wanted the President to pick him up, to come to the *Statler Hotel* to pick him up, and he hadn't even been inaugurated yet. A thing like that had never happened before in American history, and it indicated to me that not only didn't *he* know anything about American history, he didn't have anybody around him who did either. And as events developed in his administration, I guess that was about right.

"Why . . . the only time in history the President-elect hasn't come to the White House to pick up the new President was in 1801, when John Adams and Mrs. Adams left the White House before Jefferson was sworn in. And of course, Roosevelt didn't come in to escort Hoover out because he couldn't walk up the steps.

"But those were the only two times.

"Of course, you know what happened with Ike. He came to the White House to pick me up, but he wouldn't get out of the car. So I had to go out and get in. It was a

---

But Eisenhower never got specific. He never spoke those words. On the advice of unnamed Republicans in Wisconsin who persuaded him that they would be an *insult* to McCarthy, he deleted them. So much for his respect for freedom.

very shameful thing, and as you know, we didn't have much of a conversation on the way to the Capitol." *

Why do you think he was so rude?

"I think his conscience hurt him on the way he'd acted toward General Marshall. I'd let him know in no uncertain terms how I felt about it, and I think he was ashamed."

Maybe also he was nervous, realizing that he didn't know enough to be a good President.

"Maybe so, but I don't think he had the sense to know that he didn't know enough. The trouble with both of the

---

* In *Mr. Citizen*, which Mr. Truman wrote with the help of William Hillman and David M. Noyes, that ride is described as follows:

"The journey in the parade down Pennsylvania Avenue was quite restrained—as far as the occupants of the Presidential car were concerned. We began our trip in silence. Then the President-elect volunteered to inform me: 'I did not attend your Inauguration in 1948 out of consideration for you, because if I had been present I would have drawn attention away from you.'

"I was quick to reply: 'You were not here in 1948 because I did not send for you. But if I *had* sent for you, you would have come.'

"The rest of the journey continued in silence."

Also from *Mr. Citizen:*

"It was January 20, 1953, when it became my time to take part in the ceremonies of turning the office of the President over to Dwight D. Eisenhower. Washington, on that day, was cold and clear but not uncomfortable. The President-elect and I were sitting in the room of the sergeant-at-arms in the Capitol, waiting to go out through the Rotunda to the Inaugural platform.

"Suddenly General Eisenhower turned to me and said: 'I wonder who is responsible for my son John being ordered to Washington from Korea? I wonder who is trying to embarrass me?'

"I answered: 'The President of the United States ordered your son to attend your Inauguration. The President thought it was right and proper for your son to witness the swearing-in of his father to the Presidency. If you think somebody was trying to embarrass you by this order then the President assumes full responsibility.' "

candidates in 1952 and again with the same ones in 1956,
they just couldn't make up their minds about things. I
don't think the one who was on our ticket would have
been a good President, but at least he knew something
about the office. Ike didn't know anything, and all the
time he was in office he didn't learn a thing.

"I'll give you an example. In 1959, when Castro came
to power down in Cuba, Ike just sat on his ass and acted
like if he didn't notice what was going on down there,
why, maybe Castro would go away or something. Of
course what happened, the Russians didn't sit on their ass,
and they got him lined up on their side, which is what you
have to expect if you've got a goddamn fool in the White
House. He was probably waiting there for his Chief of
Staff to give him a report, and he'd initial it and put it in
his out basket. Because that's the way he operated.

"He came to see me. I invited him in not long after the
election, and he didn't want to come; I think he didn't
want to interrupt his golf game down in Florida or Georgia
or wherever it was, but he finally did come. And he looked
around a little, but I could see that nothing that was said
was getting through to him. He got there mad, and he
stayed mad. One of his troubles . . . he wasn't used to
being criticized, and he never did get it through his head
that that's what politics is all *about*. He was used to getting
his ass kissed.

"At one point he says to me, 'Who's your chief of staff?'
I held my temper. I said to him, 'The President of the
United States is his own chief of staff.' But he just could
not understand that. In all the years he was in the White
House he never did understand that the President has to
act. That's why the people of the United States elect you.
They don't elect you to sit around waiting for other people
to tell you what to do.

"Now when Castro came into power, if I'd been President, I'd have picked up the phone and called him direct
in Havana. I wouldn't have gone through protocol or anything like that. I'd have called him up, and I'd have said,

'Fidel, this is Harry Truman in Washington, and I'd like to have you come up here and have a little talk.'

"He'd have come, of course, and he'd have come to the White House, and I'd have said, 'Fidel, it looks to me like you've had a pretty good revolution down there, and it's been a long time coming. Now you're going to need help, and there's only two places you can go to get it. One's right here, and the other's—well, we both know where the other place is. Now you just tell me what you need, and I'll see to it that you get it.'

"Well, he'd have thanked me, and we'd have talked awhile, and then as he got up to go, I'd have said to him, 'Now, Fidel, I've told you what we'll do for you. There's one thing you can do for me. Would you get a shave and a haircut and take a bath?' "

Mr. Truman, whose sense of timing was as good or better than any stand-up comedian I've ever heard, waited for the expected laugh, and when it was over, he said, "Of course, that son of a bitch Eisenhower was too damn dumb to do anything like that. When Castro decided to go in the other direction for support, Eisenhower was probably still waiting for a goddamn *staff report* on what to think."

As you may have observed, Mr. Truman was often a profane, a mildly profane man to me anyway, but "staff report" were the two dirtiest words he uttered in all our talks together.

I said, *Mr. President, what happened after the inauguration in January, 1953?*

"We had lunch at Dean Acheson's house, and then we got on the train and came home, and that was all there was to it."

28

Five Weak Presidents

Mr. President, you were saying the other day that you had great faith in the future of the Republic, that we had five weak Presidents before the Civil War, and that, having survived them, you feel we can survive almost anything. Could you tell me about them?

"That was one of the very worst periods in our history, the twenty-some years before Lincoln was elected, before the Civil War. And if we hadn't had those weak Presidents, we might not have had a Civil War, although that's just a guess on my part.

"What I do know is that when you have weak Presidents, you get weak results.

"There's always a lot of talk about how we have to fear the man on horseback, have to be afraid of the . . . of a strong man, but so far, if I read my American history right, it isn't the strong men that have caused us most of the trouble, it's the ones who were weak. It's the ones who just sat on their asses and twiddled their thumbs when they were President.

"It started out . . . this whole period started out in 18 and 40 when the Whigs nominated William Henry Harrison, the old fella we talked about the other day. Harrison was another one of those who was great for getting his name in the headlines and treating the truth with considerable carelessness. He was of the same ilk as MacArthur in that regard, although not so much so.

"The campaign of 1840 was the first one in which the Madison Avenue people took over. Only, of course, it wasn't Madison Avenue; it was just that the campaign was run by people who didn't know or care what Harrison's policy was. And anyway he didn't have any policy. He wouldn't of known what a policy was if he'd seen one.

"They made a very big thing out of the Battle of Tippecanoe in Indiana, which had taken place almost thirty

375

years before. In 1811, I believe it was, and it wasn't much of a fight, just a few hundred soldiers under Harrison's command and some Shawnee Indians, and some historians seem to feel it ended more or . . . in what might be called a draw, although the Indians withdrew.

"But Harrison wrote back to the Secretary of War in Washington saying practically that he'd won one of the greatest battles against the Indians since the Pilgrims landed at Plymouth Rock.* And he said he'd defeated the great Shawnee Indian chief Tecumseh, which wasn't the case at all. Tecumseh wasn't even there at the time; it was his brother, an Indian by the name of . . . he was called the Prophet.

"Harrison got away with it, though, because there wasn't anybody around to check up on him. There's a lot wrong with the newspapers and the radio and television and all of that, and we've talked about it. But in

---

* In *The Patriot Chiefs* Alvin M. Josephy, Jr., writes of the Battle of Tippecanoe: "The number of Indian dead . . . was never known, though it was estimated to be between 25 and 40. Harrison lost 61 killed and 127 wounded, but on his return to the settlements he announced that he had won a great victory and wrote to the Secretary of War that 'the Indians have never sustained so severe a defeat since their acquaintance with the white people.' The importance of the battle was soon exaggerated beyond reality, and in the flush of excitement many of the western settlers began to think that Harrison had beaten Tecumseh himself. The facts of what had been little more than an .inconclusive swipe at a small segment of Tecumseh's followers never fully caught up with the legend of a dramatic triumph, and in 1840 the magic of Tippecanoe's memory still worked well enough to help elect Harrison to the Presidency."

I could find no sound evidence that Harrison himself claimed he had defeated Tecumseh, probably the greatest Indian chief in American history. Harrison's followers did make that claim, though, and General Harrison never denied it.

In 1813 in the Battle of the Thames River in Ontario Harrison's men actually did kill Tecumseh.

the long run, like Jefferson said, about newspapers, that is, we'd be worse off without them.*

"So as a result of Tippecanoe, Harrison got a somewhat inflated reputation as a general, and it kept him going for thirty years and finally got him into the White House, although not for long.

"The campaign slogan in 1840 was 'Tippecanoe and Tyler, Too.' I'll tell you about Tyler in a minute.

"And the people who were running the campaign claimed he'd been born in a log cabin, which was a damn lie. His family had . . . were very large landowners in Virginia, and his father, Benjamin Harrison, was one of the men who signed the Declaration of Independence.

"And Harrison himself had a big farm in Ohio, down near Cincinnati, I believe it was.

"But in the campaign that was never mentioned, and they sent out a log cabin on wheels around to various parts of the country. They also claimed he drank hard cider and wore a coonskin cap. It reminds me a little . . . and I wouldn't want this to get out . . . I wouldn't want to hurt anybody's feelings, but it reminds me of that fella from Tennessee that was aching to be President and went around getting his picture taken in a coonskin cap.†

---

* In a letter to Edward Carrington in 1787 Jefferson wrote: "The basis of our government being the opinion of the people, the very first object should be to keep that right; and were it left to me to decide whether we should have a government without newspapers, or newspapers without government, I should not hesitate a moment to prefer the latter. But I should mean that every man should receive those papers and be capable of reading them."

And in a letter to Elbridge Gerry in 1799 he wrote: "I am for . . . freedom of the press and against all violations of the Constitution to silence by force, and not by reason, the complaints or criticisms, just or unjust, of our citizens against the conduct of their agents."

† Estes Kefauver, a Senator from Tennessee, gained a national reputation in the early 1950's as chairman of a Senate committee investigating organized crime. He did a lot of cam-

"Of course the idea was that Harrison was a plain man of the people, while the fella that was President and he was a good, strong President, too, Martin Van Buren, they claimed he put perfume on his whiskers and ate on gold plates in the White House. That wasn't true either, but in that campaign, like at least one recent one that I could mention, the true facts didn't matter much.

"And, of course, Harrison won the election. He was sixty-eight years old, and on inauguration day he was showing off. It was raining cats and dogs, but he insisted on leading the inaugural parade back to the White House on horseback. He wouldn't wear a hat or coat or anything, and that was on March 4, 1841, and exactly one month later, on April 4, he was dead of pneumonia. So he . . . so I'm not counting him as one of the five. It's like he never had been President, and it's just as well. He wouldn't of had any notion at all of what to do.

"John Tyler, who succeeded him, was the first Vice President to become President, and he was the brother of my great-grandmother's father, and so he's kinfolk of mine in an indirect way. Margaret's got his nose. His picture's hanging in the family dining room, and I used to say, 'Margaret, look at your nose up there.'

"And she'd say, 'Turn that old man around; I don't want to see him.'

"Old Tyler. He was nominated for the Vice Presidency by the Whigs, although he was really more of a Democrat if he was anything. I never could figure out what he stood for, and I don't think the Whigs ever did either. I don't think they ever asked him. All they were interested in was getting Harrison in the White House. It just never seems to have crossed their minds that he'd catch pneumonia by acting like a damn fool—and die.

"Of course Tyler had been in the Virginia legislature

paigning for the Presidency posing as a kind of frontiersman in a coonskin cap. He was nominated for the Vice Presidency by the Democrats in 1956 but was defeated in the Eisenhower landslide, along with Adlai Stevenson.

and in Congress, and he was governor of Virginia and then was in the Senate. And he resigned from the Senate because the Virginia legislature wanted him to expunge a censure of Andrew Jackson from the Senate record. He wouldn't do it, and so you can't say he was . . . that he didn't have principles, but that's about all you can say for his record. In none of those jobs did he leave a record so that you could figure out what he stood for.

"And in the White House about the best thing you can say for him is that he was a stubborn cuss. The Whigs wanted him to let Daniel Webster, who was Secretary of State, and Henry Clay, who thought he ought to have got the Whig nomination in 1840 and been President . . . let those two run things. Tyler said, no; he said he wasn't about to be an acting President, and eventually he won out, and Webster resigned.

"But when that had been accomplished, Tyler couldn't seem to figure what to do next, and in the meantime the War Between the States was getting close to being inevitable, and Tyler and the ones that followed him just watched it happen. They were all one-term Presidents, and not one of them was able to fill the office they held."

I was reading about them last night, and as nearly as I can make out, they seemed to feel that if they just kept quiet and didn't rock the boat, the differences between the slave states and the free states and the opponents of slavery and the proponents would just disappear.

"That's right, and that's the one thing that won't ever happen, not in a million years. That's the *meaning* of government. If you're in it, you've got to govern. Otherwise, you're in the wrong business.

"Now Tyler, about the only thing he's gone down in history for, his wife died while he was President. He was in his fifties, and he married a rich young girl in her twenties. It was quite a scandal at the time.

"And so after those . . . after his years in the White House, he went back to Virginia, and he finally tried to call a last-minute peace conference of those other weaklings that had been in the White House. That was in February, 1861, but, of course, it was too late, and nothing ever came of it.

"Tyler finally turned up in the Confederate Congress, and that was the end of him."

Mr. President, it seems to me in the Memoirs *you spoke rather more favorably of Tyler.*

"Did I? I don't remember. . . . Well, if I did, I must have learned something since."

After Tyler came Polk.

"Yes. And Polk [James K.] was nominated by the Democrats in Baltimore in 1844. He was a real dark horse, and he was only nominated at all because the delegates to the Democratic convention in Baltimore in 1844 were deadlocked, and the Southerners didn't want Van Buren.

"Of course during Polk's administration we fought and won the Mexican War, which gave us more . . . a larger area of new territory than at any time except for the Louisiana Purchase. Polk had a good deal of trouble with his Cabinet, though; he just couldn't seem to keep it in line, and Mrs. Polk . . . she wouldn't allow any dancing or cardplaying in the White House, and they say there were times when she got it into her head that she herself was President. She was a very strong-minded woman.

"Polk . . . after his term in office he went back to Nashville, and he died within a month or so after leaving the White House.*

"The next man . . . we talked about him the other day was 'Ole Rough 'n' Ready,' old Zack Taylor, the hero of Buena Vista, and he was another of those damn fool generals that didn't know anything about politics, nothing at all in any way, shape, or form, and so Daniel Webster, who was Secretary of State, and Henry Clay ran things, and after sixteen months in office, on July 4, 1850,

---

* Polk lived a little less than fifteen weeks after leaving the White House and was buried in the dooryard of his home in Nashville; his wife outlived him by forty-six years.

he went to an Independence Day celebration, and they say he ate too much watermelon and died.

"And the fella that took his place, the Vice President, was Millard Fillmore, who had started at the very bottom and worked his way up, and I think I told you, his son was ashamed of his father's origins, and after the old man's death, his son burned all his papers.

"Not that I mean to indicate that Fillmore was much of a President. He forgot all about his origins. He'd been born in a log cabin someplace in New York State and was apprenticed to a wool carder. He married a schoolteacher and started working his way up, but at the same time he started toadying to the rich, which he continued to do all the rest of his life, including when he was President. As a result, he was never any kind of leader. He did just what he was told, and what he was told was not to do anything to offend anybody. Which, of course, meant that he ended up by offending everybody.

"But he was just a no-good; he took to having his bath water perfumed, and he surrounded himself with every kind of luxury you could think of.

"As President he was . . . well, I'll tell you, at a time when we needed a strong man, what we got was a man that swayed with the slightest breeze. About all he ever accomplished as President, he sent Commodore Perry to open up Japan to the West, but that didn't help much as far as preventing the Civil War was concerned.

"And, of course, he was followed . . . Fillmore was followed to the White House by Franklin Pierce, finest-looking man who I guess ever was President. He's got the best picture in the White House, Franklin Pierce, but being President involves a little bit more than just winning a beauty contest, and he was another one that was a complete fizzle. He signed the bill that repealed the Missouri Compromise, and that did it. That started the Civil War. There just wasn't any holding it back after that because that's when the two-state war we were talking about began, the border raids on both sides of the border that separated Kansas and Missouri.

"Pierce was a friend of the fella that wrote *The Scarlet Letter,* Nathaniel Hawthorne, and when he was elected President, Hawthorne said to him, 'Frank, I pity you from the bottom of my heart,' and that's just about right. That's about what he should of done, felt sorry for him because Pierce didn't know what was going on, and even if he had, he wouldn't of known what to do about it.

"The last of them, of course, the last of these weak Presidents that brought on the Civil War, that at the very least allowed it to happen, was James A. Buchanan, and he was just like the fella that followed me into the White House. He couldn't make a decision to save his soul in hell.

"He was an old bachelor, and the only reason he got the nomination was that he'd been out of the country; he'd been the American ambassador to England, ole Pierce had sent him over, and as a result, Buchanan hadn't made any enemies to speak of on the slavery question.

"Another reason he got the nomination, he was from Pennsylvania, and in those days the Pennsylvania election was held in October. They figured if he could carry Pennsylvania in October, he could carry the whole country in the November election, and he did both.*

"When he was inaugurated, he was sixty-five years old, and he was another one of those fellas, he'd been trying to *be* President for twenty years, but when he got it, he didn't have the first idea what to do. By the time his four years was over he was in disgrace just about everywhere, and he died a very unhappy old man.

"But there you are, five men, Tyler, Polk, Fillmore, Pierce, and Buchanan, not counting Harrison and Taylor, and the five of them coming one right after the other made the Civil War inevitable. Not that I'm saying it might not have happened if we'd had strong men in office, but there's a chance that it wouldn't.

* In accepting the nomination, Buchanan said that he was really too old to enjoy it, that ". . . all the friends I loved and wanted to reward are dead and all the enemies I hated and had marked for punishment are turned my friends."

"They were no damn good at all, but they were all honorable men. It's a most interesting study to find out that the Presidents of the United States have all up to now been honorable men, whether you like them or agree with them or not. Not a corrupt man among them."

How can we have been so lucky? Or is it luck?

"No. Luck had nothing to do with it. It's due to the fact that we've got the best Constitution in the history of the world, and one of these days I'm going to read it to you and explain how these men who met in Philadelphia in 1787 made it great."

What Ruins a Man

We were sitting in Mr. Truman's office at the library during one of the interminable waits for film to be changed in a camera. It was after lunch, and I believe he had had a "libation" or two. His eyes were a little brighter than usual, his complexion a little pinker.

In any case, without warning, he said, "Do you want to know what I think causes the ruination of a lot of men?"

I said that I most certainly did. The question is one that has occurred to me now and again.

"Well," Mr. Truman said, "I've made a great, long study of these things, as you can see up there if you've looked."

He pointed to the bookshelves, which, as I've said, mostly contained biographies and histories.

"Three things ruin a man if you want to know what I believe. One's power, one's money, and one's women.

"If a man can accept a situation in a place of power with the thought that it's only temporary, he comes out all right. But when he thinks that he is the *cause* of the power, that can be his ruination.

"And when a man has too much money too soon, that has the same effect on him. He just never gets to understanding that getting enough money to eat and getting a roof over his head is the thing that throughout history most people have spent their lives trying to do and haven't succeeded. . . . If you've got too much money too soon, it ruins you by setting you too far apart from most of the human race.

"And a man who is not loyal to his family, to his wife and his mother and his sisters can be ruined if he has a complex in that direction. If he has the right woman as a partner, he never has any trouble. But if he has the wrong one or if he's mixed up with a bunch of whores, why, then he's in a hell of a fix. And I can name them to you, the ones that got mixed up in that way. But we won't do it now.

"Those three things, though, in my opinion, power, money, and women in that order, are what most often contribute to the ruination of a man. You read your history and you'll find out."

Like a great many of Mr. Truman's maxims, it is easy to dismiss these particular observations as hopelessly corny, especially the part about women. I think it can be safely said that Mr. Truman never got mixed up with a bunch of whores, not even when he was in France during the First World War. So far as I can make out, his only erotic experience Over There was in Paris, France, where he went to the Folies Bergères, which he found, and I quote, disgusting. I hesitate even to think how he would have reacted to the carryings-on of Miss Linda Lovelace in *Deep Throat.*

No, I think his knowledge of women was limited to his mother, his sister, Bess Truman, and Margaret. He was so painfully shy with all other women that he seemed to pretend they simply didn't exist. In our first meetings one of our party was a woman who fancied herself, I guess, a director, and Mr. Truman never once looked at her or addressed himself to her. In conversations with me he referred to her as "that other one." He would say, "I hope that other one isn't coming today."

Fortunately, she didn't last long. Not only did she make Mr. Truman nervous, she was a total incompetent. Like so many others in the project, she drifted off after putting together an hour of film that was totally incomprehensible.

Jane Wetherell, whom I have elsewhere described as "a girl who dresses in clothes you'll see in next month's *Vogue,*" was coordinator of the television project, and if Mr. Truman absolutely had to address her it was as "young fella."

Ms. Wetherell is now the wife of Robert Alan Aurthur, and he described two occasions when she had to deliver material to Mr. Truman's suite at the Carlyle: ". . . he opened his door a crack, peered suspiciously at her for a moment before admitting her into the sitting room, and then very deliberately left the door wide open for as long as she was there. Both times, Jane reported, after Mr. Truman had nervously hustled her out, she heard safety bolts snapping closed behind her. A fella from Missouri never knows what kind of badger games New Yorkers will pull next."

So Mr. Truman didn't know much about women, but then during his tenure in office, Women's Lib was as outlandish as a suggestion that man might someday land on the moon. But what Mr. Truman has to say about power, its causes and effects, is both shrewd and sophisticated, and *that* was something he had to know about to be able to govern.

Mr. Truman never made the mistake of thinking that he was the *cause* of power.

The last time I was in Independence, in the fall of 1969, I talked as I had many times before to Miss Sue Gentry, who, as I've said, had been writing about Independence and the Trumans since 1929 for the Independence *Examiner*.

I said that the President must have been very upset a few months earlier when [in March 1969] Richard Nixon stopped off in Independence with Mr. Truman's old White House piano as a gift for the Truman Library.

Mr. Truman, then eighty-four, went to the library for the first time in several years, and he and Richard Nixon shook hands. The whole of the journey and the ceremony that followed must have been an effort, not only physically but mentally as well. But if an incumbent President of the United States was so crass and unfeeling as to carry out such hypocrisy, what was an old man who was an ex-President of the United States to do except go through the motions with a man he despised?

And then, to add to the insult and injury, Mr. Nixon sat down at the piano and played "The Missouri Waltz." Neither he nor anyone on his staff had apparently taken the trouble to find out that Mr. Truman hated that particular piece of music.*

Miss Gentry said, yes, it must have been a trying time for the President, but she added that Mr. Truman had been very hard of hearing in recent years and that when Nixon finished playing, Harry Truman turned to Bess and in a loud stage whisper asked, "What was that?"

It becomes increasingly difficult to know when to laugh and when to cry.

---

* In a television interview in 1962, when we still had some hope for the series, David Susskind interviewed Mr. Truman on *Open End,* and David said to him, " 'Missouri Waltz' isn't really your favorite song, is it?"

Mr. Truman said, " 'Missouri Waltz' was composed in 1911 or 12 or maybe as late as 1914 by a man from Iowa. And it was called 'Hushabye, My Baby.' And the Foster Music Company in New York bought it, changed the name of it, called it 'The Missouri Waltz,' and didn't take the words of it. You ought to read the words, and then you'd see why it's kind of obnoxious as a state song."

Susskind, "It's not your favorite number?"

Mr. Truman, "No, no. My favorite number is Chopin's A-Flat Opus 42 Waltz."

Of Painting and B. Berenson

It is easy to dismiss Harry Truman's taste for painting, nothing surprising about it. He was fond of Rembrandt's "Descent from the Cross." His favorite painters were Frans Hals, Rubens, Leonardo da Vinci, and Holbein. He liked Gilbert Stuart's portrait of George Washington. He thought as little of modern painting as he did of modern architecture. He was quoted as saying, "I love beautiful pictures, landscapes and portraits that look like people. We see enough of squalor. I think art is intended to uplift the ideals of the people, not pull them down."

Strictly George Babbitt, depressingly predictable, and yet . . . and yet. I had read that when Harry Truman and Bess were in Europe in 1956 they went to see Bernard Berenson, that awesome and feisty old man, who was then ninety-one. Incredible. Harry Truman at I Tatti? You have to be kidding.

One day I asked Mr. Truman about the visit, and he said, "Oh, yes, when we were in Europe, we just had to look him up. He was the best in his line, and if I've learned one thing in life, it's that you have to pay attention to what the experts say. You don't have to agree, but you have to listen.

"Old Berenson was one of the nicest fellows I've ever met, and he took us all over the house and explained to us what to look for in a painting. And when we got to those museums in Florence and elsewhere, we knew a little about it.

"When I found out that the Boss and I were going to be able to see him, I took the trouble to read up on him. If it's possible, I always do that before I meet somebody. The more you know about a person, the better you can judge him. Of course, you can't *always* depend on what you read. In the end, you have to make up your mind. You have to depend on your eyes and ears and your good sense, and nine times out of ten you're right. Especially if you give the other fellow the benefit of every doubt, and I've always done that, always *tried* to anyway. . . . But Berenson. He was really a remarkable fellow, and I wish I'd got to know him better.

". . . Of course I already knew a *little* something about painting. When I was a young fellow, I used to go to a museum in Kansas City, and they always had a pretty fair collection. . . . I never told anybody about it, my going there I mean. In those days that was not the kind of thing you talked about, not around here anyway."

I asked the President if during the years he was in Washington he had spent much time in the National Gallery.

He said, "When I was in the Senate, I used to go there pretty often, but after I got into that other job, I just . . . never could. In *that* damn job I couldn't even go to the bank to cash a check without a crowd following me around. Asking for autographs. And it's just like I told you. Those folks who want autographs. They're just like a bunch of pups. Once one of them pisses on a fire hydrant then they've all got to do it."

In 1963 Bernard Berenson's *Sunset and Twilight* was published, selections from his diaries for the years 1947–58. By that time he had been putting down what he thought of people for more than seventy years, and he was not easy to please. Earlier in his life he had complained that Bertrand Russell and George Santayana never really *listened;* André Gide, he felt, was too solemn and quite unwilling "to recognize me as an equal." Henry Adams was only interested in sounding off about imbecility—"his own and the world's, in that order."

And only ten days before the Trumans came to I Tatti, he had taken Mary McCarthy "to Gricigliano, back by the Sieci and along the Arno. Tuscany at its most enchanting moment, a wonder and a joy for my eye. But Mary scarcely opened her eyes to all this beauty."

But on May 28, 1956, Bernard Berenson wrote:

Harry Truman and his wife lunched yesterday. Came at one and stayed til three. Both as natural, as unspoiled by high office as if he had gone no further than alderman of Independence, Missouri. In my long life I have never met an individual with whom I felt so instantly at home. He talked as if he had always known me, openly, easily, with no reserve (so far as I could judge). Ready to touch on any subject, no matter how personal. I always felt what a solid and sensible basis there is in the British stock of the U.S.A. if it can produce a man like Truman. Now I feel more assured about America than in a long time. If the Truman miracle can still occur, we need not fear even the McCarthys. Truman captivated even Willy Mostyn-Owen, aged twenty-seven, ultracritical, and like all Englishmen of today hard of hearing anything good about Americans, and disposed to be condescending to them—at best.

On Evangelists

"It used to be you couldn't go downtown in the evening without running into a half dozen evangelists ranting and raving and carrying on; some of them put on their shows in tents or at camp meetings, and some of them just stood around on street corners and worked up a crowd. They'd stir people up for a while, but they always got over it.

"But now we've just got this one evangelist, this Billy Graham, and he's gone off the beam. He's . . . well, I hadn't ought to say this, but he's one of those counterfeits I was telling you about. He claims he's a friend of all the Presidents, but he was never a friend of mine when I was President. I just don't go for people like that. All he's interested in is getting his name in the paper."

32

An Attempted Assassination

On November 1, 1950, while President Truman was taking a nap at Blair House, the Presidential residence while the White House was being renovated, two Puerto Rican nationalists tried to break in to assassinate him. In three minutes thirty-two shots were fired, and one White House policeman was killed, as well as one of the Puerto Ricans.

I asked *Mary Jane Truman* about her memory of that day, and she said, "At the time . . . the day they attempted to assassinate my brother, I was the Grand Matron of the state in the Order of the Eastern Star, and I had two chapters to constitute down in what we call the boot heel of Missouri.

"And we had been driving that day down from Springfield, down into the boot, and we didn't have a radio in the car. So when we arrived there . . . the telephone rang just as I got there, asking for me. It was a call from St. Louis, and it was the FBI calling, but when they told me it was the FBI, I was sure they were mistaken. I was sure it was the Secret Service, and I was . . . you might say I was somewhat apprehensive, and when I got to the phone and they informed me that they . . . that an attempt had been made to assassinate Harry . . . they said it just like that, and, well, I was . . . I'm afraid I just kind of went to pieces. I was sure he had been hurt, but then they told me that he hadn't been, but they insisted on sending several guards . . . several guards were put on the place where I was. They thought . . . they seemed to think that other members of the family might be in danger, but I just pulled myself together, and I went ahead and constituted the chapter that night. And the next night we constituted another one in a little town about twenty miles from Pottersville and then went on into St. Louis from there."

Weren't you nervous?

"Oh, yes, I was nervous, but I went ahead and did what I . . . what had been set up for me to do. It certainly wouldn't have done my brother Harry or anyone else any good to worry about something that hadn't happened, and I knew that he felt very strongly about not losing sleep over that *kind* of thing.

"When they saw the guards, some of the others were much more upset than I was."

In speaking of the assassination attempt Mr. Truman told Admiral Leahy, "The only thing you have to worry about is bad luck. I never had bad luck."

I asked Mr. Truman about that remark and the assassination attempt, and he said—this was almost two years before John F. Kennedy was assassinated—"Well, I'll tell you. Getting shot at was nothing I worried about when I was President. It wouldn't have done the slightest good if I had. My opinion has always been that if you're in an office like that and someone wants to shoot you, they'll probably do it, and nothing much can help you out. It just goes with the job, and I don't think there's any way to prevent it." *

What did you do afterward . . . after the attempt?

"Why, I went and got dressed, and I went ahead and went out to Arlington Cemetery and made a speech dedicating a statue out there, and then I proceeded with the rest of my schedule. If you are President of the United States, you can't interrupt your schedule every time you feel like it. The people who put you there have a right to expect that you will carry through with the job."

Going ahead and doing your job seem to be characteristic of Trumans.

About luck Mr. Truman said, "You asked about being

* When Mr. Truman lectured at Columbia, he was asked his opinion of capital punishment, and he said, "Why, I've never really believed in capital punishment. I commuted the sentence of the fellow who was trying to shoot me to life imprisonment. That's the best example I can give you."

lucky, and I'd say, yes, I have been. To have gone as far as I did—a lot of it has to be luck.

"I told you. Around here I was never considered anything special. They never kept any records on me because they didn't think I'd amount to much.

"Around here they're like—a lot of people are like that old fella in New Salem, I forget his name, but he'd been a friend of Lincoln's, and after Lincoln was assassinated, they asked this old man what he remembered about him, and he said, 'Well, I had no idea he was going to be President, so I didn't take as much notice of him as I might have.' "

Mr. President, you may have been lucky, but you never . . . there's no point in your life when you seem to have trusted to luck.

"No, no. I was always out there pushing."

33

The Dean Resigns

I read only this afternoon that yet another book by a revisionist historian has been published, saying that Dean Acheson was a bloodthirsty cold warrior, and maybe that's true. The dean certainly believed in Russian containment and both as Undersecretary, and as Secretary of State he was an advocate of a hard-line policy against the Soviet Union.

Moreover, as you have seen, except for Harry Truman himself, no man was more responsible for the United Nations "police action" in Korea. So if, as the revisionists insist, guilt must be assigned, I guess Harry Truman and Dean Acheson were as guilty as anybody for the fix we're in, and any day now sainthood will be conferred on the late, beloved Joe Stalin, who was Christ-like by comparison.

Speaking of revisionists, Bob Aurthur has written: "It has been said that Mr. Truman reversed the Roosevelt philosophy of tolerant accommodation toward the Communist world, setting us a hard-line, anti-Communist, counterrevolutionary course, resulting in hot and cold wars, a trillion dollars spent on armaments, and a reversal of priorities that has virtually plundered and wrecked our planet. Yes, this charge can be made, if not proven, and in all of it Mr. Acheson concurred."

Yes, the revisionists may be right, although it seems to me far too early to tell, and I am always suspicious of those who would rewrite history to fit their convictions of the moment.

After reading Charles Beard's *An Economic Interpretation of the Constitution,* which takes a dim and narrowly Marxist view of the Founding Fathers and what they did in Philadelphia that hot summer in 1787, Justice Oliver Wendell Holmes wrote to his friend, the English jurist, Sir

Frederick Pollock, "You and I believe that high-minded-ness is not impossible in a man."

Mr. Acheson, a friend and great admirer of Justice Holmes, was a high-minded man.

The dean was always controversial, of course. When he was in office, he was, as I have observed elsewhere, probably more hated than any Secretary of State in our history. Of course, then his detractors were of the right. They found him not too hard but too soft on Communism and the Communists, both the domestic and the international variety. If, in fact, he was not a Communist himself.

In his own account of his years as Secretary and before, *Present at the Creation*, Mr. Acheson reports on a meeting sponsored by the National Council of Soviet-American Friendship to which he had been assigned to speak in place of James F. Byrnes, then Secretary of State.

The tone of the meeting was best indicated by the fact that the keynote speaker was the Very Reverend Hewlett Johnson, the "Red" Dean of Canterbury Cathedral. The meeting was in Madison Square Garden, and Johnson received "a tumultuous ovation as he sashayed around the ring like a skater in the long black coat and gaiters of an English prelate, his hands clasped above his head in a prize fighter's salute."

Johnson's speech "became an antiphony, the Dean shouting the rhetorical questions, the crowd roaring back the responses. After an ovation, as much for themselves as the speaker, or for him as one of themselves, my hour had come," Mr. Acheson writes.

I felt like a bartender announcing that the last drink before closing time would be cambric tea. Fortunately mine was a short speech, but between me and the end of it was a paragraph of my own devising—one of the few. It followed an acknowledgment of the Soviet Union's reasonableness in desiring friendly governments along her borders. Then this: "But it seems equally clear to us that the interest in security must take into account and respect other basic interests of nations and men, such as the interest of other peoples to choose the general surrounding of their own lives and of all men to be secure in their persons. We believe that that adjustment of interests should take place short of the point where persuasion and firmness become coercion, where a knock on the door at night strikes terror into men and women."

I hurried on, trying to outrun the pursuing boos and catcalls, tossing to those wolves a quotation from Molotov and one from Stalin. But I had shown my colors; those who took their red straight, without a chaser of white and blue, were not mollified. When I finished, protest drowned out even polite applause. At the end of the ramp, a policeman touched me on the arm. "Come," he said. "I can show you a quiet way to your car." Nothing could have been more welcome, except possibly, the quiet scotch waiting for me at the friend's house where I was staying.

Some years later, during what has come to be known as the "McCarthy period," my presence at the Madison Square meeting was adduced as evidence of sympathy for communism. This seemed to me to add a companion thought to Lincoln's conclusion of the impossibility of fooling all the people all the time, the difficulty of pleasing any of the people any of the time.

Mr. Acheson seemed to infuriate people without half trying, and while his friends insisted that he was serious, he was irritatingly unsolemn, and as we all know, a solemn man is a man who can be trusted.

As Undersecretary he was asked how it had happened that Soviet Ambassador Nikolai Novikov had been held incommunicado at LaGuardia Airport for refusing to sign a customs declaration which, as a diplomat, he did not have to sign. Mr. Acheson replied, "I will have to give you the celebrated answer of Dr. Johnson—'Ignorance, madam, pure ignorance.' He was likely to begin an address at a solemn meeting of State Department officials from this and other countries by saying, "All I know I learned at my mother's knee—and other low joints."

Once when helping with the manifesto for a United Nations program to help feed postwar Europe, he suggested that a phrase be changed from "expectant mothers" to "pregnant women."

He told the delegates, "A maiden aunt of fifty-one once told me that she was an expectant mother. What you mean here is 'pregnant women.'"

As I have said, scarcely a week went by when Senator Joseph McCarthy did not demand his resignation, and a great many less hysterical members of both houses of Congress broke into a rash at the mere mention of his name. Senator Hugh Butler, one of the Neanderthal men that Nebraska with depressing regularity seems to send to Congress, once said, "I watch his smart-aleck manner and his British clothes and that New Dealism, everlasting New Dealism in everything he says and does, and I want to shout, 'Get out, get out. You stand for everything that has been wrong with the United States for years.'"

Once at a press conference when such attacks were at their most hysterical he was asked how they affected him, and he said that he was reminded of the man found on the Western plains during the days of Indian fighting. He was brought to a fort hospital and in examination found to be scalped and, among numerous other injuries, to have an arrow sticking in his back.

As the doctor prepared to take out the arrow, he asked, "Does it hurt very much?"

"Only when I laugh," said the man.

I'm inclined to think that the historian Douglas Southall Freeman best summed up the dean's lack of easy popularity. Mr. Freeman wrote, "Acheson found it difficult to conceal his contempt for the contemptible."

When I met Mr. Acheson, it was easy to see why he unnerved a great many people. He was tall, broad-shouldered, carried himself like a British cavalry officer, wore a precisely trimmed mustache that still bore some traces of red, and had deep-blue eyes that I at first thought were cold, possibly even cruel. I later changed my mind about that. His eyes were amused more often than not, and they were extraordinarily warm when he was discussing his association with Harry S. Truman or George Catlett Marshall.

Dean Acheson's father had been the Episcopal Bishop of Connecticut, and his mother was the heiress of a wealthy Canadian distilling family. He had gone to Groton, to Yale, and to Harvard Law School, where he was graduated near the head of his class.

In confronting the dean it always gave me some slight comfort to remember that a friend at Yale and his roommate at Harvard was a witty young man from Indiana who never quite made it in the law, Cole Porter.*

One of Acheson's professors at Harvard, Felix Frankfurter, recommended him as a clerk to Louis D. Brandeis, Associate Justice of the U.S. Supreme Court, and he spent two years in that capacity, soaking up a good deal of Brandeis' libertarian philosophy as well as the liberalism of Brandeis' close friend and associate Justice Oliver Wendell Holmes.

Acheson was fond of quoting Holmes' advice on the way to achievement: "If you want to hit a bird on the wing, you must have all your will in a focus. You must not be thinking about yourself, and, equally, you must not be thinking about your neighbor; you must be living with your eye on that bird. Every achievement is a bird on the wing."

And that, he once told me, was what Harry Truman and George Catlett Marshall had in common. They lived with

---

* More accurately they were housemates. In: *The Life That Late He Led: A Biography of Cole Porter* George Eells writes of that time: "In various ways, all during his sojourn at Harvard, Cole persisted in trying to turn it into a little patch of Yale. The fall of 1915, he joined a number of Scroll and Key men from New Haven, including Dean Acheson and T. Lawrason Riggs, in renting a house at 1 Mercer Circle. To care for the place, they hired a man who cleaned, prepared one meal daily, and served tea for them and their guests every afternoon at four."

their eyes on the task at hand. He would not, Mr. Acheson said, place himself in that category; that would be presumptuous.

Most of those who knew him well would have so placed him, though, including Harry Truman. I asked Mr. Truman why it was that he, a man suspicious of Eastern intellectuals and in particular those with what he contemptuously called Ha-vud accents, had got along so well with such a one as Dean Acheson.

Mr. Truman said, "Because I knew . . . I sensed immediately that he was a man I could count on in every way. I knew that he would do what had to be done, and I knew that I could count on him to tell me the truth at all times.

"I've said this before, but when you get to be in a position of authority, which I was at that time, that's the most important thing there is. You've got to be able to count on a man's word, and if you can't, forget it. . . . I've had experience with the other kind as well, and that's the *worst* thing there is. A liar in public life is a lot more dangerous than a full, paid-up Communist, and I don't care who he is."

An odd combination those two, the plainspoken man who was a dropout after two years of night classes at the Kansas City Law School and the austere Grotty and honors graduate of Harvard Law. Mr. Acheson has written: "In the last analysis Mr. Truman's methods reflected the basic integrity of his own character. He could have said of them what Mr. Lincoln said of his: 'I desire to so conduct the affairs of this administration that if, at the end . . . I have lost every friend on earth, I shall have one friend left, and that friend shall be down inside me.'"

There is a kind of rueful satisfaction in writing those words, as I am, on the final day of John Mitchell's testimony before the Watergate Committee.

It is impossible to imagine Mr. Truman and Mr. Acheson telling less than the truth to each other.

At first Mr. Acheson refused to have anything at all to

do with the television project. He was furious when he heard that David Susskind's company was in charge of the project. Not long before David, the eternal Candide, had conducted a haphazard television interview with Nikita Khrushchev during which Nikita proved, among other things, that he was a very smart cookie. David proved that he was more than somewhat naïve where international affairs were concerned.

But, otherwise, their hardly historic exchanges seemed to me innocent enough. Not to Mr. Acheson. His eyes glowering, his mustache bristling, the dean said, "Susskind almost started the third world war with that *insane* interview. I decline to be associated with him in any way."

Bob Aurthur explained that David was not directly involved in the project, and I nodded vigorously. No matter. We were, as Bob later wrote, "sent, if not flung, out into the snow."

But two days later, after a telephone call from Mr. Truman in Independence to Mr. Acheson in his Dickensian law offices in Washington—I always felt like Pip the first time he went to Mr. Jaggers' offices in London, fresh from the country—the dean agreed to cooperate with us. After that I spent, sometimes with Bob, more often alone, several afternoons with him, mostly talking about Korea and about Mr. Truman.

I didn't tape any of those conversations; if you want the truth, I was afraid to ask for permission. But immediately after each session I hurried back to the Statler and typed up all of Mr. Acheson's stately sentences; they are not easily forgotten.

I should add that while I always apologized for taking too much of the dean's time, despite the fact that he was a highly successful lawyer, as well as a very visible social figure in Washington, he always urged me to stay just a little bit longer, and I always did. I had the feeling, very likely wrong, that he was lonely, not so much lonely for other people as lonely for the power he once had, lonely for the days when, for good or ill, he and his friend Harry had the fate of what in those days was called "the free world" in their hands, almost alone in their hands.

One thing for sure. He loved talking about those days, and I don't think that there was a single doubt in his mind that what he and Harry had done was right, that, indeed, it had saved the world, all of it, not just the free part, from total disintegration. The regrets were, as he says in *Present at the Creation,* only those of Holmes who on his fifty-ninth birthday spoke at a meeting of the Massachusetts bar, summing up his years on the supreme judicial court of that state:

"I ask myself what is there to show for this half life-time that has passed? I look into my book in which I keep a docket of the decisions of the full court which fall to me to write, and find about a thousand cases, a thousand cases, many of them upon trifling or transitory matters, to represent nearly half a lifetime. . . .

"Alas, gentlemen, that is life. . . . We cannot live our dreams. We are lucky enough if we can give a sample of our best, and if in our hearts we can feel that it has been nobly done."

To which Mr. Acheson adds:

Of the years covered in this book the first five were for me preparation for the last seven. Those seven, the period of Mr. Truman's Presidency and of the immediate postwar years, saw the entry of our nation, already one of the superpowers, into the near chaos of a war-torn and disintegrating world society. To the responsibilities and needs of that time the nation summoned an imaginative effort unique in history and even greater than that made in the preceding period of fighting. All who served in those years had an opportunity to give more than a sample of their best. Yet an account of the experience, despite its successes, inevitably leaves a sense of disappointment and frustration, for the achievement fell short of both hope and need. How often that which seemed almost within grasp slipped away. Alas, that is life. We cannot live our dreams.

I do not know if, before Mr. Truman's death, Mr.
Acheson was aware of the revisionists or, if he was, what
he thought of their conclusions.

I am sure, though, that he would have deplored their
prose. Without exception they write as if English was a
second language that they will never quite master.

Of course, the fact that they are ponderous may account
for their popularity.

One afternoon I told Mr. Acheson that I might someday
write a book about Harry Truman, and I paraphrased
Jonathan Daniels' comment that so far as Mr. Truman was
concerned, "never has so little been rewritten by so many."

Mr. Acheson said, "I have never understood why the
press did such an *abysmally* poor job in writing about the
President. . . . *That's* something you should consider in
your book. It's as if the correspondents had made up their
minds when Mr. Truman became President that he was a
country bumpkin, and I am afraid a great many of them
never changed their minds.

"I have read over and over again that he was an *ordinary*
man. Whatever that means . . . I consider him one of
the most extraordinary human beings who ever lived.

"The difference between the public image of him and
the private man that I knew was vast, greater than for any
public figure I have ever known."

Mr. Acheson had for a short time in 1933 been Undersecretary of the Treasury in Franklin Roosevelt's administration, but he had resigned over a disagreement over the
devaluation of the dollar. Roosevelt was furious with him,
although seven years later, in February, 1941, after a
lengthy courtship on Roosevelt's part, Acheson returned
to the fold as Assistant Secretary of State.*

* Mr. Acheson has written that his feeling toward Roosevelt
was one of "admiration without affection."
In his book *Morning and Noon* he adds: "The impression
given me by President Roosevelt carried much of this attitude

I said, *Mr. Secretary, was there a greater difference between Mr. Truman's public image and his private self,
greater than the public and the private Franklin Roosevelt?*

"Indeed yes. So far as I could ever discover, there was
really very little difference between Roosevelt the public
figure and Roosevelt the private man. Roosevelt was all
surface. If there were hidden depths in him, I never discovered them, although I suppose it could with justice be
said that I did not spend too much time searching for
them.

"Roosevelt had great *charm* [Mr. Acheson made the
word an epithet], but I have never thought highly of charm
in a man; for that matter, I have never thought particularly well of charm in a woman.

"I have never been an admirer of the work of Sir James
M. Barrie, and I believe him to have been wrong in what

_____

of European—not British—royalty. The latter is comfortable,
respectable, dignified, and bourgeois. The President could relax over his poker parties and enjoy Tom Corcoran's accordion, he could and did call everyone from his valet to the
Secretary of State by his first name and often made up
Damon Runyon nicknames for them, too—'Tommy, the
Cork,' 'Henry, the Morgue,' and similar names; he could
charm an individual or a nation. But he condescended. Many
reveled in apparent admission to an inner circle. I did not;
and General Marshall did not, the general for more worthy
reasons than I. He objected, as he said, because it gave a false
impression of his intimacy with the President. To me it was
patronizing and humiliating. To accord the President the
greatest deference and respect should be a gratification to any
citizen. It is not gratifying to receive the easy greeting which
milord might give a promising stable boy and pull one's fore-
lock in return.

"This, of course, was a small part of the man and the impression he made. The essence of that was force. He exuded a
relish of power and command. His responses seemed too
quick; his reasons too facile for considered judgment; one
could not tell what lay beneath them. He remained a formidable man, a leader who won admiration and respect. In others
he inspired far more, affection and devotion. For me, that was
reserved for a man of whom at that time I had never heard,
his successor."

he wrote about charm.* As he was in so much else that
he wrote.

I said—this is known as White House dropping—*I had*
substitute for intelligence in persons of both sexes. Thus,
I have always been and will remain wary of it."

I said—this is knowin as White House dropping—*I had
dinner at the White House twice while Mr. Roosevelt was
President, and it seemed to me that he was incapable of
listening. Perhaps that's unfair. He didn't seem to me to
listen. Would you agree that that was usually the case, sir?*

The dean smiled, and his eyes were very pleased.

He said, "The ability to listen is very rare. I have known
very few men, particularly men in high places, who have
been able to do it. Most public men I have known were
not accustomed to the sound of any voice save their own.
And Roosevelt was very high among them.

"I must add that Mr. Truman not only had the ability
to listen, he could *hear*, which is quite another thing. And
at the end of a conversation, he not only remembered what
he had heard, he understood and made use of it."

*Mr. Secretary, how would you define the difference be-
tween the public Harry Truman and the private Harry
Truman?*

"One difference is that the picture of Mr. Truman that
has emerged through the press is that of a man who, to
use that questionable phrase that I believe originated in
what is known as the Old West, was inclined to 'shoot
from the hip.'

"And indeed, very often in his press conferences it was
difficult to restrain Mr. Truman. Once he was asked a

---

* In his play, *What Every Woman Knows*, Sir James M.
Barrie wrote:

"*Alick.* What *is* charm, exactly, Maggie?

"*Maggie.* Oh, it's—it's a sort of bloom on a woman. If you
have it, you don't need to have anything else; and if you
don't have it, it doesn't much matter what else you have. Some
women, the few, have charm for all; and most have charm
for one. But some have charm for none."

question, he was inclined to answer it when it might have been the better part of valor to maintain silence. Perhaps, however, that was the price to be paid for his utter lack of guile. Mr. Truman was perhaps the most guileless man ever to reach such high office.

"His answers to the press were never calculated, never, for that matter, calculating. But as a result, he earned the reputation of being a *peppery* man, an impatient man.

"In his private associations with the people in his administration, he was perhaps the kindest and most patient man in my memory.

"But to me his greatest quality as President, as a leader, was his ability to decide. General Marshall, who also had that quality, has said that the ability to make a decision is a great gift, perhaps the greatest gift a man can have. And Mr. Truman had that gift in abundance. When I would come to him with a problem, the only question he ever asked was, 'How long have I got?' And he never asked later what would have happened if he had decided differently. I doubt that that ever concerned him. He was not a man who was tortured by second thoughts. Those were luxuries, like self-pity, in which a man in power could not indulge himself.

"I would say that Mr. Truman had an Aristotelian understanding of power. He had not only read the Greek and Roman philosophers, he understood them. And by understanding what men had done in the past he was able with a sometimes terrifying reality to anticipate what a man would do in the present. He had an almost unbelievable ability to judge character.

"And he was as near to being totally unselfish as any man I have ever known, with the possible exception of General Marshall.

"Mr. Truman was a good friend of Justice Brandeis, and when he was in the Senate, he used to go, almost every week, I believe, to the Justice's at-homes. On Monday evenings.

"It may have been Justice Brandeis who told him, as

the Justice once told me, that: 'Some questions can be decided even if not answered.' He meant by that that it isn't always necessary for all the facts on a given situation to be available. They almost never are, perhaps never are.

"And it isn't necessary that one side be wholly right and the other totally wrong, because that seldom happens either.

"It is enough, the Justice used to say, that the scales of judgment be tipped in one direction, and, *after* a decision is made, he would say, 'One must go forward wholly committed.'

"I have been with Mr. Truman through a great many decisions, foreign policy decisions, decisions about war, peace, whether or not to go through with a difficult, unpopular operation, and never once have I seen him pause to consider whether or not he ought to do something because of its possible effect on his electoral future or the political future of his party.

"Now I can understand that many people would think this isn't a compliment, and it isn't really meant as a compliment. It is meant as an analysis of the man.

"I suppose that a President has to remain President in order to do great things, and therefore he ought to do *sensible* things to be reelected. But I am also perfectly certain that if too many things get between the President's vision and the target he's shooting at, his vision is going to be deflected. Ambition is one of the great things that intervenes. Political considerations. Will this get me votes or will it lose me votes? That deflects the aim.

"Ego is a great deflector of aim. One of the major elements of Mr. Truman's greatness is that these matters did not get between his eye and the bull's-eye. He looked at what he was doing without the myopia of ambition or extraneous events or any of the other weaknesses of important people.

"I hope you will be able to get some of that feeling about Mr. Truman into your book.

"As you know, I have been associated with some ex-

traordinary men, but to me, of them all, Harry Truman
was the most remarkable, the most extraordinary."

*Mr. Secretary, I read someplace that several years ago
you said you had known two great men in your life and
one who was near great. And that the first two were Justice Holmes and General Marshall.* You were quoted as
saying that the third was Justice Brandeis.*

"Oh, dear, did I say that? I must say I don't remember
saying it, although I shouldn't wish to deny that I *may*
have said it. In any case, if I *did* say it, it must have been
early on, very early on in my association with Mr. Truman, and I would now amend what I may have said to
place him in the very front ranks. With General Marshall
. . . his greatness was immediately apparent. With Mr.

* In his book *Sketches from Life* Mr. Acheson has written:
"The moment General Marshall entered a room, everyone in
it felt his presence. It was a striking and communicated force.
His figure conveyed intensity, which his voice, low, staccato,
and incisive, reinforced. It compelled respect. It spread a sense
of authority and of calm. There was no military glamour
about him and nothing of the martinet. Yet to all of us he
was always 'General Marshall.' The title fitted him as though
he had been baptized with it. He always identified himself
over the telephone as 'General Marshall speaking.' It seemed
wholly right, too. I should never have dreamed of addressing
him as 'Mr. Secretary'; and I have never heard anyone but
Mrs. Marshall call him 'George.' The General expected to be
treated with respect and to treat others the same way. This
was the basis of his relationships.

". . . President Truman has put his finger on another
foundation of General Marshall's character. Never, wrote the
President, did General Marshall think about himself. . . .
With General Marshall self-control came, as I suppose it always comes, from self-discipline. He was, in a phrase that has
quite gone out of use, in command of himself. He could make
himself go to bed and go to sleep on the eve of D Day, because
his work was done and he must be fresh for the decisions of
the day to come. He could put aside the supreme command
in Europe in favor of General Eisenhower because it was his
plain duty to stay in the Pentagon dealing with that vast complex of forces which, harnessed, meant victory."

Truman it was less immediately apparent, but that did not in any way detract from its existence.

"But should we not get into other matters? I have no taste for playing God, I leave that to others. The world is filled with people who like nothing better."

Being certain that I knew the answer, I said, *Mr. Secretary, have you ever had any regrets over what you said about Alger Hiss after his conviction in January, 1950?*

Mr. Acheson must have been expecting that one because he hesitated for just a moment; then he said, and at no time had he sounded more positive, for that matter more eloquent, "I have in common, surely with all other human beings, surely this is the universal experience, even among the highest and most mighty, many regrets. Decisions that were wrong, decisions that were evaded, words that I should have spoken and did not speak, words that I did not speak that I should have.

"In short, like every man, I have many regrets, but what I said on that day is not among them. I could wish that I had said it better, but what I said came close to what I intended saying, and that is, I imagine, enough to ask.

"I had, of course, given a great deal of thought to what I would say about Alger Hiss if I were asked, and I knew I would be asked. I even consulted Mrs. Acheson on the matter, and she said, and rightly, that there are some decisions, the loneliest decisions, I suppose, the most important, that *no one* can share. And so that morning, feeling naked and most vulnerable, I said what I felt I had to say."

One of the discomforts of being fifty or so is that what I expect everyone to remember a great many people do not remember, in many cases, alas, because they weren't born at the time. Thus, for those who missed the case that was to my generation what the Dreyfus case was to that of Emile Zola, a few words about Alger Hiss.

Like Acheson, Hiss was a graduate of Harvard Law

School. Acheson received his degree in 1918, Hiss in 1929. He had been a brilliant student, and Felix Frankfurter, then a professor, recommended that Hiss become the secretary to Justice Oliver Wendell Holmes, which for a year he was. Later he was one of the young New Dealers in the Agricultural Adjustment Administration and the Justice Department. In 1936 he joined the Department of State, and he was an adviser at a good many foreign conferences, among them the one at Yalta among Roosevelt, Churchill, and Stalin. He was never, however, in the first echelon of State Department officials, and in 1947 he resigned to become president of the Carnegie Endowment for International Peace.

The next year Whittaker Chambers, a vast, untidy man who had become a senior editor at *Time* magazine, accused Hiss of being a Communist. Later he said that Hiss had turned over some confidential documents—they turned out to be of minimal importance—to him, and he in turn, he said, had turned them over to the Russians. This had all happened, if it happened, in the thirties, just when in the thirties was a matter of some dispute, but that need not concern us here. What matters is that too much time had elapsed for Hiss to be charged with espionage, but he could be and was tried for perjury.

And while his two trials were going on—the first ended with a hung jury—it was impossible to go anywhere, in Washington or New York anyway, without getting into an acrimonious discussion about whether Hiss or Chambers was telling the truth. Chambers was not easy to love. Not only was he untidy, but he had had an erratic career and was clearly far gone into paranoia.

Hiss, on the other hand, seemed to have been a model public servant. He was an outwardly gentle, undeniably brilliant, rather elegant man of whom, according to Murray Kempton,* a Harvard classmate once said, "I remem-

---

* In *Part of Our Time*, a book about the thirties that was published and widely admired in the fifties, Mr. Kempton writes: "Alger Hiss and Whittaker Chambers are two ex-

ber Alger Hiss best of all for a kind of distinction that had
to be seen to be believed. If he were standing at the bar
with the British Ambassador and you were told to give a
package to the Ambassador's valet, you would give it to
the Ambassador before you gave it to Alger.

"He gave you a sense of absolute command and absolute grace. . . ."

Even Chambers described him as having, among other,
less admirable qualities, "an unvarying mildness, a deep
considerateness and gracious patience."

As the Hiss trials progressed, those on the lunatic right,
and at the time that seemed to include a good part of the
Republican Party, became more and more persuaded that
not only were Acheson and Hiss both Harvard men, but
they were both too piss-elegant for comfort, and they were
undeniably fellow traitors.

Actually, their association, both personally and professionally, was scarcely more than casual. Mr. Acheson has
written: "I had known him since his graduation from Harvard Law School . . . but had no close association with
him until in 1946 his work in charge of United Nations
liaison in the Department brought him under my supervision. His brother, Donald, however, had served as my
assistant from 1941 through March 1944, and was, in
1949, as he is at the time of this writing, one of my
partners in the practice of law. This is the first appearance
of the Alger Hiss affair in this book. It is enough to say
of it here that at the time of the hearings [on Acheson's
confirmation as Secretary of State by the Senate Committee on Foreign Relations] what had seemed in the beginning incredible and bizarre had moved into personal tragedy. It was destined to go on to something approaching
national disaster, lending, as it did, support to a widespread attack throughout the country upon confidence in
government itself."

---

traordinary men; yet it has been their fate, accepted by
Chambers and forced upon Hiss, to be treated as typical of
the decade through barely three years of which they were
drawn together and so inextricably involved."

So much for the Hiss-Acheson connection. What concerns us here is that the second jury chose to believe Chambers, warts and all, rather than the impeccable and unflappable Hiss. On January 21, 1950, Hiss was found guilty of two counts of perjury, and at his weekly press conference four days later Dean Acheson was asked if he had any comment on the case.

Acheson said that he would not discuss the legal aspects of the case because it was still in the courts. But then with a passion rare, perhaps unprecedented in an American Secretary of State, particularly one who was the son of an Episcopal bishop, Mr. Acheson leaned forward in his chair and said, "I take it the purpose of your question was to bring something other than that out of me. I should like to make it clear to you that whatever the outcome of any appeal which Mr. Hiss or his lawyers may take in this case I do not intend to turn my back on Alger Hiss. I think every person who has known Alger Hiss or has served with him at any time has upon his conscience the very serious task of deciding what his attitude is and what his conduct should be. That must be done by each person in the light of his own standards and his own principles. I think they were stated for us a very long time ago. They were stated on the Mount of Olives and if you are interested in seeing them you will find them in the 25th Chapter of the Gospel according to St. Matthew beginning with verse 34.

"Have you any other questions?" *

_____

* On the night of January 25 Dean Acheson wrote to his daughter: "This has been one of those days easy in the intrinsic tasks, but hard and exhausting because of what was added. Today Alger Hiss was convicted and today I had my press conference. Alger's case has been on my mind incessantly. As I have written you, here is stark tragedy—whatever the reasonably probable facts may be. I knew that I would be asked about it and the answer was a hard one—not in the ordinary sense of do I run or do I stand. That presented no problem. But to say what I really meant—forgetting the yelping pack at one's heels—saying no more and no less than one

In *Present at the Creation* Mr. Acheson adds: "After the press conference was over, Mike McDermott, Special Assistant for the Press, who had served secretaries since Mr. Hull, walked with me in silence to my door. 'I am going to ask a favor of the Secretary of State,' he said, 'which I have asked only once before in my service. May I shake your hand?'

"We shook hands and parted."

Eleven years later, almost to the day, Mr. Acheson looked at me and said, "I remember that occasion very well, and I remember going to the President in the late afternoon in great despair. As I told you, I had been asked a question I had long expected, and I had answered it as I felt I had to, but I had not anticipated the . . . the intensity of the reaction. Within an hour the newspapers were filled with headlines about my statement, and I felt that I had perhaps made it impossible for me to continue in office, that quite possibly my usefulness was at an end, and so that afternoon I went to the President to offer my resignation.

"The President already knew what had happened; he had seen the ticker tape.

"He looked at me, and he said he understood why I said what I had said. He said he knew all about friendship, that not too long before he had flown to the funeral of a friend, Tom Pendergast, and he said, 'You should have seen the headlines and the carrying-on when I did that, but Tom Pendergast was a good and loyal friend, and he

---

truly believed. This was not easy. I felt that advisers were of no use and consulted none. I understood that I had responsibilities above and beyond my own desires. And all this one had to handle dependent upon the fall of some fool's question at a press conference.

"At the end of the day I am tired, but I have no idea that there was any better way, though one could have wished for better words and thoughts in that crowded and slightly hot and sweaty room."

never asked me to do a dishonest deed, and so I went to
his funeral, and, eventually, it all blew over, and this will,
too. In the long run, after all the hullabaloo is over, people
will remember that you're a man who stuck by his friends,
and that's what counts.'

"Then he looked up at me, and he said, 'Dean, always
be shot in front, never behind.' And then he said, 'You'd
better get back to work. We've got a lot of *important*
things to do.'

"And, of course, that is what I did, and the matter of
my resignation was never mentioned again."

I didn't tell the dean, but I had discussed that afternoon
with Harry Truman some weeks before, and his memory
of what was said was somewhat different. Mr. Truman
said, "When I appointed Dean Secretary of State, I said to
him that as I understood the Constitution, the President
ran the foreign policy of the United States, while the Secretary of State was his principal adviser in the field, and I
said that I assumed that it was understood between us that
that was the way our relationship would work. He said
that it was.

"And I remember I told him, I said, 'Now, Dean, if
there is an important decision to be made, always bring it
to me in the morning so I'll have time to think it over. If
you bring me a decision in the afternoon, that will mean
you've already made up your mind and only want me to
okay whatever it is.'

"Well, when he came to me that afternoon and talked
about resigning, I told him that when my friend Tom
Pendergast died, I got in a plane and flew out to Kansas
City to attend his funeral. He was my friend, and he never
asked me to do a dishonest deed, and that's what I told
Dean, and I said, 'If you think there's a big hubbub over
this Alger Hiss thing, you should have seen all the carrying-on there was then.'

"But I said these things don't last. I said, 'A month from
now, all of this won't mean a thing.'

"And then I said, 'Now, Dean, about this resignation

business, this is the first time you've brought me a decision late in the afternoon. Don't do it again.' He said he wouldn't, and he didn't."

A month after his famous press conference Mr. Acheson was asked to appear before the subcommittee of the Senate Committee on Appropriations. Ostensibly, that summons was for him "to clarify" his statement on Hiss. Actually, of course, the hope was to stir up more hostile headlines. The chairman of that particular subcommittee, Senator Pat McCarran of Nevada, was, as Mr. Acheson gently puts it, "not a person who in the eighteenth century would have been considered a man of sensibility."

Mr. Acheson made several points that afternoon, but the one I like to remember was this:

"There were . . . personal reasons for stating my attitude. One must be true to the things by which one lives. The counsels of discretion and cowardice are appealing. The safe course is to avoid situations which are disagreeable and dangerous. Such a course might get one by the issue of the moment, but it has bitter and evil consequences. In the long days and years which stretch beyond that moment of decision, one must live with one's self; and the consequences of living with a decision which one knows has sprung from timidity and cowardice go to the roots of one's life. It is not merely a question of peace of mind, although it is vital; it is a matter of integrity of character."

On the last afternoon we talked, the last before the filming on the Korean decision began at Blair House, I said, *Mr. Secretary, I once wrote that Harry Truman may be the last human being ever to be President. I know it's far too early to make any definitive judgment on that, but would you care to make any comment on it?*

Mr. Acheson thought for a moment, and then he said, "Yes, yes. On the basis of our present, very limited experience you might say that. Mr. Truman may be the most *human* person I have ever known. He is completely without artifice.

"In public life he did always what seemed to him best to do. Now in my youth and, of course, in Mr. Truman's youth that would not have been considered so unusual a quality. One did what seemed to be the best thing to do without undue regard to the consequences to one's self.

"But it seems to me, as I look around me, and this may only be a sign of increasing age, it seems to me that this quality has become increasingly rare, especially in political life.

"We are increasingly urged to do what is pragmatic, what will work, what is popular, what has been approved as acceptable by the polls. I sometimes think that many men currently in public life would be hard put to commit themselves on whether or not it was raining without first finding out what reply would be most acceptable to the electorate."

Mr. Secretary, would you say that is true of the present administration, Mr. Kennedy's administration?

Mr. Acheson smiled. "I believe," he said, "that my meaning is quite clear without elaboration."

The Kennedy people talk a good deal about situation ethics, whatever that means. How do you think Mr. Truman would feel about that?

"You'd have to ask Mr. Truman, but I seriously doubt that he has ever found it necessary to place a modifying adjective in front of the word 'ethics.' "

As I've said, I don't know whether Mr. Acheson's international policies will eventually be found to have been right or wrong. I am sure that he was an honest and courageous man. And if there are men of such rectitude —it's been a long time since I've been able to work _that_ word into a sentence—anywhere in public life today, I fail to see them.

I commend to the revisionists these further words of Mr. Acheson on the last afternoon we talked:

"I incline to go along with Winston Churchill, who said that among the deficiencies of hindsight is that while we know the consequences of what was done, we do not know

the consequences of some other course that was not followed." *

* In the *Apologia Pro Libre Hoc* to his massive *Present at
the Creation* Mr. Acheson adds this thought: "In the epigraph
Alphonso X, King of Spain, is quoted to the effect that if
he had been present at the creation he would have given
some useful hints for the better ordering of the universe. In
a sense the postwar years were a period of creation, for the
ordering of which I shared with others some responsibility.
Moreover, the state of the world in those years and almost
all that happened during them was wholly novel within the
experience of those who had to deal with it. 'History,' writes
C. V. Wedgewood in her biography of William the Silent, 'is
lived forwards but it is written in retrospect. We know the
end before we consider the beginning and we can never
wholly recapture what it was to know the beginning only.' "

On J. Edgar Hoover

Mr. President, what did you think of J. Edgar Hoover?
"To tell you the truth, I never gave him all that much thought. He was, still is inclined to take on, to try to take on more than his job was, and he made quite a few too many speeches to my mind, and he very often spoke of things that, strictly speaking, weren't any of his business, but then a lot of people do that, especially in Washington. As long as he did his job, I didn't pay too much attention to him.

"One time they brought me a lot of stuff about his personal life, and I told them I didn't give a damn about that. That wasn't my business. It was what he did *while* he was at work that was my business."

The CIA

I said earlier that Mr. Truman was not much given to second thoughts, and I learned not to expect any. But one morning as we were yet again waiting for a cameraman to change film, I said, *Mr. President, I know that you were responsible as President for setting up the CIA. How do you feel about it now?* A few days earlier we had been discussing the Bay of Pigs fiasco.

"I think it was a mistake. And if I'd known what was going to happen, I never would have done it. I needed . . . the President needed at that time a central organization that would bring all the various intelligence reports we were getting in those days, and there must have been a dozen of them, maybe more, bring them all into one organization so that the President would get *one* report on what was going on in various parts of the world.

"Now *that* made sense, and that's why I went ahead and set up what they called the Central Intelligence Agency.

"But it got out of hand. The fella . . . the one that was in the White House after me never paid any attention to it, and it got out of hand. Why, they've got an organization over there in Virginia now that is practically the equal of the Pentagon in many ways. And I think I've told you, one Pentagon is one too many.

"Now, as nearly as I can make out, those fellows in the CIA don't just report on wars and the like, they go out and make their own, and there's nobody to keep track of what they're up to. They spend billions of dollars on stirring up trouble so they'll *have* something to report on. They've become . . . it's become a government all of its own and all secret. They don't have to account to anybody.

"That's a very dangerous thing in a democratic society, and it's got to be put a stop to. The people have got a

right to know what those birds are up to. And if I was
back in the White House, people would know. You see,
the way a free government works, there's got to be a
housecleaning every now and again, and I don't care
what branch of the government is involved. *Somebody*
has to keep an eye on things.

"And when you can't do any housecleaning because
everything that goes on is a damn *secret,* why, then we're
on our way to something the Founding Fathers didn't have
in mind. Secrecy and a free, democratic government don't
mix. And if what happened at the Bay of Pigs doesn't
prove that, I don't know what does.

"You have got to keep an eye on the military at all
times, and it doesn't matter whether it's the birds in the
Pentagon or the birds in the CIA." *

---

* I should add that publicly Mr. Truman continued to uphold the CIA. This was one of the few areas in which what he
said publicly differed from what he said privately.

On a disastrous day at the Army Command and General
Staff School that Bob Aurthur described in detail in the August, 1971, issue of *Esquire,* Mr. Truman was asked about
the CIA by a young Army officer who was a veteran of Korea.
On that occasion Mr. Truman said, "When I took over the
Presidency he received information from just about everywhere, from the Secretary of State and the State Department,
the Treasury Department, the Department of Agriculture. Just
everybody.

"And sometimes they didn't agree as to what was happening in various parts of the world. So I got a couple of admirals
together, and they formed the Central Intelligence Agency
for the benefit and convenience of the President of the United
States. . . . So instead of the President having to look
through a bunch of papers two feet high, the information was
coordinated so that the President could arrive at the facts.

"It's still going, and it's going very well."

On the other hand, now that I've looked at it again, that's
pretty faint praise.

Moreover, it has recently been revealed that as far back as
February, 1947, General Marshall in a memorandum to President Truman said of the agency five months before it was set
up: "The Foreign Service of the Department of State is the

only collection agency of the Government which covers the whole world, and we should be very slow to subject the collection and evaluation of this foreign intelligence to other establishments, especially during times of peace. The powers of the proposed agency seem almost unlimited and need clarification."

Some Friends and Neighbors, Too

Eddie Meisberger, a retired newspaperman, and a veteran of Battery D: "The thing about Mr. Truman is . . . he has never changed. He never changed at all. He was the same man in Battery D and as county judge and President and after. That was one of the things you could always count on; you always knew where you stood with Mr. Truman.

"I remember one time not too long after he got to be President, and he'd just been to Potsdam and met Stalin and Churchill and all of those, and he came out here to Kansas City, and, of course, there was quite a following of the press, and they had a press conference at the Federal Building here in Kansas City, to be followed by a luncheon. I was invited to the luncheon, but I got over to the courthouse a little ahead of time, and while I was waiting, a Secret Service man came in and said, 'There's a gentleman at the other end of the building who wishes to see you. Follow me.'

"I followed him, and we went to a corner office, and he opened a door, and there was the President behind a desk, standing up. He'd been to Potsdam and to San Francisco for the United Nations, and I don't know where all he'd been, but he hadn't changed a particle.

"There were some others there, Ted Marks I remember [also a veteran of Battery D] and one or two others, and the President opened a drawer in the desk, and he kind of grinned, and then he went over and locked the door. And then he went to a cupboard and reached up and got an old tumbler. It wasn't too clean, a heavy glass tumbler. And he took out a bottle of refreshment and poured each of us a drink. We told him we'd enjoy that, but where was his glass?

"He said, 'I won't take one right now because right in the next room is a delegation of Baptist ladies from Independence, and we have an appointment in a few minutes. So I can't join you now.

" 'But,' he said, 'I feel a bad cold coming on, and I'll just put this away and take it out at home tonight and use it.' And he folded up the carton around the bottle and put it back in the desk.

"And I said, 'Well, I'm on a government payroll, you know, and I don't know whether I should take one right now.'

He said, 'Well, as President, I'll give you fifteen— fifteen minutes of annual leave right now, and you can join the others.' So we said, 'Down the hatch.'

"And he told us stories about some of the vicissitudes and the problems of the Secret Service and how being President his privacy was not what it used to be. But he said that went along with the job and he'd just have to put up with it as best he could."

I gather from what you say that Mr. Truman has remained unchanged since he came back to Independence to live after being President.

"Oh, yes. He hadn't changed a bit after being President. And I'll tell you one thing, if you didn't know he'd been, he'd never tell you. It's not the kind of thing he'd ever mention. He's not proud in *that* way.

"One day after he got back we had a lunch at the hotel here in Kansas City, and during the luncheon for some reason or another he got a Charley horse or a kink in his knee.

"And when he was ready to leave the hotel to go back home to Independence, he told us he could hardly walk. So a couple of us helped him downstairs and got him into one of the boys' cars, and we took him over to Eighth and Grand, where he had his car parked.

"When we got there and the attendant got his car out, he still could hardly walk. And we said, 'Mr. President'— because we always address him as *Mr. President* regardless of how well we know him—we said, 'We don't think you should drive this car by yourself. We're worried about you.'

"And he said, 'No. Hell,' he said, 'turn it and point the damn thing towards Independence. I'll get there.' And we put him in the seat, and off he went bound for Independence. He got there safely, and I guess he always will."

Susan Chiles, retired schoolteacher and writer: "Of course, since they got back from Washington, we haven't seen so much of the Trumans, because they don't go out much. I think they're lonely in that big house. I think they think people would treat them . . . the way you'd treat a President and First Lady, and maybe people would. It's hard to tell.

"But almost nobody goes to see them. I think people would go to see them, but when a man . . . when a couple have been President and the First Lady, you hesitate just to go and call. They've met so many people, kings and queens, and . . . people just don't seem to call the way they might otherwise.

"But I know this. There must be some satisfaction for Harry Truman knowing he has been one of the great Presidents, and I believe that has already been proven.

"Mort, you know—Mort, Junior—was a special FBI agent in Washington in the first year that Harry was President. And I visited there six weeks, and I visited Mrs. Truman in the White House, but Harry was at the United Nations meeting. So I didn't get to see him.

"But while I was there, I attended a banquet of the National League of American Pen Women, and they were discussing Mr. Truman and his attitudes and saying very harsh things about him. I took it as long as I could, and then I got up, and I said, 'Now I don't know anything about the issues, but I know that Harry Truman is honest, and whatever he says will stand the test of time,' and I sat down, and they didn't discuss him anymore.

"In the time that has passed since, I believe it can be said that I was right."

Walter Bodine, a Kansas City television commentator: "While he was President, those of us who covered the news here in Kansas City were kept at a distance from Mr. Truman. When he would come back from Washington, there were always a lot of reporters around, and there would be the Secret Service. You couldn't get to know him then.

"But we did get to know him after he came home, and I think I, like everyone else, thought that when Harry Truman came home, he would stay a brief period and then, like almost everybody else who goes to Washington, he would find some reason to go back and live there. Or maybe settle down at an Eastern college, an Ivy League college as a lecturer or something like that.

"I couldn't really believe that after all he'd been and all he'd done he'd come back and live in Independence, but he has, and, actually, I think no man ever relished being a private citizen more. He couldn't wait to start driving his own car, and I remember one day, when a newsman met him at Ninth and Grand—in those days he had an office at Tenth—Mr. Truman was carrying a briefcase.

"The newsman said to him, 'Mr. President, could I carry your briefcase for you?'

"And he said, 'No, I'll tell you something. Before we left Washington, I decided that when we got home, we were going to do everything for ourselves, and that definitely includes carrying my own briefcase.'

"The way I'd sum it up is that Harry Truman never left home, actually. He's a citizen of Independence, and I think he just commuted to Washington for a while."

Edgar Hinde, former postmaster of Independence and a veteran of Battery D: "I think when Harry came back to Independence from Washington, he sort of hoped he could live like everybody else. He'd been used to going up around our old country square here, and he always knew everyone there. But after he was President, he couldn't do that, and it bothered him. I think it still does.

"Of course, Independence is no longer a small town;

it's a small city, and everywhere Harry goes now, it's just a nuisance, with people coming up and wanting him to autograph a piece of paper and shake hands with him.

"And there are all the visitors, all wanting to take a look at Harry Truman. I guess he's our most famous local product and maybe always will be.

"And he tells me . . . he says it's even worse when he's on a trip. It just always takes all the pleasure out of it because he is never left alone. People won't leave him alone. He'd go . . . he goes into a town, and somebody always says, 'There's President Truman,' and naturally, everybody follows him.

"He was telling me about one time when he was in Indiana in a motel, and this motel owner knew him, and he promised he wouldn't tell anybody Harry was there.

"But he and Mrs. Truman went out for dinner, and when they got back, he said there were about five hundred people waiting for him in front of the motel. And he said it was the same thing all the way back to Washintgon. His privacy, he has none."

Harry Truman: "I try to live the way I did before I went to Washington, try to live like I always did, but it's a hard thing to do. When you get to be a notorious character, people are always around with curious ideas of taking a look at the fellow who's been through what I have. And I'm patient with them because I know exactly what's affecting them. But it's not very good for privacy.

"I was told by the former President, Mr. Hoover, that souvenir hunters had even taken the doorknobs off his house, had taken some of the weatherboarding off his house. And when I became President, the Secret Service had found out all about this situation, and they decided that the property where Mrs. Truman and I lived ought to be protected. So they put an iron fence around it so people couldn't come in and pick up flowers and souvenirs around the place.

"On one occasion, when the back gate was left open, some old lady drove in and began pulling up the tulips that Mrs. Truman had set out, beautiful white tulips. And she was stopped by the guard who happened to be on duty and told that it was private property and she shouldn't do that.

" 'Oh,' she said, 'Mrs. Truman won't care if I take a few of her tulips,' and kept on pulling them up. So that's the reason we have to be surrounded by an iron fence, and I don't like it. Never did like it and never will like it, but it has to be done because of the souvenir hunters. They're not real Americans. They're just people who want to accumulate a lot of stuff and then throw it away. You find most of it in the attic when they die."

Miss Ethel Noland: "My picture window here pictures the Truman house across the street. Originally it was the Gates house. It's a very old house and an interesting house, and it is certainly a fine example of Victorian architecture.

"Of course, since Mr. Truman came back from Washington, the tourists are omnipresent. They're there when I first look out in the morning. They walk down Truman Road, and they survey the house from all sides. And finally, you find them standing out in front. And one *always* goes across the street and takes a picture of those at the front gate. It seems to me that's almost an unwritten law, that they shall do this.

"Sometimes if I go out, they will come across to ask me questions. They will say, 'Do you know Mr. Truman? Does he visit the neighbors? How do they like him?' And many questions like that.

"Fortunately, we can all speak well of him. I answer their questions as if I were just a neighbor, instead of telling them that he and I are related. Harry Truman and I are first cousins, my mother having been a sister of Harry's father, John Anderson Truman.

"However, he never complains because the tourists' attitude is always quite admiring. You'd surely have to admire a person to get up at five or six o'clock in the morning to go and see where he lives and try to catch a glimpse of him. . . . That does not, however, make it any easier for Mr. Truman. Although, as I have said, he does not complain. He comes from the kind of background and has the kind of upbringing where one is publicly cheerful at all times. One does not *discuss* one's dissatisfactions with life, as seems to be so prevalent with people nowadays.

"I am sure I am quite old-fashioned. When I ask someone how he or she is, I trust that they will say to me, 'I am fine. How are you?' And I will do likewise.

"I most certainly do *not* want them to tell me how they are."

Mrs. W. L. C. Palmer: "I do not think that Mrs. Truman ever liked any part of it. She just never learned to enjoy public life in any way . . . the politics of it and some of the people that at one time or another Harry had to . . . with whom he was associated. I had that feeling here when Harry was judge and, later, when I visited them in Washington. At the White House when he was President and she was First Lady.

"I think Mrs. Truman would have been just as content with life if she had never left Independence, but I doubt that she has ever mentioned it, even to Mr. Truman. She has always been a woman of great understanding, and in recent years, since they have come home from Washington, Mr. Truman has seemed to be very much dependent on her.

"But the important thing is, being First Lady was just never anything that was *necessary* for her."

Do you suppose it was rather like Rachel Jackson who, after Andrew Jackson was elected President, said, "Well, for Mr. Jackson's sake I am glad, but for my part I never wished it"?

"Very much so. Mrs. Truman is a person who would do what she feels Mr. Truman wanted her to do, but she has always been a person of great privacy, and politics is not a life she would have chosen for herself." *

Edgar Hinde: "Of course Harry likes people, and that shows. He is very fond of people, I'd say, and he takes time with them.

"After the library was built, I took my sister over to visit him. He chatted with her; he played the piano for her, and he showed her around the library.

"Later on the way back from the library she said to me, 'I can see why Harry Truman has been so successful in politics. He takes time with people.' "

I mentioned to Mr. Truman what Edgar Hinde had said and added, *I understand you did the same thing when you were President, that you always took time with people. I wonder, sir, does that have anything to do with the fact that when you were first elected to the Senate, you had considerable difficulty getting in to see President Roosevelt at all?*

* Bob Aurthur has written of one "dinner" he had with Mr. Truman at twelve noon in Independence: "As the limousine left the parking area, Mr. Truman suggested we eat at the Howard Johnson's just outside the Library. 'I could take you home,' he said matter-of-factly, 'but the food at Howard Johnson's is much better.'

"I regretted the opportunity to have lunch chez Truman, however poor the fare, but as Mr. Truman checked his coat in the painfully familiar Howard Johnson's, Bill Hillman revealed sadly that the offer had been an empty gesture. Except for an afternoon during the shooting of the first film, Hillman and the other cronies had never been invited to the house. Other evidence gathered over my time with Mr. Truman led me to the conclusion that sometime early in their marriage Bess Wallace Truman had made a deal.

" 'Harry,' I imagined she'd said, 'be a judge if you want. Get to be a Senator, Vice-President, or even President . . . but *never* bring those people you hang around with into *my* house.'

"Or words to that effect."

When Truman first came to Washington in 1934, he almost immediately called at the White House to pay his respects to Roosevelt, but for five months he was stalled off by Steve Early, Roosevelt's press secretary. When he finally did get in to see Roosevelt for the first time, the appointment lasted only seven minutes, and nothing of importance was discussed.

The truth is that during Truman's first term in the Senate, while he supported Roosevelt and the New Deal almost totally, Roosevelt ignored him. The White House took him and his vote for granted.

At one point, having started to drive back to Independence, he was brought back to the Capitol by state highway patrolmen to break a tie on a major bill. He was in a fury, and he called Steve Early and said, "I'm sick and tired of being the White House office boy. This is the third time I've come back here to bail you guys out on a vote. You tell that to the President!"

I mentioned that incident to Mr. Truman, who said, "Oh, yes. I was angry, and I was hurt, but I got over it, and Roosevelt and I became . . . quite close.

"But the whole thing taught me a lesson. People are always very nervous when they meet the President of the United States, and they can be . . . they can have their feelings hurt if he is . . . less than kind to them. And courteous. Courtesy is the cheapest thing in the world, and it's a wonder to me that people aren't that way more of the time.

"When I was President myself, I never ran anybody out. If you're willing to work a little extra, you can see everybody it is necessary for you to see, and you can spend as much time with them as need be. There's always, almost always plenty of time. There are always twenty-four hours in a day if you make use of them. I think I mentioned that that's one of the lessons I learned from reading old Benjamin Franklin's *Autobiography*. He gives you some very good hints on how to make the best use of your time.

"The main thing isn't *time*, it's *people*, and I have al-

ways tried very hard to keep that in mind. In the White
House it was never . . . almost never that people
wanted to stay too long. They were always embarrassed
at taking my time, and they wanted to leave too soon.

"And it's the same here at the library. The main thing
I have to be concerned with is to be sure that my visitors
are at ease and not worried about whether they are going
to stay too long and that kind of thing.

"When you get into a conversation and it lasts over the
time they're supposed to stay, I always tell them to stay
and finish, and of course, that's the way it ought to be
done, and as long as I'm around, it always will be. It's
very, very easy to hurt people, and if you don't have to
do it, you should do everything possible to avoid it."

In 1964 Eric Sevareid in a conversation with Mr. Truman got on the same subject, and he quoted him as saying, "What you don't understand is the power of a President to hurt."

Sevareid added, "An American President has the power
to build, to set fateful events in motion, to destroy an enemy civilization, to win or lose a vast personal following.
But the power of a President to hurt the feelings of another human being—this, I think, had scarcely occurred
to me, and still less had it occurred to me that a President
in office would have the time and the need to be aware
of this particular power among so many others.

"Mr. Truman went on to observe that a word, a harsh
glance, a peremptory motion by a President of the United
States, could so injure another man's pride that it would
remain a scar on his emotional system all his life."

Then Sevareid recalled an episode that the President
had also told me, shortly after it happened, in the late winter or spring of 1962. He had given a lecture at, I believe,
the University of Southern California, in any case at a
college or university in Southern California; the lecture was
on the subject he loved best, the Constitution and the
Presidency.

During the question period a boy got up and said, "Mr.

President, what do you think of our local yokel?" He meant Pat Brown, then governor.

Mr. Truman told the boy that he should be ashamed of himself, that to speak of the governor of a state in such a disrespectful way, even if he disagreed with him, was a shameful thing. The boy, close to tears, sat down.

When the question period was over, Mr. Truman went to the boy and said that he hoped he would understand that what he had said had to do with the principle involved and that he meant nothing personal. The boy said that he did understand, and the two shook hands.

Afterward Mr. Truman went to see the dean to ask him to send reports from time to time on the boy's progress in school. The dean said he would and had.

I asked Mr. Truman if he had ever heard from the boy himself, and he said, "He's written me two or three times, and I've written him back. He's doing very well."

Sevareid said of the incident, "The simple point here is that Mr. Truman had instantly realized how a public scolding by a former President could mark and mar the boy's inner life and his standing in the community.

"I feel gratified to have heard this story. It has given me an insight into the responsibilities of a President that I did not have, and it has immeasurably added to my own residue of memories about the man from Missouri. He is nearly eighty now. He may live to be a hundred—his is a strong stock—but this, I know, is the specific memory that will return to me when his time does come."

Earlier Sevareid had written: "A man's character is his fate, said the ancient Greeks. Chance, in good part, took Harry Truman to the presidency, but it was his character that kept him there and determined his historical fate. He is, without any doubt, destined to live in the books as one of the strongest and most decisive of the American Presidents." *

* From *Eric Sevareid: An Unknown Side of Truman*. From the Washington *Evening Star*. February 4, 1964. Also reprinted in Cabell Phillips' admirable book *The Truman Presidency*.

Captain Mike Westwood of the Independence police department, a companion, sometime chauffeur, and longtime friend of Mr. Truman: "I don't recall the date, but it was after Mr. Truman got back from Washington, from being President, and we took a trip down south to Jefferson City. That was on Highway Forty before it was a double-lane highway. And all of a sudden Harry told me to pull over to the side of the road, and there was a woman trying to herd a bunch of hogs that had got loose, and he said, 'Let's help that lady get her hogs in.'

"So I went out and stopped traffic, and he helped her get those hogs off the road. Can you imagine a President of the United States, a former President of the United States, doing a thing like that?

"Well, when we got to Jefferson City, there was a reporter there to meet us. Someone on the highway had recognized the President and called Jefferson City saying he'd seen Harry Truman out there herding hogs. The reporter asked him, I don't think he could believe it, thought there was a mistake of some kind, but he asked Harry, and Harry said, yes, he'd done it. He said somebody had to, and he said anyway he'd been a farmer long before he got to be President."

The Library Tour

Except for the lectures in the auditorium I think what Mr. Truman enjoyed most in the years when he could manage it was taking people on tours of the library. I must have gone on the tour, say, twenty times, and Mr. Truman's comments never varied much. He just edited his remarks some when there were ladies—to him all women were ladies—and children on the tour. I am sure that in his entire life he never swore or uttered an obscenity in what he called "mixed company."

When we left Mr. Truman's private office, he would stop for a moment at the piano in the large reception room, pounding out a few chords. Then, if the company were strictly male, he would say, "My choice early in life was either to be a piano player in a whorehouse or a politician."

He would pause; as I've said, he was a skilled stand-up comic, albeit with a somewhat limited repertoire, pause, then say, "And to tell the truth there's hardly a difference."

I laughed just as heartily the dozenth time I heard that Rotarian joke as I did the first, and so did the dejuicers, Noyes and Hillman, who must have heard it many more times than that. So did Harry Truman, who'd heard it more than anybody.

On the first day and the last and on a few occasions in between Mr. Truman stopped first at a glass case in which was a mint copy of Dwight D. Eisenhower's book *Crusade in Europe*.

"That's the first copy he gave to anybody outside his immediate family," the President would say. "Take a look at what he wrote in it."

On the flyleaf the general had written to the man who was then his Commander in Chief, "To Harry S. Truman —with lasting respect, admiration, and friendship, Dwight D. Eisenhower."

"I sometimes wonder if the son of a bitch knows the

meaning of any of those words," Mr. Truman would say, walking on.

We would come to a framed copy of that issue of the Chicago *Tribune* that on November 2, 1948, had the head-line DEWEY DEFEATS TRUMAN.

Mr. Truman always looked at that headline as if he had never seen it before. He never said anything about it. No need to. He just stood there and grinned, and at that moment he never seemed to look much older than he had that memorable night in 1948. Few men in history have known such a victory, and it was all his, all, and he knew that and relished it. One of his more attractive qualities, to me anyway, was that just as he was never arrogant, he was never falsely modest either. He took the knocks, and hard knocks they were, without complaint, and he felt he was entitled to enjoy his triumphs. And he did, by God, and it was fine to see.

That first day I said, "Mr. President, were you really able to go to sleep that night without knowing for sure whether you'd won the election?"

"Of course," said the President. "I knew I was going to win. Never had the slightest doubt about it. Besides, it was all over but the shouting. What would have been the point in not getting a good night's sleep?"

How do you explain your remarkable ability to go to sleep like that?

"Because I don't drink coffee for one thing. Another thing is that whatever I've done I've done the best I can. So I don't go to bed and worry."

The President stopped at a photograph of himself, General MacArthur, and several administration officials on Wake Island.

Mr. Truman identified the other people in the picture, saving MacArthur until last.

"And, of course, we all know who that is," he said, pointing. "That's God.

"We'll talk about him some other time, but if you think I'm rough on him you ought to hear what General Wainwright had to say about him." Major General Jonathan M. Wainwright, Jr., succeeded MacArthur as commander of the U.S. forces in the Philippines after MacArthur left for Australia early in the Second World War.

"Wainwright said he wasn't any better than a common coward, and General Marshall gave me a rundown on MacArthur that was the best I ever did hear. He said he never was any damn good, and he said he was a four-flusher and no two ways about it.

"I'll tell you about the trouble I had with MacArthur. Why, hell, if he'd had his way, he'd have had us in the Third World War and blown up half to two-thirds of the world."

We walked on, and the President said, "People who think they are God are bound to get in trouble sooner or later."

One entire section of the public part of the library is filled with gifts Mr. Truman had received from various world leaders, a display of coins, medals, even a solid gold dinnerware set sent by some Arab potentate. Mr. Truman never thought any of those things were *his,* though. "They were given to the President of the United States, which is what, for a time, I was, but I never thought they were meant for my personal use. The only exception—"

He stopped in front of a jeweled sword given to the President by King Saud of Saudi Arabia, and Mr. Truman said, "The only exception. I told Bess I'd give *that* to her if she'd kick Bricker [a reactionary Republican Senator from Ohio] in the ass, but she wouldn't do it. So it's still here."

We came to a corner of the library in which were photographs or drawings of all the Presidents. Mr. Truman pointed to the picture of Abraham Lincoln.

"Lincoln was a great President," he said, "and I'll tell you why. He had nerve enough to save the Union under the most difficult circumstances. And if he hadn't saved the union of the United States, we would have been divided into half a dozen countries like those Central American countries and I wouldn't have any influence in the world. That's the reason I admire him. He had the guts to go ahead and do what he thought was the right thing at a time when he had a great big opposition. He was roundly abused for it, but he did the right thing."

How do you suppose he knew what the right thing was?

"He knew the history of this country. He'd been in the Congress, and he didn't like to serve there. And he'd also been a local politician. He knew things from the ground up. And he knew that if the United States as a country couldn't be saved it would end up in a division of the various states into various governments which would never get together and do the job. That's the reason."

The President started on, then stopped. "Lincoln was a great man all right," he said, then added: "Of course, heroes know when to die."

Was he making an analogy between Lincoln's death and that of Franklin Roosevelt? I thought so and was even more sure of it when he turned back and pointed out the photograph of Andrew Johnson.

He said, "It took about eighty years for the truth about Andrew Johnson to come out, but it finally did, and now people know what kind of President he was."

I said, "Why did he get into so much trouble, coming so close to getting impeached, by one vote, wasn't it?"

"One vote less than the necessary two-thirds in the Senate. I'll tell you why it happened. Johnson tried to carry on Lincoln's policy. Lincoln was going to treat the South not as a conquered nation but as a sinful child. Johnson tried that, and what happened was a case of the power of Congress ruining a President of the United States. Old Thad Stevens was the cause of that. He just wasn't any damn good. Period.*

"There never was a man in the White House who was more thoroughly and completely mistreated than Johnson. He was a Democrat from Tennessee. An Andy Jackson Democrat. That's what he was. So when the Republicans after their first administration found out they couldn't win

* Thaddeus Stevens was a Republican Congressman from Pennsylvania. After the war he was one of the organizers of the effort to treat the Southern states as "conquered provinces" and was a leader of the effort to impeach Johnson.

without some other approach, they set up the American Union Party with Lincoln as the Presidential candidate and Johnson as the Vice President.

"They got elected, and, of course, after Lincoln was shot, Johnson being a Tennessee Democrat was abused and mistreated, but he was a tough old guy. He didn't have any diplomacy at all, but he finally wound up at the end of his life by being reelected Senator from Tennessee. He fought from one end of the damn state to the other, and you know it was divided into three parts the way Gaul was. . . .

"Anyway, he finally won and made one of the finest speeches that has ever been made in the Senate on what a public servant ought to do. You ought to read it."

If Lincoln had lived. . . .

"If Lincoln had lived, he would have had the same experience, but like I said, heroes know when to die."

One of the tours of the library was with Bobby Kennedy, then Attorney General. It was a hurried tour, and it was clear to me, though probably not to the Attorney General, that the President wanted to get it over with as quickly as possible.

After Kennedy had left, Mr. Truman said, "I just don't like that boy, and I never will. He worked for old Joe McCarthy, you know, and when old Joe was tearing up the Constitution and the country, that boy couldn't say enough for him."

He stopped for a moment, and there was an inaudible sigh.

"The whole Kennedy family, as nearly as I can make out, about all they're interested in is *getting* the power. They don't care a hoot in hell about using it. They're afraid to use it for fear it might not be *popular*. I've told you what happens if a President worries too much about winning popularity contests every day . . . every other day or so. You simply can't do it.

"I wouldn't want this to get out, because I hope the boy in the White House will do a good job, but so far it looks to me like power for itself is the only thing that interests any of them, and they've spent the money to buy it. I don't like that. I told you the other day . . . the minute you can buy an *election,* this country is in big trouble. The biggest it's ever had.

"Now they say young Bobby has changed for the better. They never say anybody's changed for the worse. They say he's changed for the better, and maybe he has, but what I can never understand and never will if I live to be a hundred is why it takes so long these days for somebody to learn the difference between right and wrong. A man who hasn't learned that by the time he's thirty is never going to learn.

"They say Nixon has changed, too, but they'll have to prove it. They'll have to prove it to me. Where that fella's concerned, you might say I'm from Missouri."

When we finished the first tour of the library, it was late afternoon, and the sun was beginning to set.

We stopped off in the office of the President's secretary, Miss Rose Conway, who had been with the President since 1945 when he became Vice President.

Mr. Truman started toward his own office, stood in the doorway for a moment, then turned back, smiled, and said that he looked forward to seeing us the next day.

"About this television series," he said, "you fellows keep in mind that I have no idea of selling a bill of goods to anybody. I just want to give people—especially the youngsters—some idea of what a President has to do, what he has to go through from the point of view of a man who's been there."

We were silent for a time after he went into his own office. Finally, I turned to Miss Conway and said that it must have been quite an experience working for so many years with a man like Harry Truman.

Miss Conway, the gentlest of women, said that it had been.

"And in all this time," she added, "he has once to say a harsh word."

The Cause and Cure of Hysteria

Mr. President, we've talked about hysteria in the United States several times, and I know it's a subject that concerns you very much, and I wonder if we could go back to it, at least briefly, today?

"Yes, and I'll tell you why it interests me. I may already have told you. I feel that if our constitutional system ever fails, it will be because people got scared and turned hysterical and someone in power will demagogue them right into a police state of some kind. That's what I've always worried about. And still do."

Last night I was reading a statement about a man I know you admired—we've discussed him before—Justice Brandeis. It was his dissent in a wiretapping case at the time the Prohibition Amendment was still in force. I believe the government, probably through the Justice Department, claimed that in order to catch some bootleggers it had to do some wiretapping. Or else it had done some wiretapping. I'm not sure which.

Anyway, the majority of the Supreme Court went along, agreed, but Justice Brandeis dissented. I'm sure you're familiar with it, but could I read you what he said, in part anyway?

"Go right ahead. I've probably read it at one time or another because I think I've read every one of his decisions, but . . . I'm sure whatever he said was right. Because he was a man who always thought his way through to the right conclusion."

Well, sir, he wrote, "Our government is the potent, the omnipresent teacher. For good or ill, it teaches the whole people by example. Crime is contagious. If the government becomes a lawbreaker, it breeds contempt for law; it invites every man to become a law unto himself; it invites anarchy. To declare that in the administration of the criminal law the end justifies the means—to declare that the government may commit crimes in order to se-

cure the conviction of a private criminal—would bring terrible retribution." *

I really don't have to ask, but I will anyway. Would you agree with that, sir?

"Oh, yes, right down the line. You see, if you study the history of this country, you'll discover that there have always been certain people who felt that to get a certain law to work—and I think I told you the Prohibition Amendment was a big mistake, shouldn't have been passed in the first place and couldn't be enforced—but there are always people with a certain kind of mind who

---

* Brandeis' dissent was printed in Jonathan Daniels' biography of Mr. Truman, *The Man of Independence,* a book of which, as has been mentioned earlier, Mr. Truman didn't think highly. Mr. Daniels also quoted Max Lowenthal, a civil libertarian whose acquaintance with Mr. Truman went all the way back to his investigations into railroad finances during his first term in the Senate.

" 'What I think is deep in him,' said Max Lowenthal who had discovered Truman's integrity on the railroad committee, 'is a sense of the atmosphere of the American tradition. That sort of atmosphere was pervasive and a part of men's feelings for America in the eighties and nineties and 1900's when Truman was growing up. I know it of the Middle West where my own childhood and youth were spent in that atmosphere. While there was much economic injustice at the time, there was a quality of freedom—an absence of any aspect whatever of the modern police state—that some of the younger generation today may not know of except in a limited way through their reading.' "

And on the same subject Daniels quotes a man he identifies as an "old liberal":

"Nothing is more important than the grasp of fundamental American principles shared by such liberals as Truman and old-time conservatives, too. I think we find it in Truman, not because he is for liberalism in economic matters, but because he senses the spirit of the American political system. That has something to do with the way he ran his investigations. It is an innate part of his personality to be fair and to know what is fair, and to exercise restraint when he possesses great power, particularly the power to investigate and detect, and the power to police."

say that you've got to violate the Constitution or the Bill of Rights or both in some way or another to make sure some new law works or take care of some new threat.

"I've always thought that the democratic system can survive any threat at all from the folks, it doesn't matter who they are, the Jacobins, who everybody thought was the enemy in Jefferson's time, or the Communists now.

"It isn't any different now than it was when Jefferson became President. Read his first inaugural speech;* you'll see what I mean. And you must remember how young this country was then, young and didn't have too many friends in the world, but Jefferson said, I've got it right here, I'll read it to you, said, '. . . let them stand undisturbed as monuments of the safety with which error of opinion may be tolerated where reason is left free to combat it.'

"And read that letter he wrote to Henry Lee† saying

---

* At his first inaugural on March 6, 1801, Jefferson said, ". . . If there be any among us who would wish to dissolve this Union or to change its republican form, let them stand undisturbed as monuments of the safety with which error of opinion may be tolerated where reason is left free to combat it. I know, indeed, that some honest men fear that a republican government cannot be strong; that this government is not strong enough. But would the honest patriot, in the full tide of successful experiment, abandon a government which has so far kept us free and firm, on the theoretic and visionary fear that this government, the world's best hope, may by possibility want energy to preserve itself? I trust not. I believe this, on the contrary, the strongest government on earth. I believe it is the only one where every man, at the call of the laws, would fly to the standard of the law, and would meet invasions of the public order as his own personal concern. Sometimes it is said that man cannot be trusted with the government of himself. Can he, then, be trusted with the government of others? Or have we found angels in the forms of kings to govern him? Let history answer this question."

† In 1824 Jefferson wrote to Henry Lee: "Men by their constitutions are naturally divided into two parties: 1. Those who fear and distrust the people and wish to draw all powers from them into the hands of the higher classes. 2. Those who

that there always have been two kinds of people, the ones that trust the people and the ones that don't. It's been true all through the history of this country, all through the history of the world."

And wiretappers, people who want to wiretap are among those who don't trust the people, would you say?

"That's right. Any attempt to invade the privacy of a private citizen, doesn't matter what it is, is in violation of the Bill of Rights, and those who propose such a thing are more of a danger to the country than the ones they want to listen in on."

Didn't you have something to do with the consideration of wiretapping when you were chairman of a Senate subcommittee that considered all wiretapping bills?

"Yes, I was. There's always somebody around, Congress, somewhere, that thinks the country won't last until day after tomorrow unless there's a lot of wiretapping allowed. And of course, before they invented wiretapping, they depended on other means to pry into people's personal lives. And I have always been against it, when I was in the Senate and when I was President.

"I am happy to say that none of the wiretap bills ever got out of that subcommittee when I was chairman."

And as you say, you continued to feel the same way all through the time you were President.

"I did. There were all kinds of hysterical bills, legislation that the people who were so scared of the Communists said would take care of the matter and forget about the Constitution. The Mundt-Nixon bill was one, you

---

identify themselves with the people, have confidence in them, cherish and consider them as the most honest and safe, although not the most wise depository of the public interests. In every country these two parties exist, and in every one where they are free to think, speak, and write, they will declare themselves. Call them, therefore, liberals and serviles, Jacobins and Ultras, whigs and tories, republicans and federalists, aristocrats and democrats, or whatever name you please, they are the same parties still, and pursue the same object. The last appellation of aristocrats and democrats is the true one expressing the essence of all."

remember, and then there was the McCarran Act,* which was finally enacted into law over my veto, but I spoke out against things like that every chance I got. They tried to stop me; it was just before the Congressional elections of 19 and 50 I think it was, and they all tried to stop me, keep me from vetoing it, saying a veto would

* As Cabell Phillips in *The Truman Presidency* describes the bill, "What McCarran [the powerful chairman of the subcommittee of the Senate Committee on Appropriations] came out with in the end was a well-nigh undecipherable bill . . . which did *not* prohibit membership in the Communist party but *did* require that all who belonged to it proclaim that fact by registering with the Attorney General. . . . A Subversive Activities Control Board was called for to enforce these registration provisions. In addition, the bill denied employment to Communists and their 'dupes' in defense facilities; prohibited the issuance of passports to them; called for the deportation of any alien who had ever been a Communist; and provided for the detention in wartime 'of any person as to whom there is reason to believe he might engage in acts of espionage or sabotage.' This meant Communists, obviously. It could also, presumably, mean anybody whom a McCarran (or an Un-American Activities Committee chairman) found to be, by the rule of guilt by association, a sympathizer or fellow traveler of the Communists. It was a dragnet such as any dictator might envy."

The bill passed—the year was 1950, you remember—the House by a vote of 354 to 20 and the Senate by a vote of 70 to 7. It was not a brave year, 1950, but Harry Truman vetoed the bill. He said: "It's just like the Alien and Sedition Bill of 1798, and that didn't work either."

He tried desperately to have the veto sustained in the Senate, but the veto was overridden, 57 to 10.

According to Mr. Phillips, "It was a good fight, a typically Truman kind of to-hell-with-where-the-chips-may-fall fight. He had stood his ground against overwhelming odds for what he believed to be right. His enemies gloated over his defeat, but he won new respect with the more dispassionate editorial writers and columnists. And just as he had prophesied, the McCarran Act did prove to be a legalistic and administrative monstrosity, destined to be fought over in the courts for more than a decade and adding little to the net security of the nation."

cause the Democratic Party to lose votes, a lot of votes, and it may have. It may have, but just because the country is hysterical, and there was a lot of hysteria at the time, why, that is all the more reason the President has to speak out for what is right. Otherwise, he's got no reason being in the White House. The President has to do the leading in a case like that.

"I've said before, the President is the only person in the government who represents the whole people. There are some who can afford to hire lobbyists and others to represent their special interests, but the President isn't elected to pull strings for anybody. He's elected. I've said it before, to be the lobbyist for everybody in the United States. And he is, too, if he's any good.

"And when there's a moral issue involved, like any violation of the Constitution, the President has to be the moral leader of the country. Right now we've got this Birch Society, this John Birch business, and it's just another example of hysteria, and it's fooling some people, the same class that was fooled by the Ku Klux Klan and the other wild things that have come along. It'll work itself out.

"And if the politicians have got the guts, they help shape public opinion, but some of them, a lot of them, are like Mark Hanna said about William McKinley, they've got their ears so close to the ground they're full of grasshoppers. They can't tell what's going on."

Would you say, off the record, Mr. President, that that's somewhat true of the man who's now in the White House [John Kennedy]?

"Yes, I would, and I'm sorry to say it, but all the time he was in the Senate, all the time he could have provided some leadership as far as old Joe McCarthy was concerned, he never did do it, and it's a shame. I hope he learns. He wrote that book, you know [*Profiles in Courage*], and I hope he learns to be a little more outspoken about issues, but I have yet to see it."

Mr. President, early in 1948, when hysteria over the Alger Hiss case was at its height, you were asked if you

*thought the whole thing was "a red herring" to divert the
country's attention from more important matters. And you
said that you did think it was. And, of course, as you
remember better than anybody you were greatly criticized
for that remark. I wonder if in the years since you've
changed your mind.*

"I wouldn't say they criticized me for that. I've been
criticized by experts, and it doesn't bother me, but they
carried on a campaign against me that was as bad as any
this country has ever known. Those men, McCarthy and
that fella Jenner and Nixon [then a Congressman from
California], they stirred up a hysteria as bad as any this
country has ever known. We're lucky to have pulled
through it, and I'm not at all sure we're over it yet.

"But about Hiss. I never knew him, of course. I met
him once out in San Francisco when we were setting up
the United Nations, but that's the only time.* I'll tell you
something, though. They never proved it on him."

*Proved that he was . . . had been a Communist spy,
you mean?*

"That's right. They tried, twice you may remember,
they tried to do it, but they never did."

*Wasn't that because the statute of limitations had run
out so that he couldn't have been convicted on espionage
charges; so they convicted him on perjury charges instead?*

"That's what they said, but I never did believe it. I
think if they'd had the goods on Hiss, they'd have produced it, but they didn't. All it was was his word against
the word of that other fellow [Whittaker Chambers].
They didn't come up with any proof. That's the way I felt
at the time anyway.

"What they were trying to do, all those birds, they were
trying to get the Democrats. They were trying to get me
out of the White House, and they were willing to go to

---

* Actually the President saw Mr. Hiss again after the San
Francisco conference ended. Hiss, who had been Secretary
of the conference, flew back to Washington in a government
plane and presented the charter to Mr. Truman at the White
House.

any lengths to do it. They'd been out of office a long time, and they'd have done anything to get back in. They did do just about everything they could think of, all that witch-hunting that year, that was the worst in the history of this country, like I said. The Constitution has never been in such a danger, and I hope it never will be again."

Hiss's name was mentioned once again. Mr. Truman said that the best biography of Andrew Johnson had been written by Lloyd Paul Stryker, and I said that, as the President no doubt knew, Stryker had been Hiss's lawyer in the first trial.

Mr. Truman said, "I'm not a bit surprised. He was a man who was never afraid to take on an unpopular cause."

Mr. President, do you think the United States is particularly susceptible to hysteria, more than any other country, I mean?

"I don't think so. You read your history and you'll see that from time to time people in every country have seemed to lose their good sense, got hysterical, and got off the beam. . . . I don't know what gets into people. The first go-round if you remember was in Massachusetts at Salem."

Let's talk about that.

"It was back in 1692, and some of the girls up there started saying they'd been haunted by evil spirits. They wanted to create a sensation, and of course, they did. It took fire. And they even brought a defecting minister back from Maine or wherever it was and hanged him as a witch. Altogether I think twenty people were hanged, and one man was pressed to death. And they used dunking stools, that kind of thing. It was awful, what happened.

"And of course years later, back in 1954, the state of Massachusetts said it had been a big mistake, the whole thing, and they passed a law pardoning all the people that had been put to death, but that didn't do them much good. It's not much good to apologize for hanging a man after the deed's been done."

Tell me about the Alien and Sedition Laws.

"They were passed in 1798, passed by the Federalists to stay in office, and old John Adams signed them into law. That was a phase of the situation brought about by the Jacobins in the Jefferson campaign. The Alien and Sedition Laws were absolutely unconstitutional. You ought to read them. Damnedest things you ever saw. One of the first things Jefferson did was to repeal them. They couldn't enforce them."

What did they say?

"Well, it was a totalitarian approach to things. They made it a crime for a man to say anything about the prevailing powers in government, and they made it a crime for an alien to take a hand in any affairs of the American government, and that included foreigners who had been made citizens of the United States. You ought to read them. You wouldn't think it could happen in this country, but it did.

"And what lay behind it was that people were afraid, the way I said earlier, it was the fear of the French Revolution, fear of the Jacobins. And the Federalists exploited that fear to stay in office, just the way the Republicans at the time we were talking about exploited people's fears of the Communists to *get* themselves in office.

"They accused Jefferson of being a Jacobin, which he wasn't, and after he was inaugurated, one of his first acts was to free all the people that'd been put in jail because of the Alien and Sedition Laws. Mrs. John Adams was very upset. She thought people who had criticized her husband ought to be in jail. At least that's the way it looked, but Jefferson wrote her a letter that set out his feelings in the matter in no uncertain terms. You ought to look it up. It's a crackerjack.*

* Jefferson's letter to Mrs. Adams said, "I discharged every person under punishment or prosecution under the Sedition Law, because I considered and now consider that Law to be a nullity, as absolute and provable as though Congress had ordered us to fall down and worship a golden image, and that it was as much my duty to arrest its execution in every stage as it would have been to rescue from the fiery furnace

"And then when old Andy Jackson came along, he had been a past Grand Master of the Masons in Tennessee, and they organized an anti-Masonic outfit at that time, in the campaign of 1832, and the anti-Masonic party got seven votes. Jackson won by a bigger majority than the first time, of course, but they still got seven votes."

What did they have against the Masons?

"Nothing. Nothing. They claimed that some fella was going to give away the secrets of the Masons and that the Masons up in New York had thrown him in Niagara Falls to prevent it. I've got every degree in the Masons that there is, and if there are any secrets to give away, I'll be damned if I know what they are.

"But it turned out to be a situation that was made to order for the period, and it was another example of hysteria that lasted, as I say, through a Presidential campaign.

"And then those same kind of people, after the anti-Mason thing petered out, they became anti-Catholic. And they burned churches and tarred and feathered priests all over the northern part of the country.

"And then it became the Ku Klux Klan, of course, and we've talked about that. Those birds were against everything.

"And of course after the First World War there was an hysterical period. These things always seem to happen after a war. I've never quite figured out why. But after the First World War we had J. Mitchell Palmer. Woodrow Wilson had appointed him Attorney General of the United States, and it was one of the worst mistakes Wilson, who was otherwise a great President, ever made.

"Because Mitchell, instead of enforcing the law, which was his job, started seeing Communists everywhere, and people got in a panic, and everybody was afraid of everybody else. People got thrown in jail for no reason at all

---

those who should have been cast into it for refusing to worship the image. It was accordingly done in every instance without asking what the offenders had done, or against whom they had offended, but whether the pain they were suffering were inflicted under the pretended Sedition Law."

except they parted their hair on the wrong side according to their next-door neighbor.

"It was a terrible thing, a terrible thing. These hysterical periods always are."

You had some hysteria right in Independence with the Mormons, didn't you?

"We did, very much the same sort of thing. The Mormons got chased out of Illinois, Nauvoo, Illinois, on account of the polygamy situation. And when they left there, they came to Independence, and the same sort of situation developed. They even called out the militia to help chase them out, and then they went to a town called Fair Play north of the river about halfway to the Iowa line.

"And, finally, they came to Council Bluffs, Iowa, and Brigham Young marched them out to Utah, and it's the most remarkable march, I think, in the history of civilization. Some of them were pushing carts, and some of them, those that could afford it, had wagons. And they set up the Mormon state of Utah. They were exceedingly hardworking people, and they built Salt Lake City, which is one of the most beautiful cities in the country."

Why do you think people in Independence in those days hated them so much?

"People in Independence haven't changed a bit. The old people hate them just as much now as they did then. It's a violent prejudice. I don't feel that way, and a great many of the people of Independence do not, but you take the old-timers, the old Independence families, they won't have anything to do with Mormons."

Why?

"Well, why does a South Carolinian hate to eat at a table with a nigger? It's the same feeling exactly. It's a prejudice, and it doesn't make any sense, but it's there. And some people in public life take advantage of those prejudices."

Mr. President, a few minutes ago you said that the same kind of people are always behind these movements. What kind of people do you mean?

"Well, of course, a great many of them are not mentally complete, and many of them have prejudices of the kind we talked about, and with some of them it's a case of their having lost everything. You remember how in the deep Depression, when the farmers were having such a hard time, particularly in Iowa and northern Missouri, the corn belt, and a judge in Iowa made an injunction against the farmers' organization that had spilled milk on the road when they didn't get the right price for it.

"And those farmers didn't pay any attention to the injunction, and they came close to hanging the judge. But then Roosevelt came along with that lovely voice of his, and he made Henry Wallace Secretary of Agriculture, and they wrote a farm bill that worked, and the farmers calmed down.

"But what it always is, the people who are hysterical are afraid of something or other, and somebody's got to lead them out of it."

And speaking of hysteria, in your time, of course, there was a man named Joe McCarthy.

"Oh, yes, and I've told you he was just a no-good son of a bitch. And he was a coward. You take a damn demagogue, and he's always a coward. And what you have to do with a coward, you have to fight him, and I did. I cussed him out every chance I got.

"And of course, it wasn't just McCarthy. A fella like that couldn't have got anywhere if he'd been fought from the very beginning. They didn't do it, though. A man like that—it's like a sickness. It isn't going to disappear if you just ignore it. If that was the case, we wouldn't need doctors, would we?

"And the others, the people who know a man like that is up to no good but who encourage him for strictly partisan reasons. People like Taft [Senator Robert A. Taft, a Republican Senator from Ohio, father of the present Senator], he knew that what McCarthy was saying wasn't true, that he was demagoguing the issue for all it was worth, and he knew that was a dangerous thing to do because while I never did agree with him on much of anything at all, I think he understood the history of this country. But he said, you know, that if McCarthy didn't have the facts in one case, he should keep on making accusations until he got to one where he could come up with the facts.

"Now that's where the real danger comes; it isn't only the demagogues. It's the ones who encourage them, who'll do anything in the world to win an election. They're just as bad."

Mr. President, when you were at Columbia,* you were asked about the Japanese on the West Coast being relocated during the Second World War. You said that was another example of hysteria. Could you comment on that?

"They were concentration camps. They called it relocation, but they put them in concentration camps, and I was against it. We were in a period of emergency, but it was still the wrong thing to do. It was one place where I never went along with Roosevelt. He never should have allowed it."

Nobody ever suggested that Americans of German descent or Americans of Italian descent be put in concentration camps, be relocated.

"Well, it may have been suggested, but it didn't get very far."

Do you suppose it was because Americans of Japanese descent looked different?

"It may have been. But the reason it happened was just the same as what we've been talking about. People out on the West Coast got scared, and they panicked, and they decided to get rid of the Japanese-Americans. That's how it happened.

* In April, 1959, Mr. Truman gave the first Radner lectures at Columbia University; he spoke on the Presidency, on the Constitution, and on hysteria and witch-hunting. The lectures were published by Columbia University Press in a book called *Truman Speaks.*

"That's what I've been telling you. A leader, what a leader has to do is to stop the panic. I've told you a time or two before, I guess; a leader has to lead, or otherwise he has no business in politics. At least that's the way I've always looked at it.

"What you have to understand is that most people in this country are men and women of common sense, and when somebody gets too far out of line, like that McCarthy fellow, the people take charge and put him out of business.

"In the long run people with common sense always take over, and we don't have to worry about people whose opinions are out of line with the rest of us.

"And there have always been men who understood that, from the time this country began there have been. Take a look at what Jefferson had to say on the subject:

"'Reason and experiment have been indulged, and error has fled before them. It is error alone which needs the support of government. Truth can stand by itself. Subject opinion to coercion: whom will you make your inquisitors? Fallible men, men governed by bad passions, by private as well as public reasons. And why subject it to coercion? To produce uniformity. But is uniformity of opinion desirable? No more than face and stature. Introduce the bed of Procrustes then, and as there is danger that the large men may beat the small, make us all of a size, by lopping the former and stretching the latter. . . . Is uniformity attainable? Millions of innocent men, women, and children, since the introduction of Christianity, have been burnt, tortured, fined, imprisoned; yet we have not advanced one inch toward uniformity. What has been the effect of coercion? To make one half the world fools, and the other half hypocrites. To support roguery and error all over the world.'" *

I said, "I've never read that before. It's very beautiful, and I thank you for introducing it to me. Among so much else."

* From *Notes on Virginia*.

"Well, the point is we've been very, very fortunate in this country up to now; we've had men like Jefferson who were reasonable and responsible and who understood our past and been concerned with our future.

"There's been such men in the past when we needed them, and I see no reason why there won't be in the future. That's why I'm an optimist, and I think you'll agree with me that the facts bear me out."

Afterword

The last time I was in Independence, in the fall of 1969, the old man who drove me there from the Kansas City airport asked if I had come to town on business or pleasure. I said a little of both, and he said—people in Independence tell you things; you don't have to ask—"If you've come to see Harry Truman, and nine out of ten strangers, that's why they come, you won't be able to. Mrs. Eisenhower was here day before yesterday, and she talked to Mrs. Truman on the phone, but that's all. He don't see people anymore, don't even go on his walks half the time. Neither of them go out much since that sickness. Four years ago it was."

He stopped the taxi in front of the gate at 219 North Delaware. The house had been repainted the previous summer, and it glistened clean and white in the late afternoon sun. The wide lawn was neatly trimmed. A black man was sweeping the sidewalk, and there were the sounds of his broom and of copies of the Independence *Examiner* being tossed onto neighboring front porches by a boy on a bicycle. Otherwise there was silence, awesome in its way and welcome. We were only six miles from the smoke-blackened skyline of Kansas City, but it could have been a million.

The taxi driver got out, looked at the house for a moment, deposited some tobacco juice on the sidewalk, and said, "This used to be the summer White House, and there'd be reporters around. By the hundreds they were. And even when he and the missus came back from Washington, there was the tourists always around. But you don't even see many of *them* anymore. They forget. That's the damn trouble with people. They forget."

He jammed the Stetson lower on his forehead and for a moment wobbled precariously on the high heels of his cowboy boots. "You get old. It don't matter a good goddamn who you are or what you did, they don't pay you no mind. Especially the kids. Their long hair and dirt an inch thick on their faces—they can't wait for you to die. I'd like to get ahold of just one of them. I'd take him by the hair, and I'd—"

He looked at me and then, as if dismayed by the anger within him, closed the pocketbook mouth over a single yellow tooth and got back into the taxi.

"Don't usually talk that much, especially to a stranger," he said. "But I'm a friend of Harry's. Never been in the house, but I'm a friend all right. Everybody in town is, I guess, or think they are, and there isn't practically a building that don't have a picture of him, unless maybe it's the Republican headquarters."

I paid the fare, including a tip. He rejected the latter. "Can't take that, wouldn't feel right. Now you take Harry there. Harry'd understand. We're old men, the both of us, but by God neither one of us took nothing we didn't earn. And we don't owe anybody in the world."

For a while I was alone in front of the house, which may some day be a national monument like Monticello or Mount Vernon or the Hermitage, where old Andy Jackson is buried. Miss Sue Gentry of the Independence *Examiner* told me later, "No one knows what will happen to the house. It is a question no one has asked."

Just before dusk a young man and his wife and their three children, two boys and a girl, started taking pictures of the house and of each other standing in front of it. They were all blond and blue-eyed and handsome. Not surprisingly, their car had Minnesota license plates.

The young man asked if I'd mind taking a picture of all of them, and they stood in a rigid line, displaying an extraordinary number of perfect white teeth.

"Except for the Bomb, I mean his dropping the Bomb, I don't really know much about him," said the young man, "but we were in Kansas City, and I thought, what the hell, we're this close. It'll give the kids something to remember."

He glanced somewhat nervously at the house. "Are they in there now, do you think?" I said I thought they were, and he said to the children—who, if not the most knowledgeable, must have been the cleanest children ever—"Do you realize there's a former President of the United States in there? And a First Lady?" The kids nodded. So?

Finally the wife, who looked a little like the very early Ingrid Bergman, asked a question that has occurred to me from time to time. She said, "What in the world do you suppose they talk about?"

They drove off, the question unanswered, unanswerable.

It was dark now. The only light in the house was in the small sitting room downstairs. Harry Truman and his First Lady were two old people, alone, lonely. The house was peaceful at last. Harry Truman once called the White House a big white jail, but now the house at 219 North Delaware was a prison, too. Mrs. Truman was still a member of the Tuesday Bridge Club, but it had been years since she had attended, and a couple of years earlier, when she was invited to Kansas City to be done some honor or other, she said, "I can't. Mr. Truman won't go to bed until I get home."

I watched the light go off in the sitting room, and a moment or so later another one was turned on in the Truman bedroom upstairs. Finally the house was in total darkness, and there was not a sound anywhere. It was ten minutes after nine.

Independence is no longer a small town; it is a city with a population of 116,000, and, to be sure, there are the inevitable developments, Manor Oaks and Virginia Heights and Monticello with the tired modern houses that Harry Truman disliked so much. And there are the equally unlikable flossy apartment houses, most of them with the look of displaced Beverly Hills Renaissance. One has two swimming pools but not a single palm tree. And the motels; I stayed at Howard Johnson's.

But, happily, until the end of Mr. Truman's life there

was a kind of nineteenth-century oasis around 219 North
Delaware. The streets cannot be so very different from
what they were in 1890, when the Trumans moved to
town from Grandview. They are wide and lined with
trees, elm and cottonwood and oak, and on that crisp
autumn afternoon the leaves were just beginning to turn.

They are the kind of streets we remember or would
like to remember from our childhood, free of smog, free of
wars and confrontations, free of insoluble problems. Even
the names are nostalgic: Linden, Maple, Walnut, Cottage,
Liberty.

The houses are large and well kept, and between forty-
five and fifty of them were built just before or just after
the War Between the States. Houses like Miss Cammie
Johnston's, for instance, at 305 South Pleasant, built in
1850, vaguely English, in a style of architecture called
Missouri River Gothic. In the north wall is a cannonball
left from the First Battle of Independence.

Mr. Truman spent most of the last twenty years of his
long extraordinary life in the oasis, surrounded by the
houses and the people he grew up with and who loved
and respected him.

Only a block away from the house at 219 North Delaware was the site of the high school from which he and
Bess were graduated in 1901; the building itself had long
since burned to the ground. I had read that he had carried
some lines from Tennyson's *Locksley Hall** in his wallet

* The lines were:
    "For I dipt into the future, far as human
        eye could see,
    Saw the Vision of the world, and all
        the wonder that could be;
    Saw the heavens fill with commerce,
        argosies of magic sails,
    Pilots of the purple twilight, dropping
        down with costly bales;
    Heard the heavens filled with shouting,
        and there rain'd a ghastly dew
    From the nations' airy navies grappling
        in the central blue;

ever since his graduation, and one day I asked him about that.

He said, "Oh, yes, and the paper I copied it on kept wearing out, and I kept recopying it. I don't know how many times, twenty or thirty I expect.

"That poem made a very strong impression on me, because, although it was written in 1840 or thereabouts [1842], it predicted a great many things that happened during my lifetime and some other things that haven't happened yet but will happen someday. Tennyson knew all those things and wrote them, and that's one of the reasons I've always—and I hadn't ought to say this— had a lot more faith in poets than in reporters. Reporters just tell what has happened, and they don't do too good a job of it a lot of the time, but poets, some of them, they write about what's going to happen.

"Now Tennyson knew there were going to be airplanes, and he knew there was going to be bombing and all of it. And someday there'll be a parliament of man. It stands to reason, and that's what I was doing when I went ahead with setting up the United Nations and when I kept it from being torn apart by what happened in Korea. The United Nations is the first step.

"I guess you might say Tennyson had some influence on my career, such as it was, and I could have had worse examples to follow."

Did you read Morte d'Arthur *when you were a boy?*

"Oh, yes. I read the complete works. Everything he

Far along the world-wide whisper of the
    south-wind rushing warm,
With the standards of the people plunging
    throw' the thunder-storm;
Till the war-drum throbb'd no longer,
    and the battle-flags were furl'd
In the Parliament of Man, the Federation
    of the world.
There the common sense of most shall hold
    a fretful realm in awe,
And the kindly earth shall slumber, lapt
    in universal law."

ever wrote. That's what I'd do. I'd read something I liked by a fella, and then I'd go to the library and get . . . take out everything else he ever wrote and read it straight through. He wrote another poem about the same time as *Locksley Hall, The Golden Year,** it was called, and there's a lot in there about peace, too. I can't remember what it was, but Tennyson was a man very much concerned with stopping wars, and I guess you might say I was, too.

"We went about it in different ways, of course."

Mr. President, I understand from reading Mr. Citizen that you were offered a number of high-paying jobs after you left the White House and that you turned them all down.

"Oh, yes. I could have been a millionaire and then some I guess. But they weren't interested in hiring me. They were hiring an ex-President. They wanted to cash in on that, and they offered me, oh, a lot of six-figure salaries to do nothing much at all except let them use the name of an ex-President. I wouldn't let them do it, though. I'd rather die in the poorhouse than do a thing like that."

I was reading last night that when you were chairman of that committee we've talked about you turned down something like fifty thousand dollars for some lecture tours. Was that another example of your not wanting to cash in on your position?

"You've got to be careful. You've got to be careful. It was the same sort of thing. They were putting up the money for the chairman of what was called the Truman Committee, and I wasn't going to take advantage of the others who were on the committee and were working just as hard as I was and deserved just as much of the credit. It wouldn't have been fair to them.

"Besides, my job, the job I was elected to fulfill was to

---

* "Ah! when shall all men's good
Be each man's rule, and universal peace
Lie like a shaft across the land?"

do my job in the Senate, and that meant doing a lot of homework and not gallivanting around the country and being half-dead tired all the time, as well as not being prepared to ask the right questions and get the facts we were after."

Mr. President, another thing I didn't know until last night when I was reading about it in the book about the library here, you had a chance to go overseas to investigate transportation and supply, but you wouldn't do it. Would you mind explaining why?

"That's right. I could have gone, but two members of the committee had boys that were in the service over there, and I didn't. So I sent them instead. They wanted to see their boys, and I thought they ought to be able to do so."

Wouldn't you have liked to go?

"Oh, yes. Oh, my, yes. But I think I've told you a time or two. You can't always do what you'd like to do, and the sooner you learn that, the better off everybody is."

Mr. President, it constantly amazes me that you seem always to know what is the right thing to do.

"Oh, I don't think knowing what's the right thing to do ever gives anybody too much trouble. It's *doing* the right thing that seems to give a lot of people trouble."

After a moment we went on to other matters.

Mr. President, could I ask you a very personal question?

"Go right ahead. I've told you before, if I want to stop you, I'll stop you."

You said the other day that Justice Holmes attributed his long and successful life to the fact that he discovered at an early age that he wasn't God. To what, sir, do you attribute your long and remarkable life?

"Well, I never thought I was God; that's one thing for sure. I grew up wanting to be as good a man as my father was and as my mother wanted me to be. I never had the notion that I was anything special at all; even when I got that job in the White House, I didn't. And I never had the notion that there weren't a lot of people who couldn't do whatever it was better than I could.

"But that never worried me. All that ever concerned me was that I wanted to do it as best *I* could. So I guess I'd have to say to that, to your question, that I always tried to be satisfied with what I was and what I was doing. My father used to say that a man ought to leave the world a little better than it was when he came into it, and if that can be said about me, I guess you'll have to say I lived a successful life."

Did it bother you, leaving the pomp and circumstance of Washington? Of the White House?

"Never gave me any trouble at all. I always kept in mind something old Ben Franklin said at that meeting in Philadelphia we were talking about. They had a big discussion about what should be done about ex-Presidents, and Alexander Hamilton I think it was said that it would be a terrible thing to degrade them by putting them back among the common people after they'd had all that power. But old Ben Franklin didn't agree. It's here someplace . . . I've got it, what he said. . . . Here, read it."

Franklin said, "In free governments the rulers are the servants and the people their superiors and sovereigns. For the former therefore to return among the latter is not to degrade them but to promote them."

Mr. Truman smiled, and he said, "I kept that in mind when I was in the White House, and I've had it in mind ever since I got my . . . promotion."

Index

P9-CCP-593

Manner of Death

INCREDIBLE PRAISE FOR
THE NOVELS OF STEPHEN WHITE

Critical Conditions

"A superior psychological thriller." —*Chicago Tribune*

"Stephen White is one writer who never disappoints."
—*Hartford Courant*

"Compelling . . . more than just another psychological
thriller." —*The Orlando Sentinel*

"Spine-tingling. . . . In his sixth suspense novel, Stephen
White . . . comes up with another compulsive read . . .
guaranteeing anticipation for number seven."
—*Library Journal*

Remote Control

"Impressive . . . wild. . . . The pace never flags."
—*Chicago Tribune*

"Top-notch . . . a tightly constructed thriller."
—*Library Journal*

"White's finest hour . . . nonstop injections of adrenaline."
—*Kirkus Reviews* (starred review)

"Dark and fascinating . . . Stephen White writes thrillers of
the first order." —Nelson DeMille

continued on next page . . .

"Taut . . . breathless . . . great entertainment. White keeps getting better."   —*Denver Post*

"A sweaty-palm thriller . . . page-turning action . . . psychological suspense at its best."   —Jeffery Deaver

"Gripping . . . keeps the reader hooked."
                                             —*Publishers Weekly*

"Intriguing and suspenseful. . . . An absorbing thriller."
                                        —*Newport News Daily Press*

"A compelling tale of intrigue and murder as contemporary as today's headlines."   —*Abilene Reporter-News*

"Fresh and compelling . . . Stephen White expertly winds his way through the psychological suspense."
                                        —*Colorado Springs Gazette*

"Fascinating . . . colorful."   —*Sunday Oklahoman*

Higher Authority

"Sinister and scary."   —*New York Times Book Review*

"A powerful piece of storytelling . . . tense . . . chilling."
                                             —John Dunning

"Absorbing . . . intriguing . . . chilling."
                                        —*San Diego Union-Tribune*

"As intricate as it is mesmerizing."   —*Denver Post*

"A dazzler."   —*Cleveland Plain Dealer*

"Stephen White scores again . . . a captivating read."
—*Milwaukee Journal*

"An intriguing, compelling grabber."
—*Boulder Daily Camera*

Harm's Way

"Gripping."   —*New York Times Book Review*

"A genuine puzzle that should keep readers guessing."
—*Denver Post*

"Taut, tightly spooled storytelling . . . difficult to put down."
—*Rocky Mountain News*

"Engrossing."   —*Publishers Weekly* (starred review)

"Superb . . . one of the best thrillers of the year."
—*Cleveland Plain Dealer*

Private Practices

"Detective writing at its best."
—*West Coast Review of Books*

"White weaves a near-flawless web of evil."
—*Publishers Weekly*

"A can't-miss read."   —Larry King

"Intriguing. . . . Solid, satisfying entertainment."
—*San Diego Union-Tribune*

ALSO BY STEPHEN WHITE

STEPHEN WHITE

MANNER OF DEATH

A SIGNET BOOK

SIGNET
Published by New American Library, a division of
Penguin Putnam Inc., 375 Hudson Street,
New York, New York 10014, U.S.A.
Penguin Books Ltd, 27 Wrights Lane,
London W8 5TZ, England
Penguin Books Australia Ltd, Ringwood,
Victoria, Australia
Penguin Books Canada Ltd, 10 Alcorn Avenue,
Toronto, Ontario, Canada M4V 3B2
Penguin Books (N.Z.) Ltd, 182–190 Wairau Road,
Auckland 10, New Zealand

Penguin Books Ltd, Registered Offices:
Harmondsworth, Middlesex, England

Published by Signet, an imprint of New American Library,
a division of Penguin Putnam Inc. Previously published in a Dutton edition.

First Signet Printing, January 2000
10 9 8 7 6 5 4 3 2 1

PUBLISHER'S NOTE
This is a work of fiction. Names, characters, places, and incidents either are the product
of the author's imagination or are used fictitiously, and any resemblance to actual persons, living or dead, events, business establishments, or locales is entirely coincidental.

BOOKS ARE AVAILABLE AT QUANTITY DISCOUNTS WHEN USED TO PROMOTE PRODUCTS
OR SERVICES. FOR INFORMATION PLEASE WRITE TO PREMIUM MARKETING DIVISION,
PENGUIN PUTNAM INC., 375 HUDSON STREET, NEW YORK, NEW YORK 10014.

If you purchased this book without a cover you should be aware that this book is stolen
property. It was reported as "unsold and destroyed" to the publisher and neither the author nor the publisher has received any payment for this "stripped book."

To Terry Lapid,
for three decades of friendship

. . . the best liar is he who makes
the smallest amount of lying
go the longest way.
                    —SAMUEL BUTLER

ONE

Adrienne's tomatoes froze to death the same night that Arnie Dresser did.

September 27 is about a week early for a hard frost along Colorado's Front Range, but it's late for tomatoes. The only fruit left hanging on my friend's ragged vines the afternoon that initial winter cold front scooted south out of Wyoming were some hard green orbs that didn't appear likely to ripen before the millennium. Since I'd already made enough tomato sauce and salsa to fill half my freezer as well as a good chunk of Adrienne's, I didn't mourn the death of the tomatoes as much as I did the demise of the half-dozen fresh basil plants that had shriveled and blackened in response to the assault of the chill Canadian air.

Arnie Dresser's death was much more unexpected than was this first frost, but his passing caused me less initial reflection than did that of my neighbor's garden. The funeral was, thankfully, the first I would be attending in a long time, and I suspected that I would shed no tears at Arnie's services. I hadn't seen him in years, and we had never really been close friends. My presence at his funeral was indicated, I felt, so as not to show disrespect. If I had fallen down a steep cliff in the Maroon Bells wilderness and cracked my skull open on a rock before succumbing to exposure, I'd like to think that someone like Arnie would come and pay respects to me.

That's actually not true. Most days, I really wouldn't care. On insecure days, maybe. Most days, no.

Arnie—Arnold Dresser, M.D.—had stayed in touch. I had to give him credit for that.

Since our days training together in 1982 in the psychiatry department at the University of Colorado Health Sciences Center—he as a second-year psychiatric resident, I as a clinical psychology intern—Arnie always included me on his Christmas card list. Occasionally, he would send a note to congratulate me on something he had heard through the grapevine about my life, like my wedding, or to commiserate with me over some tragedy he thought we shared, like our divorces.

Arnie's professional demeanor was a bit overbearing—okay, before he died, I considered him pompous and arrogant—but away from work he was a nice enough guy who I never put much energy into knowing well. After my training at the Health Sciences Center was complete, I'd moved to Boulder to practice. Arnie stayed in Denver, enrolled in the Analytic Institute, and set up the de rigueur Cherry Creek office-cum-couch. I had often considered Arnie's congeniality toward me to be too much, even reaching the point of being gratuitous at times, but had never given much thought to understanding it.

At his funeral, I expected to see a slew of other nice people and some not-so-nice people whose faces I remembered from long ago in my training but whom I never knew well, either. That's the nature of internships and residencies. Short training rotations throw strangers together for intense interludes of manic involvement and long hours. It's no way to train quality health-care professionals, and certainly no way to develop enduring social relationships.

If I were someone who was into class reunions, though, Arnie would have been my pick for chairman. He seemed to have had a need to stay in touch with a lot of us from his training years. In annual Christmas cards, he'd fill me in on news about many of the other residents and interns from those days and tell me what had happened to them. I recalled some of the names, but the faces that went with them seemed to have composted in my memory. Other names

Arnie mentioned in his annual cards rang no bell at all. They belonged, I suspected, to people he had included through some arbitrary misstep of his own recollection, as he confused me with someone else whose card he was writing while he took his annual long Thanksgiving-weekend ski trip to Vail. Occasionally, reading the cards, I'd get momentarily somber over the news of some tragedy, or feel the reverberations of the stirring of ancient lust over the mention of someone for whom I'd had romantic, or more likely purely lascivious, yearnings. But mostly, I didn't pay much attention. And since I was not a Christmas card writer, I never wrote back.

My failure as a correspondent had never deterred Arnie, and I granted him points for persistence. So, despite the fact that a crisp September Saturday in Colorado offered an infinite variety of more enticing indulgences than attending a funeral, I decided that I would pay my final respects to Arnie Dresser.

Befitting Arnie's passion, which was climbing mountains, his services were going to be held in the high country at a gorgeous stone church outside Evergreen. The town of Evergreen meanders over picturesque peaks and valleys twenty miles west and a couple of thousand feet above Denver, just south of Interstate 70. If Denver at times seemed to yearn to be cast as a landlocked San Francisco, and Boulder auditioned for the role of Berkeley, Evergreen would line up to play a serviceable Sausalito or Tiburon. Evergreen was close enough to the metropolitan area to be a suburb, high enough to allow commuters to feel they truly lived in the mountains, and rural enough so that they could believe their domiciles were in the wild. But over the years this mountain oasis had started to attract cookie-cutter housing, which was soon followed by state-of-the-art supermarkets, and inevitably a Wal-Mart. The charm, sadly, has been tarnished.

The church was tucked away in the woods on the north side of the interstate. It was situated so that worshipers, or in this case mourners, could gaze out the big western windows behind the altar and see what God had wrought on one of His better days during that frantic week of creation. From the front row of the church's sanctuary, on a clear autumn day like this one, the Continental Divide stretched north and south farther than human vision permitted, the jutting peaks sided with glistening glaciers and framed by sky as pure as a mother's dreams.

Arnie Dresser's love had been climbing those mountains. But he hadn't been a rock climber or an ice climber. He wasn't one of those reckless types who conquered mountains while draped with enough ropes and hardware to stock a small-town True Value, inching upward toward the summit one handhold at a time. Arnie had been an avid recreational mountain climber. What he liked to do was walk up mountains, resorting to limited technical gear only when a particular rock face precluded a less determined stroll.

But on the other hand, it would be a slur to call Arnie Dresser a mere hiker. He was a proud member of the Fourteener Club, a loose assemblage of hiking-boot–clad outdoors people who had managed to ascend all fifty-four of Colorado's fourteen-thousand-foot peaks, from the diminutive Sunshine Peak at 14,001 feet to the majestic Mount Elbert at 14,433 feet. I'd trudged to the top of two of the fourteeners—Mount Princeton and Mount Sherman—so I considered myself officially one twenty-seventh of the way to membership. The fact that I'd been one twenty-seventh of the way to membership for the better part of seven years is an indication of the respect I could muster for those people, like Arnie, who had not only completed one circuit of Colorado's tallest peaks but had already completed two and eagerly gone back for more.

Arnie had come from a wealthy family, the Dressers at one time apparently controlling a sizable amount of the cable TV business in Wisconsin. I'd never before bothered to consider what lavish touches financial resources could bring to a funeral. I suppose I would have assumed that big bucks could provide the opportunity to occupy a fancier than necessary box in which to decompose, but Arnie's innovative send-off gave me a whole new appreciation of what family wealth could do to enhance a solemn good-bye.

The church service was brief, an inspiring mixture of nonoffensive liturgy from a tall laconic minister who I didn't think had ever met Arnie Dresser, and poignant Quaker-like testimony from the surprisingly large gathering of loved ones, friends, and acquaintances. Arnie's body wasn't actually present in the church; he had apparently already been reduced to ashes that were contained on the altar in a tasteful cherrywood box that looked as though it might have been designed to hold expensive cigars. The box was dwarfed by two huge sprays of freesia.

At the conclusion of the service a man younger than Arnie approached the pulpit and identified himself as the deceased's brother, Price. He invited the gathered mourners to leave the church with him and take a short hike down a dirt road through the nearby pine forest for a final good-bye. He didn't say why.

The trek through the woods ended in a clearing that was empty except for a helicopter, a gleaming black jet model that had seats for six, in addition to ample room for what little was left of Arnie.

I stood at the periphery, unsure what was going to happen next. I was secretly hoping for a lottery that would give me a chance to be one of five lucky mourners selected to accompany the pilot back up into the Colorado sky. But the passengers of the chopper had been pre-chosen. When Arnie's brother, Price, climbed in, I surmised that the fortunate few were family, with maybe a significant other or two thrown in.

I watched from across the clearing as the cherry chest was handed up into the cabin. The act was accomplished with so much reverence and ceremony that it looked overrehearsed, like a Super Bowl halftime show or the bridal stroll down the aisle at a wedding. Moments later, the helicopter lifted off with a pulsating roar and those of us left behind waved good-bye to Arnie Dresser for the last time.

Everyone on the ground was soon covered in a film of

fine dust stirred up by the big blades. I wondered if the symbolism was intentional.

The person next to me yelled into my ear that the chopper was on its way to the Elk Range to return Arnie's ashes to the place where he died.

The place where he died.

The *how* of Arnie's dying was actually more interesting to me.

The story I had pieced together from news accounts and from mutual acquaintances who were busy either cataloguing rumors or spreading them was that Arnie had been alone, climbing a steep but nontechnical section of Maroon Peak in the Elk Range near Aspen. Climbing alone was apparently standard practice for Arnie since his divorce. When the accident occurred, he was well below timberline, late September being much too late in the season to be attempting to reach the peak of a fourteener without winter gear. Members of the mountain rescue team that had recovered his body and examined his clothing and provisions were certain that this had been a mere recreational jaunt. No witnesses saw the actual fall. The consensus, however, was that Arnie must have lost his footing on a notoriously tough section of trail and tumbled back down a rocky slope for almost one hundred and fifty feet before clearing a rock cornice and soaring through the air for another hundred feet or so.

That a climber of Arnie's experience and skill might die from a slip-and-fall seemed ironic. In the days before the funeral I'd heard speculation that he had been suffering from recurring bouts of vertigo, or that his heart rhythms had been irregular, or that maybe a TIA, a baby stroke, was to blame for the loss of balance that led to the fatal fall.

But no one knew.

What we did know was that when he came to rest for the last time, he was crumpled piteously on a flat rock high on the south side of Maroon Peak. The rock shelf where he died was the size of a racquetball court, and the left side of Arnie's skull was flattened like a carelessly dropped melon.

Over the course of that night the chill Canadian air blew down from the north and stole the remaining life from his weakened body.

It was the exact same cause of death as Adrienne's tomatoes.

TWO

Lauren had decided against attending the funeral of a total stranger, arguing persuasively that life generally delivered enough grief and that she didn't see any reason to go inviting any extra. She'd never met Arnie Dresser and could barely recall the Christmas cards he'd sent that were always addressed to me, not us.

We had driven up to the mountains together. She had dropped me off at the church while she went across the valley to get pampered at the Tall Grass Spa on the other side of Evergreen near Bear Creek. By the time she came back to retrieve me at the church, the helicopter and all the cars but two had departed. The afternoon was warm, and I waited in the shade, sitting alone on a stone wall in front of the church.

September 27 was not only a little early for a first killing frost, but it was also a little late for that year's fall leaf season. Even at the lower elevations along the Front Range, the glory of the metamorphosis of the aspen leaves as they changed from sweet green to golden was already a few days past prime time. But Lauren and I hadn't been up to the mountains at all this month, and we thought we would take advantage of the location of Arnie's funeral to venture a little farther up I-70 in hope that some of the gilded splendor remained intact in the high country.

When she arrived back at the church driving my old Land Cruiser, Lauren had a warm glow about her that I associated with post-coital splendor. The spa treatments had left her sleepy and pink, and she asked me to drive as we left the church. As she got out of the car to move to the passenger side I found myself distracted by the sunshine that was sparkling off her raven hair. Lauren had recently cut her hair short for the first time since we'd met, and I was still getting used to the change. The novelty of seeing her long neck and sleek jaw exposed captivated me.

As she walked around the front of the car I checked her gait and was encouraged to see no evidence of a limp. My assessment of Lauren's health these days was an unconscious but constant concern, a kind of reflexive checking that reminded me of patting my pocket for my keys or touching my hip for my pager. I let myself feel encouraged by the evenness of the strides she was taking, though I knew damn well that the limp could be back the next time she got out of the car, whether that was ten minutes from now or five hours from now.

That's what her multiple sclerosis was like for us. I always kept an eye on it. It was a cantankerous dog that I always suspected could bite.

She asked about the funeral at the exact same moment that I wondered aloud about her massage.

She pulled a bare foot from her black clog and rested it on the dashboard. "I got a pedicure, too," she said. "That's why I was late."

I glanced over at her slender toes, with newly painted shiny violet nails. She has great feet. I said, "I like the color. It's cute. Sort of an *Addams Family* touch. Arnie's funeral was, well, different. Interesting. The service itself was unusual. Lots of people talked. It was nice."

"What was so different?"

"That came after. His body had already been cremated and once the services were over we all walked down this trail and there was this big black helicopter waiting to whisk his ashes back up to the Maroon Bells to the mountainside where he died. Somebody told me that his remains are going to be scattered from the chopper over the spot where he fell."

"Really?" She glanced over at me with a skeptical face. She wondered if I was making this up.

"Really. Big jet helicopter, six seats. Black, like a hearse. Took off from this little clearing down the road from the church. People waved good-bye as though Arnie was actually heading off to climb Everest or something."

"You wave, too?"

"No. Actually, I had been kind of hoping to be invited for a ride on the helicopter."

She said, "Oh, so you were being petulant. And what do you mean you wanted a ride? What about me? I was supposed to cool my heels while you flew up to the Maroon Bells to sprinkle ashes?"

"You were getting a pedicure, remember? You still want to go looking for leaves?"

"Absolutely. Central City?"

"No, I don't think so. I'm not up to fighting the gambling traffic."

"How about Georgetown, then? Guanella Pass?"

"Yeah, good. I'm hungry. You?"

"Famished. I didn't eat at the spa. I was in a Mexican mood. They were serving seaweed and some grain that I thought was bulgur but wasn't."

"Quinoa?"

"Maybe."

"Silver Plume for lunch, then?"

"Perfect."

I'd noticed that Lauren and I were having more and more conversations that felt like they had been scripted from a synopsis prepared by Cliffs Notes. For about a mile on I-70, I wondered what it meant.

Then I began to notice the golden leaves on the mountainsides and I didn't wonder anymore.

Our lunch destination was on the eastern slope of the Continental Divide, just downhill from the spot where I-70 burrows through the Divide at the Eisenhower Tunnel. The town of Silver Plume rests against the side of a mountain about two miles up the valley from its restored nineteenth-century mining sister, Georgetown. During the Colorado precious-mineral frenzy a hundred-plus years ago, Georgetown was gold and Silver Plume was silver. In the years since, Georgetown had been lovingly restored and painstakingly polished to a Victorian luster that probably surpasses its appearance during the 1880s. Silver Plume, in contrast, sits in rickety nineteenth-century decaying wonder, with dirt streets, wooden sidewalks, and hitching posts that actually once had animals tethered to them.

Georgetown lives for tourists. Silver Plume somehow just manages to survive. In excess of ninety-nine point nine percent of the cars that exit I-70 at Silver Plume turn south to the parking lots for the Georgetown Loop Railway tourist attraction. To get to old Silver Plume you have to turn north of the highway and weave across a suspicious-looking wooden bridge and down a couple of narrow lanes that don't look like they're going anywhere you might deliberately want to be heading. One more bend and you're heading east on the main street in town. It doesn't take a western historian to know that Silver Plume is nothing but a ghost town in training, one of the few remaining authentic vestiges of the Colorado mining west.

In the middle of Main Street, with big windows to catch the brilliance of the southern sun, was our destination, the KP Cafe.

The furniture in the cafe is as old as the building but not as well cared for. None of it matches. The attitude inside is friendly and warm. Folks who want to be left alone are left alone. Those who want to chat get chatted with. The food is just fine. When the coffee's fresh it's good, but sometimes it burns after it sits for a while on the big old Bunn machine behind the bar.

Lauren and I poked our heads in the door and said hello to the same waitress we'd had the last few times we were in. Her name was Megan. She suggested, and we gladly took, a sunny deuce by the front windows. We ate at the KP five or six times a year, always on our way somewhere else. It was sufficient frequency that we were treated like honorary regulars.

We both ordered Mexican and decided to split a beer.

Megan smiled at Lauren and ignored me. My memory was that she had done that the last time we were in, too.

Maybe thirty seconds after we ordered, another couple entered the café. I noticed their arrival because they were both in suits. Megan stopped wiping the counter because they were both in suits. His was a nondescript navy. Hers was a vibrant fuchsia trimmed with raspberry. I didn't recognize her but I knew that suit. These two had been at Arnie Dresser's funeral.

I whispered to Lauren, "They were at the funeral, too."

She glanced over. "In that suit?"

I shrugged. "I doubt if Arnie was offended."

"That's important, I suppose. But how does one offend ashes, anyway? Doesn't make it funeral garb in my book."

"I didn't know you had a book."

She punched me across the table as Megan directed the couple to a cramped table in back, near the door to the rest rooms. I assumed, with some confidence, that they weren't regulars. I watched with gossipy interest as the two of them immediately entered into a contentious discussion about something I couldn't quite overhear. Their upper bodies were leaning forward over the rickety table so far that their heads almost touched in the middle. Her voice was louder than his. I thought I heard the Deep South hibernating somewhere in it. I finally lost interest as Megan dropped a couple of menus on their table.

A minute or so later, Megan brought us our beer along with a basket of tortilla chips and some salsa that didn't come out of a bottle. As Lauren was taking her first sip of beer, her eyebrows arched. I turned toward her gaze and saw that fuchsia suit was approaching our table. I sat back on my chair.

She said, "Dr. Gregory? Dr. Alan Gregory?"

The woman wearing the fuchsia suit was apparently somebody I should have but didn't remember from long ago at the medical center in Denver. With more embarrassment in my voice than I felt, I said, "Yes, that's me. I'm Alan

Gregory. I'm sorry, do I know you from the Health Sciences Center? I think I recall seeing you at the funeral."

She fingered the lapels of her suit jacket with both hands. "Yes, yes. I was at Dr. Dresser's services. But no, I didn't do my training here. I went to Georgetown. Not the little one we just passed down the hill, here. The big one in D.C." She laughed at her own wit and held out her hand to shake mine. "I hope you will please forgive my intrusion. My name is A. J. Simes. Dr. A. J. Simes."

I wasn't sure if I was ready to forgive her intrusion. I shook the hand she offered and said, "This is my wife, Lauren Crowder. Lauren, Dr. Simes."

"Pleased to meet you, Ms. Crowder."

I was afraid she was going to ask to pull up a chair. She didn't. I hoped her visit was over. It wasn't.

She said, "This may seem presumptuous—my walking up to you like this—and after you hear what we have to say, perhaps preposterous as well, but my associate and I feel that it's essential that we have a word or two with you, Dr. Gregory. I do hope you don't mind." She tilted her head toward her companion across the room, who appeared embarrassed and wasn't looking our way.

I sighed. "Actually, we're enjoying a rare afternoon out. Another time would be much better. I'll be happy to arrange some time to see you . . . both. Why don't I give you a card?"

She shook her head in a tight little arc, almost more of a shiver than a shake. "Please don't jump to conclusions, Doctor. I'm not usually an impolite woman. Not at all. Interrupting you like this makes me easily as uncomfortable as it is making you. What we want to discuss with you just shouldn't wait, I'm afraid."

Simes looked back over her shoulder at her companion. He was studiously avoiding her, his eyes raised toward heaven. It appeared that he was either in deep prayer or was into architectural relics and was doing a thorough examination of the pressed-tin ceiling.

Megan walked up behind A. J. Simes with two large platters of steaming Mexican food that she was gripping with potholders. She had a pained smile on her face and she was dancing back and forth from one foot to the other as though she had to pee. I was guessing that the aging potholders in her hands had lost some of their original insulating capacity.

Over Simes's shoulder, Megan said, "Careful, now, you guys, these platters are hot."

I cleared space in front of me for the food and asked, with minimal interest, "And why is that, Dr. Simes? I don't even know you. Why can't this wait?"

Simes moved her feet a little—though not quite enough for Megan to pass—and faced me directly. She turned her head toward Lauren until she was certain that she had her attention as well as mine. But she spoke to me.

"This can't wait because," she said, "after quite a bit of investigation, and a significant amount of contemplation, I'm relatively certain that someone is going to try to kill you, Dr. Gregory."

Behind her, the green chili burrito platters went down with a roar. Refried beans erupted into the room like lava from the Second Coming of Mount St. Helens.

THREE

Megan said, "Oh shit. Frank, I need some help out here. Bring the mop. Bring the broom. Bring the damn trash can."

I stood to help. Megan almost shoved me back into my seat. "No, no. Sit. Sit. Your shoes are covered with green chile and crap. All of you, sit, damn it." She faced Simes, who didn't have a chair. "God, I'm sorry about my mouth. Oh, no. Look what happened to your pretty suit."

A. J. Simes didn't seem to know what to say. She turned to face her associate. His face was buried in his hands and he was shaking his head back and forth. With her back to us, I could clearly see the damage that the burritos had done to Dr. Simes's clothing. A pattern of splatters and chunks spread out like a fan from the top of her thighs to her shoulders. I thought that Henry Lee could probably do an entire lecture on the splatter pattern of green chili burrito platters off century-old pine flooring.

Lauren was dressed in black jeans and clogs. The damage to her wardrobe was, relatively, minor. She wiped her shoes clean with her napkin, stood, and slipped Dr. Simes's jacket from her shoulders. "I'll do your jacket. You'd better spin that skirt around and see what you can do with the back. I'm afraid it's not pretty."

Somebody is trying to kill me? Why is everybody so damn concerned about the frijoles? I actually looked out the window to see if there was someone coming my way with a weapon.

Dr. Simes said, "I'm so sorry. This is all my fault. I didn't handle this well." She headed to the rest room to salvage her fuchsia skirt and to try to escape her obvious humiliation.

Lauren went immediately to work on the back of the jacket with my napkin and a glass of water.

I said, "Did she say she thought someone was trying to kill me?"

Megan looked up from her catcher's crouch on the floor and said, "Damn straight that's what she said."

Lauren just nodded. I couldn't read her expression at all.

Frank and Megan made quick work of the burrito catastrophe. Lauren continued to dab at the jacket. A. J. Simes maintained her retreat to the bathroom. I'd been in that bathroom on a couple of occasions. Nineteenth-century charm ends at plumbing. Period, end of sentence. The bathroom of the KP Cafe was absolutely no place for a leisurely respite.

Without glancing up, Lauren said, "She has MS. Dr. Simes."

"She does? How can you tell?"

She shrugged. "Look at the muscles around her eyes. She forms her words a little too carefully. She's a little unsteady. I don't know. I can just tell."

I nodded. Lauren could tell. The mild form of the disease wasn't as invisible to people who lived with it as it was to the rest of us.

"What on earth do you think she was talking about? I mean, someone trying to kill me? Is she nuts?"

"I don't know. I got the impression that she was planning on telling us soon enough, though. Before the burrito thing, anyway."

Across the room, the man in the navy suit stood and approached our table. Lauren lowered the fuchsia jacket to her lap and smiled politely. I said, "Hello. I'm Alan Gregory. This is my wife, Lauren Crowder."

He held out his hand. "I know who you both are. I'm Milton Custer, by the way. Pleased to meet you."

Milton Custer was built like a redwood. Tall, thick trunk, thin limbs. His hair was salt-and-pepper, and his handshake was painful. "Call me Milt," he said. He tilted his head toward the back of the cafe and raised his left eyebrow. "But I think you should call her Dr. Simes."

Lauren asked, "What kind of doctor is she?"

"Same as your husband, ma'am. A psychologist."

Lauren seemed to be considering something, and said, "Won't you pull up a seat, Mr. Custer?"

Reluctantly, it seemed to me, Milt Custer sat, first twirling the chair around so he could straddle it. I sensed he liked the idea of having some kind of barrier between us. He removed his glasses and started to clean them. It turned out to be a complicated ritual that involved a tiny lavender cloth he pulled from inside a hard case that he retrieved from the pocket of his suit jacket.

As he polished the second lens, he said, "I didn't want to do it here. Tell you like that, you know, about what we think is going on and all. That was her idea. She was determined. First I told her I didn't think we should do it at the church—I mean, that's not right, at the church right after a funeral. I told her we should follow you home and tell you there. Where you feel more comfortable, safer, you know. But then you didn't go home, you came here, and then I didn't think we should do it here, either." He looked self-conscious. "For obvious reasons. But she was sure you guys were heading someplace overnight and insisted we better take care of things right now. Dr. Simes, she's single-minded sometimes. Maybe you might even say stubborn."

I asked, "You and she are . . . ?"

He considered the question. "Colleagues. Partners, I guess. For now, anyway."

You guess?

"And you both think someone is trying to . . . what? Hurt me?"

He reflected for a good ten seconds before answering. When he was ready to speak he stared right at me and nailed me with a glare that screamed *pay attention*. He said, "No. This guy is definitely planning to kill you. Merely hurting you would indicate failure on his part. And so far as we can tell, he hasn't failed at any of this, yet. He's batting a thousand."

A thousand? Instantly I wondered how many times the guy had been to the plate.

Lauren asked, "Who the hell are you people?"

I thought, *Yeah!*

Megan wanted to clean a little more thoroughly under our table and asked if she could move us all to a little alcove by the counter. A secondary benefit occurred to me: If someone took a shot at me over there, it wouldn't be as likely to endanger the other patrons.

A. J. Simes rejoined us a few minutes later. Lauren handed her the jacket and said, "I did the best I could."

She said, "Thanks. I'm so embarrassed."

I found myself examining A. J. Simes for indications of multiple sclerosis. Maybe there was something odd about the coordination of her eyes when she blinked. But so far she appeared to me to be just an attractive woman in her late forties who had an intriguing swirl of gray in a thick head of auburn hair.

Milt said, "They just asked who the hell we are."

Simes nodded. "Good question. May I sit?"

I said, "Please."

"I'm so sorry. That was infelicitous. Blurting that out the way I did. And I accept full responsibility. Including dry cleaning, of course."

Lauren said, "It's forgotten already."

"You are too kind. How to begin?"

I said, "I think you've already begun."

She widened her mouth into something that was either a sardonic smile or the beginnings of a snarl. "The easiest way to explain our interest in you, Dr. Gregory, is to tell you we're both ex-FBI." She lowered her chin at Milt. "My colleague is—was—Supervisory Special Agent Milton Custer, who concluded his career in Chicago. And I spent almost all my time with the Bureau in the Investigative Support Unit. Initially, at Quantico. That's in Virginia. As I said before, my name is Dr. A. J. Simes."

The "Doctor" stuff was beginning to sound pretentious. But I knew about the Investigative Support Unit.

I said, "That's Behavioral Sciences, right?"

"The name changed a few years back. A bureaucratic thing. But yes, a similar division. Most of the same responsibilities."

"Were you in VICAP?" I was asking if she had been involved with the Violent Criminal Apprehension Program, the team that profiled serial killers and sexual psychopaths, among others.

"Yes. You're familiar with our work?"

I said, "Unfortunately," but didn't elaborate about my friend Peter's murder a couple of years earlier by a suspected serial killer. I had a funny feeling that these two already knew about Peter's murder. "Were you a profiler, Dr. Simes?"

"Yes. It was one of my responsibilities. I have those skills and a significant amount of experience, and expertise, in the area."

Lauren had narrowed her focus. Her gaze was locked on Simes. Lauren, a deputy DA, was moving quickly into prosecutor mode. I was grateful. She was an astute observer and a more pointed interviewer than I was. She asked, "You said *ex*-FBI, Dr. Simes?"

Simes answered, "That's right. Ex. Mr. Custer and I are participants in a consortium of ex-agents and other ex-Bureau personnel who provide private consultation to law enforcement agencies, businesses, and, occasionally, individuals, on matters in which we might have particular expertise."

I remembered reading something about this group once. "Your organization was invited to participate in the Jon-Benet Ramsey investigation in Boulder, weren't you? A couple of years ago?"

"Some of our colleagues were asked to assist the family, yes. With one unfortunate exception, everyone who was contacted declined. We are quite selective about where we lend our resources and experience. That offer from that family was particularly easy to decline."

I said, "And now I assume you're on a different case? And you are lending your experience to . . . ?"

The two FBI types looked at each other. Simes nodded. Custer answered, "We've been given permission to inform you that we were retained by the mother of Dr. Arnold Dresser."

Given their presence at Arnie's funeral, I shouldn't have been surprised at the answer, but I was. Lauren pressed on with her earlier line of questioning. "Why did you leave the FBI, Dr. Simes?"

Simes raised her chin a little and said, "Medical disability." The way she formed her words communicated her desire that Lauren not inquire further seeking details.

Lauren said, "And you, Mr. Custer?"

"I did my twenty-five. I retired."

Lauren nodded as though their answers were somehow self-evident. "And Dr. Dresser's mother hired you to investigate something involving her son's death on that mountain, right?"

"Right," Custer said.

"Mrs. Dresser wishes for you to determine what, exactly?"

Simes replied, crisply, "She would like us to determine whether or not her son was murdered."

Murdered?

Lauren continued, "And by your earlier statement about the danger that my husband's in, I take it we can assume that you've determined that Dr. Dresser was murdered?"

Simes answered, " 'Determined'? Perhaps too strong a word for this stage of the investigation. But we've begun to assemble a body of evidence that indicates that it is possible, even likely, that Dr. Dresser's death was in fact a homicide and not an accident."

"And you are here with us, today, because you've made some connection that takes you from Dr. Dresser to my husband?"

Simes said, "We have reason to be . . . concerned. I felt— Mr. Custer and I each felt—that our concerns are strong enough and the evidence is substantial enough that it would be a dereliction of duty to fail to inform your husband that he, too, may be at some risk."

I protested, "I barely knew Arnie Dresser."

I felt Simes's gaze turn to me. It felt condescending, and I didn't like it. "If our theory is correct, the risk comes not from how well you knew Dr. Dresser, I'm afraid, Dr. Gregory, but rather from *when* you knew Dr. Dresser."

"I haven't spent any time with him for over fifteen years."

"Exactly."

Lauren looked at me and, I'm sure, saw the complete befuddlement in my face. She said, "What does that mean? 'Exactly.' What do you mean?"

Simes said, "That's the time period—the window, if you will—that appears to be important. Almost sixteen years ago. When Dr. Gregory and Dr. Dresser were in training together on an inpatient psychiatric unit at the Health Sciences Center of the University of Colorado in Denver. The unit was known as Eight East."

She had her facts right. I didn't find that reassuring, however. I asked, "Why is that important?"

A family with two small children was taking the table next to ours. Milt raised his voice above everyone's and said, "I'm not real comfortable with how all this is proceeding. Please, everyone, let's not do this here. Why don't we take a little walk, get ourselves some air?"

I hadn't eaten a bite. I wasn't at all hungry. I asked Lauren if walking was okay with her. She said it was. I threw forty dollars on the table to cover our beer, our burritos, and the havoc we'd precipitated and said, "Okay, let's walk."

The afternoon was radiant. The angle of the autumn sun and a light wind spiraling down from the Divide caused the aspen leaves on the mountain faces to twinkle like a million golden stars. Stark cumulus clouds were tugged and distorted by the winds as they floated against the blue sky. The steam whistle from the Georgetown Loop train pierced the quiet from across the narrow valley.

Milt said, "I love trains. I wish we had time."

Simes admonished him sharply, "We don't." If Dr. Simes had children, I was certain they never grabbed items off the shelf at the supermarket.

Lauren took my hand and we began walking toward the general store at the eastern end of the little town. She pointed toward the door. "Remember the bread? This place has great bread," she said to me. "We need to buy some before we leave today."

Get bread? I was beginning to go nuts inside. Two ex–FBI agents thought somebody was trying to kill me—yet everybody around me, with the exception of our waitress, seemed to be taking the news in stride.

Two more steps and I said, "Would somebody please tell me what the hell is going on?"

Milt looked deferentially at Dr. Simes. I couldn't tell whether his deference was the result of respect, or fear. She raised her chin to indicate it was all right with her that he proceed.

"Dr. Dresser had apparently been concerned for a while that something . . . odd . . . has been going on with the group of people he trained with during his residency in 1982. Specifically, he was worried about the group of interns, residents, and supervisors who were working on the . . . what? The Orange Team? Is that right? On that unit called Eight East in the hospital at the medical school. That includes you, Dr. Gregory. You did some training on the Orange Team on Eight East in the fall of 1982, didn't you? With Dr. Dresser?"

We were standing in front of a frame building that a hopelessly faded sign said had once been a livery. The structure looked as though it would fall over if I sneezed. I said, "Yes. I was one of the psychology interns on that unit then. That's when I met Arnie. He was one of the second-year psychiatric residents."

"Well, to get back to my story. Dr. Dresser was close to his mother. His father died quite a few years back and he and his mom have been real close ever since. He was kind of a compulsive letter writer and E-mailer and over the years he'd begun to express some continuing concern to her that the group of people he trained with on the Orange Team seemed jinxed in some way."

I asked, "Jinxed how?"

Lauren tugged on my hand. "I know it's hard, sweets. Be patient. Let him tell his story." My stomach growled. Lauren's tolerance for skipping meals was much lower than mine. If I was hungry, I guessed she must be famished.

Two young men in cowboy boots, Lee jeans, and worn Stetsons paused next to us for a moment. I was feeling so paranoid that I checked their hips for holstered Colt .45s. No one spoke until they passed.

I broke the silence. "Okay, go on. I'm sorry."

"It's fine, I understand. This has to be totally strange for you. Us hijacking you like this. I'm just trying to present it to you in a way that doesn't sound more off-the-wall than it is."

Milt's manner wasn't coplike. I knew a lot of cops—was good friends with one—and Milt's manner reminded me more of bad news being delivered by a kind uncle than bad news being delivered by a cop. Still, I was impatient for him to get to the end of his story.

"Let's go back to the early eighties. You remember a supervising psychiatrist on the Orange Team named Susan Oliphant?"

"Yes. She was the ward chief." Next I expected to learn that she had become a full-time proprietor of the past tense.

"Do you know she died in 1989?"

"No," I said slowly, drawing out the long vowel, assuming what I was going to hear about the details of her death was not going to be good news. Had Arnie told me about Susan's death? I didn't think so. Maybe it was in one of the cards I never bothered to finish reading.

"She was a private pilot. Did you know that about her? She died in a plane crash. A little Cessna, a 172. The crash killed both her and her twelve-year-old niece. The plane crashed into a mountainside in the Adirondacks. Clear weather. Radio contacts with air traffic control just before the impact were particularly heartbreaking, made it clear to anybody who listens to them that the plane suffered some catastrophic mechanical problem."

"I'm so sorry." And I was. I had been fond of Susan. Some of the psychiatrists on the Orange Team treated the psychology interns as though we were younger siblings who had been tethered to them by parents who didn't have a clue how much of an annoyance we really were. Susan Oliphant hadn't been like that. I hadn't heard much of her over the years, only knew she wasn't in town. Once more, I tried to recall whether Arnie's Christmas cards had notified me of her death. I couldn't remember. Was I that callous? I hoped not.

Milt continued, "After a routine investigation, the NTSB ruled the plane crash to be an accident, caused by control-linkage failure. The impact was severe, though, and destroyed most of the evidence."

"She couldn't steer the plane?"

"Basically."

I touched Lauren's arm while I asked, "Manner of death?"

From the corner of my eye, I saw a tiny smile grace Simes's face. She was pleased at my question. With my words, she had realized with visible relief that she and Milt weren't going to have to connect the dots for me.

"Accident."

I don't know why, but I faced Simes. "But you don't necessarily concur with the coroner's findings on manner, do you?"

Milt answered as though he didn't even notice the slight. "We'll get to all that in a minute. May I continue?"

"Sure. Go on."

"Dr. Matthew Trimble?"

"Yes, I remember him. Matt was a psychiatric resident. He did medical backup for me on a few cases on the unit. He's dead as well?" I was playing stupid now. I knew about Matt's death. News of his senseless shooting had spilled through the mental health community in Colorado like a flash flood through a floodplain. It had touched us all, some more deeply than others. Matt was the only professional I knew who had actually gone ahead and arranged his career so that he could try to do as much good for people as the idealistic plans of his youth said he was going to do. I wasn't his friend, but I respected him immensely.

"Yes. He died in 1991. He was the victim of a drive-by in southeast Los Angeles as he was leaving a people's-clinic–type place where he was doing pro bono work with their drug program. He—"

"That's where he was from. Compton. That's where he grew up. He went back there to work."

"Right. No arrest was ever made in the case. It's still open. Local cops said it looked random to them. A Crip who was walking with him got hit, too. L.A. had a ton of drive-bys in those days. The Summer of Blood and all that." He paused. "Manner on that one was, of course, homicide. It's the only one I'm going to tell you about where the manner of death was homicide."

"How many more?" I said. I could barely form the words.

He didn't answer. He said, "Next one was 1994. A trickier one."

My heart crashed to my toes. *No, not Sawyer.*

"Dr. Wendy Asimoto."

I'd been holding my breath. I exhaled. I didn't know about Wendy's death. Though I hadn't thought about her in years, I had no trouble remembering her. I said, "Wendy was a psychiatric resident, too, second-year like the others. She was older than the rest of us, closer to thirty. She had already completed an internal medicine residency prior to coming to the medical center for psych training. I remember her as having a healthy dose of skepticism about psychiatry."

"Very good memory, Dr. Gregory." The compliment, and a surprised tone, came from Dr. Simes.

I had an impulse to tell them both to call me Alan, but I wasn't sure I wanted that level of intimacy yet. I said, "Is she the last one?" I wanted Wendy Asimoto to be the last dead shrink.

Milt looked up at the leaves and paused to let the cut of

the steam whistle slice through the valley. He wasn't willing to give me a count, yet.

"Anyway, Dr. Asimoto dropped out of the psychiatric residency program after her second year. Decided she preferred internal medicine after all. By the time 1993 rolled around, she was working as a ship's doctor for the Cunard Line. Turns out she disappeared at sea off St. Petersburg in the Baltic on the fourth day of a twelve-day cruise in June of 1993. No one saw her go overboard. No body was ever recovered. She has since been declared dead. Manner of death on this one is still undetermined, but I think it's presumed accidental. We're not done looking into it, but there were rumors that she had begun to drink excessively."

"She was a cruise ship doc?"

"For a few years, yeah."

"And she was an alcoholic?"

"Perhaps. It happens."

"But you don't believe it? The accident part."

"May I continue?

"I'd rather that you be done."

Custer stared at me as though my impatience was concerning him. "No, I'm afraid I'm not done."

I was starting to get really nervous and I didn't want Lauren to know why. I said, "I think maybe we should go someplace and sit down."

Lauren examined my eyes, bit her bottom lip, slid her arm around my waist, and said, "In town, honey, the KP is about it, isn't it."

Simes looked weary. She said, "How about your car? It's big enough for all of us."

We started walking to the Land Cruiser. I desperately wanted a diversion. I didn't know what to do next. I didn't want to be with Simes or Custer when I heard that Sawyer Sackett was dead.

But the most troubling thing was that I didn't want to be with Lauren, either.

FOUR

Milt Custer said, "This next one is the weirdest of them all. And it's the most recent. It happened in February, this year."

The blood seemed to vaporize from my limbs and I felt dizzy. *February? This year? That's after Arnie's last Christmas card. Maybe Sawyer is dead and I don't even know it.*

I was sitting on the driver's seat of my car and had enough of my wits still about me to recognize the irony of being in that position. Lauren had climbed into the backseat to allow one of the ex-agents to join me up front. For now, this was Milt Custer's show, and he claimed the shotgun position. Simes sat right behind me; I could see her impassive face in the mirror. Suddenly I wasn't sure whether her lock of white hair was an intense shade of blond or a prematurely advanced shade of gray.

The sun was heading down for the day, spending its last minutes perched along the peaks that framed the southern horizon, and the rays were beating down on the car. I turned on the power so we could lower the windows for some ventilation. Everyone but Simes did. When a breeze rushed through the car, she touched her hair twice with an open palm, side and back.

Lauren asked, "What do you mean? All the deaths seem strange to me."

Custer scooted sideways on his seat to face her. "You're right. But there's a lag here, timewise, I mean. We're talking over two years from the previous death. This one took our guy some time and careful planning. Method is creepier, too. This victim died in a home tanning bed."

I couldn't talk. Lauren said, "What? How?"

"She had a skin condition—what's that called, A.J.?" I noted that suddenly Custer sounded like a cop. I wondered whether it was an intentional change on his part or whether he was just returning to form.

Simes frowned and said, "I don't remember. Maybe it will come to me."

"Yeah, whatever. Anyway, she had to use a tanning bed for ultraviolet skin treatment. Did it at home, the treatment, a regular type of thing. Had this big fancy, bed—you know what I mean, you seen 'em? Like in those salons? One of those clamshell-type things where the top closes over you and you get zapped by lights top and bottom at the same time. Have to wear those little goggles to keep the fluid in your eyeballs from boiling. I'm a little claustrophobic myself. No way I climb into one of those things, let me tell you that."

Please. Was it Sawyer? Please.

"Anyway, she sets the timer, climbs in, pulls down the lid, puts on the goggles, and flips the switch. Immediately, two things go wrong. One, the timer malfunctions, never ticks down, so the lights just keep on cooking. Two, one of the hinges breaks so the bed won't open back up. When those two things go wrong at the same time in a home tanning bed, you have a recipe for roasting a human being to death."

Lauren asked, "Why didn't she just pull the plug?"

"Bad design. Cord comes out at the foot of the bed. No way to twist around to get down there with the top pressing down on you."

"And the hinge couldn't be forced back open?"

Custer shook his head and said, "It was badly jammed. No."

"No way to squirm out?"

"Not in this design."

"So she died?"

"Yeah, eventually. A relative found her after almost two

days. But she didn't actually die for another thirty-six hours."

Lauren was appraising me with some mixture of pity and concern. Fortunately, she recognized my apoplexy. She asked Custer, "And, given the tenor of this discussion so far, you both suspect that the bed was tampered with?"

Custer said, "Timers fail sometimes, right? We're gonna take a look at that—the bed's still in evidence. But the hinge? Even the local cops thought that was odd. They tried to find the technician who last serviced the bed, which just happened to be the day before all this crap happened, and he was nowhere to be found. Had worked for the company for only six weeks. Disappeared right after that service call. Never picked up a paycheck. Never said good-bye."

"Did he service the hinges or the timer?"

"Wasn't supposed to. He was there to change the bulbs, that's all. The police looked hard at him. Had his photo taken for company ID, so there's that. Left a trail of paperwork, which looks to us like it's probably all false. He never lived at the address he gave to his employer. And after this lady gets toasted, he vanishes like a fart in a firestorm."

I thought Custer looked a little embarrassed about his choice of analogies. I knew Lauren was far from offended; her tongue was under her upper lip and I could tell she was busy piecing something together. Custer continued, "In case you're curious, manner on this one is undetermined, no surprise. Local cops don't like to hear about it from people like us, but the truth is that their experts can't be certain about any tampering, one way or another. Dr. Simes and I are encouraging them to pack up the whole damn bed and ship it to the FBI lab. My fear is that the guys who looked at it locally have managed to screw it up forever from a forensic point of view. For now, though, they don't have any hard evidence of foul play and they don't have the resources to track this guy down and question him."

Lauren asked, "He disappeared without a trace?"

"That's right," Milt replied. "That's not surprising, though. Our guy is good."

"But you have a photograph?"

"Yeah, but it's pretty worthless. Long hair and a big goatee. Tinted eyeglasses big enough for a clown to wear for an audition at Ringling's."

Lauren said, "So was she the last one? Before Dr. Dresser, I mean. Was it the last death?"

"Last one we know about. We found your husband easily enough, ma'am. We've identified one other staff member from the Orange Team who we feel might be at risk, as well. She's not been . . . available, so far. Out of town. One or both of us will go see her as soon as we leave Colorado."

"Who's that?" I asked, as nonchalantly as I could.

He tapped himself on the side of the head. "I'm sorry, I'm having a charley horse in my brain here. A.J., what's her name?"

"Sawyer Faire," she said without hesitation. "You remember Dr. Faire, Dr. Gregory?"

Sawyer is still alive.

I stammered, "Of course. She was, um, Sawyer Sackett then, another psychiatry resident. There were two interns and three residents on the team. My memory is that she quit. Left the program at Christmastime. Maybe this all has to do with something that happened after she left. If so, she wouldn't be in any danger at all."

With the news that Sawyer was alive, I felt like my lungs could process oxygen for the first time in ten minutes. I didn't want to talk anymore about Sawyer, so I asked Custer, "You didn't mention a name. Who was it who, uh, who died in the tanning bed?"

Simes answered from the backseat. I thought her tone was unnecessarily provocative when she said, "That was your clinical supervisor, Dr. Gregory. Dr. Amy Masters."

"Oh God." Amy Masters had been in her early fifties when she had been my clinical supervisor on the adult psychiatric inpatient service. She would have been nearly seventy when she was roasted alive in that tanning bed. "She was small, frail, she couldn't have . . ."

Milt finished my thought. "No, she didn't have a prayer of forcing those hinges open."

I stared out the windshield at this old western mining

town, watching the shadows lengthening in the dust before they melded into the darkness. This late-day choreography of light hadn't changed in Silver Plume in a hundred years.

The inside of the car was quiet until I said, "I would like to go home."

Lauren objected. "Wait a second, sweets." She spoke again, directing her question to the two agents. "First, do either of you think Alan is in immediate jeopardy? Is this danger imminent?"

Simes answered after contemplating something long enough to aggravate my discomfort even more. "No, we don't. None of these deaths, if indeed they were murders, as we suspect, were impulsive. Quite the opposite. As you know, Dr. Dresser has been dead barely a week. As far as we can tell, no two deaths have taken place closer than eight months apart. If our suspicions are accurate, we feel that the man responsible is just now beginning to plan the death of his next victim. That could be Dr. Gregory. That could be Dr. Faire."

Lauren said, "Okay, then. Are you planning on telling us what you think we should do? Or are you just planning on terrifying us with innuendo?"

Before Simes could answer, I said, again, "You know, I really, really would like to go home."

Lauren ignored me again. "Are there any law-enforcement agencies that share your concern about this series of deaths?"

I was surprised to hear defensiveness in Custer's voice. "Remember, we've only been on this five days. It's preliminary. We've done good work. We have a lot more work to do, I'll grant you that. It's just us and some chits we called in. We don't have the resources of the Bureau here."

Simes's response was more to the point. She said, "The only formal investigation that's still at all active is the tanning-bed death. That would be Dr. Masters. There were no reasons to link the others together before Dr. Dresser's mother informed us of his suspicions about his colleagues' deaths. If you follow the trail as we've done, you will discover that we're discussing different jurisdictions in widely different geographic areas, hugely different MOs, and a long, long period of time."

Lauren began to employ her devil's-advocate voice. I knew she didn't believe the protest she was making. I doubted that Simes or Custer would be able to tell, though. She said, "And so far, if I follow that trail along with you, your formulation of this case, of the danger my husband is in, is based solely on coincidence and conjecture. You hear hoofbeats, and by my reckoning you're thinking zebras, not horses."

Custer said, "No, ma'am, no. That's not exactly right. Like you're suggesting, we started off following the hoof-beats, and we did it with a healthy degree of skepticism. But what we found, as we proceeded, is we found zebra shit. And that's why we're thinking zebras."

Suddenly, I recognized what I was watching. Lauren had managed to get these two cops to take on the role of having to convince a prosecutor about the quality of their evidence. The FBI types had done it a thousand times with federal prosecutors. Lauren had done it a thousand times with various local cops.

The mutual suspicion left everything slightly constipated.

Lauren said, "I assume you've taken your suppositions back to your old employer. A series of homicides that cross state lines certainly falls under the jurisdiction of the FBI. What do they say?"

Simes said, "We have discussed it informally with the Bureau. One of my old colleagues has expressed professional curiosity. He's asked us to develop this some more and get back to him. So that's what we're attempting to do. Proof in these cases is almost always elusive."

"Is there a specific reason why the FBI is reluctant?"

Simes cleared her throat. "Cases like these are the toughest serial crimes to recognize. And they are even harder to solve, Ms. Crowder. Identifying a link between two or more murders is usually accomplished through either physical evidence or eyewitness identification. In the absence of those things, we depend on pinpointing similarities in circumstances, similarities in victims, or similarity in MO. I'm sure you know all this."

Lauren countered, "And in these cases, you have none of those things. All you have is the fact that these victims—if indeed they are victims—worked together for a few months, what, fifteen years ago?"

"That's right. If Special Agent Custer and I are correct, we are looking at a murderer who has maintained a roster of intended victims for fifteen years. He carefully plots the murder of one victim at a time. He carries out those homicides in such a way as to make the deaths seem to fit in the context of the victim's life. He varies his method each time so that his hand is unrecognizable from case to case, and devises the murders so that the deaths appear accidental, or incidental. He leaves no calling card and takes no trophies. So far, he is demonstrating more patience than Job. And with the exception of the recent murder of Dr. Amy Masters in the tanning bed, from a law-enforcement point of view, he has operated almost invisibly." She paused. "He is going from doctor to doctor, one at a time. He is, in his own ironic way, making rounds."

Lauren softened her voice. I think she wanted Simes to admit how frail this construction was. She asked, "But despite all the hypothesizing in your scenario, you're confident enough of your appraisal that you've come to Colorado to warn Alan that he is a likely next target?"

Custer shrugged and said, " 'Likely' may be a bit strong, ma'am. Fifty-fifty's more accurate."

I wondered if Simes was going to correct him, adjust the odds a little. Eighty-twenty?

Simes caught my eye in the mirror and quickly added, "We *are* here to warn you, Dr. Gregory. That's true. And I hope you pay heed to how clever your adversary is. But we're also here to enlist your help. I've come to believe that to stop this man, to keep him from killing two more people, the first task is, obviously, to identify him and to find him so that we can bring him to the attention of federal and local law enforcement. And there are only two people who can help us identify possible candidates from the Orange Team on Eight East in the autumn of 1982. One is you. The other is Dr. Faire."

My breathing was shallow as I said, "Help you how?"

I turned on my seat to face her. Although I still couldn't feel any confidence that I was seeing the subtle problems with her eye musculature and couldn't discern any oddity in her speech construction, I could see something else. In Simes's face I saw the familiar visage of the visit of the afternoon ghost of fatigue. She looked just as tired as Lauren did.

Maybe she does have multiple sclerosis.

Stifling a yawn, Simes said, "We need to identify possible suspects."

"Who are you thinking?"

She turned her head and yawned into her fist. I saw frustration creep into her expression and wondered whether it was with me or with the appearance of the afternoon lethargy. She said, "Who would you guess might be responsible? Who might have the motivation and the patience to plan the murders of the entire professional staff of a specific psychiatric inpatient unit? A group of professionals who were working together for only six months?"

I knew, of course, where she was going. "You're thinking that an ex-patient is doing it."

Simes shrugged, and I detected a shadow of a smile in her thin face. She had managed to get me to say it. As though that could make it my idea. I reminded myself to be careful, that she was probably very good at what she did.

I said, "Why would a patient want us all dead? That doesn't make any sense. And anyway, no patient would have had contact with all of the doctors. Maybe two of us, maybe three. But no way all the docs. Each patient was treated by one resident or one intern. That's all."

"There was no group therapy for patients on the unit? That's hard to believe, Dr. Gregory."

"Okay, you're right. He could have had another contact in group."

"Just one other contact? Not co-therapists running the group?"

She already knew the structure of the team. "Okay, two. There were two group leaders."

"And—correct me if I'm wrong—if a patient was being seen by a psychology intern, that patient would also be seen by a psychiatric resident for medical backup and medication consultation?"

I nodded.

"And in group therapy, a patient could have had contact with the other intern and the other resident? That's possible?"

"Yes."

"And the residents sometimes ordered psychological testing of their own patients. A psychology intern would do that psychological testing, right? Face to face with the resident's patient. That's correct as well?"

The residents certainly did order psych tests. Too many, I thought. I often suspected that the orders were purely hostile, a way of increasing the psychology interns' workload. "Yes. The psychology interns occasionally did psych testing on the psychiatric residents' patients."

"So there are ways that all the residents and interns could be involved with a single patient."

"I suppose it's possible. But what about the two supervisors? What about Dr. Masters and Dr. Oliphant?"

Simes scratched her neck with the fingernails of her left hand and let me answer my own question.

Lauren had been busy doing math. "Wait," she said. "What about the other psychology intern? Nobody's talking about him."

"Her," I said. "Her name was Alix Noel. She died of leukemia a few years after the internship." I snapped my head to face Simes. "You don't suspect . . . ?"

"No, we don't. Not at this time."

I said, "I can't help you with this, Dr. Simes. I can't provide you with patients' names."

"Why is that?"

"You know why that is. It was a long time ago. And the identity of the patients who were on the unit then is protected by privilege."

She sighed through pursed lips to indicate her disappointment. "You and Dr. Faire are potential victims. Likely victims. And you are going to let protocol interfere with helping me identify a killer who may have already killed five of your colleagues."

"Protocol? Confidentiality isn't protocol. And you're talking a purported killer. I'll grant you this: you and Milt have spun a fascinating web here today. But that doesn't mean the spiders are all black widows." As the words exited my mouth I realized I had no idea what they meant. I tried to cover my inanity by making a follow-up statement that I didn't believe. "There's no evidence of a single killer that ties all of this together. Is there?"

She shrugged. "Want to bet your life on that?"

I shrugged.

"Want to bet Dr. Faire's life on that?"

No, I don't, thank you.

I asked, "Why don't you go directly to the hospital? Get the patient records from them?"

She raised her chin a smidgen and admitted, "The hospital has already refused to let us see them."

"What about the nursing staff?"

"They don't have the detailed patient knowledge that the interns and residents had. You know that."

"There was a social worker on the unit, too. To assist with the families. Her name was—"

"We're looking for Ms. Pope. We've been unable to locate her. She may be of some help. This could, of course, be a patient's family member we're looking for. You and Sawyer Faire are more likely sources of assistance. You would know the families as well as the patients themselves."

"I assume you're about to make a Tarasoff argument to me. Did you make one to the records people at the hospital?"

"Of course we tried. The director of medical records brought in the university attorney, who quickly pointed out the defects in my argument. As far as we know, no threat has been made to either you or Ms. Faire. Therefore, no potential victim has been identified. Tarasoff, therefore, doesn't apply."

Tarasoff v. *California* was a landmark California supreme court decision that mandated that mental health professionals have a "duty to warn" potential victims of violence after a patient has made an "overt threat" against an "identifiable individual."

For some reason I felt a need to win a pyrrhic victory. I pointed out, "Probably doesn't meet the 'overt threat' criterion either." Simes didn't respond, so I continued, "But you think that, unlike the administrators at the hospital, I'll ignore the fact that Tarasoff criteria haven't been reached?"

"To be frank, Dr. Gregory, we think you have a little more motivation to cooperate than they do."

"Staying alive?"

Her eyes were half closed when she said, "Mm-hmm. Staying alive. Top-notch motivation. That's what my doctorate is in, by the way. Motivational psychology."

"Have you a motive in mind for the killer, Dr. Simes?"

"Sure. You guys ruined his life. So he's ruining yours. Or ending yours, to be more specific. I don't know how you screwed up his life. I don't know why he blames you. But when you're pondering possible motives for an ex-patient to commit these murders, please keep in mind that by definition, this group of possible suspects was not judged to be particularly well adjusted."

I swiveled on my seat and faced Lauren. I was trying to bind my terror but I was certain she could see it in my eyes. I said, "I'd like to go home. I'll think about all this a little better there."

"Hey," Milt said, trying to lighten the mood. "What more could we ask? Let's all sleep on it and talk some more tomorrow."

Simes glared at him. But she looked like she wanted a nap.

FIVE

Lauren grazed my thigh with her fingers twice as we descended the steep hill out of Silver Plume. She used a comforting tone as she said, "You know, if I were dreaming this, or if this were a movie, Simes would look like Gwyneth Paltrow and Milt would be a hunk. You know, like Harrison Ford or Michael Douglas. And we wouldn't be scared to death." I glanced over and half smiled. It was the best I could do. For a mile or so we nestled our hands together on top of the gearshift lever and didn't talk. We were insulated in our own spaces as we contemplated the unsettling news we'd received from Custer and Simes. I pulled off the highway at Georgetown and stopped at the Total station, where we used the rest rooms and picked out some junk to eat in the car to try to compensate for the burritos we'd never had a chance to touch at lunch.

Lauren was asleep before we reached the cutoff to Winter Park, as I guessed she would be. It was a rare day for Lauren when MS didn't necessitate a nap, and an afternoon as stressful as this one had been was sure to aggravate her fatigue. I wondered if Dr. A. J. Simes was asleep next to Milton Custer in the front seat of their rented Ford Taurus.

I don't recall seeing any more golden leaves as the last of the day's light leaked away in the steep canyons west of Idaho Springs along I-70. At Golden I cut off the freeway and took Highway 93 north toward Boulder. The day was over and the night was moonless and dark as I pushed impatiently past the Rocky Flats Nuclear Weapons Facility, ignoring both the speed limit and the plutonium.

It was only a little more than an hour after leaving Georgetown when I turned onto the dirt lane that led to our Spanish Hills home on the eastern slopes of the Boulder Valley. Nothing had changed. The city sparkled below and stars dotted the sky like glitter, faintly silhouetting the cutting peaks of the Front Range. The turn onto the lane where we lived felt ordinary. The view to the west was as spectacular as ever.

Our house was still too small and it still needed a coat of paint and a new roof. The windows still needed to be replaced or, at the very least, washed. Emily, our Bouvier, was bounding around in her dog run the way she always did after Lauren and I had been gone for more than an hour, especially when our sojourn took place over the dog's dinner hour.

As I parked the car, I focused all my attention on these constants, reassuring myself that the pattern of stars in the sky above still formed the same reliable constellations they always did. But a shining bright comet, as brilliant as Hale-Bopp, had entered my night sky, too.

It took all my effort not to stare and be blinded by its menace.

Emily had been alone since breakfast so I played with her and gave her some dinner and fresh ice water while Lauren went downstairs to take a bath. Once back inside the house, I flicked on the CD player and punched up some old Bonnie Raitt, raising the volume high enough so that Freebo's bass shook the loose pane of glass on the north side of the dining room. I turned the little black-and-white TV in the kitchen to mute so I could monitor the larger world for further intrusions into my peace at the same time I was caramelizing some onions for a frittata.

It appeared that Channel 4 was doing a piece about the autumn leaves. The story lost a lot of its luster in black-and-white.

Incongruously, I managed to get distracted. Things would

feel fine for a few unfettered moments and then I would remember the events of the day and let myself consider the
very strong possibility that someone with great cunning and
patience wanted to kill me.

Across the small room, an architect's latest renderings for
renovating our funky little house were spread out on the
kitchen table. One side of the blueprints was held in place
by a brass pepper mill, the other by an unopened jar of
peanut butter.

The plans as drawn were much more extensive than Lauren and I had originally envisioned when we decided to em-
bark on the often postponed remodeling. Our initial idea
had been to enlarge the kitchen by adding a room to the
north, and to tuck in a new study and master bath below it.
But Lauren's recent history with MS reinforced the need to
allow her full mobility on one level of the house, which
meant, at the very least, adding a master bedroom and bath
on the main, upper, floor. The current house was eight hundred square feet up and four hundred down. The architect's
vision almost doubled the main level to accommodate the
new spaces.

The whole prospect of turning my house over to a contractor had been overwhelming to me twelve hours earlier.
Now, it felt unimaginable. I stepped over to the table, lifted
the peanut butter jar and the pepper mill, and watched as the
pages rolled together and tumbled to the floor.

It was a meaningless gesture but I derived some satisfaction from it.

I opened a bottle of Riesling and poured two glasses. The
frittata was browning up nicely in the oven. I went downstairs to find Lauren. She was curled up on the bed, still in
her cherry-red bathrobe, her black hair in short damp ropes,
her breathing shallow and peaceful. I carefully laid a down
comforter over her, kissed her wet hair, and turned off the
light.

Her being asleep, it was okay.

I needed to think this through.

* * *

The German wine was crisp and I drank too much, or perhaps ate too little of the frittata, which wasn't anywhere near as good as it had looked while it was cooking. Regardless, I was a little buzzed by the time I carried the portable phone into the living room and punched in the speed dial number for my friend Diane.

I was busy convincing myself that Diane would understand. She'd been on the internship with me. She knew what it was like back then.

She knew Sawyer. She knew me. Diane and I had shared an office suite for years.

I listened to an annoying buzz in my ear for almost ten seconds before it dawned on me that her line was busy.

Years ago, I did a lot of court testimony as a forensics expert. Custody and abuse issues mostly, but I also evaluated accused criminals for some defense attorneys and for a few of the district attorney's offices in the counties surrounding Boulder. During depositions, or in the first few minutes of my cross-examination, I came to quick judgments about the nature of the adversarial attorneys. Occasionally I blew it, but more often than not I was able to make accurate determinations about the strengths that the opposition was bringing to the table.

Unconsciously, I had already gone through the same process with Custer and Simes. My appraisal was that Custer was the slipperier of the two. But Simes would, in the end, be a more difficult adversary.

Custer had spent a long time on the street without many scars from the road. That, in itself, was impressive. He was part good old boy, part small-town minister, and underneath, probably all cop. He deferred easily and naturally to Simes, but I sensed that it was a deference that was voluntary for him and was granted without granting any underlying status.

Simes was chippy. She knew that Custer was granting her latitude, and that irked her. She didn't want latitude; she wanted status. Maybe Lauren was right and Simes did have MS or a similar malady and that's why she'd been forced out of the Bureau on a medical disability. Maybe it had left her bitter. I wasn't sure. But I was leaning toward a conclusion that she had an overdetermined intellectual and professional arrogance that had been cemented by some monumental insecurity that she was struggling to tame as a lion tamer controls a big cat. Perhaps she could get her insecurity to sit down and stop growling, but she knew that at any time it might jump up off its perch and bite her head off.

I wondered, too, about their pairing. How had they ended up together?

Surprisingly, though, I wasn't wondering much about their conclusion regarding a serial killer at work. The pattern they had proposed seemed intuitive, easy to grasp. Once I crossed the bridge that led me from my skepticism, I also had to let go of traditional serial killer images. This wasn't Jeffrey Dahmer or Son of Sam or the Hillside Strangler we were talking about. This wasn't a sexual psychopath. If this guy was real, his closest malevolent relative was the Unabomber.

The person who was stalking me was obsessed. He was patient. He was meticulous. He was dedicated.

And he was a believer.

Add all those things up and what you have, I decided, is a psychological terrorist.

I hit the redial button.

Diane's husband, Raoul, answered the phone. He asked about my day and about the status of the leaves in the high country and we ended up chatting for a few minutes about the origins of the term "Indian summer." I tried to help him put things in a cultural context that would make sense back home in Barcelona. I'm pretty sure I failed. He also informed me that he and Diane were thinking of moving to a house in town. "Winters are too difficult up here. You know?"

A lot of snow fell sometimes in those steep canyons in the Front Range above Boulder, like Lee Hill, where Diane and Raoul had their spacious home. Winter started early and spring started late. And sometimes it seemed that spring was as much about mud as it was about flowers. Summertime could be a major burden, too. Well problems, deer problems, mountain lion worries, black bear worries, wildfire worries, flash flood worries.

I said, "Summers are hard on you guys, too. But the autumns are always special, Raoul."

"That's the truth, my friend. That's the truth. This time of year it's hard to think about leaving, but I think it's time to get urban. Maybe we'll move out east, by you. I like the views out there. But I'm monopolizing you. I assume you phoned to talk to the brilliant one?"

"Is that what she's calling herself now?"

"She guessed right about that thing that happened with Intel. We made a few dollars. Suddenly she's a wizard, you know?"

"I know. She's difficult when she's wrong, and she's impossible when she's right."

"That's my girl. I'll get her. At this moment, the brilliant one is in the kitchen, making a tart of kiwis and berries. I will be courteous until it comes from the oven. Wise, right?"

A minute later I heard a loud buzz in my ear, followed by "Hey, I'm rolling dough, so I have you on the speakerphone. You're going to have to speak as though you actually have a voice."

Diane teased me frequently about the fact that my everyday voice was soft enough to stuff a pillow.

I said, "I'll try." Then I thought better of it. "Listen, this isn't a speakerphone conversation. I'll call you back in a while."

"Oh no you don't. Hold on." The buzz disappeared and was replaced by one of Diane's admonishing tones. "You won't call back. You'll make me suffer wondering what it is I missed."

"What about the tart?"

"The dough's covered. Well?"

"I went to Arnie Dresser's memorial service today, and—"

"You were that close to Arnie?" When she wasn't in

therapist mode, Diane's tone couldn't disguise a thing. This particular intonation said, "You shittin' me?"

"No. Not really, we weren't close. Just showing my respect, I guess." I didn't want to go into the whole Christmas card thing. Diane would have a field day with that information.

"You *respected* Arnie Dresser?"

"Diane, please."

"Sorry."

"The services were in Evergreen. Lauren came up with me, got a massage at Tall Grass while I was at the church. After—"

"Was it great? I heard that place is great. Tell her next time I want to go with her. We'll do a girl thing. Get a foot massage. Tea and tootsies for the ladies."

I smiled; I couldn't help it. "Yes, she said the spa was great. After the services, we drove up to the mountains to try to find some leaves. We stopped in Silver Plume for a late lunch."

"Silver Plume has a restaurant?"

"Diane, yes, Silver Plume has a restaurant. Do you really want me to digress again?"

"Sorry."

"And it turns out that two FBI agents followed us all the way from the church to the mountains."

"*What?*"

"Actually these two who walked up to our table in Silver Plume said that they're ex-FBI. They're consultants now. One was an agent in Chicago, the other one is a retired profiler, a Ph.D. in social psychology. Motivation. They said Arnie's mother hired them. Apparently she thinks Arnie's death might not be accidental."

"Wow! A profiler? Really? Like in *Silence of the Lambs*? What did they want from you?"

I wasn't fond of Diane's literary allusion. I asked, "Do you remember Susan Oliphant, from our internship year?"

No hesitation. "Sure. She was the ward chief on Orange. Never had her for supervision myself. But I liked her more than I liked any of her residents." Diane's inpatient rotation had been on the Blue Team.

"They told me she's dead. Did you know that she had died? I didn't know. She died in a private plane crash that they think is suspicious. In the Adirondacks. Quite a few years ago."

"No, I didn't know."

"What about Matt Trimble? Remember him?"

"Yeah, the black resident? I know he died. I liked him, too. He was cute. You ever see his legs? Michelangelo would have liked his legs."

I was tempted to digress myself. When had Diane had a chance to see Matt's legs? I controlled myself. "Wendy Asimoto?"

The air was still for a few seconds. "I don't remember her."

"She quit after her second year. But she was on the Orange Team, too, while I was there. She's another dead second-year resident. She disappeared while working on a cruise ship."

"Since when do cruise ships hire psychiatrists? What was she working on—the Divorce Boat?"

I could tell her mind remained more focused on her piecrust and her kiwis than on my litany of dead mental health professionals. "Diane, are you with me? Are you sensing a pattern here?"

"I'm reminded of that old joke about what do you call three lawyers at the bottom of a lake?"

I'd heard the joke, of course. But I didn't respond. I was speechless for other reasons.

She said, "A good start. Get it?"

"I've heard it."

"Okay, these FBI types think that there may be an evil force at work. Somebody killing psychiatrists."

Diane's reflexive sarcasm was set to "high." I needed to jolt her into focusing her considerable intellect onto what was going on. I said, "Not just psychiatrists, Diane. They told me that there is some doubt whether or not Amy Masters's death was by natural causes, either."

It worked. When Diane finally spoke again, her voice betrayed quivers of shock and hollow rings of sorrow. "Oh my God. Amy? No. Murdered?" Amy Masters had been Diane's outpatient psychotherapy supervisor during our internship year. Diane had thought that Amy walked on water.

"The story they tell certainly makes it sound suspicious. She may have been murdered. These two agents are looking into it."

"What do they mean? How did it happen?"

"You know Amy retired in San Diego? That's where she was from."

"I know. How? We heard she died after an illness. She hadn't been well for a long time. But that's not what happened?"

"She had a skin condition, nothing terminal, that required UV treatment. She used a home tanning bed for the treatments. These two FBI people think someone may have rigged the bed so that once she turned it on and closed it, it wouldn't go off, and she could never open it again."

Diane framed the picture in her mind. She asked, "And it was on the whole time? She was toasted?"

"Yes."

She was quiet. I thought I could hear her switching the phone from one ear to the other. "This is truly awful, truly gross. Has there been anybody else? What's that so far, four?"

"Arnie is number five. What ties everyone together is the Orange Team on Eight East, fall rotation, the year we were there."

I heard her inhale deeply. "Sawyer was there, then, too."

"Yes, she was. They—the agents—haven't talked to her yet. They're on their way to see her."

"But they're worried? About her? Aren't they? And about you? They're worried about both of you."

"Yes. That's why they followed Lauren and me. To tell us that I may be in danger."

"Alan, we're talking Sawyer, here. Right? Brings back a shitload of memories, doesn't it? It's because this involves

Sawyer Sackett, that's why you called me tonight, isn't it? Otherwise—I know you—you would have casually mentioned something to me at the office tomorrow. 'Oh, by the way, Diane, the FBI thinks somebody's trying to kill me.' Like that, right?"

"I guess."

"Does Lauren know about you and Sawyer?"

"No. We've never been a couple that does the ex-lover, romantic time travel thing."

"Me and Raoul neither, thank God. I'm not sure I want to know every pillow that pretty head of his has ever been on. I wonder if that's denial. Hell's bells, of course it is. Have you talked with her since, well, you know?"

"You mean Sawyer?"

"Of course I mean Sawyer. Jesus."

"No. I don't even know where she went after she pulled out of the residency. She got married, I guess; one of the agents said her name is now Faire. You haven't talked with her, have you?"

She made a dismissive noise but didn't even bother to answer my question. "So you don't know why she . . . ? You still don't know why . . . ?" Her voice trailed away. Diane was rarely at a loss for words.

"No."

"What's their point? These two agents. Are they going to do anything to protect you?"

"No, that's not it. I think they want to frighten me enough that I'll want to help them put together a patient roster from that fall on the inpatient unit. For possible suspects."

She scoffed, "You can't do that."

"I've been thinking about it, Diane. Ethically, I couldn't do it even if I wanted to. But the reality is that I can't remember the names of patients from that long ago. Maybe two or three have come to mind. That's it. Could you name your patients from your inpatient rotation?"

"Of course, most of them. My own patients, anyway. But then, I'm smarter than you are. Hey, why ex-FBI? Why not the real thing?"

"These two haven't convinced anybody but me that all

these deaths are either, A, homicides, or B, connected to one another. The deaths share no similarities. On only one of them has the manner of death been determined to be—"

"Wait, what's 'manner of death'?"

"Determination of agency. You know, like who or what's responsible for someone dying. Suicide, homicide, accident, natural causes. It's a coroner's thing."

"I thought that was cause of death."

"No, cause of death is whatever results in the termination of life: the immediate *how*. Cancer, gunshot wound, asphyxiation, whatever. For example, if cause of death is 'gunshot wound of head,' the manner of death would depend on who pulled the trigger and why. Get it?"

"And what about the brains that get scrambled by the bullet? What's that?"

"The scrambled brains would be the mechanism of death. Okay?" Diane grunted. I decided it meant she got it. "Anyway, on none of the deaths but Matthew's is the manner of death even considered a homicide by the local police agencies. The five people who have died have died in five different locations. And the various things they died of—those are the causes of death—couldn't be more different."

"Other than that all the dead people are professional staff from the Orange Team in the fall of 1982?"

"Right."

"But you believe what they're telling you?"

"I guess I do. The consequences of not believing them are a little intolerable. I realize, though, that I'm looking at these two as adversaries. I'm not sure why that is. It doesn't feel exactly right. I mean, they've gone out of their way to warn me about this guy. Why would I look at them as though they're the enemy?"

Diane was silent. I knew, for her, the act required monumental effort. She wanted me to answer my own question.

"I suppose because they want me to walk them through the psychiatric records of a bunch of innocent people in hopes of finding one guy who's decided to spend his entire life killing off a bunch of doctors."

She said, "When you put it that way, it makes me think

that maybe you should narrow your search and start looking only at managed care administrators. They certainly
have impeccable motives for wanting to kill off a gaggle of
doctors."

I smiled.

She continued, "What does Lauren think?"

"I'm not sure. She was with me the whole time these two
FBI types were talking. From her questions, I think she
feels this has more merit than she's comfortable with. She
fell asleep as soon as we got home."

"Is she okay?"

"Yeah. She's fine. You know how tired she gets. This is
routine stuff."

Diane must have heard some defensiveness in my tone.
She said, "I have to ask, you know."

"I know."

"How quickly does this guy work? I mean, how imminent
is the danger to you and Sawyer?"

"Apparently, he works slowly, methodically. The two
deaths that are closest together in time are the most recent
ones. Amy Masters and Arnie Dresser."

"And that is what, eight months or so, between those?"

"More or less."

"Do you have a gut feeling about this? Who it might be?"

"No, I'm drawing a blank on that."

"Nobody you guys put on a hold tried to fight you on it?"

"No."

"Did you do any commitments?"

"Personally? Not that I recall. I remember a couple of
memorable psychotics from the unit. But no, no big hassles
over anything. But then we may not be looking for one of
my patients."

"You saw almost everyone in group, though? You heard
about everybody in rounds, and met everyone in Community Meetings?"

"Yeah. I'm sure I crossed paths with almost everybody
who was admitted for more than a day or two. Over the
course of a six-month rotation, that's a lot of patients,
though."

"In the morning when you wake up, if you still believe what these FBI agents are telling you, you're going to have to find Sawyer, Alan."

"I know."

"How do you feel about that?" She even used her best shrink-voice to ask the question.

"I'd rather not."

"See her? Or feel?"

"Diane, please."

"Did you ever stop loving her?"

"It was a long time ago."

"Don't distract. It won't work with me."

"She was your friend, too."

"Whatever. It wasn't the same."

"She crushed me, Diane."

"That's not what I asked."

SIX

Once, from a helicopter that was hovering inside an extinct volcano in Hawaii, I saw a circular rainbow. A full three-hundred-and-sixty-degree orb of color. It was miraculous.

Once, in the desert outside Taos, I saw a boomerang of lights dot a parcel of sky the size of an aircraft carrier and speed away with the velocity of elsewhere. It made no sense.

And once, after a single glance of blond hair and a fleeting look at the barest of profiles, I fell in love with a strange woman from across a crowded room.

I can't explain any of it.

I'd arrived in Denver on July first, 1982, to look for a place to live. Although the psychiatric residents began their rotation at the beginning of July, the psychology interns began a month later, on August first. I landed in town early because I wanted to get settled and to get familiar enough with my new surroundings to try to make some of my anxiety evaporate.

The housing office of the University of Colorado Medical Center was located on the south side of the campus on the first floor of an old brick building. My experience with university housing offices told me that they were of relatively little utility, but two days of classified ad hunting had left me without an apartment, so I stopped by on Friday morning to check the listings of available flats and rooms.

I wasn't feeling hopeful.

Four of five seats were taken at a long table on one side of the housing office. I settled onto the last seat on the right end and reached for the closest card file. I was flipping through it—"apartments to share"—without much interest because I'd already decided I didn't want to deal with a roommate. I clearly recall the instant I felt her presence across the room from me; I was reading a listing that was so full of acronyms I couldn't decipher what any of it was supposed to mean.

I felt her presence physically, as though a cool breeze were brushing over my bare skin. As I looked up to find the source of the sensation, I laid eyes on her. A clerk on the other side of the counter was smiling right at her, saying, "Thank you, Doctor." The woman's blond head was turned away from me, her chin tilted up and slightly thrust forward. She had a small daypack slung casually over her right shoulder. Her shoulders were bare, her skin the color of freshly oiled pine. Her sunny hair was haphazard and short, her neck tan and long. The ring finger of her left hand was naked.

I never saw her eyes that day.

I returned my attention to the index cards long enough to exhale and process my reaction. I felt a smile creep onto my face and thought, *Why not?* I dropped the card file, picked up my appointment book, and faced the room.

She was gone.

The hallway outside the office was empty. At the adjacent staircase, I listened but I couldn't hear a flutter of steps retreating either up or down. Stepping outside, I scanned for her blond head in the distance, and thought for a second that maybe I saw her crossing Eighth Avenue, but then I wasn't sure. I rushed back inside the building and parked myself outside the entrance to the women's rest room for almost five minutes.

She never came out.

The blond woman had disappeared. My feelings about her vaporizing ambushed me. I should have felt, maybe, a sense of lost opportunity, or perhaps a touch of disappointment. But I ended up feeling terribly disconsolate, as though a lover had just told me she really just wanted to be friends.

I assured myself that my overreaction was a sign of my temporary insecurity. I was in a new town, I had an internship coming, and with it new responsibilities, and new opportunities to screw up. I had no apartment and a budget that was about as flexible as my fifth-grade English teacher.

That's all this overreaction was about. That's all it was.

Twice more that day I stood still as a statue, thinking that once again I could feel her nearby. Both times I waited for the invisible breeze to pass again over my exposed flesh.

It never did.

Late that afternoon I chanced onto a small duplex that I liked on Clermont Street only a couple of blocks from where I would be working. The apartment was a one-bedroom that cost fifty dollars more a month than I could afford, but it was available immediately and I wouldn't have to drive to work or extend my motel stay, so I rationalized away the extra expense.

I made a final trip to the housing office to remove my name from the "needs apartment or flat" roster. Of course I checked the room for her. Of course she wasn't there. The only person in the room at the end of the day was a clerk, a rotund man with the blackest hair and darkest eyes I'd ever seen in my life. I offered him a smile and told him he was losing a customer.

"Found a place?"

"Yeah, a duplex on Clermont."

"Congratulations. Name?"

"Gregory, Alan."

He looked up from his pencil. "Which one's first? Gregory, or Alan?"

"Alan. Gregory is my last name."

"Just a second," he said, while he wheezed through his mouth and flipped through his card file. "Here you are. Okay, you're history. Got an address for me? For the university directory?"

I gave him my new address. In my mind, as I did, I saw

her daypack hanging from her shoulder. In my mind I remembered that it had an embroidered monogram on it.

SAS.

Once again, I thought, *Why not?*

"I'm looking for someone who was here earlier in the day. A girl, a, a woman. I don't know her name. Her initials are S—A—S. The directory you mentioned? May I take a look at it, see if I can find a match?"

"You know her initials but not her name?" His face turned suspicious. "You're what? A resident?"

"Clinical psychology intern."

"And what? You want to ask her out or something?"

"Exactly. Something."

He shivered a little, as though he couldn't imagine doing what I was doing, looked at me askance, and asked, "Got ID?"

"From the medical school? No, not yet. Psychology interns don't start until August one."

He shrugged as though he had no interest in my romantic explorations. He said, "Don't have the new directory printed yet, but you can see the typewritten list they've sent me so far." He flipped through a thick file. "Here's the S's. Maybe she's in here." He pushed the stapled pages across the counter at me and turned his attention to a big bottle of diet Dr Pepper.

I carried the directory over to the long table against the wall. The dozen or so pages had thirteen entries with the initials S.S. I was a little discouraged. Why couldn't her monogram have read KTZ?

Five of the names belonged to obvious males. I ruled them out. Of the remaining eight names, three were M.D.s and one was a Ph.D. Earlier that day the clerk in the housing office had called the woman "Doctor." I ruled out the names of the four without doctoral degrees.

Three of the remaining names had obviously female first names. The other one's first name was Sawyer.

Sawyer Sackett. Androgynous. Couldn't exclude it.

I turned and asked the clerk if I could use the phone.

He said, "Think I care?" I was pretty sure he would be listening to every word I said.

I called the work number of the first of the Dr. S.S.s, Susan Sipple, Ph.D.

I was connected to a secretary at the School of Pharmacy.

"Hello, I'm trying to reach an old friend who lives in Denver. Her name is Susan Sipple. Is—?"

"Dr. Sipple? Just a moment, please."

"No, no, no. Excuse me. I want to make sure I have the right Susan Sipple. Could you describe her for me?"

"Sure. She has brown hair and beautiful green eyes and—"

"About how old would you say she is?"

"I don't know, maybe forty, forty-five."

"I'm sorry to trouble you, but that's not my friend. Thanks."

I hung up and had roughly the same conversation with a more suspicious someone named Tammy in the School of Nursing regarding a professor named Sandra Sorenson.

My next call let me know that Sylvia Spencer, M.D., of the Department of Pediatrics was now working at St. Jude's in Memphis.

I was left with Sawyer Sackett's name. The directory listing had her living in the six hundred block of Cherry Street. Which happened to be in the general direction that I thought I might have seen the blond head disappear across Eighth Avenue. I called the listed work number for Dr. Sackett.

A voice answered, "Clinic."

Big help there. "Hello, I'm trying to reach a Dr. Sawyer Sackett. The one I'm looking for has a middle initial of A. Is this the right number for her?"

The woman responded sarcastically, "You think we have two Dr. Sawyer Sacketts on staff?"

"I just want to be certain."

"I don't know any doctor's middle initials. I barely remember my brother's middle initial. Do you want an appointment?" Her tone told me she thought I could use one.

"Is Dr. Sackett blond?"

"You want to know Dr. Sackett's hair color?"

"Please. I don't want to bother the doctor if it's not the right one."

Exasperated, the woman said, "Dr. Sackett has blond hair. May I ask what this is about?"

"I'm another trainee."

"Is this about a patient?"

I lied, "Yes."

"Well, she's with a patient. I'll tell her you called. Your name, Doctor?"

The gender finally registered. *She said "her." She said, "She's with a patient."*

Pleased, I said, "No. I'll call her back."

"Suit yourself." She hung up.

I handed the directory back to the clerk in the housing office. He asked, "You find her?"

I nodded. "Think so."

"Good luck," he said.

"Thanks," I said. "My luck wasn't too good this morning, but it's improving, I think."

The next day I moved my few belongings into my new furnished apartment. I was pleased with how bright the apartment was and delighted I could walk to work in two minutes. Twice I took breaks from my chores and made the two-block stroll to Cherry Street where Dr. Sawyer A. Sackett lived in a prim little Tudor that was camouflaged by junipers.

I didn't see her and didn't know what I would have done if I had.

I spent half of Saturday night drafting a note to her. I spent the other half convincing myself that any self-respecting woman would view my efforts as moronic or dangerous, not romantic.

The next morning I woke up at five, got up at six, gave myself a pep talk, and walked by her house. Instead of using the mail slot, I slipped the note into the Sunday *New York Times* that had been dropped onto her front walk. I hesitated about the placement of the note, finally deciding that the missive should be placed, appropriately, in front of *Week in Review*.

* * *

Most of the next week passed and she didn't call. I convinced myself she was involved with someone. Denver was hot and dry, my apartment wasn't air-conditioned, and I was regretting moving to town so long before my internship was set to begin.

I thought about Sawyer Sackett a lot. Way too much. With monumental effort, I forced myself to stop strolling past her house twice daily. I didn't really want to be spotted by her boyfriend or husband.

On Friday afternoon, my phone rang for only the second time since it had been installed. It startled me.

After I said hello, an unfamiliar, sweet female voice asked, "Is this Alan Gregory?"

My mouth turned dry. I managed to say, "Yes."

"Hi." She laughed. "It's not who you're hoping for. My name is Mona. Mona Terwilliger. You don't know me, but I'm a friend of Sawyer Sackett's."

"Oh," I said as casually as I could. "The note."

She laughed again. "Yes, the note."

"When I didn't hear from her I figured she was offended. Or at the very least, uninterested."

"Actually, she thought it was sweet. I think she did, anyway. She showed the note to all her friends. Listen, I'm having a party at my apartment tomorrow night. Just a casual thing, a couple of dozen people. Sawyer thought it might be fun if you came. You interested?"

"Yes. I am. I am interested. She'll be there?"

"She says she will. But you never quite know what Sawyer is going to do. Don't worry, the rest of us are a lot of fun. Especially me."

She gave me directions to a condo near Cheesman Park and said the party started at sunset. "You can come early if you want. The view is special."

Later, after a lot of years on the Front Range in Colorado, the Terwilliger name would feel familiar to me. Mona's family owned a fence company that dominated the industry

from Fort Collins to Colorado Springs. On every installa-
tion the company placed a burgundy tin plaque that read "A
Terwilliger Fence." Some of the considerable family income had been used to buy the tenth-floor condo on Race
Street where Mona lived with her younger sister on the east
side of Cheesman Park, just a half mile west of the medical
center campus.

I had been buzzed into the lobby and took the elevator to
the tenth floor. The door to the condo was open, so I walked
in. The place was a sea of green. Pine green carpets. Sea
green wallpaper. Lime green Formica on the kitchen counters. Appliance green appliances. No one greeted me.
Everyone who had arrived before me had assembled on the
balcony to watch the blue sky melt into the oranges, reds,
and purples of sunset.

Cheesman is one of Denver's three jewel parks. Built on
the site of a nineteenth-century cemetery, it is a large urban
oasis of grand design that is blessed with stunning views of
the mountains. The park was beautiful, but not as beautiful
as the sun setting over the distant mountains.

And certainly not as beautiful as Sawyer Sackett.

I was confident I would have radar for Sawyer, and I spotted her immediately. She was leaning back against the railing on the left side of the balcony, her hands behind her, the
contours of her chest accentuated by her posture. She was
smiling, slyly I thought, talking to two men who looked a
little older than me. I hesitated in the dining room while I
poured myself a glass of wine. I concluded that the two men
with her were physicians, real doctors, and I didn't have a
chance with her.

For a few more moments I enjoyed my anonymity, realizing that no one knew who I was. And no one knew what I
looked like.

Another minute or so passed before a tall woman with a
recent perm and a big smile walked up to me and said, "Hi,
I'm Mona."

"Alan Gregory," I said. "Thanks for the invitation."

We shook hands.

She took a half step back and eyed me. Then she moved

forward, standing no more than ten inches away, and said, "You're cute. She's gonna like that. I didn't peg you as the shy type, though. Why are you hanging out in here?"

I shrugged. "This is all pretty odd for me, Mona. What I did, I mean, with the note and everything. It's not something I've ever done before. I don't know exactly what to do next."

Mona touched a small pendant that hung at the top of her breasts, exactly where her ample cleavage was exposed. Her fingers lingered on the jewelry until she saw my eyes drop.

Point, Mona.

"You shouldn't be self-conscious about what you did," she said. "I'm sure by now everybody here has heard your story."

I laughed. "And that's supposed to be reassuring?"

"Sure. It was romantic, what you did." She appraised me carefully. "Once they lay their eyes on you and see how cute you are, all the women in the room will wish you had sent them the note. And once they see you with Sawyer, all the men will wish they had written it."

"You're quite sure of yourself, aren't you?"

"I have ulterior motives, Alan Gregory. I don't know her well. Sawyer. But what I think is this: She's intrigued by you, by what you did, what you said in your note. And my guess is that she's going to think you're gorgeous. But I think—no, I'm sure—Sawyer ultimately is going to blow you off. And I know that besides her, I'm going to be the sweetest thing you meet at this party."

She touched the pendant again. I tried not to look.

I failed.

Sawyer walked up behind her.

"So are you the one?" she asked, laughing.

"I am."

"You've got balls," she said, "I'll give you that. I'm Sawyer." She stared at me, her eyes never leaving my face.

We shook hands.

I said, "Thanks for taking the chance."

"What chance is that?" she asked.

I started to reply, but she walked past me, poured two

inches of Maker's Mark into a wineglass, speared a big shrimp wrapped in prosciutto, and took long strides back out to the balcony.

I didn't say another word to Sawyer that night but watched her from a distance as I made small talk with Mona and a few of the other guests. Darkness descended and smothered the park. Sawyer was never by herself for more than a few seconds. She attracted men the way a salt lick attracts deer. The dance she did as men approached her was unsettling to watch. She flirted, yes, but without any joy. Her eyes were daring but not inviting. Not once did I catch her stealing a surreptitious glimpse my way.

I made a quick judgment that she was wounded and that I was the perfect one to comfort her. I also decided that the other men couldn't see it—her distress. This intuition about her pain was not a benevolent assessment on my part. I met Sawyer at a time in my life when I couldn't imagine someone wanting me for who I was. I entered virtually every relationship endeavoring to decipher what I could provide to cement someone's interest in me.

That evening, it turned out, my radar about Sawyer Sackett was accurate. My assessment, unfortunately, was flawed.

SEVEN

Sawyer had left the party at Mona's condo early, arm in arm with the pair of men she had been talking with on the balcony. I tried not to let my imagination run away with me and ended up leaving shortly thereafter, first promising to meet Mona for racquetball the following week at someplace she called the DAC.

Mona was a philosophy student at Denver University who had met Sawyer at a lecture they were both attending at the Natural History Museum. Mona turned out to be as bright as she was flirtatious and as much fun as she had advertised. She was also one terrific racquetball player. She took me two out of three games on the air-conditioned courts at the Downtown Athletic Club on the edge of Denver's business district. Mona was an attractive woman and a bold, amusing companion, but nothing was clicking romantically for me with her. I thought she might be disappointed. She said she wasn't. We made plans to have lunch and to play again the following week.

But she refused to let me fish around for information about Sawyer. "I'm not telling you a thing, not that I have much to tell," she said.

"She's hurting about something, isn't she?" I asked.

Mona seemed surprised by my query. "Sawyer?" She narrowed her eyes.

"Yes."

"I don't know about anything."

"But you see it too, don't you?"

She shook her head in a way that suggested that I drop it. "You're on your own with Sawyer, just like me, just like everybody else."

"That means what?"

"She's not an easy woman to be friends with. It means what it means," she said.

In my original note to Sawyer, I'd promised not to call her unless she called me. Technically, she hadn't called me, so I kept my promise and didn't phone her. I'd been tempted, but I hadn't succumbed. I was so asinine with infatuation that I had myself convinced that this was actually my game and that I had written the rules.

The party invitation had raised my hopes that I might hear from her, but by midweek I'd decided that I'd failed the audition that Sawyer had arranged at Mona's soiree. So I was surprised on Thursday morning when I found a note in a pink envelope in the copy of the *Rocky Mountain News* I collected from my front porch. The note summoned me to a restaurant called the Firefly Cafe at four-thirty that afternoon. It was signed with a flourishing S.

I checked for perfume. None.

I arrived at the restaurant right on time.

She seemed relaxed. And happy to see me.

"I got off lucky. My brother's name is Clemens. It's my daddy's thing. He read *Tom Sawyer* to me for the first time when I was only four."

We were sitting on the little patio on the west side of the Firefly, on East Colfax, not too far from the medical center. I was trying to convince myself that this plate of soggy nachos and these cold beers on a muggy July afternoon constituted our first date. But verbalizing that to Sawyer—seeking consensus, as it were—felt both immature and foolish. From the moment I saw the back of her blond head that first time, Sawyer wasn't a "let's be friends" candidate for me.

She had to know that. I hadn't felt so erotically charged since high school.

Other than that half minute in Mona's dining room, I hadn't really been able to look at Sawyer up close When I finally had the chance, I noticed right away that her eyes danced constantly. Save for an occasional blink, they never seemed to narrow at all, instead were always open wide to everything in a way that was not incredulous, not naive, but daring and daunting. And sad, too. Heavy. I continued to feel some assurance that her sadness was going to be my entrée. The temptation I felt was to lock on to her eyes, to submerge myself in them, to count the golden specks that dotted the blue like a design for a flag for some country where I wanted to live forever. But her irises danced so incessantly that I hesitated, perhaps knowing that I was doomed to follow, never to capture them, certainly never to lead.

I know that now. That day, though, I was captivated by the chase. I was inspired by the challenge to find a way to comfort her.

I was stupid.

I said, "Besides Clemens, do you have any other brothers or sisters?"

"You mean Huckleberry and Pudd'n head?"

My face obviously conveyed the fact that I believed her. I didn't consider that she'd probably used this line fifty times previously.

She said, "I'm kidding. It's just me and Clemens."

It would have been a perfect time for her to ask me about my family, or my siblings. Or where I was from. Or what I was doing at the medical school. But she didn't ask. If I had been paying attention, it would have taught me something important about Sawyer. But I wasn't and it didn't.

The ominous gray form of an approaching thunderstorm had been looming to the west from the moment we sat down on the restaurant patio. Presaging its arrival, wind began to gust through the nearby elms and one prodigious blow actually sent a limb flying from a big cottonwood across the street. The wind died after two or three minutes. Seconds later, the first sharp crack of lightning made it difficult for me to think. A second brilliant flash preceded a roaring clap of thunder by only seconds. Hail the size of baby peas began to pelt the canvas awning above our heads.

I stood to move inside.

Sawyer didn't.

"It's just a little thunder," she said as a loud snap that sounded like a tree trunk breaking swallowed her words. I was torn between staying alive and staying in the presence of a captivating woman.

I sat back down.

The rest of the patio patrons had already scurried inside. The hail that was falling now was the size of acorns. I said, "Are you sure you don't want to go inside? We can watch the storm from there."

"People say these things pass in minutes most of the time in Colorado. It's not like back home. This is kind of fun. Let's wait it out. How many people actually get struck by lightning, anyway?"

I was thinking, very few. But I was also assuming that the statistics were heavily skewed by the fact that most people had the good sense to go indoors when lightning was illuminating their faces as brightly as a portrait photographer's flash. I figured that of the remaining few—those who insisted on remaining outside during thunderstorms—a reasonably high percentage was actually struck by lightning.

I also figured that, by and large, this natural selection tended to improve the gene pool.

I said, "You're sure?"

She parted her lips slightly and smiled a shy smile. Right then, for the first time, I began to believe my premonition that Sawyer had secrets. Immediately, I filed the thought away in a place that would make the insight difficult to retrieve.

Behind her in the parking lot, the hail was soon deep enough to shovel.

The thunderstorm was being pushed east by powerful winds aloft and it passed, thankfully, in minutes. The sky cleared first to the west. The hail turned quickly to rain and moments after that the brash sun was beating down on the ice balls that had accumulated in the parking lot. Sawyer had finished her beer. Our waitress finally decided it was safe to venture back out to the patio, and Sawyer called her over and ordered a Maker's Mark neat.

She said, "I've been curious about something. What made you think I wasn't going to read your note and decide you were some psycho?"

"I thought about it. I figured that I didn't have much to lose. Anyway, most psychos, especially your successful ones, don't leave their names and phone numbers with their intended victims."

"You think you know a lot about psychos?"

"Yeah. I think I do. Enough anyway. I'm starting my internship in clinical psychology at the hospital in a couple of weeks. I'll probably learn a little more about psychos there."

I thought I saw her jaw muscles tense. She didn't say anything.

"After I decided to write the note, I assumed you would be either offended or intrigued by it. That you would decide that my gesture had been either terribly romantic or appallingly desperate."

"Which was it?"

I decided to be honest. "A little of both, probably."

She seemed to take a moment to process that. "Why? Why was it so important that you meet me?"

"I wasn't sure at first. I felt kind of crazy when you seemed to disappear from that office before I had a chance to, to . . ."

"Try to pick me up?"

"Introduce myself. I still don't know what it was. You ever see somebody across a room and feel that your life is never going to be the same again? You ever have a day when gravity seemed to totally disappear?"

Sawyer didn't answer. Her eyes skipped away. For ten seconds or so she wasn't even in my vicinity.

The waitress delivered Sawyer's whiskey. She took a long pull, downing half of it, and said, "And?"

With that solitary word, her voice was suddenly devoid of melody. I was surprised to feel a hard surface in there, somewhere. It was as though I'd bitten into the seed of a fresh cherry that I thought had already been pitted. What did I do? I spit it out and moved on.

"Well, that was what it was like when I saw you in the housing office that first time. And, believe me, I barely saw you. I didn't see your eyes that day. I didn't see you smile." I leaned across the table in my best imitation of a flirtatious pose. "I saw your neck and your hair and the tip of your nose and your lips, maybe your lips. I saw the skin on your shoulders. I didn't even know then that you're as"—I swallowed—"as lovely as you are. I just knew that I had to try and find out exactly what had happened between us in that room."

"And what might happen later? Right? You wanted to know that, too?"

"Yes. I wanted to know that, too."

She brought her hands together as though entering into a prayer. She raised them in front of her mouth. "Nothing happened between us that day, you know. I didn't even know you were there."

"When a radio station sends out a signal, it doesn't know who's listening. Far as I can tell, that doesn't detract from the message."

She ignored my analogy and said, "So what happens now, Alan Gregory, note writer?"

"This." I waved my hand over the table as though I were a magician who could make cocktails and tortilla chips and frijoles disappear. "I get to begin the wonderful process of getting to know you."

"Do you?"

I sat back confidently. "Sure. I'll show you. Watch. What kind of doctor are you, Sawyer?"

She shook her head and pushed her chair back from the table. "No. That's not the way to know me. You'll have to find another way. You showed me you have some imagination. Really, that's why I'm here right now. You're going to have to use that imagination if you want to know me." I remember thinking that she looked playful. Though, in retrospect, I'm more certain she was looking smug.

"I can find out. I could call your work number again and ask what kind of clinic it is you work at. That's pretty easy."

"Knowing that won't tell you much."

"If I press Mona enough, she'll talk."

"Mona doesn't know."

"Doesn't know where you work?"

"Don't be silly."

"Doesn't know what, then?"

She nodded approvingly at my question. She said, "There you go." Abruptly, she leaned forward, her breasts crushed against the edge of the table, her eyes doing a private waltz just for me. "Do you want to sleep with me?"

I thought about it for the time that it took my eyes to blink. I said, "Yes, Sawyer, I do."

"Good," she said. "Now I know more than you do."

If I were truly insightful I would have recognized that Sawyer had just used sex to create a dangerous fjord between us.

I wasn't. I didn't.

EIGHT

Three relatively rare events occurred the morning after Arnie Dresser's funeral.

Lauren woke before I did.

I was hungover on good Riesling.

And I learned that the FBI was coming over for dinner.

I couldn't do anything about the first two. The last one, though, I thought I could at least influence. I could call the motel where Simes and Custer were staying and cancel the repast that Lauren had arranged while I slept in. Canceling, however, felt more petulant than prudent. My other option, I decided, was to go along for the ride and bring an objective observer to the table.

Lauren was rushing out the door for an early appointment at the courthouse but said she had no objection to the second option, so I phoned Sam Purdy before I left for my office. Sam, a detective with the Boulder Police Department, had been my friend for a long time. If you asked, he would be happy to assert that he had been on a Christmas visit to his family in Minnesota the night JonBenet Ramsey was killed, was never assigned to the case, and insisted he was "untainted" by the resulting fallout.

I explained to Sam about Arnie Dresser's funeral, the weird lunch in Silver Plume, and the two ex–FBI agents. He said it sounded like so much bullshit to him and asked me for the ex-agents' names. I told him. Then, with increased interest evident in his voice, he asked what we were planning on having for dinner. I told him I didn't know for sure but it would probably be Thai something.

"Tie something what?"

"Thai, as in Thailand. Asian food."

"Is it like Chinese?"

"No, different. Thailand, Sam. Curries, coconut milk, basil and cilantro, fish sauce. There are other Asian cuisines besides Chinese."

"Doesn't mean I want to know about them. Boulder has restaurants from countries that aren't even recognized by the UN, that serve food that isn't sold in any grocery store I've ever been in. I can't keep up, so I don't even try. I like Italian and Mexican. That's adventurous enough for me."

"I think you'll like dinner. Almost for sure, we'll have salad and chicken and noodles and rice."

His voice took on a skeptical shadow. "But it's not going to be anything like my mom's chicken and rice. Right?"

"Maybe a little spicier. Your mom's not Thai, is she?" I knew well that Sam's parents and their parents and probably *their* parents were from Minnesota's Iron Range.

"My mom thinks people from Milwaukee are foreigners."

"Don't worry, Sam, you'll like dinner. Can you do seven o'clock?"

"Yeah. Can I bring anything?"

"Just your skepticism."

"I never leave home without it. So, tell me, worldly one, do people from Thailand drink beer?"

"Absolutely. I'll get some Singha. Thai beer. Has jasmine in it."

He made some noise I interpreted as relating mild disgust. "Listen, one more thing."

"Yes?"

"Actually, two more things. Buy some Bud on your way home. And do I have to use chopsticks? I hate chopsticks."

"They're optional."

He said, *"Bueno."*

I was glad that my Monday schedule was busy. I had eight patients to see between nine-thirty and six. I didn't want a lot of free time to think about Custer and Simes, methodical murderers, and Sawyer Sackett. A full day of other people's problems was a perfect prescription for distraction from my own paranoia.

Diane's day was as frantic as my own, but she found a few minutes to come down the hall into my office for a brief visit after lunch.

"Well?"

Once Diane was in the loop, she acted as though she were the proprietress of the loop. No one else in the loop was permitted to be reticent. I knew all those rules, so I filled her in on the latest developments.

"Lauren and I are having the FBI over for dinner tonight. I've invited Sam to sit in."

"Really—a local cop and the feds at the same table. You're trying to see if oil and water really do mix?"

"I just want his take on things. He's smart. I'm kind of hoping he'll convince me that they're blowing smoke."

She seemed amused at my capacity for denial. "You thought any more about Sawyer since last night?"

I lied. I said, "No. Diane, that was a long time ago."

"So was the Holocaust. But for some reason I just can't understand, the Jews are still suspicious. Come on, certain things are hard to forget, Alan. And most of the time, they really shouldn't be forgotten."

I didn't respond immediately.

"Do I need to expound on my analogy? How about black America, lynching, and the KKK? Does that ring a bell?"

"You're being a little over-the-top, Diane. I haven't forgotten about Sawyer, but I'm not terribly eager to revisit all that, either."

"You know, until lately with Lauren, I've never considered your relationships with women to be the most mature corner of your personality, but whatever it was that went on between you and Sawyer was an absolute nadir, and certainly not a paradigm of mental health. Yours or anyone else's."

"Including hers?"

"Including hers. Maybe especially hers. You two were a pair back then. Oh my. Jesus."

"Thanks for your confidence. But I'd be lying if I told you I wasn't at least a little bit afraid it would happen all over again. That I'll see her once, and . . ."

"And, let me make a guess. Your testicles will once again swell until they're bigger than your brain?"

"Something like that."

She smiled at some idea she was having before she said, "You know, Alan, maybe . . . maybe Sawyer's gotten fat and ugly. Maybe there really is a god or a god-ette whose sole role in heaven is to exact retribution from beautiful blondes with great bodies."

"She was your friend, Diane."

"And what? I can't be jealous of my friends? What planet do you live on?"

"When I find her—*if* I decide I need to find her—how about this? I'll bring her over to your house to meet Raoul. He'll—"

"No. No, no, no. You keep Sawyer away from Raoul, Alan. The man is *weak*, I tell you, he's weak. Sawyer's a natural blonde and Raoul's currently on this Marilyn Monroe nostalgia kick that worries me no end. You haven't been over to the house for a while, but we now have Marilyn coasters in our living room and there are old *Life* magazines everywhere."

I tried to picture it. "Marilyn Monroe tchotchkes along with that big Neiman of the World Cup over the sofa? Oooh, that must be a good look. Now there's a decorator's dream."

She laughed. "I'm embarrassed to admit that Raoul bought yet another masterpiece by the God, LeRoy. This one's bullfighting, for heaven's sake. The World Cup is now in our bedroom." She glanced at her watch and warned, "Don't say what you're thinking. Listen, I have a patient to see, one whose denial, by the way, doesn't even begin to approach yours. We'll continue this later."

I checked the little light on the wall of my office that indicated that my next patient had arrived as well. "My next patient's here, too. See you."

* * *

Lauren made it home from the DA's office before I made it home from my practice. She'd been busy; she had a green papaya salad chilling in the refrigerator along with a huge platter of chicken breasts marinating in something that was redolent of fish sauce and hot chili oil and cilantro. I was left with the easy work: getting the jasmine rice started in the rice cooker and throwing together some sesame noodles with green onions.

The day had been warm, almost hot, and I suspected we would be eating out on the deck to take advantage of the evening breezes. But Lauren had stacked plates and napkins and glassware and chopsticks and silverware on top of the pool table that consumed the center of the dining room, which indicated to me that we were going to be unfolding our dining room table from its home against the east wall and dining inside.

As we struggled to move the heavy fruitwood table out into the room, I asked her why we were eating in instead of out.

"I told you. Dr. Simes has MS. She'll be more comfortable in here with the air conditioning."

"You're that sure she has MS?"

"Yes." With that she started downstairs to rest before everyone arrived. She was gripping the handrail tightly as she descended the stairs. I pulled the rice cooker from the pantry and started water boiling for the noodles.

As I hoped he would, Sam arrived before Simes and Custer. He'd driven his own car, an old fire-red Jeep Cherokee, but he was still in his work clothes, which always seemed to include a plaid shirt and pastel tie. This sport coat was green corduroy. I wasn't sure I'd seen it before and wondered if he'd actually bought new clothing.

Under his right arm, he was carrying his very own six-pack of Bud.

Emily, our Bouvier, greeted him like an old friend. Few visitors were spared Emily's usually ferocious welcome, but she'd liked Sam right from the first time they'd met.

I thanked him for coming over and took his six-pack to the refrigerator. Since one of my responsibilities in life is expanding Sam Purdy's narrow cultural horizons, I poured him a Singha instead of a Budweiser and carried it to him in the living room, where he was sitting on the sofa, talking on the telephone. He pointed at his pager and I handed him the beer.

I prayed he wasn't going to get called away before he had a chance to size up Simes and Custer for me.

After a minute or so he hung up and took a long draw on the beer. His mustache was dotted with foam. "My page? Lucy's warning me about a call. There's a house with a suspicious smell in North Boulder. She's getting a warrant so she can go in. She'll call if it turns out to be what it smells like."

"You'll have to go?"

"Yeah, I'll have to go." He held up the beer glass and smiled at me warmly. "Now, why don't you stop messing with me and go get me a Budweiser. This tastes like somebody dropped a gardenia in it." Sam's wife, Sherry, was a florist. Generally, he knew his flowers. Not this time.

"Jasmine," I corrected.

He laughed. "You're confusing me with someone who gives a shit."

Lauren came upstairs and embraced Sam, who pecked a kiss to her cheek. She looked lovely in a long rayon skirt and a small black knit shell that was supported by straps thinner than the tender noodles I was cooking in the kitchen. But Lauren also looked tired.

"You nap?" I asked.

She shook her head. "I'm way too nervous about all this."

I was surprised. "You haven't seemed nervous."

Sam interrupted, "Hey, you guys? By the way, I checked these two out. The ex-agents? They're legit, apparently. He's a—"

Emily's feet scraped the wood floor like a dog in a Disney cartoon and she mouthed two crisp barks. Her pads finally found purchase on the oak and she ran at warp speed to the front door. I told her, "Quiet," and she barked louder.

I repeated myself. So did she.

Lauren watched my charade with the dog and then, in a firm voice, said, "Emily, sit." Emily did.

"Down." Emily lowered herself to her haunches.

Reluctantly, I thought.

"Stay." Emily stayed.

Lauren looked at me and admonished, "You have to work with her if you want her to listen to you."

Sam found Lauren's comment particularly amusing.

Outside, two car doors slammed. A moment later the doorbell rang and Emily whimpered and stared plaintively at Lauren. But she stayed down.

The ex-agents stood at the front door looking like a couple that had been married a long time. Milt towered over A.J. but he seemed to soften his contours so as not to overwhelm her petite form. She was dressed in a yellow pantsuit. Actually, it could better be described as a YELLOW pantsuit. It would have had to pale considerably to approach the brilliance of a ripe banana. The woman liked color.

The two ex-FBI agents were, appropriately, more interested in Sam Purdy and Emily than they were in Lauren and me. I wondered if Simes and Custer accurately assessed that the one who wasn't growling at them was actually the more dangerous of the two strangers.

Lauren said, "Hello. Please come in. Please. That's Emily—she's more harmless than she looks. And this is Sam Purdy. Sam, Dr. A. J. Simes and Milt Custer. Formerly of the FBI."

Sam said, "Hello, Doctor. Mr. Custer." Everyone shook hands with exaggerated civility.

Simes looked at me and asked, "Is Mr. Purdy your attorney?"

I was about to ask if I needed one but was distracted by Milt. He was shaking his head as though he'd already discerned Sam's role.

Sam laughed out loud and said, "Hardly. It's 'Detective' Purdy. I'm a friend of these two. They asked me to listen in, if you don't mind. I'm just here to provide another point of view."

"You are a detective with . . . ?" The question came from Simes. She didn't say whether or not she minded that Sam was present. I guessed that she did.

"Boulder Police Department."

She nodded to herself and responded crisply, "I'm not sure I understand. None of what we are discussing with Dr. Gregory and Ms. Crowder has taken place in Boulder, Detective."

Sam shrugged, said, "Yet," and he let the word hang like a belch at the dinner table. "Regardless, I'm not here in a capacity that's any more official than yours, Dr. Simes."

With that little volley complete, Lauren suggested we all move into the living room.

Milt was wearing a sport coat, which he shed as we moved to the other side of the house. Beneath the jacket was a polo shirt that had a little logo on it and the word "Augusta." I guessed golf. Milt helped Simes onto a chair before filling one end of the sofa. Sam took the other end. Other than the size of their heads—Sam's was too big, Milt's too small—the two men were about the same size and shape.

Lauren offered wine and everyone declined. Beer? No. Anything?

No.

Lauren asked Simes whether the temperature in the house was okay, whether she was comfortable.

Simes eyed her curiously, took a deep breath, and said, "Fine. Thank you for so much for asking. And it's so kind of you to offer to feed us after the bad news we've brought your way."

Milt said, "Yes. Kind."

"If what you suspect turns out to be true," Lauren replied, "you're the ones doing us a kindness. Anyway, our brief history together in restaurants has not been particularly auspicious."

Milt laughed generously and said, "I'm glad you see it that way. It's been my experience that in these circumstances, people often prefer just to shoot the messenger and be done with it."

Sam reached forward and scooped up a handful of cashews. He began popping the nuts into his mouth one at a time. I found the activity distracting and assumed that was his intent.

I faced Simes and said, "On the phone this morning, you suggested to Lauren that you would have some new information for us tonight. Maybe we should get right to it, clear the air before we eat. This, I don't know—whole situation—is leaving us a little on the anxious side."

Sam smacked his lips loudly and sucked some nut fragments from a crevice near his upper molars. Everyone looked his way. "Hey, before we move on to new information, let's review what we know already. I'm in a secondhand position here, and I don't like being in a secondhand position." He faced Milt. "You ever like getting briefed by the briefees and not the briefers? Me neither. I prefer to hear it from the guy who develops it. The source."

Milt seemed to be taking Sam's measure but didn't hesitate long before he launched into a synopsized rendition of the tale of the dead doctors. I didn't like hearing the parable the second time any more than I had liked hearing it the first. When Custer finally finished, I expected some questions for him from Sam. Instead, Sam leaned forward and grabbed some more cashews.

Simes raised her chin toward the western sky, smiled at Lauren, and said, "This view up here is lovely. Just lovely. I don't know how you ever manage to leave to go to work."

The sun had disappeared behind the Flatirons and the splintered high clouds above the mountains were lighting up in pastels. The dark canyons—Boulder and Sunshine—knifed back into the Front Range like jutting black holes. It was lovely. I have never grown tired of it.

Sam said, "Yeah, it's gorgeous. But that's not all you got, right?" His tone was matter-of-fact, not at all confrontational.

Simes spun on him. Her eyes blinked a split second apart. She parted her lips slightly but thought better of speaking.

Sam continued, "If that's all you have, you would have spent some more time developing things before scaring the shit out of my friends. If this guy strikes the way you say he does, he strikes slowly. Time isn't the issue. Still, you follow Alan and Lauren from a funeral and spring this on them in a cafe over brunch? And you don't breathe a word to the local law enforcement authorities who might have an interest in protecting them?"

A. J. Simes seemed more irritated than defensive as she said, "We've discussed these deaths with each of the local jurisdictions where they have occurred, Detective. We've—"

"Call me Sam."

"Sam. We've met with varying degrees of, shall I say, skepticism, about our suggestion that each of the deaths may have been a homicide. We've met with even greater skepticism about our hypothesis that a single offender may be responsible for the entire series of murders. It's my opinion that the evidence becomes compelling only when it is viewed in its entirety."

Sam popped another nut. "But, by now, I'm sure you've run your suspicions by your colleagues in Virginia. My guess is that they've had the opportunity to view this in its entirety, right? Why didn't they bite?"

"Perhaps," Simes said, "they have had the benefit of sufficient experience . . ." She paused and seemed to be choosing her words with increased care. ". . . with similar crimes to recognize the inherent difficulty in connecting evidence from disparate homicides with varying MOs over extended time periods."

Sam ignored the professional dig, sat all the way back against the cushions of the sofa, shook his head, and turned to face me. "They've decided there is something you don't need to know, Alan. I'll be damned if I know why that is. Hey, is anybody hungry here but me?"

I was growing more anxious rather than less. Sam's presence was supposed to make me feel better, not worse. I reminded myself that I trusted his instincts. I said, "Chicken will take about five minutes on the grill, Sam."

"Why don't you go out there and get it started? I'm starving. Sherry says I shouldn't eat too many nuts."

I waited a moment to see if either Simes or Custer was more easily provoked than I expected—they weren't—so I stood and walked to the kitchen. Lauren and I exchanged puzzled glances. I grabbed the marinated chicken from the refrigerator and carried it outside to the grill, while she began to arrange the rice and the cold food on the table. In the middle, she placed a big galvanized bucket full of beer bottles and ice. Loudly, Sam reminded her not to forget to include Budweiser. I heard him belatedly call out, "Please."

Inside, the three cops started talking. From my vantage on the deck, I couldn't hear them. Simes had moved from her chair to a perch on the edge of the coffee table. Each was leaning forward into their tight huddle. I guessed they were engaging in conspiratorial whispers abut what it was safe to reveal to me and Lauren regarding the man who might be plotting to kill me.

The fact that I wasn't included pissed me off.

NINE

The chicken charred up beautifully, and as I carried the platter inside the aromas of jasmine and fish sauce and sesame mingled together in a wonderful Southeast Asian symphony.

I said, "Dinner is served."

Small plates of green papaya salad graced each place setting. Beers were passed around.

I drank. I picked at the papaya salad, one of my absolutely favorite foods in the world. I drank some more beer. Other than the sounds of mastication, the table was silent. I couldn't stand it.

"Okay, tell me," I said. "What the hell's going on?"

Sam smiled at the other guests and asked, "May I?"

Simes nodded.

Sam wolfed down the rest of his salad and placed his fork on the plate. I was glad he liked the salad. I had no plans to tell him that the main ingredient was under-ripe papaya.

"They didn't want to tell you yet, Alan. They would have preferred to wait, develop things a little more. Problem is that without help from one of the doctors who was there in 1982, this investigation could stall out like Sherry's minivan trying to climb up to the Eisenhower Tunnel."

"Go on."

"The social worker you used to work with—" He stopped himself and looked across the table at Simes and Custer. "Here I am doing it. One of you should tell this story."

Milt checked with Simes. She closed her eyes regally.

"The social worker on Eight East was a woman named Lorna Pope. You remember her?"

I nodded. I remembered Lorna well. The social worker was responsible for the initial family evaluations for patients admitted to the unit. All the interns and residents worked closely with her. I said, "Lorna was an interesting woman. She was dating a Denver Bronco at the time I was on the unit. A placekicker, I think. She was a sports nut; a great skier. Had a healthy disdain for the residents and interns. Refused to date them. If I remember correctly, her father was a doctor. She used to say that although they might need one in an operating room, she couldn't imagine needing one in a bedroom. Something like that. That was Lorna."

Milt said, "Once again, I'm impressed. I hope you remember as much about all the patients as you do about the staff."

"Please don't tell me that Lorna is dead, too."

Simes spoke. "We don't know. Her family doesn't know. She . . . um, she disappeared."

"Disappeared?"

"She went on holiday to New Zealand with her new husband. Her third. They vanished."

Third? "Vanished?"

"Went out one day sightseeing, never came back to their hotel. Their car was discovered in a church parking lot on the other side of the island a week later. Nobody remembers seeing them."

I swallowed some beer. "Passports?"

"In the safe in their hotel room."

"Are they presumed dead?"

"No. It hasn't been long enough yet. They're listed by the U.S. embassy as missing."

I was almost numb. I was actually thinking, *So what? What's one more?* It was easier to think of her as number six, not as Lorna. I'd liked her a lot. Lusted after her a little. To myself, as much as anyone, I said, "I'm so sorry." Like Simes and Custer, I was assuming she was dead.

Sam said, "Tell them when, Milt. They need to hear when."

Milt said, "Yeah. That's what's important. When. See, she disappeared in July. July of this year."

The meaning of those words didn't immediately register. Then I heard Lauren gasp.

I asked, "July? Two months ago? This July?"

Simes replied. "Yes, this July. Please keep in mind that we haven't been able to pin this one down at all. We're discussing events in New Zealand, not New Jersey. It could all be coincidence. We don't know."

I stated the obvious. "But if it was him, things are compressing. Timewise. Things are compressing, aren't they? That's the concern?"

Simes answered. "If it was him. Yes. If it was him in New Zealand, we're looking at a rapid, rapid acceleration in his activities. If it was him, it means that he has committed three murders in a little over seven months."

Milt said, "Four. Don't forget Lorna's husband."

"That's right. Four."

"So he could be stalking me right now. Or Sawyer. He could be planning to kill one of us tomorrow?"

Simes said, "He could. I don't think so. But, yes. He could."

I disagreed with her earlier contention. "You do want to alarm me. You don't only want to warn me, you also want to scare me into helping you."

Incongruously, Simes said, "This is fabulous chicken, isn't it, Milt? But the answer to your question is yes. The danger to you may be more acute than we revealed yesterday. We wanted to develop the New Zealand situation a little better before we discussed it with you. And the need for your assistance is, well, crucial. But I think we made that clear yesterday."

I touched my lips with my tongue. Gazed over at Lauren. I could see the fear in her eyes. It was the same wariness I saw in her violet eyes when she had the first inkling of a fresh exacerbation of multiple sclerosis, during those hours when she didn't know if she was going to be merely annoyed by the progression of her disease, or debilitated by it.

I said, "If you're looking for the names of patients, you'll need to look elsewhere. As you well know, Dr. Simes, ethically I can't start giving you the names of patients from back then. Nearly all of them are absolutely innocent. At this point in time, none of us can predict the impact on their lives of revealing their identities and their histories."

Milt said, "But we may be able to predict the impact of not revealing their identities."

Simes said, "I promise we will be discreet."

"That doesn't cut it. You know that."

She closed her eyes for twice the length of a blink. Opening them, she said, "Dr. Faire said you would say that."

With the mention of Sawyer's name, I suddenly felt a tightness in my chest and abdomen. I was afraid I was going to burp.

She said, "Dr. Faire, that's right."

"I thought you said you hadn't found her." I told myself I hadn't stammered, but I had.

"That's not quite correct. We haven't seen her. But we spoke with her this morning by telephone and will meet with her soon. She's implied that she wouldn't cooperate unless you did."

The jasmine rice in my mouth seemed to congeal into a plug of gelatin the size of a golf ball.

I couldn't swallow. Lauren asked me if I was all right. Her tone told me she already knew the answer to her own question.

No more than a minute later, Sam's partner, Lucy, paged him to let him know that the search warrant had arrived and that the smell coming from the old house on North Broadway was, indeed, exactly what everyone's nose suspected it was. He excused himself to investigate the suspicious death.

But before Sam could throw his napkin onto the table, Simes announced that they, too, should be going.

Within ninety seconds, the table was empty of guests, the lane was empty of cars, and Lauren and I were alone.

I told her I would clean up the kitchen.

She told me she would take Emily out for a few minutes and then get ready for bed.

Twenty minutes later I walked downstairs, quietly peed and brushed my teeth, took off all my clothes, and climbed into bed. The west windows were cracked open and the dry, cool autumn air left the room perfect for sleeping. I curled onto my side and scrunched the pillow under my ear. I was trying hard not to think about Lorna, and was failing.

I was trying hard not to think about Sawyer. I was failing at that, too.

I was trying hard not to think about someone trying to kill me.

I was failing at that, too.

I just wanted to sleep.

Beside me, Lauren's breathing was slow and sang the soothing rhythm of slumber. I tried to match the cadence, to be captured by whatever peacefulness she'd found. But my mind quickly crossed the Pacific, and I was wondering what part of New Zealand Lorna had been visiting when Lauren's voice startled me. She said, "You awake, babe?"

"Yeah," I said, trying to sound sleepy.

"This is really scary, Alan."

"Yeah, it sure is. I don't know what to do next. My first impulse is to call the cops, but the cops and FBI are the ones who called me."

"You have to consider helping them, Custer and Simes. You know that. This guy, he could try to kill you tomorrow."

"I know. I checked all the doors twice before I came down here. I think we'd better get an alarm installed."

"This killer, this guy, he doesn't seem like the kind of guy who is stopped by alarms."

"Still. Can't hurt."

"I have a better idea. Let's move back to my place on the Hill. I'm between tenants. There are more neighbors in town than here. That house already has an alarm installed."

"And do what here?"

"Cancel our weekend in Taos. Use the time to move out. Turn this place over to the contractor. Get the remodeling over with. This isn't the time to go away. Not with all this hanging over our heads."

"I thought going away seemed like a great idea."

"Not under the circumstances, sweets. It didn't work for your friend Lorna. It didn't work for Arnie Dresser. We have a few little problems to solve first."

I rolled toward her. Her body was cool and soft. We struggled for a moment to find a position that was right.

"You're probably right. I'm not sure how relaxing it would be to get away, given everything that's going on."

"I wouldn't relax."

"You're really ready to do the remodeling?"

"Yes. I'm tired of talking about it. We can put this off forever arguing about where to put the recessed lighting and what kind of trim to put around the windows. It's time to just do it. And I know I'll feel safer living in town until all this . . . other stuff settles. Out here it's just Adrienne and us."

She kissed me on the top of my chest, just below my collarbone. She said, "Alan?"

"Yes."

"I think maybe you should tell me about Sawyer."

"About Sawyer?" I said, startled.

"Well, yes," she said. "About you and Sawyer. What went on. Whatever went on?"

"You're sure?"

"No. I'm not at all sure. Asking makes me terribly anxious. But I think I need to know."

"Yes. I suppose I should tell you."

TEN

By the time August first finally arrived and my inpatient rotation on Eight East was due to start, I'd managed to learn a few facts about Sawyer. I had called back the clinic where she worked and discovered that it was an outpatient psychiatry clinic, the exact same clinic where I, too, would soon begin seeing outpatients.

I wasn't too surprised to discover that Sawyer Sackett, M.D., was a psychiatric resident. And since she'd been on campus longer than I had, I guessed that she was a second-year psychiatric resident. Mona Terwilliger had reluctantly confided that Sawyer had attended medical schools in Florida, and that her family still lived in Virginia, where she grew up.

I have to admit that I was disappointed to learn that Sawyer was doing her training in psychiatry. I'd pinned my hopes on pediatrics. Or family practice. Or maybe one of the surgical sub-specialties, like OB-GYN. Although I had not actually spent any time praying that she wasn't training to be a psychiatrist, I wasn't looking forward to sharing turf with her.

What else did I know about Sawyer by the time my internship started?

Not much.

I wondered about that a lot. Worried about it some. But soon the pressures of my training took almost all of my attention.

* * *

The day my initial rotations were assigned and I knew that my first inpatient rotation was going to be adult Orange Team, I phoned Sawyer at home and asked her non-chalantly—I thought—what inpatient unit she worked on.

"Eight East," she'd said. That meant the adult unit. The adolescent unit was on the seventh floor.

"Blue Team or Orange Team?" I asked.

"Orange," she said.

"Me, too," I said. "I just received my assignments. This should be weird. You'll probably be doing my medical backups."

"Probably," she said. I was trying hard to appear nonchalant. Sawyer was clearly succeeding.

The first meeting I attended on Eight East was rounds. The meeting was held in a conference area adjacent to Dr. Susan Oliphant's office. Susan was the ward chief for the Orange Team.

In addition to the ward chief, daily rounds were attended by all the residents and interns, by the chief psychologist—my supervisor, Dr. Amy Masters—by the team social worker, Lorna Pope, by the head nurse, Kheri Link, and by any of her staff who were free to attend.

Unlike the residents who are making rounds on some of the medical floors of the hospital, the trainees in inpatient psychiatry don't traipse from room to room carrying charts and asking patients questions about their condition before being grilled by their attending. Instead, we sat in an oblong circle and reviewed history and therapeutic progress, medication status, community and group process, and family meeting information on all the current patients. I also quickly perceived that we were to try to act as though we were brilliant and compassionate enough to have a prayer of helping the troubled people down the hall.

The ward chief and the chief psychologist had roles different from those of the trainees. Their job was to let us know when we were being brilliant and compassionate, and, conversely, when we were being ignorant and condescending. Occasionally they managed to accomplish this with an amount of humor and kindness that left our swollen egos unlanced. Usually they didn't bother being so delicate.

That first day in rounds, I found myself sitting in an uncomfortable sled chair between Arnold Dresser, M.D., and Wendy Asimoto, M.D., two of the three residents on the team. Amy Masters was across the room whispering something to Lorna Pope, the unit social worker.

Wendy and Arnie were leaning together in front of me, comparing notes about a seminar they had to attend that afternoon on the new CPT-IV codes. I didn't have a clue what a CPT-IV code was, but didn't want to embarrass myself by inquiring. I was sure it was something I should have already learned in graduate school and that my ignorance about it would soon cause me great humiliation.

A minute or so later, Sawyer entered the room along with a tall, thin woman with a narrow face, sandy hair, and brilliant green eyes. I tried to act unconcerned at Sawyer's arrival; I even pretended to be part of the tête-à-tête about CPT-IV codes that was occurring over my knees.

While Sawyer took a chair almost directly across from me, the woman who was with her walked across the room, fumbled with some mail that had been piled on the desk, and dropped her briefcase unceremoniously in the middle of the blotter. Her back turned to the room, she asked, "Who are we missing?"

Dr. Masters said, "It appears we're dragging one of my interns, Susan."

Arnie smirked. "He's probably lost."

Lorna added, "Susan, nursing is just finishing up a restraint. I don't think they'll be on time either."

"Who's being restrained?" Arnie asked, nervously, I thought. I didn't know him at all then, but later I would realize that Arnie's question was precipitated not by curiosity but by worry that one of his own patients was misbehaving, which Arnie would definitely consider a black mark on his record.

Lorna said, "Sorry, Arnie, I'm afraid it's Travis again. He

was threatening one of the nurses this time, had her cornered in the corridor by his room. Thought she was that Frieda person he's always talking about. He was using his toothbrush, you know, holding it like a knife in front of him. He doesn't go down easily—it was a tough restraint. He's really strong."

Before Arnie could say anything Susan Oliphant asked, "How much Navane is he on, Arnie?"

Arnie said, "I upped it to forty."

"Is it enough?"

Arnie opened his mouth. For a second, nothing came out. He said, "Given the recent history, I think—"

Susan pressed him. "Is it the right drug?"

Wendy Asimoto said, "What about Thorazine or Haldol?"

I looked around the room at the psychiatric residents. At Sawyer. At the other two. They had started on July first, so they had been on the unit a month already. A month was a lifetime in a training rotation.

They were experts.

The lexicon of medical school training said that students first see a procedure, then they do the procedure, and then they teach the procedure. Well, Sawyer and her two comrades, Arnie and Wendy, had already seen one. They had already done one. And now, with fresh blood on board— the other intern and me—they were going to be eager to teach one.

Susan Oliphant looked over her shoulder and scanned the room. "We'll deal with Travis in a few minutes. Let's get started somewhere while we're waiting for the other intern." She looked at me with mock seriousness before saying, "I don't like waiting for people, do I, Wendy?"

Wendy smiled her reply with her dark eyes. She said, "No, waiting is not your best thing, Dr. Oliphant."

Susan continued to fumble with her mail while she looked over her left shoulder at me.

"You must be Dr. Gregory. Right?"

I hesitated. I thought this might be a trick question. Technically, I wasn't a doctor, yet. I wouldn't receive my Ph.D.

until after I completed my internship. "I'm Alan Gregory," I said, sidestepping the question.

The obfuscation didn't work with Susan Oliphant. She said, "Here, on Orange Team, you're 'Dr.' Gregory. You get a temporary promotion, get to wear the figurative white lab coat. Patients in the hospital don't want to think students are providing their care. They want to believe that we're the best, most experienced damn healers who have ever set foot on this planet. They want to be treated by doctors. So for a few special months, you get a dispensation. You're Dr. Alan Gregory. Everyone, meet Dr. Gregory and introduce yourselves."

Arnie Dresser made a noise I couldn't quite interpret, but I would have guessed it had some familial resemblance to contempt.

Susan didn't turn around. She'd heard the noise too, apparently. She said, "Arnie, the best therapists are those who don't believe they are God's gift. Dr. Gregory, introduce yourself to the team."

The room took on the silence of a chapel.

I wasn't ready.

I had prepared myself for this day for four years of graduate school. Classes, seminars, patients, supervision. Reading. God, so much reading.

I had prepared myself for this moment since four-thirty that morning. I was wearing my best gabardine trousers and a wool sport coat I considered stylish but not too trendy. My shirt was white, my tie brand-new, my shoes shined. My socks were interesting.

The reality was, though, that despite all my preparation, I felt like a kid. An impostor. I was still occasionally carded in bars. If I didn't look old enough to drink, how could I possibly be old enough to provide adequate treatment to a schizophrenic?

I felt confident enough with outpatients in clinic settings. I felt that my training had left me with many of the skills necessary to help the ambulatory distressed. Psychologists are trained to use the power of the therapeutic relationship to effect change in their patients. Often, in outpatient settings, those skills sufficed.

Psychiatrists, too, were trained in the art of psychotherapy. But, in addition, psychiatrists possess medical degrees and, thus, the knowledge and authority to assess medical problems and the privilege to prescribe drugs.

Clinical psychologists have a powerful arsenal that consists of one weapon: psychotherapy. The temptation, of course, when one is carrying nothing but a hammer is to treat everything as though it is a nail.

And I feared that my hammer, no matter how skillfully I wielded it, wouldn't work here. Not with this unit full of crazies.

Amy Masters caught my eye, and with an expectant smile, nodded at me to proceed. Her face was as nonjudgmental as my grandmother's had always been. Dr. Masters had been here a long time, had seen a lot of interns come and go. She had seen the self-doubt, maybe felt some of it herself at one time. She had supervised the doubters.

And she was telling me to go on.

"Good morning," I said. "My name is Alan Gregory. I'm a new clinical psychology intern and I'm delighted to be here." Right then, having spoken my first untruth, I made the mistake of looking toward Sawyer.

She was smiling into her lap.

I was rescued by the rushed entrance of the head nurse and two members of her staff along with the other psychology intern, a young woman I'd met briefly at orientation earlier that week. Her name escaped me.

She said, "Sorry I'm late. I couldn't get my key to work."

A trace of annoyance in her tone, Susan Oliphant asked, "Why didn't you just get buzzed in?"

The intern said, "I did. Problem was I was trying to open the wrong door. I got myself buzzed into the adolescent unit. All the patients there were *younger* than me. And I thought I had been assigned to a unit where the patients were supposed to be older than the doctors. Hi, everybody, I'm Alix Noel." She smiled a brilliant smile.

Amy Masters said, "Well, Alix, you're Dr. Noel now."

Alix looked at me, then at Amy Masters. She said, "Cool. I'm a doctor now? Does that mean I skip the rest of my internship? Even better, can I, like, totally forget my dissertation?"

Everyone laughed.

Of course, none of us knew then that that day was the first time that all of the dead doctors would be together in one room.

The introductions lasted about five minutes. I was looking forward to Sawyer's, hoping I might learn something. I didn't. She stated her name, said that she was a second-year resident and had a particular interest in forensic psychiatry. She smiled at Alix, didn't once look at me.

Since neither Alix nor I had yet picked up any patients, the residents took turns reviewing their current cases. They did the reviews from scratch for our benefit. History, medical history, reasons for admission, precipitating events, treatment course, meds. Everything.

Sawyer went first.

She was dressed in a tartan skirt that reached the middle of her calves and a long-sleeved white blouse that an hour earlier I would have bet good money wasn't even part of her wardrobe. The social bluster and gaminess that was so much of what I had seen on our quasi-date during the hailstorm was absent. She was precise, professional, perhaps even a little shy. She presented her four cases with confidence and a trace of humor. She accepted compliments and criticism from Dr. Oliphant and from her peers with the same grace. Perhaps my judgments were colored by my lust, but I thought she showed surprising sensitivity in presenting her two active cases, a young first-break schizophrenic and a severely depressed woman in her forties. Dr. Oliphant was pressing for electroshock; Sawyer wanted more time to work with her patient in psychotherapy.

I realized for the first time that the Sawyer I'd met at Mona's party, the Sawyer I'd risked life and limb to have cocktails with in a thunderstorm, had either been putting on an act for me or was putting one on right then. I also realized that I didn't know which was true.

That should have warned me off.

It didn't.

It intrigued me.

ELEVEN

After rounds, Alix and I were introduced to the rest of the Orange Team staff and to the other therapists who worked on the unit. Alix rushed off to an outpatient clinic appointment. I had a few minutes to kill before I was due to meet my new supervisor in the psych ER, so I loitered outside the nursing station hoping to learn when I would be assigned my first patient.

Sawyer walked up to me and introduced herself as though we had never met. She called herself "Dr. Sackett."

I got the message.

She suggested that since we would be working together, we get to know each other better, and wondered if I was free for a late lunch at the Campus Lounge on Eighth Avenue. I said I thought I could do that.

At one-thirty she was waiting on the sidewalk across the street from the campus. In my brief stay in Denver, I'd already learned that the tacky restaurant and adjoining bar were a hangout for the medical school staff and students. I waved and she smiled in a way that made her mouth widen without the corners rising at all and said, "Hi. I forgot my appointment book. I'm lost without it. Totally lost. Why don't you come to my house instead? I'll fix a sandwich or something. Do you mind? Please."

"Not at all," I said. The levity in her mood surprised me. We hadn't been together since that night at the Firefly during the thunderstorm. I expected more of the same gaminess.

But it was absent. I considered it propitious.

We walked in silence for the block and a half to her home. With her arms crossed she held a small satchel against her chest like a schoolgirl. At her house, I followed her down a narrow brick walkway to the backyard. We climbed three rickety stairs and entered a tiny kitchen through a battered screened-in porch.

"Why don't you check the fridge, see if there's anything you want. I'm going to get out of this skirt. It's way too hot for today." She disappeared into another part of the house.

I hung my jacket over a kitchen chair and ignored the refrigerator, which was humming loudly. I used a glass from the dish drain to get myself a drink of water from a big glass bottle that was resting on a ceramic crock across the small room. The water tasted great, so I got another, and sat on one of the kitchen chairs.

Sawyer walked back in after two or three minutes. She had changed her outfit and was wearing a short-sleeved floral blouse, a lightweight khaki skirt, modest pumps, and panty hose.

She looked preppy.

I was surprised.

In her hands she held the day's mail. She smiled at me before starting to flip through it, quickly setting aside everything but an envelope constructed of good blue paper. "Excuse me," she said, slitting the letter open.

She turned her back to me, crossed the room to the sink, and started to read. I couldn't be sure, but I thought I heard a whimper or moan escape her lips. She flipped the single page over and began to read the back. Her posture weakened and she rested her elbows on the sink. Her left hand sifted through her hair.

After a minute or so she stuffed the letter back in the envelope and hiked out of the room as though I weren't there.

I was alone for a good five minutes before she returned. She stood in the doorway.

"Bad news?" I asked. "The letter."

She lowered her eyes and moved her head in a way that wasn't yes, wasn't no.

"Want to talk about it?"

She swallowed. "It's nothing. The past."

"Didn't look like it was nothing." Impulsively, I grabbed her hand as she walked by me.

When she didn't pull away from me, I reeled her closer. She hesitated slightly, but not enough to warn me off. I continued to pull until she was facing me, not more than a foot from the chair. "What is it? What upset you?" I said.

I reached for her other hand. She tensed. I could feel her weight pull against me. For a second I thought she intended to move away, but she relaxed, stepped forward, raised her left leg, and straddled me on the chair, lowering herself gingerly to my lap.

She said, "It's nothing, really. Forget it. You're feeling a little more bold today than you were the last time around, aren't you?"

"This particular situation doesn't feel as dangerous as thunder and lightning and hailstones."

Her voice was heavy. She said, "You never know."

"Maybe you haven't heard? I'm a doctor now. Like you. So I get to be righteous. Cocky."

Sawyer said, "Cocky?" and laughed softly.

The sound was pleasant and lifted my spirits. I tried to recall whether or not I had ever heard her laugh before.

She said, "You think I'm arrogant, huh?" Her tone wasn't defensive. Maybe a little mocking, I thought, as though I had badly misjudged her character with an ill-chosen adjective.

"You're something, Sawyer. I'm not sure what."

With her left hand she reached forward and grabbed the knot on my tie. With her right, she gripped the fabric below. I thought she was going to choke me. Playfully, of course. But instead she began to release the pressure, loosen the knot, and fumble with the button beneath.

I also felt her weight shift on my lap as the soft mass of her spread legs seemed to find cushion against my groin. Her breasts were only inches away from my mouth.

"Don't let the residents on the unit fool you. We were all terrified a month ago, too. A month from now you'll begin to feel invincible, too. The terror was unwarranted then, the invincibility isn't warranted now."

"I figured all that. But the bravado is . . . is so refined, it's scary."

"We have seminars on conceit in medical school. It's a required course." With these few words, I thought she wiggled just the slightest bit. But it could have been my imagination.

My tie was loose, open all the way to the first button on my shirt.

She had been looking past me while we talked. I captured her hands and slowly released them before I reached up and touched the sides of her face with my fingers. I was particularly gentle as I touched her, as though I were lifting the petal of a rose. Her cheeks were soft to my touch, all powder and tender flesh. I traced an invisible line to her jawbones and lifted her face until I captured her gaze in mine.

She permitted me to examine her eyes for only a moment and then she looked away. I moved my face and met her eyes again, maneuvering as delicately as I could, the same way I might try to corral a ladybug.

For an instant, Sawyer tried to fly away from me again, but then, to my surprise, she let me lock onto her dancing eyes for two or three seconds. The light sparkled off her speckled irises like confetti falling to the ground.

Then she was gone.

I felt even more pressure in my groin. This time, I was rather certain it had nothing to do with Sawyer shifting her weight.

She flitted a glance my way and said, "You know, you're making me uncomfortable."

"Ditto." I squirmed on the chair.

She laughed again. "That's not what I mean."

I leaned forward and kissed her on the chin. Held the position long enough to begin to memorize the sensation of her skin on my lips.

Abruptly, she turned her face away from mine, but I persisted and I moved my mouth lower and kissed her on the side of the neck below her ear. My lips were parted and as I touched her with my tongue I tasted salt and inhaled the perfumes of flowers and spice.

In the midst of a protracted exhale, she said, "I have a two-thirty patient in the clinic."

I slid my fingers up and into her hair. It was as soft as down.

I said, "I guess that means we had better hurry."

With my hands on the back of her head, I pulled her face to mine and moved my lips to her mouth. For the first time, we kissed. I tasted her breath and our tongues jousted in the neutral territory between our teeth. After three tantalizing parries, our tongues finally touched and I felt a jolt shoot down my limbs that was pure electricity.

My hands tugged at the back of her blouse and her hands were on my belt and seconds later, it seemed, her weight was off my lap and she was sliding my trousers to my knees. I slid my hand up her thigh and discovered the panty hose were only thigh-high stockings.

This outfit wasn't as preppy as it had looked. Briefly I was aware that this seduction wasn't really mine. The thought vaporized.

She reached between her legs, took me in her right hand, and lowered herself back onto me in one uninterrupted thrust. I felt the moisture and the warmth and the tightness and for an instant felt nothing else in the world. I couldn't smell, I couldn't taste, I didn't know if I was breathing. The rest of the world was gone.

She pressed down harder, until I could feel the flesh outside of her as well as in. I pulled her body to me with both my hands and tried to raise myself off the chair to meet her.

She whispered, "Don't move." Although the words were hushed, the message was not.

For a moment we were still.

Then I moved.

Her voice sad and desperate, her lips behind my ear, she said, "Please. Please. Don't move. Please. Oh, don't move."

She gasped.

I wondered if she was about to cry.

Into her hair, I asked, "What would you like, Sawyer?"

I felt her fingernails hard and sharp in the flesh of my shoulder. She answered, "Just fill me, okay? Just . . . fill me."

The next morning, Sawyer wasn't at rounds. I wondered about her absence until I was distracted by the news that I would be getting my first inpatient that afternoon, a transfer from the crisis unit at the mental health center in Jefferson County.

An hour later, I attended my first Orange Team Community Meeting—Sawyer was there this time—and for the first time I met Arnie Dresser's already legendary patient, Travis, who was fresh out of eight hours in restraints and sixteen more in an isolation room.

Travis was an incredibly skinny man. I guessed he stood around six-two yet weighed no more than one-forty. His blond hair was almost white. He was balding on the crown and his hair had receded so dramatically on his temples that what remained resembled a platinum horseshoe that someone had hammered into place high on his pale forehead. While the other patients and the staff members were finding seats, Travis began to slowly shake his head back and forth while his mouth continuously formed the word "no." The elderly woman next to him stared at him with a dull expression on her face, the whole time making the hand and face motions necessary to apply and reapply lipstick.

Of course, her hand was empty.

A quick assessment of the room found no one else who looked more disturbed than anyone I'd seen on my last crosstown trip on a city bus.

Dr. Oliphant said, "Travis?" in a soft voice. "Would you prefer to be excused from this meeting today?"

He didn't hear her, or he ignored her. I couldn't tell.

More sharply, she repeated his name. "Travis."

He looked up at her, still mouthing the word "no."

"Would you prefer to be excused from this meeting to-

day? Perhaps try again next time when you're feeling a little more in control?"

Travis raised his chin and tightened the tendons in his
neck. He said, "I'm sitting here. I'm sitting. I'm minding
my own business. My business." He stared at the ceiling
tiles for a moment before lowering his chin to his chest.

Dr. Oliphant said, "The Community Meeting isn't about
your own business, Travis. Are you prepared to pay attention
to what's going on and to participate with the community
this morning? Or would you prefer some more time alone?
It's just fine if that's what you need." Her words were soft,
an invitation to withdraw, not a threat of exclusion.

I was impressed at her manner.

Travis looked up once again, this time appearing startled
that the room was full of people. He said, "I . . . I . . . I'll
do whatever it takes, I says. I'll do whatever it takes to
makes . . . takes to makes . . . the nurses think me of a
gentleman. Kind man." The form of his words was as man-
gled as their meaning, as though he were trying to enunciate
through a mouthful of yogurt. I remembered all the Navane
he was on and assumed the pharmaceuticals were the cul-
prit. Travis was taking enough antipsychotics to stop a ma-
rauding bull elephant. Certainly enough to slur his speech.

Dr. Oliphant said, "That's fine. You're welcome to be
with us, then." With Susan's approval, Travis was going to
be permitted to participate in the Community Meeting.

Attention turned next to Olivia, the woman with the
imaginary lipstick. A nurse asked her to finish her makeup
after the meeting. With an audible huff, Olivia dropped her
hands to her lap.

I spent most of the rest of that first Community Meeting
wondering whether my first admissions would have any familial resemblance to Travis or Olivia, or whether they
would resemble one of the other members of the community. The other patients who lined the dayroom that morning appeared sadder than most, angrier than most, or more
medicated than most. But I could see myself sitting down
with any of them for psychotherapy.

But if my first patient was as psychotic as Travis or

Olivia, I figured I might just as well pack up my briefcase and go home.

I had my pants around my ankles and a length of toilet paper in my hand when I heard the commotion that started on the unit around ten-thirty that morning. The staff rest room was at the end of a narrow hall near the occupational therapy room. I finished up on the toilet, washed my hands, and gingerly made my way back down the hall toward the unit to see what the heck was going on.

Halfway back to the unit corridor, I stopped in my tracks as I heard Arnie Dresser insist loudly that Travis put down the knife.

"Now, Travis. Now. Put down the knife. Put it down." I thought Arnie sounded much more frightened than authoritative.

And what the hell was Travis doing with a knife? I figured it must be one of the little flimsy plastic jobs that dietary served with patients' meals.

I continued down the hall to the spot where it intersected with the corridor, poked my head around the corner, and tried to see what Travis was doing. Twenty feet away, his back to me, Travis was holding someone hostage in front of him. Ten or twelve feet beyond Travis, a few doctors and nurses were grouped together trying to coax Travis to release the knife. Behind them, even farther down the corridor, the rest of the staff were busy hustling patients out of their rooms toward the dayroom, away from danger.

From where I was standing, I could only see the back of Travis's head. The skin on his neck was bright red, so brilliantly red it looked sunburned.

Travis cried out, "Frieda. Frieda. Frieda."

With the plaintive voice of a street beggar, Arnie said, "That's not Frieda with you, Travis. That's Dr. Sackett. You don't want to hurt her. And you don't want to hurt Frieda. Put down the knife."

Sawyer?

I looked again and saw some wisps of blond hair protruding above Travis's right shoulder.

He had Sawyer. And he had a knife.

All of Travis's attention was directed at the posse in front of him. Either he had already decided that no one was behind him or in his current mental condition he was incapable of considering the possibility that danger might come from some other direction.

I backed into the hallway and considered my options. A fire exit behind me would sound an immediate alarm if I used it to go for help. But Travis's reaction to an alarm was unpredictable, and that unpredictability would present an unacceptable risk to Sawyer's well-being.

I assumed someone had already alerted hospital security anyway.

Okay, I said to myself, what do you know about Travis that might help?

What I knew was that Travis was psychotic. His diagnosis: paranoid schizophrenia. DSM III 295.33. Which meant Travis had a thought disorder, which meant I didn't have a clue about the current reality he might be inhabiting. I could safely assume that it wasn't the same one where I was hanging out.

That Travis had confused Sawyer with Frieda told me he was delusional. At rounds that morning, Arnie had reported that in addition to his ongoing delusions about Frieda, Travis had reported hearing auditory command hallucinations—voices telling him that he should accomplish various acts, usually not things like jogging or playing Scrabble. Travis had assured Arnie that he was ignoring the voices.

I also knew that Travis was taking forty of Navane.

All in all, this wasn't a pretty picture.

One of the hallmarks of severe psychosis is thought disorder. One of the trademark symptoms of thought disorder is ambivalence, the inability to choose between alternative actions. I wondered if I could use that to my advantage, to briefly paralyze Travis with ambivalence by giving him an alternative to ponder, anything other than slicing Sawyer with the knife he was holding to her body.

That might give us enough time to disarm him and restrain him.

Or I could do nothing. Allow the people with experience to handle this.

The doing-nothing alternative was winning my favor when Wendy Asimoto screamed, "He cut her! Oh, no, Travis. She's bleeding. Don't do that, don't do that. Oh, God."

Arnie's voice shook. "Travis, please put down the knife."

Travis said, "Blood."

I waited to hear Sawyer cry out.

But the next voice I heard was Wendy's. She screamed, "No, Travis, no, not again! NO! WHERE IS SECURITY?"

Then I heard Sawyer whimper and Travis say, "Frieda, Frieda."

Without further contemplation, I left the sanctuary of the hallway and walked briskly down the corridor as silently as I could and tapped Travis on the shoulder. I adopted a tone that was as close as I could manage to the one I had heard Susan Oliphant use that morning in Community Meeting.

I said, "Excuse me. Travis?"

He turned his head just a little.

"Travis? It's Dr. Gregory."

He turned a little more. I could see the knife now. It was a little red Swiss Army pocketknife, the kind so small you can hang it from a key chain. The shiny steel blade was stained with Sawyer's blood.

I said, "Would you like to go back to your room now? It's a little safer in there, don't you think? I think that might be a good idea."

He seemed to be considering my presence, or my words. Or something. He dropped his hand—the one that was holding the knife—until it came to rest at least six inches away from Sawyer's flesh. Doing so exposed his chest and upper body to me for an instant.

I didn't hesitate. I drove my shoulder into the small opening as hard as I could, lifting his thin frame away from Sawyer and off the floor. He came down hard against the wall, looking stunned.

Seconds later, he was being restrained by the staff.

Immediately after tackling Travis, I had grabbed Sawyer. She felt heavy in my arms as I eased her down to the floor.

Her blood was running down my fingers, down my arms, and she felt to me as though she were melting into a puddle on the floor.

When I looked up again, the staff had Travis in restraint, preparing to move him toward the isolation room.

He was moaning, yelling about his shoulder hurting, asking about Frieda.

Wendy Asimoto was a board-certified internist who was retraining in psychiatry. She took over Sawyer's care.

Sawyer's two wounds were to the side of her neck, and in the seconds that it took Wendy to get pressure bandages over the lacerations, they appeared, to my untrained eye, to be superficial.

But nobody wanted to take any chances, and the moment a gurney arrived on the scene Sawyer was helped onto it and transported with haste toward the elevators and the emergency room.

Wendy Asimoto went with her.

Arnie Dresser wanted to talk to me in the nursing station.

With a somber look on his face, he said, "Thank you so much. I can't believe what you did out there. I'm so grateful. I don't know what I would have done if Travis had, you know—"

I stopped him and tried to be reassuring. "Arnie, Travis is your patient, not your kid. You're not responsible for what he was doing out there." The reality was that if one of my first patients had attacked another doctor, I would have been so humiliated I would probably have resigned my internship.

Arnie wasn't listening. "Maybe Travis needs different meds. Maybe more isolation. I don't know. I don't know."

"Susan approved his being back on the ward. We can all learn something from this, right?"

"Whatever I can do to repay you. Anything. You let me know. You'll let me know, right?"

I didn't have the courage to tell him that I hadn't been brave for him. Or for Travis. I'd done it for Sawyer.

I had my back slapped by a lot of people in the next few

minutes. I was told I was a hero. I was hoping my accidental gallantry would earn me some credits I could cash in when I screwed up, which I knew was inevitable. The whole time I was fighting the urge to run downstairs to the ER to check on Sawyer.

TWELVE

Lauren was cool to me the morning after our Thai dinner party.

The night before, after I'd begun to tell her about Sawyer, we'd lain in bed and she'd posed a few questions that I knew she didn't really want to ask and that she knew I didn't really want to answer.

The first came after a pregnant moment when she kissed me on one of my nipples. She asked, "Did you love her? Sawyer?"

Of course, I'd considered the question many times on my own over the years. Had I loved Sawyer? The answer was that I adored Sawyer Sackett so long before I discovered whether or not she was deserving of my adoration that I probably never got enough emotional distance to love her in any manner that approached what I'd developed with Lauren.

I didn't want to admit to my wife that my adoration of another woman had been so blinding, though, so I said, "I wasn't real mature back then. I thought I loved her. Knowing what I know now, I know I didn't really. It's not anything like what we have."

I had only the dimmest hopes that those words would be palliative. So I wasn't surprised that they weren't.

She was slowly tracing her index finger up and around one of my breasts and then under and around the other. And then again. I realized she was forming the mathematical symbol for infinity.

She asked, "Do you still have feelings for her?"

"Feelings? No. I don't even know her now. I probably didn't even really know her then."

Lauren shifted her weight, and I could smell the conditioner she used in her hair. I inhaled more deeply, hoping for perfume. No.

"But there's something there, isn't there? She could still push your buttons, couldn't she? If you saw her tomorrow, it would still stir something up?"

With my fingernails, I began scratching long gentle lines from the crack in her ass to her shoulder blades. This particular caress usually made her purr.

Not this time.

I said, "You want me to be honest?"

She laughed and the ironic timbre of her chuckle chilled us both.

"No," she said, slapping me semi-seriously on my hip. "I want you to be reassuring. What do I want? I want to hear that I'm your one and only. I want to know that you haven't decided you made a mistake by marrying a woman with multiple sclerosis. That's what I want to hear. But . . . if this woman, this Sawyer, could still get you going, even after all these years, I should probably know that before we start looking for her."

"You are my one and only. And, no, I don't want to see her, Lauren. I've never been tempted to find her."

"You're not curious?"

"Let's just say that a long time ago, I came to the conclusion that she's not good for me."

She didn't miss a beat before she said, "Or for us, right?"

Which, of course, was where the money was.

"You're good for me, Lauren. I love you. Deeply. I'd marry you again tomorrow."

"You're sweet, and you always know the right things to say," she said, but she didn't sound reassured. She grew quiet for a moment, and her breathing changed. When she spoke again, her tone had taken on a rougher burr. "You know, it's a nightmare that this guy is out there, somewhere, threatening your life. It's a double nightmare that indirectly he's also threatening ours, our life together. I'm not sure we have any true choices in this. We either wait for him to try to kill you and hope he fails for the first time in his illustrious career as a serial killer. Or you have to go see your old lover Sawyer in order to try to save your life."

She paused and added, "Even if it kills us."

At breakfast she said she had decided that she wanted to build the garage we'd been so ambivalent about adding to the remodeling project. She was tired of climbing into a hot car in the summer and didn't want to face another winter of frosted windshields. She asked me if I'd think about it.

I had to admit her timing was pretty good. If she had asked me to add an Olympic swimming pool and an indoor tennis court to the remodeling project, I probably would have assented.

Right after I rinsed our breakfast dishes, I phoned the architect and ordered working drawings of the garage.

We signed an AIA agreement with our eager contractor over the lunch hour. He had informed us that he was primed to get going, and apparently he wasn't kidding. The ink on the contract wasn't yet dry when he said he wanted to begin demolition on Thursday morning.

We said we'd be out of the house by Friday afternoon. Disappointed, he asked if he could demo over the weekend.

Lauren looked at me and shrugged her shoulders. I raised my eyebrows in a "why not" gesture.

The contractor's name was Dresden Lamb. We'd heard from friends who used him that he always scheduled scuba diving holidays at the end of his big construction projects. It gave him a selfish reason to meet deadlines, a fact I appreciated.

I said, "After we're out, Dresden, you can tear it apart whenever you're ready."

He said, "Good. First, I have to get the new windows ordered. That's always a problem, getting the windows delivered on time. Then I'll get the demo boys in here. This project's gonna cook. You watch. We'll have your home torn apart in no time at all."

The metaphor wasn't lost on either of us. But neither of us mentioned that he might have plenty of help with that endeavor.

I finally reached Sam Purdy later that afternoon. He was still wrapped up in the investigation of the unexplained death on North Broadway, but he didn't think it was going anywhere important.

He said, "Sorry I had to rush away last night. Everyone's noses told them this might be a homicide."

"It isn't?"

"No. Looks more like the guy who lived in the house had a heart attack and fell down some stairs. Broke his neck. He probably just died and then stewed for a few days until he smelled bad enough to bother the neighbors. Happens sometimes."

I needed to get him talking about Custer and Simes. "Sam, what's your impression about last night? How nervous should I be?"

"About all those dead doctors you worked with? Very nervous. I think this is serious stuff. They've been thoughtful, those two ex-agents. This isn't some bullshit story they're cooking up."

It was exactly what I expected to hear from him. But by nature I'm such an optimistic guy that I was holding out hope that I'd be surprised.

In my best sardonic voice, I said, "Great. That's not what I wanted you to say, you know. I don't have a clue what to do next."

Sam laughed and said, "You know what her name is? Simes, I mean? Do you know what A.J. stands for?"

What?

"No, Sam. What does A.J. stand for?"

"Ambrosia June. Her name is Ambrosia June Simes. How's that for a moniker? I'd call myself A.J., too, if my parents planted that one on me."

I didn't want to talk about Simes's unfortunate name. "Sam, what am I going to do?"

He sighed. "I don't know, Alan. I'm thinking on it. And

I'll talk to some people I know. The whole thing is too goofy for words. With the way this guy works, I mean, I've been thinking that staying out of his way is like trying to protect yourself from mosquitoes in Minnesota in July. No matter how many precautions you take, one of them always seems to get your blood."

Huh? "This guy's a little more dangerous than a mosquito, Sam."

"True, but what do you do? Get a bodyguard? Start living on the run like a Colombian drug lord? Change your identity? How do you defend yourself against someone who is so clever at finding ways to kill people?"

"Sam, you're my expert here. You're the one who's supposed to be supplying the answers, not the questions."

"Sorry. Listen, I'm working on it, okay? For now, I'm going to ask the sheriff to spend a little more time patrolling Spanish Hills. You guys have an alarm system, don't you?"

I thought, *As though that's going to be much of a deterrent.*

"We're moving into town this week, Sam. To Lauren's old house on the Hill—you were there a long time ago; I don't know if you remember. We've been planning to do some remodeling for a while and we decided to go ahead and get it done. Lauren says she'll feel safer in town. But yes, her house has an alarm."

"Is it monitored?"

"Yes."

"Remind me, what's the address?"

I told him.

"When are you moving?"

"This week. Should be in there by Friday."

"Well, don't be surprised if you see a lot of patrol cars in your neighborhood. By the way, does Lauren still carry?"

"What?"

"That little Glock? Have you forgotten about the Glock?"

How could I forget about the damn Glock? "As far as I know, she still has it, Sam. But I don't think she actually carries it with her any longer. I haven't asked."

"Well, ask. And if she doesn't have it with her, ask her to think about it. You know how to use it?"

"No."

"It's time you learned. I'll set it up. And I'll talk to the sheriff about a carry permit for you, too."

"I don't want to carry a gun, Sam."

He snorted, not even attempting to hide his derision. "Get over it. This isn't about liberal angst, Alan. This is about self-protection. Got it? What I'm telling you is that you need to learn how to use a handgun. I'm not trying to recruit you to become a lobbyist for the NRA."

"Yeah, well, I'll think about it. That's a big step for me to take, Sam. You know how I feel about guns. Listen, while you're pondering all this, would you focus on something specific for me, please?"

"Sure. Like what?"

"Give some thought to how you would do it. If you were this guy, this killer, how would you kill me so that it looked like an accident?"

"I don't need to think about it too much. I know what I'd do."

"Go ahead."

"You're not going to like this, but after studying your lifestyle for a good, say, forty-eight hours, I'd decide to kill you on your bicycle. Run you off the road on one of those streets that go nowhere east of Boulder. Sabotage your equipment so your bike does something it's not supposed to do while you're coming down one of the canyons. I'd do something like that."

"That's what I thought you'd say."

"Don't you agree?"

"Yeah. That's what I'd do, too. You think I should stop riding?"

"For you, that's like you telling me not to follow hockey any more. I'm not sure you can do it. Could you?"

"If it means staying alive, I suppose I could."

"That gives us two things that you can do. Learning how to use a weapon. Giving up your favorite sport."

"If I stop riding, he'll just find another way, though, won't he?"

"Yeah. He will. And Alan?"

"Yes."

"You have any clues who this might be? Those two, Simes and Custer, are right, you know. It's probably a patient from that unit you all worked on. When you think back on those days, any of your patients seem capable of this? Do any of them seem homicidal?"

"I've been trying to remember them all. I've thought of a few patients who were angry enough to do it, plenty who might be crazy enough to do it, but no one who was actually resourceful enough to do it. This guy is so resourceful. We have to remember that. He's a meticulous planner. That really limits the diagnostic categories for someone in an inpatient psychiatric unit."

"Go on."

"The vengeance, too. To hold on to this sense of injustice—fury—for so long requires an immense reservoir of vengeance."

"So he's bright, resourceful, and vengeful. Work with that. Expand your list of adjectives. Every adjective you're able to add shortens your list of potential suspects."

"You're right. I hadn't thought about that."

"He's in your memory somewhere. You know that, don't you? You're going to have to dig him up. He left a scrap there, somewhere. It's like physical evidence. You know Locard's principle, don't you?"

"No."

"When a criminal comes in contact with a surface, he always leaves a trace of evidence behind and he always takes a little something with him. This is the same. He left something there for you to find. But it's psychological trace evidence. You're going to have to find it."

"I know I will, Sam. Trouble is that it was a long time ago. Memory fades."

"His hasn't. The murderer's. That's what sucks."

* * *

Simes and Custer had checked out of their motel in Boulder. I left a message at their voice-mail number, asking them to call. I didn't tell them that what I wanted was information on how to get in touch with Sawyer.

I didn't want to give them the satisfaction.

I knew that these two were actually trying to save my life, but for now they felt like adversaries. I was desperate to know who from my past might be targeting me. Whether they liked it or not, my partner on the search was going to be Sawyer, not them.

I arrived home from work on Wednesday afternoon to find two new additions to the gravel lane in front of the house. The first was a blue rollaway trash bin that looked larger than our house.

The second was an outhouse crafted of molded plastic.

It was really going to happen. Dresden and his demo boys were going to tear our home apart.

I played with Emily for a while and then busied myself packing. Lauren and I had decided to box the place up ourselves and pay someone to move the things we couldn't use into storage.

While I was tackling the clutter of the hall closet, the phone rang. I checked my watch, hoping it would be Lauren. It was five forty-five; she was due home soon.

"Dr. Gregory? Milt Custer here, returning your call. I'm kind of hoping you're about to tell me you've had a change of heart. We sure could use your assistance with this."

"Actually, no, Milt, no change of heart. But I have decided that it makes sense—that it's prudent—that I do want to compare notes with Sawyer about some things. Could you please tell me how I can reach her?"

"What do you hope to accomplish?"

"I'd like to talk about this with somebody who was there. Someone who's in the same shoes I'm in. That list has grown uncomfortably short. Right now, it begins and ends with Sawyer Sackett."

"Her name's Faire. Sackett was her married name. She's using her maiden name once again. We just did a brief interview with her."

Married? Sawyer was married when she was at the medical school?

No, Custer's information must be incorrect.

I wondered what else he was wrong about. Hoped it was everything.

"I need to consult with A.J. before we send you off to see your old friend. Make sure she's okay with it. For right now, that's her piece of all this."

"Sawyer's her piece? And what, I'm yours?"

"Hardly. A.J. is coordinating all the psychological aspects of the case. The profiles, the professionals, the scenarios. I'm taking care of the investigatory aspects. The nuts and bolts of the crimes themselves. So discretion says I should ask her about you and Dr. Faire having a rendezvous. My guess is you'll hear back from her shortly. Me, I'm on my way to New Zealand in a couple of hours."

Oh God. "Lorna?"

"Yes. Ms. Pope. A couple of bodies have been found. The local authorities have been kind enough to offer to let me observe their work."

"Is there evidence that they were, you know, um—"

"Murdered? Can't say at this point. Nothing obvious like bullet holes, but we're apparently talking some serious decomposition. The autopsies are scheduled for tomorrow in Auckland. I think I'll be there in time, but I've never really understood this international date line thing. I don't know whether the plane I'm on will be arriving in New Zealand yesterday or tomorrow. And I can't believe I'm going to be sitting in one of those crappy little airplane seats for the next fourteen hours."

THIRTEEN

"**S**he lives in Santa Barbara. You know, California? But she's not there now. At least I don't think she is."

Simes had phoned me no more than fifteen minutes after I hung up with Custer.

"You really don't know where she is?" I asked, more than a bit disbelieving. I suspected that if they really wanted to, Simes and Custer could find J. D. Salinger before breakfast, Amelia Earhart before afternoon tea.

"No. She told us she's on the road a lot for her work, but she wasn't especially eager to hand us an itinerary after we laid out our concerns."

"What's her work?"

"She's a consultant for some organization that provides psychiatric evals for prisoners in the California penal system. A legal aid type thing."

I could tell that Simes was not enamored of Sawyer's choice of vocation. I said, "Really?"

She didn't respond. Perhaps she couldn't believe I would question her truthfulness.

"Do you have her number in Santa Barbara? I guess I'll just leave her a message and wait to hear back from her."

I could almost feel Simes's reluctance to part with the information. She hugged it as closely as a mother does her baby before handing it over to a stranger. "I'm concerned that you and Dr. Faire may try to lock me out of this, Dr. Gregory. You wouldn't be planning on doing that, would you?"

"If I said no, would you believe me?"

"No, I wouldn't."

"Good, I'm glad we understand each other. So, are you going to give me the number or not? You know I'll get it from someone else if you don't."

"You may get her number but . . . you can't get there from here without us. Without Milt and me. It's crucial that you recognize that now, early. Before you make mistakes. This man is targeting one of you this very minute. He's examining your lives, assessing your vulnerabilities, planning his . . . activities."

"I'm not going to do anything with you and Milt, or without you and Milt, before I speak with Sawyer. It's that simple. We're wasting time."

Simes gave me the number and added, "I'm expecting to hear from you quite soon. As soon as you speak with her, as a matter of fact. You and I need to be on the same page about this offender. Why? Because I'm beginning to know him already. What he's doing. Why he's doing it. How he's doing it. Even what he's likely to do next. It's crucial that you do whatever is necessary to get yourself to a place where you can take the profile I'm developing and attach a name to it for me."

My reluctance to personalize this murderer was overwhelming. I didn't want to know him. I didn't want to let him be real.

I said, "Please, A.J., let's not go there right now. I need to speak with Sawyer first."

She ignored my plea. "Remember Andrew Cunanan? The man who killed Gianni Versace, among others?"

"Yes."

"He's your model, Dr. Gregory. If you want to identify this offender, start with Cunanan's profile. Anger. Vengeance. Power. *Power.* Don't forget power. Then anonymize him—take him off the cover of *Newsweek*. Increase his IQ by fifty points, maybe more. Decrease his impulsivity by a factor of a hundred. Exaggerate his feelings of being a victim tenfold. And then, then give him the luxury of time. All the time in the world. Do that and you'll have our guy. He's Andrew

Cunanan and he's Theodore Kaczynski, all rolled into one lethal package."

Her tone grew excited as she fleshed out this demon that was targeting Sawyer and me.

Right then, I realized something important about Simes. Talking with reluctant civilians—like me—wasn't her bread and butter. Anthropomorphizing monsters was. Her specialty, her love, involved doing psychological evaluations on people whom she'd never met.

"Cunanan killed himself when he was cornered."

Without the slightest hesitation, A. J. Simes said, "This guy won't. That's the difference."

"Why not?"

"Cunanan was on a spree. Compared to this man, Cunanan was an amateur on a lark. This guy is a professional. He's dedicated. This is his life's work. Remember the Unabomber, too. He didn't give up. He didn't stop."

Something else Simes said resonated long after we hung up.

Anonymize him. Comparing this man to Gianni Versace's murderer, Andrew Cunanan, she'd said I had to anonymize him.

This murderer—if he was a murderer—was not currently a fugitive from the law. He wasn't on any Most Wanted list. As a matter of fact, until Arnie Dresser's mother grew suspicious and called for assistance from Simes and Custer, no one in law enforcement had been looking for him at all. No one had even suspected him of a crime—let alone a string of murders. With the exception of the relatively sloppy murder of Amy Masters in the home tanning bed, no police agency had even bothered to look for suspects in any of the deaths.

The man who wanted to kill Sawyer and me had been enjoying the luxury of total anonymity.

The reality of serial killing is that most serial killers aren't identified until they're apprehended. But the crimes of serial killers are rarely misinterpreted as accidents or deaths from natural causes. From the discovery of the first brutalized body, the cops are usually out looking for a psychopathic killer.

And the killer, nameless or not, therefore, has to do his gruesome work while he's looking over his shoulder.

But not this guy who was after me.

He wasn't a typical serial killer. There were no sexualized or ritualized components to his atrocities.

His victims weren't strangers.

He wasn't a typical spree killer, either. There was no particular rapidity or impulsiveness to the murders. The victims weren't chosen based on serendipity or circumstance.

His victims weren't celebrities. He didn't appear to be concerned with infamy or notoriety. Quite the opposite.

And what's more, right now, today, he's not even the least bit worried about being caught.

This man thought he was so good at causing people to die that nobody was even looking for him.

As I moved to the kitchen and began to wrap dishes and glasses from the cupboards in old pages from the *Daily Camera* before packing them away in wine boxes I'd picked up at Liquor Mart, I began to puzzle about ways to use that fact to my advantage.

Lauren came home with take-out Chinese. We sat in the living room to eat. Things were still tense.

I said, "Help me figure something out, okay?"

"Okay."

"Prosecutor and wife?"

She smiled. "Sure."

"This guy"—I didn't know what else to call him—"thinks he's so smart and so good that nobody knows what he's up to, right?"

She thought for a moment, then said, "I'd say that's true. He's been at this project of his for years, with impunity so far. I'd be surprised if he thought anyone was wise to him. Yes, I'd say he's feeling pretty smug."

"So, is that good or bad? I mean, from our point of view. In terms of finding him, do we want him complacent, or do we want him nervous?"

She narrowed her eyes. "From an investigatory point of view, I think you could make an argument either way. What are you suggesting?"

"Let's say, for instance, I get a bodyguard and we build a ten-foot fence around the house. If he's watching me, he's immediately going to know something's up, right? He'll know I'm protecting myself."

"Right. If you put up a billboard like that, he'll know that you've put two and two together and deduce that we have the pattern figured out—that somebody's killing people. But that doesn't mean he's going to assume that we're on to *him*. He's a very cocky guy, remember."

"Right, I agree. Now—today—he's working under the assumption that he has at least two levels of insulation from all these murders. One is that no one in authority has concluded that any of these people was murdered. The other, of course, is that no one is looking at him as a suspect in any particular crime. If I start surrounding myself with self-protection, he'll know for certain that his first level of insulation is gone and that the second one is, at the very least, in some jeopardy."

Lauren seemed to agree. "Makes sense. The question is, How will he respond? Will he back off? Or will he accelerate his plans?"

"Yes," I said, "that is the question. Simes doesn't think he'll give up if he's cornered." I shared Simes's impression that we were looking for a morph of Andrew Cunanan and the Unabomber. "So what do you think?"

She put down her chopsticks and kissed me with moo goo gai pan breath. "If we had a clue to who he is, Alan, we might be able to make an educated guess about the answer to that question." She kissed me again, chewing lightly on my bottom lip. "So who is he?"

"I've been over it ten times, sweetie, and I don't have a clue. Nobody from back then seems to be right."

"But you don't remember them all, do you?"

"Not even close."

"It's probably someone who didn't make much of an impression, you know? Not too crazy. Not overtly threatening.

Just somebody who felt that what you all did to him ruined his life."

"That makes it even harder. I've been thinking, what about going to the press? Get everybody looking for him?"

"I thought about that, too. But looking for whom? And is the evidence so compelling that the media will think that something is actually going on? I mean, there hasn't even been enough evidence to convince a single jurisdiction that something is amiss. Simes and Custer can't even convince their old colleagues at the FBI that some criminal genius is at work. If one of your mildly paranoid patients brought this story to you, what would you think? Would you believe him?"

"I don't know. Maybe not."

"If a stranger walked into the DA's office and laid this out to us, we'd probably snicker at him after we sent him packing."

"It's funny. I hadn't thought about people not believing us. I was more worried about the consequences of the witch-hunt they would start on all those patients if they did believe us."

She reached down and scratched behind Emily's ears. "This guy, Alan, if he's killed all these people the way we think he has, don't you think he'd just view the scrutiny as another challenge? He'd still find a way to finish what he started."

"That's my take, too. He likes being the smartest. He likes the fact he's the most clever." I paused. "You're at risk, too, sweets. It's not just me."

"I know. Innocent bystanders die too."

"We can't just sit and wait for him to try to kill us."

She sat back against the seat cushions of the sofa and sighed deeply. She said, "I can't believe I'm saying this, but . . . I think the only answer is for you to go see Sawyer, damn it."

I held her gaze and dribbled rice grains from my chopsticks onto my lap. "You're sure that's best?"

"No." She shook her head with vehemence.

"You want to come with me?"

"No. I've decided to trust you with her."

I threw away the white take-out boxes and the disposable chopsticks and finished my beer before I picked up the phone and dialed the number in Santa Barbara that Simes had given me. The mailbox greeting at the other end was institutional, not personal. I was grateful not to have to listen to Sawyer's voice, yet.

At the tone I said, "Sawyer? This is Alan Gregory. Please give me a call." I left my pager number.

Lauren had been across the kitchen, filling Emily's bowl with fresh water. She said, "That's it? That's your whole message after all these years? 'Please give me a call'?"

"That's it." I touched her below the ear and leaned in and kissed her cheek. "We should have working drawings on the garage by the time the demo is over. Dresden doesn't think adding it to the project will slow him down much, if at all. He has a lot of confidence."

With her left hand she traced the line of my jawbone. "You need a shave," she said.

"Probably."

"This garage is the same one we talked about a few months ago, right? It will hold two cars?"

Puzzled, I said, "Of course. That's what we decided."

Then I understood her meaning. She was making sure I was still planning on being around to take up one of the two slots.

My beeper vibrated at eight-thirty. I touched the tiny button to still the signal and left it anchored to my hip until Lauren moved to another room.

The number on the screen was local.

I called my voice mail. A patient had forgotten the new time of her appointment and wanted to know if it was eleven or one.

I called her back, told her the appointment time, and said that I would see her the following week.

She said, "We'll talk about this, won't we? Me begging

you for a new appointment time and then immediately forgetting when it is?"

My silence allowed her to answer her own question.

Sawyer's call came in at eleven. Lauren was asleep beside me. My beeper was still set to vibrate, not chirp, and it
almost wandered off the nightstand before I was able to corral it.

The area code on the screen was 805. I didn't know where
that was. But I knew in my bowels that 805 was where
Sawyer was.

I pulled on some sweats and a T-shirt and climbed upstairs. Emily followed me. I had the sudden awareness that
this night would be the last time I would be sleeping in my
old bedroom, ever. Tomorrow night we'd sleep at Lauren's
old house on the Hill. When we came back to this house
we'd be sleeping in the new bedroom we were building
upstairs.

I carried the portable phone to the sofa and sat, scratching
Emily under her chin and rubbing her ears before I punched
in the number from my pager screen.

Maybe half a ring later, I heard, "Alan?"

My pulse was up, my breathing shallow. Her voice sang
for me the way it always had.

"Yes," I said. "Hi, Sawyer. Long time."

"I never thought I'd talk to you again as long as I lived.
Didn't think I had the right."

Was I hearing remorse from Sawyer Sackett? I reminded
myself how badly I'd always read her. "I never expected to
talk to you, either. Figured that things had changed so much
that it would just never happen. But here we are, right? And
the circumstances couldn't be more strange."

When she responded to my words I didn't notice any of
the pressure in her voice that I felt in my own. She asked,
"You've talked to those two, I take it? The FBI odd couple?"

"Custer and Simes. Yes. They're the ones who gave me
your number in Santa Barbara. Where are you now?"

"Central Coast. In San Luis Obispo. In a hotel, a quintes-
sentially weird place called the Madonna Inn. My bedroom

looks like a stall in a medieval barn. Last time I was here I stayed in the flying saucer room. I think I prefer that one. This one's harder on my allergies."

I didn't know what to say. San Luis Obispo is a couple of hours north of Santa Barbara on the coast. Simes said that Sawyer traveled for her business. "You up there on work?"

"Yes, work. One of the facilities I visit is near here. So . . . do you want to catch up a little bit or do you want to talk about all our dead friends?"

"Both, I think. How are you, Sawyer?"

"I'm . . . peaceful, Alan. Not joyful. Peaceful. Life has taken a lot of turns I never would have chosen. And I've managed to embrace this place where I've ended up. I feel good about that. You?"

What the hell did that mean? Me? "I was better a week ago, Sawyer. But things have been good for me. I'm married and . . . I have a good life."

"Kids?"

"Not yet. You?"

I thought I heard her swallow. Her next words were "Do you believe them? Custer and Simes?"

Okay, we weren't going to talk about kids.

"Yes, I believe them. Not a hundred percent, but enough to make me crazy. You don't?"

"Actually—no—I believe them as well. As you can probably guess, over the years I'd lost touch with everyone except for Susan. After she died in—when was that plane crash?—I really never knew what happened with everyone's lives. I never heard about any of the deaths."

"Did, uh, those two agents tell you about . . . Lorna?"

"No. God. Don't tell me."

I didn't.

She said, "Tell me."

I did, concluding, "Custer is on his way to New Zealand tonight to check it out. I talked with him a few hours ago. He's hoping to be able to confirm the identification and the circumstances."

Sawyer's tone became wispy, lacy. "I really liked Lorna.

She knew about us. I think she was the only one on the unit who knew what we were up to. Did you know that she knew?"

"No, I didn't. But I liked her, too. Her death hurts a lot. There are times when I don't know whether I'm more sad or more scared about all this."

She said, "Yes, I know. Lorna, God. It's just you and me now, isn't it?"

"Of the professional staff, yes. Unless you include Kheri."

"Oh no. Do you think we need to worry about her? Oh my."

"I don't know. I haven't thought about her until right now. But if he targeted the social worker, maybe he'd go after the head nurse, too."

"Do you know where she is?"

"No, do you?"

"No."

"I can check with some people at the school. See if anyone has kept in touch."

Sawyer's tone lightened. Almost playfully, she asked, "So are you going to save my life again, Alan?"

"I didn't save your life. That man wasn't going to kill you, Sawyer."

"I wasn't talking about that crazy patient with the knife, Alan."

"What do you mean?" I said, and I tried to picture her right then, in her funky theme hotel room. How long was her hair? How had she aged?

"You saving my life—it had nothing to do with Arnie's patient and the pocketknife. It was something else that you don't understand. You couldn't understand. Because I never told you."

"What—?"

"We have a decision to make, right now. You and me."

"You mean about whether to cooperate with Simes and Custer?"

"That, too. I meant about where to meet. Do you want to

come here, to California? Or should I come to where you are? Or do you want to surprise me and leave me a note in my morning newspaper and let me know exactly where it is we'll rendezvous?"

I couldn't tell whether her tone was mocking or inviting. Jesus.

FOURTEEN

Friday evening, we finished moving out of Spanish Hills and moving into Lauren's old place on the Hill.

Saturday morning, Dresden's crew began to demolish the interior of our little house.

Saturday afternoon, at 3:46, I was sitting in the exit aisle of a United 737 shuttle that was lifting off on its way from Denver to Las Vegas.

Sawyer had said she'd be waiting for me at the gate.

In my mind, of course, she hadn't aged. Her hair hadn't grown. Her body had lost none of the elasticity or allure of its youth.

In my mind, of course, she was still an enigma. She was still someone who could bring out every juvenile sexual urge I'd ever felt. She was the embodiment of every embarrassing immaturity it had taken me two marriages to outgrow.

As I waited for the jumble of passengers in front of me to clear the aisle, I reminded myself that I didn't blame Sawyer for what had happened that autumn.

I blamed myself for succumbing to her. Actually, I hadn't succumbed; I'd thrown myself at her feet.

I reassured myself that I'd grown since then. A lot. I was stronger now. I'd learned to love and not merely fall to infatuation. I'd learned to insist that I be loved in return.

I was confident that I could handle Sawyer. This time I would be impervious to her charms.

Then I saw her standing there, and for a dangerous moment, I was an intern again. Breathless.

And stupid.

She was waiting across the concourse, and she didn't rush to greet me.

Though it penetrated, I didn't avoid her gaze. Her hair wasn't as blond as I remembered and was much longer, almost to her shoulders, with a little outward curl at the ends. She stood proudly, her shoulders back, her hands loosely clasped together in front of her. She was wearing white jeans and sandals and a tight vest made of medium-weight denim. The denim was faded.

The most striking thing about her, though, was the change in her face. She'd aged, yes. But it was the difference in her smile that struck me. When Sawyer used to smile, her mouth and face had opened gloriously. When she smiled my way—and it wasn't a frequent enough occurrence—I remembered the brilliance of her front teeth and the radiance that seemed to glow from her parted lips.

Now, though, as she smiled a greeting across the expanse of terrazzo, it was a smile borne only by her eyes, which were framed by pale sunglasses of a tortoiseshell almost as blond as her hair. Her mouth didn't open at all. The smile seemed less joyful than I recalled, but somehow more sincere and serene.

I was still five feet from her when she said, "I've gotten fat and old. And look at you—there's not an ounce of fat on your body."

I shifted my carry-on bag from my left shoulder to my right and moved forward to embrace her. She hesitated.

I hesitated, too. The resulting hug was polite.

I said, "I've taken up cycling. It keeps me in shape. I don't know about you getting fat, though. I think you look great, Sawyer." I stepped back and took her in. "I only wish the circumstances were different."

Wistfully, I thought, she stared into my eyes. "That's what I was wishing all those years ago. About us. I just wanted the circumstances to be different. It's funny how things come around, isn't it?"

"What do you mean?"

"Later. Come on—I'm not sure we should linger here. We don't really know what this man who's killing our colleagues is up to."

I had promised myself that I wouldn't say anything inane. My next line, therefore, constituted a broken promise. "Your hair has gotten longer."

Her eyes widened into another smile, and she lifted her hair from her neck with the back of her hand. If Lauren had been beside me she would have been able to tell me whether or not the gesture was intended to be flirtatious. On my own, my wife maintained, I was clueless. Most of the time she was right.

"You like the flip? Or is it too retro? Makes me look a little like Doris Day, don't you think? Which is exactly why I used to keep it so short. And now the Doris Day look is back. Maybe my time has come. One of the cons I work with told me that I look like Carmen Diaz's older sister. That's not bad, right? Better than looking like her mother."

"I think you look great." I hoped she heard in my voice that I meant it but meant nothing by it. "Where are we going? Should we get a car?" I asked.

"I don't think so. Do you gamble?"

"Gamble? Like slot machines? Not usually."

"Doesn't matter. I do. It helps me relax. We just need to find a public place to talk, and the casinos are as good a place as any. Come on."

We grabbed a cab outside the terminal and she said, "The Mirage, please," to the driver.

"How was your flight?" I asked.

"My flights are always good," she said, as she swiveled on the seat to face me. "This guy? Who may have killed Arnie? I don't know about you, but I'm working under the assumption that from now on, he's following one of us. It's probably not literally true, but still, better safe than sorry, right? I'm hoping it's me he's following today, not you. There's no way he could have stayed with me today. You bought your ticket at the gate, right? No reservation?"

"That's right."

"Good."

I was occasionally looking past Sawyer out the window of the cab. I hadn't been to Las Vegas since I was a teenager, and I found myself as distracted by the glitz as I was by Sawyer and her paranoia about being followed. Las Vegas seemed to be an odd mixture of age and youth, and so was Sawyer. Yes, she had put on a few pounds, but mostly the years had made her appear less brazen.

Not Las Vegas, though. This new Las Vegas was as brazen a place as I'd ever seen.

I think she felt me hesitate at the edge of the casino. She reached back and took my hand, leading me far into the interior of the huge space. She looked around for a moment, finally selecting two stools at a five-dollar blackjack table. She directed me to the end seat on the right of the crescent-shaped table.

She laid a hundred-dollar bill in front of her. I pulled out my wallet and decided to limit my contribution to the Las Vegas economy to twenty dollars.

"The whole casino is under surveillance all the time. I have a friend who works here, at the Mirage, in security. I don't think he's here—our adversary—but if he is, we may get a record of it."

"What kind of record?"

While the dealer exchanged our bills for chips, Sawyer raised her chin toward the ceiling. "Video. Every square inch of this floor is monitored every second of every day. My friend is watching us right this minute. He's going to keep an eye on the rest of the floor, see if anyone else is watching us too."

She placed a chip on the line. I did the same.

"You know how to play?"

"I know the general idea."

"Good. The rest is easy. I'll teach you."

For the next twenty minutes, she did. I lost a few hands, won a few hands, hit a couple of blackjacks, and mindlessly cashed in another twenty. She nursed her stack of chips into almost two hundred dollars. I was impressed.

I was also perplexed. I didn't know why I was sitting in the casino at the Mirage on a Saturday afternoon playing blackjack with an ex-lover.

"Sawyer?"

"Mmm."

"What are we doing here? More to the point, what are we going to do about this maniac and these two ex–FBI agents?"

Sawyer seemed to be ignoring me as she focused on her hand. I wondered if she was counting cards. Finally, she decided to split a pair of tens. Without looking over at me, she said, "You know who it is?"

"No," I said, "I don't. You do?" I was relieved that she might have figured out the puzzle.

"I've been thinking that it might be one of two guys. Wendy had a patient, an angry, angry young man. Remember him? I think he was in oil and gas. What did they use to call themselves back then? Land man, is that it? Yeah, I think he was a land man. Kept announcing at Community Meeting how much our 'imprisonment' was costing him. Does he ring a bell?"

The dealer graciously added an ace to the first of Sawyer's two tens and a jack to the second. Sawyer cleaned up twice as the dealer busted. I'd been sitting conservatively on an eight and a six and won my hand and a tip bet I'd left for the dealer. I now had eight five-dollar chips in my pile, which meant I was even. Cool.

I didn't recall the patient of Wendy's that Sawyer was talking about. I said, "The man you're describing doesn't sound familiar. Sounds like it could have been ten different guys. Twenty."

"Okay. Let me describe him a little bit more. He was young then. Mid-twenties, and little, smaller than me, about five-five, five-six, and—oh, oh—his hair was as red as these chips. And he kept a pocket comb with him all the time, was always combing his hair."

I nodded. The comb did it. "I remember him now. He wore madras, right, had nothing but madras shirts? Wasn't he picked up by the police on I-70? If I'm remembering the incident correctly, he was on the elevated portion, wasn't he? Near the Stock Show, wandering around? Claimed he was looking for oil? Had some ritual about kneeling in front of the mileage markers?"

"That's the guy. When they found him he was barefoot, otherwise totally dressed in Bronco orange. First-break schizophrenic. Wendy got him stabilized on Thorazine right away. The good news was that the Bronco garb disappeared and we got treated to the madras. The bad news was that we all had the misfortune of viewing his underlying personality disorder. Not a pretty sight."

It didn't feel right. I shook my head. "I don't see it, Sawyer. Let's say it's him and he's psychotic again. If that's the case, he's not stable enough to pull this kind of thing off. Let's say his psychosis is under control. Even after his thought disorder disappeared, he was impulsive, just a little firecracker, right? I've been thinking that we should be looking more for a depressed guy. Or a paranoid character disorder. Maybe even a high-functioning obsessive-compulsive. Something like that."

"Maybe you're right about the little oil and gas guy, Alan. But I'm not sure I agree with you diagnostically. I don't think we should rule out psychotics. It could be somebody with a severe thought disorder or even a severe mood disorder, for that matter. What about a bipolar who's well controlled on lithium? Or just a manic who cycles slowly? You know, someone who only kills his doctors during the manic phase?"

She was making an interesting argument about patients with mood disorders. "You're making a good point," I acknowledged. "I hadn't thought about a slow-cycling manic. But I'm not convinced the oil and gas guy is the type we should be looking for. You don't think we should consider Travis, do you?" Travis was the patient of Arnie's who had attacked Sawyer with the pocketknife.

She shook her head. "No. He's too crazy and too impulsive."

I pushed my chips forward and stood up. "Would you mind cashing out. Please? This is too distracting for me.

Let's get a beer or something. Your friend can follow us with his cameras, right?"

Her eyes lit. "Almost anywhere," she said.

At her suggestion, we settled into a booth in the coffee shop. She ordered a Cobb salad and a Diet Pepsi. I ordered a turkey sandwich on wheat bread and a beer. She hadn't even glanced at the menu. I said, "You come here a lot?"

She shrugged. I wondered if she was appraising my words for the weight of judgment. I, too, wondered if there were any stray ounces there.

"What's a lot? I gamble to relax, get away. I come here sometimes—to Vegas. I go to Reno and Tahoe, too. I'm pretty good at blackjack, not quite so good at poker. Good enough that it's cheap entertainment for me."

All these years had passed and there were a thousand things I wanted to know. Our food arrived in minutes; the casino kitchen didn't want its customers spending any unnecessary time away from the gaming floor. I swallowed a bite of my sandwich and asked, "Are you married? Involved with someone?"

The tiny lines around her eyes and mouth softened and smoothed out. "There's a guy I see in L.A. And a judge in San Francisco. But not seriously, no. I did marriage. I did it twice."

"And twice is enough?"

She didn't respond. She cut a big piece of romaine into tiny little pieces and went to work on a sliver of hard-boiled egg.

"You know, I didn't know you were married when I met you. You never said anything."

She placed her silverware down and lifted her napkin to her lips. "Technically, I wasn't."

"Okay. I'll try to be more precise. I didn't know you had been married when I met you."

She lifted her fork and speared a cherry tomato. She swallowed once even though there was no food in her mouth. She raised her chin, stretched her neck back, and closed her eyes.

I couldn't fail to be assaulted by memories. Moments before orgasm Sawyer did this same thing. A throaty groan would complete the picture.

When she looked back down at me, tears were in her eyes. "I can't do this now. Not with you. Not yet. I'm not ready to go back there. Let's just deal with murderers, okay? I do that every day."

"I'm sorry if I intruded on something, Sawyer. I didn't mean to upset you."

"It's okay. You don't know about any of that. I never . . . anyway. I don't know, I'm sorry, too."

I changed the subject. "Why don't you tell me who your other candidate is? You said you had two people in mind."

She had turned her attention to a pair of televisions above the bar. One was tuned to CNN. The other was a college football game. I couldn't tell who was playing. Without looking over at me, she said, "You remember a patient of mine named Elly? You saw her for me, on a consult."

I smiled. "Of course I remember Elly. You don't suspect her, do you?" Elly had been an eighteen-year-old girl when she was admitted to the unit for depression, anorexia, and suicidal ideation. She'd been Sawyer's patient, but I'd done a psychological testing battery on her.

"God, no."

Sawyer remained focused on the TV. I tried to remember whether she was a football fan.

She said, "But Elly's the reason we can't cooperate with Simes and Custer on a patient roster."

I tried to make sense of the connection, but couldn't. "I don't get it."

"Elly's full name, if you recall, was Eleanor Trammell. Since then, she's married. Her name, now, is Eleanor Ward."

I followed Sawyer's gaze up to the television screen. The CNN logo flashed across the screen. I wasn't getting it.

"Eleanor Ward," she said. "CNN? Ring any bells?"

"Oh," I said. "*That* Eleanor Ward." Immediately I saw the face in my mind. Eleanor Ward was one of the regular anchors on *Headline News*. "You know, I always thought that woman looked familiar, but I'd never made the connection."

"No reason you should have. Her hair color is different. And she's gained twenty pounds."

The mention of weight helped me recall the details of why Elly Trammell had been hospitalized. "Your point is that if her history—I mean her psychiatric history—was made public, it could really screw up her life, couldn't it? Professionally?"

Sawyer moved her attention from the television back to her salad. She said, "Professionally. Personally. You bet it would. There are probably a dozen more people like her, too. Patients who were on the unit back then whose lives would be turned upside down if we revealed their names and what they'd been through. So we're on our own. We can't sacrifice all those people to help those two feds."

"Ex-feds."

"Oxymoron. It's like ex-Catholic. Or ex-shrink."

"What are you implying? That some learning can't be overcome?"

"Yes, I am saying that I believe there are some things in life that change people forever. Some things you can't get over. That's exactly what I'm saying."

"I don't know about that. But I'm not going to argue with your conclusion. We can't give them a patient roster. No. There're too many unknowns."

She glanced back up at the televisions. "Good. I'm glad we're not going to fight about that."

"I do have a cop friend in Boulder whom I trust a lot. He'll do what he can to help us out. I've explained everything to him already."

"We can't give him names either, Alan."

"I know that. He knows that. Don't worry about him. So who's your other candidate?"

"Actually, I was thinking of one of my own patients, a young, angry borderline guy who I didn't like very much. He spent half his time on the unit in isolation, screaming at somebody or another. I think his name was Romewicz or something like that. But in coming up with him, I've been focusing more on the anger than the capacity for planning. I think you may be right. It may be better to look for who would be capable of it first, and look for motive second."

I said, "Wait a second. . . ."

"What?"

I touched my index finger to my temple. "Do you remember the guy—what was his name—everyone on the unit called him D.B. He was Arnie's patient, I think. It was a relatively brief admission, he was—"

She smiled and her eyes sparkled with confetti. "I remember him. He was the guy who said he would tell us the identity of D. B. Cooper if we let him off his seventy-two-hour hold so he could go back to work. He even announced the deal during Community Meeting. Asked for takers."

"Yeah."

"He was admitted that weekend we were . . ." Her voice faded away, cushioned by memory.

I finished her sentence. "In Grand Lake."

"Yes. We were in Grand Lake."

I smiled at the memory. "I'm trying to remember whether I met him or not. Did you meet him?"

"We met him. We were back in time for Community Meeting the day he was discharged. We both met him."

I couldn't get a mental picture of him. "Has that guy ever been found? The hijacker, I mean? D. B. Cooper?"

Sawyer shook her head. "You know, I don't think so."

Like most Americans, I'd been fascinated by what D. B. Cooper had managed to do in 1971.

On Thanksgiving eve of that year, a man using the name Dan Cooper purchased a ticket with cash and boarded Northwest Airlines Flight 305, bound from Portland to Seattle. The man who called himself Dan Cooper was later described by flight attendants as a polite, shy, middle-aged guy who was dressed in a dark suit and a tie. He sat in his assigned aisle seat in the middle of the plane and generally attracted no attention to himself until he handed a note to one of the young flight attendants, informing her that he was hijacking the airplane.

His demands included a highly detailed request for ransom and, curiously, four parachutes.

The plane landed in Seattle, where it was delayed for refueling, for delivery of the $200,000 in twenties that Cooper had demanded, and for delivery of the four parachutes. Cooper permitted the paying passengers to deplane and chose two flight attendants who would stay aboard as hostages.

After once again taking off, the plane flew south under flight conditions dictated by the hijacker. The route Cooper specified was an indirect, slightly westward, slightly looping path toward a refueling stop in Reno, Nevada, with an ultimate destination of Mexico City.

Cooper ordered the pilot to fly the Boeing 727 unpressurized at an altitude of ten thousand feet or less, with the landing gear in the down position. He specified that the flaps should be at fifteen percent, and that the airspeed should not exceed one hundred and fifty knots.

Cabin records indicated that fourteen minutes into the flight, Dan Cooper hit the lever that lowered the airstairs at the rear of the 727, the only commercial aircraft in use in the United States with stairs that extended from the stern of the plane. Approximately ten minutes after lowering the stairs, somewhere over the wilderness drainage of the Columbia River just north of Portland, Oregon, Cooper slipped into one of the four parachutes, climbed down the lowered airstairs, and jumped into the rainy night with his ransom strapped to his chest.

He would never be seen again.

D. B. Cooper became a certified folk hero.

Dan Cooper—whose name was later mistakenly reported by the press to be D. B. Cooper—had accomplished the first criminal hijacking ever to take place in U.S. airspace. To this day, he remains the perpetrator of the only successful hijacking ever to take place above U.S. soil.

Almost ten years later, in 1980, two kids playing on the northern shore of the Columbia River recovered $5,800 of Cooper's marked booty. Despite extensive efforts, searchers found no more of the loot and no trace of the parachute. Cooper's body was never discovered.

I asked, "What was his real name? The patient who said he could finger D. B. Cooper?"

Sawyer said, "You know, I don't remember. I'm trying to remember the stories. I think he said that he worked at—what's that place called west of Denver, where they make nuclear weapons?"

"Rocky Flats. That's right, he said he worked at Rocky Flats. His thing was that he was complaining that he was going to lose his security clearance because he'd been hospitalized in a psychiatric unit. What did he do there? Do you remember? Was he a scientist of some kind?"

"No. I don't— Wait. He was in security, wasn't he? Didn't he tell everyone he carried a gun at work?"

"Yes. And he told us that D. B. Cooper was someone he worked with at Rocky Flats. And he insisted that he had proof."

We puzzled about other ex-patients for most of an hour. The fishing felt futile. None of the candidates felt right. Sawyer and I agreed that it was possible that the patient we were trying to identify might be someone neither of us knew well. Like the man unit staff had nicknamed D.B.

After a poignant silence grew into more than a minute, she said she had to get back to the airport.

We grabbed a cab outside the casino and she directed the driver to someplace called Desert Aviation.

At the unfamiliar destination, I felt a familiar feeling. With Sawyer, I was, and always had been, just along for the ride. "Where are we going now?"

"That's where my plane is. After you drop me off, the cab can take you back over to United."

"You have a plane? You flew here yourself?"

"I do. I did. I travel all over the state every week to prisons and courts. The plane helps keep me sane. My schedule would be psychotic without it."

"Something else I guess I didn't know about you."

"I didn't fly back then, during the residency. It's something I learned about ten years ago from my father. The plane was his. When he began to develop glaucoma, he gave it to me. Flying has turned out to be another one of my relaxing things."

"Your job must be stressful. All these relaxing things you do."

She glanced at me sideways before resuming a tense stare out the side window. "Stressful enough, I guess." She paused. When she resumed, the volume was barely above a whisper. "But in my life, Alan, it's not the hurricanes or the tornadoes I worry about anymore. It's the volcanoes."

"What—?"

She managed a small smile. "Think about it."

The taxi pulled up outside a modern one-story structure that was attached to a long rectangular hangar. She grabbed her bag and began to pull herself out of the car without even a simple touch for me. I wasn't ready to let her go.

I said, "He killed Susan in a plane, you know."

"I know. I'm taking precautions." Her tone amused me. The same voice a young woman might employ when assuring her parents that she is always—always—careful when she's with a boy.

I wouldn't be easily dissuaded. "He may be an airplane mechanic. He may have access."

"I have a locked hangar for my plane. And I've used the same mechanic for years. I've asked him to do all the work himself for a while. He's agreed to that. My preflight checks are . . . exhaustive. A real pain in the butt." She pulled her hair off her neck, then released it. "I'm worried, too," she said.

"Maybe you shouldn't fly again until we understand better what happened to Susan. Simes and Custer are collecting all the details. They'll be back to us soon enough."

Her tone changed. She admonished, "Maybe you should get out of the advice business."

"I'm sorry," I said, although I didn't think that my caution was anything but prudent.

"It's okay." She grabbed her bag again and raised herself

from the car. She leaned down before she closed the door and said, "Alan, what about Chester?"

I said, "Jesus, Sawyer. I never thought about Chester."

"Maybe we should."

"God, yes."

She took a step away without saying good-bye. Then she turned back to the car and said, "Alan?"

The desert wind was blowing in short intense gusts, and she was holding her hair from her face with one hand to keep it from her eyes. I had to lean sideways across the seat to assess her expression. It was, I thought, somber.

"Yeah?"

"Did you love me? Back then. Did you really love me?"

I got out of the car, walked around the trunk, took the bag from her shoulder, and lowered it to the macadam. I embraced her the way I had wanted to in the airport terminal. She was stiff at first and didn't return the hug. Finally she softened. I could feel the tips of her fingers begin to probe the muscles on my back. I could feel the pressure of her breasts against my abdomen. I could feel her cool breath caress the skin on the side of my neck.

Into her hair, I said, "The very best I knew how."

FIFTEEN

Lauren was asleep when I got back to Boulder near midnight.

I felt odd sliding the unfamiliar key into the unfamiliar lock in this house in town where I hadn't slept since Lauren and I were dating. Those recollections of that earlier autumn when I'd been falling in love with her were decidedly mixed memories. There had been the exhilaration of romantic discovery, but those faltering first days in our relationship had also been marked by a gnawing tension. I feared the return of that tension now that Sawyer had reappeared in my life.

Some of the tension back then had been Lauren's distrust of me. We blamed her mistrust, with facile ease, on her illness. Was it true then? Partially.

What about now?

Partially.

My take? She didn't feel consistently lovable. So she had trouble believing I really loved her. And she insisted on believing that her illness was the solitary barrier to her sense of security. Without it, she wanted to believe, she would be secure as a woman and we, as a couple, would be fine.

The couple part was true. We would be. I believed that.

But, deep in my heart, I also felt that even with multiple sclerosis in the equation, we, as a couple, would be okay. Not ideal. But MS wasn't the only flaw in the silk cloth that we'd woven into our marriage coverlet. In falling in love with Lauren, in committing to her, in marrying her, I took the last steps of a journey that was freeing me of my juvenile quest to find an ideal mate. In fact, when I met Lauren I was separated from a gorgeous, witty, brilliant woman I'd married after convincing myself that she was perfect.

I assumed, always, that in her life, somewhere along the way, Lauren had made the same judgments about me and my imperfections. She had determined that I had plenty of flaws and that she loved me anyway.

I fell in love with her despite her insecurities, despite her inconsistencies, despite her illness.

I fell in love with her because of her usual joy and her surprising nurturing, because of her remarkable reservoir of courage, and because of her wisdom, and her beauty.

In doing so, I thought I had found the right woman for me. Not the perfect woman, though. I no longer had that illusion.

I felt that way before I went to Las Vegas to see Sawyer. Seeing Sawyer, touching her, had unsettled me. Still, as I crawled into bed next to Lauren in her old house on the Hill, I felt assurance that I had married the right woman.

The unfamiliar city noises distracted me as I tried to find sleep. I heard cars downshifting in the distance, and closer listened as two dogs barked up some competitive tree. I listened to the wind whistle down canyons. From my other bed in my distant bedroom across the Boulder Valley I could barely even discern those canyons as charcoal slashes in the landscape. Even Emily's big dog sighs sounded different as she fought to find a corner that provided comfort and security.

Twice I thought I knew what Sawyer had meant by professing her fear of volcanoes, not hurricanes. Twice I knew that I was guessing.

I sat up in bed and looked at Lauren's bedside table for the Glock. It wasn't there. Would she keep it under the pillow? I didn't know. I hoped not.

I thought about Chester some more and knew he was now on my list for keeps.

I tossed. I turned. I didn't believe that Lauren was actually asleep beside me.

Out loud, I said, "We're fine. Don't worry. I love you."
She didn't stir.

She greeted me warily at breakfast. I embraced her longer than I normally would have.

I told her I was grateful for the bagels and coffee and fresh-squeezed juice.

"How did it go?" she asked.

Was she asking whether I'd learned something useful or how things had gone with Sawyer? I chose the more benign fork in the road. "Okay. Good. Sawyer and I are on the same page about not divulging the patient list to Custer and Simes. We came up with some possible suspects to look at. I want to talk with you and Sam about how to check them out. I don't even know how law enforcement goes about locating people, sweets. I'm sure there are ways, though. Right?"

She smiled and said, "Yes, there are ways." She found something interesting in the bottom of her coffee mug. "So how is your friend? After all these years? Did you enjoy seeing her?"

My friend? "Sawyer was a lot of things to me back then, Lauren. But she was never my friend."

"That's funny."

Her voice told me she found the revelation soothing. I was tempted to elaborate, but didn't. Instead, I said, "But to answer your question better, I, um, I think, I don't know . . . she's . . . it's like she has a limp."

"She . . . limps?"

"Figuratively. Psychologically. Being with her, it's like an old, serious injury has healed. But one leg is shorter than the other one or something. Or the scar tissue won't really allow her to move gracefully. It's like that. Being with her, she's restricted. Tight. Jerky, awkward."

"What injury?"

"She didn't say. I didn't ask."

Her eyes scorned me. "I can't believe you didn't ask. Are you attracted to her still?"

I didn't want to follow Lauren wherever she was heading. Was there a reasonable way to answer?

"If I am—so what? She's attractive, but it doesn't mean anything. I mean, I think the new receptionist in your office is pretty hot. And didn't you recently admit that you thought that attorney you creamed last week on the drunk and disorderly is a pleasant addition to the local bar?"

The scorn in her eyes flashed a frosting of contempt. "What's different is that I didn't used to date him."

"You're right."

"And you really think Trisha is hot? She has no boobs at all. I didn't think she was your type."

"The older I get the more I don't think I have a type. I'm actually becoming a more equal-opportunity lech." I didn't confess that I was constantly amazed at how many different ways women can find to be lovely.

"So she's still pretty, too? Sawyer?"

I touched my wife across the table. "Like you, Lauren, she'll be beautiful until she dies."

With a suspicious tone, she said, "You're getting smoother as you age, you know that?"

I shrugged. Saying thank you felt risky.

Lauren and I had promised each other we were going to check on Dresden's progress in Spanish Hills every day, either before we went to work or after. While she showered and dressed to get ready for this Sunday morning visit I cleaned up the breakfast things, but couldn't seem to master the controls on Lauren's antique KitchenAid dishwasher.

She jiggled the handle on the door and the machine started. "It's cranky sometimes," she said. "Like me."

Across town in Spanish Hills, we passed Adrienne and her son, Jonas, as they were heading out the lane. Adrienne honked and waved at us but didn't slow her new Suburban. Adrienne is petite. Behind the wheel of the massive Chevy, she looked like a ten-year-old driving a school bus. I felt a pang of guilt about what our construction project must be doing to her peace and quiet.

I made a mental note to send her some flowers.

Approaching our house from the lane—from the north—

nothing much looked different about it. Momentarily, I
wondered if Dresden's demo crew had actually started work
as promised. Then I noticed the debris that was already protruding from the top of the huge blue rollaway. It was over
half full. It was definitely not half empty.

Lauren and I were relentless recyclers. Every couple of
weeks we left our papers and cans and bottles out for Eco-
Cycle. Our efforts seemed ironic, and futile, as I realized we
were rather cavalierly throwing away most of our house.

It would take a lot of plastic bins full of aluminum cans
and glass bottles to make up for this.

At the meeting where we had signed the contract with
Dresden, he had warned us what to expect in terms of
progress. "Things fly at first," he said. "The simple fact of
this business is that *de*-struction is much, much faster than
con-struction. So don't be surprised at how fast we can bust
up your house at the front end of the job, and don't be too
frustrated at how long it takes to put it back together and
paint it at the other end."

I tried to steel myself for what we would find inside.

Lauren opened the front door and said, "Oh my God."

I peeked over her shoulder. The experience reminded me
of seeing my leg for the first time after it had been secreted
away in a plaster cast for fifteen weeks when I was a kid.
I knew the leg was mine—it was protruding from my hip,
after all—but I didn't recognize it as the appendage I knew
so well.

And this house was no longer the domicile that had been
my home of over ten years.

Most of the interior walls of the upper level of the house
were gone. Four-by-eight beams held the joists aloft, the
beams supported, it appeared, by four-by-fours and prayer.
Only small sections of the ceiling remained intact. Where
we had once had a small dark kitchen we now had a small
dark cavern with exposed stud walls, naked drainpipes and
supply lines, and silver snakes of electrical conduit. The
dismal space brought back memories of torture chambers
I'd seen in B movies from the sixties.

Two-thirds of the south wall of the house had been demolished. The empty space that had been created was interspersed with support columns constructed of rough studs. Sheets of even rougher plywood covered the opening. Vertical slivers of light leaked in through the cracks.

Lauren said, "It's so clean in here. I expected, you know, Los Angeles after the big one."

The orderliness of the space was not exactly my first impression. But I had to admit it was true. I said, "It is pretty neat. Dresden and his demo boys have certainly tidied up after themselves." Other than the hanging conduits and the exposed plumbing stubs, the place appeared ready for the next phase of construction, whatever that might be.

She gazed around the room in a way that worried me. When she finally spoke, she affirmed my intuition. She said, "You're not going to like this. Don't get upset, okay? But I think we should go ahead and replace those windows. Don't you think that makes sense after all?"

To save money, we had decided to preserve as much of the existing glass as we could. I sighed. "Which windows?"

She pointed toward the dining room, where we kept her pool table. But she said, "All of them, I guess. Consistency of fenestration is important."

Consistency of fenestration? Resigned to the fact that we would be placing a new window order, I said, "Everything? All of them? Even the picture windows in the living room? That's a lot of glass, sweets. It will cost thousands."

"Don't you want them to match?"

We still hadn't ventured farther into the house than the entryway. She knew, with the chaos I had just invited into our lives, that I wasn't about to argue with her about a few windows. I started walking toward what had been the living room. "Do you want to call Dresden about the change? Or should I?"

"I will," she said.

I contemplated the fact that twenty-four hours after the start of construction, we had already managed a probable fifteen thousand dollars in change orders. I was wondering if that level of impulsive largesse might get us into Guinness when Lauren said she wanted to see what they had done downstairs.

She shoved aside a sawhorse in order to descend the stairs to the lower level of the house.

What happened next took three seconds. Five tops.

I thought—I was certain—that the world was ending. At least the portion that I occupied.

A two-by-four had been jammed into the supports of the sawhorse. As Lauren shoved the sawhorse aside, the stud was pulled along with it. The other end of the stud was simultaneously yanked out from beneath a temporary support column that stood tall in the middle of the room. As all this occurred, a squeal reminiscent of a large animal dying a torturous death filled the cavern of joists and trusses above my head.

The support column fell to the wood deck with a concussion that was way out of proportion to its size.

Lauren screamed, "Alan!"

I looked up to see one end of a long ceiling joist slipping from the spot where it should have been secured to its intersecting beam by a joist hanger. The joist began to fall in a short arc toward my head. I barely had time to move before the two-by-eight grazed my arm and crashed to the floor at my feet.

I waited for more lumber to fall.

None did. Another joist sank a few inches and squeaked. Another one shuddered and groaned. But the single ceiling joist was all that came down.

Lauren rushed to my side, skipping over the fallen joist. She said, "You're bleeding. Are you okay? I'm so sorry. Did I do that? Did I make that come down? Come on, let's get out of here, it's not safe."

I figured standing still was the most prudent thing I could do. For half a minute I stared at the joists and trusses, trying to determine if anything else was about to tumble down.

I examined my biceps. I was bleeding. One of the nails that should have been holding that joist in place had slit my skin. I said, "I think I'm okay. Just a scratch. I'll probably need a tetanus shot. God, I hate tetanus shots."

"Why did that happen? Should that have happened?"

"No, that shouldn't have happened. Do you have your phone with you? Let me call Dresden."

Dresden lived in the town of Louisville, which was actually closer to our house than was most of the city of Boulder. Less than ten minutes later, he was parking his big Ford pickup on the lane.

He wanted the story again. He said, "A joist fell? You're sure?"

"Two others came loose. Go check for yourself, Dresden. Do you have a hard hat?"

I might as well have been warning one of the Joint Chiefs about the dangers of UFOs. He said, "Joists don't fall from ceilings on my jobs, Alan. I don't need a damn hard hat."

Dresden spent about five minutes inside while Lauren finished dressing my arm with first-aid supplies from the car.

Our contractor spoke even more slowly than usual when he rejoined us. "This is crazy. So tell me what happened again."

Lauren was eager to repeat her tale. "I wanted to go downstairs to see what you guys had done down there, but there was one of those things in the way at the top of the stairs. What are they called?" She turned to face me.

"A sawhorse."

"Yeah. There was a sawhorse in the way. So I slid it back a couple of feet. When I did—"

"Don't forget the stud. Somebody had jammed a stud into the brace of the sawhorse."

"Yes. And when I moved the sawhorse, that board—it's a stud, is that what you called it?"

"Yes, a stud."

"That stud moved. And then those two sticks that were holding up the ceiling fell and then that big board came down from the attic and almost hit Alan in the head. It could have killed him."

Dresden turned his head to me for help in the same polite way a politician consults a translator on a foreign junket.

I said, "The stud that was caught in the sawhorse had also been stuck under the temporary support column that was holding up the joists. When Lauren moved the sawhorse, the stud moved and came out from underneath the column, the column fell, then the joist squealed, and then it just came crashing down right next to me. Two others came loose."

Lauren clarified, "Right on top of you, you mean."

Dresden had been standing. He sat beside us on our little front stoop and removed his baseball cap. This one read "Belize." I think he had a cap from every place he had ever scuba dived. I was beginning to believe it was a large collection. He smoothed down his dusty brown hair and replaced the cap on his head. "Alan, somebody wanted to bring the whole center section of the roof down. It wasn't just one joist that was sabotaged."

"You're sure?"

"I'm sure. Listen, we didn't leave it like this. I was the last one here at the end of the day. I'm the one who put the sawhorse in place at the top of the stairs. Just as a precaution, since we'd already removed the stair rail. There was no stud anywhere near it when I left last night. No way. It was around seven, maybe six-thirty, when I left. And there was no stud shimming up that support column. No way in the world I'd use the end of a long stud to shim a column. That column was cut to length and nailed in place. Nailed to the floor, and to the beam in the ceiling." He paused. "Lauren, Alan, I don't work this way. I'm careful. I'm neat. I'm methodical.

"I would never leave a site that sloppy. No way. This was malicious."

Lauren looked at me with tears in her eyes and said, "Oh my God, Alan. Oh my God."

Dresden's face turned ashen. He thought she was upset about him.

Dresden offered to call the Boulder County sheriff to report the incident as vandalism, and he said he would wait for the deputy to arrive. I pulled Lauren off to the side, huddled with her for a moment, and then accepted Dresden's offer. We didn't tell him we didn't think he was dealing with a simple vandal.

On the way back across town, I wondered what I could conclude. I couldn't be sure that he hadn't been planning to kill me under a collapsed roof, but also had to entertain the possibility that he merely wanted to warn us. Maybe he wanted us to be looking over our shoulders, listening for the other shoe to drop. I didn't know why, though, because it didn't seem to make sense. His job—killing me—would certainly be easier if we weren't wary of his approach. I considered the possibility that he was just letting me know that he knew we were on to him, and that it didn't matter to him.

He was smarter than we were. He was more clever. He was more resourceful.

After she calmed enough to recover her usual astuteness of problem-solving, Lauren agreed with my conclusions about the incident, but she was intent that practicality, and not hypothesizing, rule the short term. She wanted to call her friend John at Alarms Incorporated and have him hang motion detectors inside the house to keep intruders out during the remainder of the construction.

Although I felt this particular adversary would be amused by that particular impediment, I didn't say so. To me, such a deterrent was akin to using a kiddie gate to hold back an angry Doberman. But she said having the alarm in place would make her feel better, so I demurred. The calculator in my head clicked our change orders up to a new total, this one a few hundred dollars higher.

I, too, had some concrete matters to attend to. Custer was in New Zealand. Which meant I had to phone Simes and tell her about the sabotage. I was aware that I would have preferred to report this news to Custer, not Simes. But before I talked to either of them, I wanted to consult with Sam Purdy and get his advice.

Sam didn't respond to his beeper, so I tried him at home. His wife, Sherry, answered.

"Hi, Sherry, it's Alan. Is Sam around?"

"Alan, hi. No. He's, um, he's in the hospital." She started to cry.

"God, Sherry, what's wrong?"

She swallowed away some sniffles before she continued. "He had some, uh, terrible pain in his back yesterday morning when he was out front playing roller hockey with Simon, and he, uh, well, I . . . I made him call the department doctor. The doctor didn't like what Sam was describing and made him come in for some tests, and they took him right to the emergency room and—"

"Sherry, is it his heart?"

"Well, they thought so at first, but they did a, a—what do you call it?—with the heart?"

"An EKG?"

"Yes, and that went okay, I think, but then he got a high fever and the pain got worse and they did another test, an IVP I think they called it, and now they say he has a kidney stone. And he's still there, at Community Hospital, getting antibiotics. I just came home to be with Simon for a while."

My own heart was pounding at the news. "So he didn't have a heart attack?"

"No, they said he didn't. The pain was from the stone."

"Did he pass it? The stone?"

"No. The doctor's going to go get it tomorrow or the next day, after they bring his fever down."

"Do you know his doctor's name?"

"I'm sorry, Alan. I'm so upset, I don't remember."

"Is it a woman? A small woman?"

"Yes," she said hopefully.

"Dr. Arvin. Dr. Adrienne Arvin."

"Yes, that's her."

"I know her, Sherry. She's great. Sam's in good hands. And she knows him from some police work."

"That's nice." I thought she sounded relieved.

"How are you doing with all this, Sherry?"

She said, "I was so scared," and again she started to cry.

SIXTEEN

I didn't bother calling Sam first. He would have told me not to come.

Lauren was ambivalent about visiting the hospital with me. Ultimately, she decided to remain at home with the alarm on, with Emily at her side and with her Glock close by. For the first time since I knew she owned it I liked the fact that she had a handgun.

At the door to Sam's hospital room I didn't knock for the same reason I hadn't called. Although the bed was situated so that he couldn't see the door, Sam apparently heard it squeal open as I entered his room. He said, "Jesus, you want more blood? Do you people drink it or something?"

I felt great sympathy for his nurse, for his urologist, Adrienne, and for the laboratory technicians.

I walked into his line of sight before I said, "No. I don't really want your blood, Sam. How you doing?"

"Alan," he said, looking away from me. "You talked to Sherry?" The unsaid part was "Damn it."

He knew I'd talked to Sherry. I nodded. "This must have been pretty scary," I said, taking in the IV and the tubing that disappeared below the sheets.

"They won't let me do much. My back is killing me. What time is it?"

"It's almost one."

"No. What time is it exactly?"

I looked at my watch. "Twelve fifty-one."

He had been watching the television with the sound turned off.

"So," I said. "Adrienne's your doctor?"

He shrugged as though the question didn't interest him much. "She said she'll get it out of there. She talks about it like it's a cavity she has to drill away, you know? Suggested I not worry about it."

"And?"

"And what?"

"Are you managing not to worry about it?"

"You ever had one? A kidney stone? She told me—your friend Adrienne—that she has women patients who have had stones and who have gone through childbirth. They prefer childbirth. I can only tell you that when the damn thing starts moving around it feels like my worst fear of being shot. Man, does it hurt."

"Where is it? Your kidney or your ureter?"

"Tube. It's in the tube." He stared at me and licked at his lips, which looked parched. He said, "I'm forty-three next week, Alan. I've got a little kid. I can't have health problems. I just can't. I've got to get back to work. Yeah, I'll manage not to worry about it."

"Apparently you do, though, Sam. Have health problems. Otherwise this is a pretty elaborate charade that Adrienne's pulling on you."

I could see his mandibular muscles constrict into tight balls the size of walnuts. "Look behind me. What's my blood pressure?"

I checked the monitor. "One-fifteen over seventy-eight."

"Pulse?"

"Eighty-three."

"And I have those numbers even with you sitting here making me anxious. My cholesterol is one fifty-eight. Not two fifty-eight. One fifty-eight. Maybe I'm a little overweight, I'll grant you that. I could lose ten pounds, twenty even. And, sure, the job is a little stressful sometimes. But how bad could this really be? I think it's a fluke. That's what I think."

He wanted a co-conspirator. Although I wanted to be

comforting, I couldn't bring myself to help him affix this psychological Band-Aid.

As casually as I could, I asked, "What's the prognosis?"

"I think I'm fine." His words were clipped and dismissive. It was as though he were describing twisting his ankle and was maintaining some fragile confidence that he'd be able to walk it off.

"When do you get out of here?"

"My fever goes down, then she goes in and gets the stone. During that part I sleep, thank God. Then I go home."

"Goes in how?"

He shivered. "Right through my dick."

I decided that confronting Sam's denial was neither in his best interest nor mine. Instead of pressing him, I asked, "What about changes? What's Adrienne recommending?"

"What changes?"

"Lifestyle changes. Exercise. Diet. Stress." Sam's appetite was prodigious. His choice of foods had always been dictated by his belief that his low cholesterol was God's way of telling him he had a license to eat plenty of saturated fat. My guess was that Adrienne was going to caution him away from calcium and tell him to exercise, reduce his stress, and drink more water.

I didn't think he exercised regularly, but when we'd bicycled together I'd always been amazed by his endurance.

"The little doctor said we'd have a chat about those things before I leave the hospital. She also said she's going to be putting something up in there for a while. A stent, I think she called it. She said I couldn't run around chasing bad guys until she took it back out."

"Adrienne actually said 'chasing bad guys'?"

"Yep." He shook his head. "So I'm going to be on leave for a week, ten days. It's going to drive me nuts."

"You know," I said, "I think I may have an idea to help you pass the time."

After I left the hospital I stopped by my office and used the phone there to call Simes's beeper/voice-mail setup and to leave a message for Sawyer. I told each of them that I

would be at my office number for thirty minutes and then
I would be going home.

Simes's call came first, five minutes later. "Dr. Gregory?
Dr. Simes."

"Please call me Alan."

"Okay, Alan. I assume this must be important."

"It is." In as much detail as I could muster, I related the
story of the construction sabotage.

She was silent for a good ten seconds after I finished the
tale. She asked, "What does your detective friend think?"

I found the question interesting. It informed me that
Simes respected Sam Purdy. That was good.

"Lauren and I live in the county, not the city. So it's
the sheriff, not the police. Sam doesn't know what happened, yet."

"You're calling me before you call him? That's interesting."

I didn't want to talk about Sam's health, although I wasn't
sure why. "What do you think? Is this sabotage related to,
you know?"

"Is it sabotage?"

"The contractor feels certain that it is. I have no reason to
mistrust him."

I could almost hear her shrug over the phone line. "There
are some problems developing with our theory. You should
know."

"Such as?"

"Your old supervisor? Dr. Masters? The local police finally tracked down the tanning bed repairman. The one who
looked so dirty? Well, now he looks clean. He's been hop-
scotching around trying to hide from an ex-wife, heard she
was getting close, asking around about him in town, so he
split. As best we can tell he's never lived in Colorado."

"Amy's death may have been an accident?"

I felt the distant shrug again. "Possibly. Or it could mean
that this offender we're pursuing is as smooth now as he
was six years ago and that he killed her without raising any
more suspicion than he did in any of the other murders. For
now, let's just say it makes it more difficult for Milt and me

to interest the various jurisdictions in collaborating on this investigation."

"And your colleagues at Quantico? What do they think?"

"This, unfortunately, fuels their skepticism. The repairman was our only solid lead."

Simes's affect remained an enigma to me. I went fishing. "Are you questioning your assumptions about all these deaths?"

"No."

"It's not a possibility?"

"You want to take this risk?"

I didn't hear the slightest waver in her tone. Was it confidence or bravado? I didn't know. "Have you heard from Milt?"

"Only that he's arrived safely in New Zealand. I expect some news later today. Milt loves E-mail almost as much as he loves golf and trains."

"Will you keep me informed, please?"

"As warranted. Have you seen Dr. Faire?"

The question came out of nowhere and caught me upside the head. I couldn't muster a lie. I said, "Yes," but wished I had just a smidgen more sociopathic blood running through my veins.

"And?"

"She and I are in agreement that we don't have any right to help compile a patient list for you. We spent some time puzzling together about some old patients who might be harboring a grudge."

"A grudge?" She laughed. "Are you kidding? This guy has a grudge like Arizona has a canyon. And who did you come up with?"

I didn't respond. It seemed less confrontational than saying I wasn't going to tell her.

"Don't make this more tedious than it needs to be, Alan. In case you've taken your eye off the ball, Milt and I are trying to save your lives."

"You know I can't tell you the identities of the patients who were on the unit back then."

"Then don't. Although I would love some names from one of you, I'm more interested right now in profile, not identity. You can give me details about potential suspects that I can compare with my working profile."

I sighed. "I'm not sure . . . I don't know."

"You're not sure what? That you trust me?"

"Actually, I'm pretty sure that I don't trust you. I'm sorry."

"Don't be sorry. I'm hoping it's a character trait of yours. Let's say your suspicions are confirmed about the sabotage on your remodeling project. What would that tell you about this man we're seeking?"

Her tone reminded me of a professor's questions during a graduate seminar. Reflexively, I tried to be appropriately thoughtful. "It raises the question of whether he's done this before. Been provocative before he actually kills someone. Do you have any evidence of that?"

"Later. It's a good question, though. Stay on that road. Let's say he hasn't. That this is new behavior, something we haven't discovered about the prior murders. What does it tell you?"

"Well, I've been puzzled by the acceleration in the time frame that it takes him to accomplish each murder. Amy Masters, Arnie Dresser, and now Lorna Pope close together. Things are speeding up. He's using less time to plan each attack. That's a significant change. Maybe this sabotage is evidence of yet another change. Maybe if this was just taunting it's indicative of a new phase."

"Maybe. Go on."

"Well, okay, say it's true. Perhaps it's a sign he's getting more and more reckless. Maybe—"

"Why? Why would he suddenly get more reckless?"

"Maybe his need to isolate his affect is becoming more determined—is, I don't know, requiring more frequency. Or . . . ?"

"Or what?"

"Maybe his underlying mental disorder is fluctuating. Maybe getting worse. Or maybe getting better. Sawyer raised the possibility that he has a slowly cycling mood disorder. Maybe there's been a change in the cycling. Maybe he's bipolar and the manic phases are more frequent."

"Don't stop."

"Or maybe it's not too complicated psychologically at all. Maybe he's running out of time."

Over the phone line, I heard a dog bark. A little yap dog. An appetizer dog. Simes said, "Perhaps you've been wasting your skill in a small-town practice, Dr. Gregory. You may have a calling here."

"Boulder isn't a small town."

"Not my point."

"I'm not at my best right now. What is your point?"

"The rules are changing. Our killer is evolving, as consecutive killers always do. He's feeling pressures we haven't yet identified. The result of those pressures is that he's changing his pattern. That may make him easier for us to catch. Then again, it may make it more difficult."

"Why more difficult?"

"Predictability works in our favor."

"So does recklessness, though, right?"

"Yes and no. Think about it."

"Don't we have to assume that the faster he kills the more mistakes he's likely to make? His obsessiveness is his salvation. His patience and planning have provided him great cover so far."

"An interesting assumption. And probably an accurate one. However, if your argument turns out to be true in the current circumstances, it only benefits the one of you who is killed second."

"I don't understand. What do you mean?"

"If he gets sloppy or careless while killing you, for example, we may well be able to use his mistakes to identify him before he kills Sawyer. Or vice versa. But one of you will die to protect the other. Although it's usually the case that subsequent murders provide new pieces to the puzzle, it's not a price I'm terribly eager to pay to flesh out my profiles."

* * *

Lauren met me at the door with a catbird-seat grin on her face. "Sawyer called. You just missed her."

Oops. "Did you get a number? I phoned her from my office to fill her in about the sabotage in Spanish Hills."

"She knows. I told her all about it." Lauren pirouetted away from me as she said those words. I couldn't see the expression on her face. I followed her back toward the kitchen.

"You told her?"

"Want some tea? I'm going to make some. She doesn't like what happened any more than we do. How's Sam?"

I wanted to hear about Sawyer but didn't want to appear insensitive to Sam's plight, so I related my impressions about him while she fixed the tea.

She handed me a mug and we moved into the little living room.

"That's too bad. I'm glad Adrienne's taking care of him, though." She ran her fingers through her short hair and said, "Sawyer seemed nice."

Nice? "You talked for a while?"

She nodded. "She was curious about me, I think. And I was curious about her. But I liked her."

"I'm glad, I guess."

She found that amusing.

"I spoke with Simes. Told her about the house."

"Is she worried about what happened?"

"It's not her house."

Lauren laughed.

"But there's some problems with the working hypothesis about Amy Masters's death. You know, the tanning bed?" I filled her in.

"That's really disappointing. I was hoping we could get some official help with all this."

"It doesn't appear to be on the horizon. I'm afraid we're stuck with Custer and Simes now that Sam's on the disabled list."

"Don't worry," she said. "Sam Purdy plays hurt. And we have Sawyer. Don't forget Sawyer. I think she's resourceful.

Oh, I almost forgot. She said she remembered the name of the guy who used to play chess all the time. And she thinks she may know how to find him."

"Chester," I said. "We used to call him Chester."

SEVENTEEN

Sawyer may have remembered Chester's name. What I recalled most clearly about him was that he needed a shower and a CARE package that included a gift set of Right Guard and a tube of Crest.

Chester arrived on the unit during the last few days of a glorious October. Although the weather was cool and clear, his reality was suffering a sleet storm of manic delusions. The primary delusion that was driving Chester had to do with God's impending visit to a cemetery east of Denver. The cemetery, out near what once was Lowry Air Force Base, is an immense forested place called Fairmount. Chester was determined that it was his duty to free God from a terrestrial prison where He was confined inside one of the graves in the cemetery. Toward that end, Chester had spent the last few days prior to admission wandering the graveyard, examining headstones, looking for signs that would tell him in which particular grave God was trapped. Somehow, Chester came to the conclusion that God would be lurking beneath the headstone of a dead person whose surname contained the name of a chess piece.

At night, Chester intended to dig up the graves of the prime candidates whom he'd identified during his daily strolls. He would do this systematically until he managed to free God from his earthly confinement. Over the course of his two-night quest Chester uncovered the mortal remains of one Samantha King, one Beverly Knight, and one man named Theodore Rook who had died in 1937 and whose loved ones had thought it fit to grace his headstone with a limerick of dubious taste.

Chester dug up no pawns.

The cops corralled Chester near dawn on the second night of his odyssey as he was meticulously clearing the sod from above Sylvester Bishop's boxed remains. The authorities brought him—Chester, not Sylvester—to the psych ER at the medical school. The admitting doc downstairs in the ER was a psychiatry resident named Sheldon Salgado. After a brief workup, Dr. Salgado assigned Chester a tentative bipolar diagnosis and told the charge nurse on Eight East that he suspected that her new admission had slept for no more than a few hours over the course of the entire last week.

The doc taking admissions on the Orange Team that night was Dr. Sawyer Sackett. After doing her own intake workup, and consulting with Susan Oliphant in rounds the next day, Sawyer introduced Chester to lithium carbonate and Haldol. After his psychosis began to abate in response to the medications, she introduced him to me.

Sawyer and I were well into our strange little romance by the time Chester was admitted to Eight East on Halloween weekend in 1982. In the months since I'd met her, I'd expected our relationship to evolve along some predictable line into a semblance of a boyfriend-girlfriend thing or to disintegrate along some equally predictable path into oblivion.

It had done neither.

What it had done was prove the law of physics about every action causing an equal and opposite reaction. Each time I edged closer to Sawyer—asking her for one too many dates, encouraging her to choose me over work, wanting to spend a night together and actually seeing what she looked like in the morning—her work became more pressing, or her fears about our relationship being discovered suffered some acute swelling. And she would quickly move beyond arm's length until I took the requisite step back.

One night she kissed me good night and shooed me out the back door of her little Tudor to send me on my way home after an evening of sex that I thought had been particularly inspirational. Together we had spent two long hours discovering some sensual oasis that I was certain no human had ever visited before.

That's how naïve I was.

To my back, as I retreated down the concrete steps into her yard, she murmured, "Don't become another of my obligations, Alan. Please."

Her tone had been soft and still freckled with the hoarseness of sex, but when I turned to see what expression was on her face, all I saw was the transient glint of kitchen light off her golden hair as the door met the jamb and the lock clicked shut. Through the gauze curtains I watched her turn away, enjoying one last glimpse of the curve of her breasts and the elegant profile of her neck.

I walked home slowly, trying to savor the afterglow of our lovemaking, trying to make it last. Along the way, I decided that Sawyer's parting words to me had been plea, not warning.

In those days I was much more adept at fathoming the depths of others' psyches than I was at plumbing the reaches of my own. By the time I had stripped off my clothes and settled naked into my double bed, I had succeeded in reassuring myself that Sawyer had been pleading with me. She had not been pushing me away.

She was asking for my patience.

Before I slept, I didn't get very far in beginning to understand the genesis of her concerns.

And I didn't spend anywhere near enough time trying to read the tea leaves of their consequences.

And by ten o'clock the next morning, the psychology I was most fascinated by wasn't Sawyer's. Or my own.

It was that of this new patient of hers, whom we'd nicknamed Chester. She'd asked me to do a psychological testing battery on him.

Psychological testing has never been one of my clinical passions. In skilled, inspired hands, the results of the process can be a fascinating glimpse into shadowed recesses of the psyche. Properly interpreted, the insight gained about the patient can be both practical and clinically useful. But the administration, the process of testing, is always—always—tedious. Over the course of my graduate school years, at least three professors had spent hours of class time trying to convince me otherwise, but the reality is that formal psychological testing is a time-consuming, mind-numbing task that I would gladly leave to my colleagues.

That Monday near noon, Chester and I sat across from each other, a laminated table between us, in a small room in the occupational therapy center on one end of the inpatient unit. I tried to engage him in an initial interview. How had he ended up here? What was he feeling? What did he think about being on the unit? What were his goals during his stay? What about family? Friends?

Chester wasn't biting.

His answers demonstrated a limited repertoire that consisted primarily of wrinkled brows, shrugs, and an occasional "I'm afraid that I'm not interested in that particular subject." Already, I was getting the impression that the projective parts of this test battery, which require active participation from the patient, were going to be accomplished with record brevity. I took solace in that.

Earlier that morning at rounds, the staff had reported that Chester had spent most of his weekend huddled over a chessboard in the dayroom. So I asked, "I understand you enjoy chess?"

His eyes widened and he opened his mouth and exhaled. His breath wafted my way. It was so fetid I had to compose myself not to react. He said, "I do," with exaggerated gravity, as though he were stating a marital vow.

"Are you good?"

"Nineteen eighty-seven," he said.

His response constituted either a loose association, a bad answer on a mental status exam question about what year it was, or some numerical fact about his chess skill that I was too ignorant to interpret.

Since his mental status had shown him oriented by

three during a morning nursing assessment, I guessed either B or C.

To camouflage my ignorance, almost always a mistake with patients, and to keep him talking, I said, "Nineteen eighty-seven. Huh."

He shook his head and snorted through his nose. He scratched his scalp with his left hand and examined his fingernails to see what interesting residue had accumulated beneath them. He flicked a couple of specimens onto the tabletop before saying, "You don't know what that means, do you, asshole?"

I sat back on my chair. I'd been on the inpatient unit for—what?—almost three months. In internship weeks, which accumulate like dog years, that made me a veteran. Actually, it left me only a couple of months shy of being an expert. I didn't have to put up with this grief from a patient. I said, "I'm getting the impression that you might be having some difficulty with our roles."

"Which means what?"

"That your hostility might reflect the reality that you don't like the fact that you're the patient and I'm the doctor."

"Or perhaps my hostility reflects the fact that I'm being asked to genuflect before a knave."

"We have a lot of work to accomplish together. Do you think we can accomplish this task with some degree of civility? I'm doing my best not to insult you. I expect the same from you."

"Is it so hard? Not insulting me?"

"That's not what I meant."

"Oh. I see. It's only what you said."

I took a deep breath. "I didn't schedule this time to argue with you. If we're unable to proceed now, we'll reschedule and do this another time. Is that what you prefer?"

"That seems to increase the probability of my spending additional time in this no-star hotel. If you simply admit you don't have a fucking clue about the game of kings, I'll be civil."

"Okay. I don't know what nineteen eighty-seven means. Does it refer to chess, or your chess skill?"

"Let's not talk about chess. The subject interests me only when the person I'm conversing with is fluent in the language."

By then, I was set up to administer the WAIS-R, the Revised version of Wechsler Adult Intelligence Scale, the most widely used IQ test of the time. I said, "As you wish. Why don't we talk about something more neutral, then? For instance," I said, and proceeded to dictate the precise wording of the first question of the Information subtest of the WAIS-R.

He replied with an equally precise answer that earned him a full score. I was surprised that he deigned to answer at all.

I tried the next question on my list. Again, he answered. Again, he answered correctly with a brevity and clarity that hinted at genius.

He stayed with me through that subtest and on to the next. I didn't know much about Chester, but I learned quickly that he thoroughly enjoyed the challenge of outwitting not only me but also the constructors of the test.

Forty-five minutes later, I knew Chester's intelligence quotient. Chester was the smartest person I had ever tested.

The projective tests that I would administer after the WAIS-R, the Rorschach and the TAT or Thematic Apperception Test, require a test subject who is willing to be verbally engaged, even effusive. At the very minimum, responsive. That did not describe Chester's demeanor that morning. We breezed through both tests in less than an hour. He was so guarded that I believed the results would be next to useless, but he did seem to take some pleasure frustrating me. That, too, was, of course, grist for the mill. I had higher hopes for the MMPI, which he would self-administer under nursing supervision over the course of the next day or two.

After the testing session was complete, I ran into Sawyer in the nursing station. I said, "Your patient is kind of bright."

"Really? I suspected that. How bright is he?"

"Sawyer, the man's IQ is one seventy-seven. I've never tested anyone whose IQ came close to that."

I let the number hang in the air between us. An IQ of one hundred was "average." One-fifty was usually considered "genius." One seventy-seven was stratospheric.

"Wow," she said, smiling. "This will be odd. Treating someone who's almost as smart as me."

I wished I knew if she was kidding.

As the Halloween holiday gave way to the beginning of November I saw little of Chester. With an on-board blood level of lithium growing sufficient to provide a buffer against the tides of his mania, he became a quiet man who kept to himself in the unit dayroom. Each day, he would choose a chair and table by the window, set up a chessboard, and work out solutions to chess problems that he created for his own amusement. Usually he refused offers to play a game. Occasionally, though, a sadistic streak would surface and he would accept a challenge from another patient or a staff member. He would beat them in no time at all, and would be certain to demoralize them in the process and taunt them at the conclusion of the game.

In therapy groups he remained sullen and condescending. His edgy demeanor was directed not only at the professional staff, but also at any other patients who stepped in his path.

Chester stayed cool with Sawyer, his psychiatrist. She told me once that their therapy sessions felt more like fencing, however, than chess. Chester didn't attach himself to anyone else on the staff, either. Even difficult patients often identify one ally among the staff. Usually they choose a nurse or a mental health assistant. Not Chester. He never chose a confidant.

On day six of his admission, the second of his two permitted seventy-two-hour mental health holds expired, and Sawyer, in consultation with the ward chief, Susan Oliphant, decided that Chester's current mental condition, although certainly not stellar, didn't warrant certification. After the second hold expires, certification is the required next legal step to hold someone against his or her will for continued treatment. Since certification involves a longer period of loss of freedom—ninety days—it is more cumbersome legally than a seventy-two-hour hold. Certifications, therefore, are used infrequently, and one would not be applied to Chester.

Chester decided to check himself off the unit and out of the hospital as soon as Sawyer notified him that his hold had expired. Although Sawyer made a valiant attempt to persuade Chester to stay in the hospital voluntarily, he wouldn't budge. He seemed to soften a little as she spoke with him and actually went through the motions of accepting a referral for outpatient follow-up with his local mental health center. Ultimately, though, his discharge was AMA—against medical advice.

We talked about him briefly at rounds the next day. None of the professional staff expected that he would take any of his prescribed lithium post-discharge. We all thought that someone on our unit or at the inpatient unit at Denver General across town would see his face again soon. How soon would he be back? There was no telling. The next time his bipolar disease cycled into mania could be next week, or next year.

I don't imagine I'd thought about Chester more than once or twice since that day after he was discharged.

EIGHTEEN

Lauren asked, "Is he a good candidate? The chess player?"

I wondered about her choice of words. "Candidate," not "suspect." I said I wasn't sure about how good a candidate he really was, but I told her what I could remember about him.

"There's not much there," she acknowledged, "other than the fact that he's smart enough and methodical enough to pull it off."

I didn't disagree with her assessment. Smart enough and methodical enough carried a lot of weight, though. "He was a bitter, resentful man. But there were quite a few of them on the unit back then. I just don't remember any of us pissing him off enough that he'd want to kill all of us."

She pulled a pillow from the other end of the sofa and hugged it to her abdomen. "From a psychological point of view, if he was doing it, killing everybody, when would he be committing the murders? Would he do it when he was sane, or when he was crazy?"

"You know, it's a good question. Given the nature of these crimes, I would say it would have to be when he's sane. The delusions he was suffering during his manic phase are too unpredictable for the kind of long-term planning necessary to carry out these murders. And violence of this kind—actually of any kind—is certainly not typical of bipolar disease. For all we know, his illness may be well controlled on lithium and he may cycle into mania infrequently, giving him plenty of time to develop his strategy and plan his next murder."

"And you don't recall anyone humiliating him, or embarrassing him? Nothing like that?"

I shook my head and simultaneously shrugged my shoulders. "Sawyer probably remembers more than I do. She spent a lot of time with him during that week. When you talked with her on the phone, did she say what his name was?"

"No," Lauren said, "she didn't." She stood and stretched and kissed me on top of the head before she added, "This doctor in the ER, the one who admitted Chester that first night, what was his name? Maybe he knows something. Have you thought of talking with him?"

I hadn't. "His name is Sheldon Salgado. He's still in town—actually he's on the faculty at the medical school. He's a pretty big deal these days in biological psychiatry. It's a good idea, sweetie. I'll call him."

But at first I couldn't bring myself to call him. Now that Lauren's suggestion had placed Sheldon Salgado on my radar, I was afraid I would learn that he, too, was already dead. That Chester or D.B., or somebody else, had covered all the bases ahead of me and knocked him off.

Sheldon Salgado was a *mensch*. A star at Harvard Medical School, he could've gone anywhere he wanted for his residency in psychiatry. But his wife, a pediatrician in training, matched at Colorado. Never considering the prestige factor, he followed her here.

I hadn't known him well during our training. Our paths had crossed on a few rotations, that was it. What did I remember about him? Sheldon was thin as a whisper, stood an inch or so under six feet tall, and had great taste in ties. Long before the rest of the psychiatric community converted, he was preaching the doctrine that psychobiology was the key to the etiology of mental illness and pharmacology was the key to treatment. Although the residency rumor mill pegged him as an average or below-average psychotherapist, even as a resident he was renowned as an astonishing interviewer. His diagnostic skills shined particularly brightly in the ER. When I was an intern, he was in the third year of his residency, and he had been appointed chief resident on the Emergency Psychiatric Service.

At the end of the year, after his training was complete, he took a teaching and research position at the school. His diagnostic acumen kept his referral practice booming with requests for second opinions and medication consultations. Over the years I'd sent at least a half-dozen of my own patients his way seeking advice on whether they might be responsive to pharmacological intervention.

Although I didn't agree with all of his prescriptions, I always learned something from his opinions.

During the course of one of the patient consultations he had done for me, Sheldon had offered me his home phone number after a frustrating week of phone tag. I jotted that number onto a scrap of paper, hoping he hadn't changed it, and called him from a pay phone at Delilah's Pretty Good Grocery on the corner of College and Ninth. I cursed my own paranoia the whole time I was walking the few blocks from our temporary house to the store.

What was I worried about? I was worried that our telephone at home was tapped. I was worried that I would be followed if I drove to Denver to meet with Sheldon. I was worried that if the killer had not already considered killing Sheldon Salgado, by getting in touch with him I would give my homicidal adversary a damn good reason to remember who it was who admitted him from the psych ER to the psychiatric inpatient unit.

Sheldon answered the phone himself. I was greatly relieved that he was alive. Weird.

"Sheldon," I said, "it's Alan Gregory."

"Hi. Hello," he replied in a way that made it perfectly clear he didn't remember who I was and was pretty certain he didn't want to be talking with me.

"We've talked before about some patients I've sent your way. I'm a psychologist in Boulder? And believe me, I'm terribly sorry to bother you at home. Especially on a weekend."

"It's all right. This is where I try to be on the weekends.

What can I do for you?" His tone was contained. He was being polite, but not gracious. People always wanted things from him. He was not always thrilled about it.

I had given some thought to what might be the most productive way to engage Sheldon's interest in my dilemma. I said, "I've recently been contacted by two ex–FBI agents who are concerned that Arnie Dresser's recent death might actually have been murder. You heard about Arnie's death?"

"Yes. Tragic."

Terse.

"Well, these two ex-agents believe that there is some reason to be concerned that a patient Arnie was seeing during his residency may somehow be responsible for his death. I'm hoping that you might have some memories of that patient, and that you might remember something, some details, that would assist us in making some sense of all this."

" 'Us'?" He paused. "Why are you calling me about this, Alan? What's your connection to Arnie Dresser?"

I was hoping he would ask that question. I used it as an entrée to walk him through the entire progression of this dark absurdity, beginning with Dr. Susan Oliphant's plane crash in 1989 and ending with Lorna Pope's recent disappearance in New Zealand.

Lorna's death seemed to have a special meaning for him. He interrupted my story and asked, "Lorna is dead?"

"Missing. Some bodies have been found. One of the FBI agents is in Auckland, now, trying to see—what? I don't know . . . to see if the body is Lorna's. To try to determine if she was murdered too."

"Lorna and I stayed in touch for a while after my training. She and my wife used to play tennis. I don't think I've talked with her in a couple of years, though. She's real sweet." The phone line crackled in my ear. Neither of us spoke for fifteen, twenty seconds. Finally, he said, "This sounds quite far-fetched, you know. This story. If what you're suggesting is true, this would be a highly atypical series of crimes for a psychiatric patient."

"Yes. I know."

"How is Sawyer? What became of her?"

His question was small talk. I didn't recall Sawyer ever mentioning a relationship or friendship with Sheldon. I guessed he was buying some time while he tried to make sense of the jigsaw I'd thrown at him. "I saw her yesterday, actually. She seems fine. She consults in the prison system in California. Competency and sanity and death-penalty issues mostly."

"Really? And she shares your concern about . . . all this?"

"Yes."

I heard a string instrument, I thought a cello, playing in the background. The same few bars, over and over. Workmanlike, and monotonous. He said, "You're calling me for more than information, aren't you?"

"I guess so. Quite simply, I'm concerned—I'm actually more than concerned—that you might be on this man's list, too, Sheldon. You, or someone else from the psych ER. If it turns out that this story has merit and it's an ex-patient from Eight East, you know as well as I do that the admission may well have come through the psych ER. I'm even frightened of leading this guy to you by making this call. I mean, if he hasn't thought of it on his own already. To be extra safe, I'm making this call from a pay phone."

"I guess I should offer my gratitude." He didn't. A long silence told me he was trying to digest my paranoia and other aspects of my mental health. "But me particularly? Why?"

"Well, yes, you particularly. One of the patients whom Sawyer and I are concerned about is someone we're relatively certain that you saw in the psych ER. Sawyer followed him on the Orange Team. I did psychological testing on him. He was a bipolar guy, a chess player, had been picked up by the police out at Fairmount Cemetery digging up graves, and—"

He chuckled. "Yes. He was trying to release Jesus from a casket or something. I remember him. I did see him before he was admitted. I'll check my consultation logs, see if I have anything useful on him."

"You'll what?"

"I keep a record of everyone I've ever seen. I've done it

since medical school. Like a diagnostic diary. Just some brief notes about everybody. Mental status, impressions, diagnosis, referrals."

"Do you keep names?"

"Just initials. You don't remember this patient's name?"

"Sawyer thinks she does. But I don't know it." Consultation logs? I'd never heard of such a thing. "You wouldn't by any chance have seen another patient we're concerned about? We don't have a name on this one. A male, late twenties, worked at Rocky Flats. He may have stuck in your memory because he offered to trade the identity of D. B. Cooper—you remember the hijacker?—in exchange for immediate discharge from the unit."

"I remember him, too. Absolutely. I must have seen him myself or heard about him at rounds or something. Wait, no, I saw him, I saw him. In fact, he made me the same offer about divulging D. B. Cooper's identity when I saw him down in the ER. I have to admit I was tempted. The whole D. B. Cooper thing has always captured my attention."

"You were tempted?"

"Kidding. Let me check my logs. When were you on inpatient rotation? When were these two admitted?"

"Fall rotation, 1982. The chess player was admitted just before Halloween. A day or two before, maybe. D.B. was Thanksgiving weekend."

He chuckled. "That's ironic, don't you think?"

"Why?" I failed to see the irony.

"That's when the original hijacking occurred. Thanksgiving weekend. Portland to Seattle on Northwest."

"I'd forgotten."

"I haven't. You remember a movie called *Brian's Song*? About Brian Piccolo, the football player with cancer? It was on TV the first time that same Thanksgiving weekend. The two things have always been linked together in my memory. D. B. Cooper and *Brian's Song*."

"I loved that movie."

"Me too. Give me an hour to dig out the right logs. I'll call you back. What's your number?"

"How about if I call you back, Sheldon?"

"You're quite serious about all this, aren't you?"

"I'm afraid so."

I didn't want to go home, so I walked down College Avenue toward the little commercial district where the eastern boundary of the Hill butts hard against the rest of Boulder. The retail establishments on the Hill exist primarily to serve students from the adjacent university. Bars, coffeehouses, music stores, and bicycle shops are overrepresented. I didn't want a drink, so I stopped into Buchanan's Coffee Pub for something warm. I was the oldest person in the place and, from what I could see, one of the few whose sole source of extraneous metal in my body was my dental fillings.

The coffee was good. The music playing in the room was not too different from what I remembered from my own college days. I couldn't understand any of the lyrics, though. I rationalized that it wasn't because I was getting old, but rather because I was out of practice.

After coffee I window-shopped and browsed for CDs. Time dragged. I people-watched from a bench on Thirteenth Street for a while, grew bored with that, and finally found another pay phone and dialed Sheldon's number again. He answered on the first ring.

"I have them both," he said.

"Great. This is great."

"You have the dates correct. The man you call D.B. is in my records under the initials C.R. I have him down as agitated, oriented, with pressured speech, and some curious obsessive/compulsive features. You know, as I read my notes, I realize he's one of those patients who I wouldn't even consider for admission these days. Not given the current managed-care environment and the advances we've made with medicine. And it says clearly in my log that he would gladly trade D. B. Cooper's identity for a quick discharge."

"Do you have a precipitant?"

"Yes. Apparently, he lost it at work. Was threatening someone, wouldn't calm down. They said he was talking crazy about a conspiracy."

"Work was at Rocky Flats?"

"Yes, that's correct. Security department."

"That's it?"

"Let's see. Well-groomed twenty-nine-year-old white married male, one child, with no previous psychiatric history. Da da da da da. No family history. Denied suicidal ideation. Denied hallucinations and delusions. Da da da. That's it."

"Diagnosis?"

"Rule out 301.40. Rule out 312.34 and 297.90."

"I'm sorry, Sheldon, I don't have the DSM codes memorized."

"Compulsive personality disorder. Rule out intermittent explosive disorder and atypical paranoid disorder. It says here that I made a call to Wendy Asimoto about him; she was up next. That's it—that's all I have on him. The other one—"

"Just a second. You sent him to Wendy? Sawyer and I recalled that Arnie Dresser treated him upstairs."

"Maybe. Happened all the time. According to my notes, Wendy was next up for an admission, but if she had already picked up a new patient—one who hadn't come through the ER—then by the time D.B. made it upstairs he would belong to the next doc on the list. In this case, Arnie."

"Oh."

"The other one? The chess player? His initials are V.G."

"How did he present?"

"Classic acute mania. Delusional. Agitated. Irritable. Grandiose. He was demonstrating flight of ideas, pressured speech, lots of clever chess associations. Cops said he was more euphoric than irritable when they first picked him up, was certain that they were there to help him dig up the graves."

"History?"

"Didn't get any. His interview wasn't coherent from the point of view of collecting reliable facts. Lorna would have followed up with his family upstairs, wouldn't she?"

I reflected that it was probably what got her killed. I said simply, "Yes. She would have contacted his family."

"I hope this helps."

"It does, Sheldon. A lot. Thank you. Listen, I don't know how to ask this next question without sounding totally paranoid. But would you like me to give your name to these two ex–FBI agents?"

"You really think I'm at risk?"

"I don't know. I don't have any way to know."

"Even if this vessel holds water, there's currently no evidence that the man you're looking for is seeking targets who never worked on the Orange Team. That's correct, isn't it?"

"For now, yes. But—"

"But it only takes one to destroy the pattern?"

"Yes, it only takes one."

"I'll be careful. For now, I think I'd prefer to stay out of it, please. And say hello to Sawyer for me. She was a special lady."

"I will. Thanks for your help. Please take care of yourself."

NINETEEN

Lauren met me at the door, one hand on her hip, the other against the wall for balance.

"Hi. I've been worried about you. You're going to need to do a better job of letting me know how long you'll be gone, okay? I was about to use your pager to check on you."

I was sensitive to the possibility that her concern might be bound tightly with criticism, but all I heard was the gentle caution of someone who cared about me. The remanding she sent my way felt sweet, and generous, like an unexpected back rub.

"I'm sorry. You're right. I'll do better about staying in touch. I walked down to the Hill for coffee, and I reached that ER doc, the one who may have admitted that patient, Chester, to the unit. To be on the safe side, I thought I should use a pay phone to call him."

She puffed her cheeks out a little and stared at the cordless phone on the hallway table as though she had just realized it could be a dangerous instrument. "I hadn't thought about that . . . that he might have the ability to do that, you know, to tap our phone. I have to remind myself how sophisticated this guy is. He's not just a schoolyard bully, is he?" She shook her head. "So you think this other doctor you talked with, he could be at risk, too?" She answered her own question. "Of course he could."

I nodded. "If I'm being watched, there's no sense marking a trail that leads to him. The good news is that he was able to remember some things that may help Sawyer and me identify this guy."

"Anything you can tell me?"

"I can tell you anything but names, hon. He just provided some information about the nature of this man's initial presentation that first night in the psych ER. Sheldon's a great diagnostician, so I put a lot of weight on his impressions. But there's nothing earth-shattering in what he remembers. At this point, though, anything at all feels like a gift. I need to let Sawyer know about it as soon as I can. Did you get a sense of whether or not she'll be home tonight?"

"She faxed this to you," Lauren said, as she grabbed a sheet of paper that was beside the phone on the hallway table. Lauren's new plain-paper fax machine occupied the lower shelf of the same table. "It's her travel plans for the next few days." She read a few lines silently and shook her head side to side. "San Diego, San Quentin, Sacramento. This woman sure gets around."

"She has her own plane. Flies from one prison and court to the next, all over California."

Lauren furrowed her brow. "That's worrisome. That she flies her own plane. Considering what happened to that other pilot doctor. Her plane was sabotaged. That's the theory, right?"

"Right. I think it's worrisome that Sawyer is a pilot, too. But Sawyer's pretty cavalier about it. Feels she's taking adequate precautions." I explained about the locked hangar and the trusted airplane mechanic.

Lauren touched me on the shoulder and said, "As far as precautions are concerned, that sounds to me, unfortunately, like the functional equivalent of the rhythm method. I think I need to have another talk with that girl."

"Speaking of that. One of us needs to clue Adrienne in on what's going on up at the Spanish Hills house. The vandalism, especially. I don't want her or Jonas walking into any booby traps."

Lauren said, "I spoke with her while you were gone. You know Ren. It didn't faze her at all. She feels pretty bulletproof in life. She'll keep her eye on things and she'll do her best to keep Jonas away from the construction equipment, which isn't too easy for a boy his age. She's pretty sure there's some link between testosterone and power tools."

"She say anything about Sam and his kidney stone?"

"Not a word. And I didn't ask."

I had to smile. Adrienne was a good friend and a wonderful neighbor, but she didn't talk out of school about her patients. "Any other calls?"

"Yes, I spoke with Sam. He's really somber, Alan. I don't think I've ever heard him this . . . I don't know, scared, maybe."

"Is he home?"

"No. The stone came out this morning. He hopes to go home later today. And he said to tell you that he likes your idea. Wonders if you'll come by around seven tomorrow morning. But he warned you the first few days, she told him he has to take it pretty easy." She paused. "It's nice of you to offer to exercise with him. He could use someone to be with now. A friend."

"It's not all magnanimous. He can use an exercise partner. I can use a bodyguard. And I may take him out to breakfast, too. Show him what saturated fat actually looks like."

"I think," she said, "you're pushing your luck. Exercise is one thing, changing Sam's diet . . . that's something else entirely." She walked up behind me and embraced me, forcing her pelvis against my butt in a pleasing rotation. "You don't have much of an ass, you know?"

"I make up for it by occasionally being an ass, though."

She bit my upper arm near my shoulder seconds before I felt her lips on my neck. "You know, the kids are asleep—"

"We don't have any kids."

"Shhh. We're not expecting any visitors."

"Almost no one knows that we live here. And certainly none that we'd welcome, anyway."

She couldn't reach my ear with her tongue, but I could tell she was trying.

Sam met me at the door to his house the next morning. He and Sherry lived in a small ranch house in North Boulder, west of Broadway, not far from Community Hospital. As he stepped out onto the compact wooden porch, I thought he looked like an old boxer who was facing the prospect of roadwork after ten years away from the ring. I couldn't tell whether his sweatshirt was older than his sweatpants, but they were both older than his only child.

"You look all right, Sam, given what you've been through. What are you supposed to be doing this morning?"

"Walk twenty, twenty-five minutes. Easy, no hills."

"You're ready?"

"No. But if I say screw it and get in the car and go get a doughnut or two, Sherry promises she'll divorce me."

"I don't have a patient until nine. Let's get some breakfast, too, afterward. I'll begin to teach you how to eat."

"I know how to eat."

"Okay, I'll teach you how to eat healthy."

"God, I'm going to hate this."

"Probably," I admitted. "North Boulder Park?"

"Sure. Me and the rest of Boulder's health nuts."

I wasn't surprised by his sarcasm, or his cynicism. I wasn't taken aback by the barely subdued anger. I was surprised, however, by the depth of his depression. He'd lost something over the weekend. Some invulnerability. He'd lost it, and at this moment he didn't expect to ever, ever get it back.

As we walked he scratched at his side frequently, just below his ribs. Nonchalantly, I thought, I asked about pain. He said he just had an itch. I didn't know whether to believe him or not. On the west side of the park, about halfway into our walk, he asked me, incongruously, about Elton John. Usually, Sam and I talked about work, or hockey, not bisexual rock-and-roll stars.

He said, "You like his stuff?"

"Yes, I do. The early stuff mostly. I haven't paid much attention since he insisted I know his sexual preferences better than I had any interest in knowing them."

Sam shuddered. Elton John's lifestyle was way out of his

comfort range. "Me, too. I like the early stuff best, too. Remember that song that has the line in it, something like 'I thought the sun was going down on me'? Remember that?" Sam actually tried to attach a melody to the lyric. I forced myself to swallow a snicker.

He scratched at his side again. I said I remembered the song.

"That's what I thought when the pain hit. I figured I must be dying. I heard that song playing in my head and I felt, holy shit, the sun is going down on me. It's, like, high noon in my life—okay, maybe it's mid-afternoon—whatever, you know. But it's early. And the damn sun's going down on me."

I said nothing but looked over so that he would know I was listening to every word.

"But then I decided that maybe what it was is that, you know, it all got dark because of an eclipse. Just some celestial event. That this wasn't really a sign it was over for me. That I didn't need to act like some ancient wiseass who didn't know why it was so dark in the middle of the day. I mean, I didn't have to rush out and start killing virgins. I could wait it out, learn from it. Be enlightened, you know."

"That's an impressive insight, Sam."

"Yeah, well, I'm an impressive guy, Alan." He looked over at me with soft eyes that I couldn't recall seeing before. "Is this kind of what it was like for you when Custer and Simes showed up and told you this guy, this old patient, wanted to kill you? Was it the sun-going-down thing? I mean, is that how you felt, too?"

We paced out another ten steps before I answered. "You know, Sam, it is how I feel, still. I feel, like, here I am, I'm trying to live a decent life, and now, at any moment, this thing, this guy—this asshole—thinks he can jump up and bite me in the jugular anytime he chooses. And when he chooses—bingo, it's over."

Sam said, "That's how I feel about my body right now. It's king. It's the one running the mortality show. Maybe it'll make another stone. Maybe it'll leave me alone. I don't know how it'll happen. I don't know when. I don't really know why. And I don't feel that there's a hell of a lot I can do about it."

"There's always eating well and stress reduction. I can help you with that."

"I think I'll let you. Within limits. And I can teach you some things that will help you with your maniac."

"Like?"

He unzipped the ass-pack that was tethered around his ample waist and pulled it open far enough that I could see the glint of light off his pistol. He said, "I need to teach you how to use one of these. For you, it will have the same pro-phylactic value as me reducing my calcium intake and low-ering my body fat percentage."

"I don't know, Sam."

"It's a package deal, buddy. You teach me about soluble fiber and yoga. I teach you about semiautomatic handguns. I guarantee you that you're getting the better part of this bargain."

Over breakfast at Marie's I introduced Sam to fresh fruit and the glories of toast without butter. He tasted oatmeal for the first time since he'd moved out of his mother's house.

It was a start.

I also caught him up on the sabotage to our renovation project, my trip to see Sawyer in Las Vegas, and my conver-sation with Sheldon Salgado.

His first comment almost caused me to choke on a crust of bagel I'd smuggled in from Moe's.

He said, "You and Lauren doing okay?"

Sam had never asked before.

"I think so," I said. "We have stresses, you know. This thing with me. Her illness. It can be hard."

He looked over at me, his spoon halfway to his mouth, and nodded. He said, "I like eggs better."

I waited for him to go on more about my marriage. And I considered asking him how he and Sherry were dealing with his illness. Instead I said, "There are some things you can do to help. Other things I think I'm going to have to do on my own."

"Confidentiality shit?"

"Yeah. Confidentiality shit."

"I understand." The growl in his voice said he didn't really. "What do you need?"

"You have any contacts in security at Rocky Flats?"

"You planning an assault?"

I told him I had a lead and that I needed to talk with the man who was head of security at Rocky Flats during the time I was an intern in Denver.

"You're piquing my curiosity."

"I bet. Can you get me the name?"

"Easier than you can get me a fat-free doughnut."

TWENTY

If I didn't have a great little shack of my own that was undergoing renovation across town in Spanish Hills, I decided that I wanted to live where Reginald Loomis lived. He had a little place that backed up to city greenbelt on the west side of Fourth Street between Iris and Juniper. His wide, unfenced backyard segued, unobstructed, into the foothills of the Rocky Mountains. His closest neighbors to the west were the wild animals that combed the ridges of the jutting hogback a few hundred feet away. In that short distance the elevation rose at least a thousand feet.

Mr. Loomis's shack did not appear to have ever been renovated. Actually, I wondered whether the siding had ever been painted. I guessed that the frame house had been built in the thirties and that Reggie Loomis had bought it for a song in the mid-sixties, before Boulder became cool and northwest Boulder became chic. The shake roof was older than I was. The windows were single-pane and probably leaked like a special prosecutor's office. The concrete walkway had more fissures than the tax code. The front lawn wasn't really a lawn at all, but rather a collection of grass and weed clumps that dotted the dusty expanse between house and street like an archipelago.

But, despite its many shortcomings, I could only dream of owning Reggie Loomis's home. I would have to win a damn good lottery jackpot to afford the half acre of ground this little shack was occupying. I suspected that at least one salivating Realtor knocked on his door each week praying he'd decided to sell.

I'd pondered my approach to Mr. Loomis from the moment that Sam had called me with the name and address of the man who had been chief of security at Rocky Flats during the early eighties. Sam had called himself and Mr. Loomis neighbors. "Only difference between us is eight blocks and about a half a million bucks." I decided right away not to approach Mr. Loomis via telephone, and I resolved to be relatively straightforward about my problems when I spoke with him. I hoped he would do the same for me in return.

The early eighties were a difficult time for anyone working at Rocky Flats Nuclear Weapons Facility. The plant, now in perennial shutdown mode, hugs a huge piece of prime, though partially radioactive, real estate not too many miles south of Boulder along the Front Range. The facility has been a source of controversy since its inception. Protests against the plant, which made plutonium triggers for nuclear warheads, were constant, and must have put particular pressure on anyone who was involved in plant security. The majority of the protesters wanted the plant shut down out of support for nuclear disarmament. A minority just wanted the damn thing closed because it had no business existing upwind and upstream from a major metropolitan area.

Reginald Loomis was retired from a tough job that had probably made him popular with very few of his neighbors.

He answered his door in a fashion I would call leisurely. I saw the light change behind the peephole in his front door from shadow to bright and back a good thirty seconds before I heard the rasp of the dead bolt being thrown. The door opened without a squeak. Given the state of the rest of the house, I was surprised at the lack of audio accompaniment to the operation of the hinges.

"Mr. Loomis? Reginald Loomis?"

He clenched his jaw. "No one calls me Reginald but strangers and my mother. And you, sir, are not my mother. Whatever you're selling, young man, I'm not buying. Unless it's youth. I'm always interested in buying a little youth."

"I'm not selling anything, Mr. Loomis. I'm hoping you will be kind enough to help me track someone down. Someone who worked for you about fifteen years ago at Rocky Flats."

Reginald Loomis was a gaunt man with white hair. Other than eyes the color of blue bank checks, his face was not blessed with much color. But at that moment, I thought he paled even further.

"You said fifteen years, right?"

"Right, actually a little longer. Nineteen eighty-two."

He seemed to get his color back. "That was a long time ago. And I had a lot of people working for me back then. In plant security, the early eighties, that was prime time. I didn't know all the staff. I'm not so sure I'd remember much that would be of help to you."

"I'd be grateful if you would try. I don't know where else to go."

"Who are you?"

"My name is Alan Gregory. Dr. Alan Gregory. I live and work here in Boulder. I'm trying to find someone I was involved with years ago. Someone whom I need to re-contact. One of the only ways I have of finding him is to use the fragments of information I recall from my brief contact with him in the early eighties. One of those fragments is that he worked in security at Rocky Flats. And that you were his boss."

He shifted his weight and his face moved farther into the shadows. "What's his name? This man you're after."

I didn't want to admit I didn't know. I said, "May I come in? Would that be all right?"

His voice took on urgency as he said, "I asked you a question. What's the man's name?"

"I wish I knew. But I don't remember his name. The best I can do is initials."

"Well, then, what are those?"

"His initials are C.R."

His lips silently formed the two letters and he looked past

me, out across Boulder toward the dry prairies that began
the sweep of the seemingly infinite midwestern plains. His
shoulders dropped an inch or two. As much to himself as to
me, he mumbled, "Why don't you come on in then?"

Maybe walking into the tent of a Bedouin ruler would
leave the same impression on me as walking into this little
North Boulder bungalow. I don't really know. But the disre-
pair of the outside of Reggie Loomis's house could not have
left me any less prepared for what I found inside.

The modest house was probably only nine hundred to a
thousand square feet, but a good half of it had been converted into a kitchen. I was speechless at how it had been
renovated.

He noticed my reaction—had, apparently, been waiting
for it. And he was proud that his house had caused it. "Don't
worry," he said. "Everybody reacts that same way the first
time. I kept a little bedroom and the original bathroom
pretty much the way they were. The rest of the house I
modified to fit my needs. Have a seat. Please. Over at the
counter."

I followed him toward the back of the house, which was
all kitchen. He sat on a stool next to a huge worktable and I
sat beside him. Almost immediately, he popped back up and
said, "Some coffee?"

"Sure."

"Espresso okay?"

"Absolutely."

He nodded his approval and moved across the room to a
piston-driven espresso machine and began to grind beans to
make us coffee.

I tried to digest the rest of the room. It was dominated by
a lapis blue enamel La Cornue six-burner range. A few
months back, Lauren had sent for a catalog from the company and had not so discreetly let me know that she coveted
one for our remodeled kitchen. I had choked, literally, at
discovering that the range cost more than every car I'd ever
owned but the most recent one.

Across the room from the La Cornue range, a big stainless
steel and glass two-door commercial reach-in refrigerator/

freezer dominated the opposing wall. The kitchen counter-tops were all made of either polished granite or stainless steel, except for one large alcove that was fitted exclusively for baking. That countertop was a gorgeous bronze marble. The pot rack suspended from the ceiling above the work-table in the center of the room was adorned with a dizzying selection of cookware, some of it oversized, most of it gleaming copper.

Reggie Loomis's voice knocked me out of my reverie of astonishment. "Can I offer you a scone? I made them this morning. They're currant and buttermilk. Perfect with coffee."

"Sounds great. Thank you."

He placed a demitasse of espresso and a dessert plate with a scone in front of me and then retrieved the same for himself.

I tasted the scone and chased it with a sip of coffee that was coated with a perfect layer of *crema*. "This is delicious. Do you, um—I don't know how to ask this—do you run a catering business or something from here?"

He laughed. The sound was contained, even self-conscious. "Hardly. How do I explain all this? Some people rot in front of the TV when they retire. I call it tube rot. Some play golf. Some people fix up old cars. I have a friend who drives around the west in an old RV. Me? I decided that I'd indulge myself during my retirement by doing what I've always loved best. And I love to cook. My momma taught me to cook. It's always been my vice. I'm never going to have a kitchen with a better view, I thought, so why not just do it here?"

I allowed myself a moment to savor the view that domi-nated to the west. The grasses on the hogback sparkled like a field of gilded wheat. I noted that the sky was the same color as my host's eyes. "Yes," I said. "Why not?"

"I outfitted this place for less than it would cost to buy my friend's Winnebago. Did most of the work myself. Even had to cut a hole in the wall to get the La Cornue in here. Do you know it's seven years old? Looks brand-new, doesn't it? It's the one thing I own in this world where I can honestly say there is nothing better. That, sir, is the finest cooking appliance on the planet. Probably in the whole solar system, but of course that's just speculation."

"It's . . . truly impressive. My wife and I have just started to renovate our kitchen. I wish I'd seen what you did here first. The range is something."

"Yes, the best. There's no better," he said.

"Are you married, Mr. Loomis?"

"Oh, was. Yep. But that ended."

"Children?"

"They moved to Texas with their mother. I was never partial to Texas. Or to Texans, for that matter. She was. Is. Good kids, though. Boy and a girl. Good." He had a wry smile on his face as he spoke of his distant family. I couldn't imagine why.

"So you just cook for yourself?"

"Lord, no," he exclaimed, patting himself on the abdomen. "I do love to eat, but I try to be cautious as well. Moderation, you know? Discipline. It makes everything possible. Everything."

"So what do you do with all the food you make?"

He appeared quite embarrassed by my question. I wasn't sure he was planning to answer.

Finally, he said, "I feed shut-ins. Sick people. Disabled people. Word gets around at church, so I find out who could use a little hand. Who needs it. Some folks donate ingredients for me. The pastor keeps a pretty fair garden behind the church in the summer, and when the Lord steers the hailstorms elsewhere, the bounty from that garden of his is impressive. I fix what I can. People seem to appreciate well-prepared food. I learned that a long time ago.

"I do breakfast on Monday, Wednesday, and Friday. Supper on Thursday and Sunday. Sunday's a tough one for the shut-ins. They appreciate the food on Sunday most, I think. So breakfast and supper is what I do. I like the mornings best. Folks aren't so tired. Each morning, I choose a different one of my guests to go to last so I get a chance to chat with everybody once in a while. I don't drive anymore, so I get some help dropping the trays by. A church lady usually.

She and her son, with one of those big Chevys. What are they called? They look like troop transports? Evening meals, the pastor sends somebody over from the church. Sometimes he and I, we do it together."

I was touched by the generosity of his spirit. "Suburbans. Those big Chevys, they're called Suburbans. It's wonderful, what you're doing here."

"Wonderful? I don't know. Sometimes it feels generous. Sometimes it feels selfish. Who's to say?" He drained his coffee. "Who's to say what's good and bad in this life? Things I was once so proud of . . . well, now." He lifted his cup, using it as a prop. "I mean, other than a fine cup of coffee and an almost perfect scone, who is to say what's good and bad in this life?"

I shrugged. "You're right, of course. Who's to say?" I paused, then added, "It sounds like you're a religious man."

"Me? Religious? Hardly. But the beauty is . . . the beauty of it is that to God, it doesn't seem to really matter. The Lord has been gracious always. Generous often. And forgiving when I've needed it. What more can one ask?"

He stood and fussed with the dishes, moving them from the worktable over to a stainless-steel dishwasher built by the same German company that manufactured my spark plugs. His back turned to me, he asked, "C.R., right? You're looking for an ex-employee of mine with initials C.R. That's a tough puzzle. Inadequate data to work with, I'm afraid. That'd be like trying to concoct a decent little coulibiac when all you've been told is that the dish contains a portion or two of wild rice."

"And that would be hard?"

"Yes, it would." He smiled warmly. "But, believe me, it would be worth it. You ever had coulibiac?"

"I don't believe I have."

"Then you haven't. You wouldn't forget that. No . . . be like forgetting your first girl."

"Maybe I'll have a chance someday."

He didn't offer to whip one up for me. Instead, he returned his attention to my request. "But I don't recall any

C.R.s in my employ. May have been a few. Odds are that there were. What did he look like?"

"He was a white male, late twenties. Normal to stocky build. Light complexion." I tried to manufacture a snapshot in my head. I couldn't. "I'd say average height, five-ten, six feet. Maybe one-eighty. Crew cut, I think."

"That sounds like a hundred guys. Half the security officers at the plant looked like that."

"No one specific?"

"Sorry. If anything jogs my memory and makes this guy pop up, I'll be sure to let you know. You have a card? A business card you can leave with me?"

I pulled one from my wallet and held it in my hand. He was still across the room. I wasn't ready to be dismissed. I wanted him to keep talking. "It must have been tough at Rocky Flats then. In the early eighties, especially in security. So much was going on, so much, I don't know, negativity. In the country, in the community. It must have been a tough time."

"Oh, it was negative, all right. The pressure was enormous. Not only from the plant management. But from the Energy Department, the FBI, even some spooks who came around who I was sure were CIA. There were the damn protesters at the fence, the terrorist threat was constant, industrial espionage was always a concern, and there was always the problem of keeping tabs on the damn plutonium a damn microgram at a time. Not to mention keeping track of all the damn dirty waste. Well, well. Employees, too. Had to keep an eye on all of them. I swear half of them couldn't be trusted to check a fence for shorts. It was a hard time. But we had no incursions. I'm still proud of that. In my eight years as chief, we had no incursions."

"Incursions?"

"Penetrations of the internal security perimeter. None of the bad guys got in to sabotage us. I considered that was my primary responsibility. Counter-terrorism. Protecting the plant from subversives."

I didn't even want to consider the consequences of the havoc a bad guy could cause inside a place as toxic as Rocky Flats. A little plutonium here, a little plutonium there . . . I was tempted to ask Loomis if any of his predecessors or successors had been less successful at protecting the internal security perimeter than he was. But I feared he would begin to realize that he was talking out of school, and shut up.

"You were chief for what years?"

"1979 to 1987. Retired in '87."

"How many years did you have in?"

"Started in '63 as a guard. Twenty-four years in all. Some of those years were better than others. I used to be a hothead, see. Thought I knew everything. Made myself miserable for a stretch there at the beginning."

"Youth," I said.

He seemed to contemplate something. "I stayed young and foolish longer than most, I'm afraid. Never too late to grow up, though. That's what I finally decided. Confucius said that the best time to plant a tree is ten years ago. The second-best time is now. That says it all, I decided. That says it all."

I said, "In 1982, this employee I'm trying to find, this C.R., apparently caused a disturbance of some kind at work. The incident at the plant, whatever it was, was serious enough that someone in authority felt the employee needed to be evaluated by a psychiatrist. He was taken directly from work to the emergency room at the medical school hospital in Denver."

As casually as I could, as I was playing my second-best card, I examined the profile of Reggie's face. He remained, I thought, impassive. Perhaps his eyebrows elevated a millimeter or two, but that was all.

"You that psychiatrist?"

"No, I'm a psychologist."

"I recall that happening a couple of times. Disturbances. Employees who couldn't cut the mustard, handle the pressure. Sometimes I think just being around the juice made some of them crazy."

"The juice?"

"Plutonium. That's what I called it sometimes. Don't recall who might have been involved in those incidents, though. Like I said, long time ago. Wouldn't have taken much to get us to ferry someone away from the site back then. We required discipline at Rocky Flats in those days. Military-style discipline. Didn't tolerate much lip."

He still hadn't made a move to come across the room for my business card, and I didn't stand and extend it toward him. I decided that the time had come for me to play my trump card.

"One more thing; I almost forgot. This next part may seem odd. One of the reasons that this particular man is so memorable to all of us who were involved with him back then is that he kept going on and on about D. B. Cooper. You know, the hijacker? Kept telling everyone that he knew who D. B. Cooper was. Does that ring any bells?"

Loomis slid his lower jawbone to the left a good inch, giving his face a cockeyed slant. Then he shifted it the same distance to the right for about ten seconds before centering it. "Oh," he chuckled, and shook his head in a disbelieving gesture. "There's a memory, isn't it? I hadn't thought about that in years, but I'm not totally surprised to hear you say it. There was plenty of talk around the plant about all that D. B. Cooper stuff. Had been for years, actually, since a few years after the hijacking at least. Rumor was that Cooper, or whoever had pretended to be Cooper, actually worked at the Flats. It was all legend. Abominable snowman stuff, as far as I'm concerned. I'm not aware of anyone ever taking it seriously."

He narrowed his eyes and asked, "You didn't? Did you?" He employed a gotcha voice.

I shook my head. "No, I just thought it was curious. Thought it might help you pin down this guy's identity for me. You know, maybe there was one particular employee who just couldn't let the whole D. B. Cooper thing go."

"Bet he even offered to expose him? The real D. B. Cooper?"

"Why would you say that?"

"Happened all the time. Someone would have a beef about

somebody and suddenly everybody wanted to know if so-and-so was working or off that Thanksgiving weekend."

"How did it get started? The legend?"

"Don't rightly remember."

"But no one employee stands out?"

He appeared thoughtful for a moment. "Sorry. Maybe the personnel office at the plant can help you with those initials you have. Narrow down your search. I'm sure they still have the records. Maybe even photographs. Maybe they'll let you thumb through the photos."

"That won't work, I'm afraid. We asked around. Personnel records are confidential."

Reggie said, "Ah," and nodded in a way that told me he already knew that. "So, um, why do you need to find, um . . . this particular man?" Something about the exaggerated casualness of his question made me think that he was trying to appear uninterested.

I found that interesting.

"Some people have been hurt. Others are in some danger. We thought he could help us sort some things out." I didn't know what else I could say.

Reggie again said, "Ah."

TWENTY-ONE

I left Reggie Loomis's ersatz catering business just in time to get to my office to see my next patient, a woman named Victoria Pearsall. By necessity, I fought to set aside my frustration about accomplishing so little during the meeting with Loomis so I could focus on the business at hand. With Victoria, that meant attending to her continuing complaints about the harassment she allegedly suffered at the hands of her boss at Ball Aerospace. I'd listened to these litanies from Victoria on and off—mostly on—for months now and I'd decided that her boss was not only not the ogre she made him out to be but was a man with angelic patience who was a viable candidate for canonization. Despite persistent and, I thought, stellar efforts on my part at reflection, confrontation, and interpretation, Victoria and I concluded the session, as we had each and every previous one, with the great majority of Victoria's plated armor intact. As I said, "See you next week," I knew that this thirty-seven-year-old woman and I still had a long, long way to go to get to the root of her problem.

Which, of course, was her.

I barely had time to pee before my next patient arrived. His name was Riley Grant. Riley had been a patient of mine for almost three years, and the difficult days of his treatment were behind him. Originally, he'd been sent to me by a Boulder County judge who offered him a choice between psychotherapy and thirty days in a concrete room with steel bars in a dull neighborhood by the Boulder airport.

It says volumes about Riley that he asked the judge if he could think about his options overnight.

His crime? After the car he was driving was cut off by a bicyclist who was crossing Broadway on a red light at the Downtown Boulder Mall, Riley sped up in order to cut off the offending bicyclist at Canyon Boulevard. Riley then climbed out of his car, a big black Lexus, and proceeded to turn the offending bicycle into a piece of modern art that closely resembled a bird's nest constructed by a condor.

When provoked, Riley used to have quite a temper. When not provoked, Riley used to be merely a bully. But that was almost three years ago.

Now he was a reminder to me of the wonder of this work I did. Riley's progress gave me hope for Victoria. And I was confident someday she would give me hope for another patient whose intractable problems vexed me no end.

I worked well into the evening. My last two patients were both men in their late twenties with relationship issues. One was a gay computer cartographer named John Fry and the other one was a straight fireman named Tom Jenkins. Neither of them had been in treatment long. And neither was doing much work in therapy. That day I found myself pressing each one of them harder than I usually did. I wasn't sure why I felt so aggressive, but it didn't seem to make much difference in either treatment. I blamed it on Victoria and reminded myself that to tear down a wall, it was necessary to remove a lot of bricks.

John asked for an extra session the following week. Tom warned me that a change in his work schedule might force him to cancel his next appointment. He said he'd call. I felt a certain symmetry at work.

The night was moonless and dark by the time I locked up the building. Diane was long gone. She'd told me earlier in the day that she was going out house hunting with a real estate agent friend of hers.

One of the casualties of being on the hit list of a mass murderer was the loss of my routine. I felt as though I'd relinquished the capacity to accomplish the mundane or the habitual. Now, every act I performed required that I contemplate the possibility of danger. It was as though I were living in a haunted house that had been set up to spook me at any turn.

Did Diane usually leave the back door to her office unlocked? No, she didn't. Since this time she had, I was forced to retrace my steps and search the entire building where we had our offices to make sure no intruders had entered through her carelessly unlocked back door.

Only a week before, turning the deadbolt would have sufficed.

Outside, I walked once around my car before I got in, immediately locking the doors after me. I winced as I turned the key to the ignition, as though wincing would offer some protection against a car bomb. Twice, in the first couple of days after Arnie's funeral, I'd actually gotten down on my knees and examined the undercarriage of the Land Cruiser, looking for explosives. I stopped the ritual of genuflecting beside my car only after I admitted to myself that unless the mad bomber had conveniently marked his package "Dynamite" or "C-4," I probably wouldn't have been able to tell an explosive device from my catalytic converter.

Lauren was at some lawyers' function that she didn't want to attend, Sam was at an early season Avalanche game with his brother-in-law and niece, and since I'd already checked on Dresden's progress with the renovation and addition over my lunch hour, I had the evening to myself. Usually, I would have enjoyed the opportunity to have a few hours alone. Now, being alone let my paranoia run unchecked. Given the current circumstances, this was not a good thing.

Conjuring up an image of Sam's kidney stone—the fantasy closely resembled Gibraltar passing through a straw—I bypassed Nick-n-Willy's and instead stopped by Sushi Zanmai to pick up some sushi for dinner. I was tempted to sit at the sushi bar and eat, but guilt about my dog motivated me to take the food home. I stuck the styrofoam box in the refrigerator while I took Emily out for an evening stroll. She was still fascinated by the novel urban odors of her temporary home, and our walk through the western edge of the Hill was anything but brisk. She demonstrated not only a need to pee on an astonishing number of mysterious odors, but also a bladder capacity that defied logic. We concluded the stroll with a shortcut home that took us through the old Columbia Cemetery on Ninth Street. Although the walk hadn't been strenuous enough to get my heart rate up, walking through a century-old graveyard on a moonless night with a price on my head sure was.

The sushi was good. I poured a beer and tried to interest myself in the fall television season. It didn't work. The fall season, I mean. I watched a little of the hockey game that Sam was attending, but the Avs were up five-zip in the second period and I quickly lost interest in that, too.

My pager went off and I picked up a message off voice mail. It was Tom Jenkins, my patient from that afternoon, letting me know he was going to have to cover an extra shift the following week and needed to either cancel or reschedule. I made a note to call him at work the next day to try to find a new time.

After considering it for a few minutes, I asked Emily if I should phone Sawyer and tell her about meeting with Reggie Loomis. I interpreted her silence to mean "Sure, why not?"

I phoned Sawyer. The line was busy.

I read the note I'd written myself about Riley Grant. Immediately, I thought about Reggie Loomis. The juxtaposition allowed me to see something that had been hovering just outside the reach of my awareness all evening long.

The two men had a lot in common.

Reggie had told me that he used to be a hothead when he was young, that he had made himself miserable. That fact alone made Reggie a lot like Riley before he and I had started to work some of it out together in therapy. I pondered the question of how Reggie had managed to quiet his own fires, and transform himself from a hothead security specialist into a culinary philanthropist with a La Cornue.

* * *

The second time I called Santa Barbara, Sawyer answered, breathless, after the third ring.

"I had a feeling it was you. It's the only reason I picked up. I'm on the treadmill; I usually don't answer when I'm working out."

She was panting. I said, "I'll call back."

"No, no. Only eighty-three more seconds. I hate the damn grades more than the speed. How are you? Take your time answering. It's easier for me to listen than it is to talk."

I spent those eighty-three seconds relaying the gist of my visit with Reggie Loomis and the urban legends about D. B. Cooper.

"I'm done," she said. "Speaking of urban legends, do you get this whole endorphin thing? I've never felt high after exercising. Not once. I only feel sweaty and out of breath and tired."

"I, uh, I like to work out. But I'm not much of a runner."

"Figures. But basically no luck with your interview?"

"Basically. I may go back and see him again. Maybe he'll be more reflective after he gets time to think about it all. What about you? Wait, maybe we shouldn't be having this conversation on our home phones."

"It's okay. I had my house swept."

"What?"

"I have a lot of contacts in law enforcement. I had somebody check my house for the presence of bugs. I'm clean. I assume you are, too. Anyway, regarding Chester? I did good. Real good. I know who Chester is. I know where Chester lives. And I know what Chester does for a living."

I was impressed. "That's great. How did you do it?"

Her breathing was beginning to slow, her words no longer punctuated by sharp gasps for oxygen. "USCF. United States Chess Federation. Given what we remembered about him, I assumed he'd be a member. It wasn't that hard to find out the information. A lawyer friend of mine is a chess player, too. He made the call to the organization for me, pretended he was a tournament director and that they owed this guy prize money. Anyway, Chester's name is Victor Garrit-

son. He's an independent software consultant. And he lives
in the desert just outside Cave Creek, Arizona."

"That's near Phoenix, isn't it?"

"Good. Yes."

"What's next for us?"

"Shouldn't we pay him a visit? I think we should pay him
a visit unannounced. See the look on his face when he lays
eyes on us. You said you take Fridays off, right? So what are
you doing this Friday?"

"I guess," I said, "I'm flying to Phoenix."

"Me too," Sawyer allowed. "What a coincidence."

Lauren looked like she had the stamina of steam-table
vegetables when she got home from her legal affair. I lit two
candles, drew her a bath, and set up a nice plate of maguro,
unagi, and shinko maki for her to enjoy in the living room
after her bath.

She was pink and grateful and smelled of vanilla and
jasmine. All of it made me happy. While she began to
eat, I shared the details of my conversation with Sawyer,
especially her discoveries about Chester—leaving out his
real name—and asked her if she would come with me to
Arizona.

"I have a trial on Friday, hon. I can't go with you to
Phoenix."

"Any chance of a plea bargain?"

"Fifty-fifty. But you know how that goes. We may not
settle until ten minutes before trial."

"Damn," I said.

"You'll do fine," she assured me.

I wasn't sure exactly what she meant by that. Was she offering some confidence about the task at hand, interviewing
Chester? Or was she making a more profound comment
about my capacity to deal with the jumble of feelings I had
about Sawyer?

Before I could inquire, she said, "How was your little
meeting today? With that patient's boss you were going to
talk with?"

"More interesting than enlightening." I told her about

Reggie Loomis and the La Cornue, about his charity work, and his lack of specific memory of employees at Rocky Flats. I also explained that he felt the D. B. Cooper thing was a dead end. That the whole theory of Cooper working at the Flats had been tossed around at the plant for years after the hijacking. "He made it sound like it had become an institutional parlor game."

Her eyes smiled softly. She was more interested in Reggie Loomis's kitchen. "I'm envious. A six-burner La Cornue? But no griddle? I'd get a griddle on mine. I'm too addicted to pancakes."

"I didn't see a griddle."

"What color?"

"Blue."

"I think I'd get green. The blue's a little bold, don't you think?"

I teased, "Apparently I haven't given it as much thought as you have."

"Maybe you should. Your Mr. Loomis sounds nice enough. And what he does with the food deliveries to the needy is truly generous."

"I think he considers it kind of selfish. The cooking. He feels he gets more out of it than he gives."

We'd begun playing footsies. "When I got home," she said, "I was so tired that all I wanted to do was sleep. Now, after all this talk about giving and getting, I'm not so sure."

"Really?" I asked. "What did you have in mind?"

"How about Scrabble?"

I leaned forward and slid my hands up her legs. "Scrabble sounds good."

TWENTY-TWO

On the way out of town to the airport on Friday, I stopped in Spanish Hills to see how Dresden's work on the house was progressing. The hat he was wearing that day came from a remote spot on the northeast coast of Australia called Hook Island. We'd discussed this particular hat before. He'd dived that area of the Great Barrier Reef once already and had told me at least three times that it was his destination again the week after our job was finished.

"We're cooking," he explained, as he showed me the footers and foundation walls for the main-floor addition as well as the foundation for the new garage that was going up on the north side of our house. "As soon as the cement is cured, we'll have these two framed and trussed in no time."

The inside of the house had already gone from the demo stage to the reframing stage, and the outlines of the newly designed rooms were taking shape in an array of studs and electrical and plumbing rough-ins. The tradespeople hired by Dresden were typical Boulder subs. The electrician on the project was a huge man with dreadlocks and a Ph.D. in art history, the plumber was a retooled engineer who liked working for himself but dressed as though he were still employed by IBM.

As I did each time we met I inquired of Dresden about any new evidence of our previous intruder.

As he did each time we met he assured me that I had nothing to worry about.

Reassuring clients was one of Dresden's many innate

skills. I'd already decided that he would have made a great nanny.

The plan I'd worked out with Sawyer had me flying into Sky Harbor Airport in Phoenix, renting a car, and meeting her at a general aviation field in Scottsdale. She said she didn't like flying into big fields, and that it would be easier for me to rent a car at Sky Harbor than it would for her to rent one at the smaller airport.

I kissed Lauren good-bye, wished her luck with her trial, and gathered a few things together for my short trip to Arizona. Just as I was leaving the house she called me back into the kitchen and said, "Look."

She was directing me to the television. A brush and forest fire was out of control near Kittredge. "That's where Gary Hart lives, isn't it?" she asked.

"Is it?" I didn't know where Gary Hart lived, but I knew that Kittredge was twenty miles north along the foothills of the Front Range, in the sharp canyons west of Red Rocks amphitheater. Which meant we were in no danger in our temporary housing on the Hill in Boulder. I was too distracted by my need to get to Denver to pay much attention to the news. "I hope they get it under control. Did you see anything about airport traffic? I need to run."

I arrived at DIA in plenty of time to answer the page that Lauren directed toward my beeper during my drive. She hadn't used our agreed-upon emergency code, so I managed to keep my pulse in double digits as I punched in our home number and said, "Hi. It's me. What's up? Miss me too much already?"

"Hardly. Didn't you tell me that that doctor lives near Kittredge? The one who saw those patients in the emergency room? You know, the one you talked to over the weekend."

"Sheldon? He lives outside of Morrison."

"Kittredge is outside of Morrison, isn't it?"

Oh no. Oh shit. "You don't think—?"

"I don't—"

"Jesus. I hope this is a coincidence. Find out what you

can. I'll call you from Phoenix, okay? Wait, let me give you his phone number. Maybe you can reach him." I dug around in my DayTimer and found the number. "His name is Sheldon Salgado. Got it?"

"Yes," she said, her voice tight. I dictated the number.

My United shuttle departed Denver on time and arrived in Phoenix early. I tried to reach Lauren as soon as I got off the plane. The home line was busy. I wasted a few minutes in an airport bar hoping to see the news of the Colorado forest fire on CNN. Instead I raised my blood pressure fifteen points watching three representatives and two senators argue that there was really no need for campaign finance reform.

Excuse me?

After trying to call home again—no answer this time; she must have been on her way to work—I took the little yellow Hertz bus to pick up my car. They had my nondescript Ford waiting in my preassigned spot. I surprised myself by not getting lost on the way to the Scottsdale airport. I arrived at eleven-thirty, fifteen minutes before Sawyer had estimated that she would be touching down.

Forest fires, even distant ones, are not uncontaminated emotional events in my life. One of my dear friends had watched people die in a voracious fire in Wyoming, and the scars from that event affected his life every day. I'd heard his brother tell the story of the ferocity of the Wyoming fire and had even flown over the skeletal remains of the forest that had been the fuel. I'd been up between Kittredge and Morrison many times and had no trouble imagining the terrain, the dry lodgepole, and the golden brush. I could see the dream homes and the don't-bother-me cabins that dotted the dirt roads. And I had no trouble conjuring the devastation that fierce wind and abundant fuel could cause to that mountain enclave after a solitary spark.

Inside the spacious waiting area of Blue Skies Aviation, I approached the counter and asked if a plane piloted by Sawyer Faire had landed yet. The man at the counter was in his early twenties but had already lost much of his hair. The embroidery on his polo shirt told me that his name was Guy.

His eyes were a distracting pale chocolate in color. After greeting me with a big smile he said they'd had no incoming this morning except for regulars. He offered to check with someone in back to be certain and disappeared into an adjacent office. A moment later he returned and told me that Gloria didn't think that my friend had been in yet. I thanked him, turned, found a pay phone and once more tried to reach Lauren, this time at work.

"Lauren Crowder," she answered, in her professional voice. I knew the voice well. She used it with me when it was time to take out the garbage or when it was my turn to perform the Tootsie Roll patrol duties around our house. Sometimes she used it during the almost-there moments of hurried sex.

"It's me."

"No good news, I'm afraid. The fire is definitely in the vicinity of his house. There's no answer when I call. Television reports said the fire started around three in the morning. So, he and his family—you said he had a family, right?"

"Yes."

"They must have been home when it started. I mean, at that hour? Unless they're out of town somewhere, they had to be home."

"I'd imagine. Any houses destroyed yet?"

"New reports are unclear. One said two 'structures' were engulfed, whatever that means. And I haven't been able to watch the news at all since I got to work. I'm real busy here—I'm sorry. You know, the trial this afternoon? There's a plea-bargain prayer blowing in the door. We're scrambling to agree on a response."

"It's okay. I'll try to find out what I can from this end. Maybe he's at work or maybe his secretary at the hospital knows something. Listen, sweets, um, do you have your gun with you?"

She hesitated and lowered her voice before she responded. "Are we going to fight about it if I do?"

"No, we're not."

"Then, yes, I do."

"Good," I said. Instantly, I couldn't believe that I'd said it.

While I waited for Sawyer's plane to arrive, I tried Sheldon Salgado's office but got a recording. I didn't leave a message. Then I phoned Sam. He was home. I filled him in on my concerns about Salgado and his home in the canyons outside of Kittredge and asked if he could learn anything through cop channels about the progress of the fire.

"Hell, yes. Give me something useful to do. I'm going nuts here. Where can I call you?"

"You can't. I'll get back to you. Say, half an hour?"

"I'll have something by then. Lauren's safe?"

"Just spoke to her at work. She has the Glock with her."

"Good. Still waiting for you to take those lessons."

"I'm thinking about it, Sam. Believe me."

"Call me back."

As I placed the receiver back on the hook, I turned and found myself looking down on the receding crown of Guy's head. I realized the floor behind the counter must be higher than the waiting area and that Guy was a good six inches smaller than I had given him credit for.

He looked up and into my eyes, quite comfortable with his height. "You know what kind of plane your friend flies, by any chance?"

"Yes, it's a Beechcraft, a Bonanza, I think she said. Is she here?"

"There's some tower talk you might be interested in. Come on over—we'll let you listen in."

I followed him to the office in back, where a woman no older than Guy was sitting behind a steel desk examining invoices. She had curly blond hair that tumbled past her shoulders. The phone she was holding had disappeared into the thicket of locks in the general vicinity of her ear. She smiled a toothy smile at me and pointed to a chair with the sharp end of a pencil. Guy remained standing.

Without another word she hung up and said, "Hi, I'm Gloria." She adjusted the volume on a radio tuned to the tower frequency. "I just got off the phone with the tower.

They have a Beechcraft Bonanza B-36, call five-six Fox-trot. Ring a bell? It's having a problem with its front gear and they have it circling the field. Does that sound like it could be your friend?"

"What kind of problem?" I hoped it didn't mean what I thought it meant.

Guy explained, "Front landing gear won't come down."

"Oh, my God."

"She has plenty of fuel, apparently. She's going to try a few things to bring the gear down."

"And if she can't?"

Guy's full lips disappeared into a tight pink line. He said, "She's going to have to scratch her belly, I'm afraid."

For some reason I couldn't understand, I knew exactly what he meant.

"What are they saying now?" I couldn't make sense of the voices coming over the tinny speaker.

Gloria listened for a moment. "They're talking to a Lear-jet that's on final. That's not your friend."

"That's Bert's plane. He's one of our regulars," added Guy.

"Aren't they going to foam the runway or something? Get ready for her? Has somebody called an ambulance?"

"Would you like some coffee?" asked Gloria in a sweet voice. She was trying not to be patronizing. "This is going to take a while to settle out. She'll probably get it to come down."

I thought of Sam and Sheldon Salgado. I said, "No, I think I need to make another phone call. Come get me if anything changes, okay?"

"Of course," said Gloria. "You won't have that coffee? I made it myself and I'm good."

At that, Guy blushed. I said, "Sure. I will, thanks."

Sam answered even before I heard the phone ring. "Alan?"

"Yes. You have something?"

"Talked to a JeffCo deputy, a friend of mine. They have two houses burned, six more are in danger. The fire is on both sides of a county road just outside of Kittredge. They're thinking arson."

"Jesus. Any casualties?"

"None confirmed. It's a big fire, though. He says it's just chaos up there, trying to get crews in and residents out."

"I don't know if it's related to the fire, Sam, but my friend Sawyer's in trouble in her plane. She's circling the airport right now. Apparently her landing gear won't come down."

"You shittin' me?"

"No."

In a voice that let me know he wasn't expecting an argument from me, he said, "If you don't have any objections, I think I'm going to go check on Lauren. I got nothing better to do today."

If this guy was trying to make me feel totally out of control, he was succeeding. A forest fire was threatening a colleague six hundred miles away and a faulty airplane was endangering an ex-lover a few thousand feet above my head. A basic tenet of psychotherapy says that if you want to know what a person is trying to communicate to you, take a look at how his behavior makes you feel.

This time it was easy. This guy wanted me to know how it felt to be absolutely out of control when everything is on the line.

He wanted me to feel vulnerable.

He wanted me to feel helpless.

He wanted me to know how it felt to know that he could rip anything he wanted from my life.

The main question in my mind right then was, did he want me to feel grief? Did he plan for Sawyer and Sheldon to die today?

I prayed not. Because if his goal was to kill them, I felt that Sawyer had no chance at all to fix her recalcitrant landing gear. And if he intended that Sheldon was to die, then Sheldon's corpse was probably already charred and curled into a fetal position in the ruins of his home.

I realized that in my mind I was granting this adversary power that seemed almost superhuman. I was feeling his presence as I might that of a malevolent god, or of some satanic force. I was feeling that he was invincible.

Outside Blue Skies I stood on the tarmac and stared into the brightness. Guy pointed out which dot traversing the airspace above the field was Sawyer's plane. He reassured me that she had plenty of fuel.

I felt like saying, "So what?" It was like telling me that somebody who was having a heart attack had a good appetite.

Gloria was inside, her focus divided between the tower traffic and, at my request, CNN. I had asked her to keep an eye out for news of a forest fire in Colorado. She was so sweet she didn't even ask why.

My pager vibrated on my hip. I'd forgotten that the pager company had told me that with my new state-of-the-art pager, I could roam. Which, the salesman explained, meant I could be reached anywhere. At the time I wondered whether or not that was a good thing.

The phone number on the screen was the DA's office in Boulder. Lauren was calling.

I raced back to the pay phone and called her.

"Sam just told me about Sawyer, Alan. Is she okay?"

"She's still up there. I can see her circling when I go outside."

"Can they do anything?"

"There is apparently a manual backup system, a crank of some kind, something that allows her an alternative way to lower the gear. She's trying it now."

"Then who's flying the plane?"

I hadn't thought about that. "Autopilot, I guess. Anything new about the fire? About Sheldon?"

"No. Sam has calls out. He's out talking to my secretary. He's waiting for his cell phone to ring." She lowered her voice. "Alan, I'm worried about his health. Should he be doing this? Isn't this too stressful for him?"

"I don't know. But my guess is that trying to get him to leave would be more stressful on both of you than allowing him to stay and—"

"Hold on a second. I hear Sam's phone ringing. I think his call just came in."

For a long minute all I could hear was background music. Then Sam speaking, and Lauren responding. Sam again.

To me, she said, "They think his house is one of the ones that burned. Sheldon's house is one of the first two that went up."

My heart felt swollen with responsibility. Had I led this animal to Sheldon Salgado's door? I'd been so careful.

"Casualties?"

I heard her say, "Sam, did they find any bodies?"

To me, she said, "He doesn't know. Just shrugged his shoulders."

TWENTY-THREE

As I hung up the phone, my mind wandered back a few mornings and I could almost feel the sensation of watching that ceiling joist descend directly toward my head in the rubble of our renovation. I tried to shake off the image as I walked outside to the tarmac and approached Guy. He was facing away from me, toward the north. I asked him to point out Sawyer's plane again. He directed me to the far side of the field, toward a speck that was on the underside of a sheer stream of clouds just above the ridgeline of some beautiful mountains. I had trouble picking it up.

He pointed again and I tried to sight down his arm.

In the distance, I heard one siren, then, I thought, two. I wondered if the emergency vehicles were coming to the airport to prepare for Sawyer's attempt to land. As I finally identified the speck in the distance that was her plane, I said a silent prayer that this whole refrain of terror was merely her ceiling joist falling; that she would duck this bullet as I had ducked that one.

Guy said, "While you were on the phone, um, before? Your friend told the tower that, uh, it wouldn't go. She said she couldn't lower the front gear with the crank. The fix wasn't working."

My knees felt weak. "So is she on her way down?" I wanted to put that off as long as possible.

"Not yet. They have a call out to the FBO at Sky Harbor and to the manufacturer. To see if the maintenance people at Beech have other suggestions."

I was about to ask what an FBO was when I heard Gloria's voice call my name. I turned to see her holding open the door that led from the tarmac to the waiting room. This was my first opportunity to see her out from behind the desk. She was wearing an incredibly short pleated yellow skirt and had the most attractive legs I had ever seen in my life. She held her hair with one hand as the wind gusted and called out, "It's the tower. The controller says she wants to talk to you. Your friend in the plane? She's going to switch frequencies. You'll be able to talk with her on our handheld radio."

Guy and I ran inside.

Gloria resumed her spot behind her desk. I tried to make sense of my temporary fixation on her splendid legs as she sat and those legs disappeared behind the black metal skirt of the desk. Couldn't. I watched her adjust the frequency on the handheld radio to 122.75 and grabbed it as soon as she offered it to me.

"The connection may not be great," she warned me. "Just push that button to talk."

It wasn't.

"Sawyer, is that you?"

"Alan? God. It's good to hear your voice. If my dad was here, he'd say I'm in a fine pickle."

The sound was scratchy. I spent an extra second processing her words. "The gear just won't come down?"

"Not yet. I think if he did me, he did me good."

"Don't say that. This is only intended to frighten you."

"It's working."

"Sorry. Didn't get that."

"I said it's working. I'm scared."

"How much fuel do you have left?"

"Twenty minutes, half an hour."

"You can bring it down, you know. You can. You'll just scratch the belly a little bit."

"It's not the belly I'm worried about. It's burying the propeller. That's when things will get dicey."

"You can do it." I didn't have a clue what it would require of Sawyer to avoid burying the propeller. I was afraid I was doing nothing more than an adequate impression of a shrink standing on the sidelines leading cheers for some psychological athletic competition.

"You know what? Time is passing pretty slowly up here and this is all reminding me of that time on the unit. That patient of Arnie's who had the knife. Do you remember?"

My reaction, which I kept to myself, was that Travis, Arnie's patient with the Swiss Army knife, was a rank amateur compared to whoever it was who had screwed with Sawyer's landing gear. I said, "Of course I remember. But I don't think I'm going to be of much help this time. You'll do fine on your own."

"Thanks for your vote of confidence." Her tone was sardonic.

I thought she was going to say something else. She didn't. The silence between us grew into seconds and felt awkward. I could think of nothing to say that didn't sound banal. She cracked it. "I'm afraid that I need to go. See if the folks at the Beechcraft factory in Wichita have checked in with any advice. I wish I knew why the manual assist isn't working. But, hey, I'll see you one way or another in about half an hour, right?"

"I'm counting on it," I said. I was aware that the circumstances were beseeching something emotional from me and I consciously fought an impulse to tell her that I loved her.

I assumed it was ancient. The impulse.

"Bye," she said.

Guy walked with me as I returned to the tarmac. We waited, staring at the sky, watching the gray dot that was Sawyer grow in size as the plane approached us then receded into the distant sky and she flew away. Once or twice I lost sight of the plane altogether. I wondered if it had exploded or disintegrated but kept the thought private, holding my breath until the sunlight again glinted off metal or glass and I could discern it in the distance.

Gloria joined us after a few minutes. I smelled her perfume before I heard her approach. She stood between Guy and me, slightly behind us. "The tower was thinking of moving her over to Sky Harbor or Williams, but she's going

to have to come down here. There's a UPS plane with a
blown tire blocking a runway intersection at Sky Harbor
anyway. They're mobilizing the emergency equipment to
get in place here."

Could anything else go wrong? "What will it be like?" I
asked. "When she comes down."

Gloria touched my wrist as she answered, "Most situations like this end up okay. A lot depends on these winds
we're having. They've been gusting like this all morning.
In calm air— How experienced is she, anyway?"

"I'm not sure. She flies all the time. It's her own plane."

"That's good. Assuming she's experienced, in calm air
she should be able to get it down okay. She's going to have
to make sure she keeps that nose up, though, to—"

"Keep the propeller off the runway."

"Yeah."

"She told me about that while we were on the radio," I explained. "But if the wind gusts?"

A tiny plane with two seats and its wing mounted above
the cabin began to taxi past us, the sharp drone of its engine
stopping our dialogue. Guy yelled in my ear, "That's a
Cessna. A one-fifty. It's not like your friend's. Hers is much
bigger than that one and has the wing below."

Gloria waited until the small plane had taxied away to answer my earlier question about the wind. "Everything about
landing is harder in crosswinds like this. Without the gear
down, her margin for error is seriously reduced because
the propeller blades are so much closer to the ground when
she actually touches down. Does that make sense?"

I nodded.

"The good news is that she'll be running almost dry. The
risk of fire if anything, you know, goes wrong will be reduced. The controllers have called a couple of senior instructors into the tower to coach her down. She'll cut all her
power at the end."

Guy asked, "Is Tom up there? In the tower?"

Gloria nodded, then explained to me, "Tom's our lead instructor. He taught both of us to fly. He's good."

Guy seconded the opinion about their instructor and then

asked Gloria something about another employee who was late showing up for work. As she answered, my mind drifted to Sawyer. Although I'd never seen her plane, I'd been in small aircraft before. I could see her in the little cockpit with the high dash, the propeller blades cutting a neat, perfectly rounded arc in front of her. She hadn't sounded that frightened on the phone. I wondered if she was terrified.

Gloria turned to leave. "Oh, by the way, nothing on TV about that fire in Colorado. Sorry." She reached back and touched me on my shoulder.

"Thanks for checking."

Guy nodded at the sky and asked, "Is she, like, your girl-friend? The woman in the plane?"

I shook my head. "No," I said, "just an old friend." To make conversation, I added, "What about Gloria? Are you and she . . . ?"

He laughed.

We stared at the sky some more.

A minute later, no more, Gloria came running back outside through the glass doors, her pleated skirt and blond waves bouncing in unison. She cried, "She's out of fuel. She's coming in without power."

What?

"She's out of fuel? I thought she said she had plenty of fuel? What the hell happened?"

"I don't know. I was inside listening to the tower traffic, and in a calm voice she suddenly reports she's losing power. Tom called over. He thinks the fuel gauges must be inaccurate."

"What now?"

Gloria said, "It means it's an engine-out landing."

"Which means what?"

"Which means that for right now she's flying a glider."

"Her plane will glide all right?"

"Yes. She's done it before; she's practiced engine-out landings. We all have. It's part of the training."

"But not without landing gear?"

"No. She doesn't have any practice doing engine-outs

without landing gear. That part's brand-new for her. But at least she won't have to worry about the propeller problem anymore."

"Why not?"

"It won't be spinning. Before, with power, she would have had to cut the engine just as she flared for touchdown in order to still the propeller blades. Now she doesn't have to worry about it. What she does have to do is pray that none of the blades stopped in the six o'clock position."

"Because then she'll bury it?"

Gloria said, "Yes. Then she'll bury it. It'll protrude below the fuselage for sure."

My heart was forcing blood into my arteries ferociously. I could hear it roar in my ears. I could feel the pressure building in my vessels. My muscles were taut and ready for my adversary. I felt absolutely ready to take on a thousand monsters.

But there was nothing I could do.

I asked, "Where will she come down?"

"Over there." Guy pointed. "On twenty-one."

"How soon?"

"Any minute."

TWENTY-FOUR

"I'd like to go over there. To the runway, where we can see her come in. Can we drive over there?"

"Not to the runway," Gloria said. "But we can drive over to Desert Aviation. They're right on the other side of the taxiway. They're in a better position to see her approach."

Guy said, "Good idea. I'll get the truck."

We squeezed into the cab of a little Nissan pickup with the Blue Skies Aviation logo on the doors and followed some indecipherable path on the tarmac to the offices and hangars of Desert Aviation. I assumed that Desert was Blue Skies' main competitor at the airport. Guy parked the truck in a lot that was out of sight of the runway. The three of us hopped out of the cab and ran around the corner of the building. Half a dozen employees were already outside, strung out like pearls on a string, watching the denouement of the events that they, too, had been following on the tower radio.

A couple of the men found Gloria's approach much more interesting than they found Sawyer's. One of them smiled at her. She seemed not to notice. He turned to her and said, "Is that one of yours up there?"

Without looking at him, she said, "No. We're just going to service it. The pilot's his girlfriend." She pointed at me, granting me the smile the other man coveted.

I didn't correct her about the girlfriend part.

Car crashes feel like they happen in slow motion. Plane

wrecks, it turns out, actually do. I remembered the video of the DC-10 somersaulting into the cornfield in Sioux City, and the fascinating tape of the 747 almost managing to belly-land just off the beach on that island off the coast of Africa.

The Desert Aviation mechanic, whose interest in Gloria hadn't waned, moved close to us. He had some binoculars around his neck. To impress Gloria, he took on the responsibility of providing a play-by-play on Sawyer's approach. His buddy fell into line doing the color.

The mechanic raised the binoculars. "Okay, she's just turning into final. I'd say she's a mile out."

"No, not that far. Is she low?"

"She's not low."

"If she's low she's screwed."

"She's not low."

"Still no gear?"

"Still no gear."

Gloria leaned over and whispered into my ear, "I think she is a little low. Not awful, but a little. I'd want to be up another hundred feet."

"What does that mean? Being a little low?"

"If she had power, it wouldn't mean anything. She'd just goose the throttle and get the altitude back. But remember she's gliding. If I'm right, she's gonna need some help from the winds to reach the runway."

I didn't like the sound of what I was hearing. "And if she doesn't get them? The winds?"

"She'll hit short. In the sagebrush. And she doesn't want to do that. There're no obstacles out there, but it's not level. And she needs level ground for this kind of landing." She squinted toward the sky. "But first, right now, she needs to fight a temptation to pull the nose up, because that will only drop her faster."

I assumed there wasn't time to remedy my ignorance about the laws that govern flight. Why, I wanted to know, would pointing the plane's nose up bring it down? I didn't ask.

"Glide path looks good," said one mechanic.

"Wrong again. I say she's low," offered his pessimistic friend.

"She's not low."

"You watch," he challenged.

In my periphery, I saw a fire truck pull into position on a taxiway almost directly in front of the tower. A hundred yards beyond it, parked in the shadows, was an ambulance with its engine running. Two paramedics stood in front of their vehicle, their hands cupping their eyes, trying to enhance their view.

Gloria touched my forearm gently, and her kindness shocked me back to attending to the sky above runway twenty-one.

The mechanic said, "She's over the highway. She's coming down short. Glide path *is* a little low. You were right, you little shit."

The little shit gleefully punched his buddy on the biceps. If any money changed hands I was going to kill one of them.

To me, Gloria whispered, "She's not doing too badly. She may still be able to catch the end of the pavement. Come on, Lord. Give her a lift, just a little updraft from the heat. Come on. Come on."

I could see the small plane clearly now. The first thing I checked was the position of the propeller blades. None of the three blades was near six o'clock. Not exactly four and eight, though—maybe three-thirty and seven-thirty. How far out was she? I couldn't tell. But I could tell that Sawyer's plane was no more than seventy-five feet from the ground and that she was descending fast. The wings were rocking up and down and the tail seemed to be scooting off to one side.

"Is she doing that? Why is she doing that to the tail?"

Gloria said, "She's crabbing. Those crosswinds I told you about? She's trying to stay aligned with the runway."

"How's her altitude?"

She squeezed my hand and said, "I sure wish she was up a little higher." Her tone was as light as helium. Almost like a prayer.

* * *

The plane was twenty feet from the ground yet seemed to be over a hundred yards from the beginning of the macadam. Sawyer wasn't going to make it.

As though she was reading my thoughts, Gloria said, "Sometimes here, in the desert, you feel it just before you touch down. A little bounce from the heat radiating off the ground. That's all she needs here. Just a little bounce from the sun gods. Just a solar push."

I reminded myself to breathe.

Guy said, "There! Look! She's up a little, isn't she?"

To my amazement, I could see it. I could see the results of an invisible hand that gently lifted the plane five feet higher, maybe ten. And it was apparent that Sawyer was fighting the controls. She brought the nose down once, then again. She jammed the tail over to the left.

"One more," Gloria implored. "We need one more bounce."

And there it was.

A bigger bounce this time. No mistaking it. A certain ten feet. Suddenly, the nose of Sawyer's plane was above the parallel stripes at the end of the runway. Everyone cheered.

Except for me. I waited for the sparks and the screech and prayed I wouldn't see the propeller blades dig into the asphalt.

And then, all at once, it seemed it was over. The emergency trucks started rushing toward the plane. The crowd was cheering. Gloria was embracing me and telling me that God was so good, so good.

I noticed that my beeper was vibrating on my hip, and I wondered if Sheldon Salgado would agree with Gloria about God's good graces.

The Bonanza had scratched to a stop and sat forlornly in the middle of the runway, just left of the center. The door on the pilot's side opened and Sawyer climbed out and stood on the wing. She waved.

Right at me.

I started to walk toward her. No one stopped me, so I started to run. The paramedics got to her first, the firefighters only seconds behind. I weaved through the crowd that quickly gathered around the plane, found her just as she found me, and hugged her tightly.

"Great job," I said. "Incredible landing."

Into my ear, she said, "I don't know about that. But I'm glad you're here. I think I need a doctor."

Behind me someone was saying it was remarkable, that there wasn't much damage.

I thought, maybe not to the plane.

My beeper vibrated again.

Twenty minutes later, Sawyer was huddled beside her plane with Guy and the chief mechanic for Blue Skies Aviation. I went back to the waiting area to find out what my two pages were about.

The number on my pager was that of Sam's cell phone.

"Alan? Where the hell have you been? You didn't get my pages?"

"No, I got them. It's been nuts here, Sam. Real touch and go, but Sawyer got down okay. I'm sure the plane was sabotaged. A real sweet job. Our guy's fingerprints are all over everything."

"Not literally, right? Can't tie him to it?"

"No, I'm babbling. Not literally."

"Well, the news isn't so good here. There are three bodies in that doctor's house. But they're too scorched to ID."

"Oh, God."

"Yeah. I'm sorry."

My reaction to Sheldon's death was going to take some time to sort out. The most pressing feelings were responsibility and anger. Fear was in there, too. I asked Sam, "You feeling okay?"

"Me? I'm fine. But nobody's trying to kill me. It's the rest of you that I'm worried about."

"Is Lauren doing all right?"

"She's upset. But she's strong, you know that. She's in a conference right now, bargaining away one of my collars, probably. A whole gaggle of suits in there with her. I think

I'm going to stick around for a while, maybe see her home, you know. Make sure that it's safe."

"Thanks, Sam."

"Listen, you're going to be home tonight, right? We're still on for walking tomorrow?"

"Yeah. I'm looking forward to it. How's the diet?"

"Don't ask."

Sawyer insisted that, despite the mishap with her plane, we keep our plans to drive to Cave Creek to confront Victor Garritson, aka Chester. Even as I drove off the airport property, I was still arguing that we accept the cards that fate had been dealing us and just fly—commercially—back to our respective homes.

"You won't get far using gambling metaphors with me, Alan. It's my territory, remember. And I don't like being intimidated."

"That wasn't intimidation up there. That was attempted murder."

"I'm not convinced."

"Wait a second. You accept that Chester or D.B. or whoever it is sabotaged your plane?"

"We looked. That mechanic and me—he's good, by the way. We couldn't find anything. No evidence of sabotage at all."

"You're saying this was a coincidence? That your landing gear wouldn't come down *and* your fuel gauge misrepresented your fuel reserves? I'm sorry, but I'm afraid your denial is out of control, Sawyer."

She folded the map she was holding with great care and said, "One of the first rules of medicine, and you know this, Alan, is that rare things happen rarely. I treat this as a mechanical problem until we see the evidence otherwise." She poked at the map with her index finger. "Next left. We're going northeast."

I pulled into the left lane.

She asked me, "Ever seen a card shark in action, a really good one? Someone who can deal off the top of the deck, or the bottom of the deck, or out of the middle of the deck, and you're watching for it and you can't see him do it and you can't figure any of it out?"

"Yes. I saw one on HBO." I didn't know where we were going with this conversation.

"What did you think?"

"I was impressed. He announced what he was going to do before he did it and I still couldn't see him do it. Your point?"

"Don't you see? Chester or D.B. or whoever it is that's after us is that clever. We know he's cheating, but he's so good we can't even catch him cheating. What's the lesson. The lesson is we can't play cards with him. Because he'll always, always end up with the aces. And we won't know how he did it."

"You're making my argument for me, Sawyer. That's all the more reason to head home. Now."

"Without seeing this Victor Garritson? No way. Alan, together we have, what, thirty-some-odd years of clinical experience? I spend half my waking hours with sociopaths, either inmates or their lawyers. We'll be able to tell. We'll know if he's the one, Alan. It takes something special, some advanced arrogance, some ultimate confidence, to do this. To cheat while the world is watching and know that they can't catch you. I want to look in Garritson's eyes and see if he has it. That arrogance."

"That's all you want to do?"

"You don't believe me?"

I didn't answer. After completing the turn I guided the Taurus into the right lane and pulled into the driveway of the first restaurant I spotted. "I'm hungry," I explained.

"Uh-oh," she responded.

Our waitress could have been Gloria-from-the-airport's little sister. Blond wavy hair and legs up to who knows where. Sawyer ordered a Coke and toast and jam. I ordered a breakfast that Sam would kill for.

Sawyer noticed our waitress's resemblance to Gloria, too. "Our waitress's twin? That girl at the airport? She's sweet on you."

"Sweet on me? What are you talking about?"

"The one with the pleats and the legs."

"Gloria."

"Yes, Gloria. I think she was yours for the asking."

"You think you know about these things?"

"Yeah. That first day I met you, when I saw you walk into Mona's party, I felt the same thing. I was yours for the asking."

"You sure didn't act like it."

" 'Act' is the operative word. You didn't do any asking."

"I was kind of shy."

"You got over it quickly enough."

I was afraid I was blushing. I said, "I'm happily married to a great woman. I'm not shopping around."

She smiled coyly, shrugged and raised her eyebrows.

I wanted to know where she was heading but not as much as I wanted to change the subject. "Before, back on the highway, when I said I was hungry, why did you say, 'Uh-oh'?"

"Because way back when, whenever you wanted to talk, you know, seriously, you always tried to do it over a meal. You did it again last week when we were in Vegas. I wanted to gamble, you wanted to nosh."

I nodded. It was an interesting observation. At first blush, I had to admit it had the ring of truth.

"This time you're right, I guess."

"I'm usually right about the little things."

"Just the little things?"

"Unfortunately." She sipped at her Coke.

I said, "I do have something serious to talk about. That call I made while you were in the hangar? It looks like Sheldon Salgado is dead, Sawyer. He died this morning sometime."

I waited for her to react.

Her eyelids drifted down and her eyes closed. A tear formed in the outer corner of each eye and her shoulders inched up. I reached over and unwrapped her hand from her red plastic glass of Coke and entwined my fingers with hers. The tears dropped one at a time. The left one migrated down her cheek in an uneven path. The right one fell to her lap.

"What happened?" she said.

Not "What did he do to him?"

I told her about the area where Sheldon lived in the foothills. About the fire overnight. About Sam's call that came with the news that three bodies had been found just as Sawyer was scraping her plane's belly along the runway.

"Three?"

"That's what my friend said."

Sawyer wanted to talk about the third of the three bodies. "You ever meet his baby? Sheldon's baby? She was born during the first week of the second year of the residency. Sheldon and Susie called her Olivia."

"No, I never met her. I wasn't that close to Sheldon. She would be, what, almost sixteen now?"

"Something like that. If she's still alive."

She stared out the window and watched as the driver of an eighteen-wheeler tried to maneuver his rig into a no-prayer space in the small parking lot. Her voice devoid of affect, she said, "She was a gorgeous baby. She didn't deserve to die. Olivia."

I said, "I know." What gorgeous baby deserves to die?

Sawyer shook her head and started to cry. I thought she might weep for a moment as the shock of Sheldon's death seeped into her. But her composure evaporated and she dissolved into grief. She lowered her face into her hands and didn't seem to be able to stop crying.

The rest of the patrons in the restaurant stared at me with rancorous glares. The waitress who resembled Gloria looked as though she would gladly stab my eye out with her pencil.

I realized they all figured I had just dumped Sawyer. I could see the irony distorted in the distance, as if through a thick fog.

TWENTY-FIVE

Sawyer wouldn't be dissuaded from continuing out to Cave Creek to lay eyes on Victor Garritson. She was actually confident that she could pick a killer in disguise out of the crush of humanity at a cocktail party. "I talk to murderers every day. I'll know him after a few minutes. Next left, we're almost there."

I turned left.

Her anguish over the death of Sheldon Salgado and his family had subsided as abruptly as it had flared. The demeanor she adopted after our brief meal reminded me of the one she had worn to keep me at bay emotionally during our training. She wasn't exactly aloof, not exactly cold. But there was no invitation in her tone, no welcome in her smile. She wasn't telling me to go away. She was telling me to stay exactly where I was.

To watch my step.

"You know, he's changing in front of our eyes, Sawyer. This man, this murderer we're after."

"What do you mean? Like a chameleon?"

"No. I'm thinking maybe deterioration, not camouflage. He's losing patience. The, um, rapidity is troubling. He used to take two years or more to plan one of these murders. Now he hits Sheldon and you in the same night. That's a radical change. He's under pressure of some kind, he must be. Why the rush? I think there's little doubt that he's starting to get sloppy. We need to take advantage of his change in mental state."

"All the more reason to confront Garritson now. We can examine that mental state face to face."

"What are you suggesting? I thought we were going to Cave Creek to 'eyeball' Garritson. What's this about confronting him?"

"Semantics," she argued, shaking the map. "Next right. That's his street."

Victor Garritson lived in a trailer park, the Red Sky Mobile Home Village. The park and its trailers had been well maintained, but were certainly a decade or more past their prime. Red Sky wasn't some contemporary community of "manufactured homes"; this was a trailer park that provided marginal housing to working people living on the margins. No double-wides here, no shiny Ford Expeditions parked beside the front doors. Red Sky consisted of a few dozen trailers, a lot of dust and sand, some mature oleanders, and a few trees that would rather be living elsewhere.

Victor lived in 103. Sawyer barked out directions to his pad as though she'd reconnoitered the place the night before. I stopped the Taurus two trailers away and examined Victor's abode from a distance.

The trailer had been in this location for a while. It was a single-wide that had once been blue and white before the desert sun bleached the aluminum shell from Caribbean Azure to the pale hue of fire-sale toilet tissue. Oleanders obscured one end of the trailer completely. A big brown Ford Econoline blocked the other end, the rust on the vehicle announcing that it had spent most of its earlier years in a locale other than Arizona, one that actually had humidity. Instead of a few steps leading up to the front door of the trailer, a switchback ramp of sun-bleached cedar led from the sandy ground to the entryway.

An air-conditioner compressor hummed loudly.

Sawyer said, "He's home."

No lights were visible. "The AC?"

"That's right."

"If he was in Santa Barbara yesterday screwing around with your plane—and if he was in Kittredge at three o'clock this morning setting fire to the forest around Sheldon's house—he made pretty good time getting back here."

"I haven't flown for two days, so who knows when, or if, somebody touched my plane. And you made it here easily enough from Colorado. He could, too. Anyway, maybe he has his own plane, like me."

"And maybe he's not our guy."

"Let's go find out."

I killed the engine and eased out of the car. The desert heat hit me in the face like a physical blow from an open hand. Sawyer didn't seem to notice.

She mounted the worn wooden ramp with determination and no apparent fear. I had barely reached the switchback when she started pounding on the door of Garritson's trailer.

After ten or fifteen seconds, I heard a reply that was almost a growl. "I'm resting. Go. Whatever it is you're selling, I don't want any. Whatever it is you want, I don't have any."

Sawyer pounded some more.

"Leave me alone, damn it."

She pounded some more.

"What the—? Shit, gimme a goddamn minute."

It was about this time that I wished that Sawyer and I had a plan. Pounding on a homicidal maniac's door unannounced didn't seem like the most prudent thing for us to be doing. At that moment, I had the sinking realization that I was along for the ride with Sawyer on this one. My memories of cocktails in the thunderstorm surfaced and I felt an uneasy feeling with my current role.

She was calling the shots again. How could I slip into such a passive place with her so easily? "Sawyer," I said, in a meek effort to raise a protest. "Doing this, you know? I'm not sure that this is such a great idea."

"He won't recognize us. Don't worry."

"What are you planning on—"

"Shhh."

I half expected a volley of semiautomatic weapon fire to pierce the aluminum skin of the trailer and slice Sawyer and me in two as though we were constructed of nothing more than perforated paper. After she quieted me, I thought I heard a groan from inside the trailer, followed by some labored breathing.

After another minute or so the doorknob turned and the door swung outward violently, almost knocking Sawyer backward off the ramp. I caught her arm and steadied her.

The inside of the trailer was unlit; the curtains had all been shut against the heat. Peering into the darkness was like looking into a cave. I couldn't see who was there waiting for us.

A voice said, "Down here, you idiot."

I looked down and saw the silhouette of a man in a wheelchair. One shoulder drooped a good six inches, and the rest of his body listed in that direction. He wore a filthy sleeveless T-shirt and had a baseball cap on his head. It was hard to be certain in the shadows, but I thought the cap was adorned with the logo of the Arizona Diamondbacks.

Sawyer was apparently as taken aback as I was by the man who was greeting us. Her tone lacked any confidence as she said, "Hello. We're looking for Victor Garritson. Are you Victor Garritson?"

He said, "Actually, I'm Christopher Reeve, doing research on a movie on what it's like to be a crip in a trailer park. Who the hell are you?"

"I'm Anton Faire," she said, without a pause. I remembered instantly that Anton was Sawyer's middle name, her mother's maiden name.

"And you want what, Anton Faire? Bill collector? You can collect all of them that you would like. Don't worry, I have plenty to spare. Child support? Perhaps you can perceive the truth, which is that I can't even support myself. Let me see, what else could you be after? I *know*. Bless you, maybe you're here to give me my daily massage. I sure as hell hope you're as flexible as you are pretty. Are you?" His mouth hung open, waiting for a reply. The man needed some serious dental work. "Come on, come on. So, what I want to know is, do you do hand jobs? I'm the odd one who prefers them to blow jobs. Some give them, some don't. I don't want any moralizing, mind you, just a woman's touch." He paused again, shrugging that one shoulder, his attention fixed on Sawyer. He was ignoring me totally. "No? Well then, I give up. What the hell do you want? Please don't tell me you want to talk to me about Jesus. Whenever I start talking about Jesus . . . no, that hasn't proven to be a good thing. No." He lowered one hand to the wheel of his chair and seemed to get lost in thinking about Jesus. Finally, he said, without conviction, "Do I know you?"

Sawyer was flustered and confused. She said, "I didn't know you were in a wheelchair."

His reply was bitter and cruel. He made a rapid clicking sound with his tongue. "Sometimes I forget, too. Just find myself walking around the house, getting on the treadmill, doing jumping jacks, taking care of business. And then I say, oops, forgot again, better get back in that chair. Can't start pretending you're not a crip, Vic. Get it? Vic for Victor, Vic for victim. Pick one, pick one."

Sawyer looked at me, then back into the tepid darkness of the trailer. "Mr. Garritson, we may have made a mistake. Coming here, I mean. I'm very sorry to disturb you."

"Does this mean no hand job? I get myself all the way to the damn door and I don't even get a little touch? Just a little woman's touch. That's all. I'm quick; it won't take long." He started fumbling at his belt with one hand. The other arm seemed beached in place by his side.

"Good day, sir," said Sawyer. "I'm sorry we disturbed you."

"Now I'm a sir. That's no good. You never get off when they call you sir."

I heard him laughing as we walked away. He cackled, "Oh, you'll be back. You've been here before."

Two or three miles later, she said, "I guess it's not him."

"No," I said, touching her hand where it rested on the edge of the seat. "I guess not."

She wasn't eager to focus on the failure, though. She wanted to strategize. "We need to find D.B. and at the same time we need to start brainstorming about other candidates."

I was less reluctant to focus on our failures. Personally, as a detective, I was feeling like a rank amateur. "I think we're way out of our league. I think we should put all of our energy into getting the FBI more interested than they've been."

"They'll want names, Alan. Everyone who was on the unit."

"Maybe our only choice is to stay alive and be unethical. The alternative is to die ethical and proud."

"Don't forget Eleanor Ward."

"That's the second time you've brought her up. Why is she so important, Sawyer?"

She looked away from me, out the side window. "Because she's an example of what will happen if we give out names." Her lips tightened and her eyes narrowed. "And because she taught me so much. That's why."

"What does that mean?"

"No," she said. "I shouldn't have said that. I'm sorry."

"Please."

She shook her head.

Her reluctance didn't feel provocative, but my patience had deteriorated a lot during those few moments on Victor Garritson's wheelchair ramp. "That's no good, Sawyer. My life depends on you right now, and yours depends on me. Don't keep things from me that may be important."

"You're doing it, too."

I made the mistake of inviting her to continue. "What does that mean?"

"You have feelings too. You're not saying anything about them. You've hardly spoken about your wife."

"My wife? What does Lauren have to do with this maniac?"

"You say you're happily married . . . but my instincts say . . . I don't know, that that's not the whole truth."

I did not want to be having this conversation. "What on earth are you talking about?"

"I think you still have feelings for me."

What she was saying was disconcerting. It may even have been true. "Don't kid yourself. Any tension you feel from me is about this situation. It isn't about us. I admit I've been waiting fifteen years to find out what happened between us. And I still want to know why you left the way you did. You took a big piece of me with you. Maybe I want it back."

"What? Me? Or your dignity?"

"I want to know why you disappeared."

She shook her head. "I can't."

"Can't what?"

In a firm voice she said, "Stop the car. Please. Stop it." She barked the last two words.

I pulled over to the shoulder of the two-lane road. Sawyer immediately popped out of the car and marched back in the direction we had just come.

I followed her. So what else was new?

"What are you doing?" I asked.

"I don't know. I'm walking."

A tractor-trailer whizzed by. I called after Sawyer, almost yelling to be heard above the droning diesel, "Bullshit. I think you always know what you're doing."

She whirled around and faced me. "Finally, the anger."

"Is that what you want? You want me mad? Okay. You hurt me. I trusted you and you trashed me. Sure I was angry."

"Was?" she asked as she walked backward, away from me. "Did I ever . . . did I ever encourage you? Did I? Did I seem to want you to need me?" Her voice seemed foreign, contemptuous. "No. That wasn't me. I liked your company. That's all."

"That's bull. You like that I was a pushover for you. You like that I'd put up with you."

She scoffed, "Don't blame me for your weakness. Despite every warning sign I put up, you leaned on me until you fell and I wasn't around to pick you up. That's not my fault. Don't blame me."

"I don't. I blame me. That doesn't excuse what you did, Sawyer. You ran. You knew that I loved you. And you ran."

"I didn't ask to be responsible for you. And you know nothing about my leaving. Nothing."

"No. You didn't ask to hold my heart. But they break when they're dropped. You dropped mine."

She turned away from the paved shoulder and pounded her feet as she headed off into the desert. She was at least a hundred feet in front of me when she yelled over her shoulder, "You don't know."

I yelled back, "Of course I don't know. You never told me anything. You never even told me you were married."

"Don't judge me. I didn't make any promises to you."

"Is that the rule? If you make no promises, you make no invitations, then nobody can be disappointed? Well, I don't like those rules. I don't remember ever agreeing to play by them."

She faced me with her hands on her hips. The sunlight sparkled in her hair. She had left her sunglasses in the car and the sun was in her eyes, but she wasn't squinting at all. I closed to within thirty feet of her before she spoke again. The words that came from her mouth were as soft as the haze on the horizon. "I wanted to believe that I could be loved without being needed. You were my guinea pig."

I stopped and said, "I guess I failed that test back then. And I'd fail again today."

"Yes," she said. "You failed." Her words weren't especially critical. Merely sad.

"Is that still what you want? You're looking for someone who'll love you without wanting anything from you?"

In a whisper, she said, "Not wanting. Needing."

"I don't get it."

She dropped her head so that I couldn't see her face. "I just want to stop being so scared."

Gracefully, she lowered herself to a sitting position in the dust, and I moved forward and held her while she cried. I cried some, too. Some old tears, some new ones. Some for Sheldon, some for Sawyer, some for me. I realized I didn't know what Sawyer had meant. Was her wish not to be so scared related to the current threats or to ancient ones?

I didn't ask. It felt good to be sitting in the sand and dust, holding her. Comforting her.

Eventually we moved back to the car, mostly just to escape the heat. I stood and looked around before lowering myself onto my seat. I wanted to be sure no other cars had stopped along with us in the middle of nowhere.

I was now officially paranoid.

I ran the air conditioner for a few moments before I started to drive away. My pager vibrated against my hip ten seconds after I pulled back onto the road. I checked the screen. Sam's cell phone number again. "It's my friend. The detective in Boulder? I need to find a phone."

She dug one out of her purse. "Here."

"Would you dial for me, please?" I handed her my pager so she could see the number. "The area code is 303."

She punched the numbers and handed me back the phone.

"Where are you?" Sam asked. "Connection sucks."

"On our way back to Phoenix."

"Any luck?"

"You told me once that you considered eliminating suspects in an investigation to be progress. If that's really true, we made progress. Chester's a definite no go."

"Sorry, I guess."

"Anything new there?"

"Not with your friend or the fire. Identification of the bodies is a day away, at least. But Lauren's fine. I'm going to see her home as soon as she's done here. I called to tell you that Custer and Simes are on their way back to Boulder. They say they'll be flying into DIA today, want to meet as soon as possible. And they want to know if you know where to find Sawyer."

"Did you—"

"I played stupid. You are coming home tonight?"

"That's still the plan, yes. Have to get back to Phoenix and see what shuttle flight I can make."

"Call me when you know. I'll pass word along to Custer and Simes."

"You don't know what they want?"

"I talked to Dr. Simes, not to Custer. If I was planning a picnic I don't think she'd tell me the weather. See you."

I punched the button to terminate the call and handed the

phone back to Sawyer. "Custer and Simes want to meet with us. In Boulder, tonight."

"Do they know I'm with you?"

"Sam didn't tell them. Doesn't mean that they don't know." I looked over at her. Her eyes were closed and her head was back against the headrest. "How do you feel about coming back to Colorado?"

"I'm not sure. I haven't been back, you know? Since . . ."

Since what, I wanted to know. I didn't press her hard. "I didn't know you hadn't been back. Bad memories?"

"No, my bad memories aren't in Denver. I didn't go back because of you. I didn't want to face you. I didn't want to see the hurt I'd caused. I didn't want to have to go through what I just went through. I didn't want to have to apologize."

Lightly, I said, "You haven't apologized."

I glanced over and saw the indentation of a dimple. "I haven't been back to Colorado yet."

"Does that mean you're coming?"

"I don't know how I feel about meeting your wife."

"That's fair. I don't know how she feels about meeting you."

"How would you feel about it?"

"Let me see. Meeting with two ex–FBI agents about some asshole who wants to kill me. Arranging a little get-together between my wife and an ex-lover. Sounds like a nice, non-stressful day to me."

She smiled. A bit too sweetly, I thought.

I drove another mile or two before I realized she had never answered my question about Eleanor Ward.

TWENTY-SIX

United didn't have two seats together on the 6:45 shuttle back to Denver. I took an aisle seat in the last row. Sawyer was in the middle in the exit row on the other side of the airplane. The separate seating arrangement was fine with me. I needed some time to think.

It surprised me that what I thought about was Eleanor Ward.

She had been a kid when she was admitted to Eight East in late November of 1982. The official records would dispute my contention that she was a kid; her chart would indicate that she was actually a nineteen-year-old freshman at the University of Denver with a history of acute weight loss and withdrawal. But she didn't look her age. Chronologically, Eleanor was too old for the adolescent unit. Emotionally, though, she was way too young to be with the adults.

Eleanor—Elly—had long sandy hair that she parted slightly off-center and let fall in waves past her shoulders. She touched her hair constantly, holding it or sifting it between her narrow fingers with the same desperate affection that an infant clutches a blanket or doll. Her skin was as pale as paint and her ghostly complexion made her blue eyes stand out starkly in her gaunt face.

She was five-five or five-six and weighed, I recalled, eighty-one pounds when I met her for the first time in Community Meeting. She was wearing a dress that reached her ankles and that might actually have fit her once. That day, though, it might as well have been a tent. She curled upon herself in the chair, and her hair fell forward so that it came together in the front of her chest to frame her face like a shawl. Her makeup was precise and abundant. She had painted the illusion of cheeks onto places on the sides of her face where I was sure she once hadn't needed to. Her lips were so full that they seemed to mock the rest of her body; they hadn't lost any of their roundness or allure.

At rounds that day, the training staff brainstormed about Eleanor. We, the trainees, discounted her obvious depression and insisted on focusing on her apparent anorexia nervosa. We discussed the state of the art for treatment of eating disorders and asked the nursing staff to assist in coming up with a plan to manage her behavior around food.

Susan Oliphant, the ward chief, let us go with our faux wisdom for a good twenty minutes before she reminded us that our colleague Sheldon Salgado had sent Eleanor Ward up from the ER for admission not only because of her acute weight loss, but also because of her depression and social withdrawal. Susan smiled at Sawyer in an affectionate way and told her that she had confidence that she would soon know what it was all about. She cautioned, "Don't get lost in the eating disorder, Sawyer. It's a fascinating piece. But it's only a piece."

Three days later, Sawyer asked me if I would do psychological testing on her young patient. Psychotherapy, she told me with significant frustration, was going absolutely nowhere and she wondered what was interfering with the establishment of an alliance. Specifically, she was concerned that her young patient had either an underlying organicity or thought disorder. And to complicate matters, Elly was refusing to allow the hospital to contact her family in New Haven to notify them of the hospitalization and to inquire about history.

My schedule had no openings for days, but Sawyer was imploring me for test results as soon as possible. I scheduled Elly for a two-hour appointment that evening at eight-thirty and another the next night at the same time. They were the only times I had free all week.

I gave up my late evenings because Sawyer asked me to, and I was an easy mark for her. But I also did it because Elly was alluring. Not sexually. Her sexuality had evaporated along with her fat stores. But psychologically, being in Eleanor Ward's presence was charged and very fleshy, full of poignancy and promise. That first night, for the first hour, all she and I did was talk, mostly, it seemed, about not talking. She told me that her doctor frightened her. She said she found Dr. Sackett to be intense and impatient and intrusive.

Sawyer, it seemed, reminded her of her mother. When I suggested the connection to Elly, she seemed shocked. That the phenomenon of transference—experiencing or treating someone in one relationship as though that person shared the traits of someone in another—was so apparent to an outsider didn't mean for a second that it was at all visible to the perpetrator.

Elly told me that in contrast to Sawyer, I was gentle. At the end of the first hour, she wondered if I could be her doctor.

During the second hour we completed the first step of the psychological testing process, the WAIS.

The next day, I told Sawyer that Elly's IQ was 127 and that the pattern of subtest scores was not consistent with any underlying organic problem. I explained that I'd know more after the projective battery, but didn't consider it likely that I was going to find evidence of a thought disorder. I recounted the results of the interview that preceded the intelligence test and suggested that there might be a transference problem in the therapy.

And maybe, I added gently, there was a counter-transference problem, as well.

Sawyer opened her mouth to defend herself, but didn't. I wasn't sure why, but psychotherapists often have a reflexive need to deny that any of their own issues might be interfering with the progress of a specific psychotherapeutic relationship. I was as guilty as anyone of defending against that aspect of my humanity.

I asked Sawyer, colleague to colleague, what might be going on in the therapy with Elly. She said she didn't know, but that whatever it was didn't feel right to her, either. She danced a little bit but ultimately acknowledged that she thought I might be right about the countertransference. She said she would talk with Susan Oliphant, her supervisor, about it.

The following night at eight-thirty, as I finished arranging the materials I would need to administer a projective battery to her, Elly asked me what I had done to Dr. Sackett.

I said I hadn't done anything other than tell her about our discussion the previous evening.

Things were different with her doctor, she said. Totally different. She told me that she had finally been able to reveal to Sawyer what had happened back in New Haven. She said she had told her everything.

And I ate dinner tonight, she said. Not all the food. But almost half. Okay, maybe a third. But much more than I've eaten in weeks.

Do you want to tell me about it? About New Haven? I asked.

No, she smiled. She didn't. Not yet. One doctor at a time.

We finished the projectives in ninety minutes and I went home and scored the Rorschach before I crawled into bed. The deep depression I expected to find in Eleanor's test responses was absent. I saw footprints of despair, deep marks where despondency had managed to leave indelible evidence. But Elly Ward had somehow escaped the darkest shadows of depression and her reactions to the inkblots showed me that she was beating a remarkable retreat from defeat.

The flight attendant asked me if I wanted more peanuts.

I didn't remember eating two bags already, but the evidence, in the form of rubbish and peanut crumbs, sat on the tray table in front of me. I smiled at her kindness, but declined. In front of me, Sawyer was walking down the narrow aisle toward the back of the plane, making her way to the lavatory. The light in the cabin, from the brilliant sun setting to the west, brightened the left side of her face, glinted off her lips, and highlighted the tan skin on her long neck. Her breasts swayed below her cotton top.

I was not unmoved.

As she passed by me she acted as though she didn't even know I was there, but her fingers grazed my scalp when she reached down to touch the top of my chair.

I heard the lavatory door open and close a few feet behind me. Then I popped the telephone from the back of the middle seat, swiped a credit card down the crevice, and punched in my home number.

Lauren wasn't surprised to hear that Sawyer was coming back to Boulder with me. Sam had told her what had been going on. She saved me a question by letting me know that Sawyer had a room reserved at the Boulderado Hotel. That's where Simes and Custer were staying.

Sawyer exited the lavatory silently. Again, I felt her fingers touch my hair and I admired her ass, mindlessly, as she returned to her seat.

The next day at rounds, Sawyer reported the breakthrough with Eleanor Ward. The precipitant for her patient's depression, Sawyer told us, had to do with the death of her baby daughter almost a year before.

Sawyer reminded us that Eleanor was a nineteen-year-old freshman at the University of Denver. Elly had spent the year between the end of high school and the beginning of college recovering from the traumatic death of her daughter in a traffic accident while she was visiting the parents of the baby's father.

After she discovered she was pregnant early in her senior year, Elly had withstood pressure from her mother to have an abortion and had decided to finish high school, and to postpone college, in order to raise the baby herself. Although the baby's father was out of Elly's life, romantically at least, by the time the little girl was born, his parents turned out to be much more supportive of Elly than her own mother was.

The day that her baby died, Elly was on a picnic with a boy she'd met from Yale, her first date in fifteen months. The baby was enjoying an afternoon with her paternal grandparents.

Tragically, the baby's grandfather died in the same crash that killed Elly's daughter. The Honda Accord they were riding in was unrecognizable after being broadsided by a police car that was chasing a suspected car thief.

Sawyer looked directly at Susan Oliphant as she offered her opinion that Elly's inpatient stay would not be brief, that the eating disorder would have to be well controlled before discharge, and that she would require ongoing psychotherapy for quite a while. Arnie Dresser argued for a while about the indications for drug therapy to treat her obvious depression. The other psychology intern, Alix, felt that Sawyer was dismissing the eating disorder in a manner that seemed cavalier.

Sawyer deflected the criticisms adroitly, looking as clinically assured as I had ever seen her.

No one even asked for the results of my psychological testing.

As the plane dropped low enough so I could see the Rocky Mountains out the left window and the flight attendants began to stow their gear in the galley behind me, I wasted a few minutes trying to figure out what time we'd actually land in Colorado. Arizona didn't subscribe to daylight savings time and it always dumbfounded me to try to figure out what time it would be when I landed there or what time it would be when I landed someplace else after leaving there. I guessed we would land in Denver at seven-ten, eight-ten, or nine-ten. Which meant I required a three-hour window to account for a ninety-minute flight.

Sometimes I was able to recognize the irony in the fact that I had been charged with the responsibility of assessing other people's intelligence.

* * *

Sawyer waited for me to exit the plane. I was the last person off, right behind a woman who had stowed her carry-on bags in various overhead compartments spaning the entire length of the 737. Apparently she thought the maximum number of carry-on bags permitted was two per brain cell. As she exited the cabin, she was juggling six.

In the concourse Sawyer was acting like a tourist, examining the spacious contours of Denver's airport. "I could actually land my plane in here with room to spare," she said. "Do they have indoor runways?"

I almost reminded her that she was temporarily planeless. But I didn't.

As we stepped onto one of the moving walkways that would take us in the general direction of the train that would carry us to the main terminal, she said, "It's odd, really odd, to be back in Denver. Especially with you. I never, ever thought this day would happen."

"This is DIA, this isn't Denver. Geographically, you're closer to Kansas than to Boulder." In my retort, I studiously ignored the especially-with-me part. "I phoned Lauren from the plane. Simes and Custer are staying at a hotel downtown called the Boulderado. She got you a room there."

"That was kind of her."

"You could stay with us, of course, but we're in the middle of the remodeling I told you about, and—"

"This is a better plan."

"The train's this way," I said. "What do you think they want this time? Simes and Custer?"

"I'm trying not to think about it. Bad news rarely warrants anticipation." She paused and turned her head toward me with a wisp of a smile on her face. "I wonder if they're sharing a room."

"Who? Simes and Custer? You must be kidding."

"No, I'm not kidding. I only saw them briefly, remember. In California. But he's not even trying to fight it. His attraction to her, I mean. She's more reluctant. But she feels the heat, too. You didn't pick it up? When he's with her, he acts like he's at his first cotillion. But Simes isn't sure he's good enough for her."

I thought about Sawyer's assessment. Maybe. I said, "Lauren thinks Simes has multiple sclerosis."

The train arrived. I led Sawyer inside. "Really?" she said. "That's interesting. What makes her think so?"

"She's good at recognizing it. Lauren's had it for years, too. MS. As long as I've known her."

Sawyer looked at me once and touched her tongue to her teeth. "Oh," she exclaimed, in a tone that said, "That explains it."

The train rumbled on, stopping once at the A Concourse and then emptying at the terminal station. I led her upstairs and across the huge tented terminal toward the parking garage and my car.

As we trudged to my car, she asked, "Should I say I'm sorry? About your wife having multiple sclerosis?"

"Sorry for me?" I asked, surprised.

"I guess."

"No. I don't feel burdened by her. Blessed, most of the time."

"How ill is she?"

"Right now she's pretty stable. The past year has been difficult at times. We're almost there."

She didn't miss a beat. "What kind does she have?"

I reminded myself that I was talking to a physician. "Relapsing-remitting. She's on Avonex, interferon. It seems to be helping, she's been more stable lately. No new exacerbations. This is my car."

"A Land Cruiser. How very Colorado of you." I unlocked the doors and she climbed in. "You need to be a little more honest with yourself, Alan. It's not easy having an ill spouse."

"You know that from experience, Sawyer?" I didn't expect her to answer.

"Boy. Do I," she said.

* * *

It was dark by the time we cleared the lines at the toll-booth plaza. Sawyer was already asleep beside me.

I gazed over at her every chance I had. I'd slept with this woman many times. But I'd never watched her sleep before. The intimacy of that moment unnerved me.

TWENTY-SEVEN

Sawyer and I arrived at the entrance of the Boulderado Hotel a few minutes after nine.

I found it odd that the green leather bag she carried over her shoulder included a stash of toiletries and a change of clothes. I had considered the Arizona jaunt to be only a day trip.

We said good-bye at the elevators and I returned to the lobby and hunted down a house phone. I hesitated. Whether I wanted to or not, I had to call either Simes or Custer to find out what the plans were for getting together. Ultimately, I chose to ring Custer's room instead of Simes's. Milt was easier for me to talk to, and I was curious about what he had learned in New Zealand.

Simes answered the phone in Milt's room.

"Hello, A.J.?" I said. "It's Alan Gregory. I'm back in town. Actually, I'm downstairs. I just dropped Sawyer off at the elevator."

"You're here already? Super. Come on up. What room is Sawyer in? We need her, too."

"She's in 311. Where are you?"

"We have a suite, 416. This is parents' weekend or something at the college. We had to beg for a room. All they had was this suite. But it's a great place to meet. So come on up."

I wanted to ask, "Is it a two-bedroom suite, or one?" I didn't. Instead, I said, "Why don't you call Sawyer yourself? I'll be up in a few minutes. I need to let Lauren know what's going on first."

I moved from the house phone to a pay phone and hesitated again. I decided I needed to reassess my strategy and convinced myself that a little alcohol would enhance the decision-making process.

I climbed the stairs to the second floor and grabbed a small table along the rail of the Mezzanine Lounge. As I often did when I visited the Mezzanine, I wished it had reclining chairs so that I could sit back and gaze in wonder at the stained-glass ceiling fifty feet above my head.

The Boulderado had been built shortly after the turn of the century as one of Colorado's frontier jewel hotels, along with the Jerome Hotel in Aspen and the Hotel Colorado in Glenwood Springs. The most distinctive feature of the Boulderado was the stunning stained-glass ceiling that rose high above the central vault of the lobby. The original ceiling had been destroyed by fire, but an exact replica had been reconstructed during renovations in the 1980s. The ceiling was an architectural extravagance that I welcomed every time I gazed at it.

A waitress came over to my table and smiled. She didn't say a word, but instead raised her bushy blond eyebrows, widened her eyes, and smiled a mannequin smile.

I smiled back. It took more effort than it should have.

With empty hands she pantomimed writing on a pad, pouring something from a bottle, and then raising a glass to her burgundy-painted lips. She swallowed with great drama.

I ordered vodka rocks, squeeze, and used words to do it.

She spun on her heels and departed. I felt as though I were being waited on by Marcel Marceau's granddaughter. But it had been that kind of day, so I wasn't too surprised.

I rested my head on the back of the settee and stared at the glass panels on the ceiling until the mime arrived with my drink. She made a scribble motion and a checkmark in the clear air with the end of her index finger. She then tried to catch the checkmark because it had, apparently, started to float away.

I paid cash. Just dollar bills. I didn't want to see what she might do with a handful of coins.

My options? Meet with Sawyer and Simes and Custer on my own and immediately relay everything they reported back to Sam and Lauren for analysis. Or invite Sam and Lauren to the rendezvous and gain the benefit of their wisdom and experience directly.

The second option was tactically superior except for one flaw. Inviting Lauren to the hotel would force the first face-to-face meeting between Sawyer and Lauren. Was I up for that?

No. I wasn't.

I downed the vodka in less than five minutes and dropped money on the table to cover the tip. I puzzled momentarily over a larger issue: whether by tipping my server generously I was violating my personal policy never to do anything to encourage a mime. I couldn't figure out that dilemma, either. I returned to the lobby, picked up the phone and invited Lauren, then Sam, to the rendezvous in suite 416.

Machiavellian concerns convinced me that I didn't want to be the first to arrive at Simes and Custer's party. I retired to the men's room and peed and washed my hands and face before phoning Sawyer's room to be certain she had already answered a summons that I assumed was as cursory as the one I had received.

She didn't answer. I made my way over the alley bridge to the modern wing of the hotel and took the elevator to the fourth floor.

Simes answered the door in a lime-colored outfit that vaguely resembled a sweat suit. I thought it looked like something an upscale Dallas housewife would have chosen from the Neiman-Marcus catalog in order to appear casual when friends dropped over for canapés. The pair of pine green cowboy boots embroidered in sequins on her chest was a dead giveaway that sweat was never intended to soil this leisure suit.

Milt was across the room in a big chair, talking on the phone. He was dressed in khakis and a white polo shirt and black socks. He waved as though he was glad I was there.

A.J. offered me a drink. I declined and took a seat across from Milt, wondering where the hell Sawyer was.

A.J. lowered herself to a settee and said, "So, you've had a busy day?"

I raised my eyebrows and nodded before recalling my run-in with Ms. Marceau. I quickly added, "So you've heard?"

"Not everything," she said obliquely.

"Ahh," I said, still wondering where the hell Sawyer was. "So what brings you two back to Boulder?"

"We thought we'd learned enough that it was time to put our heads together again."

"What did you learn?" I was trying to eavesdrop on Milt's telephone conversation at the same time I was trying to hold one myself with Simes. It was not one of my better-developed skills.

"That can wait. We ordered a few snacks from room service. Please help yourself."

"I'm fine, thanks." Milt was silent on his end of the phone call. I examined the suite, tried to decide if the design allowed for two bedrooms. I concluded that it did. Offhandedly, I asked, "Is Sawyer here yet?"

One of the doors I'd been examining opened, and Sawyer walked out of a bathroom. She said, "Yes, Sawyer's here. Where have you been?" She was wearing the same cotton top she'd had on all day, but had replaced her jeans with a black rayon wraparound skirt that did nice things for her legs.

I said, "Freshening up." It was apparent to me that she had done the same. Her hair seemed slightly damp. I figured that I looked like shit.

Milt placed the phone back on the cradle and greeted me.

"A lot's been developed. A lot," he said. Whatever the news he'd just heard was, it wasn't causing him any joy.

"A.J.?" He gestured toward one of the bedroom doors. She followed him. I detected a slight imbalance in her gait and considered whether it was from vertigo or a foot-drop.

Sawyer said, "I spoke to the mechanic in Arizona who is going over my plane. He can't find a reason that the gear wouldn't come down. Nothing. Weird, huh? He said the fuel gauge has a minor calibration problem, but there's no evidence anybody tampered with it."

"You believe him?"

"Beechcraft is flying someone out from Wichita to take a look at the gear. We should know more tomorrow or the next day."

"What's this all about?" I opened my arms to take in suite 416.

"From what I could gather, it's because of new information of some kind. I also think they missed each other."

Two loud raps echoed from the door. Since Custer and Simes hadn't reappeared, I answered. Sam walked in, nodded a greeting to me, another to Sawyer. To her, he said, "Sam Purdy. You must be Sawyer. Heard a lot about you."

"Likewise," she said.

He began examining the tray of snacks that room service had delivered. "There's not a damn thing here I can eat. You know, I'm beginning to think this diet isn't really necessary." He popped open a Coors from the minibar and sat down in the chair where Milt had been sitting. "Glad you two made it home. Sounds like a hairy day."

Sawyer shrugged and gave him an abridged version of the landing excitement. I followed with the tale of our embarrassment at Victor Garritson's trailer.

"Any chance he was scamming you? Knew you were coming and put together a little charade for you? With the wheelchair and everything?"

Sawyer glanced at me and shook her head. "Anything's possible with a con. But I don't think so."

"Alan?"

"I agree. It didn't seem like an act to me."

A trill of three quick taps came from the door. Sam looked at me. "You expecting someone else?"

"It's probably Lauren."

I noticed that, with my pronouncement, Sawyer improved her already perfect posture and pushed her hair back from her face with her left hand.

Sam got the door. Lauren entered and pecked him on the cheek. I stood and embraced her, and kissed her hello. I wanted to kiss her again. Not a hello kiss. I didn't. She smelled like flowers on the beach.

She let go of my hand and took two long strides across the room to Sawyer. She said, "I'm Lauren, you must be Sawyer. It's nice to meet you." Sawyer stood. They shook hands. I noticed they were the same height.

Lauren looked even more lovely than usual. I couldn't decide whether I was just that happy to see her or whether she had spent an extra few minutes choosing her clothes and touching up her hair and makeup.

Sawyer said, "The pleasure's mine," and sat back down.

Lauren said, "I'm so sorry about what happened today. You certainly handled yourself well."

"Thank you."

Simes and Custer rescued us from small talk by returning to the sitting area. Sam, Lauren, Sawyer and I filled the upholstered pieces, so Milt carried a couple of straight chairs over from a dining table.

Milt offered no preamble. "Lorna's brother tentatively ID'd her remains; dental records confirmed. She died with her husband in New Zealand. The local authorities can narrow down the day the deaths occurred from examining records from the lodge where they were staying." He looked my way before he continued, "Manner? I bet you're wondering about manner. Manner of death on this one is homicide. A rope bridge over a gorge was tampered with. Guy tried to cover his work with fire. Didn't play it very well. No ashes were found below the bodies in the bottom of the gorge. But there were plenty of ashes on top of them. And the fire didn't destroy enough of the rope fiber to disguise the cut marks."

"Fire? Really? You know about last night, don't you?" I
asked. "Sheldon Salgado, the forest fire?"

They both nodded. Milt said, "Yes, more fire. It's the
closest thing we have to an MO on this guy."

Simes started speaking. "There's more. The cruise ship
doctor? Wendy Asimoto? We know more about her death
than we did before. The cruise line doesn't think she went
overboard. They have a witness who saw her going from the
seventh-deck promenade into the main lobby area. That
means she was seen going from outside to inside. A few
minutes later another witness saw her near the ship's hospital. She wasn't seen after that. That was at one-thirty in the
morning."

Sam asked, "Then what do they think happened to her
body?"

"That's what I wondered. So I went down to Fort Lauder-
dale, where a sister ship of the one Dr. Asimoto was on is
docked. I asked the captain point-blank if there was a way to
dispose of a body at sea without going up to one of the decks
and pushing it overboard. He immediately said yes, and
walked me to the galley.

"The galley was this stainless-steel wonder—equipment,
walls, ceilings, everything. Seems these modern cruise
ships have advanced, environmentally sound methods of
waste disposal. Much of the waste is incinerated in these incredibly hot ovens. The organic waste, though, is ground
through this big industrial food processor and allowed to
pass into the ocean as fish food."

"You think she became chum?" Sam asked incredulously.

"Actually, no. The head chef disagreed with the captain
on the disposal method. He told me that a body would have
to have been cut into pieces no larger than eight inches in
diameter to be forced into the processor. Would have been
messy and would have taken someone without, um, experience a long time. He said if he was doing it, he would have
just used the waste incinerator. A small woman could be
placed in there whole."

"Wendy was a small woman," I conceded.

Sawyer nodded agreement.

No one said anything, so Simes continued. "I checked back with the headquarters of the cruise line. They've been cooperative. Their records don't show any inspection of the ship's incinerator after her disappearance. Their next port was Stockholm. I have a call in to the authorities there, as well, to see if they looked. But I don't imagine they did. Why would they?"

Sam asked, "How many people would have had access to the incinerator area?"

Milt smiled wryly at Sam's inquiry. "Eight total. On that particular shift, overnight, only three."

"You have their names? And, I assume, photographs from cruise line personnel records?"

"Names, yes. They've been more reluctant about releasing photos. We're increasing pressure on them through channels."

Simes said, "But for the time being we have nationalities. One was a Greek national, one a Belgian. The third was an American. But—"

Sam cut in. "You should be able to get immigration records on him. Find out when he went abroad. Address, photos, everything."

"Detective," Simes replied, "please remember we are dealing with a sophisticate. The crew member in question may well have used false documents to apply for his job. The name on his cruise ship personnel records was Trevor Elias Cash. A few phone calls revealed that the original Trevor Elias Cash died in Billings, Montana, at the age of three in a farm machinery accident."

"Dead end?" I asked.

"Hardly," Lauren said, touching my knee. She faced Milt. "You'll be able to get immigration records for passengers departing on the same day or shortly after Lorna and her husband departed for New Zealand, right? The murderer couldn't leave for New Zealand before they did in case they changed their travel plans. He couldn't leave long after they did in case he couldn't find them in New Zealand. After he killed them, he probably began his return home quickly, say within thirty-six hours. Perhaps he traveled through a third country as a diversion."

Milt said, "Very good. And the answer is yes. We are in the process of looking for an age and description match for the man we know only as Trevor Elias Cash from among the finite number of U.S. citizens who made their way to and from New Zealand in that time period."

Sawyer said, "This isn't right. He's leaving a trail for us. Why?"

Simes said, "Most sophisticated criminals want to challenge the authorities in some way. They feel we can't keep up with them. He's underestimating us—didn't imagine any of the deaths would ever be determined to be homicides. It's not atypical."

I said, "Sawyer's right. Something's amiss. It's not only the sloppiness. He used to go years between killings, but in the last twenty-four hours it looks like he's made two attacks. Milt's story says that he was sloppy in New Zealand after killing Lorna and her husband. I think he's deteriorating, psychologically I mean. He's not approaching his task the same way that he was at the beginning."

Simes ignored me. "The good news for now is that after our discoveries in New Zealand, the Bureau is interested—finally. If we can tie any of these two murders, or the recent attempted murders, together with evidence, circumstantial or not, the Bureau will come on board. Milt and I feel that the deaths of Wendy Asimoto on the cruise ship and Lorna Pope and her husband in New Zealand hold the best promise for assembling documentary evidence to support a link. We should be able to use immigration and passport data to show the same person was in both locations. I've completed a thorough review of all the earlier records and simply cannot identify any solitary piece of evidence we can use to tie any of them together."

"Other than the victims," Lauren said.

"Yes, other than the victims," Milt said.

"He's on our trail, you know," offered Sawyer. "He could be here tonight, at this hotel."

Milt said, "You'll be fine, miss. I'm sleeping in your room. You'll bunk here with Dr. Simes."

I thought I saw a look of fleeting disappointment on A.J.'s face. But two seconds later she was acting as though the move was her idea.

TWENTY-EIGHT

The next morning was Saturday. I drove Lauren to her office so that she could catch up on some paperwork and then made my way over to Sam's house so we could walk together. Lauren didn't have much to say about meeting Sawyer. Sam had a lot to say about my procrastinating about learning to use a handgun.

I didn't tell either of them that I was planning to go to Reggie Loomis's house again.

Reggie had told me that he delivered breakfast to his shut-ins on Monday, Wednesday, and Friday, supper on Thursday and Sunday. Since this was Saturday morning, I hoped to find him at home on his day off.

I pulled up to his deceptively modest house a little after nine. A late summer—or early autumn—monsoon had drifted up from Mexico, and cold drizzle blanketed the Front Range. The hogbacks were almost invisible in the low clouds.

I knocked and waited long enough to get pocked with rain. After a minute or so the front door opened. Reggie Loomis was dressed in worn corduroys and a flannel shirt. He wore no shoes on his stockinged feet.

He said, "I figured you'd be back."

"May I come in?"

"You alone?"

My heart pounded in my chest. I actually looked over my own shoulder to see if I'd been followed. I said, "Yes."

"Come in then."

We settled in at the same two stools at the kitchen counter. I smelled cinnamon and my mouth watered. But Reggie didn't offer me any refreshments. He may have expected my visit, but he wasn't happy to see me.

"Three more people have died," I said.

He nodded. "The fire in Kittredge?"

"Yes. The fire." I wondered how he knew. "You've been thinking about this some more, haven't you?"

"Yes."

"There was an attempt made on someone else's life, as well."

"But it failed?"

I thought his voice was registering surprise. "Yes. It failed."

He looked at me across his body, suddenly curious. "Tell me about it. The failure."

I relayed the details of Sawyer's near miss. Reggie asked me to clarify a couple of points. Finally, appearing relieved at my story, he offered me coffee and an apple cinnamon muffin.

"That would be wonderful," I said. "You even bake on your days off?"

"If you love what you do, you don't have days off." He busied himself with his espresso machine.

I watched his practiced movements for a minute, then asked, "How did you know? About the fire?" I was trying hard not to sound accusatory.

"I have a lot of free time. I read all the papers. You said three more people had died. That was the only recent incident I've read about where three people died. Simple deduction."

"You weren't surprised at all when I said three more people had died."

He shrugged and moved his gaze toward the greenbelt. His back was still to me when I asked, "You know who it is I'm looking for, don't you?"

He placed the two demitasse cups on saucers and turned and walked in my direction. "I have an idea. A good idea."

I waited, hoping he would be forthcoming. Instead he

asked me for more information. "You think he's killing people? This person you're looking for. This old employee of mine."

"Yes."

"How many, so far?"

"Maybe as many as eight or nine before the fire."

"Why aren't the police interested?"

"Who says they're not?"

"If they were, you wouldn't be here. They would."

Reggie was no dummy. "Until recently, the killing has been accomplished by an almost invisible hand. The crimes have been flawless. No one has even suspected that the deaths were homicide."

"But recently?"

"He's grown impatient. And sloppy."

Reggie stood back up from the counter. He'd forgotten the muffins. He shuffled across the room and placed one on a dessert plate for me. "I don't think you'll need butter," he said as he served me. I didn't doubt him. The muffin before me was the size of a softball and smelled like it came from heaven's bakery.

I waited again. My silence was lost on Reggie Loomis. It seemed to provide no impetus for him to disclose anything. The muffin was delicious. I told him so.

He smiled self-consciously and said, "Thank you."

"You seemed to react before when I said that this man I'm looking for has grown impatient and sloppy."

"Yes. Perhaps I did." He finished his coffee. "The man I've been thinking about would never—never—exhibit sloppiness. And there is not an untidy cell in his entire body. We must be talking about different people."

"People change."

"Do they? Honestly? You're a psychologist, right?"

I nodded.

His tone became challenging and slightly sarcastic. "So how malleable is character, dear Doctor? How often do you effect lasting changes on the architecture of the personality of your patients? I'm not talking behavior, mind you,

I'm asking you to reflect on alterations in the underlying structure."

I considered the question while I chewed. "Some would argue that character can be altered. There is certainly evidence to support that point of view. But I admit that there's controversy."

"Example. Can an obsessive-compulsive character ever be free of the desire for perfection? Really, truly? I'm not talking about merely lassoing impulses here. I'm wondering about effecting basic changes in human temperament."

"This man, the one you've been thinking about, he was obsessive-compulsive?"

"No, no, no. My point is that he *is* obsessive." He hesitated. "He was then . . . he is now." Reggie gestured in front of me. "Your coffee cup isn't centered in your saucer. He couldn't tolerate that asymmetry. You've dropped muffin crumbs onto my counter. It would leave him apoplectic."

I brushed at the crumbs and said, "I'm sorry."

Reggie said, "You're a supplicant. You'll always apologize for your messes. Rand . . . ? No."

Rand? That name resonated in my memory. Was that his name? Was D.B. really Rand? And what the hell did he mean by calling me a "supplicant"?

I said, "Rand. That's his name?"

"Yes. Corey Rand. Ring a bell?"

"Oh yes," I said. "It does."

It surprised me that hearing his name unlocked so much of what I'd forgotten or buried about Corey Rand.

After causing a disturbance at work, Rand had been brought by ambulance to the psych ER, where Sheldon Salgado saw him briefly. Arnie Dresser was on call that Sunday, and Sheldon paged him and asked him to the ER to evaluate a possible admission. That piece of administrative trivia was the red light Corey ran that caused his collision with Arnie Dresser.

Arnie was the second person to hear Corey Rand's proposal about D. B. Cooper. Arnie decided that the offer was compelling evidence of delusional thinking. He admitted Rand to the adult inpatient unit and took out a seventy-two-hour hold-and-treat after a frustrating attempt to assess Rand's suicide potential.

Sawyer and I had stolen that Saturday night to get away to a Grand Lake cabin that was owned by Mona Terwilliger's family. We both worked most of Saturday and drove up to the mountains and across the Divide in the dark. We got lost trying to find the cabin, and ended up staying up so late talking and screwing that I remembered watching the sky brighten in the east before I drifted off to sleep on the sofa in the living room. I woke up in time for a late lunch or early supper. Sawyer was in the shower. I joined her there. We ate, we packed up, and then we drove back down to Denver in time to squeeze in a little more sleep prior to Monday.

For a medical school trainee, this interlude constituted a vacation.

Arnie Dresser was not a good therapeutic match for Corey Rand. Arnie was an aggressive diagnostician. He probed. He palpated. He theorized. He confronted resistance wherever he spotted it, intent on stamping it out like nasty vermin in the kitchen. His style could not have been much more different from the one I was working hard to adopt, one I watched Susan Oliphant model almost daily on the unit. Her wonderfully effective style seemed to be based on patience, and listening.

But fate dictated that Arnie Dresser was Corey Rand's doctor, and by the time Sawyer and I heard about Rand at rounds on Monday morning, Corey was being portrayed by his doctor as a severely obsessive man with a teeming reservoir of anger and an underlying thought disorder. After a few questions from Susan, Arnie's supervisor, it became clear to me that most of the venom that Corey Rand was demonstrating was directed toward his doctor. Arnie would call this transference.

A more objective observer might call it something else.

Community Meeting was an interesting affair that morning, too. Census was low for the holiday weekend. The patients who could be trusted outside the unit were all out on pass. As the meeting was coming together, Corey Rand loitered by the heavily screened windows until everyone else was seated, ultimately choosing a location far from any of the other patients and far from Arnie Dresser.

As soon as Susan Oliphant started the meeting, Corey asked to address the group. I remember that his clothing seemed to have been pressed, an unusual sight on a psychiatric unit. I wondered how he had managed it. His hair was combed neatly and his face freshly shaven. His posture would have delighted an orthopedic surgeon.

She asked him to wait.

When his time came, he said that his admission had been an unfortunate combination of misunderstandings and that he would like to be released immediately. He stressed the word "immediately."

Arnie responded that they could discuss that issue in their individual session late that afternoon. I thought Arnie's tone was condescending. From the look on Corey's face, I thought it was pretty clear that he considered his doctor's tone to be contemptuous.

Corey said something like "You can't hold me here and you know it. I'm no danger to anyone. I'm not gravely disabled. My lawyer will have me out of here before I have to spend another hour with this cretin." He raised his chin at Dr. Dresser. "Save yourselves some trouble and some embarrassment. I have some information that the legal authorities want. Allow me off this unit in time to make my next shift at work, and I will divulge that information."

Arnie looked at Susan and rolled his eyes in a "Here it comes, what did I tell you?" look.

Corey continued, "I will trade the identity of the hijacker, D. B. Cooper, for my immediate release."

Susan suggested we move on to other business.

As promised, an attorney retained by Corey challenged the hold-and-treat that afternoon. At Susan's advice—and over Arnie Dresser's objection—the university attorney chose not to contest the challenge. I wasn't around when

Corey Rand left the unit that day. And I don't recall ever seeing the man again.

"What happened at work? What was the disturbance that day that got Mr. Rand hospitalized?"

"More coffee? I'm going to have another cup."

"Sure," I said.

He busied himself. "Remember, we were security analysts at a nuclear weapons facility. We were protecting national defense secrets. And we were protecting plutonium. I was senior to Corey. This was, what, 1982? Those days the facility was under constant assault by protesters, and there was a persistent fear of terrorist intrusion. We took our jobs seriously. We had to."

Reggie turned his head to face me as he said, "Corey was good at what he did. So was I. We anticipated potential weaknesses in security. We developed scenarios that outsiders might use against us.

"Corey wasn't well liked. He had a holier-than-thou attitude and thought nothing of reporting other employees for security lapses. Some major, most minor. He caused a lot of people a lot of trouble, made himself a lot of enemies. Although I couldn't prove it at the time, I think most of those guys set him up that day. They laid out a trail of cookie crumbs for him, let him think he'd discovered that a plot was afoot to infiltrate one of the labs that handled plutonium.

"He reported it to me, in great detail. I followed up immediately, of course. The plan seemed quite plausible. When I did begin to investigate what had happened, all the evidence was gone. Vaporized. The whole setup made Corey look like a fool. He lost it, accused everybody in the division of being involved in the conspiracy. Our boss. His coworkers. Everybody. The plant medical officer took one look at him, heard his story about all this imaginary evidence he'd discovered—at the time, I admit, I thought it sounded crazy, too—and had him transported to Denver."

He brought me my coffee and sat back down.

I said, "That's it?"

"Yes, that's it. Except for the sequelae."

"The sequelae?"

"The fallout. His security clearance was suspended pending review of his mental condition. He was transferred to a nonsensitive position. He couldn't tolerate the demotion. He quit."

"Then what happened?"

"I don't know. I never heard from him again. When I was promoted, I learned that he'd sued the Energy Department for damages. But that was as quixotic a quest as there ever was. He was suing a top-secret branch of the U.S. government. The damn case never went anywhere."

"What year would that have been?"

"Let me see. I imagine it would have been around 1988."

"I don't know if it means anything, but the first of the murders took place the next year. 1989."

"Was it planned carefully?"

"Meticulously. You think it might be him?"

"Who am I to say?"

Reggie stood up and walked to the back windows of his house. He stared out toward the hogback and said, "I think it's clearing a little."

"I hope so," I said.

"You have a name now—you should be able to find your man. We'll chat some more after you do."

"Why after?"

"We will. That's all."

I stood to leave. He didn't turn to see me out.

"Do you think he really knew?" I asked.

"Knew what?"

"Who D. B. Cooper was? I mean, if he was such an obsessive guy, why would he make that claim if he couldn't substantiate it?"

Reggie shrugged and faced me. "Do you think anybody would really care anymore?"

TWENTY-NINE

Lauren and I were supposed to rendezvous downtown for lunch and then drive over to Spanish Hills to see how Dresden was doing with the renovation. I wanted to talk with Sawyer about what I learned during my meeting with Reggie and see if she had any ideas on how to locate Corey Rand.

But I had at least two complications to overcome.

My first problem was that Sawyer was not only temporarily rooming with A.J. but was also being baby-sat by Custer. I couldn't figure out a ploy that would let me separate her from that formidable herd.

My second problem was that the only two people I knew who had access to public records that might actually help me track down Corey Rand were my wife, an assistant district attorney, and Sam Purdy, a cop. But I couldn't reveal Corey's name to either of them because it would violate the confidentiality of his hospital admission. I reminded myself that Sawyer and I had been totally off base in our suspicions about Chester and that prudence dictated avoiding overconfidence regarding Corey Rand.

Baffled, I stopped by my office on Walnut and checked the Boulder phone book, hoping to get lucky. There were three Rands in the local directory, but no Coreys or names with the first initial C. I tried the Denver metro book. At least two dozen Rands, easy. Again, no Coreys or initial C's.

I picked up the phone and called Reggie Loomis. "It's

Alan Gregory. Sorry to bother you again. But he was married, right? I need to know his wife's name. Corey Rand's."

I heard Reggie exhale, the sound almost a whistle. "She was a beauty. A little feather of a thing. Her name was Valerie."

I dragged my finger over the column of Rands in the phone book and spotted a listing in Wheat Ridge for a Valerie Rand. I said, "Thanks. That helps."

Reggie didn't say good-bye. He just hung up.

I punched in the number and heard a gravelly "Hello," followed by a hacking cough.

I asked for Valerie Rand.

"Speaking," she said, coughing once more, a bark as sharp as a knife.

"I'm not sure I have the right Valerie Rand. I'm actually trying to reach a man named Corey Rand, who used to work near Boulder. Could you be of any help in finding him?"

She cleared her throat in a most unattractive manner and said, "You're asking after my husband. But I'm afraid Corey is dead."

"He's dead? When did he die?"

"Labor Day 1995."

"Would you mind if I . . . ? Could I ask, please, how did it happen?"

She was silent for a moment, then broke into a series of deep hacks that must have caused her significant discomfort. "He, um, had a blood clot and a, what do you call it, a hemorrhage in his brain. It happened while he was driving. He drove into a parked bulldozer."

"I'm sorry."

"Were you a friend?" she asked through another deep cough. She placed the emphasis in such a way that I thought she would have been surprised if I was.

"No," I said. "I wasn't his friend. Good-bye. Thank you."

Lauren and I had lunch at Lick Skillet before driving east to see what was going on with our house. I wanted to talk to her about Corey Rand but couldn't think of much more to say than to tell her that I'd gone back to talk with Reggie

Loomis that morning hoping he could tell me more about his ex-employee.

She wanted to know if he could. I explained that the lead on the patient we'd called D.B. hadn't exactly panned out.

She wasn't surprised by the news. She'd been assuming all along that the killer would be someone who Sawyer and I never really suspected could be responsible for all the deaths and assaults.

Our friend and neighbor Adrienne—Sam's doctor—had left word for Lauren and me that she and her son were going to be out of town at a urologists' meeting in Florida, so we expected the lane to our house to be quiet, and it was.

The overflowing dumpster had been emptied and parked back in place and was already half full of debris again. I frowned as I looked at it; to all appearances we were throwing away much of our house.

Work had not progressed much inside the structure since my visit the previous morning. The foundation walls for the addition and the new garage were still curing, so the framing hadn't started. Our walk-through took only minutes. We were both careful about where we stepped and we both kept looking up at the joists, but neither of us said anything.

Lauren's shoulders dropped as we stepped outside. She turned back around so she was gazing toward the front door. She said, "It's going to be nice, isn't it?"

I thought, *Uh-oh*.

She continued, "Don't you think we really should have some sort of protection over the front door? It's so exposed. Look."

I didn't need to look. "I thought we'd decided not to." My protest was meek. I was playing purely for appearances.

"We're going this far . . ." She allowed her words to hang. "Anyway, the drawings are already done."

I sighed. "You liked the design with the two pillars, didn't you?"

She smiled and touched me lightly on the back of my neck, letting her fingers drift up into my hair. She said, "Yes."

"I'll call Dresden with the change order," I said, wondering what a covered entryway would cost us.

My guess was twenty-five hundred. Dresden seemed to have an affinity for that number.

On our way back to the Hill, I told Lauren I needed to let Sawyer know what I'd learned about D.B. and asked if she wanted to come to the Boulderado with me. She declined but handed me her portable phone in case she wanted to reach me.

"What about the Glock?"

"It's handy."

"You'll keep Emily with you?"

"She won't leave my side."

I dropped her off at the house and watched her walk inside and close the door before I drove away. Her gait seemed strong. That was good.

A.J. told me on the house phone at the hotel that Sawyer was out shopping, walking the Mall. Milt had gone out looking for her.

The Boulderado is only a block north of the Downtown Boulder Mall, the center of culture and commerce downtown. The Mall is a four-block-long segment of Pearl Street that was bricked over and closed to traffic back in the seventies. It quickly became the anchor of a revitalized downtown business and retail district.

I guessed Sawyer would be looking for clothes. Given what I'd seen of her wardrobe to date, and knowing what I knew about women's retail on the Mall from traipsing after Lauren, I guessed that Sawyer would gravitate to either Solo or Jila. I tried Solo first. She wasn't browsing the racks in there.

But she was in Jila.

As soon as the door closed behind me I heard Sawyer's voice from the dressing room. She and a salesclerk were arguing the relative merits of traveling with rayon. I lowered myself to an upholstered bench near the front door and waited for Sawyer to emerge. A minute or so later she paraded out wearing a long brown skirt and a short-sleeved cardigan that was the color of old blood. I watched her examine the outfit in the three-way mirror for about ten seconds before I said, "It's a keeper."

She didn't turn to face me. She said, "I knew you were there."

"No, you didn't."

"You really like it?"

"Yes, I do. The color is great."

She spun and looked over her shoulder at her butt. "I've missed this," she said. "You know how long it's been since I've shopped with a man? Heard a male opinion about stuff like this? Buying clothes together is such an intimate act, don't you think? I think it is."

I hoped the question was rhetorical. I gave both of us some room with my nonresponse. She twirled once more. To the salesclerk she said, "This skirt's wonderful. But I'll take the other sweater." She threw a coquettish smile at me over her shoulder to let me know what she thought of my taste.

"Where can we get some tea?" she asked as we stepped outside onto Broadway.

"Around the corner," I said, and led her to Bookends, a café adjacent to the Boulder Bookstore on the Mall. I asked her to hold the only outdoor table that was available in the busy café and stepped inside to the counter, where I ordered her some tea and poured myself a glass of water.

I carried a small tray to the table and sat down across from her. She proceeded to prepare her tea with an elaborate sense of ritual that sang a melody of solitude and privacy. I watched the practiced steps, feeling a little like a voyeur, and said, "Milt Custer has been looking for you since you left the hotel. And Simes isn't at all happy you insisted on coming over here while Milt was in the shower."

Finally, she sipped some tea from the cup. "Maybe she's stewing because she didn't get to share that wonderful suite with Milt last night. Anyway, think. Would you go shopping for clothes with Milt Custer?"

"I don't imagine he was exactly offering his services as a

personal shopper. I think bodyguard is more what he had in mind."

"Nobody's going to gun me down in someplace this public. It's not our guy's style."

I leaned forward and lowered my voice. "I have some news. The murderer isn't our D. B. Cooper fink from the unit, Sawyer. I went back this morning and saw his old boss. He finally told me what I think he knew all along. D.B.'s real name is Corey Rand. Ring a bell?"

Her eyes flattened, but she nodded. "Yes. Yes, it does. I remember now."

"Do you remember how angry he was at Arnie? Remember that Community Meeting?"

She was silent a moment before replying, "Yes . . . yes. But then Arnie had that effect on more than a few of his patients." Her voice sparked suddenly. "Arnie was absolutely livid at Susan for telling the university attorney not to contest the challenge that—what's his name, Rand?"

I nodded.

"—that Rand made to the seventy-two-hour hold."

"I'm not surprised it pissed Arnie off. But the truth is he probably shouldn't have been on the hold in the first place. Anyway, it's too bad. I thought he was a good match for us. This Corey Rand. The characterological structure that he brings to the table fits the profile we put together real well."

"But?"

"But Corey Rand died in 1995. I tracked down his widow, spoke with her on the phone." Anticipating Sawyer's next question, I added, "Sounds like he had a cerebral aneurysm while he was driving a car. Died."

She leaned back on her chair, holding the teacup in both hands. She was gazing up the Mall to the west, where the foothills framed the entrance to Boulder Canyon. The sky above was a dazzling blue. "Boulder certainly is pretty. How's the shrink situation here?"

I was taken aback by the non sequitur, but followed the best I could. "Congested. Like the traffic. The managed-care fungus has taken its toll."

"Too bad. Any prisons close by?"

"Just the county jail. State and federal prisons are a few hours south of here, clustered around Canon City and Florence. Supermax is there, too."

"That's what airplanes are for," she said. "Boulder does have an airport, doesn't it?"

"A little one. There's a bigger one about ten miles east of here in Jefferson County."

"Ten miles? That would work fine."

"You would actually be able to climb back into your airplane and fly again, without any real trepidation, wouldn't you? Even after what happened yesterday in Arizona?"

"I have a propensity for denial. Haven't you noticed?"

I hadn't, but didn't want to rush into that admission without some additional thought.

"So are you thinking of moving? Leaving California?" I asked, trying to be nonchalant, not even wanting to consider how Sawyer's presence in Boulder would complicate my life.

She shrugged. She wasn't looking at me. She was watching the pedestrians pass by in a steady stream on the Mall. She shook her head, a tiny smile gracing her lips. "Is there a local ordinance against unattractive people living here? But to answer your question, nothing is tying me to California. And it's peaceful here. Reminds me a little bit of Santa Barbara. I like the feel of the place."

"It is a nice town," I said, suddenly a reluctant booster for the Chamber of Commerce.

"Where do you and Lauren live?"

"The house we're renovating is on the east side of the valley. About five miles across town. Place called Spanish Hills."

Over the rim of her teacup she asked, "Why is it called that?"

"I don't have a clue."

"I think I'd like it better close to this." She waved her hand at the Mall. "In town, here. There's a lot going on."

I considered the likelihood that she was pulling my chain. Just hoping to watch me squirm.

I tried not to squirm. "I guess we're back to square one," I said.

"You and me?" she said, still not making eye contact. The sun fell behind some wind-driven clouds and a shadow swept over us with the alacrity of an omen.

I didn't know what she meant by her question. She probably knew that.

"No, I meant, you know, in regard to suspects," I clarified.

"Ah," she allowed. "There's that, too."

I didn't want to talk about Sawyer and me, whatever that meant, in a crowded public café on the Downtown Boulder Mall. I did want to know what had caused her to leave her residency, and me, without warning just before Christmas in 1982. I also wanted to know why she was so averse to a man needing her. But now wasn't the time.

I was surprised when she rescued me from my reverie by saying, "Why do you think he wouldn't tell you D.B.'s name the first time? The boss man from Rocky Flats. Why did you have to go back?"

I leaned across the table again. "This Corey Rand wasn't a flake. He sounds like he was overbearing and obsessive at work, but he wasn't delusional. Careful, precise, by-the-book. That's how he's described."

Sawyer placed her teacup on its saucer and her elbows on the edge of the table. She moved her face to within inches of mine. When I inhaled, I tasted her perfume. Sawyer saw Milt Custer strolling down the Mall from the west. He was taking a detour around a street magician who had drawn quite a crowd. She called out to him, and he returned a wave before he wandered through the bookstore and joined us on the patio. He didn't seem at all distressed that he hadn't found Sawyer before that moment. He held up a heavy bag. "You ever been to that bookstore in the next block up there?"

"You mean Stage House? Used books?"

"No, no. Mysteries. They have everything. Everything."

Sawyer was intrigued by the prospect, I could tell. I said, "The Rue Morgue. I'll show you where it is after we're done."

She said, "Milt, Alan found out that the other suspect we had is dead. Has been for a while. We can't offer you any leads."

I was hoping she wouldn't make any D. B. Cooper jokes. She didn't.

Milt was looking around as though wondering why no waitress had shown up at our table. I said, "It's counter service, Milt. What are you hungry for? I'll go get it for you."

He held up a finger to slow me down and turned his attention back to Sawyer. "If you two would just put together a patient roster for me, I wouldn't need any leads. I could merely start comparing names with the immigration records."

"You know we can't do that."

"I'm an ex-fed, young lady. I know all about rules and regulations. My feeling is that basically you gotta know when to keep them and when to bleep them. If you know what I mean."

I said, "Sam would agree with you on that."

Sawyer touched Milt on the arm and changed the timbre of her voice to something conspiratorial. "Milt, are your colleagues in the FBI still looking for D. B. Cooper?"

I'm sure I paled.

Milt laughed. "You bet. To some of the older guys, like me, he's still the biggest fish in the whole damn sea. Why?"

"No reason," she said. "Just a personal interest of mine."

"In hijackers?"

Sawyer shrugged and brushed her hair back from her face, hooking it momentarily behind her ears. She said, "Milton Custer, I want you to tell me. Now honestly, mind you. Are you sweet on A. J. Simes?"

Milt's face blushed to the color of a Winesap.

He turned to me and said, "Just coffee for me, thanks."

THIRTY

I was returning to the table with Milt's coffee when Lauren's cell phone rang in my pocket. I wasn't anywhere close to coordinated enough to answer the phone while walking with a hot cup of coffee, so I tried to act nonchalant as I strolled through the crowded dining room and then outside to the patio, the stupid phone chirping rhythmically in my pocket with every other step.

As I set the mug down in front of Milt, Sawyer raised an eyebrow and asked, "Is that your phone?"

"Yeah," I said, expecting to hear from one of Lauren's colleagues or friends as I pulled it from my pocket. I punched "talk" and said, "Hello."

All I heard in return was a loud *clunk*. The person on the other end had dropped the phone. I repeated my "hello" and waited for whoever it was to recover the receiver from the floor. I listened some more. In the receiver, in the background, I could hear a piercing *wheeep, wheeep, wheeep*. I wondered what the noise was.

Sawyer and Milt looked at me expectantly. Mostly for their benefit, I again said, "Hello?"

With astonishing rapidity my neurons started to fire.

Who knew I had this phone with me? Lauren.

What was the *wheeep, wheeep, wheeep* I was hearing in the distance? The smoke alarm.

Why had she dropped the phone?

Because she had passed out.

Oh shit. I stood up and said, "Lauren's in trouble. I think the house may be on fire. That's his thing, right? Fire. I have to go."

Sawyer said, "Wait, Alan. Call 911 first. Where's your car?"

"Around the corner, on Eleventh."

Milt threw money on the table as though we still had a bill to pay and told me to hand him the phone. I did, and one after another we jumped the wrought-iron railing and started running down the herringboned bricks of the Mall toward the corner.

I fumbled open the doors to the Land Cruiser and jumped in. Somewhere in my consciousness I could hear Milt's voice, precise and authoritative, giving instructions to the dispatch operator at 911. Finally he asked me for the address of the house. I was pulling a hard right onto Pearl Street as I told him.

"Tell them we want an ambulance, too," I yelled at Milt. In the rearview mirror I watched him nod.

I ran a red light to turn onto Ninth, cutting off a family on bicycles. The mother yelled something at me and flipped me off. I deserved it and I didn't care. The intersection at Canyon was a much dicier proposition than the one at Ninth. Running a red blind at Canyon Boulevard was out of the question. Fortunately, the light turned green just as I decided to chance it. The light at Arapahoe was green too, and I knew I was home free. Eight more blocks, no more lights.

Sawyer opened her window, and in the distance I could hear sirens, lots of them, and hoped they were heading to the house. I checked the sky to the west for smoke, but couldn't see anything.

Sawyer asked, "What did she say? Your wife?"

"She just dropped the phone. Didn't say anything. But I could hear the smoke alarm in the background. It's only a few more blocks."

Just before I turned off of Ninth, I saw an ambulance in my rearview mirror three blocks back, lights flashing. To no one in particular I said, "The ambulance is right behind us."

Milt asked, "What's your friend's number? Sam Purdy's?" I told him.

He was talking to Sam as I pulled in front of the house. A big green pumper was coming down the street in the opposite direction. I couldn't see any smoke coming from the house, and my hopes rose.

I ran to the door, Milt right behind me. The *wheeep, wheeep, wheeep* pierced the quiet neighborhood.

Of course, the door was locked. And of course, it was deadbolted. After fumbling with the unfamiliar keys I got both locks open and rushed inside. Behind me I could hear firefighters yelling at me to stay where I was.

Right. That was gonna happen.

Inside, I smelled no smoke. Nothing. I yelled, "Lauren!" But she didn't answer me.

With a fresh bolus of adrenaline, I realized that Emily wasn't greeting me at the door, nor was she trying to eat Milt Custer's leg. I said to Milt, "The dog's not here. Something's seriously wrong. She's always at the door."

I ran to the kitchen. No Lauren. Living room. No.

"Lauren!"

Bedroom?

Before I reached the door to the bedroom, I smelled vomit.

She wasn't on the bed, wasn't in the adjacent bathroom. I finally spotted her lying on the floor in front of the closet, one leg folded below her, one arm across her chest. Her eyes were closed and she wasn't moving.

Milt yelled to the firefighters, "In here. She's in here, the bedroom. Get the paramedics."

I lowered myself to her. Her heart was beating as though it were powered by hummingbird wings. Her respiration was weak. "Lauren," I said. "Wake up. Please wake up."

Behind me, I heard the clomping of at least two people's feet. To one of them, Milt said, "I think she's cyanotic."

From somewhere deep in the house, maybe the basement, I heard a baritone voice yell, "CO is over two-thirty down here. Evacuate. Get everybody out of the house, now. We need to ventilate this place. Get the fan set up out front."

The paramedics pushed me out of the way, and Milt grabbed me by the arm with a hold that had the strength of a

Doberman's jaws. In seconds they had Lauren loaded into a stretcher and were taking her outside.

The moment that the paramedic cleared the front door with the leading edge of the stretcher, she screamed, "CO poisoning. I need one hundred percent oh-two, fifteen liters. Get it ready. Set up for an IV and call for the chopper. We need to get her to Denver."

The words I'd heard from the basement finally registered. "CO" meant carbon monoxide. Lauren had been poisoned.

I heard someone say, "She must have been breathing it for a while to totally pass out." Someone else asked about brain damage.

My mind was spinning. Milt finally let go of my arm just as Sam Purdy drove up and leaped from his car. He ignored me at first, conferring with a firefighter to get the facts. Then he ran over to me and placed a hand on each of my biceps. At the exact same moment that he said, "Where's—?"

I yelled, "Emily!"

We bolted back inside past a stunned firefighter who was setting up a device that looked like a portable airplane propeller on wheels. He yelled. "No! You can't go in there!"

Sam said, "Don't worry about it, Alan. A few minutes' exposure doesn't hurt you."

I said, "I don't really care."

This house was as new to Emily as it was to me, and she didn't have favorite places picked out yet. I didn't know where to look for her. Sam and I ran from room to room calling her name. He would yell, "Not in the living room." I would yell, "Not in the kitchen."

When I ran past the door at the top of the basement stairs I smelled the pungent stink of vomit again and called, "Basement, Sam."

I barely touched the steps as I flew down. The *wheeep, wheeep, wheeep* was sharp and piercing. Apparently the carbon monoxide detector that was causing such a racket was down there somewhere.

After two false starts—one in the laundry room, one in a roughed-in bathroom—I found Emily unconscious in the furnace room, her heart beating with the same furious

rhythm I'd felt in Lauren's chest. I said, "She's alive," and
lifted her eighty-pound body into my arms as though she
weighed no more than a pile of clean laundry. Behind me, I
heard Sam's footsteps. My heart breaking, I said, "We'll
need oxygen for her, Sam. Right away."

"Don't worry," he reassured me, and preceded me up the
stairs.

I carried my dog to the ambulance at the curb. Sam took
her body from me. Calmly, he said, "I'll get her oxygen
from the firefighters. You go find Lauren. She needs you."

Lauren was already inside the ambulance, her face
shrouded by an oxygen mask, an IV running into a vein in
her right forearm. The paramedics were busy drawing tube
after tube of blood from her other arm, and they ignored me
as I climbed inside the ambulance and stepped up to the left
side of the stretcher. I took Lauren's left hand and lowered
my face to hers and kissed her lightly on her cool lips. I
thought I heard a tiny moan and felt some tension in her fingers. I told myself that was great news and fingered her
short black hair. I whispered, "I love you."

Behind me, someone poked his head into the ambulance
and said, "ETA eight minutes at Columbia Cemetery. Get
ready to fly."

"What?" I asked. "Where's she going?"

"Hyperbaric chamber in Denver. PSL. We need to super-
oxygenate her right away."

"She has MS. You should know that. They need to know
that."

"What?"

"She has multiple sclerosis. Relapsing-remitting. Tell
them that, okay? They should know."

"What medicines is she on?"

I told them as best I could, trying to remember the list,
stressing that she took interferon injections weekly.

"Any other pertinent history?"

"No."

"Out then, please, sir. We have to go."

Without hesitating, I said, "Take my dog, too. Please."

"What?"

"My dog is unconscious. She was poisoned, too. Take her, please. She'll die if she doesn't get help."

One of the two paramedics said, "I'm sorry, we don't do animals." He looked up at me quickly, then away. "But I know how you feel. I have dogs, too."

The other one, the woman, said, "What's the harm?" She gestured at Lauren. "It may help her recover to have her dog in there with her. The chamber's big as a bus—there's plenty of room in there for a dog, too."

"The chopper's gonna refuse to carry a dog."

"Maybe Christopher's flying today. I can handle Christopher. There's no time to argue. We need to roll, now."

"Can I go with you to the helicopter? Can I go with her to Denver?" My words were a naked plea.

"Follow us to the cemetery. I don't know how much room there is on board the chopper."

I called for Sam to bring Emily to the ambulance and explained that she and Lauren were heading to Denver on Flight for Life.

I jumped in my Land Cruiser and drove the few blocks to the old cemetery. At first it seemed we'd arrived at the wrong location. Within a minute, though, I began to hear the rhythmic thunder of big blades cutting through the air. The orange Flight for Life chopper approached from the southeast and landed smoothly in a dusty clearing on the south side of the cemetery. I watched the paramedics efficiently transfer first my wife and then my dog to the care of the Flight for Life nurses. Within a minute they were transferred into the cabin. Seconds later, the doors were pulled shut and the orange helicopter lifted off. A hundred feet above the ground the tail rose, the nose edged down, and the chopper accelerated back toward the southeast. The flight to Denver wouldn't take long.

The paramedics shook my hand, said they were sorry, packed up their stretcher and their equipment, and drove away. That was that.

* * *

I thought I was as alone in that graveyard as I'd ever been in my life. A breeze rustled the leaves of nearby ash trees and carried the aroma of a Saturday afternoon barbecue my way.

A headstone right in front of me was inscribed "Tobias Shunt, 1846–1902. Rancher, Elder, Man of God." Beside him, an identical stone was inscribed simply "Wife."

At that moment, I despised Tobias Shunt and hoped he'd had a painful death.

I felt hands caress my shoulders from behind and smelled Sawyer's perfume.

Milt Custer said, "I'm sorry, Alan."

Sam asked, "They wouldn't let you go with them?"

Without turning around to face them, I said, "There was an extra doc on board the helicopter, some training thing. The pilot told me it was either me or Emily. I told them to take good care of Emily." Finally, I shuffled my feet until I was facing Sawyer. Her face was pale, her lips tight, and her eyes betrayed sadness and some intense fear that I couldn't comprehend.

"What's going to happen to them, Sawyer?" I asked.

"They're doing all the right things. They got her on oxygen right away, drew the right labs. They're taking them to Denver to put them in a hyperbaric chamber that will—"

"I know that part. What's going to happen to them? I mean, what happens to someone after she breathes too much carbon monoxide?"

She moved close to me and held both my hands together in front of my chest. She adopted a cushioned tone, a compassionate doctor's voice, one I've often used myself when giving bad news to family members of my patients. "They've both had serious exposure, Alan. They could recover. There's a chance of that, depending on the level and duration of poisoning. Pray for that, okay? But . . . there is also a chance that they may both have suffered brain damage from hypoxia. The damage could be permanent. The fact that they vomited, that they were unconscious, it's not a good sign. The carbon monoxide replaces the oxygen in the bloodstream and starves the brain of the oxygen it needs. It all depends on how much carbon monoxide they were exposed to and for how long. The window of tolerable exposure is not long."

I looked down at the scraggly grass and glanced at Tobias Shunt's final resting place. My eyes drifted to endless gravestones around his. I asked, "Could they die?" I didn't feel I could form the words and wasn't sure they sounded right as I managed to get them out of my mouth.

Sawyer burst into tears and covered her face with her hands. "Yes," she said, "they could die."

The moment seemed to be monumental, a freeze-frame in time that would change my world forever.

I fixed my eyes on Mrs. Shunt's gravestone.

Wife.

I kicked the dust on her husband's grave and asked Sam to drive me back to the house.

"No," he said. "But I'll drive you to Denver to see Lauren. Milt will take care of your house. Milt?"

"Of course."

"I appreciate it, Sam, but I want you here to make sure that they find out how this happened. How he did it. Don't let them miss it."

"Lucy's on her way over. She's on it, and she won't let it slip, Alan. She'll goose the fire department investigators until they have it figured out." Lucy was Sam's partner.

Sawyer had moved to the front end of my car and was sitting on the bumper. She was still crying, hugging herself across her chest.

THIRTY-ONE

The rest of the day passed.

I decided to drive myself to Presbyterian/St. Luke's Hospital in Denver. Sam followed right behind. For the first couple of hours I waited fitfully outside the white hyperbaric facility, an L-shaped chamber about eight feet in diameter. With its portholes and gauges I thought it resembled a deep-sea exploring vessel. Lauren lay inside one of the airlocks. She was covered by a pale blue woven-cotton blanket. Her hair was still matted in places by her own vomit.

The doctor on duty explained that she had regained consciousness briefly in the helicopter. They had put tiny holes in her eardrums so her ears could tolerate the pressure in the chamber and were in the middle of a second "oxygen period" now. The hood around her head was providing pure oxygen, he said. If she didn't begin to look more lucid soon, he'd order a third oxygen period. He explained the rationale to me twice, but I still couldn't concentrate enough to understand what he meant.

He said that Emily had regained consciousness during the flight and had been transferred to a veterinary hospital nearby. "Maybe your wife will do just as well. We have people come in here who look just as bad as her, or worse, and who walk out the next day."

"What about damage?" I asked. "Neurological damage?"

"No way to know yet. She's controlling her airway.

Consciousness is returning slowly. We'll assess her as soon as we can."

"Are there long-term effects?"

"Possibly, sure. We may see some damage when she's conscious. And there may be delayed neurological sequelae. We're getting ahead of ourselves, though."

Sam tried to talk with me a few times, but I was too insulated by my grief and wouldn't let him reach out to me. Finally, I asked him to go home. I wanted to be alone. For most of an hour he ignored my pleas. But just before dinnertime he left. I didn't even have the grace to thank him. I spent my long minutes staring at Lauren through a porthole. Twice she stirred, moved her head, and opened her eyes. Each time I waved maniacally.

My shock was finally abating, and anger—no, rage—was erupting within me with the heat and force of a volcano. Occasionally I would stand and peer into the porthole and see my sleeping wife and I would feel some peace for a moment because I was in such proximity to my family. Then the rage would explode inside me again and I would feel awesome strength, as though I were powerful enough to destroy any adversary. Just as quickly that omnipotence would pass, and I would feel totally powerless because I didn't know whom to tear asunder.

The doctors told me little.

These first few hours were crucial, they said, in terms of survival. Then a day at a time, assessing for evidence of damage. I knew they meant brain damage. A young doctor, a woman with bright eyes and brand-new Adidas, went out of her way to warn me that pets and small children seem to have less tolerance for carbon monoxide than adults do. I could tell she was a dog person and didn't want me to harbor great hopes for Emily's full recovery. I could also tell that it hurt her greatly to tell me that.

Between the lines, I could read how bleak it all looked. There wasn't a single doctor who was encouraging me. None of them told me that directly, though. They hinted and obfuscated and told me stories about patients who had done well. I was sure that I looked too fragile, and too explosive, to be told what looked like the truth.

I phoned Lauren's sister, Teresa, and explained the danger her big sister was in. She agreed with me that we shouldn't tell their parents, who were both in ill health, just yet. She would make arrangements to get to Denver the next day.

After the third oxygen period, Lauren was removed from the chamber and moved to the ICU. She had regained consciousness, they said, but was sleeping. A kind nurse suggested I go home and get some rest, too. She said she had a feeling I would need my energy for the next day. I resisted for an hour but finally concurred. I contemplated checking into a hotel in Denver instead but felt a stronger need for the familiar than for the convenient.

The drive into Boulder seemed to snap by in an instant, and before I gave my destination more than half a thought, I found myself edging down the gravel lane to our half-demolished house in Spanish Hills. The cruddy rollaway trash bin was my first clue that my autopilot had failed and I'd driven to the wrong domicile.

I got out of the car anyway, paused, and glanced toward Adrienne's big house. The whole structure was dark; I remembered she and Jonas were at a conference in Florida or somewhere. The sky above was invisible to me, shrouded by a blanket of clouds that insulated the Front Range. The temperature was balmy, more like mid-August than early October. To the west, Boulder's lights danced through a misty haze.

Deep in my bones, even in the nuclei of my individual cells, I could feel how alone I was at that moment in that valley. The emptiness I felt was total. I was a parched canteen in an endless desert.

I pulled a flashlight from my car and unlocked the front door of the house. A buzzer sounded, and for a moment I thought I'd tripped a wire for a bomb. Reality finally set in. I used up almost the entire allotted forty-five seconds trying to remember the code to disarm our new burglar alarm. Finally, I got it right.

The house, of course, didn't look much different from that morning. Darker, sure.

I made my way across what had once been the living room and parked myself on top of a huge stack of Sheetrock that rested in front of one of the picture windows. I cried silently. I cried, first, for Sheldon Salgado and his wife and his daughter. I cried for Eleanor Ward and Lorna Pope. I cried for Sawyer.

Finally I cried for Lauren and Emily.

I tried to imagine my life without them and I couldn't. And so I cried for myself.

When my eyes were dry and sore I pulled a construction tarp over myself and rested my head on a bag of grout. The Sheetrock made a better bed than the grout made a pillow.

I was totally disoriented when I awakened the next morning. I heard heavy clomps, like footsteps, and tried to imagine what they were. But I couldn't even remember where I was. I sat up, startled, and below me saw Boulder beginning to illuminate for the day. Next I noticed the exposed studs of the construction morass all around me. In seconds, I felt the bone-jarring ache of having slept for six hours on Sheetrock and a grout bag.

The clomping stopped. My pulse jumped as I remembered the carbon monoxide poisoning and the maniac who was trying to kill me, and the terror of the footsteps approaching zapped through me like an electrical shock. I spun around, expecting to come face to face with the asshole for the first time.

Across the room, Sam Purdy was sitting on a sawhorse that was standing where our sofa used to be. He was wearing jeans and cowboy boots and a blue work shirt that wasn't tucked in. In a soft voice, he said, "You really should lock your doors, considering what's been going on and all."

My heart slowed enough so that I could think. I said, "Hey Sam."

He held up a brown bag. "I bought coffee and bagels from

Moe's. No cream cheese for the bagels, no cream in the coffee. *Su casa es mi casa.* And my new diet is your new diet." He gazed around at the mess. "Where would somebody go to take a leak around here?"

"Chemical toilet. It's on the side of the house."

He didn't stand up to go pee. He said, "Any change last night?"

I shook my head. "Emily's groggy but awake. Lauren was conscious but was sleeping when I left. Just a sec." I punched in the hospital number. Lauren's nurse was too busy to talk, asked me to call back in a few minutes.

He said, "Sherry said to tell you she's praying. She'll get everybody at her Friends meeting on it this morning."

I managed to say, "Thanks." The adrenaline tide from Sam's intrusion was receding, and I was so chilled that I felt my marrow had thickened in my bones. I gestured toward the brown bag. "I'll take that coffee." He stood and handed it to me. For a while I just held it between my hands for warmth. "What day is it?"

"Sunday."

"How did you find me?"

"I'm a detective," he explained. "Figured you wouldn't go back to the other house. So I guessed you'd be here."

I nodded. "You know, if I'd taken those lessons and had Lauren's Glock with me, you would be a dead man right now. I thought you were him—the murderer. And that's why I don't like handguns."

He appeared to find my attitude toward firearms amusing. But he was compassionate enough not to argue with me right then.

"News?" I asked.

"Heat exchanger in your furnace was cracked. Badly. I talked the department into opening a case file. Scott Malloy caught it and agreed to have the whole furnace removed as evidence."

"I thought you said Lucy caught it?"

"I just told you that to make you feel better. Since I know how you feel about Scott."

Scott Malloy had once arrested my wife. I had forgiven him but was having a hard time forgetting.

"Scott's officially curious now. He says he found some scratches in the brass on the deadbolt on the back door. He's wondering whether there was an intruder. He's going to have a professional look for signs that somebody tampered with the furnace. Carbon monoxide detectors are a different story, though. That's troubling."

"Did you say 'detectors'? Plural?"

"Yeah. There were two. One was unplugged, which I find a little suspicious, right? The other one, a battery-operated thing, had fallen behind the furnace. It was the one that was blaring. You know anything about either of them?"

"Nothing. We just moved into the house. It had been a rental. Lauren probably knows something."

Sam didn't comment about Lauren's unavailability to answer questions. "The neighbors, of course, didn't see shit. And we're upping the patrols by the house, for all the good they seem to be doing." He paused. "Milt said your other lead didn't pan out? The other patient you wanted to find?"

"That's right. The guy looked real good on paper. But he died of an aneurysm back in 1995."

"You're sure?"

I thought about it and considered it an odd question. "Not really. But that's what his widow said. Don't know why she'd lie to me."

Sam's face let me know he found my assertion naive. "What makes him look so good on paper?"

"Psychologically, he's a good match. Character is consistent. Has a history of resentment. He's about the right age. He has a background in security analysis, which would give him an experiential base. And he has motive."

"Tell me."

"He thinks we ruined his life."

"Did you?"

"Maybe. If the story his boss tells is true, though, we had a lot of help ruining his life. But by what we did, we certainly may have contributed to the decline. The proverbial straw that broke the camel's back, you know?"

"By doing what?"

"After he was transferred to the hospital from Rocky
Flats he was talking kind of crazy about a conspiracy-type
thing at work. The docs who saw him put him on a mental
health hold and gave him a diagnosis that ended up hanging
around his head like a ticking time bomb. Cost him his security clearance at Rocky Flats, which meant it eventually
cost him his job. He filed a defamation lawsuit or something
like that in the late eighties. Went nowhere. Don't know
what happened to him after that."

I paused. He waited. "Truth is, Sam, that in the current
mental health environment—today—there's virtually no
chance this guy ever would have been admitted to a psychiatric hospital, let alone put on a hold."

"Why?"

"The threshold has changed. Society has changed. Civil
liberty thresholds have evolved. As a culture, we tolerate
much more psychopathology and are willing to pay for
much less psychotherapeutic intervention."

"Did he need help?"

I thought for only a moment before I shook my head and
said, "Yes, probably, but not the kind we gave him. He
didn't have a problem that would benefit from a vacation in
a psychiatric ward."

"But he's dead? Your guy?"

"Yeah, for a while now." I took a long draw on the coffee.
"This is good. Thanks."

"Can you tell me his name?"

"No. What's the point, anyway?"

Sam narrowed his gaze and tightened his jaw before he
took a bite out of a jalapeño bagel, chewed it to a pulp, and
swallowed. I could tell he was thinking about something. I
knew he'd tell me what it was if he felt like it. "A.J. heard
from her immigration sources last night. They can't find a
match between the cruise ship's personnel list and the de-
partures of U.S. citizens to New Zealand in the days right
before Lorna Pope's death."

I raised my eyebrows. "Not even tentative? Nobody?"

"That's what they say."

"What does that do to their theory? Simes and Custer's?"

His upper lip puffed out as he expelled some air in a little burst. "Makes it much harder for them to get the Bureau involved. That's for sure. Other than theoretically, they're still unable to tie two of these deaths together."

My mind locked onto an image of Lauren in the hyperbaric chamber. I found myself fighting tears. "Sam," I asked, "when is somebody going to believe this is really happening?"

He drained his coffee and stared for a moment into the bottom of the cardboard cup. "My own theory on that is that they'll believe it once it's too late. And by my reckoning, given what happened yesterday, it's already too late. So I think somebody important will come on board any day now."

"You just being cynical?"

He shrugged. "You decide. Listen, as much as I like hanging out in drafty, dusty construction messes, why don't I take you to our house so you can shower before you go back to Denver? Sherry and Simon are at her meeting. You'll have the place to yourself."

Around us, sunlight was starting to seep into the dusty cavern that once had been my humble home. He gazed around at the mess. "So this is going to be nice when it's done, right?" he asked.

I laughed.

So did he.

Sam went to use the chemical toilet.

I fished the portable phone out of my pocket and phoned the hospital again. Lauren was still sleeping. "That's not necessarily bad," the nurse assured me. "As soon as she's awake, we'll assess her neurological status. If it's still compromised, she'll probably go back into the hyperbaric chamber. Let's hope she looks great, though, okay?" I translated her words to mean that Lauren was now out of the black-and-white dangers that lurked in the first few hours and had moved solidly into the shades-of-gray dangers that lurked in the next few days and weeks. She promised to call as soon as Lauren was awake.

Sam let me into his house in North Boulder, gave me a towel and a disposable razor, and showed me to the bathroom. When I emerged twenty minutes later, he was gone. A note under my windshield informed me that he had "stuff to do," and that he would call me later on Lauren's phone.

I stopped by the house on the Hill to get some fresh clothes. The place hadn't been designed to admit much sunlight, but that morning it felt particularly dark and bleak. The air inside was so crisp that I could watch my breath vaporize as I stood in the living room.

I edged into the bathroom sideways so that I could avoid looking at the spot where I'd found Lauren on the floor, but finally turned and examined it. The vomit was gone. I was grateful for that. But someone, maybe a paramedic, had left a couple of latex gloves on the nightstand. I swallowed, trying hard not to cry, while I stripped off the clothes I had slept in and pulled on clean underwear and socks, some black jeans, and a polo shirt and sweater.

I was locking the house back up when a heating contractor drove up in a big Ford van. He said Milt Custer had sent him over to do an estimate. I listened to the contractor for a few minutes as he argued persuasively against my repairing the old furnace. He was pretty excited about the new technology and focused most of his attention on the energy conservation benefits of upgrading. Given the Boulder market, it was a pretty good marketing pitch.

But I was in no mood for it. Finally I interrupted him and let him know that I wanted a brand spanking new furnace and two new carbon monoxide detectors, one in the basement and one upstairs. He went back to his truck and showed me a couple of brochures that went into a lot more detail than I wanted to know about the inner workings of my new furnace.

I asked him which one he would put in his mother's home. He said he would choose this one and poked his index finger at a Lennox model with an attractive female model next to it. The model appeared quite proud of her new furnace.

I said it looked fine and gave him the house key. He seemed pleased by my choice and informed me that he thought he could have it in by noon on Tuesday. I replied that that was fine and inquired about the cost.

He said he would write up an estimate for me, but, ball-park, he was guessing around twenty-five hundred dollars.

I smiled at the amount. I was thinking of asking him if he knew Dresden, but I didn't.

On the way into Denver, I checked my office voice mail, praying that my own personal crisis hadn't coincided with any crises for my patients. I didn't have the time or the energy to help anyone else right now.

The only message was from Sawyer.

"Alan, hi. It's, um, me, Sawyer. I'm so sorry about what happened to your . . . to Lauren yesterday. I know a little bit about how you feel right now, and, well, every beat of my heart is creating good energy for you. If being with me will help you, will comfort you in, in any way, I'd love to see you now. I'm going to stay in Boulder for a couple more days at least. I'm still at the hotel. Let me know."

I pushed the button on the phone that would end the call. I toyed with the idea of phoning her and seeking comfort.

I even started to dial the number of the hotel. Just then, though, I passed under the bridge at Wadsworth Boulevard and noticed for the hundredth time the headstone above the grave of the dog that was buried beside the freeway.

I thought of Emily and how much I was going to miss her if she wasn't okay.

THIRTY-TWO

Lauren's phone jingled in the pocket of my jacket as I drove past Federal Boulevard.

I found the little "talk" button, pushed it, and said, "Hello."

"Dr. Gregory? This is Angie, you know, at Presbyterian? Your wife's nurse? We met briefly yesterday. We talked earlier?"

I read a world of innuendo in her tone, which was as light and rich as perfect chocolate mousse. "Yes?"

"Your wife? She's awake and she's asking for you. She's looking much better. She's oriented."

"She's, uh, okay?"

"She looks . . . much improved. She's oriented. But we don't really know yet, you know? Gross neurological is good, but it will take some time."

I knew. The effects of brain trauma can be as blatant as pornography, or as subtle and difficult to decipher as fine art.

"Can I talk to her?"

"Not right now. They're drawing fresh bloods."

"I'm on my way in—I'm on the turnpike. Tell Lauren I'll be there in fifteen or twenty minutes. This is great. Thanks so much for the news."

I phoned the veterinary hospital. Emily was up and about and acting hungry.

Above me the sun was breaking through the clouds.

* * *

Lauren complained that her brain felt as if it had been processed in a Waring blender, but her mental status gave me joy, and momentarily, hope. Over the next few hours, I washed her hair and brushed it out and rubbed her feet and legs with lotion. I helped her eat and held her as she napped. I repeated to her at least three different times that Emily was recovering well and that I loved her.

I couldn't tell if she was having trouble with her memory or just needed reassurance.

We parted with great ambivalence. Neither of us voiced it, but we both knew that the reason I left was that she was much safer if I wasn't around. I promised I would check in with Sam and Simes and Custer as soon as I got to Boulder.

Sam had been busy during the afternoon while I was in Denver quietly celebrating with Lauren. I caught up with him late in the afternoon at the Boulderado, in the fourth-floor suite that had become a command post for Simes and Custer. A.J. was there with Sam, but Sawyer and Custer were elsewhere. I guessed that they weren't out shopping.

The light was fading and the western edge of town was shrouded in dense shadows. From up on the fourth floor the view of the treetops was a brilliant salad of autumn hues. Sam handed me a beer and offered me a big bag of Snyder's pretzels. I checked the label. They were fat-free. He was still being good.

A. J. Simes looked uncomfortable. With anyone else I know I would have assumed that the luminous melon-colored sweater she was wearing might have something to do with her discomfort.

Sam said, "It's great news about Lauren."

"Yes, I'm still pinching myself. She said to thank you for the flowers. She loves them." Sam's wife owned a flower shop.

"That's Sherry's doing. And Emily's okay, too?"

"She appears to be. Although I'm not sure I'd recognize brain damage in her very easily."

Simes said, "I'm so relieved for all of you."

"Thank you, A.J."

Sam munched some pretzels and finished off his can of beer. "We made some progress today."

"On what? The furnace?"

He shook his head. "No," he replied and waited until our eyes locked before continuing. "On Corey Rand."

I opened my mouth wide to stretch my jaw muscles and to keep myself from saying something I would regret.

"You didn't tell us his name, Alan," Simes said from across the room, as though that would make me feel better about having unwittingly violated the man's confidentiality.

I recalled my conversation with Sam that morning. The facts I'd offered about Rand's dismissal from Rocky Flats, and the subsequent lawsuit he filed against the plant. For a detective like Sam Purdy, it was the equivalent of marking Corey Rand with fluorescent paint and putting him under a black light. Immediately, I wondered if it had been my intention all along to give up Rand's identity.

"What kind of progress?"

Sam stood and walked to the window. "You're not planning on protesting at all? I expected a truckload of grief from you." He sounded disappointed.

"What kind of progress?"

Simes said, "It wasn't difficult. Finding him. Rand. Once we knew where to look for him."

"You mean once I led you to his door."

She smiled self-consciously.

I repeated, "What—kind—of—progress?"

Sam said, "I talked to Valerie, his widow. Went and saw her in Wheat Ridge. She have some terrible cough when you talked to her?"

"Yeah, she did. Does she smoke?"

"Like an out-of-tune diesel. Anyway, I seemed to make her uncomfortable."

"Sam, I'm sorry to disappoint you with this news, but you make a lot of people uncomfortable."

"I'll grant you that. But most of them, in my experience, are uncomfortable because they're hiding something."

"What was Valerie Rand hiding?"

"May I?" interrupted A.J.

Sam wasn't accustomed to being deferential, but he yielded the floor gracefully.

"A little history to start." She screwed the cap off a bottle of local water from Eldorado Springs and sat down on the sofa. "This is all preliminary. We've only been on it since late morning, right?"

I said, "Right. That's to be expected, since I didn't hand Corey to you until early morning."

She didn't bite at my sarcasm. I noticed that she had decided to tell her story without notes. "Once his security clearance was yanked, he left Rocky Flats. He wasn't fired, by the way. He quit after he was demoted to a clerical position that didn't require security clearance. Anyway, he struggled for a while trying to find a new career. He tried to make it in law enforcement. Was a sheriff's deputy up in . . . what's that place called, Sam?"

"Estes Park."

"Yes. Estes Park. But he never made it out of his probation. I got the impression from the sheriff that his, quote, 'style' made him a bad fit for the department. After that, he bounced around in other peripheral security-type jobs. Tried . . . aerospace, uh, Martin Marietta in . . . I'm sorry, Sam?"

"Jefferson County."

"Thank you. I don't know what's going on with me and names today. He was a security officer there. He lasted less than a year. Insubordination was the reason given by the company for denying Rand unemployment benefits."

"I'm getting the picture," I said. "He was a malcontent. It's not surprising, given the profile."

"Yes, a malcontent. After he was canned by Martin Marietta, he and his family left their home in . . . shit."

"Westminster."

"Due to foreclosure. Things got even more rotten then. His wife left him and took their son to live with her family in Wyoming, um, Cheyenne." A.J. seemed pleased that she'd finally remembered the name of a geographic location. I wondered if the concentration and word-finding problems were a routine part of her MS.

"But they didn't divorce?"

"No, as a matter of fact, they reconciled in 1990 or so. Surprisingly, he seemed to have started getting his life back together. He was managing a Radio Shack store in—oh, God damn it."

"Lakewood."

I asked, "Is this history all from Valerie?"

A.J. said, "No."

I turned to Sam for an answer. He wouldn't look at me. The nutritional label on the back of the pretzel bag fascinated him. I half expected him to inform me how much fiber there was in a handful of Snyder's.

"Where then?"

"Sources."

"Alan, it's not important," Sam said, warning me off.

"What is important, then?"

A.J. answered, "Corey Rand was five feet eleven inches tall. He had green eyes and blond hair that some people described as golden. His build could best be described as average to stocky. Records we've obtained show that his weight varied over the years from one-sixty to one-eighty-five."

The description seemed to match the hazy image of Corey Rand that I had in my memory. "Yes? So what?"

A.J. reached onto the desk behind her and picked up a single sheet of paper. She handed it to me.

I'd barely gotten over my distraction at the letterhead on the page—Department of Justice, Federal Bureau of Investigation, Washington, D.C.—when she summed up the contents of the memo for me.

"Corey Rand's characteristics match the age and physical description of the solitary American who had access to the incinerators on board the cruise ship the night that Dr. Asimoto disappeared."

It didn't seem like much to go on. "As do, what? Maybe two million other people in the United States?"

She exhaled and took a tiny sip from her bottle of water. I thought it was her method of biting her tongue.

"We can't rule him out, yet. That's what's important."

"He's dead." I knew I was arguing because a dead suspect did nothing to help me with my yearning for vengeance for the assault on my wife and dog.

"He wasn't dead back then."

I stared at Sam until he blinked, then fixed my gaze on Simes. She didn't blink. I said, "Now you've decided that you're looking for more than one killer? Is that what I'm hearing?"

Sam said, "Got to have an open mind, Alan."

A.J. recapped the bottle. She said, "What if? Stay with me here, okay? What if Matthew Trimble's death, the drive-by in L.A., wasn't part of all this? What if it was what it appeared to be, that is, a random act?"

"I'm listening."

"And what if Amy Masters's tanning-bed death was really accidental? What if the reason that the local authorities found no evidence of tampering with that bed is that there wasn't any?"

"What are you saying?"

"I'm hypothesizing that perhaps we should be investigating fewer deaths than we are. It would leave us with Susan Oliphant's death in the plane crash, Wendy Asimoto's death on the cruise ship, and Arnie Dresser's death while hiking. And, of course, Lorna Pope's death in New Zealand."

Her argument seemed weak to me. "You're forgetting Sheldon and his family. But that's not the point. I could make an argument to exclude any of them. Why choose Matthew Trimble and Amy Masters?"

"I'm hoping that you can tell us that, Alan. You were on that inpatient unit with Corey Rand. I wasn't."

THIRTY-THREE

The original litany of murder victims had been so compelling to me that I hadn't considered that any of them should be excluded from the list. But I wanted time to think about it alone.

"Do you know where Sawyer is?" I asked A.J.

"No. But they're due back soon. She and Milt."

"I'm hungry. I'll be downstairs in the restaurant getting something to eat. Tell her that, would you please? Ask her to join me."

Sam asked, "You want some company now?"

"No," I said. "Not especially." He looked more perplexed than injured at my response.

Downstairs in the restaurant I ordered a sandwich and a beer and tried to remember who had been working on the unit during the two days of Corey Rand's admission so many years before.

Sawyer and I had driven to Grand Lake for our one-night holiday and we had almost completely missed Rand's brief admission.

Had Matthew Trimble been on that weekend? I wasn't sure. He wasn't taking new admissions, though; Arnie was. Maybe Matthew was out of town and missed Rand's entire stay on Eight East. It was Thanksgiving weekend. A lot of people were taking time off.

And what about Amy Masters? She was a supervisor—my supervisor—and not a clinician. She didn't have her own patients to follow on the unit, and her involvement during off hours was rarely required. Many weekends went by when she didn't show her face on Eight East at all. I tried to recall whether she typically attended Monday-morning Community Meetings. I thought not, but I wasn't sure.

I decided it was possible that Corey Rand had never met either Matthew Trimble or Amy Masters.

Could I also convince myself that Rand *had* met all the other victims?

Susan Oliphant? Easy enough. I recalled the interaction between her and Corey as she directed that Monday morning Community Meeting. She was definitely there and was definitely involved in the decision to release him from the unit.

What about Wendy Asimoto? Sheldon Salgado had told me that Wendy was originally supposed to be Corey's psychiatrist, so she must have been at the hospital that weekend. It was even possible that Corey and Wendy had met in the ER before Arnie took over Corey's inpatient care.

Lorna Pope? In my mind, there was no doubt that if Lorna wasn't away for the holiday, she would have met Rand. Lorna, the unit social worker, would have been all over Corey and his family first thing Monday morning, assembling family history, arranging family meetings, and preparing initial reports.

Sheldon Salgado? No doubt Corey Rand and he had crossed paths in the psych ER. I'd spoken with Sheldon myself and he had the notes of his contacts with Rand in his consultation log.

Sawyer and I? Yes, we met Corey at Community Meeting.

Perhaps A. J. Simes's new theory had some merit. Maybe Corey Rand, if he was the killer, was a little more selective than we had given him credit for.

The only problem I had with the new hypothesis was that Corey Rand had been dead when Arnie Dresser and Lorna Pope were killed. And Corey Rand had been dead when someone sabotaged Sawyer's plane, killed Sheldon Salgado and his family, and poisoned my wife and dog.

What were we missing?

* * *

Sawyer showed up in the restaurant as I was asking the waitress for the check. I stood to greet her and found myself welcoming her embrace more than I should have. She held me for longer than she needed to, rubbing my shoulder blades with her open hands. I was aware of her breasts pressing against my rib cage.

"They're really all right? Lauren and your dog?"

"They seem okay. No one's one hundred percent sure. But it certainly looks better today than it did yesterday. Emily will stay at the vet hospital for a couple of days of observation."

She sat opposite me and leaned back in her chair. "I'm so happy for you. I was so scared yesterday at your house." Her eyes appeared rueful as she continued, "We've sure been dodging a lot of bullets lately, haven't we? You and me?"

I nodded. I couldn't believe how tired I was. I should have had coffee with my sandwich, not beer. "You were just out with Milt? Were you two working on something?"

"Hardly. He wanted to show me that bookstore he found. But mostly he wanted to talk about A.J. We sat on a bench on the Mall. He wanted romantic advice. He thinks A.J. is interested but he can't seem to get her to respond. Milt's wife died in a car accident four months after he retired. Can you believe it?"

Of course I could believe it. "And you provided the advice?"

She raised an eyebrow. "I'm not exactly proud to admit it, but I recognize a kindred spirit in A. J. Simes. She's afraid of Milt and what he has to offer her. Like I was afraid of you."

"You were afraid of me?" I tried not to sound as surprised as I was.

She flagged down the waitress and asked what the soup of the day was. Cream of pumpkin. She ordered tea and soup before she responded, "Yes, I was afraid of you, Alan."

"Why?"

"I was married, remember?"

"You thought I was a threat to your marriage?"

She smiled playfully and said, "Were you always this thick? Did I miss something back then?" She rearranged her silverware into perfect alignment before she said, "No. You weren't a threat to my marriage."

"What then?"

She refolded her napkin on her lap. "I need to tell you what happened . . . to me . . . before . . . I came to Colorado . . . before . . . I met you. With my first husband. You can't understand what I'm talking about unless I do."

"Okay," I said, and settled back on my chair. I hoped I was about to learn what I'd been trying to discover for so many years.

"When I met you that day at the party at Mona's condo, after you left me that note in my *New York Times,* I was a widow."

A widow? I felt stupid. Beyond stupid. "I'm so sorry. I've been— Jesus, I didn't know."

She shook her head forcefully, dismissing my protest. "How could you know? I didn't want you to know about any of that. No one knew at the school but my clinical supervisors and my therapist. I didn't trust anyone with what happened. I thought if the school knew what I was going through, they would judge me to be too fragile for the residency."

"It was recent? His death?"

"Sometimes it still feels recent. The second year of the residency started on July first. He . . . my husband . . . died . . . the previous January."

"God, I'm sorry."

The waitress delivered Sawyer's tea, and she started the elaborate ritual of preparation. She chanced a quick glance my way and read something in my eyes. Through tight lips, she cautioned, "I haven't told you much, yet." She was warning me not to jump to any conclusions. I decided to allow her to proceed without any more of my promptings or inane attempts at comfort.

"It wasn't just that he died. What happened was . . . my husband killed himself." She looked up from her tea again, but away from me, out the window. "I had told him in November, the fifteenth to be precise, I had told him that I wanted a divorce, and . . ."

Her words were halting and seemed to sweat thick beads of anguish. "He didn't take it well. He said he would change however I wanted him to. He, um, he told me he would do anything to keep me. That he couldn't live without me. I didn't take him at his word, though. No. I thought it was just his insecurity talking, and his insecurity was why I had already decided to leave him."

I was confused. How could her friends in Colorado not know about her husband? "Were you already in Denver?"

"No. I did my first year and a half of residency in Chapel Hill. In North Carolina. I thought you knew that. A supervisor there, a friend, arranged for me to repeat the second year in Colorado after . . . after . . ."

"Your husband's suicide?"

She nodded. "And after my baby died."

Her baby died? She said the words so quickly I wondered if I had heard her correctly.

Sawyer was staring at the reflections of the light waltzing off the tea in her cup. "Your baby died?" I wondered aloud, my voice as soft as her infant's skin.

She closed her eyes and swallowed. Her shoulders jumped up suddenly and then collapsed. She looked sallow and lifeless. I didn't speak. Neither did she. The sounds of the restaurant seemed to roar in my ears. I reached across the table and took her hand, gently prying it from the handle of her teacup.

She pulled it back.

"I had a baby once, a beautiful baby," she whispered in a tone that told me everything, that said, "I once had a life. A real life."

I guessed that I could jump to the end of the story she was telling, and because I could, my impulse was to close the book and walk away. I was in a mood for nothing but happy endings. But instead I waited.

"My baby was a little round bundle of love." She almost smiled. "He, um, he had her—her name was, um, her name was Simone, and . . . and she was so sweet and she was so pretty . . . and he had her for a couple of days while I was on call. That was what we'd worked out after I moved out, that he would watch her when I was on call. And . . . he, um, he killed her. He killed my little baby at the same time that he killed himself. He killed her so that I couldn't have her. And so that she couldn't have me. He wanted me to know what it was like to have something so essential ripped from his life."

The chair next to her was vacant. I moved across the table and sat on it before I slowly eased her against me. She seemed small in my arms. I waited for convulsions to rack her bones and tears to flow from her eyes, but they never came. I thought of her the day before, after Lauren and Emily were poisoned, when she was sitting against the bumper of my Land Cruiser, in anguish that I couldn't understand.

And now I could.

"When I met you, you terrified me," she said, her words so soft they were almost lost in the din of the restaurant. "You were gallant and handsome and . . . romantic. But you needed me, Alan. I could feel it. I could just . . . feel your insecurity at times. And I couldn't let that happen again. I let him need me—my husband—and look at what happened. He wouldn't let me go. And then he took my baby. He took Simone from me. I couldn't let you need me. I couldn't. It was too dangerous, and too soon."

She sat up straight, releasing herself from my embrace, turning toward me on her chair.

She touched the side of my face with one hand and then reached up with the other. She flattened both palms against my cheeks. "And now? Now I think I may have read you wrong back then. Don't you love irony?"

"What do you mean?"

"I don't know," she said. "It's all come full circle for us. Before, back then, I thought you would drag me under, drown me even. But today? Today we need each other just to stay alive. How is that for the ultimate insecurity? The ultimate dependency."

My instincts told me that something crucial had been

omitted from Sawyer's story. My mind flew back to her anguish at the cemetery the day before. "What was his name? Your husband?"

She looked at me oddly and said, "Kenneth Sackett. Kenny. He was a, um, banker. His family has a bank. Had a bank. They sold it to NationsBank a while back. I made a lot of money on the stock he left me. Even more irony, huh?" She nodded to herself as though she was acknowledging that she'd actually answered the question correctly.

"How did he do it? How did he kill himself . . . and your baby?"

Her hand jumped to her mouth as though some invisible string yanked it there. She blurted, "You already know, don't you? How do you know?"

I didn't know how I knew. I shrugged.

The waitress chose that moment to deliver Sawyer's soup. Its color was the hue of a fall sunset. The waitress's name was Kim, and she asked, of course, if everything was all right.

I answered that everything was fine. Sawyer actually giggled at the lunacy of the exchange.

When Kim had retreated out of earshot I said, "Yesterday, Sawyer. It must have . . ."

"Yes," she acknowledged. "Yes. It certainly did."

"I'm sorry."

"Just like with you, yesterday, I found them myself. I came home from work and found them. Kenneth and Simone."

"But the outcome wasn't as happy for you then as it was for me today."

"No. That's been my life. No happy endings."

She spoke with such finality I thought she was done with her story. But instead, she was just steeling herself for what came next.

"I had stopped by the house—his house, the one where we'd lived while we were married—to pick up Simone after I left the hospital at around, I don't know, seven-thirty in the evening. Nobody answered the door, but it was unlocked. I wandered around inside looking for them, cursing him for not being home. I figured he'd gone out somewhere and had dropped Simone off at her grandmother's house. Finally, I checked her room. In her crib, lying across her favorite teddy bear, there was a note that said, 'We're down in the garage.'

"That very second, I knew. I flew down the stairs and through the kitchen and yanked open the door to the garage and I . . ."

Her voice faded and she tempered her breathing. She was trying to find the strength to finish this story.

"Kenny loved his car, just loved it. It was this red Pontiac Firebird he'd had since high school. When I went in the garage, it was there. The engine was off but the whole garage smelled like exhaust. He was in the front seat, on the passenger side, slumped over, vomit all over the place.

"He had put Simone in the backseat. The garden hose from the exhaust came into the car right next to her. She was strapped in her car seat, surrounded by her toys. He'd, um . . . the shithead . . . he'd, um, taped a wedding picture of us on the dashboard in front of the driver's seat, and he'd . . . hung a picture of me over the back of the seat so that when Simone looked up before she died, she would see me. I would be the last image she ever had."

She was silent for a full minute or more, but I was sure she wasn't done. She didn't turn to face me as she resumed her story. "What, um, what galled me the most was that he left her alone to die in the backseat. He couldn't see past himself enough to even comfort her as she lay there dying. I'll never forgive him for that.

"Never."

THIRTY-FOUR

Sam Purdy walked into the restaurant, paused, and started to look around. Sawyer waved him over to our table.

She greeted him and invited him to join us as though she was delighted he was there and his presence would interfere with nothing of significance. I couldn't think of a thing to say in protest. They immediately started chatting about a cold front that was approaching Colorado after freezing cats in Montana. To my amazement, Sawyer had moved from revealing the pathos of her daughter's murder to participating in a mundane discussion about the weather with an ease that to me felt pornographic. I was tempted to ask Sam to leave us alone so that she and I could talk some more and come to something that felt like closure. But Sawyer had obviously talked enough. Or at least as much as she intended to.

Sam explained his presence. "We just decided—Milt and I, upstairs—that somebody should be with each of you all the time until this . . . thing is concluded. So I'm here to keep you company." The waitress, Kim, brought him a menu. Before he opened it, he asked me, "Should I bother? Is there anything in this place that your little doctor friend is going to let me eat?"

Sawyer said the soup was great. He looked at it and seemed to draw away physically from the creamy mixture the way a vampire might be repulsed by a bowl of roasted garlic.

I said I thought he could find something that was on his

diet. As he lowered his eyes to the pages, I stared at Sawyer, who wouldn't look back at me.

I wanted to know more about Simone.

I wanted to know why she couldn't trust anyone.

I wanted to know why she couldn't trust me.

Sam ordered an egg-white omelet and dry wheat toast. Sawyer asked for a fresh pot of tea.

I thought about things for a moment longer and announced that I was going for a walk, or something.

Sam made a face that communicated precisely how childish he thought my departure was in light of the fact that he had just volunteered to be my bodyguard. But he let me go without verbalizing a protest. I stopped in the lobby and used a pay phone to call Lauren. Her phone rang through to the nursing station, where a nurse informed me that Lauren was resting.

"How is she doing?"

"Well, she's tired. I imagine that's why she's resting."

"How was she doing before she started resting?"

"I think she was tired then, too. That's why she decided to rest."

I gave up and offered my tempered gratitude.

The woman who answered the phone at the veterinary hospital was much more forthcoming about Emily, who she said was doing "Great. She's my favorite. Is she always this much fun?"

I thought, *No, she isn't.* But I didn't say anything to dispel whatever transference was at work.

I stepped outside onto the flagstone steps of the hotel and felt the distinctive chill of autumn. That cold front that had so fascinated Sam and Sawyer was no longer approaching us from Montana; it had definitely arrived. Crisp gusts of wind were cutting through the canyons, whipping leaves from the trees, and knifing through my clothing as though I were dressed in rags. I examined the eastern sky and saw blues and blacks. When I turned to attend to the western sky, I saw strings of clouds the color of Sawyer's pumpkin soup.

Before I checked my watch, I guessed it was almost seven o'clock. But it was only 6:40.

I needed to find a place to sleep for the night. I had a plethora of bad options. One of my two available residences was a major construction zone. The other didn't have an operable furnace. Sam would offer the sofa bed at his place. A hotel probably made the most sense. First, though, I needed some clean clothes.

I found my car on Spruce Street and drove across downtown, over the creek, and up to the Hill. I parked outside for a few moments with the engine running, listening to the last few minutes of *Fresh Air* on NPR. Terry Gross was interviewing Scott Turow. Her interviewing style perplexed me, as it always did. If she were heading from L.A. to New York, she'd just as soon detour through São Paulo. But she somehow always got to her destination, and I was usually fascinated and grateful I'd gone along for the ride.

I climbed down from the Land Cruiser and made a quick tour of the exterior of Lauren's house. I unlocked the front door and stepped inside, immediately noting that the air inside was no warmer than the air outside. I prayed that this particular cold front wasn't quite cold enough to freeze plumbing and then decided not to worry about it. If the pipes froze, so be it. It wouldn't kill anyone.

The new furnace I had ordered wasn't downstairs where I expected it to be. It was sitting in a box at the top of the basement stairs. I was no mechanical genius, but I figured that the furnace had a ways to go, geographically speaking, before it was capable of generating any environmentally friendly, fuel-efficient heat for this little house. The contractor had said he'd have it up and running on Tuesday. I was now guessing Wednesday and wouldn't have been surprised by Thursday.

I avoided the bedroom for as long as I could. I swept up the dirt the rescue folks had dragged inside. I walked downstairs to the basement and found myself trying to remember what Sam had said about there having been two carbon monoxide detectors in the basement. One was made to operate on house current, but it had been unplugged. The other was operated by batteries, but it had fallen down behind the furnace.

The old furnace had been ripped out and carted away. I stared at the empty space and decided that it made no sense. Why would Lauren have installed two CO detectors in her basement? And why would one, the presumably more reliable one, be unplugged?

I climbed the stairs and went into the kitchen, picked up the phone, and called the hospital again. Lauren answered her own phone this time. The sound of her tired voice stirred me.

"Sweets, it's me. How are you doing?"

"Still a little foggy. But okay. Where's Emily? How is she?"

"Great. They love her at the vet hospital. They're threatening not to give her back to us."

She laughed gently. "You're pretty tired still?" I asked.

"Yes. I just woke up and I'm ready to go back to sleep."

"I wanted to remind you that you're due for Avonex tomorrow. You remember? I'll bring it down when I come to visit so that they can give it to you."

"Thanks," she said. She admitted, "I'd forgotten all about it."

I tried to be reassuring. "It's okay. It'll take a few days for you to sort everything out. Listen, I've been trying to make some sense of all the carbon monoxide detectors you have in the basement of the house on the Hill. There were two of them down there. Why?"

She didn't hesitate before responding. "That all happened about six months ago, I think. My tenant—remember Suzanne?—she asked me to put one in for her. I did. I originally got the battery-operated kind but when I tried to hang it on the wall, I didn't hammer in the nail hard enough and it fell off the wall and dropped and fell behind the furnace. I couldn't get back there to get it out. It was kind of stuck. I didn't know whether it was still working or not and I knew I'd never be able to change the batteries, so I went back to McGuckin and bought another one, one I could plug in. I've

been wondering why it didn't warn me earlier, you know?
Why it wasn't screaming at me when there was so much
poison in the house."

I didn't tell her that it hadn't warned her because someone had unplugged it. I said, "We're all trying to figure that
out. Scott Malloy is all over it, has somebody checking the
old furnace, and Sam is making sure nobody misses anything important. I have a new furnace going in tomorrow.
You get some rest. I'll see you sometime tomorrow. I love
you."

I hung up, wondering about the state of Lauren's
memory, gratified that she remembered the history of the
carbon monoxide detectors, and ambivalent about the fact
that she didn't show any indication that she felt that the CO
poisoning might have been attempted murder. She actually
didn't even seem to recall the whole series of events that
had followed Arnie Dresser's funeral.

Briefly, I envied her that.

I finally made my way to the bedroom to pick out some
clothes that were not only warm but also appropriate for
work the next day. The room was freezing. I toyed with the
idea of collecting every blanket, comforter, and sleeping
bag I could find in the house and burying myself under them
so I could sleep in our bed.

I talked myself out of it. Instead, I packed up some more
clothes and grabbed my appointment book and briefcase
before I began searching the house for something else. The
first place I tried was Lauren's little office. I had no success.
I tracked down her briefcase, which was locked. I shook it
gingerly and decided that what I was looking for wasn't
there. Her purse was hanging on a chair in the kitchen.
Nope. Finally, I found it in the little leather ass-pack she
carries to the health club when she works out.

The Glock.

Damn, but the thing was heavy.

The first place I tried to stash it was my jacket pocket, but
its heft totally distorted the shape of my coat. It felt way too
obvious having it there. Next, I gingerly hooked it into the

waistband of my trousers but immediately became uncomfortable at the general direction that the barrel was pointing, so I pulled it back out of my pants and stuffed it into the bottom of the little carry-on that I'd packed full of my clothing. After one last look around, I locked up the house and hopped back into my car with the knowledge that I was now officially carrying a concealed weapon. I felt fully the burden of being a felon, my eyes as much on the rearview mirror as they were on the road as I drove the dozen or so blocks to the hotel.

I had to admit, though, that the presence, close by, of that hunk of metal was just the slightest bit comforting. I puzzled over the question of whether that comfort index would increase or decrease once I actually figured out how to use the damn gun.

Parents' weekend at CU was over and the young assistant manager at the desk of the Boulderado seemed delighted to rent me a room for the night. We wasted a little too much energy haggling over price, however. I suggested to him that at the rate he initially quoted me, I'd just as soon stay at the Golden Buff on Canyon Boulevard. We both knew that his occupancy wasn't hovering particularly close to one hundred percent, and he came around to my way of thinking relatively quickly. He even feigned graciousness about offering the lower figure.

I was aware the whole time that I had a loaded 9mm semiautomatic in my luggage and wondered, of course, if it was the Glock, and not I, that had been doing the negotiating.

The thought reminded me of a conversation I'd once had during therapy, when I inquired of one of my patients what heroin was like. He warned me that horse was "so good you should never try it."

I considered the possibility that possessing a handgun was somewhat like tasting heroin. Both were artificial comforts that temporarily and unreasonably increased one's sense of well-being. Was the sense of comfort of possessing a pistol "so good" I should never have tried it?

Time would tell.

I found my hotel room, a nondescript little place on the second floor that had a stunning view of the alley. In a lesser town, that might have meant overlooking filth and mayhem. But downtown Boulder has great alleys. Neat, well lit, and paved with concrete. The choice of rooms was the assistant manager's petty revenge, I decided. I washed my face, brushed my teeth, and decided to leave the Glock in my bag while I made my way up to the Mezzanine Lounge for a drink or two.

The mime was on duty again.

Before sitting down I scouted for a location in the expansive lounge that wasn't her responsibility. But since the Broncos were playing a Sunday night game and this wasn't a sports bar she was the only waiter working the floor.

She remembered me. Instantly, I regretted leaving her such a healthy tip the last time I was in. She waved hello from across the mezzanine with that annoying arm-bent-shoulders-and-head-swaying gesture that only a mime would dare employ. I didn't wave back and actually considered fleeing through an exit before she could get all the way around the balcony railing to me.

Before she made it to the table, I heard Sam's voice in my ear. "Don't you find it goofy that these doctors will let me drink beer every day but don't want me to eat a damn hamburger? I find that goofy."

The word "goofy" was part of the residue of his upbringing on Minnesota's Iron Range. Every time he used it, he made me smile. "Hi, bodyguard," I said. "Can I buy you some carrot sticks?"

He sat on the settee across from me and followed my gaze up to the ceiling. "Nice glass," he offered in understatement as the waitress arrived. Naively, he smiled at her in welcome. She rewarded him by doing her mime thing.

He watched her act to its conclusion before he shifted his eyes to me. He stared at me incredulously, as though he'd just somehow stepped into the bar scene from *Star Wars* and he figured I was the only one who could get him safely back outside. Without changing my expression, I ordered vodka and told her I thought that Sam was doing okay with his beer.

She curtsied.

"Don't ask," I said.

"This damn town, I swear," he muttered, and moved on. "Listen, downstairs? Did I walk in on something hot and heavy with you and Sawyer?"

Sam's perspicacity ambushed me sometimes. "I'd say it was a delicate moment, yeah. But not what you think."

"What do I think?"

"Sam."

"You're not, you know, doing her, are you?"

"Sam." My voice was tired. Tired enough, I hoped, to get him to move in another direction.

"Well, sorry if I intruded. You talk to Lauren tonight?"

"Yeah. She's real tired, which the doctors seem to expect. But she seems okay. Her short-term memory has some black holes you could hide a galaxy in, but her thinking in general seems clear."

"Will she get out of the hospital soon?"

"It's day to day."

"Emily?"

"She's good. Making everybody happy at the vet hospital."

"The firefighters told me she did a smart thing. She found the cold-air feed for the furnace and lay down right under it. So she got some fresh air along with the carbon monoxide."

The story made me happy, and I promised myself I'd lighten up on the jokes I frequently made about the size of her brain. I said, "That reminds me, I asked Lauren about the two detectors." I related the explanation of why there were two carbon monoxide detectors in the basement.

"Wow. So the one with the battery that she couldn't reach is the one that saved her life?" He shook his head and smiled. "The best-laid plans, right? The asshole was good this time, Alan. Lock on the back door *may* have been picked, by the way. Furnace *may* have been tampered with. But you know as well as I do that there's no way in the world we'll get usable prints off of the other carbon monoxide detector, so who can say whether it was unplugged intentionally or not? But the killer didn't know about the other one, the one that fell behind the furnace. Couldn't have. And it's the one that stopped him."

"No leads, though?" I didn't expect any.

"None."

"How are you feeling?" I asked casually.

"Hungry. Other than that, like normal."

"But then normal apparently included a kidney stone the size of Gibraltar, right?"

He took a long swig of beer and then wiped his mustache with a napkin. "Can we talk about something more upbeat than me being in excruciating pain? Like, oh, let's say, the risk of you being murdered?"

"Sure. What do you think about A.J.'s current hypothesis? About there possibly being more than one killer?"

"It's not her hypothesis. It's mine."

"Really? You convinced her of something? She doesn't seem that . . . ?"

"Malleable. No, she doesn't."

With stealthy silence, Ms. Marceau returned with my drink. She delivered it without affectation. Sam stared at her with marked suspicion, as though he had an inkling she might be about to draw a gun, or break unexpectedly into the I'm-locked-in-a-glass-box routine.

Instead she set her cocktail tray on the table, took two baby steps backward, raised her arms, contorted her face, and tried, rather successfully I must admit, to imitate Edvard Munch's *The Scream*.

Sam lunged at her and she ran away with exaggerated cat steps. "Can you make her stop?" he implored me.

I shook my head. "You're the cop. Unfortunately, I tipped her well last time I was here. I'm afraid it encouraged her."

"Like feeding a damn raccoon." He belched politely, if that's possible. "Went like this. If this Corey Rand is so good, why throw him away? That's what I was thinking. You like him. Sawyer likes him. I kind of like him. His only problem as a suspect is that he has a damn good alibi for the killings since 1995."

"Damn good alibi is right. Major problem there, Sam."

"Not if he wasn't in it alone."

"You have an idea about his partner?"

"Not yet. Have you guessed how I got here?"

"Yeah. The change in MO between the early murders and the more recent ones. Sawyer and I have been theorizing a psychological deterioration. You're just seeing another hand at work. But the motivation doesn't work for me. Who else would have the same motive for the same killings?"

"I don't know. I admit I don't know that yet. But you can't get lost in motivation at the beginning. Think. Did someone have a motive to kill JonBenet? I don't think so. Maybe a predilection, perhaps even a need. But a rational motive? You can't start there always. Sometimes motivations are distracting at the front end of an investigation."

"Where to now?"

"I want to meet this boss of Rand's. See if he has a clue about any of this. What's his name?"

"Reggie Loomis."

"I want to meet Reggie Loomis."

"Now?"

"Why not? He's probably home watching the damn football game. I know I wish I was."

"Sam, you don't have to do this. I mean, I'm really grateful, but you should be home with Sherry and Simon, not here with me."

"That's not what I meant."

"Isn't it?"

"So you think Loomis is home."

"I doubt he's watching the football game. More likely he's making stock or preparing the dough for tomorrow's breads."

"What?"

"Never mind, you'll see." I threw six dollars on the table without bothering to ask for my tab.

Sam asked, "She won't chase us, will she? Like mimes do sometimes?"

"If she does, Sam, it's fine with me if you shoot her."

"Cool. Do you mind if Sawyer comes along with us to visit Loomis?"

"I guess not. Why?"

"Because I've already asked her."

THIRTY-FIVE

I didn't want to be chauffeuring Sawyer and Sam to North Boulder. I wanted to drink another vodka, plot my escape from the mime, retreat to my little hotel room alone, and spend some time pondering Sawyer and what had happened to her daughter, Simone. Sawyer had handed me important pieces to an old, long-incomplete puzzle, and I yearned for an opportunity to spin those pieces around, compare their contours, and see where they might fit on the board.

An unconscious corner of my awareness kept throwing Eleanor Ward's image into the mix. She had been there back then, too. On the unit. At the same time that Corey Rand was a patient.

And Eleanor Ward was the last patient Sawyer discharged before she packed up her things and left Colorado, and me, for good.

In addition, I now knew an additional fact. Eleanor Ward and Sawyer Sackett had both lost infant daughters to traumatic deaths.

Sawyer and Sam were arguing about Sawyer's speculation that a romance was simmering between Milt and A.J.— Sam said no way, Sawyer was totally sure—as I drove the car down North Broadway toward Reggie Loomis's neighborhood. I had enough self-awareness to know that I was confusing my mysteries. Part of me was consumed with understanding what had happened between Sawyer and me way back when. And part of me was consumed with solving the mystery of Corey Rand and his possible participation in these murders.

I reminded myself to try to keep my mysteries straight.

I found it odd, too, that I wished I had Lauren's Glock with me.

Sam took a break from arguing with Sawyer to ask me where Reggie Loomis lived.

"On Fourth, near Juniper."

"Which side?"

"West."

"On the greenbelt?" The edges of the question were gilded with envy.

"Yep."

"Nice neighborhood for a retired government worker."

"It's not one of the scrapes, Sam. It's one of the original houses. Looks like he's lived there forever."

"Still," he said. He was cooking something up, but as the smell drifted back my way, I couldn't tell what it was.

The front of Reggie's house was dark, but I wasn't dissuaded. Reggie Loomis didn't live for appearances.

Sawyer said, "Looks like no one's home."

"He keeps a low profile. Let's knock."

We strolled up the walk in single file and I stepped forward and rapped twice on the door.

I thought I smelled cinnamon wafting in the chill air, along with some other enticing aroma that wasn't quite registering in my memory. "I think he's here. I smell food."

Sam looked at his wristwatch as though it was important to time Reggie's response to my knock. I kept my eye on the peephole in the door, waiting for it to darken. Finally it did. Reggie was checking us out.

Sam tensed. He had noticed the shadow across the peephole, too.

After another ten seconds, Sam said, "So, is he going to open it or not? I'm not exactly warm out here."

"He's considering it."

I waited a full minute. I timed it on Sam's wristwatch,

which he held up for inspection about every ten seconds. I knocked again.

Reggie slid the dead bolt about two Sam-sighs later. He ignored my companions and looked directly at me as he said, "Yes."

"I brought some people with me, Reggie."

"I can see that."

"Are you busy? Can you spare a few minutes?" I noted that he was unconcerned with Sawyer, but had begun an examination of Sam.

"I am busy preparing tomorrow's breakfast. Cinnamon rolls? Perhaps you can smell them. Although I find them unsophisticated, I'm afraid I've become known for them. I'll be doing baked eggs in the morning and need to finish the prep work before I head to bed. Perhaps another time?"

"Those rolls sure smell good to me," Sam interjected, his voice padded with false camaraderie.

"And you are . . . ?" asked Reggie. His voice was not padded with false camaraderie.

"Sam Purdy."

"And you are . . . with?"

Sam smiled. "I'm with my friends here. You know Alan, of course. And this here, this here is Sawyer. We'd be grateful for a little bit of your time and I promise we won't stay long."

"This really isn't a convenient time for a visit. I'm sorry. I have work to do. People depend on me. Please call tomorrow, Dr. Gregory. We can find a time."

Sam said, "Lives may be at stake, Mr. Loomis."

Reggie rolled his eyes at the overt manipulation. But he said, "Then come in. If you must."

We followed Reggie into his main room. He immediately stepped over to a CD player and flicked on a clarinet concerto.

Sam's face didn't hide his disappointment at not finding the football game, though he had no discernible reaction to the configuration of Reggie's house or the splendor of the kitchen equipment. But Sawyer did.

"Wow. Nice kitchen," she said.

I explained what Reggie did, how he prepared and delivered food to shut-ins around the county.

"That's very generous of you," Sawyer said.

Sam nodded in the general direction of the La Cornue and said, "Something sure smells good."

I admonished him, "They're not exactly on your diet, Sam."

He inhaled deeply, as though he could be nourished by the aroma alone, and muttered, "Shit."

Reggie hadn't offered any refreshments, and he wasn't prompted to by Sam's infelicitous comment.

Sawyer glided slowly around the kitchen, touching the La Cornue, examining the espresso machine, and grazing her fingertips along the marble and granite countertops. She asked kitchen questions. Reggie answered in a fashion that was more guarded than I would have expected from him.

Finally, she chose a seat next to Sam and me at the counter. Reggie stood by the stove across the room. I felt a bit like a judge at a tribunal.

Sawyer stunned me by asking, "I've always wondered, Mr. Loomis. Why do you think that D. B. Cooper requested four parachutes during the hijacking? I mean, we now know that he was working alone, right? And he had things impeccably planned, so why did he ask for four?"

Sam blinked twice.

Reggie looked at me and, I imagine, saw the incredulity in my expression. "What?" he managed to ask.

Sawyer's voice was all casualness and curiosity. "Why four parachutes? You know the legend, right? After the airplane landed in Seattle, he requested two hundred thousand dollars in twenty-dollar bills, and he asked for four parachutes. Why four? Why not one? Why not two or three?"

Reggie's eyes jumped from Sam to me and then back to Sawyer. "Why . . . why are you asking me that?"

"You were a security analyst. One of your things was anticipating terrorists, right? Figuring out scenarios. Well, D.B. was like our first commercial domestic terrorist. And Alan says the whole D. B. Cooper thing was like a parlor game for the people where you worked. I'm just wondering what you guys came up with for an explanation of all the extra parachutes old D.B. requested."

Reggie backed up against the La Cornue. His voice as defensive as his posture, he demanded, "Why did you come to see me tonight? All of you?"

Sam knew what role to assume when he was in situations like this with his detective partner, Lucy. But Sawyer's line of inquiry about D. B. Cooper had apparently left him speechless.

Sawyer acted as if she expected an answer to her question. I didn't imagine it would be forthcoming.

I said, "Corey Rand is dead."

Two beats passed before Reggie said, "No. I'm so sorry. I'm just, so, so sorry to hear that." His words felt a little rushed.

Sam glanced at me. If he were to score Reggie's lie, I don't think he would have given it more than a six point five. Why was Reggie pretending he didn't know Corey Rand was dead?

I said, "You didn't know?"

He turned and squatted and lowered the oven door. The aroma of cinnamon dough almost bowled me off my stool. He fussed with the pan and finally pulled it from the oven and placed it beside the one that was already baked. "Done," he said.

"Would you like to know the circumstances of his death?"

"My—ouch!" He yanked his hand back from the edge of the pan. "My, yes, of course."

Sam kicked me on the ankle and said, "Car accident. Hit and run. No witnesses. Internal injuries."

Were I a judge of Sam's fabrication, I would have held up a card that read nine point oh.

Reggie walked across the room to the sink and started running cold water over his burned finger.

Was he going to let Sam's lie stand?

He asked, "Was it recent?"

Sawyer and I stayed silent. Sam said, "Last year, around the holidays."

He shut off the faucet before he said, "So Corey Rand isn't responsible for the recent deaths you three are investigating?"

I was about to shake my head but was able to perceive the outlines of the trap Sam was setting in time to say, "Which deaths are those?"

Reggie stared hard at me. His look was disdainful. It said, "Nice try, amateur." He dried his hands and responded, "The fire deaths, of course. In Kittredge. We discussed them, remember? The last time you were here, Doctor."

I nodded.

Reggie made himself busy cleaning the counter. Without facing us again, he said, "I'm afraid I'll need to excuse myself now. I'd like to prepare for bed."

When we were back outside, Sam commended me. "Nice pickup in there. I wasn't even sure you were paying attention to what was going on."

"Thanks. It didn't work, though. He saw it coming."

"That's just it. He did see it coming. And that tells us exactly what we need to know."

"Which is what?"

"That he knows more than he's letting on to us about Corey Rand and about all your dead colleagues." He turned to Sawyer. "And, pray tell, what the hell was all that D. B. Cooper shit about?"

Sawyer was climbing into the backseat. She settled herself and caught my eye in the rearview mirror. I shook my head just a little. She smiled.

"Sorry," she said to Sam. "I can't tell you. Confidentiality. I'm sure you understand."

Sam muttered, "No, I don't understand. And Alan will be happy to tell you I'm not much of a fan of shrinks and confidentiality." He pulled his seat belt around his waist and clicked it into place before he yanked the rearview mirror his way and focused it on Sawyer in the backseat. "And here I've been thinking that you and I were going to get along. Anybody hungry but me?"

No one was hungry but him.

I wanted to know what we were going to do next, and all Sam would tell me was that he wanted to talk to some people he knew from Rocky Flats, see if he could discover a reason for Reggie Loomis to be so slippery with us. I assumed he would learn about the D. B. Cooper rumors as soon as he started sniffing around at the nuclear weapons facility.

"When will you get final word on whether somebody tampered with our furnace?"

"I'll ask Scott. But I'm not holding my breath. If they say it was tampered with, what does that tell us that we don't already know? If they say it wasn't, are either of you suddenly going to feel any safer? I don't think so."

"It will give Simes and Custer something to take back to the FBI, though, right?"

"Wrong. The FBI is looking for something that ties two of these things together. With only one point to work with, you never get to draw a straight line."

On the rest of the short drive back to downtown, Sawyer quizzed me about property values and seemed disappointed that the desirable parts of Boulder were almost as expensive as Santa Barbara. Twice she said about Loomis's shack, "His little house would really cost that much?"

Sam muttered something about trying to live around here on a cop's salary, and Sawyer wisely dropped it.

As I parked near the hotel, Sam asked, "So where are you sleeping tonight? Is your new furnace in yet?"

"It's in the house, but it's not quite in the basement. I have a room here, too. At the Boulderado."

As I looked up, I noticed that Sawyer was staring at me in the mirror in a way that made me uncomfortable. I glanced quickly over at Sam, hoping to stifle an invitation to sleep at his house. "I'll be safe here. He's not going to take out a hotel full of people, is he?"

Sam didn't answer immediately. "Well, is he?" I repeated.

"No, probably not. A wing, a floor, maybe. Not the whole hotel. What room are you in? I'll call early tomorrow."

Before I could recall my room number for Sam, Sawyer

said, "Sam, are you with us on some kind of . . . I don't know, official basis? Don't you have other responsibilities?"

He smiled sideways at me before he responded. "I'm terribly sorry. I can't tell you. Confidentiality, you know. Listen, anybody want to do breakfast tomorrow? That egg-white thing I had for dinner wasn't half bad."

I said that I had to be at my office early. Sawyer said she was going to sleep as late as she could.

At Sam's behest, I agreed to accompany Sawyer up to the suite she was sharing with A.J. The elevator ride up was particularly awkward.

"You never told him what room you were in," she commented as the doors swooshed shut.

"No," I said. "I guess I didn't."

"Well, in case I need to reach you, where are you? You know that A.J. and Milt are going to want to know."

I felt in my pocket for the plastic card key. "Two eighteen. It's small, and dark, and not particularly charming. It may have the same address as your suite but it's certainly not in the same neighborhood."

"But then you don't have to share your room with an ex–FBI agent with an attitude who gives you the third degree every time you want to use the toilet."

"That's true. I don't."

We exited the elevator at her floor. I stopped in front of the door to the suite. "Your plane will be ready tomorrow? Is that true? They can fix it that fast?"

"Maybe. There wasn't that much damage. A little sheet metal to replace. Test the damn landing gear."

"Are you ready to go home?"

She shrugged. "Milt says I shouldn't, doesn't think it's wise. If I do go back, he wants to hook me up with a body-guard, somebody he knows from his days in Chicago. Sounds awful. I don't know what I'll do. Sometimes the night tells me things. So when my head hits the pillow, I'll be listening to the whispers."

She leaned forward slowly with her eyes locked on mine, her lips slightly parted. She moved toward me, at the last moment tilting her head to the side. She kissed me on the cheek.

I said, "Good night."

After waiting for the elevator to arrive for a good three minutes I finally realized I hadn't hit the "down" button.

THIRTY-SIX

With the curtains closed in my hotel room I was able to convince myself that I was actually ensconced on the top floor with a stunning view of the Flatirons. I wanted to end the day with another vodka, but the urge was not quite strong enough to motivate me to once again confront the mime lurking in the Mezzanine Lounge. The conundrum, I decided, was that I would only be able to find her act tolerable after I consumed more drinks than I would ever be able to tolerate her serving to me.

I could have walked over to one of the half-dozen bars close by on the Mall. I didn't. The minibar provided a tiny shot of Absolut that I sipped straight from the bottle while I flicked on the TV. I found a movie with Nicolas Cage on HBO, and stared at a nine-dollar jar of pistachios for much longer than I really needed to before I started getting ready for bed.

The bedside clock argued forcefully that it was too late to call Lauren, so I checked my pager to make sure the battery was fresh in case the hospital needed to reach me. Then I sat down next to the clock radio to make certain that the previous guest in this room wasn't a prankster who would get a sadistic chuckle from leaving the alarm set to wake me at some ungodly hour. The alarm was indeed set. The time the little jester had chosen to jolt me out of bed to the not-so-soothing sounds of KYGO was 3:48 A.M. I unset the clock, stripped off my clothes, and walked into the bathroom to take a shower.

There was a part of me that knew she would come. A part of me that welcomed her visit. Avoiding this moment would have been easy. I could have taken a room at the Golden Buff across town.

And there was a part of me that dreaded her visit. The dread wasn't actually about the visit. The dread was about how I would deal with it.

Does falling in love with one woman clean the slate and erase the love that was once so passionate for another woman? Does it?

Because I was living proof it doesn't.

Do I send her away? Tell her that her visit is inappropriate?

Because it is.

Do I tell her I'm not interested? Tell her that was a long time ago and my feelings have changed?

Have they?

Do I act as a friend might act and offer a shoulder so that she can begin to untangle her anger and unburden herself of all the feelings that are surfacing about her daughter's death?

Because a friend would.

As an intellectual exercise, I could enjoy the quandary. In fact, in my office on Walnut Street, with a patient across the room from me, I could have examined the facets of this therapeutic diamond for the full duration of many forty-five-minute hours. But as a married man naked in a hotel room with an ex-lover trilling her fingers across my door, I wasn't much enamored with the puzzle.

I was edging down the dark tunnel toward sleep when the tapping started, and it took me a while to separate the rhythmic sounds I was hearing from the comfortable reverie of pre-dreaming. Finally awake, I said, "Wait, wait. Just a minute," jumped from the bed, and immediately ran into a wall. I made my way to the closet and pulled on the robe that the hotel had provided—according to the card that was attached to the belt—for my "comfort and pleasure." Apparently, hotel management was under the mistaken impression that I would somehow be most comfortable pretending that I was five foot four and, say, one hundred and twenty pounds.

The full-length mirror adjacent to the closet let me know that three-quarter-length sleeves and an above-the-knee hem were never going to be my most alluring look in boudoir attire.

I winked into the peephole.

It was Sawyer. She was smiling, but she didn't look happy.

In my hotel room, there was one chair and there was the bed. In my comfortable hotel robe, I could sit modestly on neither. After inviting Sawyer inside, I excused myself and retreated to the bathroom to pull on jeans and a T-shirt.

She had chosen to park herself on the bed, on the side that was mostly still unruffled. She was wearing red and black animal-print tights and a matching top that accentuated her breasts. Her hair was casual and she hadn't retouched her makeup since we'd said good night earlier. She didn't look a day younger than she was, and I found her incredibly alluring.

For one of the few times in our relationship, she was as uncomfortable as I was. "This isn't, um . . . I need . . . we can go someplace else if you'd . . . I just need to talk, I think. I don't want you to . . . I mean, I hope—"

"It's fine, Sawyer. Can I get you something?" I parked my butt on the chair by the window and waved at the mini-bar as though it contained a genie ready to meet any of her desires.

"No, thank you. I'm grateful to you just for opening the door to me. It's more than I expected. More than I deserved, for sure."

The tension in the room was so dense that it felt as if it could crush the air from my chest. To lighten the mood, I said, "I need to tell you that I was, I don't know, touched— deeply—by what you decided to share with me earlier. About your marriage and your daughter."

"Simone." She spoke the word with such reverence that if

love were helium, it would have been enough to float her baby girl from her grave.

"Yes, Simone. I only wish I had known about her. You know, back then."

She fiddled with the hem of the bedspread. "I wasn't ready to grieve with everyone. With anyone, really. I knew if I told people, everyone would treat me differently. Remember that resident who had the osteosarcoma? What was his name? I don't know; it doesn't matter. But everybody had an opinion on what kind of cases he should be allowed to take. I just wasn't ready for that kind of scrutiny. I convinced myself that I needed to work, that . . . that was best for me, working, the harder the better, not thinking about what Kenny did to my baby."

I was suddenly aware of my posture. I asked, "And keeping away from men—that was best for you too?"

"No," she said, her eyes fixed on her hands. "Men were candy for me. I'd pick one and take a tiny bite and throw away any flavors I didn't like. I hurt a lot of men a little during those few months, and that felt . . . I don't like this about me, Alan, but it felt good. I loved attracting men and flirting with them and . . . nibbling at their centers and then . . . moving on. I had planned to do the same with you. And then you came along and you didn't seem to want to just play the game. I didn't feel like I was a conquest to you. You actually wanted me."

"And . . . you felt, needed you."

"Yeah, that was your mistake." She smiled to herself, not to me. "Needing me. When I felt you begin to need me, it scared me. I started seeing Kenny in your eyes and . . ."

"You left Denver because of me? I'd always assumed that your leaving Denver showed how little you cared about me."

She shook her head. "See, that's your insecurity." She shivered as though recalling an unpleasant memory. "But that wasn't it. You're forgetting about Elly." She stood up, took two baby steps, and faced the window. She parted the curtains, using both her hands. Her perfume sifted through the still air in the room and reached me, settling around me as though I were holding a bouquet of fragrant flowers. "Nice view," she said.

"Thanks. They charge extra for it, but I'm into the urban alley experience, so I figured what the hell." I stood then, too, and immediately wondered why. I figured I would regret getting up, but sitting right back down didn't feel right either. "Elly lost a daughter, too."

"Yes. Elly lost a daughter, too. She was another gorgeous baby. I doubt if you remember—why would you?—but her daughter's name was Priscilla. During those weeks between Thanksgiving and Christmas, I somehow taught Elly how to begin to grieve her loss, how to let go and move on. And, somehow, she . . . returned the favor and showed me it was okay for me to begin to grieve, too. But she was way ahead of me. After those weeks with her, I couldn't keep it in any longer—the pain, the anger. I talked to Susan about it for a long time. And my therapist, too, of course. We all agreed it would be best if I left the residency and went back to Raleigh and dealt with . . . my feelings about Simone. Maybe I'd come back and finish up in Colorado later, maybe I wouldn't."

"You didn't say goodbye to me. You never explained why you were leaving." My tone surprised me. These words weren't an accusation on my part. They were a plea for her to help me understand.

"I convinced myself that since I hadn't let anyone in the door, I didn't owe anyone the courtesy of a good-bye. That was my rationalization, anyway. The truth is sadder. The truth is that I didn't want to see how much I had hurt you. Because I knew you cared, and I feared you cared too much. And I knew I was going to hurt you, deeply. By leaving, by my dishonesty, by everything I'd done. I didn't want to witness it. Part of it was cowardice. And part of it, the bigger part, was that . . . I was too afraid of what men could do when they're hurt."

"I would never have harmed you, Sawyer."

She shook her head viciously, her blond hair flying off her shoulders. "I once believed that about Kenny, Alan. That he could never harm me. When I was having so much trouble establishing an alliance with Elly, you taught me an important lesson about transference, remember? Don't forget the lesson you taught me. God knows that I never have."

I stepped toward and embraced her from behind, my hands folded over her abdomen, my face buried in her hair. She crossed her arms over her chest and grabbed one of my arms with each hand. I felt her ass against my groin.

The room lights flickered, and I wondered how to move away, feeling desperately how much I didn't want to.

The lights darkened once again, staying off for two or three seconds before returning.

I inhaled the smell of her and filtered through a thousand memories before I thought of Lauren, and the room went dark again.

This time it stayed dark.

"Power failure," Sawyer said. "Ooooh. Where were you when the lights went out?"

I reached past her and parted the curtains. The alley lights were dark, and the traffic signals at the corner were black dots. Through the walls of the adjacent room I heard an anxious voice saying, "What? What is it?"

"It's not just the hotel," I said, pointing at the street. "It looks like this whole part of the city is dark."

She turned and faced me, our bodies now in full contact, our lips inches apart. I could taste her breath and feel the air stir as it caressed my skin. I wondered which one of us would look away first.

She tensed and looked to one side and then the other. She furrowed her forehead and said, "Oh, shit, Alan. Do you think?"

Immediately, I knew what she was talking about. I yanked her backward away from the window, and she tumbled on top of me onto the bed. Her weight on me was a comfort, and I felt the contours of her body as familiar and precious, like the memory residue of a special old aroma.

Our chests were heaving from the combination of emotions. Each inhale heightened my arousal. I stammered, "We should phone Milt."

She didn't move. She admitted, "Probably. But he'll tell us to stay where we are, don't you think?"

"Probably." I didn't know what to do with my hands. "I'm not sure this is a good idea," I said.

"Staying here?" Her voice was a murmur. She was gazing at me through bedroom eyes.

"No. Staying in this position."

She didn't move right away. She asked, "You're sure?" I felt her hips rotate and I knew I was getting hard.

"Sawyer, at this moment, I'm not even sure of my name."

She started to smile. Outside, a car braked hard, tires squealed, and time stood still as the protracted screech ended in a vicious crash. Seconds later, someone yelled, "Anybody have a phone? Somebody call 911. On no! We need an ambulance!"

I started to get up, and Sawyer rolled off of me onto her back, onto the bed. Her top had ridden up, and I could see the swell of the bottom of her breasts. She didn't try to cover herself. I turned my attention to the window, pulling back the draperies an inch or two.

"I can't see anything, the accident," I said, turning back to her.

She put her hands behind her head and her top rode up even higher. At that moment, I recalled every contour of her nipples. They were small, with aureoles no larger than nickels. They would grow hard with the slightest touch.

I exhaled, and my voice came out too loud. "I'll call Milt," I said, moving to the other side of the bed. I grabbed the phone and punched in the number for Milt's room. He picked up on the first ring, obviously groggy.

"Milt? It's Alan. The power's out in the hotel, in this whole part of town, actually. I doubt if it means anything, but I'm feeling a little paranoid."

He was quiet for a few seconds, maybe ten. I said, "Hello? Milt?"

His tone was crisp, authoritative. He said, "It's probably nothing. But get away from the window and stay where you are. I'll be down in a minute. Three knocks. Check me through the peephole."

"Okay. Um, Sawyer's here, too."

"I know," he said, his tone packed with disapproval.

Before the receiver was back on its cradle, Sawyer asked, "What did he say?"

"He said to stay put. He's coming down."

"I told you so." With her right hand she pulled her top down and covered her breasts.

For some reason I'm not sure I want to understand, at that moment I remembered I had the Glock.

THIRTY-SEVEN

Milt's nostrils kept flaring as though he were sniffing for the odors of sex.

His manner was disapproving. My guilt said it was about Sawyer and me being alone in my hotel room, but his gruffness could have been typical of him after he had been waked up to baby-sit relative strangers. He said hello to each of us without making eye contact with either of us, told us where to sit—Sawyer on one side of the bed, me on the other—and got on his cell phone, surprisingly, to Sam Purdy. He explained to Sam what was going on and asked if Sam could make a call or two to try to figure it out.

We sat in silence for two or three minutes waiting for the phone to ring again. When it did, Milt listened uninterrupted to Sam for most of a minute, before he said, "Thanks. Yeah, tomorrow."

He pinned me with his eyes. "There's a short in a transformer in a substation. Sam said something about a fried raccoon." He made a face that I interpreted as "That kind of shit doesn't happen in Evanston." He continued, "Are you two in any immediate danger? I think not. If our guy wanted you to leave the room, to leave the hotel, he would have set a fire or set off the fire alarm and waited to ambush you as you evacuated. And ambushing people in public isn't his style. I don't see how this helps him, blacking out part of the town. Do either of you see a margin in this?"

I shook my head politely, feeling as though I had been

summoned to the principal's office. Sawyer was examining her nails. She said, "No. It doesn't make sense. We overreacted."

"Then let's call it a coincidence and say we all try to get some sleep."

No one moved. Milt offered his hand to Sawyer. "Come on, Doctor. I'll see you back upstairs."

She said, "That's really not necessary."

He said, "But it will be my pleasure. Don't want to take any foolish risks, right?" I thought I saw the shadow of a smirk on his face as he turned to me. "Double-lock this door. Put out your 'Do not disturb.' Don't order room service. Keep those curtains closed."

"You mean you want me to forsake this view?" I said.

After they left I lay in the dark for half an hour, not even thinking about sleeping. The power grid came back on line in a startling flash of light, and I wasted another half hour or so flipping through the channels on the TV, trying to understand why infomercials were proliferating.

I think I managed to spend some of the remainder of the night sleeping, the rest of it wondering whether I actually would have had sex with her.

The bedside phone rang at 5:17. As I was trying to make sense of my surroundings, my dreams, my erection, and the insanely loud noise blaring beside my head, my pulse raced to a level that evolution intended only as response to the assault of a wild animal.

By the third or fourth ring, I had puzzled out that I was in a hotel room and that the phone required attention. In rapid sequence, I thought: *Hospital. Oh shit. Lauren,* and scrambled after the receiver. I mumbled a "Hello" that caught in my throat. It felt as though I would choke on the word.

"Dr. Gregory?"

Did I recognize that voice? I said, "Yes."

"Reggie here. Reggie Loomis. Hope I didn't wake you."

Thank God it wasn't the hospital.

I glanced at the clock. "It's barely five o'clock in the morning, Reggie. Of course you woke me."

He said, "Sorry," but he didn't sound it. "I have a one-time offer for you and your lady friend. But it doesn't include the cop."

How did he figure Sam for a cop? I rubbed my eyes as though greater visual clarity would help me at the moment. "I'm waiting."

"Here's the situation. My ride—the church lady with the big Chevy?—she can't help me deliver the breakfast meals this morning. Her son is home sick from school. Fever. Rash. I know you have a big car. Here's the deal. You give me a ride around to drop off food at the shut-ins, and while we're driving around, I'll tell you and your lady friend what I know about all this D. B. Cooper propaganda that you both seem so goldarned interested in."

The offer was curious. Why was Reggie suddenly so willing to spill the beans about D. B. Cooper? During my previous visits, he'd been evasive about the legend, and he certainly hadn't been responsive to Sawyer's frontal assault the night before. This was a contingency specialist; I felt confident that he must have alternative backup transportation to deliver his meals. Why did he want us? And why did he want to talk about D. B. Cooper?

I tried to remember my work schedule. My morning was free, I thought, until about ten forty-five, and then I had patients stacked like a wedding cake until dinnertime. "I need to check my calendar and find Sawyer and see if she's interested. I'll get back to you."

"No can do," he insisted. "We need to leave here by six-thirty at the latest. Yes or no?"

I exhaled and pulled the covers around me with my free hand. Did I fear Reggie Loomis? Did I even consider it a possibility that he was involved in this conspiracy that had consumed my life since Arnie Dresser's funeral?

No, I didn't.

Did I care enough about this D. B. Cooper thing to take his offer? Not really. But something was telling me that there was more to be learned from this errand than this old man's musings on the legend of an ancient hijacker. Maybe something about Corey Rand. *That* interested me.

And, I reminded myself, I'd get to do some good. Help some people who needed help.

I said, "Okay. We'll be there at six-fifteen."

"I'll have plenty of coffee, and don't worry about eating first. This shift includes breakfast, of course."

I remembered the aromas of the previous evening. "Cinnamon rolls and baked eggs."

"Not to mention fresh fruit cups with mint. I found some killer pomegranates at Alfalfa's. Pomegranate juice does things for the rest of the fruit that you just won't believe."

Sawyer climbed into my car right on schedule at 6:10.

I greeted her warmly but was careful not to touch her, keeping both my hands on the wheel. I felt awkward. She seemed serene. "How did you get away?" I asked. "Wasn't A.J. suspicious?"

She nodded, blowing warm air onto her fingers. "Does this thing have heated seats?"

"No."

"Too bad. I just told her that you and I were going to have breakfast together before you went to work. She didn't seem to be worried about it."

"If Milt had been there, he wouldn't have let you go."

She cupped her hands around her mouth again. I heard her blow through her fingers. "Milt was there, I think. A.J. closed her door behind her when she came out to ask me about the phone call. I think he was in there with her."

"Huh," I managed, momentarily trying to picture the parameters of that tryst before allowing my mind to wander elsewhere.

Sawyer asked, "So Reggie's offered to tell us what he knows about D. B. Cooper? That's why we're doing this?"

"That's the offer. I'm actually hoping to learn more about Corey Rand than about D. B. Cooper. Rand is the one who was so consumed with him—Cooper. Maybe we can get Reggie talking about Rand's fixation."

"What about Sam?"

"Reggie said the cop wasn't welcome."

"He made Sam for a cop?"

"Apparently."

She lowered her hands to her legs and slid them beneath her thighs. "Reggie could have some guilty knowledge. You thought about that?"

"Yes, I have."

"And we're delivering food?"

"To shut-ins. We're going to be do-gooders this morning, Sawyer."

She shivered. "I have two questions."

"Yes?"

"First, why on earth do shut-ins want to eat breakfast so early? Why don't they sleep in?"

"Sorry, I can't help you with that one. Second?"

"Do you want to talk about last night?"

I flicked on my headlights, checked my mirrors, pulled away from the curb, and said, "No, I don't think so."

As I drove west on Kalmia on the way to Reggie's house I glanced in my rearview mirror and saw the first glow of light in the eastern sky. The moment I turned left onto Fourth, I noticed that Reggie was standing on the four-by-four slab of concrete that sufficed as his front porch.

Sawyer and I strolled up the walk. Reggie didn't say good morning. He said, "You're late."

I pulled my left hand out of my pocket and checked my watch. The time was precisely 6:17. "Two minutes?" I said.

"Excuse me? If your patients are two minutes late for therapy, do you let them get away with it?"

The truth was that usually I did. But I admitted his argument by saying, "No. I guess not." Left unsaid was that I didn't schedule appointments with my patients on one hour's notice at six-fifteen in the morning.

Reggie huffed, "Well, we'll just have to make up the lost time along the way. Let's get these meals loaded into the car. I'm afraid that your coffee and rolls will have to wait."

Sawyer didn't make the slightest move toward the front

door. In an even voice, she said, "Don't be petty, Reggie. We get our coffee now or we don't work. It's that simple."

I smiled. This was the woman I remembered.

Reggie's catering service was, no surprise, organized with the precision of an operating room or an airplane galley. Separate storage units kept the hot food hot, the cold food cold, and the room-temperature supplies, room-temperature. Moments after closing the doors, the interior of the car smelled like a Paris café, but without the permeation of Gauloises.

"Where to?" I asked.

Reggie was riding shotgun. "We'll head south and work our way back to this end of town. We have some canyon stops to make, too."

"Broadway?"

"Yes. First home on the list is right below N-CAR."

"Is that tarragon I smell?"

"Yes. It is."

His directions were flawless. As we arrived at a nondescript split-level with a million-dollar view, he gave us the drill. "My guests are not accustomed to their homes being invaded by strangers. Mrs. Savage, my usual driver, accompanies me inside to help set up the meal and to collect the dishes from our previous visit. I would like one of you to do the same at each house. You may alternate. You should each get a feel for this work that I do."

I'd finished my coffee. Sawyer's hands were firmly wrapped around her mug. I said, "I'll do the first one."

I popped the rear hatch of the Land Cruiser and stepped around to open it. Reggie prepared the first tray, choosing a large cup of fresh fruit, a ramekin of baked eggs, and a cinnamon roll the size of his fist. He drew coffee from a big urn into an insulated pitcher and added small cartons of skim milk and orange juice to the tray. "I used to do fresh-squeezed. But I'm afraid it wasn't totally appreciated," he explained, apologizing for the carton of Tropicana.

"This is a young widow, Mrs. Levitt. Her husband was

killed in a traffic accident that caused her severe injuries.
She has been one of my guests for almost six months. By the
way, I will not be introducing you to her as 'Doctor.' I'm not
intending to diminish your stature, but for most of my
guests, presenting you as 'Doctor' would be intrusive and
confusing. I'm confident that you understand." He looked
at his watch before lifting the tray. "We continue to run a
few minutes behind schedule. I allow seven minutes inside
each house, except for the last one. I alternate which guest
comes last for each meal, and I linger there with that guest,
visiting. I've explained this to you already."

I nodded.

Reggie opened the front door with a key. Inside, he
pointed me toward the kitchen and explained I would find
the previous meal's dishes in a brown paper bag on the sink.
I was to retrieve them and wait by the door.

I heard the sounds of the *Today* show, Katie teasing Matt
about something, and Mrs. Levitt's high-pitched, excited
voice greeting Reggie. She started cooing over the breakfast tray, and Reggie began asking about her children.
About a minute later, I heard, "Mr. Gregory?"

I followed the sounds of the TV and found Reggie sitting
beside Mrs. Levitt on an awful chartreuse sofa in the living
room. Mrs. Levitt was indeed young; I guessed late twenties. She was painfully thin and pale and was covered to her
waist by a chenille blanket. A thin scar extended upward
from her right ear, across her temple, and disappeared into
her hairline. One arm hung useless by her side. She raised
the other one to shake my hand. I stepped forward and
touched it gently. "This is so kind of you," she said. "Helping like this."

"It's my pleasure to help." At that moment, it was.

"My balance isn't very good anymore. And with only one
arm . . . well, you know. Mr. Loomis is a lifesaver."

We visited for maybe two more minutes, until Reggie began a gracious transition to the door. I followed his cue. Moments later we were back in the Land Cruiser on our way
to a house just south of the Bureau of Standards. I poured
myself more coffee while Reggie and Sawyer delivered

breakfast to an elderly male inhabitant of a brick ranch that was dwarfed by junipers.

Our next two stops were tract homes in Martin Acres, followed by a cluttered one-bedroom apartment near Baseline and the Boulder Turnpike. Thus far, I realized, the stops had been no more than three or four minutes apart.

I was well aware that I had nothing in my stomach but a couple of mugs of coffee.

I was also well aware that thus far no one had mentioned D. B. Cooper.

THIRTY-EIGHT

I waited patiently, I thought, through one more breakfast stop, this one at an apartment building behind the old CU Credit Union building on Baseline. While Sawyer and Reggie delivered the breakfast tray, I went around to the back of the car and poured myself another mug of coffee. They returned right on schedule, and as soon as they were buckled back into their seat belts, I asked, "Well, Reggie, what about D. B. Cooper? You said you would fill us in."

He was gazing out the windshield to the northwest. He said, "Our next guest lives in married student housing in that complex off Arapahoe behind Naropa. You know where that is?"

"Yes, I do." I didn't start the engine.

"Well, then, scoot, scoot." He tapped his watch. "We've almost made up our lost time. If we make the lights, we'll be back on track."

I still didn't start the engine.

He glared at his watch as though it were lying to him.

Reggie sighed and said, "Okay. Okay. Drive. I'll talk."

I decided to take Twenty-eighth Street over to Arapahoe, which probably was a mistake even this early in rush hour. I missed the first traffic light and listened to Reggie punctuate my braking with a sigh.

He started by saying, "I don't know how much you recall about the Cooper legend. But it was a big deal back in 1971. Captivated the country. Divided the country, really. Seemed at the time that half of us wanted him caught and the other half were rooting for him to continue to elude the FBI and make them look like fools. You have to remember those days in the early seventies. This was right after the bombing in Cambodia, during the height of Vietnam. There was a lot of anti-government sentiment going around."

The light changed, and I inched forward, pulling up the on-ramp onto Twenty-eighth Street. We were soon stacked up behind a UPS truck halfway back from the light at College.

In a voice his ex-wife had probably detested, Reggie said, "You should have taken Thirtieth."

"Probably," I acknowledged.

He was energized as he returned his attention to the Cooper saga. "The crime itself was something special. It was innovative. No one had ever hijacked a commercial jet for ransom in this country before. It was planned meticulously. The man was so ordinary that hardly anyone remembered him well enough to describe him. He left no fingerprints on his ticket or near his seat. His escape was brazen and a work of pure genius. He actually parachuted out the rear stairs of a 727 into the mountain drainage above the Columbia River and disappeared into thick cloud cover.

"Despite the fact that the government combed his drop zone for months they never found a thing. No dead hijacker, no parachute, no ransom, no candy wrapper they could tie to him. Nothing. He disappeared into thin air."

From the backseat, Sawyer asked, "I think Alan and I know all that. But what was so captivating about him for your colleagues at Rocky Flats? Why did all of you get so enthralled?"

"We didn't. Not then, anyway. Back in '71, when it happened, I don't think we paid any more attention to the hijacking than the rest of the country did. Maybe less. The security department was busy then. I mean, we were consumed with our responsibilities. The plant was in constant danger of terrorist intrusion by outsiders. Antiwar people, anti-nuclear people, environmental people. We had to keep an eye on all of them and anticipate their incursions. We had a hell of a lot of plutonium to protect. And a ton of secrets to secure. We even had one demonstration where there was a Save the Whales banner." He laughed at the memory.

I cleared the light at College and made it halfway to Arapahoe before traffic again crept to a stop.

"In 1976, the media made a big deal of the five-year anniversary of the hijacking. You know how they do it, the TV people, on anniversaries. Overkill. They replayed all the old film, they reinterviewed the pilots and the stewardesses—they weren't flight attendants back then—and they did long pieces about all the work the FBI had done. They took crews back to the Columbia drainage and searched for evidence all over again. At the plant, we all got talking about it too, and one day someone in the department suggested that it couldn't have been just any Joe who could do it. It would have to have been someone like one of us to pull off a caper like that.

"The crime was so sophisticated, so clean, so meticulously prepared and researched. It would have taken a cop, or a fed, or a security specialist trained in counterintelligence. Well, the idea kind of snowballed and people began to talk and rumors began to spread and . . . you know how it goes."

I asked, "Was Corey Rand the one spreading the rumors?"

"Corey wasn't even there in '71 at the time of the hijacking. But he was on board five years later. He didn't start the whole thing, the Cooper finger-pointing. He never even participated in any of the coffee-machine talk—remember, he was an outsider. Nobody liked him much, even then. But he sure ran with it. He made a personal decision that he was going to figure out the whole damn crime and see what kinds of special skills and special knowledge it would've taken for Cooper to pull it off. He used to say that if you could identify what you had to know to do it, pretty soon you would know who could do it. From the list of who could, you could find who did. It became a, I don't know, an obsession with him."

The light cycled once, but we moved forward only a couple of hundred yards. Taxiing behind the UPS truck was like driving behind a brown brick wall.

Sawyer wondered, "Did he? Did Rand ever figure it all out?"

Reggie hesitated and said, "He thought he did." He grew silent.

I urged him to continue. "Go on, Reggie."

"I had become Corey's only friend in the security department. I say 'friend,' but Corey couldn't really be anybody's friend. He didn't know how. He was a difficult man to get along with, had this set of rules that he lived by that—I don't know—it put people off. He couldn't really relax and be part of the group. After not too long on the job the other guys started calling him 'Adolf,' and . . . well, things got worse and worse for him over the years. He was passed over for promotions and he grew more vindictive and things just kept snowballing. At the end he was totally isolated except for me.

"I tried to protect him for a while. Put him under my wing, so to speak. Tried to get him to recognize the difference between a rule being broken and a rule being bent, but he was more rigid than a concrete slab, and hell, to tell you the awful truth, he was just about as cold."

We finally cleared the light and turned west on Arapahoe. We were getting close to the married student housing complex.

"Then the guys set up that final sting for him. I wasn't in on it; they knew I would've put the kibosh on it if I'd known what was going on. Years later, one of them admitted to me how he and two of his buddies had set Corey up." He shook his head at the memory. "It was a good dupe they did, worthy of a bunch of security analysts, I'll tell you that. They laid the tracks just right to lure him in, and they cleaned up the tracks just right so you couldn't tell they'd ever been there. By the time I looked around, I couldn't find a trace of their scam. But I remain surprised to this day that Corey fell for it. He was a bright man, certainly brighter than they were."

The light at Folsom was green. Reggie said, "Next left. So, anyway, their plan worked. It turned out that they got rid of Corey just like they had hoped."

Sawyer asked the question that was on the tip of my tongue. "This man who admitted to you what they'd done to get Corey out of the way? What became of him?"

I glanced over and saw Reggie's eye twitch. "Funny you should ask. He died in a hunting accident in 1987."

"Let me guess," I interjected. "The shooter was never identified and the killing was ruled accidental."

Reggie started breathing through his mouth. It was the only change I could see in his demeanor. He pointed out the windshield. "This is the parking lot, Alan. And it's your turn to help," he said.

I caught Sawyer's stern face and wide eyes in the rearview mirror before I got out of the car to assist Reggie with the next shut-in. Sawyer tightened her jaw and nodded her head, once up, once down. She raised three fingers and smiled that rueful smile that left her cheeks dimpled.

Reggie refused to elaborate on either D. B. Cooper or Corey Rand during the short drive to our next destination, a tiny frame cottage near Boulder High School. While Sawyer and he were inside, I called the hospital to check on Lauren's progress. According to the nurse, she was asleep and seemed clear cognitively, with the exception of short-term recall for the time before the poisoning. There was some minor concern about changes in her liver function. She said the doctor would tell me more later in the day after the new labs came back.

She didn't sound too worried about the new liver concerns, so I decided that I wouldn't be, either.

We moved from one of Boulder's most modest neighborhoods to one of its grandest, from the simple frame house near the high school to a mansion on Mapleton Hill. I drove north across town on side streets, well aware that I would miss plenty of lights along the way. I'd already decided to allow Sawyer room to press Reggie for more information.

She picked up the ball deftly. "The 'two buddies' you talked about, Reggie. Whatever happened to them?"

"I know what you're thinking. And I don't . . . I just don't think it's . . . it wouldn't be . . ."

"The two buddies? What happened to them?"

He looked away from us, out the side window, before he spoke again. "One of them was a NASCAR fanatic named Ricky Turner. I know what you're thinking, and you're right. He died in a one-car accident in Boulder Canyon after he got blitzed at the Pioneer Inn up in Nederland. Police determined that he was doing over sixty when his car left the pavement. It actually landed on the *other* side of Boulder Creek from the road."

"Year?"

His tone irritated, he said, "I told you I was willing to talk about Cooper, not about old feuds. Anyway, it was an accident. He was drunk as a skunk." Sawyer and I waited Reggie out. "What year? Hell, I was still at the Flats when Turner died. Must have been 1988, '89, maybe '90."

"You seem to remember all that pretty clearly, Reggie."

"I was his boss. I went to the funeral."

"I think maybe I see a pattern here," I said, as I turned on Pine, which would take Sawyer and me right past our hotel.

Sawyer pressed an obviously reluctant Reggie Loomis. "The other buddy? What about him?"

"I don't think he's in town anymore. I lost track of him before Ricky killed himself in that wreck."

"His name?"

"Don't. You should just let this rest. It's not what you think."

"Come on, Reggie."

"We called him Jacko. His name was Jack O'Connell. I think he moved back to where he grew up. Some place on Long Island. Worked in security at one of the nuclear power plants there."

"Was he at Ricky's funeral?"

"You know, come to think of it, I don't remember seeing him."

No one spoke again until I pulled up in front of the stately mansion on Mapleton Hill. Reggie said, "My next guest is Sylvia Henning. Miss Sylvia. She lives alone here, if you can believe it. Has for over thirty years. She's been one of my guests from the very start."

"I guess it's my turn to help," I said.

"Miss Sylvia doesn't like strangers. Help me get the tray together. But I'll take care of her all by myself. And I'll be a few extra minutes with her. Why don't you put together some food for yourselves and eat while I'm inside?"

Sawyer and I prepared trays and carried them over to the elegantly landscaped island that separated the westbound lane of Mapleton from the eastbound lane. She examined the palatial homes and asked, "Old money up here?"

I said, "You bet." I settled onto the smooth face of a decorative granite boulder. "Sawyer, do you think?"

She was sitting across from me. "Yes, I think," she said and dug into her ramekin of eggs. I smelled a fresh burst of tarragon.

"It doesn't make sense. We're chasing a ghost, you know?"

"You mean Rand?"

"His wife told me he was dead. Why would she lie to me?"

"People lie all the time. Some of them don't even need reasons. I spend most of my professional time with people who lie with every third breath just so they can stay in practice."

"I don't know. I'm troubled by it. If Rand's dead, this is all for nothing. We can't finger a dead man for killing our colleagues."

"What else do we have?" she asked.

I ate most of my fruit salad before pausing to use the cell phone to call Sam at home. I asked him to check on the whereabouts and well-being of a Jack O'Connell, ex-Boulder, ex-Rocky Flats security, currently doing security work at a nuclear energy facility on Long Island. He didn't ask why I wanted to know, which meant he figured he already knew why I wanted to know. Sam liked people to think he was ahead of them even when he wasn't.

He said he'd get right on it.

Sawyer said, "Bet he's already dead. This Jacko guy. Want to do a wager on how Corey Rand got to him?"

"Not especially, no."

"There's good news here, too, Alan."

"What's that?"

"It's taken our minds off what happened last night."

She made me laugh. "I called the hospital while you were inside the last house with Reggie. The nurse said there's something screwy with Lauren's liver functions. Is that common after carbon monoxide poisoning?"

She swallowed and tried not to look concerned. "How screwy?"

"Doctor is going to fill me in later."

She said, "Well, I wouldn't get alarmed," which, for some reason, is one of the most alarming things that physicians can ever say to me. "But there are rare—let me emphasize, rare—cases of elevated liver enzymes after CO poisoning. I'm not sure anyone really understands the pathogenesis. It sounds to me like her doctors are just being prudent."

"Now I'm getting alarmed."

She reached out to touch me before pulling back. She looked down. "The eggs are great. Go ahead, you'll need the protein."

THIRTY-NINE

Once he was back in the car, Reggie wouldn't answer any more questions about Corey Rand. "Corey wasn't part of the deal I made with you two. You want to talk Cooper, we can talk Cooper. If not, we can listen to music. You have any Vivaldi?" he asked before offering directions to an apartment house near Community Hospital.

"No Vivaldi. Did he ever tell you?" I asked, careful not to actually mention Rand's name. "You know, did he ever tell you who it was he suspected of committing the hijacking?"

"He never told me the name, no. But he came to me once and laid out the case in some detail."

"Well, you seem like a good student of these things," Sawyer prompted. "Were you convinced?"

"The presentation," he said, "was compelling."

"But were you convinced?"

"He had identified . . . a guy. A guy at the plant, in our department. The guy made sense for a number of reasons. Crucial, of course, he was off-duty over Thanksgiving weekend that year. But that didn't tell me much. My thinking was, so what? All nonessential personnel at the plant were off over Thanksgiving weekend. Then Corey pointed out that this particular guy came back to work a day later than expected, on the Tuesday after the holiday instead of the Monday. Rand said that gave him an extra day to make his way back from the Pacific Northwest, a day Corey said he needed because of some unexpected problem.

"What problem? Well, what first focused Corey's attention on this man, apparently, is that the guy came back to work with a broken ankle. His story at the time was that he was doing some early season cross-country skiing up above Rollinsville and hit a rock on a downhill and broke his ski and his ankle."

Sawyer said, "And Rand thought that was bullshit, that the ankle break was actually evidence of trouble on the parachute drop?"

"Right. But Corey didn't stop there. Once he had this guy in mind, he locked on him like a heat-seeking missile. He went back and looked at the man's military records and found that when he was in the Marines, the man graduated from parachute school. That's important not just for technique reasons, but also because it meant that Cooper knew the safe parameters for a parachute drop from that plane. Cooper gave specific orders to the pilots. He told them to fly the plane unpressurized at ten thousand feet. That was so he could safely lower the airstairs in flight. He specified that the gear be down, that the flaps be set at fifteen percent, and that the airspeed should at no point exceed one hundred and fifty knots."

I said, "He knew what he was doing."

"Cooper didn't miss a detail. The crime was a thing of beauty. When he jumped, he waited until the plane was in the clouds so the military jets that were tracking them couldn't see him leave the plane."

I pulled up in front of the apartment house that was our next humanitarian stop, hopped out of the car, and prepared a tray. I was getting efficient at it. Reggie and I were in and out of the apartment and back in the car within the allotted seven minutes. Sawyer picked up the story as though she'd frozen the conversation in time.

"Doesn't sound like Rand had much to go on. Circumstantial, every bit of it."

"Oh, he had more. Corey kept looking at the guy. He found out where he worked before he came to Rocky Flats. Turns out that two jobs back he was employed in security at a company in Reno that did contract maintenance for

American Airlines, among others. Corey checked further. One of the planes that the company serviced for American was Boeing 727s."

"Which means he could have had knowledge about the rear airstairs, and how they operated?" I asked.

"Exactly."

I was thinking about old conversations with my wife the assistant district attorney about the components that prosecutors use to assess suspects. Means, opportunity, and motive. M-O-M. "Rand's hypothesis covers means and opportunity, Reggie. What did Rand come up with about motive?"

"I'm not done. This guy that Corey Rand was so sure about. Turns out he grew up in a suburb of Portland, not even seventy-five miles from the drop zone identified by the FBI."

"Still, as Sawyer pointed out, it's all circumstantial," I said, trying to imagine the words Lauren would use to assess the story. "Where am I heading next? What's our next stop?"

Reggie shrugged. "Rand was convinced. That's what was important to him. The last two stops are up Sunshine Canyon."

I headed west on Mapleton into the canyon. "Back to motive for a minute. How did Rand figure motive?"

"Two motives. One, of course, was money. Remember, Cooper got away clean with two hundred thousand dollars. And the second motive was retribution. Vengeance, if you will."

"Retribution?" I wondered. "Against whom? Northwest Airlines?"

"No, the FBI. Rand figured this guy wanted to show up the FBI, to . . . I don't know exactly. Maybe prove that he was better than them? Repay an old slight? Something like that."

Suddenly Reggie sounded tired. I was confused by his supposition of Cooper's motive and said, "That doesn't make sense. Why would he hijack an airplane to get back at the FBI?"

Reggie touched his fingertips together, one at a time, until all ten digits were touching. The gesture appeared childish, yet composed. At a subdued volume, he said, "Corey had a theory. I don't recall that I know what it was, exactly."

From the backseat, Sawyer apparently had missed the burp that I had seen in Reggie's demeanor. She asked, "What about the money those two kids found? When they were digging along the banks of the Columbia River years ago? When was that? Nineteen . . ."

"1980," he said, without a smidgen of delay. "The kids found fifty-eight hundred dollars in twenties while they were playing along the shore of the Columbia in 1980. The serial numbers proved that the money came from the hijacking."

"But doesn't that show that Cooper didn't make it down safely? That he crashed during the parachute drop and the money ended up in the river?"

"Nope. It doesn't prove that at all. Corey figured the missing money was all part of Cooper's planning genius. Corey's theory is that Cooper dumped some of the ransom on the banks of the river, hoping that people would come to the conclusion that he'd drowned in the river during his parachute drop and then washed out to sea with all the rest of the evidence. Ergo, everyone would stop looking for him on land. What was six thousand dollars to Cooper? Three percent of the ransom? Pretty cheap for an insurance policy that might get the search called off."

I backtracked toward Mapleton on Ninth and cut west into Sunshine Canyon. The sun was high enough in the eastern sky behind us to begin to brighten some of the curves and hollows of the twisty road. "How far up the canyon are we going, Reggie? I have to be back at your house by ten."

"Quite a ways up, I'm afraid. A neat little log cabin. I'll tell you when we're getting close. I only visit this particular guest in good weather. Almost got stuck up there once last winter. But don't worry, we'll be back on time."

The log cabin enjoyed a sunlit eastern exposure, and its ridge-top position provided an incredible view down the

Front Range. The house itself was a simple rectangle constructed of stacked ten-inch logs topped with a red metal roof. Every window was covered by iron grating. The storm doors on the front were constructed of heavy black steel.

Reggie explained. "Theodora, Theo, has grown a little paranoid since her stroke. She's remarkable, though. You'll like her."

I parked in a narrow clearing between a gleaming white propane tank and the house. Theo met us at the door. She was no older than Sawyer and me. Her stroke had severely impaired her speech, and she used a four-legged cane to get around the house. Reggie was right; I did like her. Her courageous adjustment to her stroke reminded me of Lauren's adaptation to multiple sclerosis. "You never know how brave you can be until it's your turn to be brave," Lauren had told me once.

Theo had had her turn.

Our visit lasted the prescribed seven minutes.

I waited in the car at the last stop in the canyon, a shack of a place on an old horse ranch on the canyon floor only half a mile or so out of Boulder. This was the culmination of our morning, and Reggie used his entire allotment of time for this final visit. Twenty minutes.

We were back at his place on Fourth Street, as promised, by ten. With a grin on his face, he said, "See you in two days."

"What?"

"I need your help one more time. Please. Mrs. Savage, you know, the big Chevy lady? She canceled until Friday. I'll make it worth your while, I promise. I'll tell you more about Corey. Okay? And you have to admit the food alone is worth the trip."

I said I would go. Sawyer said she thought she would have returned to California by then.

I stayed anxious all day long. Lauren's doctor finally paged me around three o'clock with good news about her liver function. It appeared the earlier tests might have been anomalous. He planned to repeat them one more time before he discharged her, hopefully the next day. Only some short-term memory problems clouded her mental functioning.

The vet hospital in Denver told me that Emily was ready to come home but they would be happy to board her until I made it back to Denver.

Sam paged me at half past four. Again at four forty-five. Once more as I was escorting my four-fifteen patient out the door.

I called him at home.

"Hi. Sorry it took me so long to return your page. I was with a patient." To Sam, I knew that would sound like an excuse, not an explanation.

"Whatever. To answer your earlier question about the employee from Rocky Flats? Well, Jack O'Connell died in 1992 in New York. He was electrocuted in his own home. The local cops thought it was suspicious, looked at it real carefully. Felt his wiring might have been tampered with. Case is still open, and manner is still pending. Now tell me how he fits."

I explained that O'Connell had been a coworker at Rocky Flats of this man who was admitted to the psychiatric unit back in 1982.

Sam interrupted. "Corey Rand?"

"Yes. O'Connell—they called him Jacko—he was one of three guys who arranged the setup that got this man Rand in trouble at work and then admitted to the hospital, and finally cost him his security clearance and his job."

"I take it the other two are dead now, too? The other guys who helped O'Connell."

"Yes. One died in a hunting accident on the western slope. No shooter was ever identified. The other one died in a one-car accident in Boulder Canyon after a night drinking at the Pioneer Inn up in Nederland. DUI."

"Get a name and year on that one? The DUI?"

"Just a second." I'd scribbled the facts in a notebook. "Ricky Turner. Late eighties. 1988, '89, maybe '90."

"Now tell me how you learned all this."

"Sawyer and I spent some more time with Reggie Loomis, Rand's old boss at Rocky Flats."

"Was Milt with you?"

"No."

"I thought we had an agreement about protection for you and Sawyer."

"Loomis said we couldn't bring you or any other cops or he wouldn't talk about . . . you know, Rand."

"Now I wonder why the hell he said that. I'm still thinking maybe that man has something to hide."

"My interest is Rand. Not Reggie Loomis's petty crimes."

He chewed on my words for about ten seconds. "You ever go out and meet Corey Rand's widow?"

"No, I just talked with her on the phone. Why?"

"I went over to her place again today." He hung his words like a night crawler on the end of a line.

"And?"

"Hell of a cough that woman has. Hell of a cough. You think maybe she has TB or something? I feel like I should wear a mask."

"Sam, please. I have another patient in a few minutes."

"Mrs. Rand lives on a nice little three-acre horse ranch in Wheat Ridge. They have a couple of real pretty Appaloosas. Summers we used to go to this place when I was a kid that had Appaloosas. I like 'em. Anyway, Mrs. Rand takes in a few boarders, I mean horses, that kind of boarder, though none of them are as nice as those Appaloosas. But a very, very nice place. I began to wonder how the widow of a ne'er-do-well Radio Shack manager might be able to live in a place like that. So I checked the records of her husband's estate. She inherited zilch, basically. But it turns out that she was sole beneficiary of the half-million-dollar life insurance policy that Mr. Rand had been paying on since 1991. When he crashed his pickup and bought the ranch, she cleaned up, and she bought the ranch, too. So to speak."

"Yeah?" I knew he wasn't done.

"Then"—he tried to sound bored as he continued—"I didn't have anything better to do, so I had the local coroner's office pull up Mr. Corey Rand's death records for me. Accident he died in was bad, included a vehicle fire. Took place on private land out at one of those gravel mines on

'93, near Golden. Body was badly disfigured at the time of the autopsy. Rand's pickup truck ran smack into a big Caterpillar front loader. The bucket almost tore the damn truck in half. Coroner eventually decided that Rand had an aneurysm that caused him to lose control of his truck. ID was made by his wife and son. I was not surprised to learn that his body was cremated the same day it was released by the coroner."

Son. I hadn't given a moment's thought to Corey Rand's son.

"How old is the son?"

I could almost hear Sam smile over the phone line. "He is almost twenty-nine years old."

I rearranged the cards that Sam was dealing. "You think the three of them faked his death?"

"Why not? If they pull it off, it gives Rand a get-out-of-jail-free card in case anybody like us ever gets a clue about all these murders. And it gives his wife and kid a bonus of a half a million bucks to refresh their not too happy lives. Not to mention that it fits right in with Rand's whole fuck-the-system-that-fucked-me attitude."

"You know anything about the son? What's his name?"

"Patrick Rand."

"What do you know about him?"

"He's a firefighter in Lakewood."

Lakewood is one of Denver's western suburbs. "That's interesting."

"Given all the fires and the poisonings we've been dealing with, yes, I'd say it's interesting. Something else, too."

"Yes?"

"One of his coworkers thinks he was off-duty when that lady and her husband were killed in New Zealand."

"A lot of people were off-duty then, Sam."

He let my skepticism drop with a thud. "Another thing about firefighters is they work long shifts and then they have long periods of time off."

"Which means what?"

"They have plenty of time to indulge in hobbies."

"Like killing people."

"Keeps them off the streets."

I continued, "So if you're right about this conspiracy, where's Corey Rand? Where's Patrick's dad?"

"Around here somewhere, buddy. Around here somewhere."

FORTY

My sister-in-law, Teresa, arrived in Denver the next morning, only an hour before Lauren was discharged from the hospital. I didn't want the two of them anywhere near Boulder, so I rescheduled my morning patients, drove to Denver, and moved Lauren and her sister into a downtown hotel. Lauren reluctantly acknowledged that they would be safer if I spent the night in Boulder, thirty miles away.

Before I kissed her good-bye I handed Lauren the Glock. I could tell from her eyes that she thought it would be prudent for me to keep it. But her rueful smile told me that she had no faith I could actually use it.

Without a word, she accepted the gun and made it disappear into her big purse.

I was feeling some apprehension that she would ask me where I'd be sleeping that night and how close by Sawyer would be sleeping. She didn't ask. In her silence, I sensed trust, and I felt strength and love that I wondered if I deserved.

Lauren trusted me more than I did.

Back in the car, I phoned the vet hospital and put off retrieving Emily for another day, then rushed back down the turnpike and fit seven forty-five-minute therapy sessions into what was left of the afternoon. At the end of the day I was surprised to find that Sawyer was still registered at the Boulderado. At the front desk she'd left me a handwritten message that the folks in Phoenix were still waiting on a part for her airplane and that it wouldn't be ready until the next day at the earliest. If it was still possible she wanted to join Reggie and me the next morning on his rounds.

I called the suite she was sharing with A.J. to let her know what time I'd be leaving for Reggie's house in the morning. No one answered. Not knowing how things stood between Sawyer and A.J., I didn't leave a message.

Like a dutiful subject, I phoned Milt and told him I was safely ensconced in my room. He answered as though my call were an intrusion. He said he already knew I was back. I asked him if he knew where Sawyer was.

"She's with Dr. Simes. Dr. Simes needed some medical attention and Sawyer was kind enough to go with her."

"What kind of medical attention?" I expected him to say something about multiple sclerosis.

"Dr. Simes is quite private about her health. I hope you will respect that." Milt's words said "hope," but his tone said "expect."

"I know quite a few people here, Milt, in the medical community. I may be able to be of some help."

"Thanks for offering. I'll pass it along." He paused and transformed his voice into something even more parental and bilious than the one he had been using. "What you did yesterday was . . . bullshit. You know that, don't you? You put yourself and Dr. Faire at risk."

I tried to respond rationally. "We learned some things. It was worth the risk, I think."

"Your friend Sam doesn't trust that man. Mr. Loomis."

"Sam was happy for the information. And you don't know Sam very well, Milt. He doesn't trust too many people."

"In our line of work, that point of view often has merit."

"Milt, Reggie Loomis is responsible for us knowing about Corey Rand. Without him we wouldn't have a clue about a possible subject. And I think he has even more that he can tell us."

"I've been busy all day on that. We're trying to access Rand's records. Especially travel. He's most vulnerable on travel. We should know more by tomorrow."

"Don't worry, Sawyer and I are being careful."

He said, "We're getting close to him, you know. Once we get the travel records sketched out we can compare his whereabouts with all the other crimes. This Mr. Rand. And I'm sure he knows we're on to him. Don't underestimate a cornered animal."

I wanted to ask which Mr. Rand, father or son, they were closing in on. But I said, "I understand the situation. I'm not planning on being a cowboy."

"No, Dr. Gregory, I don't think you do understand. Rand's teeth are bared now. He never expected to be identified. All along, he's been thinking he's been committing the perfect crimes. He expected to be another D. B. Cooper. A legend in his own mind. But now we're on his tail. He's not going to act according to form. Lock yourself in for the night. Page me if you go anywhere. I'll be out checking on some things."

Milt's warning caused me to feel the absence of the Glock. I found myself surprised at how peculiar and intimate the loss felt. It was as though I'd gone to rub my eye or pick my nose and discovered that I'd misplaced one of my fingers.

As I double-locked the door I began to wonder about the D. B. Cooper allusion Milt had used. Was he on to something about Reggie, or was that an inadvertent caution? I wasn't sure.

I tried watching the local news and got bored. I stared out the window at the alley and wished I'd paid for a better view. I contemplated confronting Ms. Marceau in the Mezzanine and getting a little drunk. I thought about going for a walk on the Mall. Ultimately, I decided to stop acting so damn paranoid and opted to go see what progress Dresden and his gang had made on our renovation in Spanish Hills.

Before I left, I called Sam at home to see if he wanted to come along. His machine picked up and I got the pleasure of listening to some cute instructions from Simon, Sam's son, about what to do after the beep. I declined. I paged Milt and left him a message where I'd be, what I'd be doing. The last call I made before I left the room was to Adrienne, my neighbor, to see if she was back home from her travels. I got her machine. I had second thoughts about heading out alone and shushed them.

I was anxious driving across town, literally trying to talk myself into believing that this silent enemy wouldn't go after me twice in the same location. Mostly, I convinced myself that although what I was doing was foolhardy, it probably wasn't any crazier than flying down Left Hand Canyon at fifty miles an hour on my road bike or skiing down Pallavicini at A-Basin on days when the moguls were bigger than Volkswagen Bugs.

I couldn't help but smile as I drove down the lane. My old house looked like a new house. Dresden and his carpenters had been busy. The main-floor addition and the freestanding garage were not only framed but also sheathed with insulating sheets, and the roofs had already been decked and tar-papered. For a few minutes I stood outside on the lane and admired the profile. Dresden had roughed out the new front porch, too, and I felt an odd sense that for the first time in my adult life I'd be living in a house that looked like it might actually be inhabited by a grown-up.

Although Lauren and I had mentioned it cautiously and only in passing, standing there with my hands in my pockets and my feet on the gravel, I felt a crystal-clear awareness that this new structure was large enough for a family. It was actually meant for a family.

I unlocked the front door and extinguished the alarm before I flicked on a light switch and was astonished to see the new recessed cans in the ceiling beam brilliantly down on me.

Houston, we have power.

A short hallway that led to the new main-floor bedroom was framed and Sheetrocked, effectively separating the front of the house from the back for the first time ever. The new bedroom felt huge, and the tall corner windows framed the Flatirons just as our architect had promised they would. The master bathroom seemed to have enough plumbing rough-ins for a family of eight to use individual fixtures simultaneously.

I meandered back toward the original structure into the space where the old kitchen had gone through a strange mitosis. Doubling once and then, somehow, once again, the new space had been mysteriously reclaimed from someplace in the house where I wasn't going to miss it. I stared at the spot where the new range would be installed and promised myself I'd pick up some extra court-ordered evals for a year or so and see about the La Cornue that Lauren coveted.

I sighed and felt a shiver up my spine. Looking around this space, I felt my future with Lauren as precious and real, as though I already held our first baby in my hands. Conceptions would happen here. First steps. Many tears. All the joy that life promised and all the sorrow that life delivered would happen within these new walls.

Without hesitation, I was eager to get started with her.

But first, I reminded myself, I had to stay alive for a few days while Sam and Milt found the Rands.

I was impatient to settle back into the house. My eyes flew around the shadowy space. The Sheetrock needed tape and mud. The whole place needed trim. There wasn't a fixture to be found in the bathroom or kitchen. A lot of tile was yet to be laid. And the painters would be here for weeks. Weeks.

But I felt my future in this place. It felt satisfying, a fullness I associated with sitting back after a fine meal. I wanted to digest it awhile.

Like for a lifetime.

I stopped for dinner at Tom's and sat alone in a booth. I ate a complete meal of foods that were discouraged on Sam's diet. I considered taking in a movie, but decided not to. I actually convinced myself that Milt and Sam and A.J. were hot on the Rands' heels and that the bad guys were on the run.

The dark sky was spotted by flurries the next morning as Sawyer and I made our way to the car. On the late news the night before, the weather folks had promised that this little disturbance approaching from the west was nothing to worry about. They promised we would get a "light dusting," unless, of course, that nasty little upper-level low over New Mexico slid a tad farther north than anyone expected it to. If that happened, well, then we'd be talking upslope conditions, and all bets would be off.

Stay tuned.

As Sawyer snapped her seat belt she smiled at the storm and said, "I miss the snow. This is pretty."

I admitted that it was but didn't caution her about the possible consequences of the migrating low-pressure system. Instead I asked, "How's A.J. doing? Milt told me she was ill last night."

Sawyer made an apologetic face. "She asked me not to talk about it, Alan. I'm sorry. We saw a specialist last night. I think she'll be okay."

"Was it, um . . . you know? I mean, because of Lauren, she and I know the best neurologists in town. We'll be happy to make contacts for her."

She touched me on the arm. "Let's just leave it that your wife has good antennae, okay? But we didn't need a neurologist. I think A.J. will be fine." I saw Sawyer's breath in the cold car. She rubbed her gloved hands together and said, "I wonder what Reggie cooked up for us this morning."

I felt calm beside her. She had no way of knowing about the clarity that I had found while visiting my home the night before. She had no way of knowing that her special place in my heart had altered its orbit a few degrees. She had no way of knowing that our pasts might always touch, but our planets would never collide.

We were silent for the next few minutes until we arrived on Fourth Street. Reggie waited impatiently on his little porch, anxious to get to work. Sawyer ignored his exhortations and made a beeline for the coffee before she lifted the first cooler.

Compared to our earlier effort only two days before, we loaded the car with the breakfast goodies in half the time.

*   *   *

Reggie wasn't chatty. Twice I tried to steer him to resume his tale about D. B. Cooper and Corey Rand. But each time he shook his head a little and closed his eyes, shutting out my questions. I feigned patience, as I would during therapy, reminding myself that we had a lot of time.

We kept our roles from our earlier delivery route. Reggie didn't want his guests to have to deal with any more new faces, so Sawyer and I delivered trays to the same homes that we had two days before.

The breakfast from Chez Reggie was simple but elegant. A fruit salad of late berries and perfect crescents of early Satsuma tangerines. Fresh brioche that had been transformed into tantalizing baked French toast. Coffee and juice. And a puffy croissant. "This is for later," Reggie would tell each guest as he offered the croissant. "Just a little snack to hold you over. I made the preserves myself from last summer's Palisade peaches. I think you'll like them."

We squeezed in a couple of extra stops. One of the new guests had been hospitalized two days earlier, the other had been out of town. Our new efficiency allowed us to absorb the minutes into our schedule with ease.

Sawyer and I once again ate while Reggie alone delivered the tray to Sylvia's mansion on Mapleton Hill. This time, however, we ate in the car. The flurries were beginning to transform from charming into storming, and the car offered protection. The French toast was the best I'd ever tasted. I decided my reward for the morning was going to be the recipe.

Sawyer asked, "I wonder if we'll still go up the canyon. Given the weather."

"The little ranch where we ended up the other day is close to here, only half a mile or so. I don't think that's a problem. But Theo's log cabin is way up there, halfway to Gold Hill. I hope Reggie doesn't want to try to make it."

She nodded at my assessment. She looked away from me briefly before locking her eyes onto mine. Her voice cracked and she said, "So what happened yesterday? You decided you could live without me?"

Her words could have been framed by levity, but they

weren't. I sipped some coffee before I replied. "More, I think, Sawyer, I decided I couldn't see my future without her. Without Lauren. I love her." I glanced down only after I was done speaking.

She was facing away from me. "Ironic, don't you think? I mean, look who's insecure now. Look who needs who now. It's no prettier when I see it in the mirror than it was when I saw it in you years ago."

"That's not it, Sawyer. I'm not afraid of you needing me. I made the right choice with Lauren. I feel my future there. You've shaken me up a bit by showing up again. It's left me feeling stronger. More certain about things with her."

"She allowed that, didn't she? She let you see how far you would go?"

"She trusts me, I guess."

Sawyer laughed, the sound gilded with irony. "Oh no. That's not right. You don't quite get it. Lauren crossed her fingers about you. About you loving her enough to come back. The person she's been trusting since I showed up and confused things . . . is herself." She cupped her chin in her gloved palms. "Maybe I can learn something from her, too."

I'd been busy patting myself on my back for how strong I'd been in resisting Sawyer's temptations. It wasn't easy accepting the proposition that the true show of strength had been Lauren's, not mine.

But I knew what Sawyer was saying was true.

Reggie hopped back in the car and said, "Hurry. Let's do the ranch. Theo's our last stop today."

"A lot of snow coming down, Reggie."

"We'll see how the canyon looks after we do the horse ranch. This has four-wheel drive, right?"

"Right," I admitted. I didn't tell Reggie that I didn't consider it license to be reckless.

FORTY-ONE

The decrepit little horse ranch on the floor of the canyon was Sawyer's stop. I stayed in the Land Cruiser with the engine running, trying to keep warm. By my reckoning, a good half inch of snow fell during the seven minutes that Reggie and Sawyer were inside.

After he climbed back onto the front passenger seat, Reggie seemed to hesitate about proceeding farther up Sunshine. He fidgeted with his gloves and raised and lowered the zipper on his jacket. Finally, he said, "Let's give Theo's place a try. She really doesn't get too many visitors. This may be my last chance to visit with her for a while."

Through the windshield I watched the profile of a pickup truck as it slithered up the canyon road. The snow continued to fall in curtains, and the flapping windshield wipers made rhythmic traverses across the glass. I said, "If that's what you want to do, Reggie, I'll head up the canyon. But if it gets bad, we'll turn around."

"Deal," he said.

He was silent for the first mile or so up the canyon. My focus was locked on the slick surface in front of me and on my fervent desire to stay halfway between the often difficult to distinguish shoulders. Once I edged over to the right to permit a Mazda Miata to float by on its way to town. Seconds later I was distracted by the high beams of a truck that was parked up a driveway perpendicular to the canyon road. The truck's engine was running, steam rising to envelop the cab in fog. Reggie stared at the parked truck, too. Then, without preamble, he rotated on his seat and faced Sawyer in back. He said, "There were two reasons Cooper took four parachutes."

When she didn't reply immediately, he continued, "You were wondering about that, remember? D. B. Cooper's rationale for demanding four parachutes."

"Yes. Yes, I was." I chanced a glance in the mirror. Sawyer's eyes met mine. Hers were narrowed and cautious. Behind her in the distance I thought I spotted headlights on the road. Just as quickly, the orbs of light were gone.

"Well. The first reason Cooper insisted on four parachutes was because he didn't want the authorities to know whether or not he was acting alone or whether he had unknown accomplices on the plane. Obviously, if the FBI was forced to consider the possibility that he had accomplices, then their contingency responses became more limited. By requesting more than one parachute, he forced his adversaries to consider the possibility that he was not acting alone. Make sense?"

Sawyer nodded. I checked the mirror again for headlights. Nothing back there. I slowed.

"Second reason. Cooper obviously suspected that the authorities might try to booby-trap the parachute they were providing for him. Had he asked for only one, I'm sure that they would have given serious consideration to doing just that. But by asking for four, and by keeping two stewardesses in reserve as hostages, he left open the possibility that he not only had accomplices, but that he might force one or both of the stewardesses to jump from the airplane with him. With that risk in place, the authorities, of course, couldn't take the chance of sabotaging one of the parachutes. The possibility existed that it would end up being worn by a hostage."

I asked, "Did Corey Rand figure all that out?"

Reggie replied, "It wasn't hard to figure. It doesn't take a genius to figure out why somebody did something after the fact. That's just hindsight. The genius is in the anticipation. Remember, we were contingency planners. Our job was to avoid getting caught in traps like the one that Cooper set."

For a pleasant moment I realized that Reggie had described the challenge of psychotherapy with an elegant precision. Any average therapist could help any average patient understand why the patient had done something maladaptive. The genius came when therapist and patient could anticipate the next trap, so the patient could avoid getting caught by the same circumstances again.

Sawyer said, "I hadn't thought of that, Reggie. That's an interesting theory."

"It's not a theory," he said, his voice hollow. "It's the way it was."

I smiled at the assurance I was hearing but quickly moved my attention back to the narrow, glassy road. The shoulders had disappeared beneath the shroud of fresh powder and I was thinking hard about turning back.

"Do either of you see anyone behind us? I thought I saw some lights a way back."

They both turned and gazed out the almost opaque rear window. Sawyer said, "So? Maybe we're not the only ones crazy enough to come up here in this weather."

Reggie said he didn't see anything, but his tone told me that my concerns were resonating with him. "One passed us earlier. A pickup truck," he added.

Sawyer and Reggie didn't resume their conversation about D. B. Cooper.

The storm paused, and for a few moments I was driving uphill toward a thin ribbon of blue sky that was barely visible through a break in the clouds. Again I checked for lights in my mirrors. Nothing. I figured we would be at Theo's cabin in less than five minutes. I considered dropping the four-wheel drive into low but decided that the Land Cruiser was doing okay, considering.

I asked, "So where's the parachute?"

Reggie pulled his gloves from his hands and took out a little tub of lip gloss. He smoothed the wax over his lips. "Buried," he said.

"Isn't that risky? Why not carry it out?"

"Too bulky. He buried it in a hole he pre-dug before the crime. He had stashed a motorcycle for his getaway close

by. Easier to hide from a search helicopter in a motorcycle
than in a car. He wouldn't have had room to take the parachute with him."

"The jump was that accurate? That he could hike to his
motorcycle? Even with a broken ankle?"

"The jump was that accurate."

A thin plume of smoke snaked from the tin chimney of
Theo's cabin. The scene was a postcard, the cleared ground
around the cabin carpeted by five inches of white powder,
the roof frosted, the windowsills dusted. The joints between
the big logs were etched with white. I parked the Land
Cruiser halfway between the big propane tank and the
front door.

Reggie said, "This is why she won't move to town. I've
offered to help her out, help her find a place. But she loves
it up here. The serenity, she says. She can't leave the
serenity."

"That's not much of a fire she has going, considering how
cold it is," Sawyer observed.

"Theo burns coal, not wood, to save money on propane.
There's usually not too much smoke from the chimney. I'll
stoke it when I get inside. This is the last stop, Alan. Help
me with her tray, and then give me my time with her,
please."

I checked the fuel gauge to make sure I had enough gaso-
line and told Sawyer to leave the engine running for heat.
Reggie and I pulled the tray of food together, covered it, and
trudged the twenty feet or so to Theo's door. Behind us, a
pickup truck sliced through the snow on the road. Reggie
paused, too, and watched it pass. I thought it was the same
truck that had driven past us when we were parked at the
horse ranch at the bottom of the canyon. How had it gotten
behind us?

Reggie's eyes followed the truck until it disappeared
toward the west. He turned and rapped twice on Theo's door
with his gloved hand. The dull sound was swallowed by the
insulation of the storm. He removed a glove and tried the
knob on the security door. It turned in his hand.

"That's funny," he said. "Theo's usually pretty security-conscious. Mmm." He yanked the door open and tried the latch on the plank door behind it. That lock was unlocked, too.

"I hope she's okay," he said as much to himself as to me. "Maybe she left it open for me. Theo? Theo?" he called. "It's Reggie Loomis."

I held the security door with one hand, the tray in the other. Reggie kicked the snow off his boots and padded inside. The interior of the cabin was freezing, barely warmer than the air outside. I followed him in, closing the two doors behind me to try to ward off the chill.

"Theo? Theo?" Reggie whispered, almost apologizing for the intrusion. He immediately took long strides toward the back of the cabin, where a door was propped open. He barely avoided tripping over a bucketful of coal that was spilled just this side of the threshold. He slammed the door shut and again called Theo's name. His voice caught as he exclaimed, "Oh, my God," and broke into a run toward the far side of the main room.

I looked over Reggie's shoulder and saw streaks of bright red in a shadowed corner and lowered the tray of food to a nearby table. The red was so plentiful that at first I imagined that I was looking at a plaid blanket that had been carelessly tossed out of the way.

In seconds, Reggie was on his knees at Theo's side. He was remarkably composed. In a steady voice, he said, "I think she's still breathing. Cover her, okay? I need to get Sawyer. Sawyer's a physician, right? We need to get Theo down to town fast." He stood and ran from the cabin as I pulled a crocheted throw from a dusty old velvet sofa. I lowered it over her.

The left side of Theo's head was sliced down the side in three or four parallel tracks, and her neck was splayed open so widely I could see tendons and tissue and blood vessels. A huge chunk of flesh was missing from the biceps of her arm. Fresh blood pumped weakly from the exposed vessels. Her beautiful blond hair was matted flat by her own blood.

Sawyer rushed inside and looked past me at Theo. "Oh,

no. Oh my God. Who did this to her? Oh, Jesus." She made fists with both her hands. "I don't even know what to do. I'm a damn psychiatrist. She needs a trauma surgeon."

Behind me, I heard a creaking sound. Without bothering to turn, I said, "Reggie, call for more help. If she doesn't have a phone here, there's one in the car." I wondered whether Flight for Life would fly a chopper in this weather. Probably not. I felt so helpless. I wanted to patch Theo up as I would repair a disintegrating snowman or a broken doll. But she seemed to be missing so many pieces.

The next noise I heard wasn't Reggie seeking help on the telephone. It was another creak accompanied by a low bass rhythmic rumble—a primal warning—that caused me to freeze.

The sound I heard was a growl.

Sawyer whispered, "What was that? Does she have a dog in here?"

I turned slowly, raising myself to my feet. "I don't know," I said.

The cabin was small. I saw no dog.

Sawyer said, "I don't see a dog."

My eyes climbed a wooden pole ladder to a loft that Theo had probably used as a bedroom in the days before her stroke. At the top of the ladder, in the darkness near the rafters, I saw two orange circles the size of dimes. "Look up in the loft," I whispered to Sawyer.

"What is it?" Sawyer asked.

"It's a cat," I said.

"A cat?"

"Yes. A big cat." My voice was as soft as the snow outside. "I think it's a mountain lion."

FORTY-TWO

Sawyer asked, "What on earth is it doing in here?"

My first thought was that it was dining. But after that momentary irreverence passed, my mind trailed quickly to the pickup truck on the canyon road. Could the Rands have something to do with this? I said, "It looks like it came in when she was outside getting coal for the stove. She had the door propped open."

The cat was perched above us as still as a painting. Although those luminescent orange disks were, I was certain, taking in every move Sawyer and I made, I couldn't discern even the slightest flicker of life in the cat's eyes. Yet I knew that with a quick tensing of some powerful muscles that cat could be flying through the air toward either Sawyer or me in less time than it took me to blink.

I forced my mind to recall every news story I'd ever heard about human–mountain lion confrontations along the Front Range. Confrontations were rare. Dead humans were even rarer. But they happened. A young boy had been killed recently in Rocky Mountain National Park.

This cat, I had to assume, was hungry. And by the looks of the wounds on Theo, we had interrupted it quite early in its meal. Sawyer and I were now, unfortunately, standing like sentries between the cat and its kill. Probably not the safest place in the world to be.

Where's Reggie?

The news stories always gave the same advice on how to survive a confrontation with a mountain lion: Stay together in a group. Act big. Make noise. Don't approach the animal in a threatening way.

"We need to move a little so we're not between the cat and Theo. Don't look it in the eye. Don't be threatening. But we need to act big."

"I don't know what you mean. How do you act big?"

"First, step sideways a little, right after me. Stay close so we look bigger together." We moved in lock step until we were three or four feet away from Theo. The act felt cowardly. I wasn't ready to sacrifice Theo to the cat, although I didn't see how she could possibly survive her injuries. But I knew I had to convince this mountain lion that it didn't have to protect its kill by coming through us.

"Now slowly unzip your parka," I said to Sawyer. She did. So did I. "Good. Now raise your arms above your head. Do it *slowly*. Stand as tall as you can." Sawyer raised herself up on her tiptoes.

Beside me was an aluminum and canvas camp chair, the collapsible kind that people take car camping. I reached down and lifted it up and handed it to her. "Here. It will make you look bigger," I said.

She grasped it as though she had fallen overboard and I was offering her a lifeline. Quickly, she suspended it between her two raised hands.

Where's Reggie?

My eyes were adjusting to the darkness near the rafters. In my peripheral vision I watched the predator watch us. The cat was as beautiful as a creature could be. Its coat was full and plush for winter. Its profile was all strength and grace. And it still hadn't moved a muscle from its crouch. From it, though, I felt as much potential danger as I might if I were traversing an avalanche field in a snowmobile.

I wanted a weapon in my hands and longed for Lauren's Glock. My hands felt behind me on the wall for an elk rack that Theo had mounted for decoration. I lifted the rack into my hands and immediately wondered whether I had just succeeded in masquerading as this cat's favorite food. I held onto the sharp antlers anyway.

Where's Reggie?

Sawyer whispered, "Will it let us out the door?"

The door was in the general direction of the cat. I didn't have a clue how the cat would interpret us approaching the door. "We'd have to get two of them open," I said.

"Do we have a choice?"

"Where's Reggie?" I finally said out loud.

"What could he do?"

"Open the doors for us, if nothing else," I said.

"Could we run for it?"

"We can't outrun that cat if it decides to chase us. I was actually hoping it might choose to leave if the doors were open."

She made a noise that was appropriately skeptical. "How do you know so much about mountain lions?" she asked.

"I don't," I said.

FORTY-THREE

With my admission of ignorance about its habits, the cat finally moved. It was as though it suddenly understood how defenseless we were.

The first movements were a raised paw and, on the opposite side, a simultaneously cocked ear. Sawyer sucked in air and I held my breath before finally hissing, "Act big. Don't look at it." She raised the camp chair above her head and I shook the rack of antlers above mine. Our unzipped coats widened at our trunks. The cat moved another paw and raised its body an inch or two from the floor of the loft.

I felt the strange awe I'd had once when I chanced upon some barracuda while snorkeling in the Mexican Caribbean. The combination of beauty and danger was almost paralyzing.

The paw closest to the pole ladder reached down and felt gingerly for the first rung. "It's coming down," Sawyer said. "It's coming down."

The cat rose on its haunches and raised its head in our direction, temporarily unconcerned with its bloody kill in the corner. The other front paw felt for the upper rung on the ladder. My eyes scanned frantically for another weapon. Theo was security-conscious enough to have bars on her windows and doors—she must have a weapon handy to protect herself. The cat lowered a paw another rung. The back legs felt for purchase at the edge of the loft.

Sawyer said, "Oh my God."

I saw it, finally. Theo's gun. Her final protection was a

shotgun. I counted two barrels, side by side. The huge gun was resting lazily on the sill of the window between us and the door, mostly hidden by some gingham curtains. Unfortunately, the barrel end, not the trigger end, was closest to me.

"Have you ever fired a shotgun, Sawyer?"

"Why? Do you see one?"

"Yes, on the windowsill right by me."

"My dad had one."

The cat felt for another rung.

Sawyer's father had taught her how to fly; I sure hoped he had taught her how to shoot. "Give me a quick lesson."

"I guess we need to assume it's loaded, huh?"

"Yes."

"Theo lives alone. Pray that it's ready to go. There's probably a safety you need to release. After that, just point in the general direction of the cat and fire. You don't have to aim very well."

"I can do that," I said, unconvincingly. "Walk with me toward the window so I can reach it."

We shuffled sideways.

The cat growled and bared its fangs.

"Jesus. Oh God." I think the prayer I heard was Sawyer's. Though it might have been mine.

Holding the elk antlers in one hand, I reached out with the other and grabbed the barrel of the shotgun. The steel I touched was as cold as a snake's heart.

Where's Reggie?

The cat leaped down to the foot of the ladder and landed with a muffled thud that mimicked the sound of the blood pumping through my ears. The lion was now closer to Theo than we were. But it was closer to us than it was to Theo. I wasn't breathing and didn't think Sawyer was either.

Outside, I heard a car. The cat did, too. Its ears twitched. Seconds later, voices. Outside. Male voices. I thought, *Reggie got us some help.*

The cat's eyes widened; its jowls moved.

I maneuvered the shotgun so the barrels were no longer pointing right at me and felt along the side of the weapon for the safety. My fingers found a steel lever and I pushed on it until it stopped moving. I felt for the trigger guard, slowly inserting my index finger and caressing the curved steel of the first of two triggers. I felt a chilling awareness that if this damn gun wasn't loaded and cocked, either Sawyer or I, and perhaps both of us, were going to be mauled by this cat.

The cat was again absolutely still, staring right at Sawyer. I slid closer to her. The arm above my head supporting the antlers was almost numb. I needed to put them down to fire the gun.

The voices outside grew more distinct. The handle turned on the security door.

The cat leaped at Sawyer.

With a rush, she lowered the camp chair to protect herself and I raked the space in front of her with the antlers, trying to keep hold of the shotgun at the same time. We struck the lion together and managed to deflect it to the side, where it landed on its flank between Sawyer and Theo.

I couldn't shoot it there. I might hit Sawyer. And I'd definitely kill Theo if she wasn't already dead. Blood trickled from the lion's ear. It shook its head and righted itself.

The latch clicked on the inner door, the plank door, and a huge man in a black parka and a fur hat filled the entryway to Theo's cabin.

I said, "Careful. There's a mountain lion in here."

"What?" he said, his voice disbelieving.

The cat hissed.

The big man said, "Oh, shit." Pause. "I've seen that cat around here. Did it kill Theo?"

"It attacked her. Do you know her well?"

"Yes. I'm her neighbor."

"Is the gun I'm holding ready to fire?"

"Definitely."

"Then I think we need to get the cat away from Theo so I can use it."

FORTY-FOUR

"**S**omebody was outside with you?" Sawyer asked the big man.

"He's still out at the road, waiting to direct the ambulance. Said something about a pickup truck, said you'd know what he was talking about."

The man surveyed our dilemma and said, "Let's all slide away from him, toward the loft. You'll have a clear shot."

We started to slide, trying to be the biggest animals in the world. The cat seemed focused solely on the smallest prey in the room, Sawyer. As she slid away, it actually feinted toward her.

Across the room, beneath the loft, I heard a mechanical clicking. So did the cat. The lights on a VCR flickered and the TV came on. The opening credits for *Guiding Light*. Theo had timers set to turn on the TV and to videotape a soap.

The noise from the TV seemed cacophonous, and the cat edged cautiously toward the sound. I tracked its every deliberate step with the barrel of the shotgun. The moment it was clear of Theo, I fired.

The TV imploded.

I was unprepared for the recoil, which almost blew me over. For many minutes afterward it seemed as though everyone around me was whispering.

An ambulance arrived soon after the cat died, and the attendants found Sawyer kneeling over Theo, crying quietly, pronouncing her dead.

I used Lauren's cell phone to call Sam Purdy and told him what the sheriff was going to find in this quaint log home up Sunshine Canyon, and asked him to run interference.

Sawyer and I left our business cards with Theo's neighbor at the cabin. We assumed that the sheriff's investigators would want to talk with us at some point. We concluded that we could leave before the authorities arrived because Theo's cabin wasn't actually a crime scene. After all, could a mountain lion be charged with B&E or homicide? Neither of us had any faith that the investigators would ever find any evidence that the Rands had managed to lure the lion inside the cabin.

Both Sawyer and I were skeptical anyway. They were too savvy to rely on a predator to do their work.

Reggie was cocooned in a shell of grief as we drove back down the mountain. Despite compassionate prompts from both Sawyer and me, he didn't say a word the whole way back, though he did make a point of constantly checking the passenger-side mirror.

I never spotted the pickup truck again.

Sawyer was rattled too. She wanted to get back to the Boulderado and make final plans to return to Phoenix to get her plane. She planned to take Milt up on his offer to find someone to provide her some protection. She agreed to page me if she was leaving before tomorrow. For now, I had to get back to work. I had patients scheduled and I wanted to see them, maybe even needed to see them.

Sam and the two ex–FBI agents were going to stay busy looking for the Rands.

Back at my office, I checked in with Lauren and her sister. Teresa answered the phone, said Lauren was sleeping and seemed well. I didn't tell her about Theo's cabin and the cat, didn't see what good it would do.

My day at the office started as had a thousand before it. I reveled in the routine of seeing familiar patients at familiar

times and listening to their familiar dilemmas. I was surprisingly serene with Victoria Pearsall as she ruminated
about her shitty boss. I stayed a step behind Riley Grant as
he further consolidated his gains. Each forty-five-minute
session was a comforting bracket that seemed to insulate me
further from the morning's terror. I did six sessions in six
and a half hours. Diane was kind enough to bring me a couple of empanadas and some lemonade for lunch. I wolfed
the food down but didn't taste a bite.

Midday, I got a page from a sheriff's investigator who
wanted to talk about the mountain lion and Theo.

I didn't call back. I didn't want to think about anything
other than my patients' problems, which felt much more
mundane than my own.

As four-thirty rolled around, the end was in sight. I had
two more sessions to go—my two resistant young men in
their twenties—before I would drop by the Boulderado to
say good-bye to Sawyer and drive to Denver to be with Lauren for the night. She and I would have to talk about getting
bodyguards.

Diane and I worked our office suite without a receptionist. When a patient arrived, he or she flicked a switch
marked with either Diane's name or mine in the waiting
room. The switches lit a red indicator light in the corresponding office. My red light flicked on right on schedule at
4:28. I expected to see my regular four-thirty appointment,
Tom Jenkins, the man in his late twenties whom I'd been
treating for a few months for relationship issues and anxiety. Usually I found his stories tedious, his resistance to my
intervention fatiguing. But I had to concentrate when I was
with him, so he would most definitely be distracting.

Before going out to retrieve him from the waiting room I
went to the bathroom and peed, then to the little kitchen,
where I poured myself a fresh mug of coffee, which I carried back to my office and placed next to my chair. I made
the short walk toward the front of the house and opened the
waiting-room door.

The waiting room is roughly square, with seating on only

two of the four walls. From the doorway, I can see only one of those walls, which is furnished with a burgundy sofa that Diane picked out during a recent Crate and Barrel phase. Sawyer was sitting on the sofa, looking nervous.

I was surprised to see her. "Hi. Are you on your way home already? I wish you had paged me; I have two more patients to go."

She didn't speak, but I watched her eyes flit briefly toward the wall I couldn't see from where I was standing. I took one step into the room, turned, and recognized my four-thirty, Tom Jenkins, sitting in one of the three uphol-stered chairs lining the wall. I said, "Hello, Tom. I'll be with you in just a minute. Come on back, Sawyer."

Tom stood but didn't face me. His voice was apologetic as he said, "I'm afraid she's with me, today." He showed me a handgun. He didn't point it at me, just pulled it from his jacket pocket and held it out in front of him. I thought it resembled Lauren's Glock. Not identical, but equally menacing.

I said, "Oh, damn."

Sawyer nodded twice, slowly, and arched her eyebrows in an "I'm sorry. What could I do?" exclamation.

Months earlier, Thomas Jenkins had been referred to me by his internist, a man I'd never heard of. Maybe that should have made me suspicious. It hadn't. I didn't pretend to know every internist in the metro area. Tom had come in to see me for the first time maybe three months before Arnie Dresser ever went for his final hike in the Maroon Bells. Long before A.J. and Milt intruded on Lauren and me dur-ing our lunch in Silver Plume.

Tom wasn't an atypical patient. He was an isolated man who called his loneliness "solitude." He described a history of jealousy and possessiveness in a long series of brief, im-mature romantic relationships. He described symptoms of anxiety that temporarily had me ruling out panic attacks. The only odd part of his presentation was that he was a self-pay patient in the brave new world of managed-care headaches.

But, of course, that made him more attractive to me, not less.

Oh yes. He had told me he was a firefighter in Longmont, fifteen minutes down the Diagonal from Boulder.

A firefighter. Just like Patrick Rand. Though Patrick worked in Lakewood, twenty miles away.

I shouldn't have been ambushed by him like this. But I was.

I said, "Your name isn't Tom, is it?"

"Why don't we go back to your office?" he suggested. "All of us." He turned to Sawyer and said, "Doctor? After you."

She stood and walked past me into the hallway that led toward my office. He moved across the room and turned the dead bolt on the entry door of the house. "You next, Doctor," he said to me. I wondered if Diane was still in her office, and that thought precipitated chilling snapshot memories of the last time I'd seen a gun in these offices.

God, there had been a lot of carnage that day. I lost a moment trying to date the memories.

As though he were reading my mind, my patient said, "Your partner is gone for the day. Lucky for her."

We marched down the hallway to my office. Inside, he closed the door and moved toward the chair where I always sat. He said, "Coffee smells good. I always wondered why you never offered me any."

Sawyer and I sat side by side on the gold and gray couch that was directly across from him. I said, "Should I call you Patrick? Or Mr. Rand?"

He didn't react. "I wouldn't be here like this if I didn't know that the game had gotten risky, Doctor." He rested the pistol on his lap and rubbed his eyes with his hands. "But I have to tell you—that mountain lion today? Can you believe it? That cat saved some lives, I'll tell you what." He half smiled and shook his head.

"I don't think I know what that means," I said. The words, I recognized, were therapist's words.

"It means today wasn't the first time I followed the three of you to that cabin."

"That was you in the pickup?" It was hardly a question.

He raised one eyebrow in surprise and admiration. I decided to point out his failure and try to milk it. "You were sloppy. Your father would never—never—have allowed us to spot him."

The words caught him mid-blink and he held his eyes shut for three or four seconds. My gaze wandered to his pistol.

He nodded and opened his eyes, catching me staring at the gun. "You're right. He was much better at this than I am. I'm afraid I almost blew it for him, all that he had worked for. But my plan at the cabin was good, considering the circumstances. I was going to blow the propane tank. Either the explosion or the fire should have engulfed your car and the cabin, gotten the two of you no matter where you were. But the cat, hell, now there's a wild card for you. Damn cat shows up and pretty soon half the emergency equipment in the county is on its way up there. Even though it didn't work, you have to admit my plan was sound. I did that whole thing—reconnaissance, planning, execution—in one and a half days. My father couldn't have done that, what I did. No. No way." He grew silent, reflecting on something. "I've mentioned him some to you, haven't I? He was such a weird character. He'd plan his meals a week in advance, right down to how many slices of bread he'd eat on Friday night along with his three fish sticks and whether or not he'd use jelly on the bread. A day and a half to get that whole plan in place? Not a chance. Sometimes I think it took him a day and a half just to decide to move his bowels."

Sawyer asked, "How were you going to set the propane off?"

He smiled and blinked, didn't answer. He was a magician protecting the secret of his best trick. "Did the lady die? The one who lived there? Did the cat get her?"

"Yes," I said, waiting for him to react to the news. He didn't seem to care. Theo's death wasn't particularly consequential to him.

"You tell me, then, so how did those two get on to me? The FBI types? Why did they suddenly show up to help you out?"

"Dr. Dresser had noticed that a lot of his old friends were dying. He was a journal writer and E-mail nut. He kept his mother apprised of his concerns. When he died too, she got suspicious. Involving the FBI was her idea. And her money."

"How did they find me?"

"They didn't. We did." I looked at Sawyer. "We tracked down your father through our memories of old patients. Had some false starts. But we put it together from there."

"Did Loomis help?"

I lied. I said, "Not really."

He fingered the gun as though it were a hypodermic full of truth serum he could employ anytime he chose.

"Well. He helped me. But then I had a little leverage with him. Ironic, though, about Dr. Dresser's writing tripping me up. It was my father's notebooks that got me going in the first place."

Tom, or Patrick, seemed to want to talk. I was surprised how much this felt like his usual therapy session. Except for the gun, of course. And Sawyer. Through my anxiety I was trying to decide how much of what I knew about this young man was psychologically accurate and how much of it had been act. I quickly decided that he wasn't sophisticated enough to fool me about his character and I could expect those traits to endure through this encounter.

I could have reflected back to him the juxtaposition of his mention of Reggie Loomis and his father's notebooks in the same breath. I didn't.

Sawyer did. "You're talking about your father's specula-tion about D. B. Cooper, aren't you?"

"Speculation? You know, I don't think so. You should see the case on paper in black and white. Dad had Loomis down cold for that hijacking. But he liked Loomis. Respected him. Emulated him, even. Dad wouldn't ever have turned Reggie Loomis in to the feds for that hijacking. Reggie doesn't know it, of course, but I wouldn't have turned him in either. The threat was good leverage, though." He shook his head. "Damn cat got in the way, that's all." He smiled. "My father used to hold up his index finger sometimes and make these important pronouncements. He called them 'life lessons.' Well, here's a life lesson for you." He held up an index finger. "You can't plan for everything. No matter how hard you try, you can't plan for everything."

In my therapy voice, I said, "I don't understand something. Why did you decide to take up your father's work? Why not just leave it alone?"

He scrunched his face up in a consternated way I'd seen in his previous visits to my office. As he relaxed the muscles, he said, "Couple of reasons. From the time I was little, I learned to share his hate for all of you for what you did to our family. That was one. Second, I wanted to prove something to him, I guess."

With obvious disbelief, Sawyer asked, "So your father isn't dead?"

Patrick widened his eyes and smiled at the question in a manner that increased my already swollen discomfort. But he didn't answer. "Did I blow it in New Zealand? I shouldn't have done that, should I? Gone overseas?"

I answered, "The FBI agents are confident that they can use immigration and airline records to identify you. Eventually, anyway."

"You know, I knew that. I *knew* that. But I did it anyway. Jeez. Stupid. Sorry, Dad."

"Your father went overseas once, too. The cruise ship killing. It appears that he had a false passport, though. You didn't?"

He shook his head. "That was my favorite. Of all the notebooks of the killings, that was my favorite. He planned it forever. Do you know how he did it? How he made her disappear?"

"Yes," I said. I knew he was talking about Wendy Asimoto's gruesome end, and he seemed oblivious to the fact that he was sitting with two people who might have cared about her. He only wanted to talk about the ingenious way

his father had disposed of her body. "Your father incinerated her body on board the ship."

He clapped. "Bravo, bravo. You figured that out? Perhaps
I underestimated all of you."

"Did your father do the drive-by in L.A.?"

He looked embarrassed. "He wasn't proud of that one. He
called it a 'duck shoot' in his journal. Vowed not to use guns
again. No matter how well planned."

I stared at the pistol. "But he broke his vow with the hunting accident?"

Patrick raised his eyebrows. "You have the order wrong.
The hunting accident came first."

Sawyer said, "You didn't sabotage my plane, did you?"

He shook his head. "Your plane? No. What happened to
your plane?"

She told him.

"No, I wouldn't have done that. Sabotaging landing gear
isn't lethal enough. Any good pilot could do what you did.
That would be an even more lame attempt than what I did
with Dr. Gregory's furnace. And anyway, that would have
been copying. I didn't want to copy him. I wanted each of
mine to be original. Each one of his killings was original. I
wanted mine to be, too. Life lesson," he said in an odd baritone voice as he raised the index finger of his right hand.
"Always avoid a recognizable MO."

He stared at me. His eyes were warm. "You're a better
therapist than Dr. Dresser. I actually think you helped me a
little. Do you know he wanted me to take Zoloft? I pretended I was. It made him feel better. The right medicine always makes the doctor feel better." He smiled bashfully.
"Thought you might want to know."

"You were Dr. Dresser's patient, too?"

"Yes. Getting to know each of you first was particularly
cool. Dad couldn't have done that part, of course, but he
would have appreciated it. The panache."

"Was I going to be your next victim? Or was Sawyer?"

"If the feds hadn't shown up, you mean? You were next.
Then I was going to go to California, live there a while, get

to know Dr. Faire a little, and take care of her and that other lady."

What? "Other lady? What other lady?"

He widened his eyes. "I'm sorry, but I'm bad with names. She's older, I guess, uh—"

"Dr. Masters? Amy Masters?"

"Right, that's it. Don't tell me she's already dead?" He made a tsking sound with his tongue and the roof of his mouth.

Sawyer nodded.

"I guess I can cross her off my list, then."

"You didn't kill her?" I asked, feeling relief she hadn't been murdered.

"I would have. But, no, I didn't."

"How were you going to kill me?"

"You mean if things hadn't gotten so rushed?" He waited for my nod. "Your bike. It would have been a piece of cake. You know that route you do in Left Hand Canyon? Where it's real steep on the downhill?"

"Yes." I did that ride a couple of times a month when the weather allowed. When the conditions were perfect, I could fly.

"You seem to do it pretty regularly. I figured I'd precipitate a little rockslide when you were going about fifty. There's one curve where I figured you would lose control for sure and go over the edge. It's two hundred feet down, maybe more."

"You know, I guessed you would use my bike. The other stuff you did, the beam falling on my head? The carbon monoxide? Those were impulsive? You were improvising when you did those things?"

"Yeah. The beam especially. But you have to admit, despite my lack of planning, you were pretty damn lucky. One of the guys at the station said he heard from a friend in Boulder that you guys had two CO detectors instead of one. Who has two CO detectors? What are the odds of being tripped up by that, huh? Dad would have forgiven me that one, I think. No amount of planning can overcome something like that. And that beam in your house? That was my fault. It was supposed to be the whole damn roof that came down. My engineering skills are rusty."

"What about me?" Sawyer asked.

"Sorry. So sorry. Hadn't got there yet. Life lesson: One at a time. One at a time. Don't try to plan two murders at once. Each one requires tremendous creativity. Actually, when you think about it, it's an art. Murdering people and not arousing any suspicion. None. Imagine? It's an art."

He looked at her. Then at me.

"Really," he insisted. "It is."

FORTY-FIVE

He lifted the gun with both hands and hefted it as though he wanted to assess its weight. "Since I know they're watching me, I have to be careful what I do next. It's why I bailed out with the propane. Too many possible witnesses. This next one has to be pretty believable if I want to get away with it. Dad always said life's performances are hardest when you have an audience."

"Who is watching you?" Sawyer asked.

"You don't know?" He examined her eyes, then mine. "Really? The FBI guy and that Boulder cop—the one who seems to be your friend, Dr. Gregory. They have my townhouse staked out right now. Which tells me they don't have a warrant, not that they'd find anything even if they did. But that means that they really don't have any evidence tying me to anything. Not yet, not enough to take to a judge. Despite their suspicions, I could still walk. My first goal, of course, was never to be identified as a killer. My secondary goal was never to be convicted. That one's still within reach, I think." He threaded his finger through the trigger guard. "As long as you two don't survive."

Sawyer and I both reacted physically, the g-forces of fear forcing us back against our chairs.

"Don't worry. I'm not going to shoot you unless you get stupid. Dr. Gregory, would you please get Dr. Faire a piece of paper? A blank one?"

I did.

"I need a prescription from you," he said to Sawyer.

"Make it for . . . Xanax. Good. Put my name on it, my real name. Good. Sign it. Date it. Good. Oh, almost forgot, your DEA number, too. Yes. See, now you're one of my doctors, too. I like it like that. Things feel complete. Hand it over to me, please."

He folded the paper carefully into quarters and tucked it in his shirt pocket. "Now we go." He stood and swept my keys off my desk. He waved the gun as though he were a theater usher directing us to our seats with a flashlight. "Out the back way, I think. We'll be taking your car, Dr. Gregory. I'm afraid you two are about to have an unfortunate accident. But I really do have a nice place picked out for you to die."

A door leads from my office to the backyard of the old house. My car was parked on the adjacent driveway. The snow that had been so persistent up at Theo's cabin that morning had never really amounted to anything down here. The ground was dotted with leaves from a nearby ash and debris from our neighbor's linden, but there was no snow remaining on anything.

I had already decided that I might as well do something desperate here in town. Lauren had taught me once that no matter what immediate jeopardy it caused, you should never let a kidnapper take you someplace where his control over you increased. My best location for a last-ditch effort was here in town, on my own property.

I caught Sawyer's eye and hoped she could see my determination. Patrick Rand apparently did. He kept the pocketed handgun focused on her, not on me, underlining what the consequences would be if I tried anything. "Don't be foolish," he warned. "I want you to drive, Dr. Faire. Dr. Gregory, you ride up front. I'll be in back. We'll go straight up into Boulder Canyon."

Lamely, I said, "Your father did Boulder Canyon for a car crash. One of his coworkers from the plant. You don't want to repeat that, do you?"

"Nice try. You *have* pieced a lot of this together, though. You're both quite resourceful. I respect that and I'll keep it in mind. But we're not going to have a crash in Boulder

Canyon. Actually, we're going to turn up Magnolia. There's a lovely place up there that I want to show you."

He never took his eyes off me or his gun off the middle of Sawyer's back as he spoke. His calm demeanor chilled me. I was absolutely certain he would shoot Sawyer if I tried to escape.

"Take those damn catering things out of the back of the car, please. Stack them over there. We'll need a lot of room. If I see you open a single case to search for something to use as a weapon, she's dead."

I followed his instructions to the letter.

In a minute we were on our way.

The road up Magnolia cuts off Boulder Canyon not too far from town. But the foothills of the Rocky Mountains rise precipitously west of Boulder. By the time we got to Magnolia, the cliffs were already steep, the road was already treacherous, and the possible isolation was almost total. On these winding roads I couldn't figure out how Rand was going to get us to crash at a high enough speed to kill us and still manage to ensure his own escape.

I couldn't piece it together. Was he going to jump from the car?

Dusk was blacker in the canyon than it was up Magnolia, where the light of a moon that was only two days past full shimmered off the fresh snow and the golden grasses of the high meadows. Sawyer actually commented on how pretty it was.

He directed her to take a turn off Magnolia down one dirt road and then down another. The congested housing that was clustered on both sides of the main road was quickly behind us. The road we were on was narrow, twisty, and in ill repair. There was no way he was going to engineer a crash up here that would guarantee two fatalities and one survivor. I began to question his judgment.

He ordered another turn, and then another. The last one took us from the road up a steep driveway marked by a sign from Mock Realty. The sign informed us that we were driving onto 6.3 acres with a great building site and a well. The long driveway had been badly rutted by runoff, and the big Land Cruiser listed hard to the left as we climbed.

"Keep going," he said. "Careful, now. Don't want any accidents, do we?"

At the top of the driveway, which probably extended almost a quarter of a mile, we reached a relatively flat clearing. The day's light was almost gone, but it was apparent that this building site commanded stunning views to the south and east. Far in the distance, the sky above Denver glowed as though irradiated.

I grew even more nervous as he said, "Pull straight ahead. Go on."

Sawyer urged the big car forward across the clearing and slowly approached the edge of a cliff. The cavern below us was dark. I couldn't tell how steep the incline was. I couldn't tell how deep the fall would be.

I figured plenty steep and plenty deep.

Five feet from the edge, he said, "Stop."

She did. He said, "No, a couple more feet." I heard her sigh as she gingerly edged forward. I wondered if she had worked out in her mind what was about to happen.

"Kill the lights. Turn off the engine for now. Good." He opened the door to the backseat. Chill air filled the car. "Don't move."

I didn't need to look; I could hear what he was doing behind us. He was lowering the sections of the backseat so they would be flat with the cargo area.

"Okay," he ordered, his voice crisper now. "Now undress. Both of you."

We stared at each other. I saw sorrow, not fear, flood Sawyer's face and imagined she was thinking about two other deaths staged in another car. He said, "Come on, everything. Take everything off."

Sawyer didn't look surprised at Rand's order. Maybe she had discerned what was coming. I tugged off my sweater in a swift motion. She was wearing a suede coat. She struggled out of it. I helped her get it off her arms.

"Come on. Don't procrastinate. Dad hated procrastination."

As we unbuttoned our shirts, I pondered whether I

wanted to take my chance going over the cliff in the car, or if I preferred to risk death at the hands of this man and his semiautomatic handgun.

Methodically, in the least erotic manner I could ever have imagined, we removed the rest of our clothing. It took a couple of minutes and then I was naked beside Sawyer and, except for her socks, she was naked beside me.

"Start the car now, Dr. Faire. It's way too cold for two old lovers to do it up here without heat, right?"

"No," she said, without conviction. I glanced over at her. She was covered in gooseflesh. Her tiny nipples were as hard as the steel in our murderer's hands.

"Do it," he said. "And the second you do, I want to see your hands on your heads. Both of you."

She hesitated for a good twenty seconds, then reached out and turned the key. The car obeyed the command; the engine rumbled to life. We raised our hands as instructed.

"Now," he said. "Climb into the back. Don't get out. Climb right over the console. One at a time."

While Sawyer moved gracelessly to the back of the car, I watched Rand, hoping for an opening. The barrel of his gun never left her. I could throw open my door and run into the night. I might actually make it. No way Sawyer would.

Defeated, I followed Sawyer to the back of the vehicle.

"Now, start. Go ahead. You know you want to do it. I might even let you finish before I . . . well . . . whatever. You won't know when the end is near. I'll be quiet. Enjoy. Go on. Go on." His voice was encouraging, generous.

Obscene. He was managing to rape both of us at the same time.

The whole thing could not have been more incongruous. Sawyer sat next to me, naked. I could smell her. Almost taste her. The view was heavenly. The setting serene. And all I wanted to do was run.

Suddenly, she reached up and hooked my neck with her elbow, pulling me down to her.

"No," I said, resisting. "No." She clutched me tighter to her.

My face was buried in her hair. "Somebody's here," she

whispered. "Get ready to open the back." With that she kissed me, pulling me sideways, upright, then over, so that our heads now faced the back of the car and not the front. I could feel the fabric of her socks against the top of my feet and the weight of her breast against my arm. With my left hand, I groped randomly for the latch on the back hatch door.

I whispered, "Got it." *Please. Whoever is out there. Say something. Do something.*

Stop this.

The sounds almost overlapped as Rand simultaneously closed the rear passenger door and opened the driver's door. I raised my head to see what he was doing.

"Uh-uh," he warned. "Ignore me. Focus, now. Enjoy. She's very pretty. It's a good way to go."

All he had to do now was reach into the car with one leg and one hand. Put his foot on the brake, slide the gearshift into drive, and release his foot from the brake. Those simple movements were all that was left between life and death for Sawyer and me.

FORTY-SIX

Rand was watching us. I could feel his eyes.

His father, I was certain, would not approve of his taking a respite from the task at hand to quench his voyeuristic thirst.

I pushed Sawyer's shoulder back away from me, exposing her chest to his view. Instantly, she seemed to understand what I was doing, and she raised her leg onto my hip, angling her crotch for his appraisal.

Time, I thought. *We need time.*

"Go on. Go on," he urged.

I touched her neck and she slid her hand to my side and let it migrate down between my legs. She touched me almost chastely.

Go ahead, keep watching, asshole. Keep watching.

He did, for a good minute. I stayed limp in Sawyer's hand.

Suddenly, the weight of the car shifted, and I knew the time had come. He was moving toward the gearshift and the brake. I threaded my fingers under the latch of the door and pulled it hard. The noise was distinctive as the mechanism released and the hatch door popped open two inches, then stopped.

He barked, "No!"

A gunshot, crisp and frank, pierced the air. Sawyer and I ducked. I held my breath as though my inflated lungs could deflect a slug.

The balance of the car shifted again and Rand yelped. He

seemed to be trying to swallow the sound of his own scream. The car lurched forward a few inches and tugged, like a big dog straining against its leash. The engine raced again as Rand hit the gas pedal with his foot while he was searching for the brake. Another gunshot rang out, accompanied by a loud thud.

I pushed the hatch door up with my forearm. Sawyer and I were fighting to untangle from each other so we could scramble out the back of the car before Rand sent it over the cliff. I heard a familiar sound—*clunk*—as he dropped the gearshift from park into drive.

Finally the heavy car began to ease forward as Rand's foot came off the brake. Gunshots filled the air, ringing out in rapid order. At least two guns, maybe three. I couldn't tell. With all my strength I pushed Sawyer toward the open hatch, my efforts throwing me back farther into the car.

I felt the incline change, gravity's new tug pulling all the blood from my heart. The clearing we'd been on was rapidly becoming cliff. I pawed at the carpet, climbing the cargo bed as though it were a ladder, desperately clawing to get to the still-open hatch door.

My mind jumped to thoughts about Lauren and the baby we'd barely talked about having.

With a sudden shudder the car angled down farther. I figured the incline was now close to forty-five degrees. I managed to hook my fingers on the frame of the back door but I couldn't get enough purchase with my bare feet to propel myself out against the steep incline. Hands suddenly clamped onto my wrists. One, then another.

A woman, not Sawyer, ordered, "Let go, Alan."

I did, feeling that with the release of my curled fingers, I was giving up any hope of escaping the car. I was dying. But the hands on my wrists held firm and, as though in slow motion, I felt the car drive out from under me. My chest cleared the bumper first, and a split second later so did my legs. I fell in a heap into dust and rock.

Below me I heard a crash like a minor traffic accident, and then two seconds later, a horrific crunching sound echoed through the canyons around Magnolia as my Land Cruiser found the bottom of the cliff.

A. J. Simes and Reggie Loomis had arrived up Magnolia in a yellow cab, which was still waiting at the bottom of the long driveway. Sawyer and I made the driver's day by climbing into the backseat of his cab nearly naked.

He didn't even try to pretend he wasn't staring at Sawyer. He asked, "Were those gunshots I heard?"

I said, "I didn't hear anything." Sawyer was wearing A.J.'s coat, this one a shade of teal that would probably be dangerous around people with seizure disorders. It barely reached her thighs. She was shivering. I was wearing Reggie's blue denim workshirt. I was shivering, too. "Could we have some more heat, please?" I pleaded.

"Sure," he said. Feigning nonchalance, he added, "Where to?"

"The Boulderado," I said.

"They must have relaxed their dress code."

I wasn't in any mood for his comedy. "On second thought, just run the meter. I have a feeling we should stick around for a few minutes."

A few minutes became ninety. Although they were treating us like victims, not offenders, the sheriff's investigators proffered plenty of questions neither Sawyer nor I wished to answer. The cops also had blankets, though, and that was good.

The gunshots that had felled Rand had come from A. J. Simes's weapon. That fact made her the center of attention. Sawyer and I waved to her as she was moved into a sheriff's car to be transported somewhere for questioning.

Reggie Loomis was nowhere to be found. Disappearing was apparently one of his best things.

A deputy sent the cab on its way and drove us down to town and the Boulderado. Getting from the hotel entrance to our rooms was awkward. Wrapped in borrowed blankets, we sneaked in a side entrance and used the house phone on the second floor to ask that room keys be brought our way. The explanation that the bellman extracted from us for why we didn't currently have clothing or identification was long and mostly fictional. Fortunately, he recognized Sawyer, and we got the keys. Once inside my room, which momentarily felt like a palace, I phoned Lauren and reassured her that our biggest problem appeared to be over but I wouldn't make it to Denver tonight. She said she'd been worried and asked why I wasn't coming down. I told her that I'd had some trouble with my car and I'd explain more tomorrow.

I paged Sam and waited a few minutes for him to return the call. He didn't.

I showered until the chill left my skin.

Sawyer and I rendezvoused, as planned, under the stained-glass roof in the Mezzanine Lounge forty-five minutes later. The mime wasn't on duty. I figured it was an omen, a good omen. Sawyer had arrived before me, her hair still wet. I noted that her clothing could not have been more demure. She'd already ordered a bottle of champagne and some diet cola.

The wooden staircase from the lobby to the mezzanine of the Boulderado is grand in design and permits a grand entrance. The one we witnessed next was special.

I heard Milt's voice before I saw any of them, but as their heads cleared the tread of the top step, I could see all three. Milt and Sam were cradling A.J. between them, as though she were a queen on a portable throne. In my mind, I was assuming that she was being carried up the stairs because climbing that long rutted driveway to save our lives had cost her whatever precious energy she had left in her legs.

Sawyer and I jumped up and ran to meet them.

"These two sprung me," she said, her voice girlish. Milt said he hadn't done anything. Sam shrugged.

Sam said, "He's dead. Rand. They're getting a warrant now for his truck and his townhouse. The truck was parked about a quarter of a mile from where he tried to kill you two. Let's hope he's left some evidence behind that will tie him to all of this."

A.J. said, "Turns out I only clipped him. Twice. Leg and

shoulder. He got his foot caught in the car, though, and he went over the cliff with it. Rolled on top of him a couple of times. He died in the crash." She sounded disappointed that her shots had only wounded him.

"You saved our lives," Sawyer and I said, virtually simultaneously.

"I'll be happy to take some credit for that," she said, beaming. "But I have to share it with your friend Mr. Loomis. He tracked me down this afternoon at the hotel and dragged me over to your office to warn you about young Mr. Rand. Loomis doesn't have a car. And I don't . . . drive anymore. When we pulled up to your office in a taxi, we saw you and Sawyer coming down the driveway with someone in the backseat of your car. We figured that we were already a little late with our warning. So we improvised and followed you into the mountains in the cab." She shook her head and laughed at the memory.

"Where did Reggie go afterward, A.J.? After the shooting?"

"Told me that there were some good reasons for him not to be associated with any of this. Before the sheriff showed up, he was gone."

"And where were you two?" I asked Milt and Sam.

Milt answered, "Rand tricked us. Left word at work he was on his way home from a hiking trip to Rocky Mountain National Park. One of his colleagues at the fire station was helping us out, and he let us know Rand's plans. We spent all day staking out his townhouse, waiting for him to get home." He faced A.J. and said, "Sorry. Got duped."

She touched him affectionately on his wrist and allowed her fingers to linger. "It all turned out fine," she said.

The waitress delivered three more champagne glasses. Sam eyed her suspiciously until she actually spoke. Sawyer raised her Pepsi, and she and I toasted the cops. All three of them.

Sam went along politely with the toast. Then he ordered a Budweiser.

FORTY-SEVEN

Our celebration ended near midnight.

Sawyer was leaving for Phoenix on the first shuttle the next morning, and, with an audience of law enforcement officers, she and I said our final good-byes. I think she preferred that our parting be public and not sentimental. I whispered in her ear that I'd never forget her. She whispered back that she'd always remember me. We never spoke a word about our last evening naked together.

Before meandering back to my little alley-view room, I thanked the three cops who had helped save my life.

In the alcove beside my hotel room door, a man sat on the floor, his knees up, his head resting on his folded arms.

Reggie.

"Hello," I said. "I wondered when I'd see you again. I think I owe you some serious gratitude."

He raised his head and said, "Least I could do after leading you into that ambush up at Theo's house."

I shook my head to indicate I didn't get what he was talking about.

"That truck? Up the canyon? The one you were worried about? I spotted it again when I ran out of the cabin to get help for Theo. The pickup?"

"It was Rand. He was going to blow up the propane tank. That's what he told me."

"I wondered about that, thought he might be up to something. That's why I stayed outside and sent Theo's neighbor in. I was afraid it was Rand and thought I should keep an eye out for him. Anyway, when I got back down to town, I had an old colleague of mine run the license plates on the pickup for me. Sure enough, it was registered to Corey's widow."

"What convinced you it was Patrick and not his father?"

He shrugged. "Corey was a perfectionist. The truth is that if he was after you, you'd be dead. Anyway, Corey's kid called me to tell me he'd found some of his father's things. Just before he asked me if I needed help with my food deliveries."

I nodded.

"I said I didn't. He asked if the same folks who helped me yesterday were going to help again the next time."

"And you said yes."

This time he nodded. "I wasn't thinking," he said. Reggie had a padded envelope in his hand, a large one, big enough for a book. He noticed me looking at it. "Got this in the mail today." He nodded toward my door. "Do you mind if we go into your room?"

I used the card to let us in. He took the chair. I sat on the bed and offered him the splendor of my minibar. He declined.

From the envelope he slid a marbled black and white notebook, the kind that school kids have toted for a hundred years. "Rand sent this to me today. The kid, Patrick. But the notebook was put together by his father, Corey."

I didn't reach out for it. "Is that the D. B. Cooper notebook?"

His eyes asked, "How did you know?" He picked the book up and smacked it on his thigh. "It's actually the Dan Cooper notebook. A reporter copied the name incorrectly off a manifest early in the investigation. The hijacker originally checked in calling himself 'Dan,' never 'D.B.' Corey knew that, of course."

He lifted it toward me. "You want to see it? A lot of interesting stuff in here."

I lowered my eyes to the notebook before raising them back toward Reggie. I shook my head. "No, not really. I don't think so."

He nodded. "Think Sawyer does?"

"I doubt it. She's leaving town tomorrow. My guess is that she has better things to do."

He exhaled through pursed lips. "Want to know where I grew up?"

"No."

"If I was in the service?"

"Not especially."

"If I had parachute training?"

"Not curious. Sorry, Reggie. Listen," I said, "you and I both have lives to get back to, people who count on us. Let's say we do it."

"Just like that?"

I sensed a shiver shimmying up my spine. I said, "Doesn't feel like 'just like that' to me."

FORTY-EIGHT

Dresden finished our renovation right on time and took off for his scuba trip to Australia. Lauren and Emily and I moved back into the Spanish Hills house over a long weekend at the beginning of December.

Despite a paucity of furniture our home was lovely. We enjoyed a late Thanksgiving dinner feast and promptly decorated for Christmas.

Lauren and Emily seemed to have recovered completely from the carbon monoxide poisoning.

No one was trying to kill any of us.

And Lauren and I were busy trying to make a baby.

Adrienne had removed the stent from Sam's plumbing, and, as expected, he gradually repressed the pain and dread that had erupted from his brush with kidney stones. His new diet resolution became a curious memory long before the New Year.

Sawyer called frequently. She'd speak, happily, to whichever of us answered the phone. Lauren commented after one conversation that Sawyer was busy finding new reasons to have a life instead of gilding old reasons not to. I found the words sage.

I left Patrick Rand's four-thirty psychotherapy appointment open for a while. I did it on purpose. Each week I used the time to drive up Magnolia in my new car and ponder all that had happened and the vagaries of the cards that fate had dealt.

The line between lucky and unlucky in life is so thin, I knew, that it is often carved with a laser.

ACKNOWLEDGMENTS

As always, I asked for and received plenty of instruction, guidance, and assistance on the way to completion of this novel.

Over the years Tom Faure of the Boulder County Coroner's Office has been an ever patient teacher. Hopefully, I've finally learned my lesson, and I will never again need to beseech him to explain the difference between "cause of death" and "manner of death." Stan Galansky, M.D., and Terry Lapid, M.D., offered medical support and, more significantly, friendship. Cathy Schieve, M.D., provided a curbside consultation, literally. Earl Emerson assisted me with my research by doing what he does so well: he told me a great story. Bob Holman answered a battery of questions while he showed me around in his Beechcraft Bonanza, even generously permitting this retired pilot to take the controls for a while.

There are always family ties. I'm grateful to Colin and Amy Purrington for being romantics and to Sara Dominguez for being so darn sweet. My mother, Sara Kellas, sells so many books she should be on commission. Rose and Xan, you've been there every day. What else can I say?

Elyse Morgan, Mark Graham, Harry MacLean, Tom Schantz, Karyn Schiele, Alison Galansky, and Rose Kauffman read the manuscript during its development, and the final version benefited greatly from their observations. Patricia and Jeff Limerick have provided support over many years in many ways. In New York, Al Silverman, Lori

Lipsky, Michaela Hamilton, Elaine Koster, Phyllis Grann, and Lynn Nesbit each left their professional mark on this book. I couldn't have been in better hands.

I'd like to acknowledge an old debt, too. Years ago Dr. Bernard Bloom was my dissertation chair at the University of Colorado. He taught me many enduring lessons, most of them by example. Virtually every day he demonstrated that the most essential thing a writer does each day is put his butt in the chair. Bernie, thanks for that and for all your graciousness and wisdom.